# HISTORIC CAMDEN

PART TWO
## NINETEENTH CENTURY

BY
THOMAS J. KIRKLAND
ROBERT M. KENNEDY

Southern Historical Press, Inc.
Greenville, South Carolina

This volume was reproduced
from a personal copy located in
the Publishers private library

Please direct all correspondence and book orders to:

www.southernhistoricalpress.com
or
SOUTHERN HISTORICAL PRESS, Inc.
1071 Park West Blvd.
Greenville, SC   29611

southernhistoricalpress@gmail.com

Originally printed: Columbia, SC   1926
:ISBN #978-1-63914--027-5
All rights reserved
Printed in the United States of America

# TABLE OF CONTENTS

|  | PAGE |
|---|---|
| Prefatory | V |

### Chapter I.
"Kirkwood" ..... 1

### Chapter II.
Localities Around Camden ..... 11

### Chapter III.
Pen Pictures—Commercial, Social, Economic ..... 14

### Chapter IV.
The War of 1812 ..... 57

### Chapter V.
LaFayette's Visit ..... 64

### Chapter VI.
Nullification Times ..... 83

### Chapter VII.
James Blair ..... 91

### Chapter VIII.
Pilgrims—Abram Blanding ..... 100

### Chapter IX.
Stephen D. Miller ..... 107

### Chapter X.
Exodus—William McWillie ..... 114

### Chapter XI.
The Seminole War ..... 120

### Chapter XII.
The Kershaw Volunteers in the Mexican War ..... 124

### Chapter XIII.
Irrepressible Conflict ..... 139

## Contents

| | PAGE |
|---|---|
| *Chapter XIV.* | |
| Thos. J. Withers | 151 |
| *Chapter XV.* | |
| War Times in Camden | 159 |
| *Chapter XVI.* | |
| Pantheon | 176 |
| *Chapter XVII.* | |
| Slaves | 187 |
| *Chapter XVIII.* | |
| Reconstruction and Red Shirts | 196 |
| *Chapter XIX.* | |
| The Iron Man | 227 |
| *Chapter XX.* | |
| The Court House | 251 |
| *Chapter XXI.* | |
| Schools and Schoolmasters | 262 |
| *Chapter XXII.* | |
| Churches | 277 |
| *Chapter XXIII.* | |
| Newspapers | 300 |
| *Chapter XXIV.* | |
| Liberty Hill | 309 |
| *Chapter XXV.* | |
| Notes from Nature | 314 |
| *Chapter XXVI.* | |
| Miscellaneous | 328 |
| *Chapter XXVII.* | |
| Curiosity Shop | 337 |
| *Chapter XXVIII.* | |
| Family Histories | 350 |
| *Appendix.* | |
| Confederate Soldiers from Kershaw County | 451 |

# PREFATORY

The first volume of HISTORIC CAMDEN covering the Colonial and Revolutionary periods was published in 1905, twenty-one years ago. Much has occurred since then to delay the completion of the second part, which is devoted mainly to the eighty-odd years subsequent to 1800. Some subjects of an impersonal nature have been brought down nearer to the present time. It was not possible to follow any hard and fast line.

This attempt to recount the annals of Camden grew out of a suggestion from Mr. Caleb Ticknor of Massachusetts, when about the year 1900 he became proprietor of the "Court Inn". What was first proposed as a mere sketch has expanded with research until it has been difficult to restrict it within bounds.

We have retained on this volume, as on the first, the figure of King Haiglar, which, as emblematic of Camden, we claim to have been the first to adopt.

In thus reaching the end of our labors we are moved to exclaim with the Spirit in Comus:

"Now our task is smoothly done
We can fly and we can run."

THOS. J. KIRKLAND,
ROBT. M. KENNEDY.

July, 1926.

> "And if chance thy home
> Salute thee with a father's honour'd name,
> Go, call thy sons; instruct them what a debt
> They owe their ancestors."
> —*Mark Akenside.*

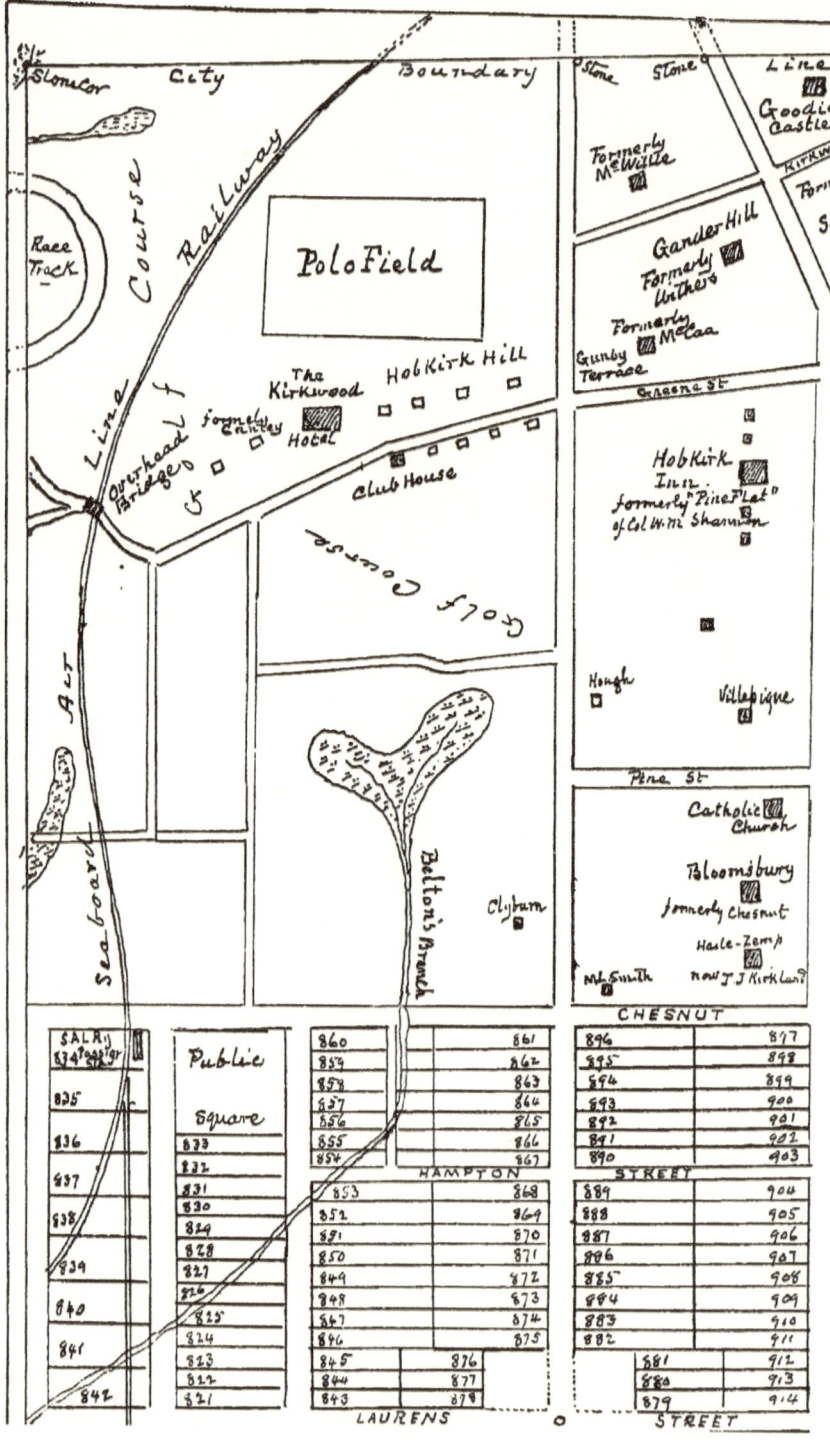

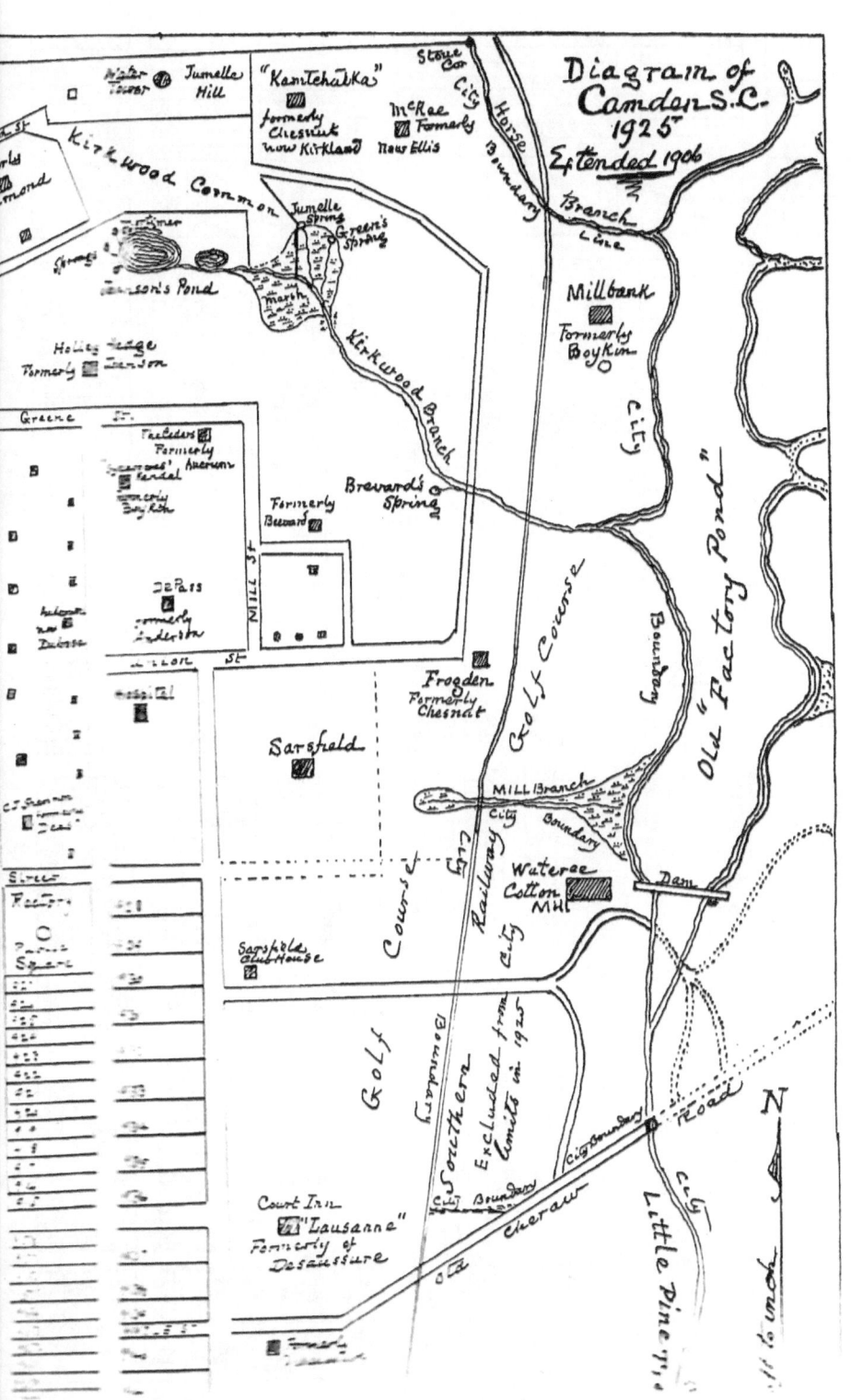

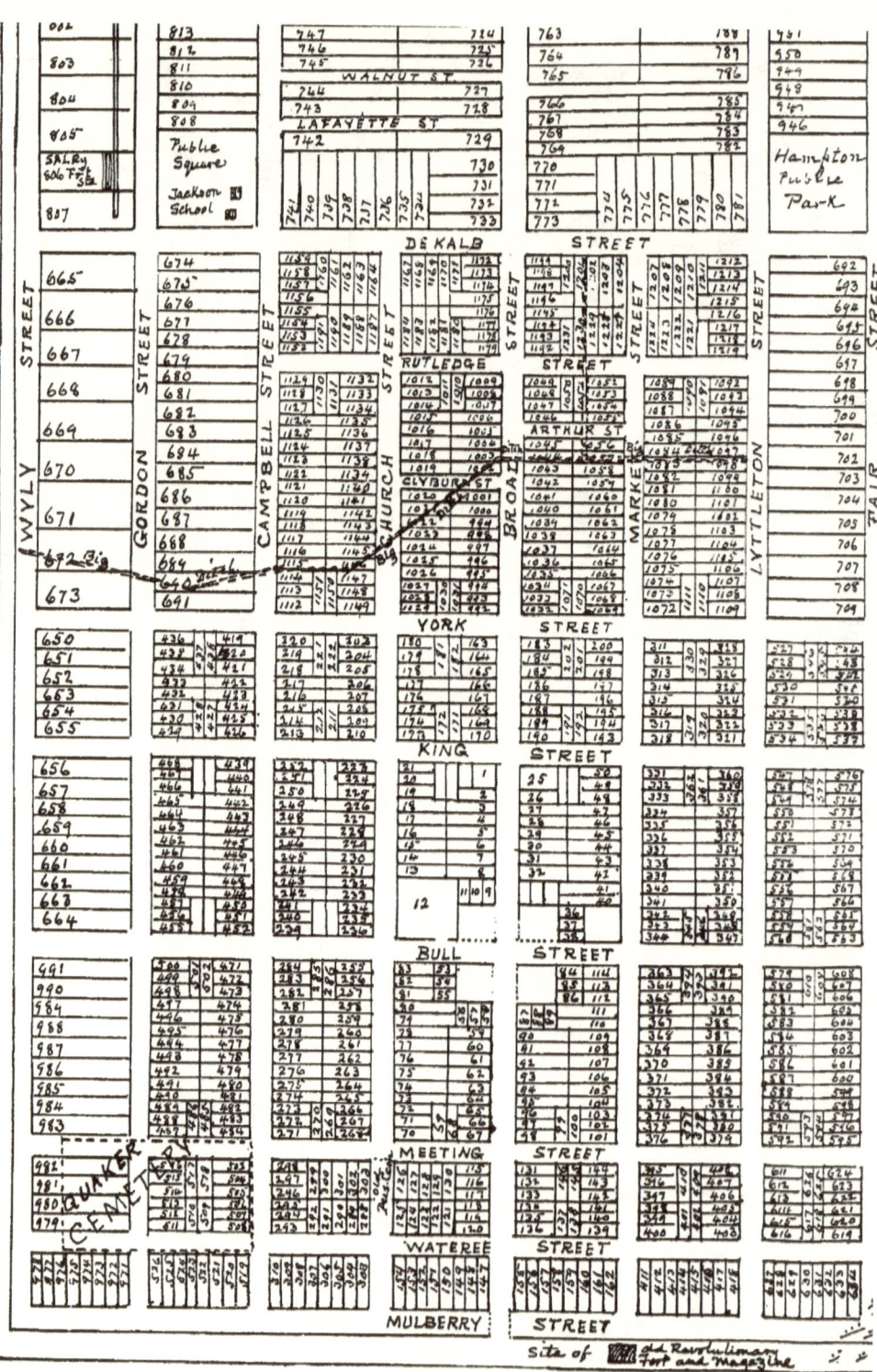

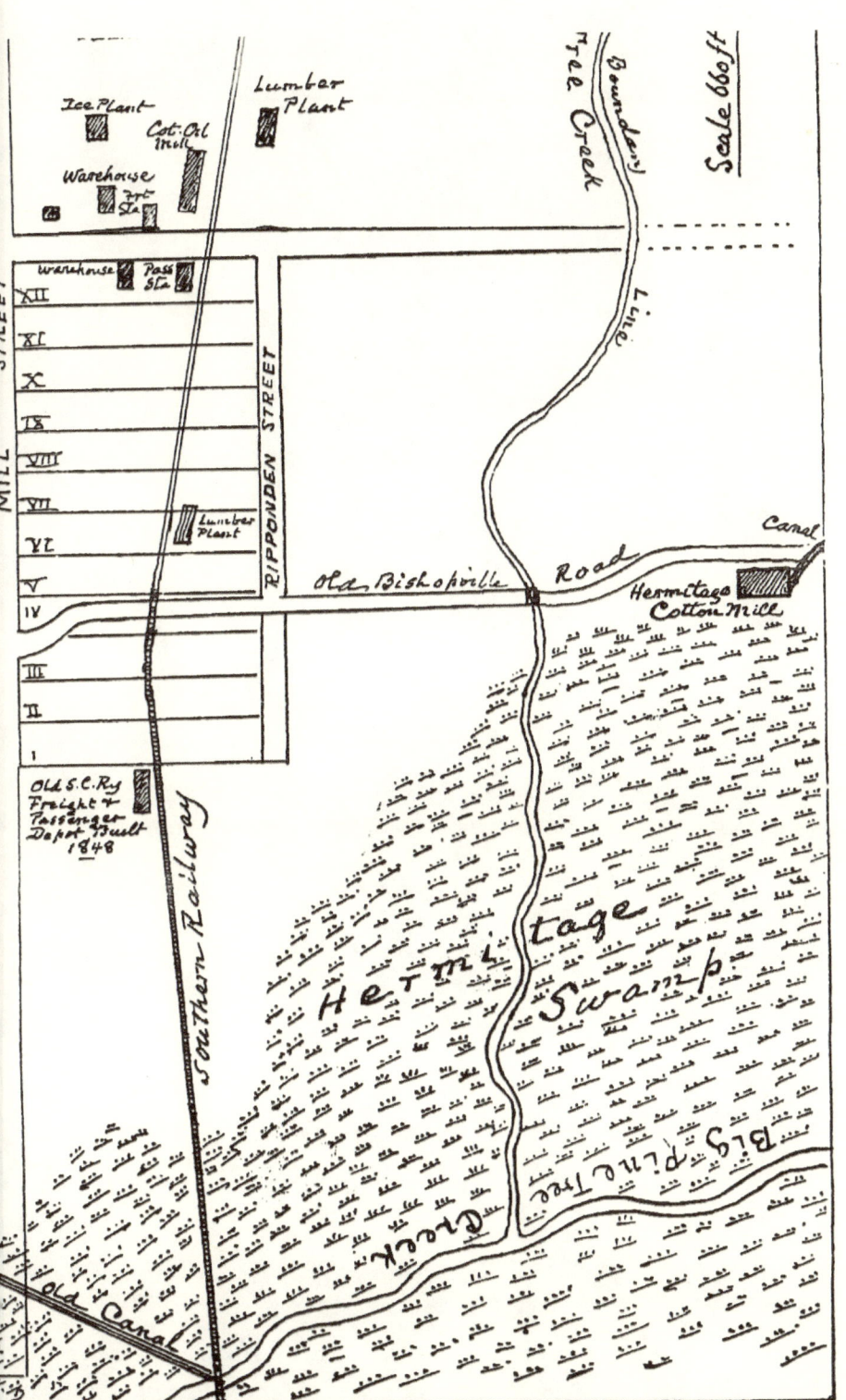

# HISTORIC CAMDEN

## CHAPTER I.

### "Kirkwood".

Since 1818 that district extending about three-fourths of a mile north of Old Boundary, now Chesnut Street, has been known as Kirkwood. In 1872 Camden was enlarged by legislative enactment so as to embrace the Kirkwood territory but in 1878 was reduced to its former limits. Again in 1906 these limits were extended northwards as in 1872 to the old stone land marks set up in that year by Mr. Colin McRae, and eastwards to the run of Horse Branch and high water mark of Pine Tree Creek.

In 1925 in accordance with result of a vote on the question, about 30 acres, including Wateree Cotton Mill, lying between Mill Branch on north, Railroad on west, old Cheraw Road on south and Pine Tree Creek on east, were released from City limits. (See folded map.)

The terrain of Kirkwood rises from Chesnut Street northwards by easy ascent to the crest of a low sandy ridge which extends east and west for about a mile. This ridge is crossed near its middle point by Lyttleton Street, that portion lying to the west being known as Hobkirk Hill; that to the east terminating in what is known as Jumelle Hill, on which is situated the stand pipe of the City water works. Along this ridge was fought the battle of Hobkirk Hill between Greene and Rawdon, April 25, 1781.

Kirkwood seems to have been practically devoid of residents until the northeast section was laid off into lots by John Kershaw in the year 1818. The plan of this village is of record in the office of Register of Deeds at Camden, Book "I", page 333, and is here reproduced (Diagram No. 1), including Kershaw's written declaration, from which it appears that the name was bestowed in honor of Capt. Robert Kirkwood of the Delaware troops who fought there so well in 1781. The lots, it will be noted, all fronted on a "Common". The

# HISTORIC CAMDEN

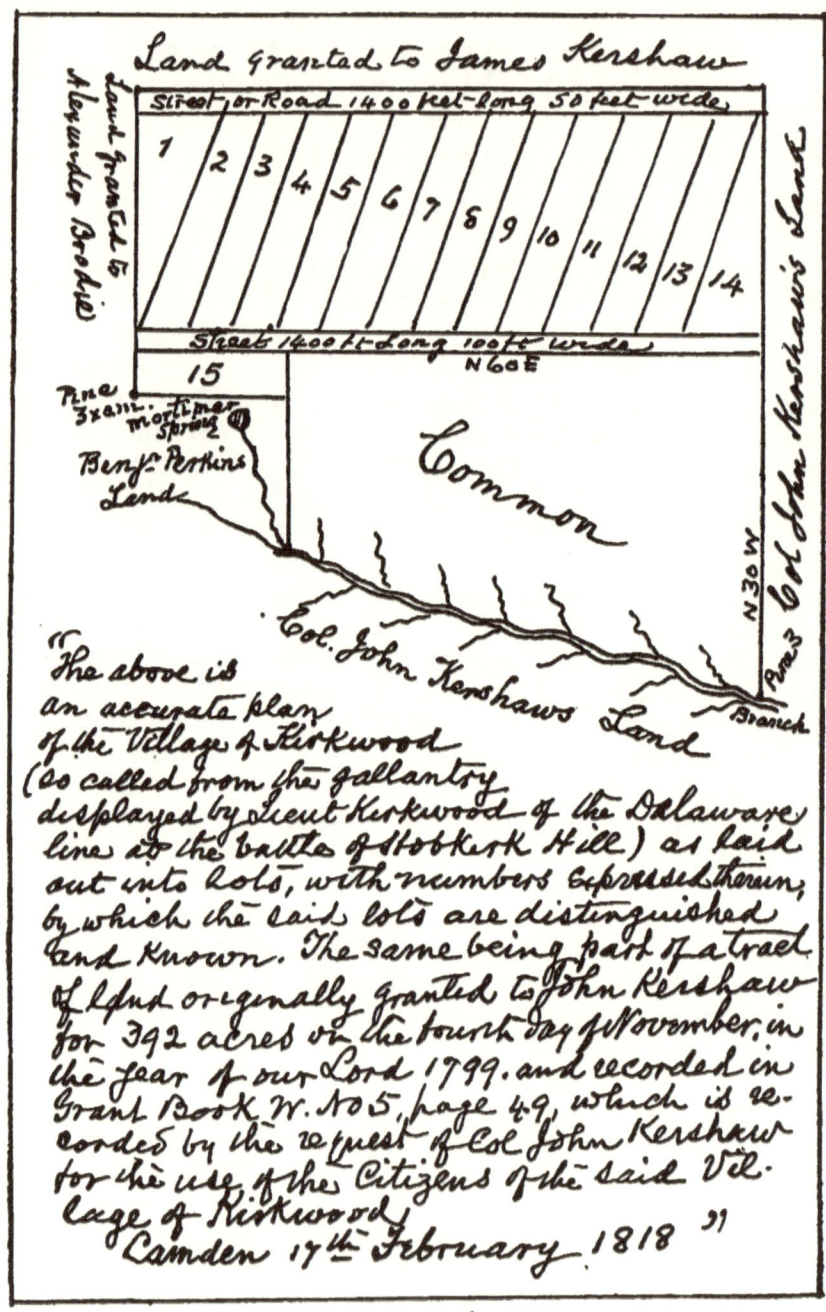

Diagram No. 1.

## "KIRKWOOD"

southern boundary of the Common was Kirkwood Branch, originally known as "Martin's Branch", which took its rise at Mortimer Spring.

Having at hand an article in the *Charleston News and Courier*, reprinted in the *Kershaw Gazette* of June 7, 1876, adopted by Col. W. M. Shannon as No. 8 of his "Old Times in Camden" and which he asserts was written by a "prominent Citizen of Camden", we are happy to invoke that anonymous author for the following narrative:

"About the year 1789 Edward Mortimer, a young Charlestonian, came to Camden seeking the lady who was afterwards his wife. This gentleman on the occasion of some convivial meeting at the Spring, in the heart of the breezy pinelands, concealed a bottle of something good to drink, wine or probably cognac (whiskey was not in use then), with the intention of returning with a few chosen spirits to refresh themselves. He was detected and, of course, found nothing but the empty bottle. The laugh was against him, but he bore it good-humoredly and the spring was called for him. This is the story as we got it from old Col. Chesnut, who remembered the incident.

"Hobkirk Hill and Mortimer Spring remained in the condition Greene and Rawdon had found and left them. Camden pent up next to the River had not broken bounds. No house stands there now built prior to 1800. The year 1816 proved a very sickly one, and malarial fever of a fatal type showed itself in town, many of its oldest inhabitants dying from the effect of it. As a consequence we find in a copy of the *Camden Gazette* of June 30, 1817, the following notice:

'The subscriber is willing to dispose of a few lots of land, one acre each, lying southwardly from the summit of Hobkirk Hill, with the perpetual use of the Spring on the South side of Mortimer's Spring Branch.
JOHN KERSHAW.'

"Dr. Edward H. Anderson, who was authority on all matters of hygiene in those days, and for a long time advocating Kirkwood as a summer retreat, with the merchants and professional men, purchased lots and built on them in easy access to the Spring, in what they called the Village of Kirkwood. Dr. Anderson had an uncle in the Maryland line at the battle of Hobkirk Hill.

"For many years Kirkwood was a village of small houses, suited only for summer, their occupants coming out in June and going back to town in October or at the first hard frost. Finally the town houses were given up and more permanent residences built, and Kirkwood soon became a recognized locality, giving its name to all the surroundings. The old name of Mortimer Spring has become extinct."

The malady above mentioned must have affected the brain of its victims and may account for the dismal production of "Peter Plunderbottom", appearing in the *Camden Gazette* of 1817, only a portion of which is here inflicted on the reader:

"THE VATICIDE, *ALIAS* LOCAL VAGARIES."

AN ODE.

Oh Camden, Camden, 'mortalized in story,
From head to foot, bedecked with Whig and Tory,
Attend, attend, below the mighty steeple,
That's to say, I mean the Camden people.
Think not, 'cause grandfather, saucy Peter,
'Neath a great tub hid me, can't shine in metre.
The time has come—merrily I'll dance and sing,
Shake off dull care—quaff th' ambrosial spring—
Lo, then be it known, our monstrous town,
By dire pestilence and want invaded,
Thought proper to import a cunning clown,
Who had the monarch death—evaded. Etc., etc.

Peter was not allowed to go unrebuked, and in a succeeding issue of the *Camden Gazette,* one styling himself "Cynicus", retorts in equally ponderous lines of which the following few are specimens:

## "KIRKWOOD"

### TO VATICIDE

POET LAUREATE TO THE GODDESS OF DULLNESS

Dear Vaticide!
Sudden you dipped your pen in ink,
Then filled your glass and took a drink;
Scribbled a line,—threw down your pen,
Then filled your glass, and drank again.
And now the fumes of grog arose
Into your brain, your fancy glows,
And harsh as croaking raven's bode,
Your discordant numbers flowed.
Now hoarse and hoarser, rolls along,
The burden of your mystic song,
And copious nonsense streams around,
With uncouth rhyme, and stunning sound. Etc., etc.

There will probably be no dissent in awarding the laurel to Peter in this literary contest. We may remark in passing that Peter's allusion to the "mighty steeple" gives us puzzle. What steeple in 1817 stood in Camden? Our only solution is that Peter imported the steeple by poetic license merely to rhyme with "people". We have been always under the impression that the first steeple in Camden was that erected in 1822 over the Presbyterian Church, and one later in 1825 over the old market.

On July 17, 1818, Kirkwood lots were purchased from Col. John Kershaw by Thomas Salmond, Abraham DeLeon, Alexander Young and Dr. E. H. Anderson. On ground just west of Lot No. 1 Salmond built the large residence now known as "Goodie Castle". The premises adjoining the village on the east, some thirty acres, were purchased from Kershaw in 1820 by William Lang. Here Gen. James Chesnut, the succeeding owner, about 1854, built the residence still standing to which he gave the name of "Kamtchatka".

Benjamin Perkins established the village of South Kirkwood adjoining Col. John Kershaw's village on the south, and in 1827 sold lots to Royal Bullard and Wm. E. Johnson. A plat of South Kirkwood, dated 1831, by Joseph Kershaw, grandson of the first Joseph, is in our possession. The "Old Spring" in the upper corner is Mortimer Spring, which name had then, it seems, become obsolete. On Lot No. 27 today stands "The Hobkirk Inn" a tourist resort (the first) established in Camden by F. W. Eldredge, the main building of which was formerly the residence of Col. W. M. Shannon, which he called "Pine Flat", from the forest of large pines which there abounded.

By degrees Mr. W. E. Johnson acquired all of South Kirkwood east of Lyttleton and north of Greene Streets. He devoted all of his leisure and a large part of his ample means to the creation here of gardens and grounds of notable beauty, for an adequate portrayal of which we must resort again to the old chronicler quoted above:

"The wilderness around the spring was bought out by a single proprietor (W. E. Johnson) and elegant grounds laid out, with fish pond, terraces and shrubbery, and the wild battle-field of nearly a hundred years ago is today one of the most attractive spots in the Southern country. The old Mortimer Spring with half a dozen others, cleared out and fitted up, pour out streams of the clearest water sufficient to make a small lake, that with its vines, shrubs and trailing roses make up a scene of rare beauty. Some years ago, after its embellishment, it was the writer's duty to show Mr. Bancroft, the historian, over the battle-field. He was then going over the Revolutionary fields of the South with a view to their description. We were rather proud of exhibiting this, the show place of the up-country, to one of the solid men of Boston, and watched him curiously as he stood, note-book in hand, conjuring in the mind's eye all the features of the fight; the red-coats in front pushing through the dense thickets, their bayonets gleaming, driving before them the pickets back upon the reserves—Kirkwood and his Delawares who stop the rush and give them something to think about—Gunby, Howard and Williams rapidly forming their line of battle across the crest of the hill. But the real scene then before the historian was so different. The still waters of the lake, reflecting a thousand shadows, the rush of the waterfall, the song of birds made up a scene from Arcady. The seer's vision seemed troubled. 'Sir', said he emphatically 'they have spoiled the battle-field'. Landscape gardening was then at a discount with Mr. Bancroft."

## "KIRKWOOD"

In Diagram No. 2 it has been attempted to show the changes produced by a century of time in the plans of North and South Kirkwood. The old demarkation of lots as first laid out have been merged, mingled and consolidated until now completely obliterated. The

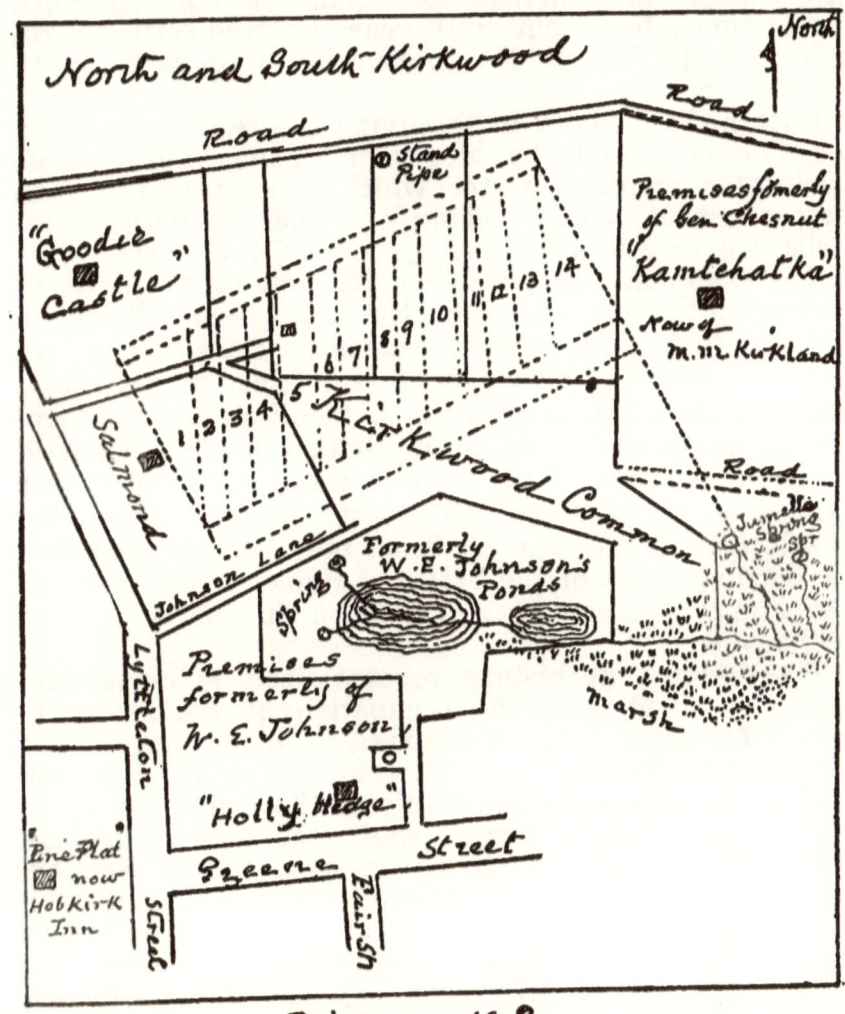

Diagram No. 2

dotted lines show precisely the location of North Kirkwood and the Common as originally planned. By a process of absorption of some parts and addition of other parts the shape of the Common has been greatly modified. In 1859, pursuant to permission granted by deeds from owners of the abutting lots and from descendants of Col. John Kershaw, a portion of the Common along Kirkwood Branch was enclosed by Mr. W. E. Johnson, and has remained under fence until now. So, other small sections have been acquired by other abutting owners in exchange for equal areas added, until the Common for about sixty years has the settled form indicated in Diagram No. 2, covering approximately 10 acres.

Within the memory of the living the residents around the Common used the Mortimer Spring and Jumelle Spring for drinking water which was carried up the long slope in buckets along well beaten paths. Jumelle Spring was on the very edge of the western line of the Common (Diagram No. 2), but by the drift of sand from the hillside and neglect it has been obliterated.

About fifty yards further east is Greene's Spring, enclosed by blocks of brown stone (see folded map of Camden). This name arose from a tradition that General Greene was here flanked by the British in 1781. General Chesnut once owned the premises and his grandfather figured as a patriotic resident of Camden during the Revolution. Hence the tradition may well be true that the opening shots of the battle of Hobkirk Hill occurred here and that Greene was present on this end of his line at the time.

The adage that history repeats itself is being constantly verified, and the occupation of Kirkwood by armed forces in 1781 re-occurred in 1865 when it was completely in possession of Sherman's troops. It is even possible that the episode of July 3, 1830 might be again duplicated. That occasion was the festival of the "Glorious Fourth", which in that year fell on Sunday, and was celebrated in Kirkwood apart from Camden. A copy of the *Camden Journal* of that day survives to tell the tale. We learn that the ladies were conspicuous in the Kirkwood event, preparing a sumptuous banquet, and that the Camdenites were quite piqued at the "Kirkers" for acting so independently. At 3 o'clock a party of some sixty or eighty were seated at the table of Dr. E. H. Anderson who presided. Among the toasts indulged was one on Kirkwood, quite neatly turned in these words: "Classic ground, consecrated by the blood of him whose name it bears, his devotion to liberty pure

## "KIRKWOOD"

as its air, our gratitude unceasing as its springs." At 5 o'clock the party was aroused by the sound of a bugle from the woods, followed by the clatter of Capt. McRae's "Camden Dragoons". William J. Grant, a member of the troop, presented himself at the head of the table and delivered himself of a grandiloquent speech on the sentiment: "The soldier's homage to beauty—his incentive and his reward." That evening was given over to a ball, in which the belles and beaus of Camden and Kirkwood combined in revelry.

The local bard who produced the following gallant attempt at a charade on Kirkwood, found in the *Kershaw Gazette* of 1876, doubtless in his boyhood took part in those pompous ceremonies of 1830:

### 1

"In olden time with pike and sword
All sternly gathering there,
To guard the banner of the Lord
Fierce men had knelt in prayer,
And now within my "first" doth raise
The true heart's solemn song of praise.

### 2

Come wander then along with me,
Beneath the old oak's kindly shade,
Here well might be the "trysting tree"
Where Robin and his men have laid,
And Friar "Tuck" and "Little John" and "Marian".
A child now could
My "second" tell you if he would.

### 3

The bending pine responsive calls,
In murmurs floating through the air,
My whole where yon fountain falls
Sounding the soft name everywhere.
A name amid the sudden rout
And fierce attack, a battle shout.
Hark! to the cry, 'tis ringing yet,
You cannot sure that name forget."

Since publication of the first volume of *Historic Camden* the following named citizens have served as Mayors of Camden:

| | | |
|---|---|---|
| 1906 H. G. Carrison | | 1918 S. F. Brasington |
| 1908 F. M. Zemp | | 1920 W. J. Dunn |
| 1910 F. M. Zemp | | 1922 H. G. Carrison, Jr. |
| 1912 S. F. Brasington | | 1924 H. G. Carrison, Jr. |
| 1914 S. F. Brasington | | 1926 C. P. DuBose |
| 1916 C. H. Yates | | |

# CHAPTER II.
## LOCALITIES AROUND CAMDEN

(Distances from Camden are estimated from the Court House, corner of Broad Street and Lafayette Avenue.)

*Battlefield of Camden.*—About eight miles north of Camden, marked by a granite block erected on spot where Baron DeKalb fell.

*Cool Springs.*—About three miles north of Camden. This name traces back to early days and occurs in the original grant of this property to Sarah Nesbit in 1767. Here John Boykin built in 1832. His residence was, in 1853, enlarged and remodeled by Reuben Hamilton, architect, for James B. Cureton. It is a notable structure with its extensive porches and sixty-four columns.

*Knights Hill.*—About six miles northwest of Camden. It's name runs as far back as 1781 in which year we find it mentioned in the Diary of Samuel Mathis.[1]

*Marengo.*—About six miles northeast of Camden, a mill site established in 1801 by Duncan McRae, the great victory of Napoleon being then of fresh impression—hence the name: this according to a statement by Mr. Colin McRae.

*Hyco.*—About seven miles northeast of Camden, an old name probably derived from the Indians. A spring near the highway marks this locality and near by is the station of Shepherd on the Seaboard Railway.

*Trent Hill.*—About four miles east of Camden on road to Marengo Mill. The name probably derived from Dr. John Trent who figured in Camden prior to 1800.

*Malvern Hill.*—About two miles east of Camden quite an eminence overlooking the town. This name occurs in James Kershaw's Diary under an entry in 1808 in which year he notes moving to this spot from Lucknow.

*Paint Hill.*—About two miles southeast of Camden. It is an old tradition that the Indians here obtained colorings from the various clays of the bluff with which to paint their bodies. This name is of long standing

---
[1] See Vol. I, *Historic Camden.*

and is found in John Boykin's map of Kershaw County executed in 1820. We have heard the statement of an old resident that the Indian name for this locality was "Patapatagoodoo."

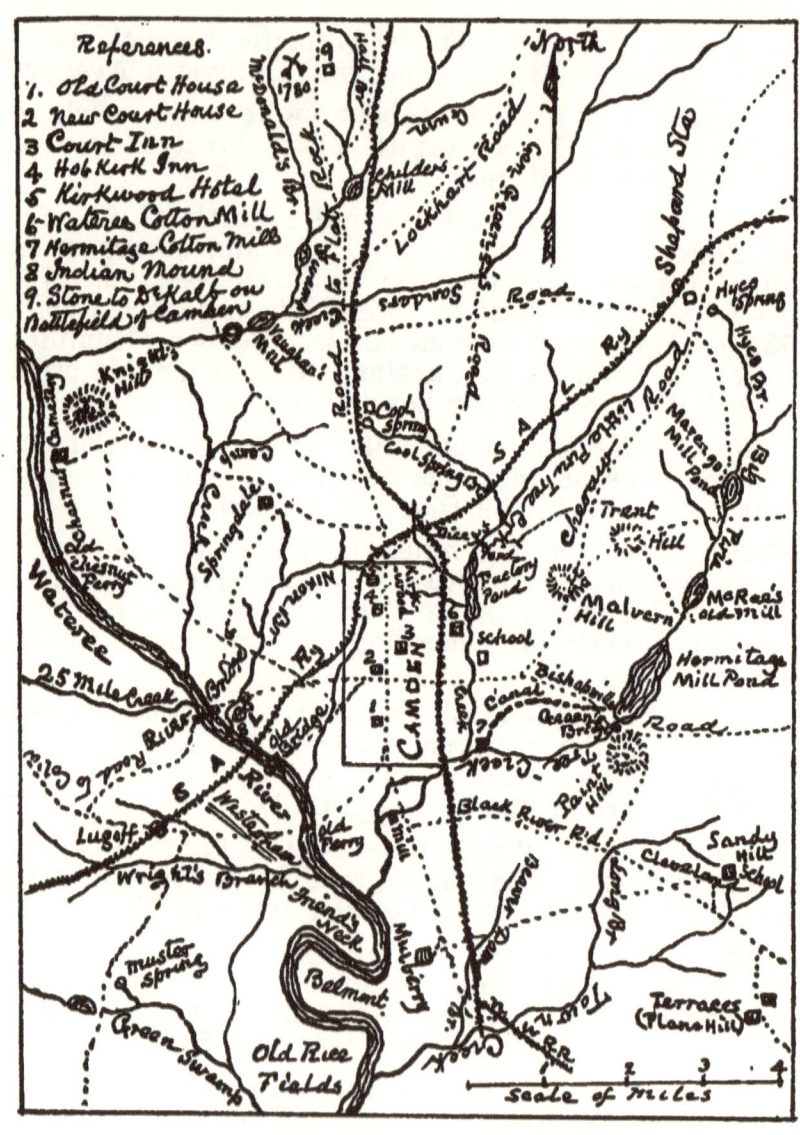

Localities Vicinity of Camden - Diagram No. 3

## Localities Around Camden

*Terraces.*—About seven miles southeast of Camden. This was the residence of Governor Stephen D. Miller, 1828-1830, called by him "Plane Hill" which name it bore until recent years. It was later the home of A. Hamilton Boykin, who is said to have constructed the Terraced Garden from which the modern name arises. It is now the Charlotte Thompson School.

*Mulberry.*—About four miles south of Camden. This large brick mansion was built by James Chesnut in 1820, and is still occupied by his descendants. Its exterior is plain, the interior handsome. The broad expanse of park and massive oaks give to this old homestead an air of grandeur perhaps unequalled in these parts.

*Muster Spring.*—About seven miles southwest of Camden (across the river) at foot of Stony Hill. This is the boldest spring in Kershaw County and was probably the scene of military musters in by-gone days.

*Springdale.*—About three miles northwest of Camden, on the road to Knights Hill. This was the home of the old Adamson family—removed from a point nearer the river. It has lately been converted into a Country Club House.

*Flat Rock.*—About fifteen miles due north of Camden. A high plateau and hillside of granite around which settlement a group of staunch and steady families have resided since Colonial days. Here in old times was the scene of many a military muster and political debate. The Rock is pitted with small circular basins, which doubtless suggested the tradition that when the American Army was in flight along the road from the disastrous battle-field of Camden, some miles to the south, barrels of liquor were emptied into these natural bowls to attract the fugitives to rally here, but after a hasty dram they kept on at accelerated speed.

# CHAPTER III.

### PEN PICTURES—COMMERCIAL, SOCIAL, ECONOMIC

1756.—Jervis, in his "Ceramics", states that, as early as 1756, clay was exported to England from South Carolina and was quite extensively used by Wedgwood and other potters. "Mr. Lloyd", of Charleston, South Carolina, says he, "sent a box of porcelain earth from the Cherokee Country to the Earl of Hyndford, who deputized Mr. Goldney, a very serious gentleman, to make experiments on the principle of Chinese porcelain."

This was evidently John Lloyd, a brother-in-law of Richard Champion, one of the great English potters, who, at Mr. Lloyd's instigation, settled in Kershaw County in 1784, with a view presumably to the utilization of the superior pottery clay found near Camden, though he does not seem to have carried such ideas into effect.[1]

That experiments had been made with the Camden clay is evident from the letter of Josiah Wedgwood to his patron, Sir W. Meredith, 1766: "Permit me to mention a subject of a public nature which greatly alarms us (the Staffordshire potters). The bulk of our manufactures we export to the Continent and islands of America. We send them an amazing quantity, our home consumption in comparison is very trifling. We are apprehensive of losing this trade, as pot works are set on foot in Carolina (Bartlam, at Camden), and they are at this time hiring a number of our hands for the establishment of these same works. They have every material there, equal, if not superior, to our own, for carrying on this manufacture."

Jervis says further that Wedgwood sent out an agent by the name of Griffiths, under heavy bond, who shipped him much clay from the neighborhood of Camden. The Revolution, says he, put a stop to all fear of this threatening competition.

1760.—Prior to the Revolution, Joseph Kershaw's mills on Pinetree Creek were turning out "Fine Carolina flour" as early as 1760.[2] Colonel Kershaw also operated saw and grist mills, indigo works, a tobacco warehouse,

---

[1] See "Champion" in *Historic Camden*—Part I: Colonial and Revolutionary.
[2] South Carolina *Gazette*.

## Pen Pictures—Commercial, Social, Economic

a distillery, and a large store in which, at different times, his brother Eli Kershaw and John Chesnut were partners.

Samuel Wyly's store antedated Kershaw's as a centre of trade in and about Pinetree Hill (Camden).

1771.—Robert Milhous' widow offers for sale his tan yard, bark mill, utensils, etc., at Camden; also "one negro man used to the tanning and shoemaking trade."[1]

John Adamson and Thomas Charlton were also merchants here at this early period.

1772.—The *South Carolina Gazette and Country Journal* of May 5, 1772, relates that "His Excellency, Lord Charles-Greville Montagu, our Governor" had set out the previous week, "with his Lady" on a tour to Camden and other "Back Parts of this Province," and, in the issue of May 19, states that they had safely returned.

1781.—Samuel Mathis, in his Diary,[2] mentions the following places of business in Camden:

> Murkeson, the Taylor.
> Castello, Shoes.
> Thompson, the Blacksmith.
> Bettie, Knives, etc.
> Adamson & Co., General Merchandise.
> Mrs. Dinkins, Butter.
> Downs, Rum.

1786.—An advertisement in the Charleston paper offers for rent in Camden "the large store on Broad Street, upwards of sixty feet in front (formerly Kershaw, Chesnut & Co.), where about forty wagons have been dispatched in a day, in compleat order for a Dry Goods Store."

Elkanah Watson, a northern veteran of the Revolution, visiting Camden in 1786, says, in his "Memoirs", that, at that date, the town had fifty dwellings, and that it commanded a valuable interior trade in tobacco, flour, deerskins, indigo and beef. These commodities were transported to Charleston "by a circuitous and expensive water carriage, down the Santee and by Bull's Island."

---

[1] *South Carolina Gazette.*
[2] See *Historic Camden*—Part I: Colonial and Revolutionary.

1790.—*The American Gazetteer* (London, 1798) gives some facts about Camden based on the census of 1790. It is spoken of as a "post-town", containing about one hundred and twenty houses, among them an Episcopal church,[1] a Courthouse and a gaol; "the navigable river" on which it stands enabled it to do "a lively trade with the back-country."

1791.—Washington, when at Camden, 1791, notes in his Diary, that the staple agricultural products about the town were corn, tobacco and indigo: also that vessels carrying fifty or sixty hhds. of tobacco came up to the Ferry there, where there was a tobacco warehouse.

Colonel Shannon, in his *Old Times in Camden*[2], attributes the great prosperity of the place just after the Revolution partly to the splendid flour mills established on Pinetree Creek by Broome and "other Virginians of Lee's Legion", partly to its location at the head of navigation on the river. For a long period it was the most important town in the interior of the state. The districts of Chesterfield, Darlington, Sumter, Fairfield, York and Chester of South Carolina, and the counties of Cabarras, Monroe, Mecklenburg and Union of North Carolina, traded in Camden. "By the close of the century, the rapid importation of slaves, the invention of the cotton gin, the consequent rapid spread of the cultivation of cotton" increased the wealth and importance of the town. "An old lady still living" (1872) recalled that in her youth the ordinary employment of the evenings for the ladies and children was separating the seed from the cotton.

1801.—Mills ("Statistics") informs us that, in the year 1801, 40,000 bushels of wheat were consumed at two or three flour mills within one mile of Camden, and that the product in flour was six thousand barrels of a superior quality, much of which was exported. The introduction of the cotton gin about this time led to the early abandonment of wheat as a staple crop.

Mills says also that the castor oil plant was being successfully cultivated. Mr. Rudolph of Camden had several years earlier planted fifty or sixty acres of it, the yield being one hundred to one hundred and fifty gal-

---

[1]Presbyterian, doubtless: no record of any other at that time.
[2]A series of articles contributed to a Camden paper.

## PEN PICTURES—COMMERCIAL, SOCIAL, ECONOMIC

lons to the acre of cold-drawn oil, which was quite equal to the imported article.

The influence of cotton raising on the institution of slavery is interestingly told by the following census reports:

|      | Free Whites | Kershaw County Slaves | Free Negroes |
|------|-------------|-----------------------|--------------|
| 1792 | 4,000       | 1,456                 |              |
| 1800 | 4,606       | 2,530                 | 104          |
| 1820 | 5,628       | 6,692                 | 112          |

1802.—Drayton, in his *View of South Carolina*, says that Camden, in 1802, contained two hundred dwelling houses and that it was somewhat larger than Granby, a town on the Congaree, of which there is now not a vestige except the old burying ground. Columbia, a mile from Granby, then had less than one hundred dwellings. There were in the vicinity of Camden three excellent flour mills, by which the growth of wheat in the Waxhaws settlement and even North Carolina was much encouraged, and "superfine wheat flour" was exported from this place. The salary of the "arsenal keepers and powder receivers", at Camden, Georgetown and Beaufort, was fifty dollars each. Dancing, horse-racing, ball-playing and rifle-shooting were the amusements of the time, gentlemen often shooting for prizes, such as a beef, instead of raffling. Citizens were famed for fine horsemanship, boys of seven or eight riding back and forth to school and, shortly after, learning the use of a gun. Before the Revolution, says he, young men went to England to school, but, since the War, to the Northern and Eastern colleges, after completing the courses at the local Grammar Schools "of which the notable ones are at Georgetown, Beaufort and Camden."

1804.—Mrs. Phineas Thornton, in her *Reminiscences* (mss.) says that when she first came to Camden, in 1804, there were only six houses above the Court House[1]— one at the "Nixon Hotel corner" opposite, two small houses on the same square, and a two-story house "occupied by Dr. Joe Lee's father" at the "Holleyman Hotel corner."[2] Above this was a swamp or marsh, often im-

---
[1] Corner of Broad and King Streets.
[2] Corner Broad and York Streets.

passable, wet and muddy and, after rain, full of water. The sixth house was "an old one, piazza looking as if ready to fall, where the McLelland house now stands, and, indeed, that is the same house, often repaired and enlarged.[1] Above this, somewhere between Dr. Lee's present residence[2] and the McClelland house, was a small log cabin, or house, which gave to this portion of Camden the name of Log Town." All around these scattered houses were woods, and, in the marsh mentioned, "ducks in the pond were often killed."

The "square" opposite the Court House, says she, was "filled up with beautiful houses, all nearly constructed alike, stores below and family residences above, with a parlor downstairs in the rear, or side, of the storeroom." Among these houses were Dan Carpenter's and Reverend Isaac Smith's. "The Ladies Store, or Fancy Store, kept by Alexander Matheson, was just opposite." The Court House was a wooden building, "later used by Drucker for a store." She had often heard preaching in that building.

1807.—The wife of the first Dr. Isaac Alexander, who was Sarah Thompson of Connecticut, writing in 1857, has left (mss.) a most graphic and delightful account of the Camden that she came to as a bride half a century earlier. She asks:

"Who among you recollects Dinkins' Tavern, the last house in town, opposite the dwelling of Dr. Alexander? Who now living can say, there in Dinkins' Long Room many a pleasant hour have I spent in 'tripping on the light fantastic toe', where it was not unusual for all Camden to assemble who were not so old as to have lost all the springs of youth, or whose religious scruples did not forbid the innocent pastime?

"In speaking of the social customs of that day, we hesitate to draw the comparison between the past and present. Whether the ladies of that day, dressed in calico or gingham at a party, enjoyed less the hilarities or festivities of the time than they of our day, stiff in their silks and elaborate flounces, is a matter that might admit of much argument. There was at least one advantage in those days: their minds were not occupied in

---

[1]Now the Baptist Parsonage, moved back from its old site on Broad Street, where the new Baptist Church stands.
[2]Now the Baum place, town lot No. 720.

care for their apparel, and, should they chance to sustain any damage, the cost and time would be less to repair it. The careful fathers and mothers found less disturbance in their purse strings. It was not necessary then to have more time than from morning to evening to prepare for a ball or tea party. The young gentlemen would send out cards in the morning for a ball at night at Dinkins', and some they would call on where intimately acquainted, and a verbal invitation was just as acceptable as any. Mrs. Dinkins was celebrated for her entertainments: she had no need of confectioners. She, as well as all the ladies of that day, could beat up a pound cake and prepare a whip syllabub at short notice: a pound cake, some wafers, broiled venison, ham and a cup of tea was ample viands. Occasionally the large china punch bowl went around among the ladies. If the gentlemen had anything stronger in the side room, their conduct in the ball-room did not betray it: perfect respect and politeness marked their manners among the ladies. All ranks and degrees mixed freely: the rich and the poor all met and exchanged the courtesies and civilities of life, with no respect of persons, except where vice had drawn the barrier." At all such functions, including "quiltings", there was "no slandering or backbiting or uncharitable constructions." In politics, there was perfect accord, all having too recently escaped from a common danger to be dissatisfied with a government of their own creation. "Abolitionism" and "the ranting demagogue" were unheard of. And, as if this were not Arcadian enough, she continues: "Steam cars and telegraphs were never dreamt of: the cows grazed quietly in their pastures without disturbance from the whistle or fear of being crushed beneath the wheels, and people were content to travel in the stage to Charleston at the rate of three miles an hour and plunge through Nelson's Swamp, be it high or low water, happy if they got there in a week with life and whole bones."

Mrs. Alexander locates a few stores and residences for us (in 1807). John Adamson's residence, later moved to Logtown and "modernized", was on the southwest corner of the Central Public Square (Lots 56, 57, 58). Next below it was his store, which some years later, became the Post Office. Opposite Adamson's residence was Major Joseph Mickle's dwelling, with store in front. Other residences looking on the Square were those of "Esquire Brown, Esquire Mathis, Mr. Lang, Lawyer Blanding and others." A public pump was on the Square, and a Revolutionary cannon stood, "as a post", on the corner near Blanding's. From Dinkins' up to Logtown was reckoned a mile and the street was closely built with stores and dwellings up to the "big ditch". The jail stood opposite the Court House, on the site of the later Market House. It, with most of the town, was destroyed in the great fire of 1813.

We must again quote her language for a very clever and amusing character sketch: "On the side of the ditch next Logtown stood one solitary house, the residence of a Frenchman by the name of Barillon, . . . who for many years held the office of Constable, Magistrate *pro tem*, a baker, a collector, and one who was an awful terror to negroes, whose backs could bear testi-

mony to his tender mercies. Should any property be missing, you had only to send for Barillon. He would present himself with his large cane, and the Grand Marshal of France never bore himself more pompously than this official armed with a little brief authority. If it was a possible thing, the goods abstracted were forthcoming and the criminal punished as sure as fate. For upwards of thirty years he held his baton of authority and ruled despotically, but, alas, like all other sublunary things, he has gone and none has ever filled his place since as did the redoubtable Christopher Barillon."[1]

[1]Christopher Louis Barillon's bold signature attached to his petition for citizenship, of date Camden, Nov. 8, 1802, is in the author's hands.

## PEN PICTURES—COMMERCIAL, SOCIAL, ECONOMIC

Mrs. Alexander informs us that, about the year 1817, "a spirit of migration began to agitate the houses. Sickness had driven the inhabitants to seek out summer resorts and the buildings took a notion they would not be left behind, so they, one moonlight night, started up of Logtown, . . . and in a short time there was nothing left but the land. Ancient Nineveh has been found and many relics discovered, but of the Camden of Revolutionary days naught remains." Alas, too true!

The following extract proves this witty chronicler a prophet as well: "Judging Camden by its present locomotive propensities, those who live a few years hence will see it perhaps on the top of Hobkirk Hill."

Of the period between the Revolution and the War of 1812, Colonel Shannon says: "Many of the founders of the best society of the District came to Camden at this time." A very fine set of young men came to the front during the first years of the 19th century. Though older than himself he was associated with most of them. "They lived to be prominent citizens and did much to complete the good work laid out by their predecessors in giving form, shape, tone and finish to a society unequalled in the interior of the state. We never saw a purer, higher, nobler society than Camden owned at this period. For lofty bearing, high courtesy, generous hospitality, manly independence and individuality, indeed for all the virtues which adorn the citizen, we have never seen them surpassed anywhere and never known any one community in which was gathered such a proportion of excellence."

As examples, he names: Colonel James S. Deas, Colonel John Boykin, Governor McWillie, General James Blair, Colonel Chapman Levy, General James W. Cantey, Major John Cantey, Major John Whitaker, Dr. William Whitaker, Mr. Wm. W. Lang, Captain Thomas Lang, Dr. Alfred Brevard, Colonel John Chesnut, Mr. Charles J. Shannon, Major Benjamin Elmore, Colonel Henry G. Nixon, Colonel William O. Nixon, Colonel John Carter, Mr. James C. Doby, Dr. John McCaa, Dr. Edward H. Anderson, Dr. Abraham DeLeon, Mr. Lemuel Boykin, Mr. John J. Blair, Mr. William E. Johnson, Captain John McRae, Mr. Thomas Hopkins, General Wm. Hopkins.

1815.—The *City Gazette and Daily Advertiser* of Charleston states that the ladies of Camden had subscribed liberally for the purchase of a service of plate to be presented to the Hero of the West, General Andrew Jackson. The "rich and elegant silver vase" was duly presented the next year. General Jackson in his will says that the vase was given him "by the ladies of Charleston." (?)

1816.—The *Camden Gazette* of April 4, 1816, states that Broad Street was one mile long and contained one hundred and twenty dwellings, stores and shops. There were thirty stores, "wholesale and retail". Four religious denominations were represented, all but the Episcopal having "convenient houses of worship". The Society of Free Masons had a handsome brick Hall. Other public buildings were "a large framed Court House, an elegant brick market and Library Room, a large wooden building originally intended for an Academy belonging to the Orphan Society, a handsome brick Arsenal, a jail and two fire-engine houses". Seventeen or eighteen districts in which cotton was the chief staple, between the Yadkin River in North Carolina and the Broad in South Carolina, were tributary to the town. The only drawback was the want of banks. Cotton was selling at 23-25 cents, corn $1.50, bacon 13-15 cents, tallow 16-18 cents, beeswax 25 cents.

## BUSINESS DIRECTORY: 1816-24.

(From advertisements in Camden papers.)

1816-24—Phineas Thornton, Groceries, Garden Seed, Raccoon Skins, etc. (one door below Market, on Broad).

J. B. Mathieu, Groceries, also profiles taken (above ditch, near DeKalb Street).

Josiah Smith, Postmaster.

Henry Abbott, Dry Goods, etc. (upper part of Camden, in new building opposite Mr. James Clark's residence).

A. & M. DeLeon, Drugs.

Frank A. DeLiesseline, Lawyer.

W. Blanding, Drugs.

Charles and John Meugy, Dry Goods, etc.

Kohler & Miller, Tan Yard (formerly of James Clark).

Lee & DeLeon, Dry Goods, Groceries, etc.

William Brown, Dry Goods.

PEN PICTURES—COMMERCIAL, SOCIAL, ECONOMIC

Jumelle & Young, Patent Medicines.
Francis S. Lee, Sheriff, Kershaw District.
William Brasington, Jailor, Kershaw District.
Samuel Mathis & Co., Dry Goods, etc.
Jonathan Eccles, Groceries, etc.
James K. Douglas & Co., Dry Goods, etc.
Mrs. Carpenter, Mould Candles.
Hugh McCall, Dry Goods.
Shannon & Ballard, Dry Goods, etc.
Coleman & English, Dry Goods, etc.
Alexander Young, Patent Medicines, Jewelry, etc.
J. Lyon, Dry Goods.
Robert Mickle, Dry Goods.
E. M. Bronson, Tinware.
Francis & John Cook, Bricklaying & Plastering.
James Clark & Co., Dry Goods.
Levy Solomon, Fancy Goods, etc., (at Mr. McKain's house near Big Ditch).
Uriah Blackmon, Wines, Crockery, etc.
B. Carter, Tan Yard.
Joseph Thornton, Dry Goods.
William C. Adams, Hair Dressing & Shaving.
Peter Warren, Shoes, etc.
William Parker, Gold & Silver Work (at "Magazine").
Allen Jones & Drury Campbell, Gin Making (King Street next to Printing Office).
William Atkinson & John Workman, Saw Gins made and Repaired (at sign of Sheaf, Rake & Hoe).
Trapp, Patterson & Wilie Vaughn, Dry Goods.
General Cantey's New Store.
Latta & Foster, Merchants.
J. & F. Blair, General Merchandise.
Gilkeyson & Blair, Taylors.
Samuel Lopez & Co., Merchandise (corner Broad & DeKalb).
Hodges & McCaa, Dry Goods, Cognac, Brandy, etc.
William Matheson, New Store (two doors from Masonic Hall, opposite J. & J. W. Cantey).
Latta & Kilgore, Merchandise.
H. Levy & Company, Merchandise.
C. Emile Catonnet, Fruits, etc.
John Kershaw, Lumber Mills.
George Forbes, Bookbinding, Stationery.
Abram Blanding & James G. Holmes, Lawyers.
John B. Morin, Hair-Dresser, Hair-Worker & Barber ("lately from Paris: teaches small sword practice at Havis' Ball-Room").

Camden Medical Association: A. DeLeon, William Blanding, E. H. Anderson, B. W. Carter, Alfred Brevard, John McCaa, W. B. Whitaker.
Ilai Nunn, Dancing.
MacFeat & Thompson, Furniture.
Thomas E. Baker, House & Sign Painting, Gilding.
A. Matheson & Co., Dry Goods, etc.
J. White & Co., Boots & Shoes.
W. E. Johnson & Co., Merchandise.
Murray, Robinson & Co., Merchandise.
W. Olds, Boots & Shoes.
E. Hurley, Dentist.
Alex. Rodgers, Auction Room.
H. R. Cook, Carriages, etc., Made and Repaired.
I. Wood, Tailor.
William Blanding, Drugs, Wholesale & Retail.
Charles A. Bullard, Lawyer.
A. Burr, Boots & Shoes.
John Workman, General Merchandise.
L. F. Breaker, Boots & Shoes, Wholesale & Retail.
Dr. S. Blanding, Physician.
William B. Hart, Lawyer.
Charles Jugnot, Groceries.
Henry G. Nixon, Lawyer.
Jonathan S. Jenkins, Vocal Music (over Market).
"Camden Book Store".
Coe & Strong, Penmanship (in Council Room).
"Camden Candle Manufactory".

1822.—Long before the advent of modern water works, a tax on water was imposed in Camden, as we see by this published notice: "All persons owning occupied tenements within the town of Camden (not having wells thereon in good order) are hereby required to pay their well-tax to the recorder, on or before the 1st of April next.   WILLIAM G. O'CAIN, Recorder."

1824.—*The Southern Chronicle and Camden Aegis* says that Camden had seemed dead from 1818 to 1823; but the establishment of the Branch Bank of the State in 1822 and the building of the Orphan Society Academies and the Presbyterian Church on DeKalb Street, in 1824, marked the beginning of better times. Seven boats with cargoes of various descriptions arrived on December 28 and other boats were engaged from Columbia and elsewhere to "carry off the large quantities of cot-

## PEN PICTURES—COMMERCIAL, SOCIAL, ECONOMIC

ton filling the stores and streets". Camden was drawing cotton from within sixty miles of Charleston.

1825.—LaFayette's visit to lay the corner-stone of the DeKalb monument is treated in another chapter.

Cotton sold at thirty cents on June 4 of this year.

1826.—Mills ("Statistics") says that, in this year, river lands near Camden were selling for thirty to sixty dollars per acre, best uplands from five to ten dollars, while pine lands near Camden would bring scarcely fifty cents per acre. The new court house building at Camden "will be superior in its design to any in the state, both for convenience of accommodation, beauty and permanency"[1]. The town hall, containing a market place and a subscription library, was across the street. The high tower of this building, ornamented with a clock and surmounted by a conspicuous spire, gave "an air of importance to the place". The consummation of the great public works on the Catawba River—the Wateree and Rocky Mount canals—"will open great facilities of communication with a rich and extensive back country", extending into North Carolina. Twenty thousand bales of cotton were purchased in Camden during 1825. Subscriptions were raised for the "Jefferson Relief Fund": Thomas Jefferson was about to lose "Monticello".

1827.—Census of Kirkwood: Whites 45; Blacks 59.

1828.—The *Camden Journal*, of December 6, states that Broad Street had for several days been literally choked with wagons, carts and all the various vehicles ever made use of in the conveyance of produce and merchandise. "On Wednesday, eighty-four wagons were counted at one time, loaded with cotton, corn, wheat, flour, iron, etc., and upwards of one hundred and fifty arrived during the course of the day. Thirty-three river boats arrived on Tuesday." A boat load of Camden flour sold in Charleston at six dollars per barrel; twelve thousand, nine hundred bales of cotton were purchased in Camden from September 1st to December 27th.

1829.—This was the year of the great fire; eighty-five buildings burned.[2]

Postage rates, as published, were: Letters, thirty miles, six cents; eighty miles, twelve and one-half cents; one

---
[1] Robert Mills himself was the architect of this building, as of the Presbyterian Church and the DeKalb Monument.
[2] See *Historic Camden*—Part I.

hundred fifty miles, eighteen and three-quarters cents; four hundred miles, twenty-five cents; newspapers, to any point in the state, one cent.

The "Independent Fire Engine Company," white, volunteer, incorporated.

1830.—The *Camden Journal* in an editorial on *Camden—A Tale of the South*,[1] understood to have been written by "a gentleman from Kentucky", says: "Here have we the moss-grown graves of the gallant Marylanders . . . and the redoubts where the chivalry of Merry England intrenched itself." These graves were doubtless on Hobkirk Hill, a reference to their supposed location being made in our first volume. The remains of one of the redoubts in the lower end of the town are still to be seen. The earthworks near the cemetery are also probably referred to.

1831.—A prosperous year. The same paper calls attention to the building of a "beautiful church for the Episcopalians, a large and splendid hotel", several capacious brick stores and many residences, two of which were "large and expensive mansions".

The "Handel and Haydn Society" meets: D. Carpenter, Secretary and Treasurer.

1833.—A gloomy year in business. The *Camden Journal* remarks that, if Columbia succeeds in getting a branch of the railroad to that place, Camden will be ruined.

Temperance Societies were very active at this time.

1834.—This was the period of the great wave of migration to the southwest, an account of which is found in another chapter.

1835.—Many handsome residences were built in Kirkwood, by persons seeking immunity from fever during the heated season in the lower part of the town. The paper states that Kirkwood was first settled seventeen years before at "Kirkwood Spring", but that it "now extends from Hobkirk Hill on the left to Carter's Mill on the right".

Plenty of fruit that year; fine peaches were selling at twelve and one-half cents per bushel.

Twenty thousand bales of cotton were shipped. The need of another bank was very great, the two already here—"The Agency of the Planters and Merchants

---

[1] We have vainly tried to find a copy of this book.

Bank" and the "Branch Bank of the State", not being sufficient for the business done.

Eight hundred people (white and black) passed through the town in one week going westward—three hundred in one party.

1837.—C. J. Shannon, A. Matheson and Alexander Young were sent as delegates by the town to Augusta, Georgia, to try to establish direct trade with European ports.

1825-40.—Of the generation of young men who came along in the late 20's and 30's, Colonel Shannon says that they made in the fine social record of the town a "frightful gap, a sad, gloomy and desolate picture, due to the demon, rum". This he attributes partly to the great wave of prosperity following the War of 1812 and partly to the political excitement and its round of barbecues, public dinners, suppers and night meetings. Habits and tastes were formed in such scenes that were never shaken off. Reared in luxury and idleness, the youth of the day made pleasure the business of life, and "passed off the stage of action leaving at best for their record a void, not even presenting at last the original 'talent wrapped in a napkin' ". This, he adds, is the only blot on Camden's history and a terrible lesson.

It may be noted that, in an effort to counteract this deplorable condition, temperance societies were formed and were very vigorous for many years. The leading temperance advocate of the day was John Belton O'Neall. He was a frequent visitor and lecturer on the subject in Camden, and one of the Societies had an oil portrait made of him, which hung for years in their hall.

1841.—Celebration of the 13th Anniversary of the "Camden Debating Club": elegant dinner "without wine"; J. C. West, orator; Dr. James H. Carlisle, then at school in Camden, proposed a toast.

"A cold water man" suggests, in the *Camden Journal*, that "the bell" be rung at 10 p. m., instead of earlier, from May 1st to October 1st, in order that people having to get water from a distance may do so without passes: a hint of "Run, nigger, run, the paterol'll catch you!"

"The Wateree Agriculture Society" was organized at Swift Creek Church: President, Colonel James Chesnut; Vice-Presidents, Thomas Lang and William Sanders; silver cups and other premiums to be offered; annual exhibits of stock, produce, etc., to be held.

1842.—(From the *Camden Journal*: bard unknown)
Lines on seeing the beautiful Miss M—— walking up Broad Street without a bustle.

> Refreshing sight! That these degenerate days
> Can boast a woman, with a soul that scorns
> To follow Fashion in her monstrous ways
> Where she disfigures that she would adorn;
> Who, standing as the champion of her sex,
> Throws off the horrid incubus which has
> So long maintained its sway upon the backs,
> Making of fair proportion one huge mass:
> She has the thanks of one, (a poor reward),
> Who, in this *bustling* world, has not lost
> His love of nature, but who, with the old bard,
> Thinks "beauty unadorned adorned the most".

1843.—At a meeting of the Dialectic Club, composed of pupils of the Male Academy, W. B. Carlisle proposed the toast (in cold water): "The merchants of Camden—For intelligence, uprightness and integrity, they may proudly compare with their brethren anywhere and everywhere."

The "DeKalb Lyceum" met at the "New DeKalb Hall on Church Street; large and brilliant audience".

1844.—Temperance agitation continued very marked: William McWillie was president of one temperance society, A. M. Kennedy of another.

The town, as it appeared to a young man fresh from Scotland (the late Robert M. Kennedy), who arrived that year and spent the remainder of a long life as a citizen, is interestingly described by him in an article which he contributed to a local paper in 1894, entitled "Camden Fifty Years Ago". Only a few extracts can be given:

"Camden in those days had no railroad, and passengers got off at Gadsden. Arriving at that place, I found a stage run by Mr. James McEwen waiting for the mail and travellers. The driver was something of a curiosity to me. He had a very sallow complexion, sandy hair, broad-brimmed hat, and drab overcoat cut in French fashion, short waist and long skirt, with two huge buttons between the shoulder blades.

## Pen Pictures—Commercial, Social, Economic

"I was the only passenger, and, unaccustomed to rough roads, thought my Jehu made a point to strike every stump and run into every rut. Pitched and jolted beyond endurance, I found refuge in the straw between the seats, managing in this way to reach my destination about midnight, with whole bones.

"The town had a quaint look, with its dingy frame buildings and sandy streets. The sidewalks, innocent of brick or flagstone and fringed with grass which was a receptacle for cigar stumps and trash, were interlaced with projecting gnarled roots, no lamps to light the path, and, when the trees were in leaf and the stores closed at night, it was Egyptian darkness. Hogs, horses and cows roamed at will through the streets.

"There was no apparent effort to make the stores attractive. They had low ceilings and small windows, and large dry goods boxes were placed in front to accommodate idlers and loungers, who passed their time whittling and gossiping. Inside these same stores, however, the shelves were filled with the products of the looms of Britain, France and Germany. The merchants were shrewd, substantial business men whose credit in the northern markets was second to none. The citizens were well-to-do and looked it, enjoying life in a rational way.

"The young gentleman of the time had his clothes made in Charleston or Columbia, and looked well in a French broadcloth suit costing from sixty to seventy dollars, a seven dollar hat, ten or twelve dollar boots, and a four or five dollar dress shirt. Add to these several hundred dollars invested in watch and jewelry, and you have a rather expensive ornament of society as it was at that time. The dandy wore long hair tucked behind his ears, very tight pumpsoled boots, gold-headed cane, diamond breast pin, finger ring and a three-button flashy vest."

Speaking of the annual review of the militia, a momentous occasion, he says:

"On that eventful morning, the roads leading to town were filled with vehicles of every description from the fine carriage down to the ox-cart, equestrians astride all sorts of four-footed animals, from the blooded Arab down to the two year old ox minus a saddle.

"The town was in excitement. Drums were beating, small boys in their glory, men busy here, there and everywhere. Officers from the fourth corporal to the captain felt their importance.

"In due time the companies were formed and filed out to Magazine Hill, where they were marched and counter-marched under a blazing sun for about two hours, when the colonel dispatched his aid to inform the reviewing officer that the regiment was ready for inspection. Presently down came the Governor, or Adjutant General, as the case might be, followed by a brilliant staff, mounted on splendidly caparisoned steeds; gorgeous in cocked hats and nodding plumes, blue coats with buff facings and buff breeches, gilded epaulettes, buttons, spurs, and bridle bits, high military boots and gauntlets up to the elbow, steeds curveting and prancing, they were 'the observed of all observers'.

"The regiment formed in line, the men armed to the teeth with swords and muskets down to hickory sticks and corn stalks. After cantering round the line, which had in sections a decided rams-horn tendency, the reviewing officer doffed his hat and made the usual speech, complimenting everybody on their fine appearance and military bearing. The glorification was followed by a grand hurrah from the crowd and a flourish of handkerchiefs from the fair sex in carriages. The reviewing officer and staff disappeared, as they had come, in a gallop, and the privates broke ranks to their great relief. Alas, many of them realized in after years what it was to be a soldier".

"The good old town then was rated third in the state in commerce and wealth."

1845.—Cotton four to six cents; corn forty-eight to fifty cents; bacon seven to seven and one-quarter cents.

1845.—Business Directory (from advertisements in local papers).

W. Anderson & Co., General Merchandise.
C. Matheson, General Merchandise & Bank Agent.
A. M. Kennedy, Dry Goods.
J. F. Sutherland, Furniture, manufactured by himself (opposite Baptist Church, above DeKalb Street).
E. W. Bonney, General Merchandise & Bank Agent.
A. Young, Books, etc.
William E. Johnson, General Merchandise & Bank Agent.
N. A. F. Brewer, Jewelry.

## Pen Pictures—Commercial, Social, Economic

H. Bartlett & Co., Shoes, Hats, etc.
M. Drucker & Co., General Merchandise.
William Rosser, Auction & Commission Business.
James L. Brasington, Tailor.
John Workman, General Merchandise & Bank Agent.
G. Alden, Pianos, Shoes, etc.
H. Wilkes, Gunsmith.
N. S. Punch, General Merchandise.
Chesnut & Carlisle, Attorneys at Law.
N. B. Arrants, Blacksmith & Wagon-Maker.
McDowall & Shannon, General Merchandise & Bank Agents.
H. Levy, General Merchandise.
J. R. McKain, Druggist.
J. D. Murray, Cotton Gins, etc.

1846.—Cotton eight and one-quarter to nine and three-eighths; "flour from the wagons", four dollars to four and one-half dollars per barrel; corn forty-five to fifty cents a bushel; "salt very scarce and high."

1848.—Dr. W. J. McKain and Dr. C. J. Shannon established an Infirmary for Chronic Diseases; terms: for medical treatment, including diet, etc., sixty cents per day; operations extra. This does not seem to have lasted very long. There was a strong prejudice against hospitals at that period.

1849.—A year of great prosperity, owing to the completion of the railroad to the town.

The Camden Debating Club, twenty-five years old, was revived after a long recess.

The Cadets of Temperance, composed of boys between twelve and eighteen, was organized by F. L. Villepigue, K. S. Moffat and W. E. Hughson.

Mr. Charles Perkins offered for sale a bale of wool weighing six hundred forty-five pounds raised in the county.

Mr. E. Sill completed the census of Kershaw District; males 2,421, females 2,523, total 4,944 (a gain of 1,000 since 1839). Population of Camden, including Kirkwood and Factory Village, 1,165.

### *Cotton Mills.*

From an editorial in the *Camden Journal*, June 30, 1849, we get some exceedingly interesting information about DeKalb Factory, at Camden, which for a time used negro operatives. "The stock is divided into four shares: Thomas Lang, Thomas J. Ancrum, and William Anderson, owning each a share; the fourth is owned by A. Young and William Gardiner, the skilful superintendent, whose personal attention is constantly given to the various branches of the establishment. The factory was established in 1838, with one thousand spindles for making yarn, but up to 1846, they were gradually increased so that now they nearly double that number, sixteen hundred and eighty spindles, forty looms, now run daily, making yarn and cotton osnaburgs, and consuming cotton equal in amount to a mill of three thousand or four thousand spindles, according to calculations usually made at the North."

The annual consumption of cotton was three hundred and sixty thousand pounds. "Last year over one thousand bales were consumed, and during the past month ninety-nine bales were worked up, making 8,205 pounds yarn and 47,935 yards osnaburgs. The osnaburgs weigh one-half pound to the yard and are well known in the Northern and Southern markets, and we learn from one of the company that they always command a higher price than those made at the North."

The monthly expense of the mill was a little less than nine hundred dollars; twenty weavers were employed, all white females, each one attending to about two looms, one or two to more, each receiving twelve to twenty dollars per month.

"For several years past, blacks were the principal operatives, except in the department of weaving, but white operatives are now generally employed, because they are less difficult to procure. The blacks have been discharged, except about thirty that belong to the company. The white operatives number now seventy-two, male and female. We are informed that the experience of the company is, that the blacks as operatives can compare favorably with the whites, and under some circumstances may be preferred.

"We believe the Company have never realized less than ten per cent upon their capital, but they have constantly invested the profits in additional improvements, so that the sum now invested is above double the original stock. Their immense water-power is used also to drive other machinery.

Pen Pictures—Commercial, Social, Economic

"A Grist Mill brings to the Company one thousand bushels of corn in toll, and the mill to grind bark supplies an extensive Tannery at hand, where large quantities of good leather are prepared. In connection with the tannery, a Shoe Factory has been in operation for some years, where an excellent article of negro shoes, pegged and sewed, is made, of which thousands are sold annually, far superior to the Northern made shoe sold at the same price. The workmen belong to the South and use leather tanned at their very door."

The factory village was pleasantly situated, the one hundred and fifty-four white inhabitants living in neat cottages, with thriving gardens, "indicative of comfort and refinement".

The village had a day school during the week and a flourishing Sunday School attended by old and young. The town preachers took turns in holding services every Sabbath evening in the "newly erected place of worship".

The editorial concludes: "We are told that this little village can well compare, in point of morals and good order, with any in the Union of the same size, and doubtless much of it is attributable to the interest manifested by the churches in town in their spiritual welfare."

The DeKalb factory stood at the western end of the dam of the Factory Pond, near the site of the present Wateree Cotton Mills.

It must have been an ultra-modern institution of its kind in the South for its day, bearing comparison in its social welfare features with the most advanced cotton mills of the present.

It was burned just before the Civil War.

The second cotton factory in Camden was the Camden (now Hermitage) Cotton Mill, incorporated in 1890.

It is located on the site of McRae's flour and grist mill, which in the early days was quite famous, wheat being brought to it from North Carolina and even, occasionally, from Tennessee. The old canal, no longer used, conveying water to it from McRae's pond, a half mile distant, was dug in 1811. A much larger canal was completed in 1892.

In colonial days, there was an Indian camp on the same situation, charted on some of the earliest maps.

The presidents of the Camden Cotton Mill were, successively, A. D. Kennedy, H. G. Carrison, Sr., P. T. Villepigue, E. Miller Boykin and F. M. Zemp.

In 1905, this factory was sold to a new organization, incorporated as the Hermitage Cotton Mill, with H. G. Carrison as president and C. H. Yates, secretary. In 1911, Mr. Carrison was succeeded by the present incumbent, R. B. Pitts.

This mill started with 10,000 spindles, 300 looms and 150 employees. At present, 1926, there are 16,000 spindles, 390 looms with complete electric drive, and 250 employees. About 3,500 bales of cotton are consumed annually. A high grade of unfinished print cloth in the grey is manufactured.

In 1900, another cotton factory was incorporated under the name of the DeKalb Cotton Mill, with E. Miller Boykin, president, W. B. Smith Whaley, vice-president, and Dr. J. W. Dunn, Frank M. Zemp, T. C. Duncan, directors. It was built very nearly on the site of the old DeKalb Factory, which gave its name to the adjacent Factory Pond.

The plant was capitalized at $144,000.00. It started with 12,500 spindles and 300 looms. The model little village contained seventy houses.

On the death of Mr. Boykin, in November 1903, the mill went into the hands of a receiver and remained idle for over a year.

The company was then reorganized, with T. C. Duncan as president, under the title of the Pine Creek Mill.

Four years later, the factory passed into the hands of the Parker interests.

It continued under this management until 1916, when it was purchased and operated by Lockwood, Greene & Co., of Boston, for H. P. Kendall, who took over the active control of the plant himself in 1922. It is now known as the Wateree Division of Kendall Mills, Incorporated, and enjoys the reputation of being one of the most progressive mills in the South.

There are now 21,316 spindles, and 492 looms, and the village has been much enlarged. The plant is run by hyrdo-electric power. It turns out a fine quality of print cloth.

J. L. Williams managed the mill until 1916, when he was succeeded by H. K. Hallet. A. Stanley Llewellyn, the present manager, took charge in 1924.

PEN PICTURES—COMMERCIAL, SOCIAL, ECONOMIC

The following other manufacturing plants in Camden may be mentioned.

The Cotton Seed Oil Company, built in 1902, is a branch of the Southern Cotton Oil Company. It is capitalized at $90,000.00 and employs 57 men. It turns out crude oil, meal, hulls and linters, and besides gins about 2,500 bales of cotton a year.

The Camden Milling Company, organized in 1914, grinds 30,000 bushels of corn annually. Its products, meal and hominy, supply far more than a local market. R. L. Moseley is owner and operator.

*Transportation*

Camden, like many other colonial towns, owed its early commercial importance to its location at the head of navigation of a considerable waterway, just below the falls.

1756.—As far back as 1756, the General Assembly of the State was appropriating money to make the Wateree navigable.

1772.—In 1772, the Grand Jury at the November term of court in Camden presents the commissioners of the Wateree River, viz.: Joseph Kershaw, John Chesnut, Andrew Allison, Robert Stark, Isaac Ross and others for neglecting work on said river and partially gathering the fines and forfeitures, according to law, "whereby the poor Resident on the river is greatly oppressed and the navigation of the great River, our grand canal of commerce, is rendered almost impassable".

1773.—The next year, the Grand Jury complains that "the expense of clearing and preserving the navigation of the Wateree River is assessed only upon those inhabitants living within ten miles of the banks on each side of it, such inhabitants being liable at the same time, if directed by the Road Commissioners, to work on the several highways to which they belong. And, as the navigation of said River is a matter in which the province in general is interested, we earnestly recommend that the preservation of the same be made a public expense, especially as the clearing of the said navigation frequently endangers the lives of those slaves that are liable to work thereon".

From the early Charleston and Camden papers we get our authority for most of the following statements.

## HISTORIC CAMDEN

1786.—In 1786, Samuel Mathis, of Camden, gives notice that he will run two boats between Camden and James Mouzon's store, near the mouth of the Santee River, and that Mouzon's Schooner will carry goods back and forth from that point to Charleston. This was to avoid the delay and danger of crossing Bull's Bay with open boats in bad weather. Mathis' boats ran once a month.

Advertisements of "Camden-built" boats, capable of carrying one hundred twenty barrels of rice, or fifteen to twenty cords of wood, appear at different times from 1787 to 1795.

1792.—Timothy Pickering, Postmaster General of the United States, advertises in the Charleston paper for proposals for carrying the mail on the following "Post-road": from Peterborough, Virginia to Fayetteville, North Carolina; thence, via Cheraw, Camden, Columbia and Cambridge in South Carolina, to Augusta, Georgia, the mail to leave Fayetteville every Tuesday at 4 a. m., reaching Augusta the next Saturday at noon; returning, to leave Augusta every Thursday at 5 a. m., reaching Fayetteville the next Monday at 8 p. m.

1794.—No mail received in Camden from October 1st until after November 4th; "reported that the gentleman who had contracted for transporting it from Petersburg to Augusta was sick on the road."

1797.—Another long lapse in the mail, owing to the horse throwing the mail-rider and falling on him. Terrible congestion of mail at Camden. Finally a "carriage" was sent up to bring in the mail, but, as there were at the time "four horse-loads for Charleston" and "only a single horse twice a week" to carry it, no immediate relief was in sight.

There is a notice this year of a boat constructed by "Mr. Chesnut of Camden, on a plan directed by Colonel Senf", for passing through the Santee Canal, "at half the expense and in half the time of those that go round by mouth of the Santee". This boat would carry nine hundred bushels of corn, or two hundred barrels of flour, or thirty-five hogsheads of tobacco.

Seven boats were built at Camden in 1800 for this inland navigation.

1798.—In 1798, in pursuance of an act recently passed by the legislature, a company was organized at Camden

## Pen Pictures—Commercial, Social, Economic

for the purpose of clearing Pine Tree Creek and cutting a canal from it up into the town. This, it was announced, was a great thing for planters and merchants, saving "a waggonage of near two miles between the town and the different landings on the river". This scheme seems never to have materialized.

1805.—In 1805, the "Catawba Company" advertises for a superintendent to have the canal finished from Graves Shoal to Rocky Mount. Remains of this old Catawba Canal are still in existence, showing a vast amount of solid masonry. Colonel Senf, the engineer, died in 1806 and lies buried at the Great Falls. Pole boats carried cotton and other products through the canal to Charleston, from points twenty-odd miles above Camden.

1816.—Arrangements were made with the General Post Office to have mail carried twice a week between Camden and Charleston.

Private mail routes were established from Camden to Sumterville and to Beaver Creek, once a week, the latter stopping at Garlick's Store (later Liberty Hill).

Other private mail routes were operated to Lancaster and to Winnsboro, each subscriber to a newspaper en route to pay one dollar, the rest of the cost to be met by subscription.

The first steamboat in South Carolina waters arrived in Charleston from Savannah in 1816.

1818.—In 1818, a meeting was held at Camden to organize the "Wateree and Santee Steamboat Company", to operate a line of boats from Camden to Charleston. The first steamboat put on by the company made its initial trip in 1835—seventeen years later.

1819.—Mr. Abernethy, contractor, was engaged in cutting a canal around Mountain Island (*Camden Gazette*, July 15, 1819).

1821.—A "Team-boat"[1] was completed to run between Camden and Charleston, "an invention of a Mr. Hart

---

[1] Ulrich Phillips, his *History of Transportation in the Eastern Cotton Belt*, says that from 1816 to about 1827 attempts were made to complete with steamboats by the use of horse-power in boat transportation. Horses were hitched to a beam on the main deck and driven in a circle, the power being "transmitted from the pivot of the beam through gearings to paddle wheels like those on the steamboats." This did very well on ferries where the stabling could be done on land, but did not work in through traffic, and the team-boat soon passed out of existence. They were tried on the Savannah River in 1820 and on a ferry at Charleston as late as 1827. There are no further references to them in the Camden papers.

of Connecticut, the enterprise due to the public spirit of our townsman James S. Smyth". The first experiment was made at the Camden Boat Yard. The boat proceeded up the river about five miles in less than an hour. It drew two and one-half feet empty, four feet loaded. Mr. David Gorrie was killed on this trial trip by falling from the wheel (*Camden Gazette*, March 29, 1821). In the same journal of May 3, 1821, we find this announcement:

"The Team-boat, Prior Eagle, worked by eleven mules, which left Camden for Charleston about April 1st, made the trip successfully. She made the return trip against high freshet and violent current in ninety-three working hours, towing a boat containing two hundred forty bales cotton, herself carrying one hundred ten bales. She crossed Bull's Bay against wind in two hours."

1824.—Mr. McLane, proprietor of the "Camden and Charleston Stage Line", announces that his stage will start from the "Camden Hotel" every Sunday and Wednesday, making the trip in two days: "The citizens of this section of the country will now find one of their great wants supplied—an easy rapid means of conveyance to Charleston."

The local paper says that it is informed that the Superintendent of Public Works has made his contract for the completion of the Wateree Canal and the first section of the Rocky Mount Canal.[1]

1828.—The "new" bridge made free to wagons loaded with cotton. Thirty-three river boats arrived in one day.

1831.—Crops were damaged to the amount of three hundred thousand dollars, by an unprecedented freshet in the river. An epidemic of bilious fever raged in Camden; many deaths.

"The Charlotte and Camden Stage" announces a fare of six and one-quarter cents per mile, or five cents per mile each way for the round trip.

The following advertisement appears in the *Camden Journal* of January 29, 1831.

---

[1]The State of South Carolina expended nearly $95,000.00 on the Wateree Canal in the four years between 1823 and 1826, and nearly $200,000.00 on the Rocky Mount Canal between 1823 and 1828, according to Phillip's *History of Transportation in the Eastern Cotton Belt*. With the coming of the railroad, these uncompleted canal projects were abandoned.

Pen Pictures—Commercial, Social, Economic

"Railway and Steam Carriage.

"The Ladies and Gentlemen of Camden and its vicinity are respectfully informed that a Circular Railroad will be laid down in the Old Methodist Church, giving the public a specimen of the Liverpool and Manchester Railroad, England. On which a Steam Engine will be placed and put in operation by steam, and draws a splendid car, sufficiently large to carry two. . . . The patronage bestowed on this machinery in Richmond, Virginia, and Raleigh, North Carolina, this winter, are its best recommendations; and, while the attention and capital both of England and America are absorbed in Railways, the proprietor takes much pleasure in informing the public on a subject entirely new to this community. . . . Admittance to ride on it, fifty cents; children, half price."

1834.—A meeting of citizens called by council to consider the proposition of a railroad from Camden to Charleston.

1835.—An editorial in the *Camden Journal* suggests that steam-boats be used to the forks of the Congaree and Wateree and that the (Santee) Canal be abandoned; says it takes a boat eighteen days, sometimes three months, to make the trip to Charleston by the canal, and the cost of "passing and repassing" the canal for a boat carrying one hundred bales of cotton is forty dollars.

Later in the year, the arrival of the first steamboat, from Charleston, the "Cheraw", is announced. It drew five and one-half feet of water; "the experiment" was pronounced a great success.

1836.—Commissioners appointed to receive stock at Camden of the "Louisville, Cincinnati and Charleston Railroad" (never built).

1837.—The steamboat "Congaree" leaves Camden with five hundred twenty-two bales of cotton for Charleston.

1838.—Steamer "Thomas Salmond" makes "quick trip" to Charleston in sixty hours; returns on third day loaded with cabin passengers and cotton.

1840.—(From the *Camden Journal*, January 1840) "Despatch Extraordinary—A sensation produced by arrival here of Boyd's Boat 'Belle' from Charleston" in the "unprecedented time of one hundred forty days on the trip". Is this sarcasm?

HISTORIC CAMDEN

The steamboat "Camden" sunk "again" by a snag. Had on board two hundred thirty-three bales of cotton and a quantity of yarn and osnaburgs from DeKalb Factory (Camden).

The same year, a steamboat, the "Serpent", constructed by E. C. Bellinger of Barnwell, drawing only two feet of water when loaded, navigates the river above the bridge, easily passing over falls and bars.

1842.—The railroad from Charleston to Columbia was completed. "The trade of Camden is jeopardized," cries the local paper. A meeting was called to discuss a railroad from Camden to Gadsden to connect with the above. Five delegates were appointed to meet in Charleston with the stockholders of the "Charleston, Louisville and Cincinnati Railroad".

1843.—James McEwen advertises the "Camden and Gadsden Line of Stages, the best way to Charleston". Trip to Gadsden in eight hours.

Editorial mention is made of the "fleet of pole-boats", still operated between Camden and Charleston by William Kennedy, despite the competition of the steamboats.

1845.—Two hundred thousand dollars subscribed in Camden to extension of railroad from Gadsden to Camden.

1846.—Location of proposed depot discussed at meeting of citizens; they recommend that it be put "south of King Street, at or near the point designated as the Old Fort or Redoubt".

1845-7—Several meetings held to secure "The Metropolitan Railroad from Raleigh to Camden, "which will soon be built by Boston capitalists", and a railroad from Charlotte, via Camden instead of Columbia. In the latter project, Council took seven hundred fifty shares, afterwards raised to one hundred thousand dollars, on condition of the Camden route being selected. Neither road was built.

1848.—The trestle over the Wateree was completed, four miles in length, "longest in the United States". Merchants and countrymen were advised to haul their goods to the Manchester depot, "only twenty-seven or twenty-eight miles from Camden", and to ship thence by rail. Branch road completed as far as Stateburg on May 31.

PEN PICTURES—COMMERCIAL, SOCIAL, ECONOMIC

November 1, 1848, the railroad reaches Camden. First schedule: leave Camden 6 a. m., arrive Junction 8:15 a. m.; leave Junction 2:45 p. m., arrive Camden 5:15 p. m. Fare to Columbia, three dollars.

"The Telegraph is now opened to Raleigh, and communications have been received from that city, Fayetteville and Cheraw."

1849.—January 31. Streets crowded with wagons. Upwards of two thousand packages of merchandise received at the railroad depot in one day. Thirty thousand bales of cotton "already" shipped by the railroad, besides what the steamboats carry and "it is thought this amount will be at least doubled".

A new postoffice established on railroad nine miles below Camden called "Boykin's Depot".

Fare to Charleston four dollars and twenty-five cents.

This branch line of the old South Carolina road, connecting later with the main line between Columbia and Charleston at Kingville, was the only rail communication that Camden and Kershaw County had until the "Three C's" was constructed in 1887, continuing the line northward from Camden to Marion, North Carolina. The Southern Railway took over this road on a 99 year lease in 1902.

The Seaboard Airline Railway, putting Camden on a through line from Northern points to Florida, was completed in 1899.

The Northwestern Railway, connecting Camden with Sumter, known as the "Wilson Short Cut", now owned by the Atlantic Coast Line, was built by Colonel Thomas Wilson in 1900.

*Water Powers.*

Much the greater portion of Kershaw County lies in the sandy region which crosses the middle of the state from Hamlet in North Carolina to Augusta, Georgia. The streams of this section are clear, lively and permanent, shrinking little in dry spells. This is owing to the great depth of porous soil which absorbs all the rain-fall and furnishes a steady output of water to springs and wells, nor do these streams overflow except in very excessive rains. Thus the creeks of the county afford many mill sites of some ten to fifteen horse-power, developed by low dams not exceeding eight or ten feet in height.

Therefore in the days before steam power the Camden mills did a large business in grinding wheat and corn during dry seasons for all the extensive clay regions of North and South Carolina and even eastern Tennessee. By means of a dam about twenty feet high and a canal near a mile long Big Pine Tree Creek has produced one hundred and fifty horse-power at the Hermitage Cotton Mill.

The Wateree River, the name of which changes to the Catawba about twenty-five miles north of Camden, is never quite limpid but usually tawny from the blood-red clay of the upper districts through which it passes. Along the course of the Wateree-Catawba a series of power plants have been constructed. The greatest of these and the farthest down stream is that located in this county about eight miles northwest of Camden (in a due line), established by the Wateree Power Company and put in operation in October, 1919. This plant bears the name of "Wateree". Here the river is impounded by a massive concrete dam seventy-eight (78) feet in height. Its eastern end is anchored to the rocky bluff of "Eagles Nest" and its western end on which the power house is situated abuts the steep hill formerly a part of the Gettys place. This dam creates a considerable lake some twenty miles long which greatly enhances the views from the rugged hills on either side. At the Wateree plant are installed five twenty thousand horse-power turbines, and the output averages yearly 180,000 K. W. hrs. Power lines radiate from Wateree, connecting it with the Great Falls plant about twenty-five miles above and other developments still further up stream and also with power plants on the Yadkin River in North Carolina. Camden industries and the municipal lighting system derive power over these inter-connecting lines.

*Banks.*

The first Bank in Camden was established in 1822, as a branch of the State Bank. Its officers were: Thomas Salmond, president; Lemuel Reed, cashier; Joshua Reynolds, teller and door clerk.

Directors: James Chesnut, James Clark, Benj. Bineham, J. K. Douglas, E. H. Anderson, W. B. Whitaker, Wm. Blanding, C. J. Shannon, Lewis Ciples, John Carter, Wm. Lang, James Spann.

PEN PICTURES—COMMERCIAL, SOCIAL, ECONOMIC

Upon the death of Thomas Salmond in 1854, C. J. Shannon succeeded as president and served until his death in 1863, being in turn succeeded by his son, W. M. Shannon.

In 1857 Dan'l L. DeSaussure died after twenty years service as cashier. His successor, Joseph W. Doby, died in 1863, and his successor, Neil W. Baxley, in 1865. In the same year occurred the death of Jesse S. Nettles, who had served for thirty years as discount clerk.

Only a single report of the condition of this Bank has been found, in a Camden paper of 1857, showing resources of $515,198.93 with corresponding liabilities. In the complete collapse of the Mother State Bank in 1865, this and all other branches met the same fate. Specimens of its old notes are not uncommon and circulated at par until suppressed by the result of the Civil War, and even then would have had substantial value had not all the State's assets upon which they rested been embezzled by the Carpet-baggers of Reconstruction.

In October, 1836, another independent bank was established with title of "Bank of Camden", on the northwest corner of Rutledge and Broad Streets. Its first president was William McWillie. He served until his removal to Mississippi about 1850. His successor, Wm. E. Johnson, served until the general bankruptcy in 1865, resulting from ruin wrought in the South by the Civil War. We can find no surviving records of this Bank and can only mention a few of the capable officers connected with its management, which was always of the highest order of efficiency. W. J. Grant was cashier in 1850. Alexander Johnson who died in 1853 had been a director since 1836. In 1860 W. H. R. Workman was cashier.

Camden was without an organized bank from 1865 to 1888, in which latter year the present Bank of Camden under a new State charter was established, under the presidency of H. G. Carrison, who has served as such until the present (1926).

In the year 1899, the Farmers and Merchants Bank, under the presidency of E. Miller Boykin, was established, terminating its operations in 1903.

The Commercial Savings Bank and Trust Company opened in 1904 under the presidency of E. S. Vaux. After his death in October of that year, C. J. Shannon, Jr. became president in January 1905, and the name was changed to the Commercial Savings Bank, and this was in the year 1908 converted into the present First National Bank of Camden, Mr. Shannon's presidency continuing to the present.

The Loan & Savings Bank was established in 1911, with L. L. Clyburn as president. He was succeeded in 1913 by Thos. J. Kirkland, who is still acting in that capacity.

*Taverns, Inns and Hotels.*

*Dinkins Tavern*, 1794.—The earliest tavern in Camden of which we can find record; established by John Dinkins. It was two blocks south of the old Court House, lots 96 and 97, near the northeast corner of Broad and Meeting Streets. Here Minister Genet was entertained in 1794.

*Nixon Hotel*, 1804.—Northeast corner Broad and King Streets; four story brick building; built and run by Colonel Wm. Nixon. Lot No. 190.

*Eagle Tavern*, 1816.—John Havis, "Brick house lately occupied by Mr. Doby next to Colonel Nixon's". Lot 188 or No. 189.

*Public Entertainment*, 1816.—John Havis, (formerly Colonel Wm. Nixon's and later of J. Hughson). Lot No. 190.

*Planters Hotel*, 1817.—Ballard and Dye, "next to Colonel Nixon's brick building". (Same as Eagle Tavern above).

*Travellers Hotel*, (At the Sign of the Heart), 1818.— J. B. Matthieu, "in the upper part of Camden". Probably on Lot No. 1196 or No. 1197.

*Sign of the Buck*, 1819.—Welsh and Smythe, "House lately occupied by Mr. Havis". In 1820 the "Sons of Pilgrims" advertise a celebration at Welsh and Smythe's Long Room. Lot No. 190 (?).

*Sign of the Eagle*, 1820.—John G. Ballard, a few doors south of old Court House, formerly of Uriah Blackmon. Lot No. 5. This Tavern was conducted in 1822 by Henry DuBose, and again by Ballard in 1823. (Not same as "Eagle Tavern" of 1816.)

*Sign of the Bell*, 1821.—McAdams and Drakeford, "one door north of Colonel Nixon's; lately occupied by Mr. Ballard". Probably Lot No. 5: Nixon owned Lots

PEN PICTURES—COMMERCIAL, SOCIAL, ECONOMIC

No. 4 and 5. (H. A. McAdams ran the Stage line to Charleston.)

*Eagle & Harp*, 1822.—M. M. McCulloch. "Northwest corner Broad and King Streets; lately occupied by Colonel F. A. Deliesseline". Lot No. 170.

*Camden Hotel*, 1823.—Thomas Welsh, northeast corner of Broad and King Streets, "four-story brick house lately occupied by Colonel Nixon". Lot No. 190.

*Bell Inn*, 1826.—Hiram McCants, northeast corner York and Broad Streets. Lot No. 1032. (Formerly kept by Welsh and Smythe.)

*Camden House*, (Sign of the Cross Keys), 1826.—John Bailey, "near Court House; formerly kept by McAdams and Drakeford". Probably same as "Sign of the Bell", 1821.

*Mansion House*, 1827.—John MacColl, "just south of Court House—In dwelling known as residence of Wm. McWillie". Lot No. 2.

*Golden Ball* or *Goodman's Hotel*, 1828.—Joseph Goodman, northwest corner of King and Broad Streets. Same as Eagle and Harp of 1822. Lot No. 170. (Destroyed in fire of 1829.)

*Jackson Hotel*, 1828.—Thomas Welsh, northeast corner of King and Broad Streets. Lot No. 190: burned in great fire of November 23, 1829. (The old Nixon Hotel.) After the fire Welsh reopened in the old "Mansion House". Lot No. 2.

*Cross Keys*, 1829.—Wm. McKain, southwest corner DeKalb and Broad. Lot No. 1172. (Not the same as "Cross Keys" of 1826.)

*Golden Ball*, 1831.—Joseph Goodman, opens again on Lot No. 170. (Rebuilt.)

*McAdams Hotel*, 1831.—A. R. Ruffin "reopens". Lot No. 5 (?).

*McAdams House*, 1833.—Mary McAdams opens Hotel on northeast corner of York and Broad, Lot No. 1032 ("Bell Inn" of McCants in 1826.)

*Sumter Hotel*, 1838.—A. R. Ruffin, corner Broad and King, Lot No. 170. Same as "Golden Ball" above, renamed for General Sumter.

*Camden Hotel*, 1847.—R. P. Boyd, "large brick hotel contiguous to Court House". Lot No. 2. (Not same as "Camden Hotel" of 1823.)

*Planters Hotel*, 1848.—Corner of York and Broad Streets, Lot No. 1032, same as McAdams House of 1833 and "Bell Inn" of 1826 (Not same as the "Planters Hotel" of 1817.)

*Temperance House*, 1850.—J. B. F. Boone, southwest corner of Broad and DeKalb, same as "Cross Keys" of 1829. Lot No. 1172.

*Kershaw House*.—This old building, which seems to have been first opened as "Cross Keys" by McKain in 1829, was burned in the great fire of January 1874. A rough cut of it shows the pump in the centre of the intersection of Broad and DeKalb Streets. The hotel was on the southwest corner. E. G. Robinson ran it for several years just before the war.

### KERSHAW HOUSE.

### Camden, S. C.

*DeKalb Hotel*.—A three story brick structure on the northeast corner of Broad and DeKalb Streets, erected by the Camden Hotel Company in 1860. This under various names served as a transient hotel until 1914, when it was demolished and replaced by the U. S. Post Office. A. S. Rogers was proprietor for a number of years.

### Tourist Inns.

*Hobkirk Inn*.—Located near the middle of the ridge called Hobkirk Hill, scene of the Revolutionary battle,

## Pen Pictures—Commercial, Social, Economic

the former home of Colonel W. M. Shannon, known as "Pine Flat". This, the first Camden tourist hotel, was established by F. W. Eldredge in 1884 and conducted by him until his death in May, 1912, since when it has been under the management of H. G. Marvin.

*Uphton Court.*—Now "Court Inn", located at the eastern terminus of Laurens Street, formerly "Lausanne", built in 1830 by John C. McRae, later for half a century the home of Major J. M. DeSaussure, purchased in 1884 by Mrs. C. J. Perkins and by her opened as a tourist resort in 1889. After her death in February, 1898, it was purchased, by Caleb Ticknor, who in 1900 opened it as the "Court Inn", making extensive additions from time to time. Since his death (1921), his son Benj. D. Ticknor has continued to conduct the hotel.

*Kirkwood Hotel.*—Located on the western extremity of the Hobkirk Hill ridge; formerly the home of Major John Cantey. This hotel for tourists was opened in 1903 by the Camden Land Improvement Company. The Camden Country Club established a club house and developed golf and polo grounds on the extensive surrounding fields. T. Edmund Krumbholz was manager of the Kirkwood until his death in May, 1923, being succeeded by Karl P. Abbott.

### *Rural Inns.*

The map of Kershaw District in Mills' Atlas (1825), made from surveys by John Boykin of Camden in 1821, shows the following taverns in the county outside the town:

*Carwell's Tavern.*—Just above Hobkirk Hill, near the fork of the Lancaster and Liberty Hill roads. (The graves of the Carwell family are still marked in the woods across the road. "Cool Spring" is charted on this map as "Carwell's Cold Spring". It is about a mile north of the old tavern. David Carwell then owned this land.)

*Love's Tavern.*—On "the road to Hanging Rock", between Sanders and Granny's Quarter Creeks. "Mrs. Love's Tavern" is indicated a short distance north.

*Noxe's Tavern.*—On same road; just above Big Flat Rock Creek.

*Burge's Tavern.*—On same road, a few miles north.

*Miller's Tavern.*—On same road, at junction with "old Georgetown Road".

*George Miller's Tavern.*—On "Old Georgetown Road", just below the North Carolina line.

*Mrs. Aldridge's Tavern.*—On old Liberty Hill Road, just above Granny's Quarter Creek.

*McKinnon's Tavern.*—On "road to Harrison's Ford", at crossing of "Old Georgetown Road". Another tavern of the same name was on "the road to Evans", about ten miles east of Camden.

*Cuzack's Tavern.*—On Winnsborough Road, near the Fairfield line.

*Hughson's Tavern.*—On the old Columbia Road, in West Wateree, about six miles from Camden.

*Nickle's Tavern.*—In Southeastern corner of the county, near "Mrs. Schrock's Mill".

*Holliday's Tavern.*—On Columbia Road, near White Pond, about twelve miles from Camden.

*L. Peebles Tavern.*—Very near the last-named.

*Holland's Tavern.*—About ten miles slightly northeast of Camden, on "the road to Evans".

*DeBrule's Tavern.*—On same road, near the last-named.

*Dixon's Tavern.*—On same road, near the Chesterfield line.

*Sander's Tavern.*—Very near the last-named.

*Tavern.*—On "Salisbury Road", near Big Swift Creek, in the Boykin neighborhood below Camden.

*Eagle Tavern.*—Kept by John Fletcher, "twenty-one miles above Camden and eighteen from Lancaster"; not on the Mills' map but advertised in the Camden papers of 1827.

There were, of course, many others of these country inns of which the records have not come to our attention, in the years before and since 1821. They passed with the stage coach.

*Military.*

Kershaw County furnished companies of volunteers for every war in which this country has been engaged, from the Revolution to the World War.

It is impossible, were all the data available, within our limits, to give sketches of all these organizations.

## Pen Pictures—Commercial, Social, Economic

Colonel Joseph Kershaw's regiment in the Revolution was doubtless recruited from this section, though unfortunately the rolls are lost and this cannot be substantiated. Eli Kershaw's company, of which we published the names in our first volume, was raised in Camden District.

After that successful struggle for independence, it was natural that the military spirit was strong. We can name only some of the organizations of that early period as we cull them from old diaries and newspapers.

1791.—"The Troop of Light Horse", Captain James Kershaw (1791), attended Washington on his visit to the town. This company, in 1841, with a new name, the "Camden Troop of Cavalry", is spoken of in the local paper as having "originated warm from the Revolutionary Struggle". Thomas J. Ancrum was then elected Captain in place of Burwell Boykin, resigned, and the statement is made that the troop would henceforth be "mounted infantry".

1794.—*The City Gazette and Daily Advertiser* (Charleston), July 14, 1794, notes the election of the following officers for the "Kershaw County Regiment" at Camden (646 votes attending): Zachariah Cantey, Lieutenant Colonel; Willis Whitaker and Thomas Ballard, Majors. There was a flurry with England at this time for seizing French supplies on American vessels.

The same year, the "Camden Company of Militia" was officered as follows: David Bush, Captain; James Brown, Lieutenant; James Cain, Ensign.

1798.—In 1798, James Kershaw, in his Diary, extracts from which were published in our first volume, mentions a parade of Artillery, Cavalry and Infantry companies at Camden and states that the Artillery Company was organized in that year.

1809.—The "Rifle Company, Captain Coleman", was in existence in 1809. The captains of this company after Coleman were, successively, Chapman Levy, Thomas Lang, Daniel Kirkland, John A. Kennedy.

1812.—The companies in Colonel Adam McWillie's regiment that served in the War of 1812 are listed in another chapter.

1816-18.—The papers of 1816-18 mention the following companies:

"Beaver Creek Republican Sharp Shooters",

"Camden Beat Company", Postell McCaa, Captain,
"Camden Rifle Company", Chapman Levy, Captain,
"Camden Artillery Company", R. W. Carter, Captain,
"Beaver Creek Troop of Cavalry", John Fletcher, Captain,
"Camden Light Infantry", James Cantey, Captain,
"Camden Troop of Horse", J. C. McRae, Captain,
Colonel of the Regiment, Thomas English.

The *Camden Gazette* (1817) advertises for ten steady young men as a Magazine guard, pay fifteen dollars per month, "a blue coat, one pair of pantaloons and a hat" found them.

1822.—In 1822, James S. Deas is in command of the "Troop of Cavalry", John Boykin of the "Light Infantry", Thomas Lang, of the "Riflemen", Meugy, of the "Company of Militia".

1824.—In 1824, an additional company is mentioned, the "Camden Dragoons", M. M. McCulloch, O. S.

Captain John M. Doby, of the "Camden Beat Company" is, that year, elected Major, 2nd Battalion, Regiment of Militia.

1825.—In 1825, the following officers were elected for the "Camden Light Infantry": Charles J. Shannon, Captain; Thomas Hopkins, 1st Lieutenant (later killed in a duel with Nixon); Joseph Kershaw, 2nd Lieutenant; Columbus J. Nixon, 3rd Lieutenant. This Joseph Kershaw was a son of George Kershaw, therefore first cousin to General Joseph Brevard Kershaw.

1828.—A general muster of Kershaw County troops was addressed by Generals Earle and Blair; Colonel Deas' Regiment of Cavalry was complimented.

July 4th; "Captain McRa's troops" were entertained by Colonel Deas, at the "Hermitage".

1829.—July 4th; the various companies dine at the "Old Arsenal", the salute being fired by McWillie's artillery.

1836.—See chapter on The Seminole War for roster of Company from Kershaw.

1837.—July 4th; the "Kershaw Florida Volunteers", John Kershaw, Captain, have a barbecue: J. W. Cantey, Brigadier General, 5th Brigade, present.

The same month, the brigade encamps at "Camp DeKalb", near "Cool Spring", three hundred strong, and is reviewed by Governor Butler.

PEN PICTURES—COMMERCIAL, SOCIAL, ECONOMIC

In November, the same year, the "Riflemen" barbecue at "Magazine Spring, near the old Star Redoubt".

1840.—In 1840, one of the most famous of the old companies came into being, "The DeKalb Rifle Guards", J. P. Dickinson, Captain; Joseph W. Doby, 1st Lieutenant; Keith S. Moffatt, 2nd Lieutenant; A. M. Kennedy, 3rd Lieutenant; Thomas E. Shannon, Ensign and Judge Advocate.

The next year, this famous troop, Joseph W. Doby, Captain, have a grand barbecue in celebration of the Battle of New Orleans: parade one hundred strong: brilliant illumination and ball at "Gifford's Hall". The troop is spoken of as "the flower of the District".

On March 27, the same year, Governor Richardson holds a grand review of the 22nd Regiment, and, from the DeKalb Monument, presents to the company a silk flag in behalf of the ladies of Camden.

1842.—On July 4, 1842, the following companies parade:
"DeKalb Rifle Guards",
"Camden Beat Company",
"Marion Cadets" (T. J. Warren, Captain),
"Kershaw Troop of Cavalry"; attended by the
"DeKalb Amateur Band" and some "surviving soldiers of the Revolution."

1843.—In 1843, the "DeKalb Lyceum", a literary society composed of members of the "DeKalb Rifle Guards" and of the "Alarm Corps" (whose duty was to patrol during the Christmas holidays) was organized at the "new DeKalb Hall on Church Street", James P. Dickinson, President.

In May, of the same year, the local paper says of the review of the 22nd Regiment, that there was a "fine turnout" but "more drunken men were on the streets of Camden than for fifty years past".

1844.—In 1844, there is a petition for a revival of the "Patrol System", the "regular guard of four" not being efficient.

The same year, on Dickinson's elevation to the Lieutenant Colonelcy of the Regiment, Keith Moffat becomes captain of the "DeKalb Rifle Guards".

1846.—In 1846, the Guards tender their service to the Governor for the Mexican War, and are enlisted as the

"Kershaw Volunteers". (See Chapter on the Mexican War.)

1847.—In 1847, the paper notes the death of the last Revolutionary soldier in Kershaw District, Major Samuel Jones, at his residence on Lynch's Creek, in the 91st years of his age. He was buried with military honors.

The glorious record of the Kershaw County troops that entered the service of the Confederacy is told in other pages, with full rolls of the several companies.

To the future historian must be left the recital of the very honorable part played in the European War (1914-18) by the men from Kershaw.

It may be stated here, however, that, from as yet uncompleted official records, 433 young men of the county saw service overseas, in the 30th, 81st and Rainbow Divisions. Of these 87 enlisted; 346 were inducted. Many were wounded and disabled; some made the supreme sacrifice, either from disease or on the field of battle.

Of the total seventy-eight Congressional Medals awarded for extraordinary heroism, six were conferred upon South Carolinians, and, of the six, two were won by Kershaw County boys, Richmond Hobson Hilton and John Cantey Villepigue. Many others from the county won citations for bravery or meritorious conduct.

## The Turf.

"The Sport of Kings" has been a popular one in Camden from perhaps its earliest days.

James Kershaw in his Diary, (see our first volume), mentions the "Camden Races" as occurring in January 1802 and in other years up to 1812, the last year of his records.

The *Camden Gazette* in 1816 records the election of the following officers of the Camden Jockey Club: President, General Z. Cantey; Treasurer, Mr. C. Shannon; Secretary, Mr. A. Hodges; Stewards, Captain J. S. Deas, Captain Postell McCaa, Major J. Cantey, Colonel W. Nixon, Captain J. Doby, and Mr. John Boykin, Senior.

In a publication entitled *The South Carolina Jockey Club*, Charleston, 1857, we find a glowing tribute to "that venerated patriot, citizen and sportsman of the old school", General Zack Cantey. After lauding his hospitality, courtesy and sterling qualities as a man, it says:

"He had a stock of horses well bred, and always trained one or two for the Races at Camden and Stateburg, and generally won a purse. If successful, he never put into his own pocket what he won but gave it to one or other of the churches in Camden, or to the Orphan Society."

The Canteys were for generations conspicuous among the breeders of race horses and patrons of the turf in the state.

In January, 1832, the local paper states that the Camden Races were interfered with by the bitter cold, the ground being frozen hard. The usual ball had to be postponed, but there was a "big supper at Mr. Ruffin's Long Room". Horses were entered by Colonel Spann, Mr. Smith, Dr. Ellerbe, Colonel Singleton, Dr. Goodwyn, Major Cantey, Colonel Moore and others.

THE CAMDEN RACES will commence on Wednesday, the 10th of January next, and continue for two days. Free for all horses, mares or geldings, on the continent.

*By Order of the Club.*
Camden, Nov. 30, 1820.        -31-6-

☞ The Richmond Enquirer, Southern Patriot, and Columbia Telescope, are requested to publish the above three times, and send their accounts to this Office.

After that the races seem to have been held in November.

The advertisement in the *Camden Gazette* in 1818 of a house and lot for sale "on Littleton Street facing the Race Ground" confirms the statement of the late Captain James I. Villepigue that he could remember the first race course in Camden, which ran around the blocks now bounded by Lyttleton, DeKalb, Mill and Laurens Streets, the grand stand being about where Henry Savage's house now stands on Laurens Street. (Lot No. 936.)

The old Warren house on DeKalb Street (Lot No. 945), erected in 1828, still standing, was the first residence built in that territory. It was therefore abandoned as a race track about that time.

A later course was on the west side of the Lancaster Road, about a mile above Kirkwood, between "Springdale" and "Cool Spring". This was known as the "Hawthorne Course".

Still later there was a race track immediately west of the Seaboard station, Camden, on what is now the lands of Henry G. Carrison. This was in use long after the Civil War, within the recollection of many now living.

The sport has recently been revived to a limited extent at the Riding and Driving Club, which maintains a half mile track, used chiefly for training.

### *The Camden Hospital.*

This benefaction was made possible by the gifts of two men.

The late John Burdell, formerly chief of police of Columbia, settled after the War in West Wateree and acquired large holdings of valuable timber and farming lands.

By his will, he provided a handsome sum for the alleviation of the suffering in Kershaw County.

As a consequence of this legacy, a movement was at once set on foot to erect in Camden a much-needed hospital.

At this point, Bernard M. Baruch, of New York, who was born in Camden, came forward with a gift of $40,000.00 to erect a building for the hospital as a memorial to his father, Dr. Simon Baruch, a former beloved physician of the town, who had won a high position in his profession in New York City.

The Presbyterian Manse on Fair Street, with its extensive grounds, was purchased, and, with a brick veneering and added wings, was converted into a modern hospital.

The equipment was supplied by the people of Kershaw County, and the interest on the Burdell legacy was devoted to the support of the institution.

The aged Dr. Baruch and his distinguished son, the donor, were present at the opening, December 13, 1913.

The Board of Directors at that time were: Wm. M. Shannon, President; Dr. J. W. Corbett, Vice-President;

L. A. Wittkowsky, Secretary; Dr. S. C. Zemp, Dr. W. J. Burdell, Rev. J. C. Rowan, H. G. Carrison, and W. R. Hough.

The main building was destroyed by fire January 28, 1921.

Bernard M. Baruch again came forward, with an additional gift of $25,000.00. The citizens of the county and Northern tourists raised the remaining funds necessary to rebuild, and in 1922 the new and improved hospital rose on the ashes of the old.

The maintenance is from the Burdell fund, small contributions from city and county, and receipts from the pay wards. A large part of the work is, as intended, a charity.

The present directors are: Dr. J. W. Corbett, President; L. A. Wittkowsky, Secretary; W. M. Baruch, Treasurer; W. R. Zemp and R. M. Kennedy, Jr.

*The Camden Library.*

In 1805 the "Camden Library Society" was incorporated. Its books were housed in the old Market, or Town Hall, on the corner of Broad and King Streets, opposite the old Court House.

In 1820, the Society purchased the private library of Chancellor DeSaussure, for $1,200.00, and added it to its collections.

In 1830, we learn from their minutes, the Camden Orphan Society bought the books of the "Camden Library" and installed them in a "library room" in one of the Academies on DeKalb Street, for the use of members only. The *Camden Journal* in 1831 advertises that the "Orphan Society Library" is open daily from 3 to 5 p. m., Sundays excepted. C. A. Bullard acted as librarian from 1826 for several years.

In 1837, it is recorded in the minutes, the "private catalog of the library" enumerated 723 volumes, "the partial cost" being $656.59. This was a great deterioration in the number of volumes or in value.

John C. West was librarian in 1840.

In 1843, the library, "about 1300 volumes", was loaned to the DeKalb Lyceum, a literary society incorporated in that year, and was removed to the hall of the DeKalb Rifle Guards, the Orphan Society students and their parents being allowed free access to it.

The next year it was returned to the Orphan Society Academy, the Lyceum presenting its own books to replace lost and mutilated volumes.

In 1851, it was agreed, according to the Orphan Society minutes, to sell the library to the revived (?) "Camden Library Society", 742 volumes, for $600.00.

This sale does not seem to have been consummated, for next year it is recorded that the library was sold (apparently to James Dunlap and John M. DeSaussure) for $240.00. The collections must have sadly dwindled and Mr. DeSaussure probably wished some of the books that had been bought from his father in 1820. Thus ended the old Library, and we find no further reference to the Camden Library Society.

A few of the books, quaint little volumes on all subjects, bound alike in sets, one of which was labeled "Family Library", found their way back to the shelves of the Graded School Library, which in 1912 contained about 1,400 books. They were destroyed when the High School, temporarily housed in the Reynolds mansion, was burned in 1921.

In 1900, the "Camden Library Association", a new society, was organized and established a subscription library in a room over the store on the southeast corner of Broad and DeKalb Streets. This building was destroyed by fire in 1912 and the collection of about 3,000 volumes was lost.

In 1915, largely through the efforts of Mrs. E. C. Von Tresckow, the Carnegie Corporation of New York was induced to give $5,000.00 for the building of a free public library. It was erected on Monument Square, and continues to function actively, containing, in 1926, about 4,000 volumes. Miss Louise Nettles has served continuously as librarian since 1900.

# CHAPTER IV.
## THE WAR OF 1812.

The causes of our "Second War for Independence", it may not be amiss to restate, however familiar, were Great Britain's insolent disregard of the neutral attitude assumed by the United States in the Napoleonic wars and her assumption of the right to search American vessels for seamen of British birth, who were treated as deserters from His Majesty's service even though they had become citizens of this country. More than 1,600 cases of this intolerable impressment are said to have occurred before Congress declared war, June 18, 1812.

At its outbreak, the war fever was hottest in the South, which was least concerned except in principle. New England, fearing injury to her shipping and commerce, was in opposition. Most of the fighting, it is true, was done near the Canadian border, on the Great Lakes and off the Northern coast.

Some brilliant, though minor, naval engagements took place in Carolina waters, for rather brief accounts of which consult Simms' *History of South Carolina.* They are treated somewhat more fully in Roosevelt's *Naval War of 1812.*

Fortifications were thrown up around Charleston, including Castle Pinckney, and at other points along our shores where a landing by the British might be attempted. These precautions were by no means useless, as the enemy's cruisers several times appeared before the harbors of Charleston, Beaufort and Georgetown, and landings were actually made on Dewee's Island and at Hilton Head, where considerable damage was done to neighboring plantations.

To revert a little: a correspondent from Camden, under date June 26, 1812, thus writes to the *Carolina Gazette* (Charleston):

"For the satisfaction of all who feel for the dignity and honor of the American name, I beg leave to give a short account of the display of the feelings of the citizens of this place. Yesterday evening, an express arrived here from Washington, on his way to New Orleans, carrying the tidings of a Declaration of War against Great

Britain.[1] The citizens immediately assembled and reared the national flag, and fired eighteen rounds from a four-pounder, in celebration of the event.[2] Every man appeared to be animated by one sentiment of patriotism. Division and party feeling seemed to take its flight and its place was usurped by the spirit of '76. The feelings of every one were roused to enthusiasm when they beheld amongst their number many of the heroes of the Revolution. They seemed to rise superior to the infirmities of age and appear again in the full vigor of youth. Whilst this sentiment reigns in the hearts of our countrymen, what have we to fear from the attacks of outward foes?"

James Kershaw records in his Diary that there was a "draft of the militia in Camden", August 12, 1813, and that he delivered seventy-five pounds of powder to Colonel Richardson on August 16th. These were probably flurries of excitement due to threatened descents upon the coast.

Charleston was blockaded in October, 1813. Again, in September, 1814, an attack upon the city seemed imminent. Great consternation prevailed among the inhabitants, and the state troops, then enlisted in the service of the United States, were ordered to her defense by Governor David R. Williams. Washington city had been taken on August 24, and the Capitol and White House burned.

Camden and Kershaw County acted promptly and with the usual spirit. The *Camden Journal* of February 13, 1836, says editorially: "During the last war with Great Britain, when men were wanted from this regiment, when the call was made for volunteers, *all, every one* in the line marched forth."

Two companies, enlisted in and around Camden, and commanded respectively by Captain Chapman Levy and Captain Francis Blair, left Camden on October 6 for Charleston, accompanied by Douglas' and Montgomery's companies from Lancaster.[3] They were a part of the

---

[1] It will be noted that it took a week for the news to reach Camden.

[2] From a plat of the lower end of the town, made in 1811 by James Kershaw, we learn that the "flag staff" stood on the old Central Square, northeast corner of Broad and Bull Streets, south of old Court House. At the intersection of these streets was formerly buried a small cannon, perhaps this very four-pounder. It was afterwards taken up in improving the street.

[3] James Kershaw's Diary (Historic Camden, Part I). He states that he "painted a flag for Levy".

## The War of 1812

2nd Regiment, commanded by Lieutenant Colonel Adam McWillie of Kershaw.

The regiment, 1,200 strong, reached the city October 20. The *Carolina Gazette* commented upon its fine appearance and equipment, and stated that it was escorted into town from the Four-Mile House by the Charleston Riflemen amidst the acclamations of the citizens. The entire body were halted on Broad Street and treated by the Honorable John Geddes to a refreshing draught of spirits and water. The complimentary notice concludes: "To the honor of Carolina, three-fourths of the above troops are volunteers who have left their peaceful homes and comfortable firesides to meet the foe upon the shore, and, should he have the temerity to land, they will dispute with him every inch of ground with that spirit and daring which belongs only to freemen."

The regiment went into encampment at Haddrills Point. The foe did not have the temerity to land, and even the mosquitoes were too chilled to attack. The only enemy encountered apparently was hunger, as we gather from the following extracts from a spirited letter addressed by Colonel McWillie, October 25, to Major General Pinckney:

"This day, sir, have the rations of beef fallen far short, as has been the case at different times during the past week, and this day, sir, every ounce of bread that was furnished the troops has been consigned as food to the scaly tribe.

"The health of the troops is dear to every officer under whose charge they are placed, and the lovers of our country will shortly witness the ranks of our patriot army disheartened and broken, not by the sword of the enemy in battle but by the pestilential influence of unwholesome bread and the scarcity of food necessary for their sustenance, unless some means are used to correct the abuses of which we now complain. Bosoms glowing with patriotism will at length lose their enthusiasm, and these men who voluntarily abandoned the sweets of domestic life to encounter all the perils and privations of war in defense of the dearest rights of freemen, will retire at the expiration of their term with disgust from the service of their country and volunteers will not readily be found to embark under leaders whose agents may be disposed to practice fraud and imposition upon the defenders of our country's rights.

"I suggest these things, sir, from a sincere desire that abuses may be corrected which may ultimately prove disastrous to a cause that is dear to me, and which, I presume, is equally so to you."

This energetic protest, suggestive of the embalmed beef scandals of the late Cuban War, effected a speedy correction.

The treaty of Ghent was signed December 24, 1814, ending the war. Captain Levy's company seems to have been mustered out on December 7, 1814; Captain Blair's on March 7, 1815.

The *Camden Journal* of September 5, 1849, states that many of the "veterans" of this war had passed away, but that those who remained remembered vividly the sufferings from cold and stinted provisions. "The glories of an active campaign lay not before them", but "they dwelt with delight upon memory of their handsome appearance and the promptness with which they discharged every duty".

Colonel Shannon says[1] of Levy's command: "The *esprit du corps* of this company and its admirable material not only gave it a high reputation in the regiment, but enabled it to wield a powerful political influence in Kershaw District for many years after the close of the war."

From the *Recollections* of Edwin J. Scott,[2] we get an intimate glimpse of the war spirit in Camden: "I well recollect the rejoicings, illuminations, torch-light processions and paradings around the liberty pole that stood on Main Street, a little south of Havis's Tavern, at the news of every victory over the British, and particularly at the proclamation of peace. An affecting scene was presented at the separation from their families and friends of the Volunteer regiment on its departure for the coast under old Colonel McWillie of Lancaster,[3] with his son, William, my schoolmate, as adjutant. Camden contributed two companies to this regiment—the Rifles, Captain Chapman Levy, and the Artillery, Captain

---

[1] *Old Times in Camden.*
[2] *Random Recollections of a Long Life.*
[3] Colonel McWillie's lands were partly in Lancaster County.

## THE WAR OF 1812

Blair, not the General and member of Congress of the same name."

The news of peace did not reach Camden until February 20, 1815, when "minute guns were fired in Camden and Columbia", says James Kershaw.

The following "Muster-roll of Captain Chapman Levy's Company of Riflemen of a Regiment of South Carolina militia, in the service of the United States, commanded by Lieutenant Colonel Adam McWillie, from the 29th day of October, 1814, when last mustered, to the 7th day of December, 1814" is copied from the *Camden Journal* of September 5, 1849, which adds: "The certificate of C. Levy, Captain, and Wm. Bootz, Inspector General, that it is a true statement is endorsed December 7, 1814, at Camp Haddrill."

*Roll.*

Chapman Levy, Capt.
Robt. Singleton, 1st Lieut.
Joshua English, 2nd Lieut.
Duren Graham, 3rd Lieut.
A. Blanchard, Ensign.
H. H. Lenoir, 1st Serg.
Geo. Graham, 2nd Serg.
Benj. McCoy, 3rd Serg.
John Parker, 4th Serg.
Wm. McKain, 5th Serg.
John Teem, 1st Corp.
Thos. Smyrl, 2nd Corp.
Eli Adkins, 3rd Corp.
John Miller, 4th Corp.
John Marshal, 5th Corp.
Thomas Cussack, 6th Corp.

*Musicians.*

Samuel Lane
John Ballard

*Privates.*

Aaron Adams
Geo. Ashley
Laban Brock
David Bradford
Deveraux Ballard

John Ballard, Jr.
James Brown
John Burge
Sam'l Bradford
Joseph Burnsides
David Ballard
William Baker
Thomas Bradley
Robert Busby
Thomas Ballard
John Baltone (Belton)
John Baker
Ransom M. Collins
John Collins
John Cook
Sam'l Carpenter
John Clanton, Jr.
Wm. Cockran
Ely Cook
James Clanton
Peter Crim
John P. Clanton
David Clanton
John Canady
Michael DeBruhl
Robert Davis
James Denton

## HISTORIC CAMDEN

Jesse DeBruhl
Wm. Dunlap
Charles Ellis
Rolley Ellis
James Fletcher
William Fletcher
Wiley Fort
Andrew Falkenberry
Henry Gerald
John Gaskins
Reuben Gardner
James Gardner
Peter Holliday
John Hunt
James Harrison
Jacob Hughes
Wm. Hamilton
Jesse Hindson
Wm. Hunt
Hardy Horton
Jonathan Horton
Reuben Horton
John Jenkins
Wm. James
John Knox
James Love
Robert Love
John Love
Peter Logan
Joseph Loring
Gideon Lowry
John Lisenby
John Mackey
Joseph McCoy
John McCoy
John McKain
Hiram McAdams
Taskill McCaskill
Humphrey Muse
Hugh McDowell
Robert McDowell

John McDowell
John McCaskill
Malcolm McCaskill
John Mims
George Nettles
Ransom Nighten
Preston O'Neal
Bryant O'Quin
Wm. O'Cain
Daniel O'Quin
John Payne
James Rasberry
John Robertson
Abram Rowan
Sam'l Rowan
David Russel
*Jarvis Reeves
Stephen Reeves
George Sanders
Daniel Shiver
Elisha Shiver
Charles Seals
James Seals
Abel Stafford
William Shy
John Scott
Bryant Spradley
Samuel Sloan
Hugh Thompson
George Turner
Lewis Teem
James Turley
William Thompson
Samuel Wilson
William Williams
Wilson West
John Webb

*Servants.*

Big Jacob
Little Jacob
Isaac

Total 128

*Died in service.

# The War of 1812

## *Captain Francis Blair's Company.*

(From an old pay-roll, which states that the company was "mustered in at Eutaw Springs, the place of rendezvous, October 12, 1814, and mustered out at Camden, March 7, 1815.)"

1. James S. Smyth
2. John Spears
3. Jonathan Eccles
4. Drury I. Campbell
5. Henry Schrock
6. Archibald Smyth
7. John Kirkpatrick
8. Willis W. Alsbrook
9. Jehu Bates
10. Caleb Berry
11. William Burge
12. Thomas Burchmore
13. Jessee Bales
14. Nathan Campbell
15. John Cook
16. Edmond Campbell
17. Burwell Carter
18. Abram Cook
19. John Doherty
20. Alexander Doke
21. William J. Diggs
22. John Erwin
23. Dempsey Erwin
24. Benjamen Franklin
25. Elias Ford
26. I. B. Fulton
27. Daniel Gardner
28. Thomas Gaskey
29. Jonathan Hayes
30. David Hunter
31. Charles D. Hunter
32. John Tarbett
33. John Jemison
34. John Kelley
35. Daniel Kelley
36. William Langford
37. Anthony Lowry
38. Robinson Lyle
39. John Lankford[1]
40. Aaron Martin
41. Call Murphy
42. John McNiel
43. James B. McRadie
44. Patrick McGuire[2]
45. James McBride
46. Joseph W. Owen
47. Francis Pullam
48. William Russell
49. James Russell
50. John Robinson
51. David Reese
52. Nicholas Robinson
53. Samuel Shearman
54. Abram Shiver
55. William A. Scott
56. Thomas Spears
57. David Schrock[3]
58. Thomas Trapp
59. John Taber
60. Henry Williams
61. Daniel Watson
62. James Logan
63. Wilie Vaughan
64. Dan'l McLean
65. George Campbell[4]
66. Daniel Swilley[5]

[1] Died February 10, 1815.
[2] Discharged at Charleston, December 4, 1814.
[3] Paymaster.
[4] Died November 5, 1814.
[5] Died November 15, 1814.

# CHAPTER V.
## LaFayette's Visit.

Rarely, if ever, has the gratitude of a republic been more signally displayed than in the long series of honors and ovations tendered the Marquis de LaFayette during his long stay in the United States, as the guest of the nation, in 1824-5.

His progress through twenty-four states was triumphal. Enthusiasm knew no bounds and devotion, it seemed, could not adequately express itself. The romantic figure of LaFayette, next almost to that of Washington among the heroes of the Revolution, appealed to the popular fancy, and his later sufferings in the cause of liberty and humanity in his native France had all the more enshrined him in the hearts of Americans.

If, as Jefferson said, LaFayette had a "canine appetite" for popularity, it has been observed by another that no man ever strove harder to deserve it; and he enjoyed it to a remarkable degree both in this country and in France, where he is said to have retained the confidence of the people longer perhaps than any other man.

He was twice our national guest, first in 1784 for five months; again, for one year and two months, from July 1824 to September, 1825.

Congress voted him $200,000.00 and a township of land, and, on his return home, he was conveyed on an American man-of-war.

During this second visit, accompanied by his son, George Washington LaFayette, and his secretary, Levasseur, he visited nearly every famous battlefield of the War for Independence, of whose general officers he was an almost solitary survivor. In some places old soldiers are said to have fainted from emotion on grasping his hand.

Few, perhaps, of the countless invitations he received touched a more responsive chord than that from the town of Camden, to perform the pious office of laying the cornerstone of a monument to the Baron DeKalb. It was with DeKalb, and ten other companions, that he had set sail in a vessel, fitted out at LaFayette's own expense, from Bordeaux in 1777 to offer their services to Congress. He and DeKalb had landed together on the coast of South

## LaFayette's Visit

Carolina near Georgetown and been entertained by Major Benjamin Huger. Later they together tendered their swords to Washington, and both had attained high rank and distinction in the American armies.

The committee of arrangements, who signed the invitation in behalf of the citizens of Camden, was composed as follows: Benjamin Carter, Thomas Salmond, Edward H. Anderson, William Blanding, Lewis Ciples, Abraham DeLeon, John Doby, John Kershaw, Benjamin Bineham, James S. Deas, James Chesnut.

The just completed residence of Congressman John Carter on Broad Street was selected as his quarters; and, as was the custom of the period, the various households of the community vied with each other in furnishing it with their best plate and mahogany. Colonel Chesnut sent up from "Mulberry" his accomplished Philadelphian housekeeper, Miss Baldwin, to preside over the establishment. A set of china was made especially for the occasion, a few pieces being still in evidence.

The following amusing advertisement is taken from *The Southern Chronicle and Camden Literary and Political Register* of March 5, 1825:

"Look at This!

"The Subscriber is now on his way from the North for Camden and will be here positively on Monday or Tuesday, where he will open, at Mrs. Levison's Millinery Store, a variety of LaFayette Ladies' or Gentlemen's Ball gloves: D° Badges for soldiers and private gentlemen; D° Ladies Belts and D° sashes.

All of which will be sold low for cash.
Abrahams.
N. B. The above articles has been greatly admired at the North."

A few of these badges are still preserved as heirlooms. They are of white silk, with a heavy gold fringe, and are stamped with an excellent likeness of LaFayette at that time. He was then sixty-eight years old.

On his journey southward, General LaFayette was met at the South Carolina line by a corps of cavalry, composed of the companies of Captains Partridge, D. R. Williams and James S. Deas. He was here welcomed to the state by the golden-tongued William C. Preston, the representative of Governor Richard Manning, and he and his suite were transferred to two handsome carriages, drawn by four horses each, which had been put at their disposal by the Governor.

The imposing retinue moved on through the sandy region that extends across the districts of Chesterfield and Kershaw. Lynch's River was passed at DuBose's bridge, and the company camped for the night on Lovick Young's place[1] on Lynch's Creek.

Levasseur, the private secretary, has recorded, in his *LaFayette in America in* 1824 *and* 1825, so many interesting details of this part of the tour that we shall let him tell the story for us.

"Twenty-four hours after our departure from Fayetteville, we met, in the midst of a pine forest, the deputation from the state of South Carolina, sent to meet General LaFayette.

"This meeting took place on the boundary of the two states. Our good and amiable travelling companions of North Carolina delivered us to the care of their neighbors, showing lively expressions of regret at a separation which cost us as much as themselves; and we proceeded on our way in new carriages, with a new escort and new friends, to Cheraw, a pretty little town, which had hardly four houses three years ago, and now contains above fifteen hundred inhabitants. The route which we had to travel the next day was long and difficult: often, indeed, it was almost impassable. In some places, we found it entirely cut off, by the overflowing of streams; in others, we were able to cross the swamps, only by moving slowly over a causeway formed of the trunks of trees, badly enough placed, side by side. At length, we proceeded at so slow a pace, that night overtook us on the road, and grew so dark, that many of the horsemen belonging to the escort strayed from the road, at a place where it was hardly traced upon the sand, and lost themselves in the forest. The carriages of the party, indeed, soon began to be separated; and, about ten o'clock, Mr. George LaFayette and myself discovered that the one in which we were travelling was a great way behind. A few moments after, we felt a violent jolting, and heard

---

[1]It had been planned to stop at Benjamin Perkins' home nearby, but Mrs. Perkins, a daughter of Joseph Kershaw, was too ill at the time.

## LaFayette's Visit

a loud cracking. The pole of the carriage had broken, and we were left in the midst of a morass. Our situation was indeed disagreeable, and we should have had much difficulty to extricate ourselves but for the assistance of two dragoons who had not left us, and who compelled us, in spite of ourselves, to mount their horses; with which, in a short time, we got in sight of the bivouac fires kindled around the house which was to serve as our asylum, and in which the General had already been for nearly an hour. The house stood entirely alone, in the middle of the forest. We were very cordially received; an excellent supper and very good beds were offered us, and we should probably have slept very well, had not trumpets been sounded all night to call in the wandering horsemen. . . . .

"At a signal given by the trumpets (next morning), we set out again, through pine-sands, for Camden, where we were to sleep. During the night the weather had changed, and our progress was favored by a clear sky. Although it was only in the month of March, we severely felt the heat of the sun; and everything around us had the aspect of a forward spring. On approaching Camden, where a great number of gardens are seen in a perfect state of cultivation, we were greatly astonished at finding the trees in blossom, and the air perfumed with the fragrance of plants, as in France in the month of June.

"Camden is not a town of much size, containing, at the utmost, not above 1,200 inhabitants. We, however, found a large collection of people assembled from eighty miles around to receive General LaFayette, and to witness the laying of the first corner-stone of a sepulchral monument which was to be erected to the Baron DeKalb."

William C. Preston, in his unpublished "Autobiography", the manuscript of which is preserved at the University of South Caroilna, particularizes still more, as far as he goes, all too briefly, on the subject, in a little digression from an account of his visit to Paris in 1820:

"The hospitalities I received from the illustrious old gentleman" (in Paris), "I was in some sort able to return, or rather to manifest my sense of them, upon his visit to the United States.

"Governor Manning assigned to me, as his chief aid,

the command of the escort to receive him at the North Carolina line and conduct him to Columbia, the Capital.

"As the North Carolina cortege brought the General to the line at the head of our column, the General extended his hand to me and said, 'I am too happy that your good Governor has thought proper to confide his authority on this pleasing occasion to one whom I remember with so much pleasure in Paris. Please, Colonel Preston, if your duties permit, take a seat with me in the carriage and we will have a talk of old times".

"I had a squadron of cavalry under the immediate command of Colonel Deas, several companies of light troops and many militia companies, tapering off into a countless multitude of men, women and children. All should welcome LaFayette and pressed to gaze upon his beloved person.

"Our sluggish movement threw us late at night when we got to Cheraw. The road for miles was lit up with bonfires casting their lights among the tall pines. When we got near Cheraw, General David R. Williams met us with a large concourse, and said, 'We have not been able to find a Revolutionary soldier to head this procession, so the people brevetted me one and sent me as a representative.' 'Alas', said the General, 'my brethren-in-arms are almost all gone; but I am happy to see their children.' 'And their children happy to see you,' said Williams, and the shout extended away off into the darkness which covered the end of the line.

"From Cheraw our next encampment was at Lovick Young's on Lynches' Creek, where every tree and bush, as far as the eye could reach, was illuminated. The feasting and shouting and reveling had not subsided when at midnight Colonel Deas, an officer of punctilious military etiquette, came in and enquired, 'At what hour in the morning is it your pleasure that the tents be struck?" 'Please take your orders, Colonel Deas, from General LaFayette.' The General said, 'As it is but a short and smooth march to Camden, we will begin it as late as nine o'clock, that the troops may have time to make themselves comfortable.'

"But I am ahead with the episode; *revenons a nos moutons*. That is being interpreted, let's from the piney woods of South Carolina five years back to Paris."

## LaFayette's Visit

So the episode is left dangling, uncompleted, like the autobiography, to the general regret.

Camden was reached on Tuesday morning, March 8, 1825. Outside the limits, LaFayette was received by the Intendant, Thos. Salmond, and took his seat in a carriage furnished by the town.

The booming of cannon announced the arrival to the expectant multitude assembled on the Green in front of the Cornwallis House, where he was joyously welcomed by citizens, civil and military, including some officers and soldiers of the Revolution, while "a national salute was fired from the old star redoubt, in plain view from the Green".[1]

The cortege then proceeded, with great military pomp, through Broad Street, to "LaFayette Hall", as the Carter residence was ever after known.

Brigadier General James Blair was military officer of the day, with Major John Cantey as chief marshal, assisted by William McWillie, Esquire.

Near the Hall, the column halted, opened ranks and faced inwards, making a path through which General LaFayette and his suite passed to the gate leading into the grounds. Here an address of welcome was made by the Committee, and, as the old gentleman proceeded up the brick pavement to the house, his path was strewn with flowers by the young girls of the Female Academy, while they chanted the following ode:

> "Welcome, mighty chief, once more,
> Welcome to this grateful shore:
> Now no mercenary foe
> Aims again the fatal blow—
> Aims at thee the fatal blow.
>
> Virgins fair and matrons grave,
> Those thy conquering arm did save,
> Build for thee triumphal bowers;
> Strew ye fair his way with flowers—
> Strew your Hero's way with flowers."

The names of a few of these girls are preserved; to wit, Misses Ann Cook (Mrs. Dr. Edward Salmond); Louisa

---

[1] *Southern Chronicle*, March 19, 1825.

Salmond; Elizabeth Doby (Mrs. James Dunlap); Mary Young; Abathia Thornton (Mrs. S. W. Capers); Sallie Chesnut; Hester Clarkson (Mrs. Jos. Cunningham); Annie McCown (Mrs. Jesse Nettles); Catherine Clark (Mrs. Dr. Joseph Lee). There were many others. Not one of them now survives.

Miss Young, who died in 1901, vividly recalled the impressive ceremonies. The girls, said she, were in spotless white. One boy alone was with them, young James (later General) Chesnut, he alone having the white trousers and black coat required by Reverend Jonathan Whitaker, the principal of the town schools. She thought LaFayette one of the homeliest men she had ever seen: he was still red-haired and quite lame, leaning heavily, as he walked, on the arm of his son, George Washington. She recalled the only unpleasant incident of the day, the ejection from the lines of the old Tory, Jones, by Captain Starke.[1]

On the wide piazza, the few surviving veterans of the War were introduced to their former comrade-in-arms; and, after light refreshments had been served within the house, we are told that the venerated hero returned to the portico, where he listened attentively to the eloquent address of Camden's gifted young orator, Colonel Henry G. Nixon, from which we give brief extracts. If the style seems inflated and perflorid, let it be remembered that the speaker was only twenty-five years old, if indeed, he sinned any more than his elders of the time.

"General, in the days of youth, when the fancy is apt to be captivated by the splendor and pageantry of palaces and courts, you cast your eyes across the Atlantic and beheld, in the wilds of America, a people struggling to be free. Destined by Heaven for sublime purposes, you left family, country, wealth and nobility, to engage in the storms of a doubtful revolution. The pen of the historian was suspended to solve the enigma of your motive; it has been solved, and confirmed, by the stern consistency of a long life evincing under every vicissitude a Heaven-born love of liberty and man.

"You consecrated our soil at Brandywine, in your first battle, with your blood. You exhibited at Monmouth decision and bravery in battle. At Jamestown you arrested the gallant impetuosity of Wayne and his division, and we can never forget your gallantry in storming the redoubt at the investment of Yorktown.

---

[1] Johnson's *Traditions* (p. 502) relates the story.

## LaFayette's Visit

"After acting as the Champion of Freedom in the New World, you returned to the land of your sires, covered with the laurels which your valor had won. The echoes of our deliverance and joy had scarcely ceased before France caught the flame of revolution from this side of the Atlantic. The prayers of America did not prevail. The Genius of Freedom was doomed to weep over the tomb of liberty in France. The spirit of our people followed you with intense anxiety through all the vicissitudes of a second revolution, from the Assemblage of the Notables to the proclamation of the Duke of Brunswick and the triumph of the Jacobins. It followed you into exile; sympathized with you at Luxembourg; wept over your chains at Wesel; mourned with you in the gloomy dungeon of Madgeburg; cheered you in the poisonous dungeons of the Castle of the Jesuits; rejoiced with you at the treaty of Campo Formio; and inspired one of the gallant sons of Carolina[1] to risk his liberty and life to redeem you from Olmutz.

"General, your visit to Camden excites sublime emotions: we live over in fancy the scenes of its early history; though no splendid edifices, no 'gorgeous temples', no 'cloud-capped turrets', meet your eye, still there are associations connected with it more inspiring than them all. It is seated on classic ground. Its haunts are consecrated by the shades of heroes; its plains honored by their dust. Monuments of the Revolution on all sides remind us of the deeds of our fathers. In its bosom reposes General De-Kalb, your friend and companion in arms.

"I know, Sir, it will afford you a melancholy pleasure to pause and drop a tear at the hero's grave; his spirit and your Washington's will commune with you there.

"Friend of my country and of Washington, Welcome, Thrice Welcome! We greet you with our hearts!!"

### To this General LaFayette replied:

"Sir:—The congratulations of my friends, on this happy visit to the State of South Carolina, cannot at any time or place be more affecting and honorable to me than when offered by you Sir, in the name of Camden and its vicinity, on this classic ground, where, in several battles, my revolutionary brethren have fought and bled; and where, even on unlucky days, actions have been performed which reflect the highest honor on the name

---

[1] Colonel Francis R. Huger, then (1794) a young man of twenty-one years, travelling in Europe. He was a son of Major Benjamin Huger, who had entertained LaFayette and DeKalb on their arrival in America. Huger and a friend, Dr. Bollman, tried to rescue LaFayette when out driving, by arrangement, near Olmutz. Both were imprisoned and narrowly escaped execution.

of which we are justly proud—the *name* of an *American soldier.*

"Such have been, Sir, the able conduct as a commander, the noble fall as a patriot, of General DeKalb. Among my obligations to you, I gratefully acknowledge your kindness in associating me to the tribute paid to the memory of a friend, who, as you observe, has been the early confidant and companion of my devotion to the American cause.

"You are pleased to allude, in terms the most flattering, to several circumstances of our contest—namely, when I had the advantage to name the gallant General Wayne among the officers of the Virginia campaign; and when a redoubt was stormed, in which that accomplished patriot, an honor to Carolina and to mankind, Colonel Laurens, bore a conspicuous part. I have also to thank you for your sympathizing mention of my *Carolinian generous deliverer*, and for your honorable and affectionate recollections of the vicissitudes of my life.

"I shall only say that, as an introduction of American principles, not only on this whole hemisphere, but also on the other side of the Atlantic, has been the object of my continued desire and my fond hopes; so the powerful animadversions excited by those feelings I am far from deprecating and shall never forfeit.

"As to the effect you are pleased to attribute to my filial love for our great and beloved chief, be assured, my dear Sir, that, on the contrary, at the court of Germany in those times, as well as at the court of France, my own best recommendation has been the boast I was entitled to claim of being *Washington's adopted son.*

"Now, gentlemen, I find myself in your good town of Camden, surrounded by beauty in its youngest bloom; by my old *Seventy-six friends*, as it was the year of my enlistment in our noble cause; by the intermediary generations, all so very kind to me: and I am happy in this opportunity to offer you my affectionate and respectful acknowledgments."

Immediately after the conclusion of these addresses, a *feu de joie* was fired by the Infantry in front of the mansion, which was succeeded by a "national salute" from Hobkirk Hill.

The morning's exercises closed with the personal presentation of ladies and gentlemen present to their affable guest.

At four o'clock in the afternoon, General LaFayette, who, like Washington and DeKalb, was a conspicuous Mason, was waited upon by a deputation of past masters

## LaFayette's Visit

of that ancient order, who conducted him to Masonic Hall, where he was received, in open lodge, by a large concource of members and visiting brethren. Worshipful Master Abraham DeLeon delivered the address of welcome and the guest of honor replied saying, among other things, "Amidst the gratification and favors which have been heaped upon me at every step of my happy visit to the United States, the welcome of the Masonic Fraternity has been particularly pleasing."

A sumptuous banquet followed,[1] and at eight o'clock the entire gathering escorted the old gentleman to his lodgings.

Two hours later he appeared at a brilliant ball given in his honor at the Long Room of the Camden Hotel.

The late General Kershaw used to tell the following anecdote of this notable function. As each gentleman was presented, LaFayette would ask, "Married?" If the reply was yes, he would exclaim "Ah, happy fellow, happy fellow!" If no, he would cry, with a sly wink, "Lucky dog, sir, lucky dog!"

The simple account of the reinterment of DeKalb's remains and the laying of the cornerstone of the monument to his memory, as published in the *Camden Southern Chronicle* of March 26, 1825, can scarcely be improved upon and we reproduce it almost in its entirety.

"General LaFayette having stated that any hour on Wednesday (March 9th) would be agreeable to him, the procession was formed at twelve o'clock, in the following order:

Military escort on the left
Band
Masonic Body
Remains of
BARON DEKALB
War Horse
General LaFayette and Suite
Officers and Soldiers of the Revolution
Field Officers
General Blair and Suite
Superintendent of Public Works
Architect
Masons employed on the Monument
Monument Committee

[1] In one of the Orphan Society Academies. (From Minutes of the Society.)

Students of the different schools and their Instructors
General Committee
Federal and State Officers
Intendant and Municipal Officers
Citizens
Cavalry

"The remains, supported by six revolutionary officers, Colonel Anderson, Major Whitaker, and Captains Mayrant, Nettles, Starke and Brown, as pall bearers, in procession with General LaFayette and the Masonic body, were received through the ranks of the military escort with a salute, and formed on their right; when the escort reclosed ranks and marched by columns from the left up Broad Street to the site of the monument in front of the Presbyterian Church. Here a prayer was offered to the Throne of Grace by the Reverend Robert McLeod, and, the remains being deposited in the vault, the grand Masonic honors were paid by Kershaw Lodge and the visiting brethren.

"Immediately after the performance of the funeral rites, the Master of the Lodge presented to the General the appropriate Masonic implements and the dispensation, signed by John Geddes, Grand Master of the State."

After the General had laid the cornerstone in due Masonic order, he returned the tools to Robert Mills,[1] Esquire, the architect, expressing the confidence of the Committee in his talents and zeal in the direction of the work; to which the architect replied:

"Illustrious Brother: The recollection of the worth and services of him to whom this monument is dedicated, and that the cornerstone has been laid by the hands of one whom the virtuous throughout the world delight to honor will prove a sufficient stimulus to the performance of these duties which are entrusted to me as architect."

The Superintendent of Public Works, Abram Blanding, then approached the stone prepared to cover the vault, on which this inscription was engraved:

---

[1] Robert Mills, as stated in other pages, was the architect of the old Court House and the Presbyterian Church at Camden. He was appointed Architect and Engineer of South Carolina in 1820. He built the Charleston and Hamburg Railway, the first railroad of any extent in the world. He was the constructor of the Washington monument at Baltimore, the National monument to Washington at the Capital, and many other great public works. He was the author of the famous *Statistics of South Carolina* and of an excellent atlas of the state.

## LaFayette's Visit

>"This Stone
>was placed over
>the remains
>of
>Baron DeKalb
>by
>General LaFayette
>1825"

and delivered a short address.

To which LaFayette replied:

" 'The honor now bestowed upon me, I receive with the mingled emotions of patriotism, gratitude and friendship; and, like other honorable duties which await me in the more northern parts of the Union, I consider it as being conferred on the Revolutionary army in the person of a surviving general officer.

" 'In that army, Sir, which offered a perfect assemblage of every civic and military virtue, Major General Baron DeKalb has acted a conspicuous part. His able conduct, undaunted valor, and glorious fall, in the first battle of Camden, form one of the remarkable traits of our struggle for independence and freedom. He was cordially devoted to our American cause, and while his public and private qualities have endeared him to his contemporaries, here I remain to pay to his merits on this tomb, the tribute of an admiring witness, of an intimate companion, of a mourning friend'."

"While the stone was slowly descending to close the vault, the General bending with deep humility and great emotion over it, followed it with his hand to its place, and a funeral dirge increased the awful solemnity of the occasion.

"The ceremony then closed with the usual military honors.

"The Portico of the Presbyterian Church, during the ceremony, was crowded with a brilliant assemblage of ladies, who witnessed with profound attention the interesting scene that was passing before them."

In a letter to the "Camden Journal", dated Kirkwood, Mississippi, July 6, 1873, Dr. E. H. Anderson, an old Camden "boy", indulges in the following pleasing reminiscences:

HISTORIC CAMDEN

"One incident that happened when I was about eight years old, and that forms an interesting epoch in the history of Camden, has just occurred to my mind, viz., LaFayette's visit in 1825 and the laying of the cornerstone of the DeKalb monument. It is as distinct to my recollection as if it had happened but a day or two since. The coffin said to contain the bones of DeKalb was placed in the yard of the Lower Bank, that old and honored citizen, Thomas Salmond, then being president, and I witnessed with much interest the preparation of the cerement in which the bones were placed. I recollect their going to the Presbyterian Church, where the crowd was so immense that I climbed a tree opposite Henry R. Cook's residence to witness the ceremony in the churchyard, the Masons with the Marquis de LaFayette at their head officiating. I then went to LaFayette Hall, where I heard Henry G. Nixon deliver his welcoming address[1] and I recollect how well pleased he seemed to be with the duty he had to perform. I recollect too the seeming pleasure with which LaFayette heard him; and finally I remember going to the window of the Hall and seeing my father[2] seated and conversing with LaFayette. I walked in to get some lemonade, when my father called me to him and presented me to the General, who patted me on the head and said something to my father which I did not hear. I got away as quickly as possible to get more lemonade, but I still feel the impression of that pat on my head."

The next day, the party, still under the escort of Captain Deas with his troop of cavalry, moved on to Columbia.

Baron DeKalb's body was first laid to rest in the lower part of the large field on the north side of Meeting Street, half way between Church and Broad Streets, just back of the Blue House, where he expired. The exact location of the grave is marked in red on the map of Camden made in 1798. (See diagram No. 4, "Historic Camden, Colonial and Revolutionary.")

From the "Random Recollections" of Edwin J. Scott, we learn that, as a schoolboy at Camden in 1811, he "played frequently on the grave of Baron DeKalb, in the

---

[1]Nixon's address was delivered the previous day. Dr. Anderson's memory was a little confused.
[2]Colonel Richard Anderson, a veteran of the Revolution.

middle of a lonely old field at the southwestern part of the town. It was surrounded by a plain brick structure three or four feet high, covered by a white stone slab, with an inscription eulogizing his character and services."

This original tablet was discovered in 1901 by the authors in the basement of the Presbyterian Church, where it had probably lain forgotten during the past seventy-six years. The inscription, written by the historian Ramsay, is identical with that on the present monument.

When this first memorial was reared is uncertain. Elkanah Watson, a northern veteran of the Revolution, who made a tour of the South in 1786, says in his "Reminiscences": "I saw, at Camden, the tomb, enclosed by a decent paling, in which reposed the ashes of the gallant De Kalb and several British officers." He probably meant by the "tomb", simply the grave, as Washington, on his visit to Camden in 1791, records in his "Diary" that he "visited the grave of DeKalb", but does not mention a monument, as he would likely have done had there been one, with his disposition to particularize.

Weems, in his "Life of Marion", first published in 1805, says of DeKalb. "Congress ordered him a monument, but the friend of Saint Tammany still sleeps 'without his fane'. I have seen the place of his rest. It was the lowest spot of the plain. No sculptured warrior mourned his low-laid *head;* no cypress decked his *heel.* But the tall corn stood in darkening ranks around him, and seemed to shake their green leaves with joy over his narrow dwelling."

Then, in the very next paragraph, which may have been added in the edition of 1824, or earlier, he inconsistently adds: "The citizens of Camden have lately enclosed his grave, and placed on it handsome marble, with an epitaph descriptive of his virtues and services, that the people of future days may, like Washington, heave the sigh when they read of the generous stranger who came from a distant land to fight their battles and to water, with his blood, the tree of their liberties."

From all which we infer that the slab must have been placed sometime between 1805 and 1811, when Edwin J. Scott "played" on it.

Dr. Ramsay, who wrote the epitaph, died in 1815, and Parson Weems in 1825.

That it was erected by the Masonic Fraternity, we learn from a communication (writer unknown) published in the "Baltimore Sun" in 1886.

"During the Revolutionary War, at the Battle of Camden, South Carolina, where brave Baron DeKalb fell at the head of the Maryland line, there were six of the officers[1] who were Masons. Among these were several from Maryland, and Major Benjamin Nones of Philadelphia. After the death of DeKalb, who was a Mason, on the 19th of August, 1780, the brethren assembled and buried the remains with Masonic ceremonies. Many years afterwards, the brethren of South Carolina, with a commendable fraternal feeling, determined to do all in their power to pay proper respect due the memory of a deceased brother and patriot. They undertook, at considerable trouble and expense, to discover the resting place of the deceased brother, in order to mark the spot with some memento of a Mason's appreciation of a brother who gallantly fell in the cause of freedom.

"This caused search to be made, but without effect, as nothing could be seen to mark the spot. A committee was appointed to make further search and elicit all the information possible to carry their intentions into effect. The chairman of the committee, Dr. A. H. DeLeon, of Camden, South Carolina, addressed a letter of inquiry upon the subject to Mr. Nones, of Philadelphia, who, as one, and perhaps the only one, of the survivors, might be supposed, notwithstanding his great age, to have some recollection of the spot where the body had been interred. Mr. Nones, who still retained a vivid recollection of the circumstances in his memory, dictated a letter describing the spot as nearly as possible, and, within a few feet of the place designated by him, the remains were found."

Dr. E. M. Boykin, writing on the same subject to the "Baltimore News" (1886), says: "Miss Hettie Cummings, an old English lady, who had remained when the British army left, knew about where it (the body) was, and, by digging rectangular ditches, it was found.[2]

[1] Prisoners in Camden, presumably, after the battle.
[2] Dr. Boykin dates this incident at the time of the re-interment (1825)—but the difficulty of locating the remains must have been when the first stone was raised, prior to 1811.

## LaFayette's Visit

The desire of the people of the state to erect a more suitable memorial to DeKalb took definite form in the early 20's, and, by 1824, the funds had all been raised. Matters were hurried in order that General LaFayette might lay the cornerstone, while on his tour through the South.

The granite for the foundations and pediments of the structure was quarried at White Oak, sixteen miles above Camden, on the old Ciples plantation. Colonel Abram Blanding furnished it free of charge, and the planters of the vicinity hauled it down, without pay, in fourteen wagons.

All was in readiness for the placing of the cornerstone, when LaFayette arrived.

DeKalb's body was exhumed.[1] Of this interesting event Dr. Boykin says:[2] "He lay, it seems, in the 'custom of knighthood', as last of his race, buried in his armor; that is to say, his helmet, his sword and his spurs were in the grave with him. My relator (an old slave of Mr. Lewis Ciples) went on to say that, when the body was taken up, old Captain Carter, who, to use the old man's expression, did what he pleased—(the old Captain had fought under DeKalb and was lame from a wound received during the war)—said he meant to take the helmet, and that they might keep the sword and spurs; and he did take it.

"At this point, Dr. James A. Young, was applied to, who well remembered the reburial and the laying of the cornerstone of the monument by General LaFayette, and remembered that he was buried with sword and spurs."

The aged negro, Wash Carlos by name, went on to say (according to Dr. Boykin), that, at the death of Captain Carter, who was a bachelor, "old Kalb's muster cap", as he called it, was appropriated by Mr. Ciples, who was then living on Hobkirk Hill.[3] After Mr. Ciples died, the helmet was knocked about as a piece of old iron, and Dr. A. W. Burnet, who later occupied the place, found it in an outhouse on the premises. Only the visor remained: it was formerly complete, the old negro remembering

---

[1] This work was superintended by Captain Warren, Captain Carter and Mr. Ciples.

[2] Letter to the "Baltimore News" (1886).

[3] This house, remodeled, was later the home of the late William M. Shannon, just north of Hobkirk Inn.

that his sister and himself, as children, used to "slap it backward and forward" (the visor on the morion, or headpiece).

The "muster-cap" was presented by Dr. Burnet to Dr. E. M. Boykin, at whose death it came into possession of his widow and, through her, into the hands of her son, John Boykin, who, on request, expressed it to be exhibited at the Charleston Exposition (1902). It never reached its destination, and, though diligent investigation was made, it has never been found.

Dr. Burnet remembered hearing his father say that he had seen at "Middleton Place", on the Ashley River, near Charleston, what was said to be the "armor" of DeKalb. Writing to Mr. Middleton, at Dr. Boykin's instigation, Dr. Burnet was informed that the armor, except the helmet, had been in the possession of the Middleton family, (how and why was not explained), from a "few days after the Baron's death" until the spring of 1865, when it was stolen and has never since been seen. Mr. Middleton must have meant a few days after DeKalb's body was dis-interred, if we are to believe that the armor, as averred, was found in his grave in 1825.

\* \* \* \* \* \* \* \*

The DeKalb monument was not completed until 1827. It consists of a base of twenty-six massive granite blocks surmounted by an obelisk of white marble.

On the cornerstone is engraved
Foedus
EstoPerpetuum

On twenty-four of the other foundation stones are cut the names of the twenty-four states then composing the Union. The twenty-sixth block covers the remains in the vault.

The superstructure bears the following inscription by the historian, Ramsay:

Here
lie the remains
of
BARON DEKALB
A German by birth,
but in principle
a citizen of the world.
His love of liberty

## LaFayette's Visit

induced him
to leave the Old World
to aid the citizens of the New
in their struggle
for
Independence.
His distinguished talents and many virtues
weighed with Congress
to appoint him
Major General
in their
Revolutionary Army.
He was second in command
in the battle fought near Camden
on the 16th of August, 1780,
between
the British and Americans,
and
there nobly fell
covered with wounds,
while gallantly performing deeds of valour,
in rallying the friends
and
opposing the enemies
of
his adopted *country*.
In gratitude for his zeal and
services, the citizens of South Carolina
have erected this
monument.

\* \* \* \* \* \* \* \*

The historic trowel used by LaFayette in laying the cornerstone of the DeKalb monument was made for the purpose by Mr. Alexander Young of Camden. It has since been used in the dedication of many other monuments, among them the memorials to Jasper, Sims and Moultrie at Charleston, to the martyrs of the Revolution at Cowpens and King's Mountain and to the Confederate dead at Camden.

For a great many years it was in the possession of the Salmond family, who sold it, in 1893, to the Grand Lodge of Masons of South Carolina. The price paid, it is said, was $400.00. It is perhaps the most treasured relic of the Masonic Order in the state.

The blade is of solid silver, with an ivory handle, and it bears this inscription: "Made for Brother LaFayette to lay the cornerstone of DeKalb's monument, 1825."

LaFayette Hall, a large and imposing mansion, was for more than three-quarters of a century one of Camden's historic shrines. It stood on Broad Street not far above DeKalb. It was built by Henry R. Cook, it is said, who sold it before completion, in 1824, to John C. Carter, who conveyed to James B. Cureton. In 1842, it passed into the hands of James Dunlap, whose family occupied it for more than fifty years. In 1901 it came into the possession of the late Baron von Tresckow, who added a considerable wing and rented it as an hotel; he also cut a street, now known as LaFayette Avenue, through the northern part of the grounds. In 1903, the old landmark was consumed by fire, and, two years later, the new County Court House was erected upon the site.

A cedar tree, set out with others to ornament the front grounds on the occasion of LaFayette's visit, took root and still stands.

# CHAPTER VI.
## NULLIFICATION TIMES.

"The time will come when truth will prevail in spite of prejudice and denunciation, and when politics will be considered as much a science as astronomy and chemistry."
—*Calhoun.*

The rise and progress of that phenomenon known as "Nullification", marks the period between 1825 and 1835 as perhaps the most picturesque in our annals, and also marks the origin of those differences which culminated in secession. The intensity of the controversy developed a constellation of talented men, several of whom belong to Camden.

The doctrine of "Nullification" arose out of opposition to the protective tariffs and internal improvements by the Federal Government. The agricultural South bitterly resented tariff taxes as a bounty to Northern manufacturers. Stephen D. Miller put the case thus, "Have not the manufacturers laid hands on our rights in violation of the Constitution, and seized the keys to our liberty? Let Southern cuck-olds adjust their horns and shout hosannas to the Union. For my part while I believe the silver dollars of the South are poured into the lap of the West as the wages of prostitution to the Tariff, I will not join the chorus."

Internal improvements, viewed as bribes to the West for support to the tariff, became equally odious. Hence the petition in 1830 for Federal aid to the South Carolina Railway, was presented to Congress by Daniel Webster, the South Carolina senators refusing to do so.

The tariff of 1824, which at this day would seem a trifle light as air, kindled a flame in South Carolina. Public meetings in protest were held throughout the State, and the iniquities of the tariff were the burden of every speech. In the legislative session of this year Stephen D. Miller offered a resolution in the State Senate, adopted after strenuous debate, declaring that Congress had no power to levy duties for protection of manufacturers or to make internal improvements. This resolution made his political fortune.

Dr. Cooper, President of the South Carolina College, in 1825, in a pamphlet on the tariff used this phrase: "It is time for us to begin to calculate the value of the Federal Union", which furnished the text for Webster's reply to Hayne. James Blair, of our district, a leader of the Union party, and Dr. Cooper fell afoul of each other. Blair termed Cooper "that old political prostitute" and Cooper retorted by allusion to Blair's exploits recorded in the Criminal Court of Kershaw County.

The increased tariff of 1828 added fuel to the flames of the tariff conflict. While this measure was pending in Congress, a large public meeting was held in Camden, August 1827, to protest against its passage, especially the tariff on woolens. The youthful Henry G. Nixon was the principal speaker and delivered a learned discourse on the subject. James Chesnut, Sr., as chairman of committee, submitted a memorial to Congress, declaring the proposed measure hostile to farming interests.

The animosity aroused was such as to cause boycotting of Northern-made goods. Gov. S. D. Miller was inaugurated in a full suit of homespun; Geo. McDuffie declared the protective tariff to be "robbery and plunder", and gave his broad cloth coat of Northern manufacture to his servant, saying it was fit livery for slaves only. Judge Huger refused to eat Northern grown Irish potatoes.

The Legislature of 1828 ordered printed a report of some fifty pages, the acknowledged production of J. C. Calhoun, which thenceforth became the authorized version of the doctrine of nullification. It asserted the right of the State to interpose its Sovereignty and declare *null and void*, within its borders, an unconstitutional act of Congress.

The sentiment of the State, while practically a unit against the tariff, was becoming more and more discordant over the question of the nullification remedy. The extreme proposal to nullify an act of Congress presented difficulties. A strong element balked at such a proposal as too extreme and unpractical. State's Rights became the one topic. The press and the platform teemed with elaborate disquisitions on the principles of government.

Opinion in the State was pretty evenly divided up to 1830, when the Nullifiers gained the ascendant in the election of James Hamilton as Governor. The Unionists, though a minority, could boast of able leaders. In this district they always maintained a majority, and in their ranks were such men as Wm. McWillie, James Blair,

## NULLIFICATION TIMES

H. G. Nixon, James Chesnut, Sr., Chapman Levy, C. F. Daniels, C. J. Shannon, Abram Blanding. As leading exponents of Nullification may be mentioned Stephen D. Miller, T. J. Withers, Jas. S. Deas, John Boykin, Wm. E. Johnson, Joseph Patterson. The controversy between these factions was fierce and relentless. The Unionists were taunted as "Submissionists", and the Nullifiers in return were dubbed "Nullies".

The debates of 1829 and 1830 in the United States Senate, between Hayne and Webster, were but summaries of arguments used at every cross-roads in South Carolina. Never were popular discussions in politics so metaphysical. Out of the confusion emerged a proposition for a convention to consider and determine the State's course of action. The suggestion seems to have come from our own Henry G. Nixon. At any rate he was the introducer of the first resolution for such a convention, and his last legislative effort, in December, 1828, on the eve of his fatal duel, was made in its advocacy. The legislature of 1831 did call a convention for this purpose to meet in November 1832. A convention in 1828 would have eventuated very differently from that of 1832.

The elections of 1832, which were to determine the complexion of the convention and ensuing legislature, were crucial. The Nullifiers carried the State, but Kershaw County remained staunch Unionist. Chapman Levy, John Chesnut, Everard Cureton and Chas. J. Shannon were elected to the Convention over the Nullifier's ticket, Brevard, Whitaker, Cantey, Nixon. The vote for members of the Legislature resulted as follows:

*State Senate.*

| Union. | | Nullification. | |
|---|---|---|---|
| James Chesnut, Sr. | 556 | Jas. S. Deas | 358 |

*Representatives.*

| | | | |
|---|---|---|---|
| Thos. Lang | 603 | John Boykin, Sr. | 341 |
| Wm. McWillie | 596 | Benj. T. Elmore | 330 |
| Wm. O. Nixon | 583 | Jos. Patterson | 290 |

Two newspapers were then published in Camden, *The Journal*, Unionist, edited by the witty and able C. F. Daniels, and *The Beacon*, established to combat *The Journal*. Their mutual denunciation was venomous beyond parallel.

*The Beacon* poured out such expressions as the following: "When we have spoken of such wretches as the editor of the *Camden Journal*, whom we know to be a hollow-hearted hypocrite in politics"; "The servile whiffler of the *Camden Journal*", etc.

At the banquet given by the Union men at Camden to General Jas. Blair in 1832, the following was one of the toasts: "*The Tariff and Nullification*: The one unjust, inexpedient and unconstitutional; the other dangerous, inefficient and suicidal. In avoiding Scylla let us not be destroyed in Charybdis. Air: 'Go to the devil, and shake yourself'."

Daniels of *The Journal* ignored these personalities, and fired missiles into the ranks of the Nullifiers, in the following fashion:

"A grosser humbug, a more abominable deception than the Nullification party is endeavoring to play off upon the people of South Carolina never disgraced the annals of Revolution. It deserves the wrath and vengeance of an insulted community—a desperate and bloody demagogism—a very shallow attempt to gullify some portion of the people whom they have found it impossible to nullify."

The rancor of the contest was thus depicted by John Boykin, who wrote to the *Beacon*: "Our once harmonious and united district is now unhappily an arena where all the angry passions have their full scope, and those whom I had ever known as thinking and acting together are now arrayed in fierce hostility against each other. We have reached a crisis, and he must be blind indeed who does not recognize it."

Chief interest centered in the candidacy of Col. Jas. S. Deas and Col. James Chesnut, Sr., for the State Senate. Col. Deas had for eight years represented the district as Senator, and was a man of great charm and popularity, but he was decisively beaten in the election as the above figures show. His wife was a sister of Colonel Chesnut, and their families had been closely intimate. This contest, however, caused a complete breach between them, and Colonel Deas shortly after changed his residence to Mobile, Ala., where he spent the rest of his life. His son, Zack Cantey Deas, afterwards a Confederate General, was once a Camden boy.

The memorable convention met, and on November 24th, 1832 passed the ordinance of Nullification, whereby the

## NULLIFICATION TIMES

tariff acts of Congress were pronounced *null* and void, and collection of all tariff duties within the State after February 1st, 1833 prohibited. All officers of the State and jurors in all cases were required to subscribe an oath to support the ordinance. Appeal to the Federal Courts was forbidden in cases involving the validity of the ordinance.

Here was open defiance of Federal authority. Andrew Jackson had just been re-elected President, although South Carolina, his native State, had cast her vote for Governor Floyd of Virginia, a rank Nullifier. With a vim "Old Hickory" drew forth the pen and the sword also. On December 10th, 1832, after adoption of the ordinance he issued a proclamation of no uncertain sound:

"The laws of the United States must be executed. Those who told you that you might peaceably prevent their execution deceived you, they could not have deceived themselves. Their object is disunion. Be not deceived by names; disunion by armed force is treason."

But South Carolina did not waver. The Legislature, then in session, provided for 20,000 volunteers and arms to defend her ordinance. Jackson sent federal troops and vessels to Charleston, where the State forces also assembled. A collision seemed imminent.

The women of Carolina were roused. A correspondent of the *Camden Journal* of February 2nd, 1833, signing "Kershaw" tells how, at a muster in Clarendon County, a number of ladies volunteered, and begun military practice by pulling triggers and firing guns. He suggested that "gun holders" be furnished for each of these Amazons." The tension to which political lines were drawn may also be judged from the fact that in January 1833, the old officers of the Bank of Camden, who were of the Union persuasion viz.: Jas. Clark, Chas. J. Shannon, E. H. Anderson, C. Matheson and John Chesnut, were replaced by Nullifiers as follows: Jas. S. Deas, Jos. Patterson, Wm. E. Johnson, Abram D. Jones and John J. Winn.

The crisis was relieved by the Clay-Calhoun compromise in the spring of 1833, whereby a progressive reduction of the tariff was agreed upon. But Congress, along with this compromise act, passed the "Force Bill", which authorized the use of arms by the president to enforce the new, compromise tariff measure, as its acceptance by South Carolina was not yet assured.

Another convention was assembled in South Carolina in March 1833. It did rescind the nullification ordinance. But to save its principles and its face, as it were, the convention declared the "Force Bill" null and void. This amounted to nothing more than an abstract declaration, for opposition to the tariff being withdrawn, there would be no occasion to apply the Force Bill. General James Blair likened this proceeding of the convention to "an idiot nullifying the whirlwind."

This convention created further trouble by an ordinance to the effect that the allegiance of the citizen is due to the State, and obedience, not allegiance, to any other power or authority. The Legislature in conformity with this ordinance required of all civil and military officers "oaths binding them to allegiance to the State paramount to all other allegiance." Senator Stephen D. Miller vigorously opposed this Test Oath in the convention. The defeat of his effort may have been one inducement to his resignation from the United States Senate.

This provision was viewed by the Union party as aimed at their destruction. The *Camden Journal*, March 16th, 1833, expressed it thus: "The Nullies, now that they have settled with the Federal Government, wont settle with us—they are preparing more test oaths for us. The Nullifiers only want to oppress the Union party."

In various meetings the Unionists expressed their defiance in terms of which the following is a sample, adopted by the people of Taxahaw section of Lancaster County:

"We must either consent to be the humble slaves of d spotism, or resort to the dire alternative of civil strife, but if it must come we are ready for it. We never will obey any officer who will take the test oath, or wear the Palmetto button or anything like it. We will go to the very death in defence of any officer we may by our own free suffrage elect to command us. If any Union man is imprisoned on account of the Military Bill, we will at all hazards release him."

The *Camden Journal* of June 18, 1834, said: "Their offices are scorned, but the time must come when the blood of freemen which courses through our veins will refuse any longer to be governed by the spirit of long suffering and forbearance, and then to act will be our duty, if it be but to rush upon the extended bayonets of our ready executioners."

A Greenville meeting declared: "We will regard any attempt to enforce the Military Bill as an act making leaden bullets current coin."

John C. West, the head of a prominent family of Camden, which afterwards like so many others migrated westward, had been elected Sheriff of the County. He refused to take the test oaths in qualification, and published his reasons as follows: "I cannot conscientiously subscribe the oath, because it requires that I should at the same time swear to support and maintain to the utmost of my ability the laws of the United States, and to obey, execute and enforce the ordinance to nullify a portion of the very laws which I am swearing to support." He was again elected by a decisive majority.

Thomas Lang offered a curious example of the old saying that extremes meet. He was elected by the Union party to the Legislature at the head of their ticket. To their amazement he voted in favor of the test oath. The act was entirely conscientious on his part and in accord with his principles. He seems to have been identified with the Union men, not because of any disapproval of the States Rights doctrine, of which he was an extreme advocate, but for the reason that he disapproved the purpose of the Nullifier to remain in the Union and at the same time to nullify its laws. On State allegiance he was really with the Nullifiers, but was more radical and consistent than they. Colonel Shannon has said: "He cast his vote sternly, quietly, with calm dignity, and gracefully retired, knowing that the act closed his public life."

Fortunately a truce was called pending submission of the validity of the test oaths to the State Court of Appeals at Columbia. Here the foremost talent of the State was arrayed in its discussion. Of the great legal trio opposing the oath, Petigru, Blanding and McWillie, two were from Camden. The Court, composed of O'Neall, Johnson and Harper, declared the oath unconstitutional. Harper dissenting. The following Legislature abolished the Court and re-enacted the oath, but extended an olive branch by a resolution that the oath was *not intended to be inconsistent with the obligation and allegiance to the*

*United States.* Thus the strife was pacified, and the hot political fires burnt to ashes. The clouds of abolition had already begun to loom on the horizon, and the new menace diverted attention from old issues and operated to unite the warring factions.

Looking down the avenue of time, we can see the germs of Nullification in the "Virginia and Kentucky Resolutions" of 1791, whereby the doctrine was announced, that when Congress assumes undelegated powers, its acts are *null* and void, and of no binding force upon the States.

In reviewing this period a local anonymous character must not be forgotten, one who signed himself in the *Camden Journal* of the day, "A Plain Man". He contributed a series of forcible articles to that paper, and was doubtless some one of the notable men then residing in Camden. As a memorial to him this chapter will close with an extract from his pen which statesmen will do well to bear in mind:

"Liberty depends upon public opinion. It lives in the spirit and intelligence of the people. From the moment they cease to be worthy of a good government they are sure to have a bad one. The glorious right of revolution, Sir, this is the only safeguard of liberty. As Mr. Randolph once said: 'You may entrench yourselves in parchment to the teeth: a fig for the Constitution, 'tis the heart, Master Page, 'tis here'."

## CHAPTER VII.
### James Blair.

"In shape and gesture proudly eminent."

James Blair was a conspicuous figure in South Carolina politics during the days of Nullification, and leader of the Union party in this District. He was endowed with notable powers of mind and body, and with more mental ballast would have fulfilled a higher destiny.

Colonel W. M. Shannon, who was a boy in Blair's prime, has left us, in his memoirs, this graphic picture of the man. "Few men have made so strong an impression on us in our 'salad days'. We have sat upon his knee, admired and loved his gentle, winning manner, his emotional expression and noble face, and yet an hour after would be somewhat afraid of the other General Blair, whom we would see on the streets or on some public platform. General Blair was one of nature's noblemen, cast in heroic mould, six feet six inches in height, of imposing proportions. Forest born, when he came out among the men of the outer world, he towered above them as he had done among the native growth of the back woods."

We have little or nothing in regard to his early days. He was born, about 1790, in the Waxhaws, Lancaster County, that nursery of strong men, which sent forth Andrew Jackson, Stephen D. Miller, Marion Simms and others. His parents were William and Sarah Douglas Blair. Francis Blair, an elder brother, commanded a company under Colonel Adam McWillie in the War of 1812. Geo. D. Blair, another brother, practiced law in Camden for some years, and with a sister Dorcas removed to Shelbyville, Tenn. in 1834. General Frank P. Blair of Sherman's army was related to the family and camped with his troops in February, 1865, on Red Oak Camp Creek in this County at the Blair mansion.

In March 1818, when twenty-eight, Blair was elected General of the eighth brigade of State militia, being at the time Sheriff of Lancaster County. This was a distinction at his age, as the military was then the main avenue to public promotion, also a pastime that filled the place of base-ball and foot-ball in these days.

## Historic Camden

But the muster was not all parade. Here feats of wrestling, boxing and "gouging", were indulged in, often ending in serious affairs. The candidate for popular favor had to win his spurs. Blair was a perfect Hercules in all such encounters, and stood without a rival. It is related how the champion of North Carolina muster fields, hearing of the Waxhaw giant, came down to tackle him on his own ground and rode straight to his home. He found his man ploughing in the field, and on brief acquaintance insisted they have a round right then and there. "Well", said Blair "let me unhook my mule." The result of the grapple was that the champion was flung clear over the high rail fence, and so badly bruised that he had to recuperate in the hospitable Blair home.

About 1820 Blair moved to Kershaw County, where he married Charlotte Rochelle and settled on Red Oak Camp and Lynche's Creeks about twenty-five miles northeast of Camden and six miles north of the present town of Bethune. He became at once a leader in County politics, and his popularity never waned. To quote Colonel Shannon again: "His noble presence, hearty manners and bold sincerity fastened his friends. Bland and conciliatory towards opponents, he disarmed prejudice. He gave studied attention to his dress. His rich blue-cloth suit, ruffled shirt and gold headed cane were in keeping with his grand bearing."

In 1821 he was elected to Congress for the district composed of Kershaw, Lancaster, Chesterfield and Sumter Counties, over Judge Brevard and James Postell. It is sufficient evidence of his talents that he should have won the place against such opponents, at the age of thirty-one, and the next year, with only the training of a planter, have taken creditable part in the debate in Congress on such measures as the Bankruptcy bill. In July 1822 he resigned his seat, stating that his "private concerns were such as to leave no discretion on the subject."

The next six years he spent on his extensive estate on Lynche's Creek, but he must have been studious, judging by the quality of his speeches and writings. He was also a devotee of horse, hound and horn. His faithful attendant was one "Chunky Bone", a very tall Catawba Indian, who lies buried, 'tis said, in the Blair cemetery

## James Blair

on Lynche's Creek, where a phenomenally long grave is pointed out as his.

Unfortunately the General indulged to excess in strong drink, and at times played the ruffian. One of his wild freaks is matter of tradition and also of record. A neighbor, Lovick Young, had incurred his dislike. An old affidavit in the Court files exists, to this effect: "that on June 1st 1825, about dark, James Blair accompanied by his man Dave, entered the house of Lovick Young *on horseback* terrifying Mrs. Young and the children, that he did beat, bruise and ill-treat Abraham Lamb, and as the said Lamb was getting away fired a gun after him." Tradition adds that Blair leapt his horse over the infant's cradle, and that during this procedure, the said Lovick Young was hidden under the house.

It was inevitable in such times, that he should have figured in brawls and duels. Several were averted on the eve of the event, such as that with James H. Hammond (afterwards Governor and United States Senator), which ended with drinks instead of shots, after principals and seconds had met at some place in North Carolina. That with Thos. P. Evans actually occurred. Evans was very small, and wore a coat much too large, which saved him, for Blair's ball passed through the coat without touching Evans, who had no valid excuse for missing so huge a mark as the General. Evans said that the muzzle of Blair's pistol looked as big as a flour barrel.

Such exploits enhanced rather than impaired the General's popularity. In 1828 he again stood for Congress and defeated Richard I. Manning of Sumter. From that time he became the recognized head of the Union party in the district, it may almost be said, in the State; and we may rather wonder that, with his hot-spur temperament, he should have adopted the conservative side. He acquired and retained the support of such men as Wm. McWillie, Chapman Levy, C. F. Daniels, C. J. Shannon, and James Chesnut, Sr., and was re-elected to Congress in 1830, 1832 and 1834.

Some extracts from his speeches are here presented. In Congress, 1830, he said: "Sir, there are but few states in the Union that would have submitted to the shears of the manufacturers as South Carolina has. Had old Massachusetts, a state I shall always venerate, been affected by your tariff as South Carolina has been, she would long since have taught you to respect her rights, or she would have taken care of them herself, and indeed, as it is, some of her leading men had like to have kicked up a confounded dust about the molasses."

From a letter to his constituents, 1830: "As to nullification or 'peaceful resistance', have we not had too much gasconading already? If the evils we complain of are no longer to be endured, why shrink from energetic and effective measures at once? Whenever the people in their wisdom, or in their madness if you please, determine that the crisis has arrived when they must redress their own wrongs, I care not whether it be nullification, seccession, or open rebellion. I am prepared to keep even 'with him that goes farthest'."

The following are fine sentiments: "It is the sum of human prowess to temporize when the judgment dictates that to temporize is wisdom. It requires a Fabius and a Washington to be able to do it. They conquered by their wise delay and manly resistance to hasty opinions that would have goaded them to hasty action."

Again, "None of us are so high as not to look up to mighty truth, whether from Hayne or Webster. Her radiant finger alone can point us to our Constitutional highway."

Letter to Constituents July 30th, 1833:

"Having lost their hobby on nullification of the tariff, and knowing that their political existence depends upon keeping up excitement on some topic they (the nullifiers) have resorted to the question of emancipation. They are fully aware of the impolicy of the premature noise about the 'negro question', and nothing but dire necessity, and alternative of neck or nothing, could induce them to resort to it.

"They pretend that the North is disposed to invalidate our title to a certain descripiton of our property. I am as sensitive on that subject as any honest slave holder ought to be. The most of my property consists in negroes, and I have already said in Congress that whenever the tenure by which we hold that property is seriously mooted, it is a question we will not debate in the halls of Congress. *That we will decide it on the embattled plain, where musket and artillery will be our orators, powder, ball and steel the argument.*

"The curse of slavery was fixed upon our ancestors by the policy of the British Government. The Northern people I am sure, have no intention to disturb this question. I believe a majority of the Northern people would march to the South, were it necessary, to put down a servile insurrection and quell the negroes.

"The Union for better or for worse, and what Heaven has joined together none but the devil or a nullifier would wish to put asunder."

It was written in the stars that Blair should collide with that extraordinary man, Dr. Thos. Cooper, President of the South Carolina College from 1821 to 1833, during which period he exercised a potent influence in the affairs of the State. As an advocate of the radical doctrine of State Sovereignty and nullification he was in advance of Calhoun, and for a long time exceedingly in favor with the prevailing political sentiment of the State. Born in England, educated at Oxford, he emigrated to Pennsylvania in consequence of threatened prosecution for his published revolutionary views. Rising to a seat on the Federal Bench as District Judge, he was indicted and convicted upon a charge of libel upon President Adams. Through Jefferson's favor he then became professor of Chemistry in the University of Virginia, from which he was forced to retire because of his unorthodox ideas on the subject of religion. He then came to South Carolina College as professor of Chemistry and later became President.

His opponents, stung by the election of Stephen D. Miller, an extreme Nullifier, as United States Senator succeeding Wm. Smith, and imputing Miller's triumph largely to Dr. Cooper's management, vowed his destruction and began to assail him in a vulnerable point.

Blair opened the attack in the form of a letter to Rev. Reuben Tucker, published in the *Camden Journal* of January 1831, in which he denounced Dr. Cooper as the reputed author of a pamphlet signed "Layman", circulated in Washington, terming it "blasphemous". Among other things he writes: "I believe his tampering in the late intrigues by which Judge Smith's re-election to the United States Senate was defeated is no secret to anybody. If he is to be allowed to go on instilling heterodox ideas and infidel doctrines into the minds of his pupils, South Carolina may soon claim the palm from Revolutionary France on the score of immorality and atheism."

Cooper replies expressing astonishment at Blair in the role of "Defender of the Faith", congratulating the Clergy on their new acquisition, points out that Blair's letter is prompted by politics and declines controversy with one of "General Blair's character."

Blair now returns to the charge with unbridled fury, terms Cooper an "Old political prostitute" who has disgraced the seat of Justice and soiled the Ermine.

Cooper rejoins that Blair is angry because he (Cooper) declines to father the anonymous pamphlet; that while General Blair calls him (Cooper) many hard names, he gives himself a very excellent character, and alludes to the indictments against Blair for his exploit at the home of Lovick Young and the General's inebriety. In a still later article Cooper defends the pamphlet from the charge of infidelity and alleges that it is not more heretical than the tenets of the Quakers.

Thus a hue and cry was inaugurated against Dr. Cooper and the papers teem with severe strictures upon him, signed "Farmer", "Citizen" and the like. Finally Cooper is run down and in 1833 at the age of 74, retires from the South Carolina College. His ability was recognized however, and he was chosen by the Legislature to compile the laws of the State, a task which he performed with signal ability. By nature a daring agitator and storm centre wherever he went, this brainy old petrel died at Columbia in 1840, age 81.

September 7th, 1832, must have been a proud occasion for General Blair, for he then received a tribute from Kershaw County accorded to few if any other of her sons, native or adopted. On that day a banquet was spread in his honor. Seven hundred guests were seated in a structure raised for the purpose. Colonel James Chesnut, Sr. presided, and Wm. McWillie, Thos. Lang, Chapman Levy, Everard Cureton, Joseph Mickle, Wm. Nixon, A. McCaskill, Joseph Cunningham, were vice-presidents.

The leading toast was "General James Blair, our Representative in Congress, worthy of the soil of Hickory. Well done thou good and faithful servant, you voted against the Act of 1828, the vote of two Senators and six representatives to the contrary."

## JAMES BLAIR

As General Blair rose to respond he received an enthusiastic ovation, and the band played "Hail to the Chief".

We are informed by the *Camden Journal* of that date that he made a "masterly argument, with sallies of humor and happy turns of conversational ease and concluded with this sentiment: "Kershaw District, may she ever exercise that prudence and patriotism which characterized the distinguished officer of the Revolution after whom she was named."

Colonel Chesnut, Sr. spoke and condemned both the tariff, and the remedy, nullification.

A local anonymous bard, broke forth into verse in his honor, to the tune of "All on Hobbies", some stanzas of which are herewith reproduced.

"Come attention pray give, while of hobbies I sing,
  For each has his hobby from cobbler to king.
  The hobby of poets is verse to write,
  And those who cannot may doggrel indite.

"The political hobby the demagogue strides,
  And over the people he gallops and rides.
  For States-rights he goes, for convention he trots,
  At tariff he kicks—but for Jackson he stops.

"The hobby of Miller is to Congress to go,
  Expecting some great things the people to show,
  But when the rebuke of Forsyth he received,
  He thought of Judge Smith and was very much grieved.

"But the Nullies they had their hobbies to rue,
  And these are their Test Oaths and Ordinances too,
  For tremble they did when Jackson observed,
  The Union it must and shall be preserved.

"The hobby of *Blair* it delights us to sing,
  For it bends not to Master or office or king,
  In the place which he holds and so well deserves,
  Supported he'll be by the people he serves.

"Their cause he defended and property too,
  With spirit of one both fearless and true,
  And he who his courage or honor would doubt,
  Must make up his mind to fight or back out.

—*Camden Journal, August 24th*, 1833.

But his star was soon to set. He was addicted to drink and morphine to allay the sufferings of rheumatism, becoming crazed thereby. At the Washington Theater one night in March 1834, something in the play displeased him, and in a fit of aberration he fired a loaded pistol at the actors. He was arraigned before the city Court, but was fined only five dollars, upon the testimony of his physician that he was under the influence of brandy and opium taken to alleviate his suffering.

This was the precurser of his last desperate act. On April 1st, 1834 he lay in bed depressed by sickness, at his boarding house on A Street, Capitol Hill. His intimate friend Governor Murphy of Alabama called to see him and read to him at his request a letter just received from his wife. As soon as Governor Murphy departed, Blair got his pistol and shot himself through the brain.

Just after this event an appreciative friend thus wrote of Blair in the *New York Courier and Enquirer* of April 1934:

"He was ardent and excitable and unhappily addicted to stimulants. He tried harder than most men to conquer the propensity and he did conquer it for long periods, and had lately made up his mind to do so entirely. He had joined himself to the Methodist Church and determined upon a change of habit. We know him very well and we know that a nobler spirit never inhabited human bosom. He was brave to the very verge of utter indifference to fear. He never knew or understood the meaning of fear, and was at the same time bland and gentle in all the relations of life. He was more thoroughly and decidely popular than any other man who ever lived within the district he represented in Congress.

"He was a man of gigantic person, being about six feet six inches in height and of symmetrical proportions, and notwithstanding his great weight, 350 pounds, he was active, as well as powerful.

"He was born very near the spot which gave birth to General Jackson, and about forty-four years of age.

"It has been a matter of astonishment to friends as well as enemies that he could write as well as he did upon subjects with which an uneducated man like himself could hardly be supposed to be conversant, but there was a native genius in Blair that rose above all disadvantages."

General Blair left an only child, his son L. W. R. Blair, whose name figures in subsequent pages of this volume.

# CHAPTER VIII.
### Pilgrims—Abram Blanding.

For several decades after the Revolution, Camden received not a few accessions to its citizenship from New England. For some time these settlers formed a distinct group and certainly contributed a valuable element to this community, from which, while their family names have all disappeared, they are represented by descendants through female lines.

Among the earliest of these arrivals was Benjamin Perkins, of Connecticut, who came not later than 1787, and was one of the first resident lawyers in Camden. His descendants here are represented by the DuBose family. A sketch of him and his lineage will be found in the first volume of this work.

Another acquisition from New England was Abram Blanding whose career in this state was noteworthy. Born at Rehoboth, Massachusetts, November 18th, 1776, he was on both sides of Pilgrim descent. His mother was an Ormsbee. His father William, with four brothers and three maternal uncles served in the Revolution, under Colonel Carpenter, whose mother was a Blanding.

Abram graduated from Brown University in 1797, with second honor, Fisher Ames taking first. His roommate, David R. Williams, afterwards Governor of South Carolina, induced him to come South. He located at Columbia, S. C., in 1797, where he taught school and studied law under Governor John Taylor. In 1799 he settled in Camden where he completed his law studies with Judge Brevard. Here he began practice in 1800, and advanced steadily to the head of the profession in this state.

In 1806 he was elected to the Legislature from Kershaw County, but not for the succeeding term. His service was marked by the authorship of a measure which adjusted the long and bitter controversy over representation between the upper and lower sections of the state. In the eyes of that day and generation this question was of vast importance and the credit for its settlement a matter of dispute. By some it was claimed for Wm. Lowndes. Colonel Chappell, who was a member of the Legislature at the time declares: "The honor is

ABRAM BLANDING

## PILGRIMS—ABRAM BLANDING

great to whichever of these gentlemen it belongs and if it could be divided is sufficient to ennoble each." How quickly oblivion dims many a shining light and burning question.

Blanding's opposition to the General Suffrage bill of 1809 was unpopular with his constituents, yet they knew his worth and re-elected him in 1810, when he repeated his vote against the measure. Although a staunch Federalist and opposed to the War of 1812, he volunteered his troop and became Colonel of a cavalry regiment. Again he defied popular favor by his ridicule of President Madison for abandoning Washington to the British. The Democratic air of this District was highly uncongenial to his Federalist principles. But he never flinched from loyalty to his convictions, which he boldly proclaimed without equivocation. The following extract from a letter of his to Wm. F. DeSaussure, dated August 1815, will illustrate his attitude and the divisions of sentiment then prevalent: "The fall of the French Emperor has been more sudden than was expected. Indeed it is strange that a people who have suffered so much from his ambition should entertain any other than sentiments of detestation for him. The Democrats here are quite at a loss how to dispose of him, or how to fill the vacant throne. They would no doubt invite their favorite to this 'asylum of oppressed humanity'. If he comes, I hope he may be quartered on his good friend Jefferson, and both be set to writing the history of their own times."

His first wife was Elizabeth Martin, a daughter of Dr. James Martin of Camden, a surgeon during the Revolution, in the South Carolina line.

Blanding's second wife was Caroline, a daughter of Chancellor DeSaussure, to whom he was married in 1815. He had risen to front rank in the legal profession and had evinced great public spirit. He established the Camden Public Library which was one of the best in the state. In 1819 he was elected with General Davie and Joel R. Poinsett on the State Board of Public Works. In 1822 he was elected Chief Superintendent of these works, the Board having been abolished. This led to his change of residence from Camden to Columbia. He served in this capacity 'till 1827 with great efficiency, and constructed the State Road from Charleston to and over Saluda Mountain, N. C., the Wateree, Santee and other navigation canals of the state. These canals were rendered obsolete by the development of railroads but were nevertheless monuments to his energy and ability.

In 1825 as Superintendent of Works and Grand Master Mason, he officiated with Lafayette in laying the corner stone of the DeKalb monument. He constructed a system of water works for Columbia out of his private funds. This outlay was only refunded to his heirs, in bonds at a great discount, in 1878.

He also, though a Baptist, initiated the Presbyterian Theological Seminary at Columbia. In 1831 he was a leading organizer and first President of the Commercial Bank of Columbia, which, until the general smash consequent on the Civil War, maintained the highest credit. It sent from its desk six presidents and cashiers to newly organized state banks. Blanding Street was doubtless named in his honor.

In 1833 he, with Jas. L. Petigru and Wm. McWillie, was chosen by the Union party to argue before the State Court of Appeals in opposition to the notorious Nullification Test Oath. Of his effort Judge O'Neall, one of the Court has said: "It is as fine a specimen of forensic argument as can be found. If Colonel Blanding had never made any other argument, this would have given him immortality. He was conceded to be first in his profession for fully twenty years." From that argument we have room but for one sample paragraph, all compact with words of wisdom:

"I blame no man for changing his opinions, and I am bound in charity to believe these changes are the result of honest conviction. But it will be perceived at once, that if the political dogmas of one day may be embodied in test oaths,—at another day, when honest changes of opinion have taken place, even the authors of the test may become its victims."

In 1836 he was one of the chief promoters of the Charleston, Louisville and Cincinnati Railroad. Robert Y. Hayne was elected President of the road, and Blanding President of the Southwestern Railroad Bank, established at Charleston, S. C., to finance the project, the magnitude of which was too great for execution in the midst of the great financial stringency resulting from the political contest over the United States Bank.

## PILGRIMS—ABRAM BLANDING

Added to these difficulties was the fearful yellow fever scourge which ravaged Charleston in 1839. Blanding, despite the plague, remained at his post there to keep his Bank from suspension of specie payment, to which all others had been driven by the panic, produced by or coincident with President Jackson's removal of government deposits. He succeeded, but lost his life from the fever on September 20th, 1839. He lies buried at the Circular Churchyard in Charleston. A stone was placed to his memory in our Camden Cemetery, which has unfortunately in some way become mutilated. These words of Judge O'Neall are sufficient voucher to his merits: "His memoir testifies to his great, his excelling worth. Few men, in a life of sixty-three years, accomplished so much or earned such a deserved reputation."

William Blanding came to Camden some years later than his brother Abram. Here he conducted an extensive medical practice. His cottage now burned, stood facing south on Monument Square, east of Broad Street. Being a devoted scientist and naturalist, he gathered here a large collection of birds, insects, animals, notably an 18 foot alligator from McRae's pond, also many curios and antiquities. Would that some of them remained to us, but he moved away with them in the '30s to Philadelphia, whence his Quaker wife had come. There, with no children and a comfortable income, he spent his time in the Academy of Sciences, of which he was a member. In the '40s he returned to the old family Homestead at Rehoboth, Mass., which had descended to him through seven generations of Williams from the first who came over in the Mayflower. There he died in 1857, as we read on a stone to his memory in our Cemetery, erected beside the grave of his wife, Susan Willet, who had died at the age of 27 in Camden, in the year 1809. John S. Willet, a lawyer in Camden about that time, was probably her brother. He married Miss Eliza Richardson in 1814.

Beside Abram and William, two other Blandings, probably their brothers, Shubel and Samuel, figured for many years in Camden. Of them little is known. They too, probably, like others of the family, moved away. The name of Shubel appears as foreman in some old grand jury returns. Samuel was long a leading druggist here.

Mrs. Lucy Carpenter, a sister of Abram Blanding,

moved to Camden about 1820. Her son Penuel was in the mercantile business as partner of Eli W. Bonney, until his death in 1836, after which Mrs. Carpenter moved to Columbia where she lived a while with her brother Abram, and then returned to her old Massachusetts home. Thus did the last of the Blanding family depart from this community.

The same story of departure is to be told of another once prominent family here, the Bullards, of Massachusetts origin. Chas. A. Bullard and Royal Bullard, brothers, were admitted to the bar in this state in 1814. After that they appear in connection with important cases in the Camden Court records. Charles, in 1826, established the *Camden Journal.* His wife, Margaret Douglas, died in 1821, as appears by her grave stone. He left Camden for Columbia in 1828 to take charge of the *Telescope,* then a leading state newspaper. Nothing is known to us of his subsequent career. His brother Royal Bullard, was Intendant of Camden in 1820. In 1822 he advertises his property for sale, and probably moved away in that year, after which all trace of him is lost to us.

A connection between the families of Bullard and Adams is discoverable from an old deed, bearing date 1813, from which it appears that one Wm. Adams, of Camden, deceased, had been the owner of a certain tract of land near Camden, which from him descended to his uncle Joseph Adams, of Litchfield, Connecticut, and his aunts, Elizabeth Bullard, wife of John Bullard, of Pepperell, Massachusetts, and Sarah Richards, wife of Giles Richards, of Boston. The Wm. Adams referred to was doubtless a relative of the Rev. Thomas Adams, of Massachusetts, who prior to 1800 officiated in Camden as minister of the gospel, and whose wife was Dinah Wyly.

The Warrens, Peter and Thomas, likewise came to us from the region of Bunker Hill. Peter was Intendant of Camden in 1809. Thomas Warren died in 1833, age fifty, a native of Newport, Rhode Island, for twenty-five years resident of Camden. Also Phineas Thornton and his wife came from Massachusetts about 1804 and long dwelt here. From them trace the Zemp and Capers families.

PILGRIMS—ABRAM BLANDING

C. F. Daniels of Connecticut, came to Camden in 1828, remaining with us about five years, long enough to make a lasting impression. Frequent reference to him will be found in other parts of this volume.

The foregoing names have been selected as typical of the New England colony of which Camden boasted in the olden days. Others could be mentioned were this a mere catalogue, and there were certainly others whose names have been overlooked. It was inevitable that they should draw together and form a Society, of which we have some authentic record found in the *Camden Gazette*, of January 4th, 1821, which reports a meeting and dinner of the "Sons of Pilgrims", held at "Welsh and Smyth's Long Room" on December 22nd, 1820. From this we gather that Dr. Wm. Blanding was President, Captain Peter Warren, Vice-President, Charles A. Bullard, Secretary. The Rev. Joyce and the Rev. Hill invoked blessing. A pyramid in the midst of the table capped by a fragment of Plymouth Rock and an Indian Calumet pipe. Various toasts were offered, of which the three following are samples:

"Yankee Prejudice: Their rough corners are smoothed down when observation sheds its light into the mind.

"South Carolina: The beam of its sun, its genius and its hospitality are alike warm.

"The United States: They are linked together by their true interest and blasted be the wretch who whispers disunion."

The occasion was concluded with a song by Andrew J. Kennedy, the verbiage of which evinces the highest poetical intentions. Another celebration called by C. A. Bullard was held December 23rd, 1822 at McAdams and Drakefords "Long Room".

We catch in the toasts above cited traces of the discordant notes of Nullification and Abolition, which shortly arose and terminated all movement from New England hither. How deplorable the loss to this community of such additions to its thrift, enterprise and culture!

While sectional strife barred our gates to further income of Pilgrims, the sons of those who abode with us became staunch advocates of the Southern cause, and were some of the best soldiers of the Confederacy. A notable instance is that of Captain Thos. J. Warren who fell at

Gettysburg, leading a Confederate regiment and whose father came to Camden from Boston.

Another is that of Colonel James D. Blanding, son of the above mentioned Abram Blanding. On the field of Gettysburg he led the 9th South Carolina Regiment and carried evidence of the fact in shape of a permanent lump on top of his head quite as large as an egg. He bore also three other scars, one of the Mexican War. In 1824 he begun the practice of law in Camden, but removed to a neighbor town of Sumter in December 1843, where he afterwards resided. He was always a frequent visitor to Camden. When here once in his latter years, being then nigh eighty, but still sprightly as a boy, he was induced to repose for a time in the writer's office and to unfold some of his reminiscences. He then furnished many of the data used in the foregoing sketch of the Blanding family. When asked about his experience in the Civil War, with his peculiar gesticulation he pulled off his hat and bowed his head forward saying: "Here's what the d——d Yankees did for me at Gettysburg," displaying the lump above alluded to. Just at that moment a veritable Massachusetts Yankee, who had lately settled in Camden, entered the door and catching the Colonel's remark joined in the merriment produced thereby. Of Camden in his younger days he gave us this social item in his own words:

"While a resident of Camden I was a member of the "Herd of Stags"—"Stag Hall" during the summer being in the DeSassure house on Hobkirk Hill. Its sole function was to entertain the girls by escorting them in the afternoon horseback rides, with a dance at least once a week, and as much oftener as they pleased to dictate. James P. Dickinson was head of the "Herd", and Jim Lang was colored caterer. It might not be proper to name the other stags. It however should be added that it was always a big dinner on Sunday and plates laid for any of the "B'hoys"—dubbed as "Hounds"—who pleased to come up and partake. Jas. Dunlap's account at the end of the summer showed that the bills of fare of dinners and suppers were the best the season and market afforded."

# CHAPTER IX.
## Stephen D. Miller.

At the age of forty-three Stephen D. Miller had reached the highest honors in gift of the state, then attainable only by real ability. Though not a native of Camden he belongs to us, for in this county was his home, at "Plane Hill" during the zenith of his career, and his principal law practice was in the Court at Camden. He was born in the Waxhaws, Lancaster County, May 1787, son of William Miller whose wife was Margaret White, both of Scotch-Irish stock. He was related in some way to Wm. Crawford of Georgia, of national prominence in his day.

He was schooled under a capable teacher and drilled in the classics. He learned to repeat rapidly and accurately almost any part of the Scriptures, which in his Court arguments he quoted with great effect. His father died when he was quite young. Three slaves which he inherited were sold to provide his education. He graduated at the South Carolina College in 1808. In person he was of medium stature, but excelled in strength and athletic feats, of which he was very fond even after his elevation to dignified offices. His maternal grandmother is mentioned by the historian Ramsay as an instance of great longevity.

After his college course he entered upon the study of law in the office of John S. Richardson, at Sumter, and was admitted to the bar in 1811. Later he settled in Stateburg about eighteen miles south of Camden. His old residence there is still standing. The records show that he was engaged in most of the important cases in the Camden Court for a number of years.

In 1814 he married Miss Dick of Sumter. There were three children of this marriage: Elias Dick, John Richardson and William Smith. The two latter died in infancy. The eldest, Elias, a promising youth, died of lockjaw in 1832, at the South Carolina College. It was the year following the death of this son that he resigned his seat in the United States Senate.

Miller had been elected to Congress in 1814. Soon after beginning his term he was summoned home to Stateburg by the illness of his wife. Owing to her condition he did not stand for re-election and in 1818 was succeeded by Joseph Brevard. When a candidate for the United States Senate in 1830, he was assailed in a political circular for absenteeism from his seat when a member of Congress fourteen years before. From his reply we gain a bit of interesting autobiography:

"The only matter in the hand bill which I deem worthy of notice is the charge of absence without leave from January 16th to April 14th. This, I admit and submit the facts from which this absence arose. I received a letter from home informing me that my wife was at the point of death, that her physician pronounced she would not live. I read this letter to a friend and immediately jumped into a stage. I never stopped until I arrived at home, when I learnt for the first time that my wife was still alive, but exceedingly feeble. I remained until Mrs. Miller was able to travel, and I took her with me to Washington, and there soon after published my determination not to offer again for Congress at the next election. The ill health of Mrs. Miller, her disease being a pulmonary one, absolutely forbid my continuance in Congress, while it caused me to spend my time in Washington in the most painful apprehension."

During this term in Congress he met intimately his kinsman, Wm. H. Crawford, who was Secretary of the Treasury in President Munro's Cabinet, and Judge William Smith, then in the Senate from South Carolina. He accorded with their radical free trade and states rights principles. Calhoun, then Secretary of War, was at that time of opposite tendency, and decidedly antagonistic to this trio.

His wife died in 1819, and in 1821 he married Miss Mary Boykin of Kershaw County. For some years he continued to reside at Stateburg, then seat of Claremont County. In 1822 he re-entered politics and was elected to the State Senate from Claremont County, which later was with Salem County formed into Sumter District. He tells us his first act was to vote for return of his friend Wm. Smith to United States Senate, and says: "In 1824 I introduced into the State Senate the resolution which first laid the foundations of the States Rights Party." The next year they were passed by the (State) House of Representatives under the leadership of Wm. Smith, who after his defeat by Robert Y. Hayne for re-election to the United States Senate, had been elected from York County in 1824 to the State Legislature, where he was a leading light in the House as was Mil-

STEPHEN D. MILLER

ler in the Senate. These resolutions, extreme to the point of revolutionary, met with strenuous opposition, but probably voiced the prevalent sentiment of the State. Their championship by Miller was the key to his rapid advancement. While he rode a popular horse, his ability must have been excellent to stand the grilling conflicts of those days. William Smith and Stephen D. Miller, in so far as it may be traced to any individual source, have a strong claim to authorship of the States Rights creed in the State. Yet, historically, Calhoun stands as its great exponent and founder. It was but his adopted child. The proposed remedy of "Nullification", the logical or illogical consequence of the doctrine, is perhaps more properly attributable to him, although Judge O'Neall tells us he heard Chancellor Harper claim it as his invention.

But history shows that revolution runs over its promoters if they attempt to restrain it. So it was with Wm. Smith. He balked at the Nullification extension of his States Rights doctrine. The result was that in a few years he was beaten for the United States Senate by his pupil Miller, who had kept on with the procession into the fastness of Nullification.

Miller was Chairman of the Senate Judiciary Committee and continued to serve in that Chamber until his election as Governor in 1828. At this time he removed to "Plane Hill", now known as "The Terraces", in Kershaw County, about seven miles southeast of Camden.

He would doubtless have had a re-election to the Governorship had not the Constitution of that day forbidden a second term. He therefore aspired to the seat in the United States Senate occupied by his old friend, Wm. Smith. In the Campaign of 1830, which resulted in Miller's election, he delivered many speeches, some extracts from which here follow and are an index to the astounding temper of the times: This is his speech at Stateburg, September 19th, 1830, in reply to Judge Richardson:

"In replying to the distinguished individual (Judge Richardson), I consider myself as one of the voters of Claremont County. I neither regard him as a Judge, nor myself as Governor. Our official relations are lost in this primary meeting of the people.

"I sustain the principles laid down by the resolutions adopted by our Legislature in 1825. You stand pledged to the declaration that Congress have not the power to adopt a system of internal improvement, nor to lay a tax to protect manufacturers. The official relation I now bear to you, is perhaps founded more on the part taken by me in establishing this doctrine than on any other claim to public favor.

"Whenever it is thought expedient to abandon the ground assumed in opposition to the encroachments of the General Government, I should not advise you to assemble together to make a formal annunciation of your submission, but rather to hide in your native swamps and in lonesome sullen silence acquiesce.

"There appears to me something revolting to every lofty and dignified feeling in gathering the people together to tell them that they are oppressed—unconstitutionally and arbitrarily oppressed—and then require them to adopt resolutions declaring they will abide by that tyranny and sustain the government that denounces and denationalizes them. Let not the Dominico be substituted for the "Game Cock".

"Any person living in the Southern States who has paid the least attention to the progress made by the General Government in subverting their interests and confiscating without authority their property may rely with perfect certainty that the time will arrive in which no difference of feeling will exist south of a given line as to the motives which prompt and the baneful effects resulting from Congressional legislation.

"An issue is now pending between South Carolina, as a state, and Congress. We assert no new power, we claim our ancient rights, conceded to us since the formation of the government.

"The resolution proposes to submit the controversy to the assembled wisdom of a State Convention. The assertion in Convention that the Tariff of Protection is void would carry sufficient weight to make every Carolinian submit to it, or leave the country.

"It is impossible to enforce a law of Congress where the great mass of the people believe it founded in fraud and enacted against the Constitution. There are three and only three ways to reform our Congressional legislation, familiarly called, the ballot box, the jury box and the cartridge box."

He then points out how the jury box would bar the execution of a law which the State had declared in Convention to be void, inasmuch as jurors would not sustain it with verdicts and proceeds.

"The time has passed when high toned aristocrats can from the bench cram their notions down the throats of the juries of the country. Our juries must be convinced by argument and good sense, not by a knitted brow or a haughty menace.

"That man who would still live in Carolina and refuse obedience to the deliberate and solemn expression of the sense of the State ought not to be permitted to recover damages for a personal indignity. He ought to be treated as a reprobate and an outlaw. The remedy is in your own hands, if you do not creep like toads in the twilight of your hopes and fears.

"It is said every movement we make is putting the State in danger. Every controversy supposes danger in carrying it on. It is with governments as with individuals, those who fear to defend their rights have none.

"The convention decides nothing, but that South Carolina does not abandon opposition to the Tariff. It will embarrass your adversary; it is a check at least, not a useless one; the King must move or give up the game.

"You will search in vain in history for a people disgraced by gallantly contending for their liberty. The blood of one martyr to religious or political effort, is worth more than the eloquence of a Demosthenes. If standing on our rights the General Government puts one South Carolinian to death, we who are now weak will then become strong."

"The three boxes—the jury box, the ballot box and the cartridge box" became Miller's slogan, and a few weeks after the foregoing speech, which must have been relished by his audience, he was elected to the United States Senate over his old preceptor Judge Smith, by a vote of eighty-one to seventy-seven.

It was only by a narrow margin he vanquished the old Roman, who for twenty years had done honor to the State on the bench and in the United States Senate. After this Judge Smith left the State and went to Alabama.

After his election Senator Miller resided in Camden. His senatorial career it is said was cut short by ill health and was too brief for any notable achievement. He resigned in November 1833 after serving but two years. Before retiring however he gave some proof of his metal in one of those tilts with which the arena of the Senate edifies the country. The subject concerned the appointment of Martin Van Buren by President Jackson as Minister to England. Miller opposed it on the ground that Van Buren had shown bad faith towards South Carolina. Forsythe of Georgia severely arraigned

Miller for alleged desertion of his former associates, especially Jackson and Judge Smith. It cannot be claimed that Miller failed in this combat of repartee and retort. Van Buren was rejected.

Senator Miller and General James Blair, being at that time the conceded leaders of their respective parties in this district, came in the course of their controversies to the verge of a duel. By the good offices of Wm. Drayton for Blair and Geo. McDuffie for Miller, the matter was adjusted without an encounter.

Judge O'Neall tells us he was at the same hotel with Senator Miller attending the State Convention of March 1833, which met to rescind the ordinance of nullification. A caucus of the Nullifiers was held preceding the convention, Miller being a member. The proposal of ordaining a "Test Oath" of allegiance—that parent of violent controversy—was adopted. After the caucus, Miller, when asked by Judge O'Neall what had been done, replied: "They have made it a d——d sight worse than it was before." In the Convention Miller opposed the proposition. He was overruled by a small majority, but would have prevailed had not some of the Union members absented themselves.

In 1835 he purchased lands in Mississippi and moved there with a large number of slaves. To a large planting enterprise he applied the same energy and ability exhibited in his other pursuits, despite the ill health that afflicted him. His motto was to wear out, not rust out. At the age of fifty-one, on March 8th, 1838, he died at the home of his nephew, Major Chas. M. Hart, in Raymond, Miss., and there his remains lie. The people of Raymond met and paid tribute to his memory.

Banquet toasts, complimentary or hostile, furnish no safe criterion of the measure of a public man, still they are to some extent significant. Here are several touching Governor Miller.

At Camden, July 4, 1829. "His Excellency Governor Miller—A bright example for imitation of youth. His course has demonstrated what unassisted talents, integrity and industry will attain, the highest honors in the gift of a discerning people."

This satirical thrust was gotten off at the Union meeting in Greenville, 1828. "The Honorable Stephen D.

## Stephen D. Miller

Miller—Too wise for a legislator, too learned to be comprehended, too brave for a warrior and too sarcastic for a wit, may posterity assign him his place among mankind."

At a celebration in Camden, July 4, 1830, Governor Miller present, this toast was proposed—"The Governor of South Carolina.—Like the Wateree River, he has always pursued the same course"—The Governor responded and as the report states was received with the most deafening and reiterated applause."

The painting of Governor Miller in possession of his grandson, D. R. Williams, a photograph of which is inserted herewith, is a poor piece of portraiture, yet shows a face of intellect and refinement. Rising to eminence amid political storm, it was impossible for him to escape the bitterest aspersions. He must have possessed merit of high order to have emerged with honor, unscathed and unstained.

Judge O'Neall says of him: "When I first came to know Governor Miller intimately (about 1820) he was in full and successful practice. His voice was not a pleasant one, and in his speeches fell rather harshly on the ear. His flow of words was easy and abundant. He was entirely argumentative. Nothing of fancy entered into his speeches."

Edwin J. Scott, an old Camdenite, in his "Random Recollections" mentions Governor Miller's celebrated toast—"The three boxes—the jury box, the ballot box, and the cartridge box. He by the bye, was inaugurated as Governor in a full suit of homespun, and when speaking earnestly made most awfully ugly faces, as if suffering intense torture."

Governor Miller left three children by his second marriage: a son Stephen D. Miller, who lived and died in Alabama; a daughter Kate who married David R. Williams; and a daughter Mary who married General James Chesnut. His widow survived him nearly fifty years and lies in the Chesnut Cemetery at Knights Hill.

# CHAPTER X.

### Exodus—William McWillie.

The advent of the Railway ushered in the modern age of rush, and gradually relegated to the rear the stage coach and many another slow process hallowed by time immemorial. Such innovation could but lead to great changes. A wave of migration from this state westwards begun about 1830. The lure of new lands, the impetus of the steam engine, the embitterments and feuds of Nullification, combined to break thousands loose from their old moorings here.

In the *Camden Journal* of February 22, 1834, we find the following item:

"The rage for migration southwesterly has we think increased during the past year beyond all calculation. We daily see extensive caravans of movers, many of whom carry with them a considerable portion of the needful. In the course of one short week we observed nearly two hundred from North Carolina and the upper part of the State. From our own district the number is really so great as to make one melancholy, whole families disposing of their possessions here for little or nothing and migrating to the West with the hope of improving their condition. The majority of these are persons too who from their pecuniary circumstances we would suppose able to live comfortably anywhere."

The same paper of November 28, 1835, mentions, "the tremendous tide of emigration flowing westward. During the week not less than eight hundred persons, white and colored, passed through Camden, three hundred in one party, and worst of all many of them are our own people, friends and neighbors."

The contagion of this movement swept away important branches of almost every family in this community and in many cases the whole family. None of these departures was more deplored or caused such loss to Camden as that of William McWillie and his family.

Wm. McWillie was born twenty miles north of Camden near Liberty Hill, November 17, 1795. His early schooling was in that neighborhood. He was preparing for college at Camden, when interrupted by the War

WILLIAM McWILLIE

## Exodus—William McWillie

of 1812. In 1814 he joined the regiment commanded by his father, Colonel Adam McWillie, serving as Adjutant. The war over he entered the South Carolina College, graduated in 1817 and next year was admitted to the bar. In 1818, he married a daughter of Joseph Cunningham of Liberty Hill. In 1820 he formed a partnership in law with Chapman Levy. At the Camden bar he encountered on even terms such distinguished talent as Abram Blanding and Stephen D. Miller. In 1825 he dissolved with Levy, and entered partnership with Wm. B. Hart, this firm lasting until the death of the latter in 1831. Hart was a young lawyer who came to Camden from New York.

It was inevitable that he should be drawn into the political vortex. He was among the recognized leaders on the Union side, which always held a majority of the voters of the county. In the election of 1830 he led the ticket for the Legislature, his colleagues being Thos. Lang and Chapman Levy, and in 1832 was re-elected. It may be mentioned in passing that in 1829 he, with Governor John Lide Wilson, acted as seconds to the unfortunate Nixon in his duel with Hopkins.

As to the abilities displayed by McWillie in public debate we have the opinion of a contemporary, Judge Benj. F. Porter of Alabama, who in a reminiscent letter wrote as follows:

"When I first began the practice of law I settled at Chester Court House (S. C.). There I saw Judge Smith. A very large assemblage was gathered to meet Stephen D. Miller, then a candidate for Governor (1828). The anti-tariff excitement was at its height, and Mr. Miller appeared in full suit of domestic jeans. Mr. McWillie took ground against the resolutions and made a speech so plain, so full of historic fact, so persuasive, that its effect was powerful on my young mind and carried away every vestige of the anti-tariff notions, which, like most of the youth of the time, I had adopted. To carry the resolution Judge Smith left the chair, and made a most violent declamatory effort. The profound wisdom, perfect good temper, clear thought and admirable expression of Mr. McWillie's effort, have ever stood in my recollection as the finest model of a speech I ever heard."[1]

---

[1] O'Neall's "Bench and Bar", Vol. I, p. 114.

## HISTORIC CAMDEN

Such eulogy will not seem extravagant when we turn to his public addresses, some of which have been preserved. The following quotation from his speech delivered in the Legislature on January 25, 1833, against passage of the "Test Oath"[1] manifest great force and felicity of expression:

Perhaps the strongest objection that can be urged against the proposed law arises from the agitating effect which it will produce throughout the State. It will not, cannot, be received kindly. It must be met in the spirit of opposition. It is and will be considered as tyrannical and oppressive by a portion of the people of this State. It is a stain upon their honor as men—upon their loyalty as citizens; for it is in vain to attempt disguise; no man on this floor doubts its purpose. It is unwise, it is cruel, it is tearing open afresh wounds that have scarce ceased to bleed. For some time past, I have witnessed with delight, a return of the home feelings, 'The good old feelings of friendship and brotherly kindness'.

"Pass this law and you blast the fruit that was blooming so fairly. You set neighbor against neighbor, brother against brother, and in many cases children against their fathers. I scarcely know a family which on this subject is not divided. *If you pass this law you will send from your borders thousands of your people and millions of your wealth.* Their minds are already turned too strongly to the rich, the golden West, and though they are attached to their homes, they are still more attached to freedom of opinion—to the rights of conscience.

"I trust God, South Carolina will never act so unwisely. If she should oppress and proscribe, we would be unworthy a glorious ancestry, did we submit. We must, we will abandon her. For where liberty is there is a freeman's home."

Despite this splendid protest, of which the foregoing is but a fragment, the measure was enacted into a statute. The most intense opposition was aroused and its validity was brought in question before the State Court of Appeals. Each party selected its ablest talent for this great forensic battle. For the Union party appeared McWillie, Petigru, Blanding and others. Of all the arguments in this famous case that of McWillie is the least technical and by far the most moving and eloquent. The following extracts from it, taken at random, will bear out the assertion:

[1]Requiring all officers civil and military to subscribe an oath of paramount allegiance to the State, as a prerequisite qualification.

## Exodus—William McWillie

"I presume it will not be denied that this is the true issue between the two great parties in this State. The Nullification party believe they owe allegiance to the State exclusively, and the Union party believe that they owe allegiance to the United States as well as to the State.

"I will now proceed to show that the citizens of South Carolina do owe allegiance to the United States. The greatest difficulty which presents itself to my mind, in relation to the proposition is that I am at a loss to find anything more certain by which to demonstrate it. I may say that it is a truism, that in our national and state politics, it is an axiom. I might as well under the full blaze of the meridian glories of a noon-day sun, be asked for the proof that we were in the midst of light. None but the blind could ask the question, and even they perhaps might feel the heat, if they did not see the light. It is with hesitation that I argue this branch of the case. I am unwilling that others should know the hallucination with which our State is afflicted.

"The term allegiance is expressive of the relation existing between a king and his vassals, and the framers of our constitution showed their good sense and good taste by rejecting it. If I would consent to follow I might be led through a labyrinth of mataphysical reasoning and disputation as to the meaning of the terms allegiance and sovereignty, their unity and divisibility, worthy of the casuistry of the best days of the Jesuits. But splitting hairs is a business that wont pay, and I am unwilling to embark in it. That allegiance is due the State we all agree, and that it is due to the United States I flatter myself is proved.

"It was only in the year 1828 that the celebrated exposition and protest, (which I have heard aptly called the book of the Gospel of Nullification), was published to enlighten the people on the subject of their sovereignty. This was written by Mr. Calhoun and printed and paid for out of the people's money. This was the beginning of our mataphysical political philosophy. I fear too much learning has made us mad."

We regret that we have not space for more extended quotation from this splendid effort.

The Test Oath experience must have chilled his interest in politics which, in 1834, he laid aside for business. In 1836 he was elected President of the Bank of Camden, established in that year on the northwest corner of Rutledge and Broad Streets. He filled this position for nine years, up to the time of his departure from the State. Judge O'Neall has remarked how much better he was suited to the bar "than to be cooped up in the walls of a banking house."

In 1840 he returned to public life and was elected in that year to the State Senate from this County and re-elected in 1844. In the *Camden Journal* of November 1841 "Looker On" writes of him with enthusiasm: "Mr. McWillie has a high reputation and but for his modest and retiring habits would long since have occupied a more conspicuous place in the country. His mind is one of superior cast. It is bold to originate and yet cautious. A fluent, graceful speaker, very concise, occasionally impassioned, his usually soft voice becomes high and commanding. His great integrity of purpose, amiable and lofty character, render him one of the most estimable citizens of whom our State can boast."

As State Senator he carried through a measure for state aid in construction of the Camden branch of the South Carolina Railroad. In the advocacy of this proposition he captivated his constituents and was thus extolled in the *Camden Journal*: "Old Kershaw may well be proud of her Senator. We understand that seldom has there been such an able speech in the walls of the Senate Chamber as he delivered in advocating the memorial to the State to build a branch railroad to this place."

In January 1845 a great celebration was given by the citizens of Camden in compliment to the Legislative delegation, McWillie and Dickinson. Processions, dinner and speeches marked the occasion. McWillie received an ovation as the main figure. A phrase of Chesnut's was to this effect, that McWillie "with his strong arm and keen broad axe, blazed out the entire length of the road."

With this event closes his career as a citizen of South Carolina. On October 1, 1845, the Camden paper announces that Wm. McWillie had moved to Mississippi, adding: "We have lost one of our best citizens." Of his departure Judge O'Neall says: "The removal of no citizen created more universal regret. For I hazard nothing in saying that he was the favorite son of an honored mother; and if he had thought fit to remain she would have given him honor and office to any extent he might have desired."

## Exodus—William McWillie

With him went the family of Dr. E. H. Anderson, whose daughter, his second wife, he married in 1831. Dr. Anderson's wife was a daughter of Chapman Levy. McWillie's new residence in Madison County, he called "Kirkwood", in memory of his old summer home in that suburb of Camden. Here his life was that of a planter. His abilities were also recognized in Mississippi. In 1849 he was elected to Congress and in 1857 Governor of that state. His son, Captain Adam McWillie, born in Camden, led the Attala guards in the Mexican War and fell leading the same company at the first battle of Manassas.[1]

On March 3, 1869, at Kirkwood, Miss., he died at the age of seventy-four.

We cannot resist inserting here the following inimitable pen portrait of Colonel McWillie to be found in the celebrated "Black Book" of Mrs. Anne Royall:

"Whoever has visited Camden, remembers Colonel McWillie,—if they forget everyone else, they never fail to repeat the name of McWillie. He is a young, tall, portly figure, but his countenance and manners, for modesty and sweetness of expression, ease and elegance, would defy the ablest pen. If I were a judge, I would say he was a model of grace, beauty and manliness. His face is fair, rather oval, his eye dark, soft and bashful, glows with a soul-searching kindness; but the innocence of his smile, his smooth, satin voice, and the modest sweetness of his countenance is unsurpassed by the babe; to all this he unites loftiness of manners, adorned with inimitable grace and warmth of feeling. He certainly is the most captivating being in the South."

From 1830 to 1845 Colonel McWillie was President of the Camden Temperance Society. An intimate friend of his paid this tribute to his character:

"Man and boy for fifty years I have known him, and I have never known him anywhere else than on the side of virtue; his physical, mental and moral stature was truly grand."

---

[1] Captain Jas. I. Villepigue once related to us that at the battle of Second Manassas his command hurriedly pitched their camp at dark and on entering the tent found it covered the grave of Adam McWillie, marked by a headboard on which his name had been cut.

# CHAPTER XI.

## The Seminole War.

In 1835, during the second term of Andrew Jackson, war broke out in Florida with the Seminole Indians, who refused to be moved to the territory set apart for them west of the Mississippi. From the impenetrable swamps of the peninsula, the Indians prolonged hostilities until 1842.

A call was made upon South Carolina in 1836 for a regiment of infantry to do three months' duty in Florida. Governor McDuffie asked for one company of mounted men, seventy-six in all, from Colonel John Chesnut's regiment, Kershaw District. The response was enthusiastic.

The regiment was paraded on the morning of February 8, and Brigadier General James W. Cantey read the order for a draft, if a sufficient number did not volunteer. After patriotic speeches by Colonel Chesnut and Major William McWillie, "Old Glory" was planted a few paces in front of the line, and all who wished to enlist were asked to advance and dress by the flag. The entire regiment, with the exception of about twenty, at once came forward. As the *Camden Journal*, from which our reports are obtained, proudly exclaimed in its next issue: "There never has been, and we trust, there never will be, a time that such a resort (a draft) shall be necessary here." Colonel Chesnut himself volunteered and was elected Captain.

That afternoon, a meeting of the "elders" of the community was held at the Court House, to furnish the patriotic youth with equipment for the campaign, to provide for any families of volunteers left without support, and to raise funds for conveyance to the rendezvous at Purrysburg. Subscription lists were opened and, in a few moments, 23 horses, 19 sets of equipments and $855.00 in cash had been raised—the money by a note on the Branch Bank of the State in Camden, the entire assemblage pledging their faith for its payment, should the amount not be reimbursed by the United States Government.

## The Seminole War

That evening the company, well mounted, set out in high spirits, being accompanied as far as the river by a large number of citizens, including many ladies.

Arrived at the seat of war, Captain Chesnut's company saw little actual service. Under orders from General Eustis, they burnt the villages of Abram, who is described as a "Negro-Indian", and of Micanopy, the head chief of the nation. From Volusia they were sent to Peay's Creek, below Tampa Bay, and, returning, were honorably discharged at St. Augustine, on May 1. Here they chartered a steamer, by private contract, and came to Charleston, reaching Camden about the middle of the month. A public dinner was tendered them by the people of the town, at which a handsome sword was presented Captain Chesnut by his old company.

Not a man had fallen during the brief campaign, but many later succumbed to the effects of the deadly unhealthfulness of the Florida Everglades. Saddest of these losses directly due to the war was that of the much-beloved commander of the company, which occurred December 27, 1839.

Captain Chesnut had contracted measles in camp and, as a result of exposure, a pulmonary trouble resulted. All efforts to save this valued young life proved in vain. A trip to Europe with his brother James was tried as a last resort, but, a few weeks after his return, he died at "Mulberry".[2]

John Chesnut, by his amiable and virtuous character, seems to have won, to an unusual degree, the love, respect and admiration of his fellows. A former Camden friend, C. F. Daniels, in the course of a beautiful eulogy, thus speaks of him in his paper:[1]

"A member of one of the wealthiest, and, in all respects, most respectable families in the South, he was at the same time one of the finest specimens of republican blandness and simplicity to be found on the face of the earth. Every honorable man, whether rich or poor, was his peer, and none other, whether he rolled in poverty or riches, shared his favor."

---

[1]The *New York Gazette*. Mr. Daniels had formerly edited the *Camden Journal*.

[2]This fine old home of the Chesnuts below Camden is now owned and restored to its former elegance by David R. Williams, great grandson of the builder.

## HISTORIC CAMDEN

He was the eldest son of James and Mary Cox Chesnut, and was born December 23, 1799. The only political position that he filled was a seat in the State Senate, to which he was elected in 1836. His planting interests were extensive.

He married Ellen, daughter of Thomas Whitaker. Six children were the issue of this union, of whom one only now[1] survives, James Chesnut of Alachua, Fla. Another son, John, was a gallant young captain in the Confederate service; he died, a mere youth, in 1868, and lies, beside his parents, in the family burying ground at Knight's Hill.

Two of Captain Chesnut's daughters, Serena and Mary, married respectively, Thomas and Edward, sons of Benjamin Haile. They too, with their families moved to Florida in the "Fifties".

Captain Chesnut's death drew forth, from an unknown Camden poet, signing only the initial "N", an elegy[2] both heartfelt and graceful, from which we extract a few lines:

> "How swiftly Time flew o'er thy happy home!
> Around thy board bloomed opening buds, so fair,
> Thy hopes of future happiness! But then,
> Ah! then, thy country call'd; love, ease and home,
> All, all, by thee resign'd. The tented field
> And soldier's fare, how cheerfully endured!
> E'en had thy mortal frame gigantic been,
> Beneath the efforts of the soul within,
> It must have fall'n. The path of duty found,
> The inward man led on, till nature sank.
> But—thou hast liv'd, to gain the hearts of all!
> To meet in every eye affection's glance,
> From every lip, the wish to thee, of weal—
> To reach thy sun's meridian height, undoomed
> In night to set. But, better far, eclipsed in Death,
> Remember'd now, as brilliant to the last!"

---

[1] In 1906.
[2] *Camden Journal*, December 24, 1839.

# The Seminole War

### Roll of Captain Chesnut's Company.

1. John Chesnut, Captain
2. Burwell Boykin, 1st Lieut.[1]
   (Thomas Lang)
3. John D. Mickle, 2nd Lieut.
4. Lewis J. Patterson, Ensign
5. James D. Stewart, 1st Serg.
6. John D. Murray, 2nd Serg.
7. T. L. Dixon, 3rd Serg.
8. Ben Gass, 4th Serg.
9. J. S. Nettles, 1st Corp.
10. D. Kirkland, 2nd Corp.
11. J. W. Arthur, 3rd Corp.
12. J. B. Mickle, 4th Corp.
13. Wm. Kennedy, Clerk
14. Jno. A. Boykin
15. Jos. G. Bruce
16. Wm. Baskin
17. John Bowen
18. James Baskin
19. James M. Coker
20. Thos. Creighton
21. W. R. Catoe
22. D. J. Childers
23. E. W. Creighton
24. Roderick Cameron
25. J. B. Childers
26. Wm. Dunlap
27. Jas. C. Doby
28. R. W. Dunlap
29. Jas. P. Dickinson
30. Wm. Nixon
31. Kirchem Exum
32. Isaac Gay
33. W. Garner
34. S. Gunn
35. U. Gilbert
36. S. Gibson
37. M. Giles
38. G. Gerald
39. T. M. Gaskins
40. Nat Gay
41. D. Graham
42. B. Haile, Jr.
43. B. Jones
44. Wm. Kirkland
45. Bryant King
46. Duncan Lang
47. John McCoy
48. A. G. Marshall
49. O. M'Haffey
50. J. R. McCain
51. ———— Clanton
52. Allen McCaskill
53. James McCorkle
54. R. Moseley
55. M. McDonald
56. Allen Moore
57. F. Matheson
58. R. Pettigrew
59. M. Naudin
60. H. Arrants
61. Wm. Rosser
62. S. A. B. Shannon
63. J. Smyrle
64. J. M. Spears
65. Jos. Smith
66. Samuel Shiver, Jr.
67. J. Thompson
68. ———— Lodowick
69. T. E. Shannon
70. W. B. Watkins
71. R. L. Whitaker
72. T. Whitaker
73. H. Whitaker
74. James Woods
75. Burwell Buford
76. Albert Buford
77. Daniel Buford

[1] Lieutenant Boykin being too ill to march with his company, his father-in-law, Thomas Lang, by permission, took his place. Lieutenant Boykin joined the command in a few days.

# CHAPTER XII.

## THE KERSHAW VOLUNTEERS IN THE MEXICAN WAR.

Texas declared her independence of Mexico, March 2, 1836, and applied for admission to the Union. The heated discussions in Congress and throughout the country induced by this action have been treated in another chapter. The Southern element prevailed and the Lone Star was added to our constellation June 23, 1845.

A dispute with Mexico at once arose over the southern boundary of Texas, and both governments attempted to occupy the region between the Rio Grande and Neuces rivers.

The attack by Mexicans on a small body of troops near Point Isabel, a depot of supplies established by General Zackary Taylor on the northern side of the Rio Grande in the disputed territory, precipitated war. This was on April 26, 1846. In regard to the incident, the *Camden Journal* (W. B. Johnstone, editor) observed at the time:

"There is but one course left now for the American Government to pursue towards Mexico, and that is, no longer to undervalue her military prowess, or to treat her as a very weak enemy; but promptly and efficiently to put an end to this war by bringing a force into the field, sufficient not only to drive her army from our soil, but to obtain redress for the long black list of grievances now standing against her."

President Polk on May 11, proclaimed the existence of hostilities and the Act of Congress authorizing him to accept the services of not more than 50,000 volunteers for the prosecution of the war.

The DeKalb Guards[1] of Camden had the honor of being the first company in the State to offer its services under this call. This they did on May 20, before any requisition had been made upon the Governor for troops. One hundred and five men volunteered in the Guards, under Captain Keith Stuart Moffat. They were not called into action until seven months later, when, as the "Kershaw Volunteers", they were embodied in the Palmetto Regiment and mustered into the service of the United States, on December 23, at the Washington

[1] A select military company organized June 20, 1840.

## THE KERSHAW VOLUNTEERS IN THE MEXICAN WAR

Race course, Charleston. There were 85 names on the roll, with the following officers: Keith S. Moffat, Captain; J. B. Kershaw, 1st Lieutenant; James Cantey, 2nd Lieutenant; J. W. Cantey, Jr., 3rd Lieutenant. Not a man was rejected, and the inspecting officer declared that it was the best volunteer company he had ever received. James P. Dickinson had been elected Lieutenant Colonel of the Regiment on July 8 preceding, and here James Cantey was chosen its Adjutant.

The long tedious journey to the seat of war was begun on January 6, 1847; from Charleston, by rail, to Griffin, Ga.; thence an overland march of 115 miles to Nolasulga, Ala.; by rail again to Montgomery; from this point, by steamboat, to Mobile; at which place ship was taken, the first landing being at Lobos Island, near Tampico, Mexico. The Regiment arrived at Vera Cruz in time to take part in its siege and reduction, March 10-27. Colonel Butler, in reporting this action, says: "All were exposed to the fire from the city and castle, but Lieutenant Colonel Dickinson's command more so, from being farther to the right. All behaved with a coolness not to be expected among volunteers." Here ten men in the Kershaw Company were killed and Colonel Dickinson was severely wounded in the breast.

The victorious march of the American army under General Scott from Vera Cruz to the City of Mexico, a distance of nearly 300 miles, was spectacular in its many bloody engagements, the Mexicans gamely contesting at every point the progress of a foe far superior in all but numbers. The route of the South Carolina troops, who were in the brigade of General Shields, attached to the division under General Quitman, was via Jalapa, Perote and Puebla. From this point, their advance has been so graphically described by Adjutant James Cantey (later a distinguished General in the Confederate service) that we shall let his abler pen tell the story for us. His letter, to a friend in Camden, was published in a contemporary Camden paper.

"National Palace of Mexico, Oct. 27, 1847.

Dear ———: After an interval of five months, an opportunity is at length afforded us of communicating with our friends at home. * * * When ——— left us early in June, the diseases of the climate had just begun to rage. The muffled drum and measured tread of the funeral escort could be heard from morning till night; and soon the summons of death was so oft repeated that it became impossible to render the unfortunate dead the sad compliment of a military burial. When we marched from Puebla on the 8th of August with the invading army, one hundred sick were left at that place, and three hundred muskets were all that could be marched upon the bloody plains of Contreras and Churubusco, on the morning of the 20th. The sympathy of the whole state must be mingled with the admiration bestowed on us by the entire army when they learn that, out of that number, one hundred and thirty-seven brave but unfortunate men were left upon the field consecrated by the life blood of the brave, the gallant, the lamented Colonel Butler, who had only risen from his sick bed the evening before, to lead his command on one of the most severe and trying marches that men ever encountered, over mountains and hills of congealed lava, broken by deep chasms and rugged steeps—the night dark and stormy, and the rain pouring down in torrents.

"It was one o'clock in the morning before we reached our position around the fortifications at Contreras. * * * At daylight the charge was sounded and in less than twenty minutes we were all in the forts of the enemy, capturing and killing all but about one regiment of lancers who escaped towards the city.

"The whole army then moved forward and encountered the enemy in immense numbers, drawn up, fortified, and strongly intrenched, at Churubusco. They seemed determined to make a stubborn resistance to our further progress. Every housetop, hillock, bridge, or mound, was fortified and defended by cannon. The strife was tremendous and the conflict deadly—but, poor fellows, they were unable to resist the impetuosity of men determined to enter or die upon the field. An armistice was concluded that evening, when our troops penetrated to the suburbs of the city. * * * On the 12th September, the bombardment of Chapultepec was commenced, as it was deemed necessary to the assault of the city. On the 13th, the sound was again heard that announced the storming of that fortress that knows no superior in the world for strength. We had been directed, in general orders, that our little fragment of a regiment should be in the rear as a supporting column. But, before we had gone 200 yards from Captain Drum's battery, where we lay during the 12th and the night following to protect it during its play upon Chapultepec, the column was halted, and the noble Shields ordered us to the front. When we had reached the advanced position assigned us, General Quitman, pointing to a stone fortification just under a stone wall 15 feet high, and lined with 5 or 6 12-pounders and supported by about 2,000 muskets, raised in his stirrups and said to Major Gladden, that the fate of the day depended on carrying that breastwork and wall, and that the Palmettoes were the boys to do it. If ever there was a proud and ennobling moment of a South Carolinian's life, it was that in which this fragment of a regiment, numbering only 150 muskets, with wounded and lame men in its ranks, heard this address of the gallant Quitman. Immediately Major Gladden said, "Come on, boys, we will try it"—and every man moved forward with a firm step and unflinching determination to succeed.

"Our way lay over an open plain cut up by many deep ditches; through a fire from the fort in front crossed by another from the right. The Regiment moved forward and gained the wall *without discharging a musket.* But, alas, many who started for that goal of distinction failed to reach it. It was crossing the plain near the wall, that Lieutenant James Willis Cantey, poor fellow, received his wound while leading a detachment of two companies in advance of the Regiment. He was as noble and generous a spirit as ever lived, and as brave and gallant a soldier as ever bore a sword; his conduct was the subject of remark by the whole Regiment. The death of no man, nor excepting our good, noble Colonel, was more regretted, for he had endeared himself to every officer and private by his generous and estimable conduct and virtues and his last act of gallantry won the admiration and esteem of the whole division, for the charge was made in the face of it. * * *

"As soon as the castle was taken, the army moved on towards the gates of the city, every inch of the ground disputed. To undertake to describe the difficulties and slaughter consequent upon the charge at the taking of the city, is beyond my power. I could not see how it was possible for a single man to escape alive. The housetops were covered with infantry—the streets and avenues lined with cannon and musketry, firing grape, cannister, bombshells and roundshot from every quarter. Our Regiment, which had been joined promiscuously by the mounted Rifle Regiment, were the storming party and were the first troops to enter the great capital of the Mexicans—and our flag the first that floated over the gates of the city. Night put an end to the conflict, and when the morning came, the broad stripes and bright stars were floating from the battlements of the National Palace, Santa Anna and his troops having taken their departure during the night. This was the last of the five hardest fought battles of modern times, and with it falls the Mexican Republic. * * * General Shields is a man of the most dashing gallantry in the army, and perfectly infatuated with and devoted to our Regiment; much of its high reputation is due to him and old Quitman, the ablest general in the service."

The lava beds alluded to flowed from the extinct volcano of Ajusco, and extended to Lake Chalco, on which was located the old convent of Churubusco, six miles southwest of the Capital. Contreras was a temporary fortification, near the village of San Angel, about three miles northwest of Churubusco, and covered the road from Tchalplain, General Scott's headquarters, to Chapultepec. It is marked now solely by a farm-house and a break in the lava-bed. Chapultepec is about two and one-half miles west of Mexico City. In strength it never compared with such strongholds as Gibraltar. It is now the seat of the President's summer palace and of the National military academy—the "West Point" of Mexico.

At Churubusco, Lieutenant Colonel Dickinson fell. His wound was not necessarily fatal, but, owing to the season and the hardships of the camp, proved so thirty days later. His death was a severe loss to the army.

The conspicuous conduct of a private of the Kershaw company at Chapultepec should also be noticed. Says a correspondent from the scene of war, December 10, 1847: "Levi Bradley is, I fear, a cripple for life. He is a gallant fellow and behaved like a hero on the field of battle. I saw him wounded, and, after he was shot in the leg and fallen, though unable to stand, he refused to leave the field and I saw him kneeling on one knee and firing, until he was separated from the Regiment by their advance, when the charge was sounded.[1] * * * In fact, our whole company did so well that it is difficult to discriminate."

What higher tribute to the splendid services of the Palmetto Regiment could be paid than the fact that, though reduced from 1,100 men to an effective force of only 140, after the taking of the Mexican Capital, General Scott refused to allow them to leave, as, to quote his words, he "could not spare his veterans". Or this: that, when the Americans were finally ordered to evacuate San Angel, the Mexicans themselves requested that the last troops to leave might be the South Carolinians, who, "by their gentlemanly behavior, had won (their) confidence and admiration."

Before its disbanding, Keith Moffat was elected Major, and James Cantey, a captain, of the Palmetto Regiment.

On July 12, 1848, after a most arduous and gallant service of eighteen months, the Kershaw and Lancaster Volunteers returned to Camden, with only thirty-nine men in both companies, officers included. War and disease had wrought terrible havoc. They were met at Stateburg, the terminus of the railroad, by a committee of citizens and brought in carriages to Camden, where, a few days later, there was a great demonstration in their honor, at the Academy Grove (DeKalb St.). The papers tell us that the streets were thronged with citizens of this and adjoining districts, cannon boomed, bells pealed merrily, and that over a thousand people partook of the public dinner, at which, after the usual custom, toasts were drunk to the local heroes of the campaign—Butler, Dickinson, Willis Cantey—to the officers and rank and file of the Regiment and, last, to the two following Spread Eagle sentiments that deserve immortality:

1. "Mexico—We made a breakfast of her; I pity the country that provokes us to dine!"

2. "The American Eagle has soared to the heights of Popocatapetl and rested on the tall summits of Orizaba. May he continue to gaze undazzled on the sun until his wings have overspread the kingdoms of the earth."

---

[1] Levi Bradley died in 1879 at the age of 64, leaving several descendants. Though crippled, he was a useful and highly respected citizen of the county.

HISTORIC CAMDEN

Swords were presented to Major Moffat and Captain James Cantey,[1] and the movement started to raise the public monuments to Dickinson and Willis Cantey.

*Keith Stuart Moffat*, who served with distinction throughout the entire Mexican campaign as Captain of the Kershaw Volunteers and, at its close, was elected a Major in the Palmetto Regiment, was the son of William Moffat, a native of Dumfriesshire, Scotland, who came to Camden and died here at the age of thirty-eight, "leaving in a strange land", according to the rather pathetic inscription on his tomb, "a widow and five helpless sons".

Mrs. Jannet Moffat, the widow, survived until 1858 and raised at least three of the boys to manhood, Robert, Keith and John.

Robert moved to Mobile where he engaged in business as a commission merchant and is rated by those who remember him, "a first-rate man". It was he who placed the substantial monuments to his father, mother, and brother (Keith), in the cemetery.

Keith was born at Newton-Stewart, Scotland, in 1817, came to this country in 1821, and died, unmarried, at Orange Springs, Fla., in 1855. At the time he was a warden of the town of Camden. So far as we know, he never otherwise rose in civil life above the position of clerk in one or other of the stores of Camden, another instance of the capable but untrained citizen—soldiery, of which our War between the Sections afforded so many notable examples. In this latter struggle, one of the Kershaw companies paid Keith Moffat the honor of taking his name—The Moffat Rifles, 7th Battalion.

*James Willis Cantey* was the son of the then Adjutant General of the State, James W. Cantey, and Camilla Richardson, his wife.

Born in 1822 at the family home in Camden, and a graduate of the South Carolina College, in the class of 1843, he sacrificed his knightly spirit on the altar of his country at the early age of twenty-five, as graphically described in the letter quoted from his cousin, the late General James Cantey.

---

[1] James Cantey was elected colonel of the Palmetto Regiment in the City of Mexico, beating Major Gladden by 22 votes, but declined to serve, having promised to support Gladden. (The *Camden Journal* is our authority for this statement).

COL. J. P. DICKINSON
(His orderly T. E. Shannon alongside)

## The Kershaw Volunteers in the Mexican War

Though third in command of his company on leaving for the war, he was, by circumstances, first at Churubusco and Chapultepec. In the former battle, Captain Moffat was wounded just before the charge, and Lieutenant Cantey, who had just risen from a long and serious illness, immediately placed himself at the head of the company, and was the first man to reach the entrenchments of the enemy, thirty yards in advance of his men.

"At the storming of Chapultepec", says a correspondent from that field, "he was placed by Major Gladden in command of Companies C and K (which was the first to cross a large ditch running through the meadow through which the Regiment had to pass to gain the wall, and whose officers were absent, sick, or wounded), and ordered to advance with them. When far ahead of the Regiment and near the wall, he received the wound which terminated his existence. He lived long enough to see his detachment gain the wall and drive off the enemy."

Six months later, his body was brought to Camden and the honor of a public funeral, very similar to that accorded Colonel Dickinson, was his.

Partly by popular subscription, a monument—the handsomest in the old Quaker Cemetery—was raised as a tribute to his heroism.

The *Camden Journal* of October 27, 1847, lamenting his death, says:

"Another gallant son too our community mourns. Lieutenant J. Willis Cantey was killed in that dreadful but splendid attack upon Chapultepec; and never was purer spirit breathed out upon the battlefield. With the sincerity of a child and the warm affection of a woman, he had combined in him the highest attributes of the sterner sex. In the bloom of youth he has been cut down, early in the career he so well loved, but not before he had added high honor to his soldier name."

*James Polk Dickinson* was born in Camden, January 21, 1816. His father, Henry H. Dickinson, was an Englishman, from Bermuda, whose naturalization papers were taken out about 1802, at Camden, where he resided until his death in 1826.

His mother was Martha, daughter of Dr. Ephraim Brevard, reputed author of the disputed Mecklenberg

Declaration of Independence and brother to Judge Joseph Brevard of Camden. His maternal grandmother was of the well known Polk family of North Carolina and Tennessee, and is said to have been a very beautiful woman.

He had an uncle, his father's brother, living in Bermuda, a wealthy merchant and planter, whom in his youth he visited. When ten years of age, being left an orphan, he was taken to the home of his cousin, Dr. Alfred Brevard, in Kirkwood, by whom he was raised to manhood.

His entire academic education seems to have been obtained under Henry P. Hatfield, at the Camden Academy.

His training in the law was received in the office of John M. DeSaussure. Before admission to the Bar, he served under Captain John Chesnut in the Florida War.

As a youth he is described as having been proud, high-spirited, restive under control.

When the DeKalb Rifle Guards was organized in 1840, he was chosen Captain, with Keith Moffat as 2nd Lieutenant.

About this time occurred his duel with Major Smart, which has elsewhere been discussed.

In 1842 he was elected to the Legislature where he remained for six years.

But it was not in the Forum that the finest talents of the man were to be displayed. His opportunity offered at the call to arms for the Mexican campaign in 1846. His old company, as stated, was the first in the State to volunteer, and Dickinson, then a Colonel, and James Cantey a Major, of militia offered among the first to enlist as privates in the ranks.

On the formation of the Palmetto Regiment, in July of that year, Pierce M. Butler was elected Colonel and James Polk Dickinson Lieutenant Colonel.

The energy and enthusiasm of Colonel Dickinson at this period were extraordinary. On the second call of Governor Johnson for volunteers, he stirred the whole county by his appeals. His speech on December 2, from the base of the DeKalb monument, when enlistments had not been so spontaneous as he wished, seems to have been a master-effort and to have marked him as an orator of no mean rank. The audience is said to have been fairly electrified by his burning eloquence.

## The Kershaw Volunteers in the Mexican War

Men likened him to MacDuffie. One passionate utterance survived, to be later engraved upon his tomb: "I want a place in the picture near the flashing of the guns!" The ranks of the Kershaw Volunteers were soon filled, even grey-haired men offering themselves, and to Dickinson alone, the local paper attributes the credit of maintaining the honor of the District "in her hour of trial."

Colonel Dickinson's career is an inseparable part of the glory bequeathed by the Palmetto Regiment to South Carolina.

We are told that, having squandered his estates by prodigal generosity and extravagance and being submerged in debt,[1] Dickinson saw in the battle-clouded plains of Mexico a path by which he might rise to the summit of his great ambition for military renown and commend himself in the eyes of his relative, President James K. Polk.

Be that as it may, whatever the motive, he must have been a very magnificent figure on the battlefield. Of splendid physique—he was six feet four inches in height—he is described by correspondents and editors of the Camden papers in terms of most extravagant eulogy, as "the gallant, chivalrous and accomplished Dickinson * * * majestic in intellect as in appearance"; "a very Incarnation of the Spirit of War", having "on fields of carnage, an aspect of grandeur and sublimity like the fabled heroes of antiquity", and, where the fight raged fiercest, inspiring all about him by his calmness, "like the serene angel that rides in the whirlwind and directs the storm", and so on. In less hyperbolic strain, one editorial says:

"He has ever sought the post of danger and honor, and all who know Colonel Dickinson know that a braver man never unsheathed a sword."

Casting aside the halo about his head in the popular imagination, he still stands forth a picturesque "beau sabreur", of great dash and natural ability, if of somewhat too dramatic instincts.

On the weary march from Atlanta to Montgomery, he performed the gallant deed of placing a tired boy from

---

[1] An amusing anecdote is told of his effrontry to a long-suffering creditor: "James ———, your duns positively disgust me. If you send me another bill, I shall cut your acquaintance." Rare old days, those!

Fairfield on his horse and marching in his place for a whole day on foot.

At Vera Cruz, though severely wounded in the shoulder, he continued to lead two companies against a large body of Mexican Lancers.

At Churubusco, when the standard bearer of the Regiment was shot down, he seized the colors and carried them in advance of his men, though in his hands they were torn into rags and tatters by a storm of bullets.

In this engagement, owing to the death of Colonel Butler, Dickinson succeeded to the command of the Regiment. Fifteen minutes later, having received a ball in the ankle, he also fell, handing the flag and his sword to Major Gladden, with injunctions that the honor of the State be maintained.

He might have recovered from the wound, not a bone being broken, but amputation was ordered by the surgeons and this, from vanity it is said, Colonel Dickinson would not allow. A low typhoid fever set in, and, after lingering for thirty days, he died, at the village of Mixchoac, September 12, 1847.

He was only thirty-one years old. A very promising military career, barely unfolding, was cut short. The coveted distinction, a high place in the United States Army, would doubtless have been his, had he survived.

His remains were brought to Camden and interred in the old Presbyterian cemetery, January 22, 1848. The town has perhaps never witnessed so large and impressive a funeral. Minute guns were fired from "the old redoubt adjoining the Presbyterian Burial Ground."[1]

Grace (Episcopal) Church being far too small to seat the vast concourse, estimated at 3,000, a desk covered with black was put upon the base of the DeKalb monument, from which Dickinson had made his impassioned appeal for volunteers, and here Rev. Thomas F. Davis (later Bishop) pronounced an eloquent oration on "How are the mighty fallen in the midst of the battle". The long procession to the grave included numerous military and civic organizations, a band of music, and Colonel Dickinson's war horse, lead by his faithful body-servant, Jim Lang,[2] following the remains in an immense black

---

[1] *Camden Journal*, January 26, 1848.

[2] Only recently deceased. Spare, erect, of somewhat soldiery bearing, he felt immense pride in the part he had borne under his old master in the war.

## The Kershaw Volunteers in the Mexican War

leaden box, on a draped bier, drawn by four grey horses with appropriate trappings.

In 1856, the body was transferred to its present resting place in the central park of the town, then known as Log-town, now as Monument, Square. By popular subscription a very handsome shaft of Italian marble was, the same year, erected over the grave, on which are inscribed, at some length, the glorious deeds and virtues of the sleeping soldier. The top of the shaft is surmounted by a helmet and wreath of laurel. On the faces are four shields, one bearing the name "Dickinson", a second the coat of arms of South Carolina, the other two, respectively, "Vera Cruz and Contreras", and "Churubusco". A heavy iron railing forms an enclosure.

From the epitaph we quote a few lines:
"How inspiring his words and manly bearing,
When, addressing his regiment for the last time,
He seized the banner of his old company,
The DeKalb Rifle Guards,
Hastily unfurling its proud and glorious
Motto to the breeze, and planting it firmly in front exclaimed,
'Here, soldiers, is your standard, you once
Pledged your sacred honor never to desert it,
Come, redeem the pledge,
Rally around, and thrice honored be
The name that tops the list'!"

Colonel Dickinson left no descendants. His wife was Miss Emma Dyson, a niece of General James W. Cantey. She, with General Cantey's daughter, Emma (Mrs. P. H. Nelson), were the two handsomest women in Camden, perhaps, of the period, and rival belles. Mrs. Dickinson later became the wife of Warren Nelson, of Stateburg.

Roll of the DeKalb Guards who, as "Kershaw Volunteers", left Camden for Charleston, en route to Mexico, on December 9, 1846.[1]

| | |
|---|---|
| Keith S. Moffatt, Captain | †Michael P. Belcher, 1st Serg. |
| Jos. B. Kershaw, 1st Lieut. | Jonah R. Holmes, 2nd Serg. |
| James Cantey, 2nd Lieut. | †Sam'l J. Young, 3rd Serg. |
| James W. Cantey, Jr., 3rd Lieut. | †Zach Cantey, 4th Serg. |
| | W. N. Robinson, 1st Corp. |

[1]Copied from the *Camden Journal* of December 30, 1846.
Those marked † discharged from *wounds* and *disability*.

# HISTORIC CAMDEN

J. M. Gay, 2nd Corp.
†W. R. Clanton, 3rd Corp.
†Jno. B. Tilman, 4th Corp.

*Privates.*

Francis Ballard
Benj. F. Perry
Thomas Bullard
†Benj. Baskin
A. B. McCaskill
*Jackson Bradley (Lancaster)
Finley McCaskill
James Riddle
William Nelson
J. White
Robt. White
Wm. F. Hunter
Joseph Dean
Alfred Love
John Harrall
B. F. McCrummon
John Jordan
Jackson Nelson
H. Tedwell
L. B. Bright
Lewis B. Thompson
H. Gibbons
John Dunlap
Dennis Sizer
J. R. Marshall
James Herron
Anderson B. Sizer
Columbus Shiver
John Villepigue
†Levi Bradley
R. Ford
Reuben Roberts
James Dunlap
Wiley Malone
J. W. Bowns
Amos Moseley
Marshall Moseley

W. Robinson
W. Hopkins
John M. Caton
J. C. Bennett
James P. Rosser
John Creighton
*Jackson Johnson (Sumter)
Eli B. Brewer
†Peter Ciples
Ransom Logan
Charles K. Brewer
George W. Gilman
*Charles H. Moorefield (Va.)
Ivy Rape
George Waters
B. F. Spears
*Charles Douglas (N. Y.)
*A. McManus (Chesterfield)
John Caine
*Jackson Hill (Chesterfield)
G. W. Baskin
*Pleasant McManus (Chesterfield)
H. D. Richardson
†Z. H. Blanchard
*J. P. Durden (Chesterfield)
*E. B. Durden (Chesterfield)
G. R. Kirk
H. A. Rollins
*Thomas Hill (Chesterfield)
George McCorkle
*R. B. Harrison (N. C.)
J.H. Harrall
†Stephen Meggs
John Dyson
John G. Wooten
*William Page (N. Y.)
†Matthew Stratton
*S. J. Lucy (Chesterfield)
*John Wilson (N. Y.)
†James Jennings

Those marked * deserted since mustered into service.
Those marked † discharged from *wounds* and *disability.*

# The Kershaw Volunteers in the Mexican War

*Officers on Return of Regiment from Mexico.*

Keith S. Moffat, Captain
J. B. Kershaw, 1st Lieut.
James Cantey, 2nd Lieut.
K. S. Billings, 2nd Lieut.
Jno. M. Gay, 1st Serg.

George McCorkle, 2nd Lieut.
Finley McCaskill, 1st Corp.
Lewis B. Thompson, 2nd Corp.
Sanford Horton, 3rd Corp.

*Privates Who Returned.*

1. Francis Ballard
2. Eli B. Brewer
3. Chas. K. Brewer
4. L. B. Bright
5. Thomas Bullard
6. John Creighton
7. Joseph Dean
8. John Dyson
9. Chas. T. Darby
10. James Herron
11. Wm. F. Hunter
12. Geo. R. Kirk
13. Ransom Logan
14. B. F. McCrimmon
15. Wiley Malone
16. Columbus Shiver
17. Benj. F. Spears
18. Hiram Tedwell
19. Jno. S. Wooten
20. James Wilburn
21. Samuel Caston
22. Wm. N. Conner
23. Ransom Gardner
24. Jno. W. Gent
25. S. A. Garry
26. Elisha Humphries
27. Z. Huggins
28. Jno. W. Knight
29. Joshua Knight
30. Amos McManus
31. Davis Phillips

*Recapitulation.*

| | |
|---|---:|
| Commissioned Officers | 3 |
| Non-Commissioned Officers | 5 |
| Privates | 31 |
| Total | 39 |

List of Deaths in the Kershaw Company, from time of leaving Camden to November 1, 1847. (Furnished by Sergeant Belcher.)

At Vera Cruz: James Dunlap, John Jordan, Owen Poston, A. B. Sizer, Jas. White, Robert White, W. L. Weeks, Amos Moseley, Marshall Moseley, John Dunlap.

At Jalapa: (B. F. Perry), J. W. Bounds, A. Collins, W. Hopkins, Wm. Robinson.

At Perote: Wm. M. Robinson, Robert Ford, H. A. Rollins, H. R. Gibbons.

At Puebla: J. R. Holmes, John Broadnax, G. W. Baker, J. M. Catoe, John Cain, Thos. Fitzsimmons, G. W. Gilman, Jos. H. Howell, Alfred Love, J. R. Marshall, A. McCaskill, Wm. Nelson,

J. S. Powell, Ivy Rape, James Riddle, Dennis Sizer, J. P. Rosser (on his way home, wounded).

At Churubusco: John Villepigue, M. S. Caton, W. B. Hilton, W. McFarland.

At Chapultepec: Lieutenant J. Willis Cantey, J. C. Bennett.

At City of Mexico: E. F. Warlick, John Smith, Geo. Waters (wounded at Contreras).

Hiram Rials was killed near City of Mexico.

Jackson Nelson, stabbed in the city by one of his own Regiment. Died of wound.

James Harrell died at Charleston, S. C.

Reuben Roberts crushed to death by cars at Atlanta, Ga.

# CHAPTER XIII.

## IRREPRESSIBLE CONFLICT.

The framers of the Federal Constitution attempted no radical solution of the slavery problem, but passed it on to posterity. This root of discord was never dormant. By the year 1820 its menacing growth became manifest in the struggle over the admission of Missouri, as free or slave state. The celebrated compromise of Henry Clay, whereby it was admitted as a slave state, but slavery barred all north of latitude 36.30, merely deferred the issue.

Abolition sprang up in the wake of the compromise. The appearance of *The Liberator*, published by Wm. Lloyd Garrison and Benj. Lundy, marks the advent of the organized anti-slavery crusade. The welcome given to the *Liberator* in Camden may be gathered from comments of the *Camden Journal* of February 5, 1831, then edited by C. F. Daniels, a native of Connecticut, who had been branded by the *Liberator* as a "renegade". Says Daniels:

"A controversy with the *Liberator!* 'Well, buzzards are excellent for chicken pye, and that's the real truth on't'. This scandalous and incendiary budget of sedition we hereby give Mr. Garrison notice against introducing into this State. He may find himself 'dancing on nothing and holding on by the same'."

Abolition societies and publications continued to excite violent indignation at the South, and even in Boston itself, where Garrison, led with a halter round his neck, was barely saved from an incensed mob. An exhibition of the sentiment in Camden is furnished by the resolutions of a public meeting in August 1835, framed by a committee consisting of Thos. J. Withers, Chairman, Wm. McWillie, W. W. Lang, W. J. Grant, J. C. Vaughan, J. M. DeSaussure, A. DeLeon, W. E. Johnson, John Cantey, Thos. Salmond. This proclamation, savoring of the Chairman's pen, runs in part as follows:

"That the abolition of slavery, whether immediate or remote or any interference, by non-slave holders in our sister states or elsewhere, with the relation of master and slave in South Carolina, are not questions for discussion; upon such proposition we hold ourselves ready for defensive *action* only, and that prompt and efficient.

"That slavery, as it exists with us, we deny to be an evil, and that we regard those who are now making war upon it, in any shape or under any pretext, as furious fanatics, or knaves and hypocrites; and we hereby promise them upon all occasions which may put them in our power, the fate of the Pirate, the Incendiary and the midnight assassin.

"That we shall regard any attempt on the part of Congress to abolish slavery, suddenly or gradually, in any State, Territory or District where it now exists, by appropriation of the public funds or by other means, or any resolutions or Act of Congress adverse to slavery, as a reckless violation of our Constitutional compact, as a wicked and direct infringement of our rights and as involving the certain and speedy dissolution of this Union."[1]

Disapproval is expressed of any one who takes or reads an abolition paper; committee of Vigilence, numbering nineteen, appointed.

In 1838 *The Emancipator*, published by the American Anti-slavery Society, requests to exchange with Southern papers. To this invitation the *Camden Commercial Courier*, M. M. Levy, Editor, responds:

"We would request them to keep clear of our threshold, intercourse would be pollution.

The same paper says:

"Congress is not the place to which we should refer the arbitrament of this question. We rely upon the Constitution which we believe able to protect us. If however, the shafts of fanatacism pierce through that shield, we would look for support to our own strength."

Abolition continued to advance with steady, if not rapid pace, despite the disfavor of a strong element of the North. In 1844 it gained an important point. Hitherto, by a rule standing since 1790, Congress excluded all anti-slavery petitions. This rule was now rescinded by a vote of 108 to 80. At last toleration had been gained. As to this step Calhoun said: "If the party who got up

---

[1] In a similar strain runs an address of Geo. McDuffie to the South Carolina Legislature in 1835, in which he said: "Domestic slavery therefore instead of being a political evil is the corner stone of our republican edifice. No patriot who justly estimates our privileges will tolerate the idea of emancipation at any period however remote on any conditions of pecuniary advantage however favorable."

the petition should succeed in getting Congress to take jurisdiction, agitation would follow which would in the end, if not arrested, destroy the Union."

This action of Congress produced a retaliatory spirit in South Carolina. A law of this State, enacted in 1820, provided that any free negro brought into its ports upon any vessel, should be imprisoned and sold into slavery. In 1844 the Honorable Samuel Hoar of Massachusetts was sent to Charleston, where a negro on a vessel from that state had been imprisoned, to contest in Court the constitutionality of the law above mentioned. Threats arose against him, and demonstrations so violent that he had to be escorted around by leading citizens, who advised him to leave. We find it related in the *Camden Journal* of the time, that at the Legislative session following Mr. Hoar's visit, McWillie, Chesnut and Dickinson, members from Camden, advocated in the presence of crowded and applauding galleries, a measure, which became law, making it a criminal offence for any one coming into the State, or any one in the State, to question or hinder the operation of its slave laws. The act further required the Governor, at that time Jas. H. Hammond, to expel from the State any agent coming upon any mission concerning the slave laws.[1]

The subject of the annexation of Texas reopened the questions settled by the Missouri Compromise. New England was alarmed at the addition of so great a slave state to the South. The *Boston Atlas* of July 1844 says: "We shall certainly consider the annexation of Texas or any other foreign state to this country, as a virtual dissolution of the Union, and that such a vast addition to our territory would absolve the dissenting states from any further obligation under the original contract."

Town Council of Camden called a meeting of citizens in May 1844 to consider the annexation of Texas. An able committee, Wm. McWillie, Chairman, with such associates as J. P. Dickinson, John Cantey, J. M. DeSaussure, J. B. Kershaw, among whom however we miss the names of Chesnut, Withers, and Johnson, reported fav-

---

[1]On January 28, 1860, in the United States Senate, Chesnut and Hammond, then Senators from South Carolina engaged in angry controversy with Senator Wilson of Massachusetts, over the incident of Mr. Hoar's visit of 1844, and the very extreme law passed in consequence.

oring annexation. The report was adopted and forwarded to Congress. At the fourth of July celebration that year, this was the leading toast: "The Union and Texas, or Texas and disunion. Let the opponents of this great American measure accept the alternative."

But inasmuch as Henry Clay, then candidate for the presidency, had adherents in Camden, it is assumed that they, like him, were opposed to the admission of Texas. The *Camden Journal* was very tart and hostile towards Clay. A meeting of citizens, however, in February 1844, through a committee of three, T. J. Withers, Burwell Boykin and C. Matheson, invited Clay to visit Camden on his contemplated trip to this State. The invitation was not accepted.

The great territory conquered from Mexico, with California and its gold added fuel to the controversy: Shall slavery enter here? Or be wholly excluded? Or shall the Missouri Compromise line be extended, across this new region, to the Pacific, which would give to the South, Texas, New Mexico, Southern California and more. In Congress the conflict raged with utmost ferocity.

The local agitation is manifested by a large meeting, which assembled in Camden, March 7, 1849, notable among the many of which those times were so prolific. As usual the resolutions adopted were drafted by a committee, composed of Jas. Chesnut, Jr., Chairman; Wm. M. Shannon, J. B. Kershaw, Thos. J. Ancrum, B. Boykin, J. T. McKain, L. L. Whitaker, H. Levy, A. D. Jones, C. Matheson. Some paragraphs are here inserted:

"Do they allow us the benefit of the compact, when their furious and fanatical mobs are permitted with impunity to assail and beat off our citizens and even murder them when going among them to reclaim such slaves?

"Is it good faith on their part to assail us at every point, to attempt to break down every barrier of the Constitution raised for our protection, to trample on our rights, to outrage our feelings, to pray for our misfortunes, to hold us up to the world as a bye-word and a reproach? All this done by those we call countrymen, yea, sometimes brethren.

"We must determine and hold it as binding upon us as our religion, to risk all—life, fortune, the Union—to preserve the sovereignty and political equality of the States. These yielded, nothing worth preserving is left.

## Irrepressible Conflict

"Abstract principles are of the highest importance, let unthinking babblers sneer at them as they may. They are expressions of truth, and furnish us with just standards of action. We must stand upon principle, 'snuff tyranny afar off in the breeze'—our fathers did so and were successful."

A proposition of non-intercourse is then set forth:

"We must go up behind the politicians and address ourselves to the people of the North—not by reasoning, for that would be absurd, but by a course of conduct that they can readily appreciate. Their living depends upon the scope of their markets, and we of the South are their best customers.

"If therefore we cease all intercourse, sell them not a pound of cotton, buy nothing that is made north of Maryland, manufacture among ourselves all that we need, we shall bring upon their heads a disastrous infliction. We shall be the gainers. The mechanic arts will flourish among ourselves, factories will stud our streams, our merchants and farmers prosper.

"That beyond the Constitution, the Union, if it exists at all, must be a Union by force or by fraud, and the Government one of Usurpation."

A committee of safety numbering fifty was constituted as follows:

Colonel Jas. Chesnut, Sr., Colonel Jas. C. Haile, Captain W. A. Ancrum, Major John Rosser, Colonel L. J. Patterson, Dr. E. A. Salmond, Major A. H. Boykin, Colonel Tilman L. Dixon, C. Matheson, Dr. John Milling, Jas. B. Cureton, L. W. Blair, Colonel Jas. Chesnut, Jr., Captain Benj. McCoy, Major D. B. Kirkland, Major John Smart, Captain B. Jones, Major John M. DeSaussure, Dr. John McCaa, Wm. B. Fletcher, Paul T. Villepigue, John P. Knox, Colonel Jos. B. Kershaw, Colonel Wm. J. Taylor, Benj. Perkins, Jas. Team, General Jas. W. Cantey, W. B. Watkins, John Workman, Captain H. Summerville, L. L. Whitaker, Hayman Levy, Kenneth McCaskill, John S. Cunningham, Dr. Jos. Lee, Jesse Kilgore, Jas. Love, Honorable T. J. Withers, Wm. M. Shannon, Wm. E. Johnson, Major John D. Murray, Captain W. Kennedy, Captain Thos. J. Warren, Captain A. M. Kennedy, J. R. McKain, Jas. Tiller, Colonel W. Drakeford, Captain Wiley Kelley.

In 1850 Clay again poured oil on the troubled waters, and by the "Omnibus Bill" effected his third celebrated compromise. By its terms slavery was debarred from

California and the Mexican territory, but to appease the South a stringent fugitive slave law was enacted. In his last words debating these propositions Calhoun declared: "The South asks for simple justice. She has no compromise to offer but the Constitution, and no concession or surrender to make."

"The oil of compromise" allayed the other Southern States, but took fire in the hot atmosphere of South Carolina and produced the violent agitation of 1851. The State has seldom passed through a more tense situation. There were three elements, Secessionists, dubbed "Fire-eaters", in favor of separate and immediate secession, "Co-operationists", opposed to secession except in concert with other slave states, and a small number of Unionists, whom the extremists branded as "Submissionists".

In the *Camden Journal* of 1850 we find such editorial expressions as this: "It is now demonstrated that the South can no longer remain in the Union upon equal terms." "We calmly appeal to the Southern people to attempt to abolish Yankee newspapers in the South. Will you pay an abolition Yankee to cater your political food?" "If no other state will secede South Carolina must alone. Our very tree, the classic palmetto, points to our remedy. Every leaf it bears is a sword, as if to remind us that even nature bore arms for us."

In a speech at Camden this year James Chesnut, Jr. said: "The South is not desirous to surrender the institution of slavery; it has proved beneficial to the African race, a source of refinement and Christian benevolence. Freedom of slaves must be purchased, voluntary or forced, either proposition delusive. We owe the Union a rational not a blind devotion; it has been perverted from its legal object. These grievances give us a right to abolish a government insufficient to our wants. We regard some things worse than disunion."

In Camden, as in all other parts of the State, a Southern Rights Association and Council of Safety were formed, John Cantey, President, and such members as Thos. Salmond, C. J. Shannon, A. M. Kennedy, L. H. Deas, J. B. Kershaw, D. L. DeSaussure, Thos. Lang, Benj. Perkins, Wm. A. Nettles and many others as well known. The year 1851 fairly bristled with meetings, debates and conventions. The following is from an utterance of Geo. McDuffie of this date:[1]

In February 1851 an election was held for members of a Convention to determine the policy of the State. Three fire-eating secessionists were elected by this County, John Cantey, Thos. Lang, L. J. Patterson. Of the total convention membership three-fourths were of the same stamp, with a handful of "Submissionists". Of these latter the *Camden Journal* said: "Poor fellows, we pity them. We hope when they come to mix with men who were not born to be slaves and determined to defend their rights, they will remember they are Carolinians."[2] But the marvel was presented of a complete reversal of sentiment between the election and meeting of this Convention, the date of its assembly being dependent on call of the Legislature. During the interim, in October, occurred another election of delegates to a still more important convention of the Southern States, James Chesnut and Jno. C. Preston were the Co-operation candidates for membership of this Southern Convention, from this District; Dixon Barnes, of Lancaster and Wm. A. Owens of Fairfield, Secessionists.

Judge Withers cast his influence with the co-operation element. Expression of his views was invited from all parts of the State. In addressing the people of Lancaster he said:

"If the Secessionist mounts into heroics and proclaims that it is becoming in South Carolina to drive into the glories of martydom, to play the part of Sampson by seizing, in a fit of desperate revenge, the pillars of the Temple and burying in common ruin herself and her enemies, suggest to your friend that the fury of his indignation may have blinded his judgment. It is of the last importance not to mistake the question. It is this: How shall slave owners provide new guards for their security? All the world external to them is malignant against them. All the slave power combined is not too strong for the contest. Shall we offer ourselves in detail to be cut off as an easy prey?"

[1] "When I hear a Northern man say the 'glorious Union' methinks I hear the bugle blast of the robber band; but when I hear a Southern man cry out 'glorious Union' methinks I snuff treason in the tainted gale."

[2] So sanguine of the Independence of South Carolina was Chas. A. Price, associate editor of the *Camden Journal*, that he launched forth a new paper: *The Southern Republic*.

Chesnut wrote to the Greenville people:

"If we secede now, without the concurrent action of other states, or some of them, is it probable that they would follow us within such time as would enable us to reap the benefits that ought to arise from secession? Look at Georgia and North Carolina, for example. They have already decided the question, each for herself. Before we can expect them to move with us, or soon after us, their decision must first be reversed. How can they be reversed? By our leaving the Union? I think not. There exist now in those states sullen and overwhelming majorities against us, our cause and our Southern Rights friends."

Such arguments were effective. At that era perhaps no two public men in the state carried more weight than Chesnut and Withers.[1] The tide had turned. Chesnut and Preston, Co-operationists, were overwhelmingly elected, and so throughout the State, except in the Charleston District. This election practically settled the question, and the convention, State and Southern, became mere matters of form. No record is found of their meeting. The fever abated. Truly had Calhoun spoken: "It is a great mistake to suppose that disunion can be effected at a blow. The cords which bind these states together in one common Union are far too powerful for that. Already agitation of the slavery question has snapped some; if it goes on it will finally snap every cord, when nothing will be left except force."

The nine years following the turmoil of 1851, though full of moving events throughout the Union, if we may judge from the files of the *Camden Journal*, were unusually devoid of any local demonstration. It may almost be termed the tranquil era. Yet we know the still waters ran deep. In this quiet interval we may pause to inquire: What lay at the root of the inevitable conflict? What say the sages and statesmen? To Jefferson emancipation was the "sacred side" of the question, and slavery the cause of "unquiet consciences". Said Seward:

"Wherever a slave exists he is the subject of two distinct and opposite ideas, the one that he is wrongly, the other that he is rightly, a slave." Calhoun declared: "Every portion of the North entertains feelings more or

---

[1]Withers had been elected to the Bench in 1845, and could not go further than reply by letter in response to various calls for his views.

less hostile to slavery, a vital part of the social organization of the South. The more hostile regard it as a sin, and themselves under the most sacred obligation to destroy it. The less opposed regard it as a crime against humanity, and, though less fanatical, feel bound to effect the same object. The least opposed view it as a blot on the nation, and bound to give it no countenance. On the contrary the South regards the relation one which cannot be destroyed without subjecting the two races to great calamity, and the section to poverty, desolation and wretchedness." John Rutledge in debating the Federal Constitution said: "Religion and humanity had nothing to do with this question. Interest alone is the governing principle with nations." Said Jefferson Davis in 1850 in the United States Senate: "The cause of this hostility would at last be found in the fact that the South held the African race in bondage, being the descendants of those who were mainly purchased from the people of the North." In writing the history of the great conflict, after it was over, he says: "No moral or sentimental considerations were really involved in either the earlier or the later controversies which so long agitated and finally ruptured the Union. They were simply struggles between different sections, with diverse institutions and interests. The question was merely whether the slave holder should be permitted to go with his slaves into territory (the common property of all) into which the non-slave holder could go with his property of any sort."

Whether moral or selfish motives produced the conflict, we need not believe that the Northern conscience was inherently superior to that of the South. Differing interests were certainly potent factors in producing different doctrines. Many Southerners of New England descent were among the staunchest defenders of Southern ideas on slavery. The same strain of colonists developed in the North abolitionists, in the South slave-owners. Slaves were the bulk of Southern wealth, witness this table of valuation of Kershaw County property, assessed by A. M. Kennedy, March 14, 1862, for Confederate taxes.

| | |
|---|---:|
| Real estate ............................. | $1,636,336 |
| 9,371 slaves ............................ | 4,552,110 |
| Merchandise ............................ | 129,425 |

| | |
|---|---:|
| Bank Stock | 450,000 |
| Money at interest | 1,567,864 |
| Other values | 146,820 |
| **Total** | **$8,482,555** |

To the Southerner, slavery had the sanction of the Bible, of the fathers, of the Constitution, and of custom. The institution to him seemed benevolent, for the slave was, in general, happy and devoid of aspiration for freedom. The exclusion of this property from territory acquired by the blood of the South was deeply resented as an affront and wrong.

Uncle Tom's Cabin, Squatter Sovereignty, Bleeding Kansas, the Dred Scott case, lead up to the crisis. Referring to the John Brown raid in the United States Senate on December 7, 1859, Chesnut makes these utterances:

"Because in a common territory, belonging to us all alike and in common, we choose to consider that we have a right to hold our property, they denounce and meet us with the bayonet; forsooth because we assert our rights, and nothing more than our rights under the constitution we are held as trespassers, as agitators.

"Yes, gentlemen of the South, you have an institution obnoxious to the philosophical, sentimental humanitarianism of the day, you must give it up. If you do so at our request all will be well and easy with you, but such is the urgency of these motives upon us that if you do not, we will do it by violence. Most magnanimous, gracious and merciful masters, we thank you for the privilege of choice.

"The honorable Senator who last spoke asked, what mean these recent ebulitions? Sir, they mean that the heart of the Southern people has been stirred to the bottom, they mean that they have borne it as long as it is a virtue to bear, and they mean that they will not forfeit the character of freemen.

"We cannot permit the Union to be a mere badge of servitude. Call it treason, gentlemen, and make the best of it. We say that we will sunder the Union, pull it to pieces, column, base and tower, before we'll submit to be crushed by a government which is our own as well as yours; to which we contribute as well as you; and which we will defend with our life's blood as well as you, so long as it shall be a Government securing to us, as to you, equality, life and liberty."

## Irrepressible Conflict

The election of Lincoln, proclaiming that the Union "could not permanently endure half slave and half free", and the passing of the Government into abolition control, snapped the last cord of Union. South Carolina acted first. Her two Senators, Chesnut and Hammond, at once sent their resignations to the Governor. A convention was promptly called, through which means alone the Sovereignty of the State could be exerted, and on December 20, 1860, was adopted at Charleston the momentous ordinance of Secession, every member present and subscribing. Among its signers appear the autographs of the three members from Kershaw County:

T. J. Withers, Jas. Chesnut, Jr., J. B. Kershaw.

The awful shadows of the tempest had fully gathered. In the Presbyterian Church at Camden, November 11, 1860, Rev. S. H. Hay spoke as follows:

"A party, small in its beginning, and universally despised a few years ago, raised its horrible head in the Northern States of the Confederacy. Drawing its maxims, not from the word of God, but from the infidel ravings of revolutionary France, it proclaimed liberty and equality to all. As the spark which falls upon the western prairie, when fanned by the breeze rapidly ignites, and soon spreads into one vast sea of flame, so has the pestilent heresy advanced. Blown upon by the hot breath of fanaticism, it has swept with burning fury over the great masses at the North. Trampling under foot the Constitution which our fathers have bequeathed to us, ignoring the teachings of God's word, they proclaim an exterminating war against an institution acknowledged by both, and upon which our existence as a people depends. If they succeed in their dread purpose, our beautiful South will be converted into a wilderness, a servile war will devastate our land, and the horrors of St. Domingo will roll like a flood tide over us.

"We all may soon be called to witness scenes at the mere contemplation of which humanity shudders. God, my beloved hearers, is a refuge, a very present help in all time of trouble. Fly to Him before the winds blow and the storm bursts in fury upon you. Dangers may thicken before you, a bloody winding sheet may be wrapped around you, but all will be well."

A large crowd on our public square was thus addressed by Thos. J. Warren, editor of the *Camden Journal*, long an ardent champion of Southern rights, and one who in the test lived up to his words:

"Young Carolinians, nerve your hearts and bare your arms to strike for your altars and your fires, be prepared to do your duty.

"I have no ambition gentlemen to figure as a warrior, I would rather not fight if it can honorably be avoided, but war is sometimes a necessary evil and if it must come let it come, and I feel profoundly impressed with the belief that I shall for one do my duty.

"If amid the shock of contending armies, where the battle tide rages fiercest, we are called upon to die upon the altar of our country, it would be as near the gates of the celestial city from that post of duty as from any other. So with our trust in God we shall

"As victors exault or in death be laid low,
With our backs to the field and our feet to the foe;
And leaving in battle no blot on our name,
Look proudly to Heaven from the death-bed of fame."[1]

At half-past four A. M., April 12, 1861, the guns of South Carolina opened on Fort Sumter, after efforts for peaceful solution had failed and the arrival of a hostile fleet at the harbor mouth. The bombardment continued through the night of the 12th and was heard in Camden. The following is from the *Camden Journal* of April 16, four days after:

"It is a well ascertained fact that the sound of the cannonading was distinctly heard in Camden and ten miles above. From the market steeple, on Friday night, between eleven and twelve o'clock, we saw what was supposed to be repeated flashes from the volleyed thunder of Charleston harbor.

"After an agony of suspense our community were relieved on Saturday afternoon (April 13) at about three o'clock with the glad tidings that Fort Sumter was surrendered to the South Carolinians—A thrill of joy went through every heart and the streets of Camden rang with the loud acclaim, 'Fort Sumter is ours'."

"The bells were rung with an earnest will and the cannon fired louder, if possible, than ever before. At night a magnificent illumination of the stores and dwellings took place. We observed with infinite pleasure that the young ladies of Mrs. McCandless Seminary had illuminated their building and over the gateway festooned a most beautiful transparency bearing the chaste and appropriate motto, 'Our youthful hearts unite'."

[1]Warren was killed by a bullet in the forehead at Gettysburg, while leading his regiment against Little Round Top.

## CHAPTER XIV.
### THOS. J. WITHERS.

Thomas Jefferson Withers[1] was born in 1804 at Ebenezer, near Rock Hill in York County. His father Randolph Withers and his mother Sarah Bailey Withers (a daughter of Captain Thomas Bailey) were both from Virginia and lie in the cemetery at Ebenezer. Here they reared a family of nine children of whom Thomas was the eldest. It is related that when he and his brothers were put to work in the garden, by mutual agreement he would sit on the fence and entertain the others with humorous stories while they did the grubbing.

As a boy he attended a good school at Ebenezer and graduated from the South Carolina College in 1825. In the summer of 1828 he took editorial charge of the *Telescope,* then an important newspaper, published at Columbia. This he conducted for two years, during a period of intense political acrimony. Whilst connected with the *Telescope* he formed an intimate friendship with Stephen D. Miller, then an aspirant for the Governorship, and a bright star in the political firmament of that day. From his correspondence with Miller the following is chosen as an example of the independence of spirit evinced at the early age of twenty-four, and exhibited in the highest degree throughout his career:

Columbia, S. C., August 16th, 1828.

"I think my relation to the *Telescope,* of which I have been editor for a few weeks past, may render some reply to a suggestion which we lately received from you agreeable.

"You have probably observed a hasty sketch of the principles which I lay down for myself in this my new capacity, published in a late number of the *Telescope.* I know you will approve the doctrines themselves, however you may esteem the ingenuity, industry or ability with which they may be advocated. I believe they have long been the landmarks of your own career, and for

---

[1]Much of the material in this chapter has been derived from an article on Judge Withers contained in the *Bench and Bar of South Carolina,* compiled by Colonel U. R. Brooks and published in 1908. As we prepared the article on Judge Withers for Colonel Brooks, which he adopted verbatim, we felt free to make use of it for this chapter, with corrections of such errors as closer research revealed.

myself I cannot but rejoice that there is a coincidence of views between us. I have delivered entirely and solely my own sentiments, without advice or consultation with any human being * * * The paper will not forego its radical propensities, but must henceforth speak editorially my own language only. Better that the editorial head be consistent, though weak, than variable and ever so energetic. A committee of gentlemen will scarcely manage the affair successfully and usefully. I am entirely open to advice—not at all to order.

"Yes, sir, if circumstances (and you and your friends must judge) require the use of our columns, they will be yielded to any reasonable extent, but I would not choose to enlist the paper in the contest for Governor at all. It has become unusual heretofore, I believe, to canvass for Governor in the newspapers, but it is perhaps most likely that the present occasion will furnish an exception.

"I did not publish my name as editor, not for the purpose of avoiding responsibility, but because I thought the signature of so young a man, and one so little known, would detract from the prospects of the establishment.

"I am, Sir, your friend,
"T. J. WITHERS."

In 1829, at the appointment of Governor Miller, he made the stage coach journey to Washington as bearer to Congress of the memorial adopted by the Legislature of South Carolina protesting against the Tariff Act of 1828. He writes to Governor Miller the substance of his interviews with men of national prominence. In 1830 Governor Miller was elected to the United States Senate, continuing his intimate correspondence with his young friend Withers, who in 1831 was married to Elizabeth Tunstall Boykin, a sister of Governor Miller's wife. Upon his marriage he moved to Camden and entered upon the practice of law, having been admitted to the bar in 1828. The one-room wooden building, the last on the west side of Broad Street, south of the old Court House, occupied by him as an office, still stands, one of the few relics of the Camden of a century ago.

In 1832 he was elected Solicitor of this Circuit over Geo. W. Dargan, afterwards Chancellor. In this position, to which he was re-elected several times, he manifested an ability which brought him a large and lucrative legal business. His first four children, were taken off by scarlet fever, a stroke which impaired his health

THOMAS J. WITHERS

and caused him to resign as Solicitor. He shunned the enticements of a political career, for which he doubtless realized that he entirely lacked the necessary pliancy.

In 1846 he was elected one of the Common Law Judges, who also sat as Court of Appeals—a post he filled for twenty years until his death. His Judicial opinions, preserved in the earlier Law Reports, manifest the decisive and trenchant quality of his mind.

During the bitter agitation which shook the State in 1850 for separate secession (ten years before the actual event), he was emphatically opposed to such isolated action by South Carolina, without co-operation of other States. From various counties in the State he received requests to attend and address public meetings. These he declined, owing to his judicial position, but expressed his views in writing which were read at these assemblies. From his letter to the Edgefield Committee, the following extract is given as a sample:

"If I felt at liberty to participate in debating the great question of the day, I know not where I should seek an audience more to my mind than one composed of the citizens of Edgefield; for, although I repudiate the tricks of adulation towards individuals or communities, I am nevertheless impelled, by all that I know of your people, to acknowledge and declare that I entertain a very favorable opinion of that manly spirit and intelligence which prevade the general population of Edgefield, and which alone will ever lead a people to independence of judgment and inspire them with a love of truth and intrepidity in following its lead.

"You ask my views 'on the great questions that now agitate the State, and especially on the dangers and difficulties which must necessarily attend separate State secession.' * * *

"Allow me to invite your attention to what I have said to the people of Greenville, of York, and of Darlington, as comprising what I believe touching the matter you suggest. My letters addressed to committees in those several districts have been published; they contain my true sentiments, in language which I hope is undisguised and intelligible, and will exhibit, more at large than is possible for this occasion, the advice, which, when asked for it and in all modesty, I would fain give to the people of this State. The true question for us is, how shall we sustain African slavery in South Carolina from a series of annoying attacks, attended by incidental consequences that I shrink from depicting and finally from utter abolition? That is the problem before us—the naked and true point."

When ten years later the State did actually secede, he and James Chesnut and Joseph B. Kershaw were sent as delegates from Kershaw County to the momentous Convention which adopted the Ordinance of Secession, and their signatures are subscribed to that document, the original of which hangs in the State House lobby at Columbia. By the Secession Convention he was chosen as one of the six delegates from South Carolina to the Convention at Montgomery, Ala., which organized the Confederacy of Southern States. When this Convention, owing to the emergency, resolved itself into a provisional Congress of the Confederacy, Withers was chosen one of the two Senators from South Carolina, the other being C. G. Memminger. The other four delegates served as members of the House of Representatives. In the work of Dr. J. L. M. Curry on the Montgomery Convention, Withers is named in a short list of the really strong and able men of that body. From a memorandum of the debates at the Montgomery Convention the following epitome of a discussion between Robert Toombs and Withers may give some idea of his style and calibre:

"Mr. Toombs offered an amendment to the effect that after the President appointed the head of a department, such head should be a member of either House of Congress, provided he was elected as such by the proper constituent power.

"Mr. Withers, of South Carolina, opposed it. He declared in unaffected sincerity, that he lamented so frequent a conflict of opinion between himself and the distinguished gentleman from Georgia. But this was a free conference; no man was excusable, before his constituents, or his country, in hiding his light (though it be a farthing candle) under a bushel.

"The gentlemen had drawn many observations from the ample fund of a Washington experience; in that species of knowledge, Mr. W. was deplorably deficient; but when the gentlemen discoursed, historically, of and concerning the remarkable fortune of many Presidents—misfortunes it should be called—from Polk inclusive, to wit, that they found themselves in a minority upon meeting the second Congress of their respective terms, he attributed this remarkable development, as he considered it, to the absence of cabinet officers from the floors of Congress, Mr. Withers would venture to refresh the memory of the distinguished gentleman as to what he must also have observed at Washington (and he would be happy to think it had been and was confined to Washington), to wit, that when the dispenser of the spoils began his career—when the lord of the flesh-pots of Washington had begun to administer to the appetites of his followers—he always found that only so many guests could be seated at his table, and that as if by magic, every crumb had been appropriated and swallowed. To his consternation, he saw yet an army of hungry wolves yelping and ferocious for coveted baits; he saw crowds of eager vultures flocking to hunt for the consumed carcass. Surely then, it is not surprising that by the time the second Congress assembled such busy patriots should be found enlisted under a new and unfriendly banner. Does the gentleman think that cabinet ministers, though in full blast upon the floors of Congress, could counteract or modify, a course of events so inexorable—flowing from causes as enduring as corrupt human nature itself? If, then, we have found a cause adequate to produce a result, it satisfies the teachings of sound phylosophy, and we need explore mysteries no further.

"Subsequently, Mr. Toombs withdrew his proposed amendment."

Before the close of the Montgomery Convention he returned to Camden, resigned his position as Senator in the Confederate Congress, resumed his duties as Judge and wrote to Governor Perry:

"My liking for actual service in State affairs does not increase, though it may grow on what it feeds on. I am not in the ways of tough politicians and you know it is hard to teach an old monkey new tricks. My place is about the hearth stone, as I think and strongly suspect my colleagues in political adventures will testify."

In his *Reminiscences of Public Men,* Governor B. F. Perry gives a sketch of Judge Withers, the more worthy and life-like coming from the hand of a contemporary and personal associate. We therefore insert here a number of paragraphs from Gov. Perry's article:

"Judge Withers was a man of distinguished talent and ability. His intellect was as keen and bright as a Damascus blade, and he wielded it on all occasions, in public and in private, most effectually. Every word that fell from his lips in conversation, on the Bench, or in public speaking, had a telling effect. No one was ever left in doubt as to his meaning when he discussed any question. He had moral courage in a high degree, and cared not whom he pleased or offended. He was very sarcastic and bitter in his denunciations of men and measures. No one ever possessed less of the demagogue than Judge Withers. No one ever more conscientiously did what he thought was right, regardless of consequences. He was in bad health all his life, and somewhat misanthropic. He never courted popularity, and scorned the base means which others resorted to for this purpose. The high public offices which he filled were conferred on him for his talents, ability and honesty, and not on account of any personal popularity which he possessed. There was a spice of malice in his composition which delighted in wreaking itself on unworthy men and measures. He was as open as the day, and if he disliked anyone, he showed it in a manner not to be mistaken. Frankness was his character."

"The Judge told me of a piece of malice and passion on his part, which I did not think altogether right. He was going from Camden to Sumter Court in an old sulky. It was late in the evening and raining very hard, the weather, too, was quite chilly, and he thought he would stop for the night at the next house. He drove up, and the gentleman, who was pacing back and forth in a long piazza, took no notice of him till he asked if he could get to stay all night with him. The gentleman replied promptly that he did not keep a public house, and continued his promenade. This cold, inhospitable reception nettled the judge, and he said to the gentleman, "I did not mistake your residence, sir, for a hotel, but I thought your kindness and humanity would prompt you to give shelter in such weather as this, to a wet and suffering fellow-creature like myself. If there had been a public house anywhere on the road, I should not have called on you." By this time the gentleman ascertained who he was, and very politely asked him to alight, and said he would be happy to have the pleasure of his company for the night. "No", said the judge, "I will drive in the night through the rain to Sumter Court House, before I will take shelter with such a man as you are," and he drove off. "This fellow", said the judge, "was a wealthy man, and a shining light in the Presbyterian Church. He afterwards became a candidate for the Legislature, and I took great pleasure in telling about his inhospitable conduct, which damaged his election considerably, and he was defeated."

"Judge Withers married the sister-in-law of Governor Miller, a Miss Boykin, who owned a valuable plantation in Kershaw District, and a large number of slaves. His treatment of the slaves, and management of the plantation, was so kind, indulgent and humane that it displeased some of his neighbors, who said it was a bad example in the neighborhood, and demoralized the slaves on the other plantations. This determined the Judge, as he told

## THOS. J. WITHERS

himself, to sell out and invest the proceeds in bank stocks and bonds and mortgages. With all of his temper and irritability, Judge Withers was a very kind-hearted gentleman, and most indulgent and affectionate in all the relations of life. His house servants did pretty much as they pleased, and he did not pretend to watch over them. On one occasion he told me that his carriage-driver, in whom he had placed great confidence, was caught in a theft, and he thought it was a good opportunity of having a general confession of all his roguery and rascality. He asked the fellow if he had not been stealing his corn and fodder and selling it. The boy declared that so far from having done so, he did, on one or two occasions, when the judge was short of fodder, steal a few bundles of one of the neighbors to feed his horses with!"

"Judge Withers was a man of great wit and humor, and most scathing sarcasm. He told me an amusing incident between him and the pastor of his church. The reverend gentleman applied to him to receive into his house a young teacher, for twelve months or so, whom he represented as amiable, accomplished and pious, really a most lovely and charming person. The judge said to me, the idea of making a stranger a member of his family was what he could not think of for a moment. He hesitated what to say, and at last, the idea suggested itself of turning the application into a joke. He replied very seriously: 'Ah! I see what you are after, you want to make mischief between me and my wife'. The clergyman was so much shocked at this interpretation that he simply bowed and passed on to seek quarters for his protege elsewhere.

"Judge Withers was a gentleman of ordinary height, delicately slender, with Grecian face and features in character with his mind, sharp and keen. He was a great talker and talked well."

The following letter from Judge Withers to General Chesnut will afford an intimate personal glimpse of its author:

"August 4, 1856.

"My dear Sir: Your reply to me was duly received, and I expected to provoke a futher reciprocation epistolary by prompt writing; but, like many greater men, I have had the misfortune to suffer an attack a tergo. I am yet disabled. I have not been out of the prison of my four-acre limits for more than two weeks. I could have enlarged my motions, but have not felt the inclination. One who knows how little I depend upon the exchange of language for my means of making life tolerable will not be surprised to hear that this solitude, or rather, this exclusion from the outer world, has worked no punishment—that I am content to hear my dead companions through their books, or indulge my reveries in view of my black-jacks (more euphoniously called *quercus ferruginus*).

"Meantime I have finished the oration of Cicero for Milo (who was charged with murder), having piloted Tom through it, and have read two of his four speeches against Cataline. Life, immortality, soul, eternal punishment of the wicked, the admission of the good into Heaven (which the Greeks call the Milky Way, says Cicero), the origin of the world, and the soul from the divine power of Almighty God (Jupiter) and His providence, are ideas distinctly set forth by Cicero, as proved in the last sentence of his first oration against Cataline, a passage of a letter to Appius ("as for me, I must think of the life to come, and no more of this short and fleeting existence,") and that celebrated passage in *De Republica*, the last dream of Scipio, the younger, When we discover these doctrines in Cicero, and find Plato furnished the Logos *eo nomine*, and suggested two other forms of manifestation employed by his Deity, can an honest mind refuse these 'heathens' a just praise for helping us to the theory of our religion?"

In line with a common custom of that day the Judge used snuff and a red bandana handkerchief. We can recall the trumpet of his sneeze heard half a mile away.

The Civil War of course destroyed the greater part of Judge Withers' estate. After a brief illness he passed away on November 7, 1865, before age had in the least impaired the vigor of his faculties.

# CHAPTER XV.

## WAR TIMES IN CAMDEN.

On Tuesday afternoon, April 9, 1861, the "Camden Volunteers", Captain J. D. Kennedy, boarded a special train in time for the opening guns at Fort Sumter. The passing of this first contingent for the front was marked by great enthusiasm. A throng of citizens preceded by the boy cadets of Professor Peck's Academy, escorted them to the train, cheering madly as it pulled out.

On April 11, the "Lancaster Greys", Captain J. D. Wylie, started from Lancaster for Charleston, and reached Camden that afternoon, marching the distance of forty miles in one day. They too were met by the boy cadets and a concourse of citizens wearing palmetto cockades, and escorted down town, which was decked in bunting and flying the Confederate flag from the market steeple. So impressed were the Greys by their reception in Camden that a member of the Company, writing in appreciation, styled it "The Cockade Town", and another immortalized the occasion in the following stanza:

> "When death's dark stream we ferry o'er,
> A time that surely shall come,
> In Heaven itself we ask no more
> Than just a Camden welcome."

On April 24, the "DeKalb Rifle Guards", Captain T. L. Boykin, set out for Virginia, under its company flag, of Mexican fame; and on the 28th, the "Flat Rock Guards", Captain C. C. Haile, passed through on the same mission, attended by the same ovations.

These advance companies were closely followed by others, until within a year some eight hundred out of one thousand voters had volunteered. A little later these were increased by two or three hundred more, until more than eighty per cent. of the entire white male population above the age of eighteen had enlisted. As well expressed in the *Camden Journal* of 1861, "the question was not who shall go, but who shall stay at home." Those under and over age and all physically unfit, were organized as home guards, into "Beats", to control the slaves. Even this slender force at the last came under fire from the invading enemy and gave them parting shots. Of course there were some shirkers, who had to be conscripted and hunted down, and one is known to have been shot, just north of Camden.

Only by excluding the slave from military service, and keeping him at the plow, could such a large quota of white soldiery have been furnished or supported. Yet many if not most of those at the front, not a whit less earnest, were not slave-holders. Thus many a family was left without a head or means of existence. But they were not forgotten, and early steps were taken for their relief. On May 4, 1861, a meeting was organized at Camden, Major J. M. DeSaussure, chairman, to provide for these families. Committees in various parts of the District were charged with this work, which was never neglected. The same year further provision was made by law and a money tax levied and Boards of Relief established to collect and distribute it to the wives and children of soldiers. As the currency fast depreciated and the needy became more numerous, this tax was replaced by one of three per cent in kind on the gross products of farms and mills. Added to this was an eight per cent tax on products, payable in kind, and other severe levies by the Richmond Government.

In the desperate struggle for national existence, no sacrifice was too great—the only concern being to find the means. Ports were closed, commerce stifled and factories few. Southern agriculture was mainly confined to cotton. Provisions and live stock had been largely imported. To escape famine the fields must be turned to food crops. By law the planting of cotton was restricted to three acres and finally one acre to the hand. This new method must be tried with few to manage the ignorant labor.

Dearth of necessities grew apace. Wooden soled shoes were devised for the slaves. Magazines of salt had to be established. The soil under old houses was scraped for manufacture of salt-petre, essential to gunpowder. The bells of the Camden churches were taken down for casting cannon.

In spite of all efforts the armies were in dire straits. The Ladies Aid Society, formed at Camden in January 1862, with branches over the district, did Trojan work to alleviate distress, and made and gathered articles of

## War Times in Camden

all sorts for camp and hospital. This society also provided a solders' Rest. Camden, then a railroad terminus, came to be an asylum for many a worn and weary sojourner. The sick and wounded arrived in growing numbers, requiring a hospital, which was established in a large wooden building, an old hotel, then standing immediately north of the old Court House, northwest corner Broad and King Streets, now a cultivated plot. A newspaper item of 1864, states that in December of that year, two hundred were received into this hospital. It is a curious fact that among the attending surgeons there was Dr. Todd, a brother-in-law of President Lincoln. Dr. Todd married Miss Lyles of Camden, and lies buried in our cemetery.

But no adequate impression of those years could be conveyed save by one who endured them. Such we have in the reminiscences prepared in 1911 by Mrs. F. Bruce Davis. We need only to quote, as follows, from her incomparable article:

"I was a schoolgirl of sixteen when the war began and I well recall the excitement when Lincoln's election was announced and the jubilant feeling when the bells rang out the secession of South Carolina. It seemed only a gala-day, and we joyed in the valor of our little State. Without understanding it at all, we had unconsciously imbibed state sovereignty from our very cradles.

"Without one misgiving or premonition of coming evil we entered on the four years of war. Jauntily we donned the blue cockade of the "minute men" and made them for our boy friends, and fashioned dainty palmetto badges for our hair and hats. I have one of these still. We could not understand why our Northern teachers, bright young college graduates, grew pale and trembled when, from time to time, the bells rang out that another and another state had gone out of the Union. It was a trying year for those same young teachers, but they braved it out until July when, just before the first great battle in Virginia, they were safely passed across the line. I remember with what difficulty our Principal, Mrs. McCandless, gathered the gold to pay their salaries. All was bright and hopeful that first year and we saw fathers, brothers and friends don the grey and march away thinking they would soon be back and all be well.

"First came the bloodless victory of Fort Sumter and we distinctly heard the guns that April morning. 'The pride, pomp and circumstance of glorious war' were soon to give place to its horrors, and in July of that year we realized this when the wires flashed the news of the battles of Bull Run and Manassas. Though they were victories for us yet many gallant soldiers laid down their lives on those bloody fields. Throughout our Southland a bitter cry went up—lamentation, weeping and mourning for the sons that were not. That cry was not to be stilled for four long years and oh! the sadness, the pity of it! In those four years there were but few homes in our community to which there came not the fearful tidings of a loved one killed, wounded, captured or missing. The women lived on the mails and gathered round the bulletin boards to read the last news from the front. Anxious hearts sought relief in working for the soldiers. Aid Societies were formed and wayside hospitals established where the passing soldiers, wounded, sick or on furlough, were tenderly cared for. The ladies took turns day by day to minister to them and carry to them food and delicacies. Young and old learned to knit socks, and it was unusual to see any one without knitting in their hands. Some became so expert that they could knit a pair of socks in a day. I remember we even undertook to uniform a whole company. The suits were cut out by a tailor and distributed to the ladies—and how we labored over those sent us! We knew nothing of tailoring, for we had neither father nor brother, but fortunately we secured the help of old Mrs. Ford, an experienced tailoress and, working with her, we accomplished the unaccustomed task.

"Of course, as the years went on there were privations and lack of luxuries, but this made little impression on the young and strong. Only for the old and feeble we missed these things.

"There was much sociability among the young people, reading clubs, riding clubs (until the horses were impressed), walking parties, house parties and picnics, and, when a young soldier came home wounded or on furlough, how we feted and enjoyed him. Darker and darker grew our future but we *could* not believe that we could fail. We clung with abiding faith to the righteousness of our cause. Many of the incidents of those years are dim closed pages of memory, and I do not often try to unseal them for it is not good for the soul, but some events stand out vividly and need no effort to recall. Among these is our first contact with the enemy, when a corps of Sherman's army swept through Camden on his march of destruction. On the morning of the 17th of February, 1865, we heard terrific explosions and knew that Sherman had reached Columbia. That night the Western sky was lurid with the glare of the burning city and we felt that in twenty-four hours Columbia's fate might be ours. We sent off most of our silver, buried our jewelry and watches, also a canister of tea and sugar (all we had), and to our lasting regret we burned our letters and journals. In fearful suspense we waited. The next day wagons and carts brought refugees from Columbia. There were days when nothing seemed steadfast but our most holy faith. We seemed to 'draw nearer day by day, each to the other, all to God'. Every afternoon there was a united service of prayer at one of the churches and with one heart and one mind we committed our cause, our soldiers, our homes, our all to our Heavenly Father's care. Each morning a scout would come in and tell us the enemy had passed us by, and each evening another would come to say they were on the way and would be here by morning, and we would watch and wake through all the night hours of that cold rainy week."

This graphic depiction is here suspended for insertion of a statement found in the Camden *Journal and Confederate* of March 10, 1865, which we abridge as follows:

We deem it unnecessary to apologize for three weeks suspension of our regular issue, the natural consequence of the invasion and occupation of our town by the enemy,—especially as we, like others, removed the most valuable portion of our material to the swamps and sand-hills, only to have it pillaged and burnt by the enemy. We have merged the two papers, until we can procure additional type, having lost the larger part of both offices by the incendiary torch applied by our late unwelcome guests.

The storm has at length burst upon us; the anticipated blow has fallen, and Camden has been made to undergo, in her turn, all the horrors of invasion.

Most of our citizens having sought refuge in the neighboring swamps, from which they are only now venturing to return, and bodies of the Yankees being still reported hovering near the town, render it somewhat unsafe to stir abroad.

The enemy made their first appearance in our midst on Thursday evening February 23rd, having crossed the Wateree River at Peay's and Jones' ferries, about twenty miles above Camden. They were in small number—some thirty—and formed near Major John Whitaker's residence about one mile north of the town. There our company of militia composed of old men and boys, under Colonel Burwell Jones, confronted them. After a few shots were exchanged the enemy withdrew, wounding and capturing Captain R. C. Drakeford of the militia. The enemy returned the next day, Friday, and entered the town from the north, about 2 P. M. The force consisted of two detachments of cavalry and one of infantry—some two hundred and fifty men. The main body proceeded down (Broad) Street into the heart of the town. The remainder stopped to plunder and more or less thoroughly pillaged every house on the way.

The advance body, on reaching Jungbluth's Hotel (northeast corner of Broad and DeKalb Streets, site of present post office), there established headquarters, and began the work of destroying Government stores and public buildings. They first fired the freight and passenger depots; then the Cornwallis house, also the Commissary store house on the southeast corner of Broad and DeKalb Streets. From this latter building the fire spread south and consumed all the structures on that square fronting Broad Street, down to Rutledge. They also burnt Mr. Geo. Douglas' store, cotton sheds in rear of Gerald's and Bell's stores, and the Bridge over the Wateree River, the Masonic Hall and adjacent buildings. They broke and pillaged all stores, took what goods they wanted and threw the rest into the streets, whence it was carried off by the negroes, who were encouraged to appropriate whatever they needed or fancied.

After the cotton and stores had been burned the majority of the Yankees dispersed over the town in small squads to rob on private account. Nearly every house in Camden and Kirkwood was visited, besides those in the vicinity of Bishop Davis' residence before which a guard was placed. In some instances, rare ones, they are reported to have behaved with courtesy. In others, and those by far the larger number, they seem to have run through the gamut, from impertinence to outrage, from pilfering to wholesale spoliation. Many families have been stripped of everything they had in the world. In one neighborhood, where they unearthed buried liquor, they were specially riotous and fired houses with wanton cruelty.

The detachment first entering Camden was followed by others, and large forces were camped in the suburbs. In fact the whole of Sherman's army was within twenty miles of us. They left the town Saturday night, but stragglers are still to be seen.

Further contemporary testimonial exists in the form of a letter by Captain J. H. Devereux, to Miss Kate Meroney, dated Florence, S. C., June 3rd, 1906. The original is before us, and it was sent in answer to a letter from Miss Meroney (written at our suggestion) inquiring of Captain Devereux whether he had caused the burning of the Cornwallis House.[1]  This inquiry affords the Captain an opportunity to write a vivid memorial of that day in Camden, where he was in authority as a commissary officer.  We here condense his statement, preserving his verbiage:

"Well you want me to say I was a House-burner.  My orders were, as shown in the Records of the Rebellion, over the signature of no less a person than General Lee, that all stores should be destroyed, if necessary to keep them from falling into the hands of the enemy.  I had witnessed the burning of Columbia, and determined if possible to save Camden by giving them no excuse for firing the Depot of supplies on Main Street, near the Hotel, and moved all the stores to the Cornwallis House, isolated from the town.  I had sent away to Hardee's army all stores that could be loaded on the wagons available.  On the morning of February 24th the impression prevailed that Sherman would follow Beauregard and Hampton up the line of railroad towards Charlotte, and that thus Camden would escape.  But Sherman, as he told me after my capture, decided to swing across country to cut off Hardee from Cheraw, and thus took in Camden with his right wing.  Early in the morning of the 24th I had scouted five miles up the Lancaster Road and found no Federal troops.  I was certain that Sherman would give us the go by, and returned to town.  I had been in the Hotel but a few minutes when I stepped out to see Mrs. Sutherland who was in great distress at my sending her husband off in charge of the wagons.  While trying to quiet her, I heard shots on the street.  Stepping to the side walk I saw a body of United States Cavalry, the 29th Missouri, firing down the street at some of our people, who were returning the fire, among them I think Mr. Shannon and Mr. Hanckle.  I learned that Captain Colclough's company had fought them from Hobkirk Hill into town.  I gave the order to cease firing, and our men obeyed and threw up their pieces.  One near me asked what was my reason.  I told him they might kill the women and children who were running about the street screaming and crying.  In the melee I mounted and rode off, on DeKalb Street, taking a volley without receiving a scratch.  I held up to call to my wife, who was at a window with the baby in her arms, to lie down on the floor out of range of the guns.  My next

[1] The mooted question as to whether the Federals or Confederates burned the Cornwallis House, an old Revolutionary building, is treated in the first volume of *Historic Camden*, pages 279, 280.  The conclusion we then reached, that the Confederates burned it, has been shattered by later evidence, the substance of which we here introduce.

thought was to destroy the stores, and ordered *either John S. Meroney, or some one else set fire to the Cornwallis House*—and so you have the story. General Sherman told me next day, after my capture near Hughes's (Adams's) Mill, that he had a great mind to have shot me for destroying 600 hogsheads of sugar and three million rations. I suggested that would not get back the stores and begged him to postpone it, which he did, else I would not be able to prove that your father set fire to his own house to keep the Yankees from getting the stores."

But has the Captain proven it? Were his alleged orders carried out? Indeed they were not. What are we to believe in the face of the statement made to us on Friday, May 3rd, 1901, by Mr. Meroney himself, that the Federals burned the Cornwallis House, which was then in his possession, temporarily used for army stores. To the same effect is the statement, made to us in 1906, by Mr. K. S. Villepigue, which we reduced to writing at the time:

Said Mr. Villepigue:

"When the Federals entered Camden, about 3 o'clock in the afternoon, I was near the corner of Main and Rutledge Streets. Was then eleven years old. They came in sight on the hill up Broad Street just above the present Court House. Dr. Thos. Salmond, at corner of DeKalb and Broad, was firing at them with a pistol. He, Captain Colclough and a Colonel Boyd took to their horses, and were pursued through town by the Federals who were firing at them. To get away from this shooting, I went to my home, corner of King and Market Streets. Soon after I reached home, Captain Devereux came down Market Street at full speed horseback, two mounted Federals after him and firing at him. The two Federals gave over the chase, stopped at our house and threatened to burn it, but were dissuaded by my grandmother. They then went on to the Cornwallis House which was in full view from our home, standing alone in the midst of an open field. A young negro woman, Rose Withers, pointed it out to them, and they took her there with them, she sitting horseback behind one of them! I saw the fire break out, and saw it burn immediately after these two Federals went there. It was about 4 P. M. My grandmother said to the Federals: 'You will regret burning the old Cornwallis headquarters'. They said they did so because government property was in it. The fire lasted a long time—so much meat and tallow stored—For weeks after

## WAR TIMES IN CAMDEN

Sherman left, people would get meat out of the ruins, and eat it. Seven Federal prisoners, one an officer, had been taken that morning to the Cornwallis House, which was guarded by Campbell, Alex Matheson, Conway Bell, and Robert Man."

This evidence leaves no escape from the conviction that Captain DeVereux's *supposition* that the Cornwallis House was burned in accordance with his orders to *some one* is entirely unsupported. He really knew nothing as to its burning.

We cannot refrain from inserting here the following extract from a paper entitled, *Slavery as I Knew It*, by Miss A. E. Davis, a daughter of Bishop Davis and a sister-in-law of Mrs. Esther S. Davis, read before the "Camden Historical Society" in 1905 and later published in the second volume of *South Carolina Women in the Confederacy*. It is unrivalled in its vivid portrayal of the invasion of Camden:

"The next day—Oh, day of terrors!—they were in our midst. Its horrors are never to be forgotten; but I am not to tell of that, but of the servants in this hour of supreme temptation. The long line of soldiers marched down the street, were disbanded at the corner, and in an incredibly short time swarmed everywhere. They were in every yard, in every house—but ours. What restrained them we have never known, nor why we were so spared. Of course they were in the yard, asking the servants to cook for them, tempting, threatening, cursing, swearing, shouting, singing, but never crossing our threshold; and as the morning passed I went out on the upper piazza for a moment to find out what was going on below us in the street and well remember the comfort of seeing the cheery faces and hearing the undaunted voice of our opposite neighbor: 'What are they doing to you over there? They are running about my house like ants in an ant-hill', and immediately several closely cropped heads and blue shoulders were thrust out of her window and a jeering laugh greeted her sally.

"Columbia, Camden, Cheraw—all the central part of the State had become a sort of store house for the valuables of the low-country, and vacant rooms, out-houses and attics were filled with goods or cotton; these were at once objects of cupidity or vengeance. Doors and windows were broken open, boxes were smashed, goods thrown into the street; all portable articles, such as silver and gold, hastily selected by the soldiers; pockets and knapsacks rapidly and unblushingly filled, in the presence of the owners; and what they could not carry away was given to the negroes, who were told it was their wages for long wageless years. The crowds increased continually on the streets and spread the tale of Yankee generosity and unlimited looting. They will give you just what you please. They tell you to help yourself, etc., etc.

"It was now getting towards the afternoon, and the younger servants, wearied with carrying their babies—three in number yet afraid to put them out of their arms, brought them into my mother's room and begged to lay them on pillows under her high old-fashioned bedstead, fully persuaded that now they would be secure where 'Miss' was—then flew down the main street to see. Again and again they went and returned to the house laden with their spoils. 'The soldiers gave them to us. May'nt we put them in the parlor for fear they will take them back again?' Evidently this was no time for a moral lesson and permission was given. The room became a museum of the most useless things to them: Portraits, engravings, mirrors, a miniature, china, glass, books—everything that took their fancy; and we were invited to take what we pleased!

"And so at last night came, with its terrible yells, its uncertainty, its burning houses, its darkness, unless the lurid glare of the fires could be called light. It was with great difficulty that they could burn the houses, for we had had a week of incessant rain, and that alone we believed saved us from the fate of Columbia. As it was, the glare was so intense that with every shutter closed, reading was easy in the tiniest pocket testament; and we knew not what was happening to our friends, or what would happen to us the next moment."

A memorial of Sherman's occupation of Camden is afforded by a document written by one of the invaders narrating their methods of procedure. It consists of a letter found at the time (February 1865) by an old colored woman on Hobkirk Hill and delivered by her to Miss Floride Cantey (afterwards wife of Rev. John Johnson) and is here reproduced from the Camden *Journal and Confederate* of April 7, 1865.

## War Times in Camden

South Carolina—Camp near Camden,
Feby. 26th, 1865.

My dear wife: I have no time for particulars. We have had a glorious time in this state. Unrestricted license to burn and plunder was the order of the day. The chivalry have been stript of most of their valuables. Gold watches, silver pitchers, cups, spoons, forks, etc., etc., are as common in camp as blackberries. The terms of plunder are as follows. The valuables procured are estimated by companies. Each Co. is required to exhibit the result of its operations at any given place. One fifth and first choice falls to the chare of the Commander-in-chief and staff; one fifth to the corps Commander and staff; one fifth to Field Officers of regiment and two fifths to the company. Officers are not allowed to join in these expeditions without disguising themselves as privates. One of our corps commanders borrowed a suit of rough clothes from one of my men and was very successfull at this place. He got a large quantity of silver (among other things an old time silver milk pitcher) and a very fine gold watch from a Mr. DeSaussure at this place. DeSaussure is one of the F. F. V.'s of S. C., and was made to fork out liberally. Officers over the rank of Captain are not made to put their plunder in the estimate for general distribution. This is very unfair, and in order to protect themselves, subordinate officers and privates keep back everything that they can carry about their persons, such as rings, earrings, breast pins, etc., etc., of which, if I live to get home, I have about a quart. I am not joking, I have at least a quart of jewelry for you and the girls, and some No. 1 diamond rings and pins among them. Gen. Sherman has silver and gold enough to start a Bank. His share in the gold watches and chains alone, at Columbia, was two hundred and seventy five (275).

But I said I could not go into particulars. All the general officers, and many besides, have valuables of every description. We took gold and silver enough from the d——d rebels to have redeemed their currency twice over. This (the currency) whenever we came across it we burned, as we consider it utterly worthless.

I wish all the jewelry this army has could be carried to the "Old Bay State". It would deck her out in glorious style; but alas it will be scattered all over the North and middle States. The damned niggers, as a general rule, preferred to stay at home—particularly after they found out that we only wanted the able bodied men (and to tell you the truth, the youngest and best looking women). Sometimes we took off whole families and plantations of niggers, by way of repaying some influential secessionist. But the useless part of these we manage to lose. Sometimes in crossing rivers, sometimes in other ways.

I shall write to you again from Wilmington, Goldsboro, or some other place in North Carolina. The order to march has arrived and I must close hurriedly.

Love to grandmother and aunt Charlotte. Take care of yourself and children. Dont show this letter out of the family.

Your affectionate husband,

THOS. J. MYERS, Lieut.

P. S. I will send this by the first flag of truce to be mailed; unless I have an opportunity of sending it to Hilton Head. Tell Sally I am saving a pearl bracelet and ear-rings for her. Bob Lambert got the necklace and breast pin of the same set. I am trying to trade him out of them. These were taken from the Miss Jamisons, daughters of the President of the S. C. Secession Convention. We found these ladies on the trip through Georgia.

The ruffianism of the Federals in Camden, was not without shining exception. The conduct of Lieutenant John A. McQueen of the 15th Illinois Infantry will ever be appreciated in this community. He it was who protected the homes of Bishop Davis, Mrs. Reynolds, Mr. R. M. Kennedy and others. It so happened that these very same beneficiaries of his kindness were able to repay him very handsomely soon after; and one of them, Mrs. E. S. Davis, has preserved his romantic story in the memoir from which we here resume quotation:

"On Friday morning, February 24th, we were really not expecting them, when suddenly we heard rapid firing on Laurens Street and we saw a company of cavalry dashing by. There seemed to be no order but they rode as for life into every yard, up to every door. Throwing the reins on their horses' necks a party of them dismounted at our back door, rushed into the house,—from room to room—upstairs and downstairs and into the basement. In wild haste they broke open doors and drawers and desks, calling for silver, for watches, for wine and arms. They seemed wild with the lust for booty, and so afraid that others would get ahead of them that they sometimes overlooked valuable articles. We gathered in our breakfast room our mother and we four girls—and I think my mother aged in those few hours and her hair grew greyer. One rough soldier as he dashed by her, said, 'Old woman, don't look so frightened we are not going to kill you'. I looked and the agony on her face is stamped upon my memory. That party of soldiers had soon ransacked our house, taking all the silver and jewelry they could find, towels, knives, etc. Then in hot haste they ran off for the next house. Party after party came and went disappointed that they were not the first. A wagon was brought to the door of the smoke house and the year's supply of meat carried off. Of it all I remember one joint alone was left. Everything eatable, that they could lay their hands upon, was taken. It was said they timed their entrance into town just as dinners were being prepared. Our faithful cook tried in vain to smuggle something into the house for us, but it did not matter, we were too frightened to want anything. Slowly the day crept on and we dreaded the night. In my mother's room upstairs we gathered with doors left open, we dared not lock them and knew we were surrounded by thousands of hostile lawless soldiers, and as utterly cut off from friends as though miles away. Each household met the ordeal alone. For almost twenty-five hours there was no communication with even the nearest neighbor.

"Our cook, Mary, did not desert us but sat with us around the fire through all the long night. We saw the flames of burning houses, stores, mills and cotton in every direction, and heard the shouts and yells of drunken soldiers and negroes on Broad Street where high carnival was held. The stores were broken open, the contents taken, given to the negroes or thrown into the streets.

"From time to time we threw ourselves on the bed for a little sleep and I remember when all was quiet Ella and I heard our good Mary come to our bedside, fall upon her knees and pray so earnestly for 'Missis and her children'. It was comforting to feel that the fervent prayer of that righteous one was going up to God for us. Slowly the dawn came, and again party after party of soldiers came searching for valuables. About ten o'clock a knock—the very first—was heard, at the front door. My mother opened the door and an officer stood there. He was Lieutenant McQueen of Howard's Command, and said he brought messages from Dr. Wm. Reynolds, our uncle in Columbia, and had promised to protect us.

Through the efforts of Lieutenant McQueen, the house, which my uncle's family occupied in Columbia, had been saved from the general conflagration, and for weeks and months forty homeless ones found shelter there.

"Lieutenant McQueen said he was sorry his regiment had not reached Camden the day before that he might have given us a guard. From that time we were unmolested. He or his ranking officer, Captain King, came and went throughout the day, and when Lieutenant McQueen was obliged to go elsewhere he left his belt and pistols on the hall table and said, if we were disturbed, to show them and say they were his and he was in charge. A troop of fifteen soon after dashed up the avenue and, dismounting, came into the piazza and hall demanding 'wine and watches'—Mother showed the belt and pistols and gave the Lieutenant's message—Forthwith the leader turned and said: 'Come boys, we can do nothing here'. Lieutenant McQueen, at my uncle's request, had gone to Mrs. Capers' on DeKalb Street to inquire for his (Dr. Reynolds') sister-in-law, Mrs. Capers, Jr., who with her children had fled from Columbia as the army entered that city—making the journey in an open wagon that cold rainy day. She reached her mother-in-law (in Camden) very ill and lived only a few days. Arrangements had been made for her burial but were interrupted by the coming of the enemy, and they were preparing to bury her in the garden when Lieutenant McQueen offered his horse for the hearse. He and Mr. Thomas Davis, rector of Grace Church, carried her to the cemetery and laid the weary Christian to her rest.

"From house to house Lieutenant McQueen went carrying comfort and aid. Late in the day (Saturday 25th) he and Captain King came to say they were ordered out, and that by night not a soldier would be left. They were young men and could not refrain from twitting us about 'our boys'. Lieutenant McQueen said, 'Your boys are always going to meet us at the river, now they say they will meet us at Lynches Creek'. Ella replied, 'I hope they will', and they went off laughing.

"The next day there was a skirmish at Lynches Creek and the brave Lieutenant was wounded and captured and it would have fared ill with him but for letters my uncle, Dr. Porter and my mother had given him. We sent him what we could of luxuries for the sick, and when later

## War Times in Camden

he was brought to the hospital in Camden he was well cared for. My uncle and Dr. Porter came over from Columbia and arranged to carry him to Chester where he was exchanged. He recovered and returned to his home in Elgin, Illinois. We have heard from him from time to time and a few winters ago he was at Southern Pines, N. C. and expected to visit Camden but was prevented."

Some further detail as to Lieutenant McQueen and the military operations in Kershaw County may be added, on the best of authority. We here condense an article by Colonel Zimmerman Davis, reproduced in part from the *Kershaw Gazette* of April 24, 1884. He says:

"Among many brilliant exploits of General M. C. Butler was a morning attack upon one of Sherman's wagon trains on the west side of Little Lynches Creek in Kershaw County, February 22nd and 23rd.[1] The night before was dark and rainy, when he marched his command boldly between two corps of Sherman's army, in sight of their camp fires. His men were in the saddle before dawn, drawn up in fours ready for attack. When a part of the enemy's wagons had been hitched up, and driven into the road, the bugles sounded the charge, waking the forest echoes, and away we dashed, shouting, firing and hewing with sabre. In a few moments we had two hundred prisoners, and nineteen splendid army wagons laden to the top with corn and bacon, each drawn by six fine mules clad in such harness as Confederate teamsters had not seen for many a day. These were driven over into the angle between Little and Big Lynches Creeks, where they were safe from rescue. While we were in the road, drawn up in fours to resist an expected counter charge and prevent recapture of the wagons, I observed a horse running through the woods without a rider. Private McElroy caught him and brought him in to me. The new English bridle and martingale with which he was equipped I transferred to my horse, also a new saddle pouch. One side of the pouch was empty, the other contained only a book, which on examination proved to be the 'Diary of Lieutenant John A. McQueen', covering the march from Chattanooga to within a few days before it thus came into my possession. This diary showed its writer to be what you found him—a Christian gentleman—At this distance of time I recall

---

[1] Evidently Colonel Davis writes from memory and places these dates three or four days too early. Butler's attack was certainly after February 24, on which date Sherman's men entered Camden, and Lieutenant McQueen was in the town on February 25.

very little of its contents, though it was frequently discussed by General Butler, Colonel Aiken and myself for the next day or two on the march. I believe I quote his very words recorded of Columbia: 'It was heartrending to see the destruction of property, and the insults visited upon the defenseless women and children by our Union soldiers. I did all I could to prevent it but was powerless'. And this tone seemed to prevail throughout the entire book. I kept it until the morning of the 25th, when my impression is it was left upon the table at some farm house on the road to Cheraw where I procured a hasty breakfast. How little did I suppose that only the night before I had strangely interferred with the future plans of the writer!"

Few words can be spared to recount the last flickers of the war in and around Camden. After Sherman's departure, a small band of home guards, boys and old men, mixed with a few furloughed veterans, some of whom came from the hospital, were gathered in the vicinity of Camden in an effort to embarrass a greatly superior Federal force again threatening the town. Among the officers who directed these defenders we note the names of General Wm. Elliott, still suffering from recent wounds, Colonel W. M. Shannon, Captain Kennedy, Captain Conner and Captain Colclough. The Federals under General Potter entered Camden from the south about twenty-five hundred strong, Tuesday evening, April 18, 1865. They broke into the banks and safes and did desultory damage, but were restrained from general pillage of residences. They departed hurriedly the next morning owing to the menace in their rear from the above mentioned home guards, who had been joined by some five hundred Kentucky cavalry of Generals Lewis and Hannon, and who had occupied the roads and crossings over Swift Creek along their line of communications. This little force contested the ground at Boykin's Mill, nine miles south of Camden; but, after considerable firing, being outnumbered and outflanked, fell back to Dinkin's Mill, and on to Stateburg, where they dispersed. It was high time for them to get back to their homes, for Lee had surrendered and the war was virtually over. There were some fatalities among the Federals and resulting graves on the ground of their skirmishes. For lack of space we must adopt the closing words of a communication to the *Journal and Confederate* of April 24, 1865, written by one who participated in these final scenes: "As always the case in campaigning, there are many incidents we would like to record and preserve, but we have neither space nor time; 'while the funny incidents we hope to laugh over on some happier day. In this dark hour of our country we cannot pen them'."

# CHAPTER XVI.

## PANTHEON.

Camden contributed six generals to the Confederate armies: Cantey, Chesnut, Deas, Kennedy, Kershaw and Villepigue, the three first named grandsons of John Cantey, one of the early settlers of Camden. On May 10, 1911 a monument in the center of "Rectory Square" (now Kershaw Square) was dedicated to their memory. It consists of six columns supporting a pergola now mantled with trumpet vines and ivy, a column with bronze tablet commemorating each of the six.

JAMES CANTEY, son of John Cantey and Emma Richardson, was born at Camden, December 30, 1818. He graduated at the South Carolina College in 1838 and practiced law in Camden until his departure for the Mexican War as Adjutant of the Palmetto Regiment. In 1847 he settled in Alabama. He entered the Confederate service as Colonel of the 15th Alabama Infantry. He served in Stonewall Jackson's famous campaign of the Shenandoah Valley, and received the praise of that exacting commander. In 1863 he was commissioned General of a brigade which he piloted from Dalton, Ga. to the end in North Carolina, passing in the retreat through or near his old haunts in Camden. After the war he led the life of a planter at his home on the Alabama side of the Chattahoochee River opposite Columbus, Ga. Here he died in 1873.

JAMES CHESNUT, son of Colonel James Chesnut, of Mulberry and Mary Cox of Philadelphia, was born in Camden, January 18, 1815, at the family residence, which in those days was in the extreme south of Camden on the northeast corner of Meeting and Broad Streets, now an open field. His father was known as James Chesnut, of Mulberry, so called from the name of his residence built in 1820, about three miles south of Camden. In 1837 he graduated from Princeton University and practiced law in Camden. In 1840 he was elected to the Legislature where he acquired a reputation for eloquence and ability. In 1858 he was elected to the United States Senate from this State. Along with his colleague, Jas. H. Hammond, he resigned from the Senate, when his State adopted the Ordinance of Secession.

Above: JAMES CHESNUT
Left: JAMES CANTEY; Right: ZACK C. DEAS

Together with Thos. J. Withers and Jos. B. Kershaw, he was a delegate from Kershaw County to the Secession Convention which met in December 1860.

It was inevitable that Chesnut and Sumner should collide in the perpetual debate on the question of slavery. On April 9, 1860, Chesnut addressed the Senate on that subject in a tone of moderation when compared with the ferocity usually displayed in such discussions. John Brown's raid had occurred only a few months before. On June 4, Sumner replied in a vitriolic speech, splendid in diction, as will appear from the following paragraphs:

"Mr. Paxton tells us 'the best blood in Virginia flows in the veins of slaves'; and fugitive slaves have been latterly advertised as possessing 'blue eyes', 'flaxen hair', and as 'escaping under the pretense of being a white man'.

"It was the often quoted remark of John Wesley that slavery was the 'sum of all villianies'. It is wrong not merely in the abstract, as often admitted by its apologists, but wrong in the concrete also. It is nothing less than a huge insurrection against the eternal God, being practically the grossest lie and the grossest Atheism.

"Say, Sir, in your madness, that you own the sun, the stars, the moon, but do not say that you own a man, endowed with a soul that shall live immortal, when sun, moon and stars shall have passed away."

"Slavery paints itself in closing the gates of knowledge, which are also the shining gates of civilization.

"Slavery paints itself again in the appropriation of all the toil of its victims. It is robbery and petty larceny under the garb of law.

"Bad as slavery is for the slave, it is worse for the master. The slavery on which men live, in all its fivefold foulness, must become a part of themselves, discoloring their very souls, blotting their characters, and breaking forth in mortal leprosy."

As spokesman for the Southern Senators who appraised Sumner as innately pusillanimous despite his eloquence, Chesnut made the following contemptuous retort.

"After ranging over Europe, crawling through back doors to whine at the feet of British aristocracy, craving pity, and reaping a rich harvest of contempt, the slanderer of states and men reappeared in the Senate. We had hoped to be relieved from the out-pourings of such vulgar malice. We had hoped that one who has felt, though ignominiously failed to meet, the consequence of a former insolence, would have become wiser, if not better, by experience.

"Mr. President, in the heroic ages of the world men were deified for the possession and exercise of some virtues—wisdom, truth, justice, magnanimity, courage. It has been left for this day, for this country, for the Abolitionists of Massachusetts, to deify the incarnation of malice, mendacity and cowardice.

"Sir, we do not intend to be guilty of aiding in the apotheosis of pusillanimity and meanness. We do not intend to contribute by any conduct on our part, to increase the devotees at the shrine of this new idol. We know what is expected and desired. We are not inclined again to send forth the recipient of punishment howling through the world, yelping fresh cries of slander and malice.

"These are the reasons which I feel it due to myself and others, to give to the Senate and the Country, why we have quietly listened to what has been said, and why we can take no other notice of the matter."

During the greater part of the war, General Chesnut served on the Staff of President Davis. At Fort Sumter and First Manassas he was aide-de-camp to General Beauregard. In 1864 he was appointed to Command of the Reserves in South Carolina, with rank of Brigadier General. After the war he took an active part in all efforts to retrieve the calamities which had befallen the State.

Prior to the war he built and occupied "Frogden" (see map of Camden); later, about 1853, he constructed the large residence on Kirkwood Hill, which he called "Kamtchatka". After the war he lived at "Mulberry" until about 1873, when he built "Sarsfield" where he resided until his death, which occurred February 1, 1885.

In his address on Memorial Day (May 10) 1878, under the old oak in our Quaker cemetery, he closed with these words: "When the hand of peace was stretched out to us across the bloody chasm, we took it; and having accepted the situation we will keep the faith. We will look to the future and, as far as honest and true men can, forget the past—except its sacred memories and its spotless glories, which we will strive to make immortal." His last moments, which we witnessed, were serene, and it is no figure of speech to say that he passed away as one who "lies down to pleasant dreams".

He lies in the family cemetery at Knights Hill. He left no descendants.

We shall here attempt merely to mention Mrs. Chesnut (Mary Boykin Miller) to whom the General was married April 23, 1840. She was a daughter of Governor Stephen D. Miller and Mary Boykin. As the wife of General Chesnut she moved in the social centers of the Confederacy and acquired the material for her fascinating "Diary from Dixie." She died November 22, 1886 and lies beside the General at Knights Hill. Mrs. Chesnut has left her own monument in the "Diary", which holds a notable place in Southern literature, and renders eulogy or comment from us wholly useless.

ZACK CANTEY DEAS, son of James S. Deas and Margaret (Chesnut) Deas, was born in Camden, S. C., October 25, 1819. In 1835 he moved to Mobile, Ala. with his father's family. There he engaged in mercantile business. He served in the Mexican War. At the beginning of the Civil War he was on the Staff of General Joseph E. Johnson. In the fall of 1861 he raised a regiment, the 22nd Alabama, and equipped it. With $28,000.00 in gold of his own he purchased for his men 800 Enfield Rifles, and led them at the battle of Shiloh where he was severely wounded, having two horses killed under him. In 1862 he was promoted to command of the Alabama Brigade, which at Chicamauga lost over fifty per cent of its members, and fought heroically at Missionary Ridge and at Franklin. After the war he lived in New York, where he died March 6, 1882, age 63.

JOHN BORDENAVE VILLEPIGUE, born in Camden, July 2, 1830, graduated from West Point in 1854. While he was engaged against the Indians in Utah under General A. S. Johnson, South Carolina seceded, and he rode horseback to Montgomery, Ala., and entered the Confederate service. He was assigned as Colonel of Regulars at Pensacola, Fla. where in holding Fort McRae under heavy bombardment, he suffered a wound, and received the praise of General Bragg who commended him as "an educated soldier possessing in an eminent degree the confidence of his officers and men. He had been specially selected for this service. The result fully vindicated the fortunate choice." Later he was put in charge of Fort Pillow on the Mississippi, which he vacated only on positive orders, remaining behind with 20 men to blow up the works. He then joined the forces of Van Dorn under whom he fought in the battle of Corinth, which was conducted contrary to his judgment. His exertions as rear-guard in protecting the retreat, while suffering from malarial fever, caused his prostration and death at Port Hudson, La., November 9, 1862. On November 17 his remains reached Camden, escorted by his staff, and with great ceremony, attended by a large concourse, were interred in our cemetery on the 18th. His family possess a sword presented to him as "the most gallant officer of Beauregard's command."

In an argument before a Federal Military Commission in June 1868, in defense of Isaac Owens, charged with murder of two negro prisoners, Colonel W. M. Shannon, quotes the following from a letter which he received from General Villepigue in 1861, disclosing in noble words the feelings with which he renounced his allegiance to the Union for service under the flag of the Southern Confederacy: "As the sunset gun fired, I stood under the stars and stripes and as the last rays of the sun gleamed upon its glorious folds, I turned away from it forever. Will you wonder that my chin sank upon my breast and that the tears coursed down my cheeks as I bade farewell to the flag I loved so well?"

Colonel Shannon comments in his argument: "Who will believe as his heroic form flashed at Shiloh, ever at the head of his brigade, he struck at that flag? You may deem him mistaken, you may deem him in error, but you cannot deem a pure immaculate spirit like his a traitor. The soldier leaves such epithets for the politician whose fight commences when the war is over."

JOSEPH BREVARD KERSHAW: The noted record of General Kershaw and his command in the Civil War, have been so fully treated in numerous military histories that we shall attempt only the merest outline here. In this we shall have the benefit of an address by General Kennedy to Camp Hampton of Confederate Veterans in 1895 which he devotes to a review of the career of General Kershaw, whom he succeeded step by step in

Above: JOSEPH B. KERSHAW
Left: JOHN D. KENNEDY; Right: JOHN B. VILLEPIGUE

promotion from Captain to Colonel to General of the famous "Kershaw's Brigade".

General Kershaw was born in Camden, January 5, 1822, and was educated entirely at home where he began practice of law in 1843. Says General Kennedy: "He was a born soldier and a fondness for the military was instinctive. When scarcely of age he was a member of Governor Hammond's Staff; then in 1846 a lieutenant of the company raised in his native County for the Mexican War, in which he participated until failing health necessitated his return home before the capture of the city; then Colonel of the 22nd South Carolina Militia and Captain of a superb volunteer company in Camden."

With James Chesnut and Thos. J. Withers he represented Kershaw County in the Convention which passed the Ordinance of Secession on December 20, 1860. Eight regiments were at once organized by the State and Kershaw was elected Colonel of the 2nd composed of four companies of which Company E. commanded by J. D. Kennedy was one. This Regiment was present at the bombardment of Fort Sumter in April 1861, being brigaded on Morris Island at the time under the command of Colonel P. H. Nelson.

After the fall of Fort Sumter, Kershaw returned for a few days to his home at Camden, which he left for Richmond on April 28, to revisit it but once afterwards on a brief furlough during the entire war. At Richmond he was met by his four companies to whom were added a large accession of forces, and thus was organized the 2nd Regiment of the First Brigade of the First Division, of the First Corps of the Army of Northern Virginia, "ever first in the fray, the last to quit." At the Battle of Bull Run in July 1861, Kershaw's regiment was part of the brigade commanded by General Bonham. The conduct of Kershaw and his troops in this their "first baptism of fire" gave them a great reputation in the army, and on General Bonham's resignation Kershaw was promoted to General of the Brigade and Kennedy to Colonel of the Regiment. From that time forward this command and these two commanders participated with renown, and associated in every crucial engagement of the war. In the attack upon Harpers Ferry this brigade marched along the ridge of South Mountain from six in the morning until twelve at night in hot September without a drop of water to drink, fought and captured the Ferry next day, and immediately marched fifteen miles into the thickest of the fight at Sharpsburg. Here, says Kennedy: "The second became at once hotly engaged, while Kershaw led the other regiments of the brigade to the right of the Church in the open, riding in front of the line, cap in hand, waving them to the onslaught, a sight which those who witnessed, will never forget, as his figure seemed to rise in grandeur and he looked a demigod of war. After placing these troops he galloped down the line toward the left, amid a storm of cannister and small arms, and as he passed one of his regiment commanders who was wounded, he ordered one of his staff to dismount and give him his horse to assist him out of the fight."

Kershaw's ride horseback during the crisis of battle at Fredericksburg down the slope of Maryes's Hill to the stone wall, is pronounced by Kennedy, "as bold a feat as was performed during the war". Through the fiercest of the fray at Chancellorsville, Gettysburg, Chickamauga, the Wilderness and throughout the war he passed unscathed, having been struck but once by a spent grape shot at Sharpsburg and a small fragment at Fredericksburg, neither of which produced even a contusion.

At the battle of the Wilderness in 1846 where he commanded McLaws division, while riding with Longstreet and his staff the party was by mistake fired upon by their own men. General Longstreet was desperately wounded in the neck, General Micah Jenkins and Marcus Baum and Alfred E. Doby of Kershaw's Staff were killed. Kershaw was untouched. It was in this same Wilderness that Stonewall Jackson had fallen by the same mischance.

In January 1865 Kershaw's Brigade then under Kennedy, was detached to South Carolina at urgent request of Governor Magrath, to help stem the tide of Sherman's march. Kershaw continued in Virginia in command of the remainder of the division and was captured at Five Forks in April 1865 giving up his sword to General Custer. His son John (later rector of St. Michael's Church in Charleston) then a mere youth was captured with his father and both imprisoned at Fort Warren.

After the war General Kershaw returned to practice of law at Camden. In 1877 he was elected to the Circuit Court Bench, which he adorned until his resignation in 1893. His death occurred April 1894. It was our privilege to know him during the last twenty years of his life and well we recall his eagle eye, resonant voice, and erect carriage, the embodiment of grit, the very model of a commander. It was clear at a glance that his prestige as a soldier was well deserved. The photographic portrait of which copy is here inserted seems to us sadly inadequate.

Inseparably linked with the name of General Kershaw is that of Richard Rowland Kirkland, associated together as they are in the celebrated incident of watering the wounded at the Stone Wall of Fredericksburg. Fortunate indeed that it may be told in the authentic words of General Kershaw himself, who thus narrates it in a signed communication to the *Charleston News and Courier* of February 6, 1880, reproduced in the *Kershaw Gazette* of February 12, 1880. It is here inserted in full:

"Camden, S. C., January 29th, 1880.

"To the Editor of *The News and Courier*:

"Your Columbia correspondent referred to the incident narrated here, telling the story as 'twas told to him, and inviting corrections. As such a deed should be recorded in the rigid simplicity of actual truth I take the liberty of sending you for publication an accurate account of a transaction every feature of which is indellibly impressed upon my memory.

"Richard Kirkland was the son of John Kirkland, an estimable citizen of Kershaw County, a plain substantial farmer of the olden time. In 1861 he entered as a private, Captain J. D. Kennedy's Company E of the Second South Carolina Volunteers, in which Company he was a sergeant in December 1862.

"The day after the sanguinary battle of Fredericksburg, Kershaw's Brigade occupied the road at the foot of Marye's Hill and the grounds about Marye's House, the scene of their desperate defense of the day before. One hundred and fifty yards in front of the road, the stone facing of which constituted the famous stone wall, lay Sykes Division of Regulars, U. S. A. between whom and our troops a murderous skirmish occupied the whole day, fatal to many who heedlessly exposed themselves even for a moment. The ground between the lines was nearly bridged with the wounded, dead and dying Federals, victims of the many desperately gallant assaults of that column of 30,000 brave men, hurled vainly against that impregnable position.

"All that day those wounded men rent the air with their groans and agonizing cries of 'water! water!' In the afternoon the General sat in the North room upstairs of Mrs. Stevens' House, in front of the Road, surveying the field, when Kirkland came up. With an expression of indignant remonstrance pervading his person, his manner and the tone of his voice, he said:

"'General, I can't stand this.'

"'What is the matter, Sergeant?' asked the General.

"He replied:

"'All night and all day I have heard those poor people crying for water, and I can stand it no longer. I came to ask permission to go and give them water.'

"The General regarded him for a moment with feelings of profound admiration and said:

"'Kirkland, don't you know that you would get a bullet through your head the moment you stepped over the wall?'

"'Yes, Sir', he said, 'I know all about that, but if you will let me, I am willing to try it.'

"After a pause the General said:

"'Kirkland, I ought not to allow you to run such a risk, but the sentiment which actuates you is so noble, that I will not refuse your request, trusting that God may protect you. You may go.'

"The Sergeant's eyes lighted up with pleasure. He said 'Thank you Sir' and ran rapidly down stairs. The General heard him pause for a moment and then return, bounding two steps at a time. He thought the Sergeant's heart had failed him. He was mistaken. The Sergeant stopped at the door and said:

"'General, can I show a white handkerchief?'

"The General slowly shook his head, saying emphatically:

"'No, Kirkland, you can't do that.'

"'All right, Sir', he said, 'I'll take the chances.'

"With profound anxiety he was watched as he stepped over the wall on his errand of mercy, Christ-like mercy. Unharmed he reached the nearest sufferer. He knelt beside him, tenderly raised the drooping head, rested it gently upon his own noble breast and poured the precious life giving fluid down the fever scorched throat. This done he laid him gently down, placed his knap-sack under his head, straightened out his broken limb, spread his over-coat over him, replaced his empty canteen with a full one, and turned to another sufferer. By this time his purpose was well understood on both sides and all danger was over. From all parts of the field arose fresh cries of 'Water, water, for God's sake, water!' More piteous still, the mute appeal of some one who could only feebly lift a hand to say, here too is life and suffering.

"For an hour and a half did this ministering angel pursue his labor of mercy, nor ceased to go and return until he had relieved all of the wounded on that part of the field. He returned wholly unhurt. Who shall say how sweet his rest that Winter's night beneath the cold stars. This incident occurred during a bitter cold spell in December when the thermometer fell to zero.

"Little remains to be told. Sergeant Kirkland distinguished himself in battle at Gettysburg and was promoted Lieutenant. At Chickamauga he fell on the field of battle in the hour of victory. He was but a youth when called away and had never formed those ties from which might have resulted a posterity to enjoy his fame and bless his country; but he has bequeathed to American youth, yea, to the world, an example which dignified our common humanity.

J. B. KERSHAW."

General Kennedy of whose Company E, Kirkland was an original member, also testifies that "the enemy, as soon as they divined his mission ceased their fire and cheered."

The body of Richard Kirkland was brought home and interred in the family cemetery on White Oak Creek, where his grave was marked by a wooden head piece on which some forty-eight years ago could be plainly traced the initials R. R. K. His remains were later removed to the Camden Cemetery and marked by a massive granite stone and his name honored by a fountain on Broad Street.

JOHN DOBY KENNEDY, son of Anthony M. Kennedy and Sarah Doby Kennedy, was born in Camden, January 5, 1840. He entered the South Carolina College at the age of sixteen and was admitted to the bar in 1861. He volunteered among the first at the call to arms, as Captain of Company E, which formed part of the Second Regiment. The story of his splendid military career has already been largely told in the foregoing sketch of Kershaw, and necessarily so, for like the twin brethren, Castor and Pollux, they rode from beginning to end, the one but one grade in rank below the other, separated for brief periods by the chances of war. It ony remains for us to note some of these divergencies in their fortunes.

While Kershaw passed through the tempests of shot and shell unhurt, Kennedy was six times severely wounded and struck fifteen times by spent balls. Being robust, vigorous and young his recovery was always rapid and in time for the next important fight. While Kershaw's immunity was marvelous, equally so was Kennedy's recuperation from serious injuries. During his absence produced by wounds, received in the battle of the Wilderness, his brigade formerly Kershaw's, was commanded by General James Connor. When promoted to command of this Brigade, Kennedy was only twenty-four years of age, probably the youngest Brigadier in the Army.

As above stated Kennedy and his Brigade was detached in January 1865 to join Johnston's army, with which it surrendered at Greensboro, N. C. in May 1865.

As a veteran at the venerable age of twenty-five he returned to the difficulties of so called peace aggravated by ten years of reconstruction. The State being finally redeemed from the Carpet-bagger, after a struggle in which he took a conspicuous part he became a prominent political figure and in 1880 was elected Lieutenant Governor on the ticket with General Hagood. It seemed that at the following election he would be promoted to the Governorship, but in this ambition he was defeated by the log-rolling and intrigues of the Nominating Convention of 1882, to the great disgust of a large following.

From this time until his death on April 14, 1896 he devoted himself exclusively to the profession of law at Camden. In 1884 he was appointed by President Cleveland, Consul General at Shanghai, China, where he spent four years.

The General was of powerful physique and handsome countenance, of ruddy complexion, ever buoyant and hearty. His portrait here inserted is a speaking likeness, and beyond any words we can use, gives an impression of him most true to life.

# CHAPTER XVII.
## SLAVES.

After the public mind of the South had become inflamed on the subject of slavery by the Abolition agitation between 1830 and 1860, no resident of Camden would have been so bold as to utter in the public print such sentiments as those of Dr. William Langley found in the *Camden Gazette* of December 1816 from which we take the following short extract:

"The influence of slavery extinguishes the glowing spark of religious fervor and produces cruelty to which is super-added its pernicious effects in a political point of view. It begets idleness, voluptuousness and a thirst for power. It endangers our safety and destroys domestic tranquility. If it were not for slavery we should be consolidated as a people. I would not have it understood, however, as has been unjustly reported, that I am an advocate for emancipation. I am now regretting, and have always lamented, that the policy of our country has not been to remove, instead of introduce, domestic enemies."

It will appear from the foregoing that the worthy Dr. Langley was impressed as much by the dangers as by the evil of slavery. His state of mind is better understood when we learn that in July of the same year in which the above was written, the town of Camden narrowly escaped the horrors of a slave insurrection. In the *Camden Gazette* of July 4, 1816 we read:

"Considerable alarm has been excited in Camden and vicinity on account of a conspiracy that has just been detected among the slaves. Their ringleaders, to the number of fifteen or twenty, are in custody. Their intention was to have fired one end of the town distant from the arsenal, to draw attention from that quarter where their hopes were centered. After securing arms and ammunition the reader can imagine the course that would have been pursued. The promptitude and vigilance of the authorities have happily dissipated present dangers. Several executions will probably take place."

The same paper of July 11, states that seventeen leaders had been arrested and tried and five condemned and executed; that "upon trial every one who was most deeply implicated manifested the greatest apparent innocence, but upon conviction acknowledged the correctness of the Court's decision, nor did they evince the least compunction for having conceived and matured the design. It is melancholy to reflect that those who were most active in the conspiracy occupied a respectable stand in one of the churches, several were professors and one a class leader."

The foregoing is confirmed by the original record of the trial of these slaves which we found among some old documents. From this it appears that an inquiry was held July 2 by the Town Council, then consisting of Abram Blanding, Intendant and R. W. Carter, John Reed, William Langley, and Wyatt Stark. Several of the suspected slaves were apprehended upon warrant and subjected to examination by Council; a transcript of their testimony in Blanding's handwriting, is in the record, of which we here give a condensed abstract.

"SAM, a negro fellow belonging to William Lang: About a fortnight ago Jack, a fellow belonging to Thos. Lang requested him to join to raise an army and fight the white people. Said they were to fight with guns but did not tell him where they were to be got. I promised to meet him at his master's on Saturday night last, but did not go because I did not wish to join them."

"JIM, a fellow of Thos. Lang: Isaac, belonging to Thos. Lang asked me if I had heard that the black people below wanted to rise against the white people. I told him that it was of no account. I said I will have nothing to do with it. He said they were to meet last night at the old yard where Mr. Lang used to live. I asked him who they were but he would not tell me.

"ISAAC, Mrs. Sarah Lang's, a drummer for Captain Levy's company: March and I were at the brick-yard. He asked me to join them. I said for what. He replied that a party of them were a-going to take the Magazine. I said I would have no hand in it. He would sometimes stop black people and take them aside and talk to them."

"SPOTTSWOOD (McRae's): Mr. Lang's Isaac said he had a notion to get a parcel of men and go and fight the white people. I don't recollect whether I agreed to join or not. Isaac said if I told he would have me killed. Told me to speak to as many as I could and get them to join."

"ISAAC (Thos. Lang's), drummer for Captain Levy: He never engaged in any plan for rising. It has been mentioned to him by others. I have said to George, Cameron and Sam (Mr. Levy's), that I thought it would be a good scheme if they would get through with it, but that negroes were so deceitful that it would not do.

"CAMERON denies that any person ever talked with him about any scheme of rising."

"JACK (Thos. Lang's): Says he never heard anything about a rising. He never mentioned it to Wm. Lang's Sam, never spoke with Levy's March about it."

"MARCH (Chapman Levy's): Said he never heard anything about rising until now."

The drumhead Court, composed as provided by law, of Justices of the Peace, Thomas Salmond and John Kershaw, Justices, and five freeholders, Benjamin Bineham, Joseph Brevard, Burwell Boykin, Benjamin Carter and Thomas Whitaker, met at the jail on July 3 and proceeded to trial with the following results: MARCH was first tried and convicted, being doubtless the ringleader. He, together with CAMERON, JACK, ISAAC and SPOTTSWOOD were hung on July 5 and one NED on July 12. STEPHEN was condemned, but pardoned just before execution after all preparations had been completed. BIG FRANK was condemned to be imprisoned in irons for a year and sent out of the Country. Nine were discharged.

It is a matter of family tradition, confirmed by record, that this plot for insurrection was revealed to Colonel Chesnut by one of his slaves who came to the Colonel's room and warned him that his family would be murdered the next night. Colonel Chesnut's residence was then in Camden not far from the Arsenal. The State Legislature by statute in 1817 appropriated eleven hundred dollars to purchase the freedom of this slave whose name however is not mentioned, and granted him a yearly stipend of fifty dollars.

William Langley's warning is again heard in a presentment of the grand jury signed by him as foreman at the November term 1816, from which the following is quoted:

"We present the abuse of retailing spirits to negroes; also the pernicious tendency of introducing into our state the slaves of another. It is unnecessary to recur to the evils arising from an overgrown black population. The history of South Carolina furnishes abundant proof of the impolicy of encouraging a great numerical increase of that class of people. The affair of July 4th last ought to convince every reflecting mind of the necessity of adopting prohibitory measures."

The "Magazine", or "Arsenal", above mentioned which the plotters intended to seize was built by Joseph Kershaw in 1780 on Mulberry Street near the edge of the creek swamp. Its site may be still traced by the old mound and broken bricks. We learn from James Kershaw's diary that he fired it in 1794 and moved the bricks. From tradition we learn that the bricks were used to reconstruct the "Arsenal" located at the old southeast corner of Fair and Bull Streets. Here were kept stores of powder and arms. In the *Camden Gazette* of December 19, 1816, a "Citizen" warns the authorities of the unguarded state of the Arsenal, "the grand central depot of arms for the interior of Carolina"; that there was danger of a St. Domingo massacre as a result of the security of the whites. In its last stages this structure was used as a theatre. Here, in 1830 Clara Fisher, noted in her day, gave a performance and Captain James Villepigue told us that he remembered witnessing her performance. The site of the Arsenal is now a field. The bricks were said to have been used in 1836 in building the Bank of Camden (Branch of State Bank), corner of Rutledge and Broad.

An item in the *Camden Journal* of 1823 tells of the pursuit and killing of negroes in the swamps of the Wateree and Santee Rivers, among them Colonel Nixon's Isham. The head of one negro was cut off and stuck on a pole as "a warning to vicious slaves."

The settled attitude of the South is voiced by the following resolution of a conference of the Methodist Church South, which is commended by the *Camden Journal* of July 17, 1844:

"It is the deliberate conviction of the Quarterly Conference that slavery as it exists amongst us is not an evil but is sanctioned and the relative duties of master and servant fully unequivocally set forth by the Holy Scriptures which we hold the only and sufficient rule of our faith and practice."

To us now, removed by more than sixty years from the days of slavery, the code of laws applicable to that institution seem grotesque enough. On trial for homicide a slave could not plead self defense, but only mischance or defense of his master. If a slave presumed to strike a white person except in defense of his master, he was punishable, short of death, in discretion of the Court, and for third offense was punishable by death. It was a capital crime to attempt or to incite insurrection.

## Stop the Runaways.

LEFT the subscribers Plantation on Little Lynches Creek, on the 29th ultimo, three negroes, viz: SILAS, a fellow about thirty five years of age, stout and well made.

DINAH, a wench about eighteen years of age yellow complected. DARKE, a wench about twenty years of age, very black Took with them a considerable quantity of Ladies very fine clothes, silk dresses, shawls, &c. &c.

Any person or persons apprehending the said negroes, or any of them, and delivering them to the subscriber, or confining them in any jail so that I can get them, shall be reasonably rewarded.

Margaret Exum,
Lynches Creek.
August 3, 1819.   73-tf—

It was unlawful to teach a slave to write. Slaves were forbidden to wear "any sort of apparel finer than negro cloth, duffils, kerseys, osnabrugs, blue or check linen, or coarse garlix." No slave could go beyond his master's plantation without a passport, and any white person had a right to examine him for his pass. It was punishable to trade with a slave without written permit from his master, and many indictments for this offense are found in our Court records, among these the conviction for this offense of J. B. Mathieu, he who fashioned the old weather vane of King Haigler now on the turret of the Opera House.

Deeds manumitting slaves were quite common prior to 1820, several being of record in Kershaw County. But in that year the freeing of slaves was forbidden by the Legislature except by its own edict.

Specimens of advertisements of fugitive slaves in the *South Carolina Gazette* of November 28, 1775 (published in Charleston), are here inserted:

"Brought to Camden Gaol, the following runaways:

Feb. 4, 1775, a new negro fellow, who says his name is Freer, but cannot tell his Master's name: he is 5 ft. 6 in. high, of the Mandingo Country, and had with him an osnabrugs shirt, negro cloth breeches dyed yellow, a red cap, and a pair of boots, one red and the other white—and an old blanket: he is about 26 years of age.

Sept. 15, 1775. A new Negro Fellow: says his name is Joe and his Master's name Casher Gibbes: he is 5 ft. 3 in. high, about 40 years of age and has a scar on his breast and another on his left elbow, and marks on both calves of his legs, with several other scratches, and brought with him an old white Negro cloth Jacket, Robin, Trowsers and a Cap.

Sept. 16, 1775. A new Negro Fellow of the Congo Country: says his name is Jemmy and that he belongs to one Patenner who lives in Virginia: he is 5 ft. 10 in. high and about 30 years of age; a stout well-made fellow, with two large holes in his ears, and several marks on his back, supposed to be done by whipping: has on an Osnabrugs shirt and Trowsers.

JOHN RUSHBROOK HUTCHINS,

Gaoler."

In the annexed facsimile of a notice published in the old *Camden Gazette* of 1819 will be noticed in the background the outline of a gallows and dangling fugitive.

The Patrol Ordinance of 1831, found in the town Minutes, provided that the Recorder should select from the Registry of those liable to patrol duty, companies of not less than four and not more than sixteen to serve for each day in the year, the most prudent and discreet member to act as Captain. A company was to patrol through the town for twelve hours. They were to suppress any mischievous designs of free negroes or slaves authorized to carry weapons; to apprehend

## SLAVES

all slaves beyond the owner's premises under suspicious circumstances; to correct moderately with switch or cow skin those abroad without permit, lashes not to exceed twenty and to commit to jail. No compensation was provided for patrol service, which might be suspended by Intendant and Recorder. The writer recalls the refrain of an old negro song:

"Run, nigger, run, or the patrol 'll get you."

After various futile attempts at insurrection the slaves became apparently reconciled to their condition and when well treated exhibited an attachment and devotion to their masters, deserving a monument in every community. The writer's personal recollection extends only to the two last years of slavery, but covers all the period since. Among all the old darkies who figured in Camden long after Emancipation, three stand out as calling for special memorial.

JIM LANG was a model valet. He remembered Lafayette's visit in 1825 and lived to the age of ninety or more. His father, Jim Lang, was the property of Mr. Thos. Lang and was one of those slaves whose testimony in the trials for insurrection in 1816 is given above. He was not, however, one of the suspected but was implicitly trusted. Jim (the son) acted as body servant to Colonel J. P. Dickinson in the Mexican War. He brought home from Mexico, the bodies of Colonel Pierce Butler and of his master, Colonel Dickinson, whom he followed closely into the battle in which both the Colonels fell. During the Civil War he served as hostler to General Beauregard. Jim has told us how he attended upon the Federal General Prentiss who was captured at the battle of Shiloh and detained at General Beauregard's tent. Jim was a diplomat of the highest order, invariably suave and polite, and was never known to be in trouble. His long career and service became joined with much of Camden's history and he will be found mentioned in other chapters.

MONROE BOYKIN was born in 1819 as a slave in the Boykin family. He lived until the year 1904. Judge Withers, through his marriage with Elizabeth T. Boykin, acquired the ownership of Monroe. He was the Judge's devoted man servant and drove him on his circuits, which in those days were ridden mainly by horse and buggy. Monroe was at his best in times of emergency and on the spur of the moment. He was the devoted nurse of members of Judge Withers' family in their last illness, and would offer the most fervent prayers at their bedside, for he had a gift of native eloquence. He was sent to Richmond in 1864 to attend upon Wm. L. Kirkland, the Judge's son-in-law, who had been desperately wounded in battle, and served upon him ardently to the end.

After Emancipation two tracts of land were donated to Monroe by heirs of Judge Withers, now subdivided as Monroe Boykin Park. About the year 1888 Monroe established the colored church on the northwest corner of Broad and York Streets. His name, always with credit, will be found mentioned in other connections in this volume.

ELEVEN ROBINSON, a slave of Jesse Kilgore on White Oak Creek, about fifteen miles northwest of Camden, was a typical plantation darkie, and likewise a comic genius. On his visits to Camden he never failed to create a furor of fun and to draw groups around him which he kept in a constant roar of laughter. The boys would pay him a nickle or dime for one of his prolonged laughs. He could be heard several blocks away and his expansion of mouth was something stupendous. In this way he would reap quite a harvest of coin. With humble apologies we attempt a faint outline of his "Possum Hunt" story:

"Isom Hammond lib on de Collin's place next to Red Hill where I lib. He come up one day an' say:

'Lev ole fellow, I got a new 'possum dorg, bes' you ever seed. Let's go out tonight.' I say:

" 'All right.'

"Dat night we went out in dem woods cross de Marler bottom. Atter while Isom' dorg hit a trail. Isom say:

" 'What I tell you 'bout dat dorg?' Speak to 'im, nigger.'

"Twan't long 'fore he treed. When we got dar he was barking up a poplar tree wid a bullace vine growin' up in it. I say:

" 'You gwine cut de tree down?' He say:

" 'No, sah, I never cuts, I allus climb for my dorg.'

"So Isom scuffle up de tree, and when he got to de top he holler to me:

" 'Hole de torch 'roun dis side. Wot I tell you? Here he is, hangin' by his tail. Look out down dere, I gwine knock him out.'

"Wid dat he haul' off and jam his arm into a hornet' nes' up to de elbow. Down he tumble' an' hit de groun' covered wid hornets. Dat dorg run up and grab de nes' and shake it. But lemme tell you, he lit out from dere, yellin' fur's you could hear. Isom lay at the foot of dat tree hollerin' and fightin' hornets. You bet I stan' off a piece. Den Isom 'gun to groan and atter while he stop and I thought he was dead. I crep' up and say:

" 'Isom how fur you fall from?' He say:

" 'Jis fur's you see dat tree trim up dere.'

"At las' when all de hornets quit, I toted Isom home.

"Nex' mornin', jes' sun up, I went roun' to see how Isom gittin' on. He was settin' by de fire wid his face all swell' up so he couldn' see a wink. He say:

" 'Lev, you see anything o' dat dorg?' I say:

" 'Yas, he out here in de yard'. He say:

" 'Lev, retch me dat gun outen de corner, and hole one o' my eyes open so I kin see how to shoot dat damn' fice.'

"While I held open one of his eyes, he rais' dat gun and blowed dat fice to pieces."

# CHAPTER XVIII.

### Reconstruction and Red Shirts.

While it was not until April 2, 1866, that President Johnson formally proclaimed the "insurrection at an end", the war may be regarded as practically closed on May 10, 1865, on which date appeared in the *Camden Journal* Governor McGrath's announcement of Lee's surrender and the suspension of the Confederate Civil and Military Government.

The Camden *Tri-Weekly Journal* of June 16, 1865, contains the following item:

"TOWN OF CAMDEN GARRISONED.—Many negroes and others of our people, who were curious to see a Federal soldier, congregated on the public square on Wednesday evening (June 14th.) where their hearts desire was comforted in ogling two companies of the 25th. Regiment Ohio Volunteers, under command of Capt. C. W. Ferguson, who arrived early in the afternoon. Capt. Ferguson, assures us that it is not his purpose to interfere in anywise with law abiding citizens, and that he would prefer to see all kinds of business resumed. On the second page of our paper will be found several orders issued by the commandant of the post."

The orders of Captain Ferguson required all horses, mules, wagons and other property covered by terms of surrender to be reported; forbid sale of liquor without permit; proclaimed as outlaws bands of marauders who were depredating the country, and prohibited wearing of the Confederate uniform.

The soldiers returning found the season too far advanced for starting a crop, no animals, and labor demoralized. Military authorities required the planters to take oath of allegiance before the provost-marshals, and to submit all contracts of employment to the local commanding officer for approval.

In these dismal conditions a note of cheer is sounded in the *Camden Journal* of June 2, 1865. From this article signed, CINCINNATUS, the following is a paragraph:

"Many speak of abandoning the country wholly and forever. Does not this look like pure despair? Is not this land that gave us birth too fertile, healthful and desirable a heritage to be tamely yielded up to negroes and foreigners? Let us recognize the sad change in our circumstances, yet let us not yield to apathy or indolence or recklessness. On the contrary let us go to work one and all, actively as possible. The crisis tests our manhood, and our energetic capacities for self government, and true independence. Let Southern men fill up all gaps, and answer all requirements, except directly servile ones. The Country will still be our own, and will gradually, under God's blessing upon our efforts, get itself to rights."

Military headquarters were in the Council Chamber and the Town officials had to seek other quarters. To obviate the complete dearth of money the Town authorities began in May 1865 the issuance of a local currency and continued the process until 1877. It always circulated at par, and was fully redeemed. After twenty years' search for a specimen of this old currency we finally found a faded dollar bill in possession of our friend Mr. L. A. Wittkowsky.

On May 29, 1865, President Johnson issued the Amnesty proclamation, extending pardon and restoration of rights to all who had participated in the "rebellion", upon their taking oath of allegiance, excepting those worth above twenty thousand dollars, and officials of the Confederacy who were required to make special application to the President. Citizens pretty generally subscribed the oath before the Marshals, and the President granted pardons to all applicants with a free hand. A friend showed us one of these old documents issued to Wm. E. Johnson, a notable citizen of long bygone days upon which, in his hand, is endorsed the following comment:

"Nov. 15, 1865.

"It is expedient and proper to accept this pardon under the circumstances, and I have therefore written the Secretary of State this day that it is accepted, but I am not conscious of any criminality but on the contrary am entirely satisfied the measure of Secession was the exercise of a legitimate sovereign right, and the cause for exercising it was adequate, and all that has since been done on the part of the U. S. strengthens my conviction on this point.

WM. E. JOHNSON."

On July 12, 1865 a meeting in Camden, Dr. L. H. Deas presiding, adopted resolutions presented by Colonel W.

M. Shannon, declaring that those of Kershaw District who had subscribed the oath of allegiance had done so with purpose to preserve it inviolate and desired restoration of Civil government, the only existing regulations being such as the meagre military garrison prescribed; that all industry was paralyzed and social life in chaos; that President Johnson be requested to appoint a Provisional Governor and re-establish Civil Government. Indeed the President had already several days before appointed B. F. Perry, Governor, an excellent choice, but doubtless owing to the destruction of railway and telegraph lines the news seems not to have then reached Camden.

The first garrison of Ohio troops in Camden was replaced by two companies (70 men) of the 30th Massachusetts under command of Captain E. A. Fiske, who was succeeded later by Captain Sam'l Place. Captain Place was later Sheriff of Kershaw County. On January 6, 1866 an immense concourse gathered in Camden at Call of Captain Fiske who addressed them and read the military orders regulating labor contracts. The *Camden Journal* of that date says:

"On Saturday last we saw the largest gathering of sable gentlemen and ladies that our eyes ever rested on. The open square in front of the Court House and site of the old Market and the spacious cross streets were packed with a living mass of colored people. We observed present also many of the largest planters. The orders were read and explained to them. Capt. Fiske's address was clever and unexceptionable. John Chesnut and Harmon Jones, two intelligent freed-men, also made addresses and repeated the good advice they have given on several occasions. Let us hope the delusions so fondly cherished by the freed-men, that the government intended to give them land or support them in idleness have been dispelled."

President Johnson soon evinced a purpose to uphold white government in the South. On July 20, 1865 he ordered that a State convention be held to frame a new Constitution, composed of delegates to be chosen at an election in which only those could vote who were qualified under laws in force *prior to the war*—which of course confined the ballot to white males. This convention met on September 13, 1865. The two delegates from Kershaw County were Major L. W. R. Blair and

Colonel A. D. Goodwyn. In two weeks they completed a Constitution which recognized emancipation of slaves, repealed the ordinance of secession, but excluded the negro from right of suffrage.

An election was held under this new Constitution for State and County officers, in October 1865. General J. B. Kershaw was elected State Senator, W. Z. Leitner and W. L. DePass, Representatives from this County, and J. D. Kennedy member of Congress from this, then the First Congressional District. The Legislature met in October 1865, ratified the Thirteenth Amendment and by what was termed the "Black Code", established the domestic relations of the former slaves, conferring upon them rights of property and inheritance, but declared them not entitled to Social or political equality with the white people," and excluded them from the militia or the right to bear arms without permit.

The sort of Reconstruction thus proceeding under the auspices of President Johnson was highly obnoxious to the fanatic element then controlling Congress, bent upon imposing negro suffrage and equality upon the South. To effect this purpose they required two-thirds majority to override the President, and this majority could only be established by refusing to seat the Congressmen lately elected from the South, who were accordingly excluded and by act of Congress full suffrage, social and political rights were bestowed upon the negro.

The act of Congress, passed in 1867, over President Johnson's veto, created each of the "Rebel States" a district subject to a military commander, whose authority was supreme. None of these States were allowed representatives in Congress until they had adopted Constitutions framed by delegates chosen by all the adult males *without regard to color*. General Canby was appointed September 1867 to command in South Carolina, succeeding General Sickles. Acts of the State Legislature and decisions of the State Courts were subject to be nullified by Canby. The registration of votes and election of delegates to the Constitutional Convention were under his supervision.

In July 1867 the "Union Republican" party was organized in this State by a Convention composed of fifty-three blacks and fifteen whites. It declared for "cautious" restoration of rights to those "lately guilty of treason". All darkies were sworn into clubs called "Loyal Union Leagues".

On November 6, 1867 the whites met in Convention at Columbia, James Chesnut, President, Wade Hampton and J. D. Kennedy, Vice Presidents. They could only make protest and issued an address from which the following is quoted:

"The enforcement of military power under the guise of negro voters and negro conventions, cannot lawfully reestablish Civil Government in South Carolina. It may for a time hold us in subjection to a quasi-civil government backed by military force, but it can do no more."

The registration of voters for the Convention showed for the State 46,346 whites and 78,982 blacks; for Kershaw County 859 whites, 1,765 blacks. In November an election was held on the question of holding the Convention. The whites generally abstained from voting. Result; for Convention 68,876 negroes, 130 whites; against Convention 2,081 whites, negroes none. This shows that *only* 130 *whites in the whole State transgressed the color line.*

Election of delegates to this Convention ensued in December. The membership of 124 was solidly "Union Republican", composed of 48 whites and 76 blacks. Kershaw County contributed these three members: Justus K. Jillson (of Massachusetts), white; S. G. W. Dill (origin unknown), white; John A. Chesnut (freedman), colored.

The Convention met in Charleston, January 14, 1868, credentials of membership being signed by General Canby. Among the resolutions seriously proposed in this body was one to expunge from the vocabulary of South Carolina the words, "Nigger", and "Yankee", making their use punishable by fine and imprisonment, a proposal too absurd even for those solons. The *Charleston Mercury* dubbed this the "ring-streaked and striped Convention", giving occasion for our S. G. W. Dill to make the following remarks:

"The *Mercury* calls us a ring-streaked and striped convention. I admit it is all that, but who made it so? Just such men as conduct the *Mercury*. Here in Charleston I have resided for forty years and have been out of it only three years. Here in the streets I have been asked: 'Mr. Dill, what are you doing in that damn nigger convention?' My reply was, 'I have always

been a poor man, and always known to be on the side of the poor'."
(Proceedings of Constitutional Convention 1868, pp. 612, 638.)

The Constitution produced by this body conformed of course to Congressional requirements, conferred full suffrage and civil rights on the negro, and was ratified by popular vote April 6, 1868, the whites being powerless to vote it down. At the same time State and County officers were elected. The newly enfranchised mass of negro voters and the sprinkle of white renegades who led them were henceforth designated "Radicals"; they elected Robt. K. Scott of Ohio, Governor, one B. F. Whittemore, Congressman from this District, and the following from this County to the Legislature: Justus K. Jillson, Senator; S. G. W. Dill, John A. Chesnut (Col.), Jonas Nash (Col.), Representatives.

In the parlance of the day native white Radicals were branded as "Scalawags", and were far more detestable than the "Carpetbaggers" who came from beyond the State and had most of them entered with the invading Federal troops.

It is not surprising that the Spectre of the Ku-Klux-Klan now arises. Something of that nature is the following enigmatic resolution of the "Fraternal Democratic Club of "Harmony" in May 1868:

"Resolved: That it is the spirit and duty of every Carolinian who yet remains uncontaminated to give all possible aid to those of 'political proclivities' who may be in indigent circumstances. That no member of our Fraternal Club shall employ anyone who has enlisted under the vicious, unjust and detestable Banner of the 'Loyal Union League'."

About the same time this item is found in the *Camden Journal* of May 28, 1868:

"A considerable commotion was created among some of our 'citizens' on Monday last by a report that the K. K. intended paying a visit to Camden on that night. There was quite an excitement and preparation to give them a reception as warm as the regions from whence they are said to hail, but they did not appear, to the disappointment of some and gratification of others."

In the neighborhood of "Harmony" which is in the western part of this County, resided the above mentioned Solomon George Washington Dill. As head of a "Loyal League" his home was a rendezvous for the cold members, who would drop their plows in the field to hear him expound the doctrine of "forty acres and a mule". The Leaguers would guard his house, for he was apprehensive, and he had pledged them that if his blood was shed they would avenge him upon the whites from the cradle up. The newspapers of that date relate the following occurrence: After dusk on or about June 1, 1868, a few days after the Harmony resolution, one of the League, old Nestor Peay, sat with musket on guard at Dill's door. The yard dog gave alarm. Nestor called: "who goes there?" The answer was a volley of bullets under which Nestor and Dill fell dead. Mrs. Dill within the house received a ball in her thigh. One Taylor, another white inmate, escaped by the back door and scampered through the field on all-fours, and by thus using his wits, being mistaken for a calf, got away.

Federal troops scoured the country and made many arrests, but the actors were never discovered. Some twenty suspected citizens of the county were held imprisoned at the Citadel in Charleston for sometime, without extorting from them any admissions, and no one dared divulge any information.

The bodies of Dill and Nestor were brought to Camden and it is said were interred in the respective white and colored cemeteries, attended by a concourse of Leaguers. Some of the Loyal came later to visit Dill's grave and found it empty. For years it is said, Dill's skeleton served in Camden as an anatomical model, in the office of a local surgeon.

The Legislature of 1868 was composed of 134 "Radicals", of whom 88 were black and 46 white; and 20 "Democrats", all white. In the Senate we note "Dear" Josephus Woodruff installed as Clerk; in the House, Franklin J. Moses, Jr., Speaker; A. Osceola Jones, Clerk; on the floor worthies such as Elliott, Crews, Whipper, Neagle and others of that crew, whose exploits must be briefly recounted in order that we may understand the significance of the local events of that time.

These gentry without delay began the quest for spoils. The treasury was empty. The quickest resource was to borrow on credit of the State and thus draw booty from the pockets of outsiders. Hence Statutes were promptly enacted creating a "Financial Board" composed of

Governor Scott, Attorney General Chamberlain, Treasurer Parker, Superintendent of Education Neagle, with power to issue bonds of the State, and to sell and pledge the same through an agent resident in New York. They chose "Cherub" Hiram H. Kimpton as their New York agent. This Board constituted the heart of the Corrupt Ring which throughout the Reconstruction Era engineered those infamies the incredible enormity of which served for a time to conceal them, and which were not fully disclosed until absolutely proven years later by the Frauds Investigating Committee.

The honest debt of the State contracted prior to the Civil War was about Six Millions, when the act of March 1869 was passed, authorizing the "Board" to issue "Conversion" bonds to refund this indebtedness. By another Act, adopted a few days later, the "Board", through Kimpton agent, was directed to obtain loans upon pledge of *any bonds* of the State. Kimpton forthwith borrowed a vast sum and pledged the entire Six Millions of Conversion bonds without refunding a dollar of the old debt. These funds as shown hereafter were all squandered in riotous living by the Legislators.

The acts of March 1869 and 1870 provided for still more bonds, to be juggled by the "Board", from the proceeds of which lands were to be purchased for the State by one C. P. Leslie, Land Commissioner, and to be resold on easy terms to the "needy", whereby the long deferred hope of "forty acres and a mule" might be realized by the faithful. It was the same Leslie who had declared: "The State has no right to be a state unless she can take care of her Statesmen." Needless to say, the bulk of this land fund was appropriated by the eminent "Statesmen" in charge of it. The State got several thousand acres of poor land, much of it in Kershaw County, which was subdivided into forty acre lots and disposed of at a loss to the State.

The steady issuance of these bogus bonds soon depressed their selling price. Fearing the New York market had been over-played, fresh woods and pastures new were sought. The Act of March 1871 authorized "Stirling Bonds" in denominations of English money, to be sold by a "Financial Agency", in London—on pretext again of refunding the State debt. Half the issue had been executed with the great seal of the State attached, when the "bovine" Bowen (Senator from Charleston) saw an opportunity, and raised a hue and cry that the former "Conversion" sham was about to be repeated. His disclosures led to a hurried Cancellation of the bonds by Legislative resolution. For his patriotic service Bowen claimed and the Legislature granted him twenty-five hundred dollars reward!!

Still pursuing this virtuous and profitable course, in the Winter of 1871 Bowen introduced articles of impeachment against the "Board" (Scott, Chamberlain, Parker) for defrauding the State in the bond transactions. As the price for withdrawing these articles of impeachment Bowen demanded a sum which was larger than Scott would pay. Bowen continued to press the impeachment. Scott and his clique had concluded it was cheaper to buy the Legislature. Fictitious warrants on the Treasury were issued in favor of the purchased Solons. Speaker Moses afterwards admitted receiving fifteen thousand dollars. Thus the impeachment was killed by vote of the Legislature. This affair was afterwards fully ventilated before ths Frauds Committee. Here is a bit of testimony before the Committee by J. B. Dennis, a Ring henchman:

"I was a member of the Legislative Session 1871-1872 when impeachment articles were presented against Scott, Chamberlain, and Parker. One day I was in the office of Parker (State Treasurer) while the articles were before the House, and Parker said to me: 'What in the hell do those fellows up-stairs mean? Do they think they can beat that Machine?', pointing to the Safe."

These State bonds now in bad repute on the market, in the panic of 1873, fell into utter collapse. This shrinkage in supplies caused the greedy Legislators to create a committee of inquiry, of which Whittemore was Chairman. Their report in the words of Judge Hudson, in the *Bond Debt Cases*, 12 S. C., 238, was "full and unsparing, evincing a candor somewhat surprising considering the actual complicity of its authors."

These exposures brought about the act of December 1873, whereby the "Conversion" bonds, some six millions, were totally repudiated. The remainder, about twelve millions, including the old debt; were refunded, good, bad and indifferent, at fifty cents on the dollar. By this act the bond debt of the State was contracted to its original proportions at the expense of the holders of the old debt which was all *bona fide* and thus scaled to fifty cents on the dollar.

The true amount realized from sale of these fraudulent bonds was known only to the "Board" and Kimpton, and it is certain they got more than they revealed, pocketing the difference. Not a cent of the proceeds was ever applied to the purpose expressed in the Statutes under which the bonds had been issued, nor to any public purpose whatever, but, as we shall see, were entirely pocketed by officials and Legislators.

Not a particle of the State's assets escaped plunder. The State held large blocks of Railroad stocks. To capture these would be to control the roads. The scheme to accomplish this was the Machination of Chamberlain. Here enters "Honest" John J. Patterson, Carpet-bagger from Pennsylvania, who, doubtless by means of the State stock voted by the Ring, which was the "Financial Board", had contrived to become president of the Greenville and Columbia Railroad. The act of March 1870 created the "Sinking Fund Commission", in personnel none other than the same "Financial Board" with authority to "sell the unproductive property of the State." This burglarious measure was secured by the usual methods of bribery as absolutely proven by testimony such as the following:

J. L. NEAGLE.—The Sinking Fund Bill was prepared by Chamberlain who so informed me. The money paid to members of the Legislature for their votes was furnished by Kimpton. I was ex-officio member of the Commission.

JOHN B. DENNIS.—It was thought that Moses, Speaker, was fighting the Bill. When its passage seemed hopeless Patterson came to me and said: "Go ask that damned scoundrel how much he wants." As requested I went and asked Moses, who replied: "Ten thousand over and above the twenty-five thousand previously offered."

F. J. MOSES.—Patterson and Neagle offered me $25,000.00 if I would assist in passing the Bill. While the Bill was hanging in the balance, Patterson sent Dennis to me at the Speaker's stand offering to pay me ten thousand dollars additional if I would push it through that night. I sent word he must put it in writing, which he did and entrusted it to Joe Crews.

On the very day after passage of this measure the Commission met and without advertisement sold the

R. R. stocks of the State to a Syndicate which was composed of themselves and a few others admitted to the outer rim of the Ring.

The money used to buy the Legislators and to purchase this stock was none other than the State's own money, proceeds of bonds, sold through Agent Kimpton and concealed by falsification of accounts. It is now perfectly obvious that the Act of 1872 authorizing the "Financial Board" to make settlement with Kimpton in regard to all bond sales, was to enable these culprits to cover their tracks. To substantiate these statements the following from the Frauds Committee is submitted:

"The most cursory examination of the Journals of the General Assembly and the testimony annexed to this report must satisfy all that these measures (the same above alluded to) were adroitly concocted by the same persons for their joint personal benefit and by combination forced through the General Assembly by the most shameless bribery of Senators and members. The evidence of many members set forth with particularity that Patterson, Neagle, Kimpton, Scott, Parker and Chamberlain aided these nefarious measures by Counsel and advice and the actual purchase of votes with large sums of money, having full knowledge of the stealage and corruption intended to be perpetrated by such legislation.

(Report Frauds Committee, pp. 613, 614.)

Scott of course sought a second term as Governor. In an effort to defeat him, the whites, that is to say "Democrats", met in Convention at Columbia, June 15, 1870, Colonel W. M. Shannon of Camden, Chairman, and organized the "Union Reform Party". Its policy was to divide the Radicals and to coax away some of their darkie support. Therefore the delegation to this convention were mixed, and that from Kershaw County composed as follows:

WHITE.—James Chesnut, E. M. Boykin, J. B. Kershaw, John D. Kennedy, W. L. DePass, W. M. Shannon, J. M. Davis, T. H. Clarke, W. A. Ancrum, T. F. McDow, W. Z. Leitner.

COLORED.—Frank Adamson, Austin Lloyd, Clayborn Hamilton, Henry Carlos, David Jenkins, John Miller.

The Platform denounced the "incompetent, extravagant, corrupt administration of the Government," and accepted "the recent changes in the constitution and laws of the State as accomplished facts," and appealed to *all honest men* to "aid in establishing a just, equal and faithful administration." Judge R. B. Carpenter temporarily disgruntted Carpet-bagger, was named for Governor, General M. C. Butler for Lieutenant Governor, General J. B. Kershaw was Chairman of the State Executive Committee. A mass meeting of white and blacks at Camden named a Legislative ticket composed of both colors, which the white voters pretty generally supported at the polls, though a few refrained in disgust. General Hampton said: "Differ as we may about the platform of the new party, I see no alternative but to support the nominees."

It was in this campaign that the aforementioned Neagle declared in a speech at York: "Matches are cheap". Addressing the negroes at Laurens the aforesaid Joe Crews told them they had earned the land by their labor; if hungry to take corn from the fields and to use fire. The fusion ticket was defeated and the "Radicals" carried the State overwhelmingly, the vote standing Scott 85,071; Carpenter 51,537, with similar results for County officers.

At this election a fracas occurred on the street in Laurens between a white man and one of Governor Scott's constables. The negro militia company defiantly fired a volley on the public square. The whites gathered and with sticks, stones and pistols chased the militia to the armory, wounded several and disarmed the company. Joe Crews escaped by flight.

The Laurens incident shook Scott's faith in negro militia. He called upon President Grant for Federal troops and several companies were sent into the State. The State militia termed "National Guards" were composed of blacks, with an occasional white officer, and were organized into some fourteen regiments of one thousand each. Events showed they were utterly unfit to cope with ex-Confederates. Besides the militia were "State Guards", a constabulary force of imported roughs, who roamed about the State as political emissaries and rounders. The following is a dot from the Statement of J. B. Hubbard, Chief Constable:

"Thirty-two men were brought from New York by Gov. R. K. Scott and stationed in Union County. Gov. Scott in my presence threatened to bring in sufficient of this class to intimidate white voters. I don't think it possible to have found a more ngerous lot of men in any city. The Governor became frightened after they had been here a time and anxious to get them out of the State."

The foregoing explains why the Ku-Klux became active in Union County. There Matt Stevens, one armed Conferedate soldier, was beaten and shot on the highway by a Company of Scott's colored Militia. The infuriated whites captured thirteen of the company, executed five and put eight in jail. Application was made to Judge Thomas to release them on Habeas Corpus, but before the writ could be issued an army of a thousand or more Ku-Klux mounted and masked took the jail and executed the eight prisoners.

On the jail door they posted the following grim announcement, which bespeaks the hand of an unknown literary genius:

*To the Public.*

K. K. K.                      Taken by Habeas Corpus.

In silence and secrecy thought has been working, and the benignant efficacies of concealment speak for themselves. Once again we have been forced by force to use Force. Justice was lame, and she had to lean upon us. Information being obtained that a "doubting Thomas", the inferior of nothing, the superior of nothing, and of consequence the equal of nothing, who has neither eyes to see the scars of oppression, nor ears to hear the cause of humanity, even though he wears the judicial silk, had ordered some guilty prisoners from Union to the City of Columbia, and of Injustice and Prejudice, for an unfair trial of life; thus clutching at the wheel spokes of Destiny—then this thing was created and projected; otherwise it would never have been. We yield to the inevitable and inexorable and account this the best. "Let not thy right hand know what thy left hand doeth" is out motto.

We want peace, but this cannot be till Justice returns. We want and will have Justice, but this cannot be till a bleeding fight for freedom is fought. Until then the Moloch of Iniquity will have his victims, even if the Michael of Justice must have his martyrs."

In Camden on July 4, 1871 two colored companies, Sandy Stratford and C. Shiver, Captains, paraded the streets. John Smyrl, Marshal of the police, arrested a disorderly member. The companies pursued the Marshal and his prisoner into Crosby's bakery, swearing to kill the "damn Whites". Paul Wilson, ex-Confederate soldier, stood in the doorway with his walking cane beating down the bayonets by which his arms were scratched. Monroe Boykin an old ex-slave stood beside him, pleading with the rabble to desist. The one-legged veteran, Major Leitner, drove up in his buggy, and these three barely succeeded in preventing the street from flowing with blood. Some of us could feel the wave of excitement arising that day even in quiet Kirkwood.

During these times the Ku-Klux in some Counties engaged these colored militia in mid-night battles. Grant sent more troops to the State. General Chesnut among others, was called to testify before a Congressional Committee of inquiry at Spartanburg in July 1871. From his statement we can insert only a brief excerpt:

"As to secret associations of men who commit violence he had no personal knowledge. He did not know that he ever saw any individual belonging to such association. His information was derived from current report and newspaper accounts. He felt sure they did not exist in his County (Kershaw). He did not sanction them, but asked the committee to remember such associations arose under all despotic governments. The people of South Carolina lived under an absolute and atrocious despotism composed of villainous men from the North, and ignorant and vicious men at home."

In an interview printed by the *New York Sun*, General Kershaw was reported as declaring the Ku-Klux "an organization for defense against negro outrages." The *Daily Union*, a Radical paper issued in Columbia, referring to the Union incident, said: "These thirteen colored people were brutally murdered by the followers of Gen. Kershaw." There was nothing however beyond such assertions to connect General Kershaw with that organization which never operated in Kershaw County, unless the Dill tragedy be so construed.

On May 9, 1871 the Tax Payers Convention met in Columbia, James Chesnut and W. M. Shannon members from Kershaw County. Strange to say D. H. Chamberlain, who attended, supported a proposal of General Mart Gary to amend the election laws so as to allow "cumulative" voting which would have enabled the whites to overcome the negro majority. Notice to the

World was given by the following resolution of this Convention to beware of the State bonds:

"That bonds heretofore issued without legal sanction, the so-called "Sterling bonds" or any other bonds hereafter issued by authority of the State, as at present constituted, will not be held binding on us. We deem it our duty to warn all persons not to receive, by way of purchase, loan or otherwise, any bonds or obligations hereafter issued purporting to bind the property or pledge the credit of the State."

A Standing Executive Committee was established, James Chesnut Chairman, of which Colonel E. B. C. Cash was a member.

In recognition of his "bad eminence", Franklin J. Moses, Jr. was nominated for Governor by the Radicals, in August 1782, and R. H. Gleaves (Col.) for Lieutenant Governor. At their convention bitter dissension and exchange of accusations resulted in a bolt, led by ex-Governor Orr, whose membership in such an assembly was a subject of marvel. The "Bolters" named for Governor one Reuben Tomlinson and one Hayne (Col.) for Lieutenant Governor. The "Democrats" put up no ticket but in half-hearted way supported the Bolters. Moses won, 69,839 to 36,553 for Tomlinson. In this County the Radical Regulars won, electing Frank Adamson, A. W. Hough, R. D. Gaither (all colored) over the Bolters, Scott Brown, J. A. Chesnut and Wm. Boykin (all colored).

"Honest" John Patterson procured his seat in the United States Senate, as Successor to Sawyer, by the now well-established process of purchase. His defeated rivals, Scott and Elliott, caused the arrest of Honest John for bribery. The versatile Judge, T. J. Mackey granted him bail. Governor Moses removed the incumbent Jury Commissioner of Richland County and appointed in his place the reliable J. B. Dennis for the purpose of "fixing" the jury before whom Patterson would be tried. Dennis himself so testified. The indictment of course evaporated. The title "Honest" was explained by one of his associates with a sense of humor, who said: "Patterson will do what he says. If he promises to pay you he'll do it; if he promises to steal for you he'll do it."

The testimony of Frank Adamson, a colored Representative from Kershaw, would however indicate that Patterson was sometimes forgetful. Says he:

"I voted for the election of Mr. John J. Patterson to the United States Senate. Nobody ever offered me any money for voting for Patterson, *except Mr. Patterson himself*. He said if I voted for him he would give me a handsome present, and at another time, a hundred dollars. I voted for Mr. Patterson, but he never paid me the money. I have never applied to him for it and would never have done so if I had been staying in the same room with him."

Report Frauds Committee, p. 928.

Having above indicated some of the devices for raising funds let us follow their application. At the Legislative session of 1870 the "Carolina" Printing Company was chartered, composed of Scott, Chamberlain, Parker, our familiar "Financial Board". The Legislature empowered Josephus Woodruff and Osceola Jones, Clerks of Senate and House to contract with this "Company" for all the public printing. Thereupon the most fabulous and fictitious claims for printing were fabricated which Legislators would approve on condition of sharing the proceeds. For greater convenience the "Carolina Company" was replaced by the "Republican Printing Company", the latter consisting of clerks Woodruff and Jones, who could then contract with themselves. These arrangements entailed upon Josephus the burden of manufacturing the claims, collecting and disbursing them to the "Wolves". As may be imagined, his life was hell upon earth. A record of his woes he kept in a Diary, fragments of which have been preserved for the gaiety of nations. As the recipient of innumerable and sundry billet-doux from statesmen demanding their price, he became known to fame as "Dear" Josephus.

As to this printing business the Frauds Commission and Josephus will speak. Says the Commission:

"The vast sum of $385,866.99 was paid to State officers and Legislators as bribes and in contributions to the two Republican Newspapers. For the year 1872-1873 the public printing cost the State $450,000.00 exceeding the cost of like work in Massachusetts, New York, Pennsylvania, Ohio and Maryland combined by $122,932.13. In two years the State printing bill reached the colossal sum of $835,000.00."

Among the beneficiaries of this fund the receipts show items such as: Governor Moses, $20,000.00; Whittemore, $5,000.00; and to the members of the Legislature from Kershaw items ranging from $40.00 to $500.00.

The following are random items from the Diary of Dear Josephus:

"This Legislature has a hard set. I expect to be the most unpopular man going now. To disburse money and not be able to save any as it goes through is pretty rough on Josephus.

Jones agrees to pay Neagle $10,000.00 more.

Suppose by the time the Legislature adjourns the wolves will scent more keenly for Jones and Woodruff. They are all a set of damned wolves. I suppose they will unite against us for blood."

But the half has not been told. We will let the Frauds Investigating Committee report upon the subject of supplies, or "Gratifications": "History fails to cite an instance which can be compared with such a carnival of fraud and extravagance as has been held in South Carolina by and through the purchase of supplies for the members of the General Assembly. We not only make the assertion but present the proofs, substantiated by evidence no one can doubt. If the statement were made that members of the Senate and House were furnished everything from cradle to coffin, brogans to chignons, finest extracts, wines and liquors, all paid for by the State, it would create a smile of doubt and derision. But when we prove it by witnesses and the records themselves, all will with sorrow admit the truth.

"Supplies were furnished under the head of "Legislative expenses, sundries and stationery" and included groceries, horses, carriages, dry goods and furniture of every description. Vouchers in the Treasury show expended under this head in one session exceeding three hundred and fifty thousand dollars ($350,000.00).

"A room in the State House was fitted up wherein were served eatables, wines and cigars to Legislators and friends at all hours of the night. This room was visited by Judges, lawyers, editors and citizens generally, irrespective of party. The porter says the best cigars and wine were served, and that he could not keep a supply on hand as many visitors filled their pockets with cigars and often carried off a bottle of wine.

"We find paid out within four years for furniture for the State House over two hundred thousand dollars

($200,000.00), of which there is on hand only seventeen thousand dollars worth. Committee rooms were furnished every session. As soon as the Assembly adjourned the furniture would disappear. Members who received only six dollars per day furnished their rooms with Brussels carpets and oriental spring mattresses. Sixty-eight thousand dollars ($68,000.00) was paid out for stationery in one session, which cost not more than two thousand ($2,000.00) dollars. Gold pens at ten dollars each, finest pocket knives and jewelry were all dispensed at expense of the State."

The bills rendered for these supplies were by the facetious clerk, Osceola, filed as "Queer Accounts"; by Josephus as "Myths". Another item from the Diary of Josephus will serve as a sample of many: "Collected certificate for $945.00 and paid Hayden for Whittemore's watch. Gracious Goodness! Whittemore will have somewhere about ten thousand dollars this session. That ought to be satisfactory. He is always after more."

Elected to Congress from our District in 1868, Whittemore once frequented Camden where he was a familiar figure. He came as Chaplain of the 30th Massachusetts, a detachment of which garrisoned this town. Of fine physique, flowing beard and resonant voice, he exerted great power over his colored audiences. For selling cadetships he was expelled from Congress, was again returned at a special election, but was again rejected upon motion of General Logan. His Constituency then elected him to the State Senate from Darlington County where he had taken up his abode.

Justus K. Jillson appeared in Camden about 1866, in connection with the Freedman's Bureau. In 1869 along with F. J. Moses, Thos. J. Robertson and others he was a member of the Board of Trustees of the South Carolina College. This board ordered that colored students be admitted to domicile and dine together with the whites, which resulted in the college remaining closed for some years. Jillson was among the very few carpetbaggers against whom corruption was neither discovered nor alleged.

The Tax Payers Convention again met in February 1874 and prepared a memorial to the authorities at Washington setting forth the monstrous grievances of the State Government. General Kershaw was one of the

Committee entrusted to present this memorial. The Committee waited upon General Grant, receiving cold comfort. One whose memory is excellent assures us that a report of the interview was published in one of the newspapers of that time to the effect that when Grant met the Committee he curtly remarked: "Be brief, I am sick."

Symptoms of the coming storm of popular wrath can now be discerned. Such we rate the following from James R. Magill, of Russell Place, afterwards Senator from Kershaw County, in the *Camden Journal* of July 16, 1874:

"To your tents O Israel".

"Nine long wearisome years you have borne with patience the hand of the oppressor. Wrongs unparalleled in the annals of history have been inflicted upon you. Your endurance in peace has equaled your valor in war. You must no longer call (and call in vain) on Hercules to rive your fetters. You must meet the issue fairly and no longer offer to compromise with thieves. There is no compromise between truth and falsehood. Let our orators take the field and with burning words of eloquence urge the people to action."

The profligate Moses must have scented danger in the breeze. For on a moonlight night in August as he, Honest John Patterson and others of the Ring, sat at the Governor's table, the sound of horns and clattering hoofs came from the distance. The rumor started that the Ku-Klux were coming. The Governor and party expecting to be visited took panic and hurriedly ordered out the militia to discover that fox hunters just across the Congaree River were the cause of alarm.

The Radicals in September 1874, after a bitter fight, nominated Dan'l H. Chamberlain for Governor, over one John T. Green, by a vote of 73 to 40. The following glimpse of that Convention is from the *Camden Journal* of September 17.

"There sat John J. Patterson, derisively named Honest John, with villany and astuteness written all over his Pecksniffian face, lieutenanted by Bigamy Bowen, Oily Elliott, deceitful Cardozo, the pious Whittemore, and impudent Tim Hurley, whose pomposity is on a par with his huge proportions; and lesser satellites, reminding one of a solemn conclave of buzzards holding counsel over a carcass. These vultures were of course for Chamberlain, who is cold, shrewd and calculating. Patterson knows his man and woe to South Carolina if he is elected."

The minority Radical faction bolted and nominated John T. Green for Governor on what they called the "Independent Republican" ticket. The Taxpayers Convention, at call of General Chesnut, in October (1874) decided to support Green. Again the compromise policy was adopted. General Kershaw, who had entered the field for Congress from this District, was called before the Convention and enthusiastically received. General Chesnut made an address, the tenor of which will appear from this brief specimen:

"If the Republican Convention now in session will place in nomination a man of intelligence and integrity I for one will consent and will advise that there be no counter nomination. If honest men are put in the field for office we do not intend to oppose them, no matter where they come from or by whom nominated."

Between 1868 and 1876 Chesnut and Kershaw were the political leaders of the State. It fell to them to thoroughly test and prove the futility of the Compromise and Fusion policies. They had to grope in the dark, amid hopeless conditions, until the time was ripe for the bugle call to a "Straightout" struggle.

The following analysis of Chamberlain is from the pen of L. W. R. Blair, in the *Kershaw Gazette* of September 23, 1874, which he then edited:

"As usual the friends of the Republican nominee (Chamberlain) are busy putting the sheep skin of private purity upon their wolf. We have no desire to impugn their testimony, nor to assail the private character of that gentleman. His private life may be blameless. His public record is certainly bad enough for any assailant. Since his *avatar* into the politics of this unhappy state, he has been prominently connected with the most corrupt government that ever existed.

"Has he not simply taken the place of Moses as the gonfalonier of the same thieving and plundering horde? Is the horde less corrupt today than it was two years ago when Moses was chosen as the standard bearer? And can Mr. Chamberlain hope, as the chief of this horde, to carry his private integrity (if he has any) into his public administration? If an arch-angel of purity and wisdom could be entrapped into such a position by a conclave of "Honest Johns" his high endowments could not serve him otherwise than prompt him to "git" up and "git" out of such a connection."

In the election of 1874 the vote for Governor resulted, Chamberlain, 80,403, Green, 68,818. General Kershaw was defeated for Congress by "Buttermilk" Wallace, the vote standing: Wallace, 16,445, Kershaw, 14,439. Well do we remember the storms of jeers and execration that drowned out "Buttermilk" when he attempted to speak in Camden from the porch of the old DeKalb Hotel which then stood on the corner where the Post Office is now situated. Regular Radicals, all colored, were elected to the Legislature from this County, viz.: Frank Carter, R. D. Gaither, Senator; Stephen Gary and Eben George, Representatives. Of the 2,088 colored voters in the County, 1,983 voted the regular Radical ticket. "Fusion" brought over not more than 100 to the cause of "Reform".

Chamberlain was the brains of the Ring which preyed upon the State, possessed of really first rate ability, indicated by a towering bald head. His diction, spoken and written, was finished and lucid. By professing purity and assailing corruption, he deluded many of the best white citizens to believe that to support him would be the surest way to rescue the State. The following is a clause from his inaugural address:

"The work which lies before us is serious beyond that which falls to the lot of most generations of men. It is nothing less than the re-establishment of society in this state upon the foundation of absolute equality of civil and political rights. The evils attending our first steps in this work have drawn upon us the frowns of the whole world. If we who are here today shall fail in our duty others more honest and capable will be called to our places. Through us or through others freedom and justice will bear sway in South Carolina."

His policy evidently was, while adhering to the Radical organization, by cauterizing its flagrant corruption, to win over a large element of whites to his support. His culture and intellect must have recoiled from the gross depravity of his associates. Many of the leading white citizens believed him honest and sincere, and some still do, despite the exposures of the Frauds Investigating Committee.

RECONSTRUCTION AND RED SHIRTS

The Legislature of 1874-1875 elected R. B. Elliott, Speaker, of lustrous black hue, superb physique, acknowledged as ablest of the negro politicians. It is proven that he took $10,000.00 bribe money in the Bowen impeachment swindle.

The "Big Bonanza" and "Little Bonanza" Bills distinguished this session, two measures passed over the veto of Chamberlain, validating certificates issued in payment of notoriously fraudulent claims, to the amount of a million dollars or more, in excess of funds in the Treasury and held by the minions of the Ring. The *Daily Union*, Chamberlain's organ, characterized the Bonanza Bills as "schemes of plunderers led by C. P. Leslie." Thompson, the editor, was arraigned before the House for publishing these uncomplimentary remarks. After some parley he was released.

The year 1875 was full of ominous incidents. The home of General Butler was burned by an incendiary, one Ned Tenant, who confessed. His arrest led to riotous resistance by the negro military company which he commanded. Hardy Solomon's Bank at Columbia, which throve like a mushroom by shaving "claims", failed with loss of a large amount of State funds. Joe Crews was shot and killed from ambush on the highway in Laurens.

Possibly the lowest stage of degredation was reached when in December the Legislature elected as Judges ex-Governor Moses and Whipper, the latter a negro. No comment could exceed in severity that of Governor Chamberlain. Said he:

"Their election has sent a thrill of horror through the whole State. It is a disaster to the State and Republican party—a calamity infinitely greater than any which has yet fallen on this State or any part of the South. Unless the universal belief among all classes of the people in this State is mistaken, he (Moses) is as infamous a character as ever in any age disgraced and prostituted a public position. Of Whipper it can be said that he seems to have lacked only opportunity to prove himself the equal of Moses in infamy."

At a public meeting in Sumter, Moses' home, Mr. Moise spoke as follows: "Should F. J. Moses, Jr. by any legal trickery attempt to ascend the steps of the Court House to take his seat as Judge, I am ready to unite with any band of men and with muskets defend that temple of justice from such desecration."

Chamberlain refused to commission Moses and Whipper, on the ground of illegality in their election. In this position he was sustained by the State Supreme Court, the Chief Justice of which was Franklin J. Moses, Sr., father of the notorious Junior. The father's integrity was never impugned.

By such bold strokes Chamberlain gained the cordial support of a great many white citizens.

The crucial year 1876 opens with leaders of the whites still leaning to "Fusion". The Democratic State Committee in January issued a call for the formation of precinct clubs, proclaiming, among other things, that:

"The Committee recognize and appreciate the value of what Governor Chamberlain has done in promoting reform and retrenchment during the past year, and applaud his conduct in undoing the infamous judicial election."

At a County Convention held at Camden in January, largely attended, General Chesnut, Chairman, Colonel W. M. Shannon introduced this resolution:

"We cordially endorse and approve the manly, patriotic course of his Excellency, Gov. Chamberlain, regarding Moses and Whipper, and also his general administration. We join hearts and hands with him in rising above party and give him assurance of earnest and admiring support.

This resolution was seconded by General Kershaw, advocated by General Kennedy and unanimously adopted by the Convention. Yet the following letter to the *Camden Journal* better voices the real sentiment of Kershaw County, than the above unanimous resolution:

"Tillers Ferry, S. C., April 4th, 1876.

As the call to organize "precinct Democratic Clubs" has apparently been unheeded by us in this locality I thought I would give you some of the reasons. In the first place we are "straight-outs", and the journals we read have not advocated that line, and those who are the leaders hint at "Chamberlain and coalition". Now, sirs, if you want Lynche's Creek to fall in just raise an unmixed, unadulterated Democratic war cry; and we are in. Does not the past teach us that it is the only policy? In a caolition scheme it is plain we will be beaten if we win and beaten if we lose. Shall we swap our chances of ruling the State for a political partnership that will still leave us in a wretched condition? Answer now! Choose this day whom you will serve. There are those who would bow at the feet of Chamberlain. I advise all such to look up some newspaper of two years ago, read the editorials and speeches then made about this same saint, prophet, god, Chamberlain. So far as I know he has done more for his party and less for the people than Moses.

Some say all this is a beautiful theory; and that it is right if we could do it, but we can't. Well, I say, if it is just and right and beautiful, it will win *if we try*. *We do not know that it would not win, we have not tried it.* Would to God I were competent and had the power to ring out these sentiments so loud that they could be heard from seaboard to the mountains, till every son of old South Carolina would be waked up to the issues at stake.

STRAIGHTOUT."

On the strength of the foregoing utterance and that of "J. R. M." above quoted we claim Kershaw County as first and foremost in the "Straightout" movement.

The Democratic State Convention of May (1876), General Kershaw, presiding, hesitated to cross the Rubicon. The delegates from this County were J. B. Kershaw, J. D. Kennedy, W. D. Trantham, L. C. Thompson, W. L. DePass. The following resolution was offered by General Gary:

"That the Democratic party of South Carolina, when they make nominations put a Straightout ticket in the field." This was defeated, 70 to 42. Not even yet such men as Kershaw and Hampton could discern the signs, else they would not have so discouraged mention of their names as candidates for Governor in a straight fight of white against black plus the Federal bayonet—an apparently hopeless experiment likely to involve wholesale bloodshed.

July 4 marks the turning point. At Hamburg, opposite Augusta (now North Augusta), as two white men on that day were driving through the town, they were held up by a company of colored militia, cursing and rattling a drum at their horse's head. Doc Adams, the captain, and several of the men were arrested. A crowd gathered for the trial. General Butler tried to induce the accused to apologize and avoid trouble. The militia were defiant and gathered at their armory. Fighting ensued. The militia volleyed, killing young McKee Merriwether. A small piece of artillery brought hastily from Augusta was opened on the armory, which brought the inmates out. Five were captured and executed.

Chamberlain in a public address termed the Hamburg affair a "Massacre". In a bitter reply Butler said: "Many things were done on this terrible night which cannot be justified, but the negroes sowed the wind and reaped the whirlwind."

Hamburg was decisive. Even then however in the Democratic State Convention of August 66 votes were cast by "Conservatives" against 80 by the "Straightouts"—The delegates from Kershaw were W. L. DePass, J. Duncan Shaw and L. B. Stephenson, all straightout. With wild acclaim, General Hampton was named for Governor. From that moment the whites became cemented, and the zeal of "Conservative" or "Coalitionists" was not less frantic than that of the "Straightouts". Hampton's word became absolute, and fortunate it was, for his counsel of restraint and forbearance alone prevented a general massacre. Such was narrowly averted in the Ellenton riot, in September, where two whites and fifteen negroes were killed; and at Cainhoy, in October, when the negroes from ambush killed six and wounded sixteen white men at a political meeting.

Chamberlain on September 13, was renominated for Governor by his party and along with him, despite his opposition, three negroes: Elliott for Attorney General, Cardozo for Treasurer, and Haynes for Secretary of State, all tainted with rankest fraud and bribery. The course of events had driven Chamberlain into the arms of the gang whom he had flayed unmercifully, and into reliance upon the negro vote alone. The only alternative was his defeat and retirement, which his vaulting ambition could not brook. To keep the skeletons in his closet covered also required him to fight for control in his party. His scruples had to be thrown to the winds. Resourceful and wiley, backed by Federal bayonets and a heavy negro majority, with election machinery in his hands, the chances were all in his favor and the Straightouts faced a thorny proposition.

The whites now armed and organized Rifle Clubs. Conditions then existing cannot be better stated than in the following address by the Tax Payers Union:

## Reconstruction and Red Shirts

"A conflict of races has only been avoided by the uniform forbearance of the Whites, from a regard for peace and good order and a desire to avoid conflict with the Federal authorities.

"The negro is taught to consider the Rifle Clubs lately formed for social and defensive purposes, the evidence of incipient rebellion. The fact that almost the entire militia of the State are negroes and white companies have not been accepted by the State authorities may have caused this opinion.

"The negro militia are commanded by turbulent officers, are armed with fire arms, and abundantly supplied with ball cartridges, as if their services in actual conflict might any day be required.

"The negro is taught to believe that the whites design not only to deprive him of the right of suffrage, but even to reduce him to his original condition of slavery. He is taught to regard the U. S. Troops as intended to keep down the Whites.

"The carpetbaggers, by which term we mean the dishonest political adventurers who now infest the State, by incendiary speeches inflame the blacks against any of their own color who dare to vote, as they call it, against their race."

On October 7 Governor Chamberlain issued proclamation that "combinations in all counties of the State known as 'Rifle Clubs' engaged in committing open acts of lawlessness are illegal and strictly forbidden by laws of the State", ordered all such to disband in three days and declared that State and Federal forces would be used to compel obedience.

The Democratic Committee rejoined that the Governor's sole object was "to provoke collisions as excuse for appeal to the Federal garrisons in the State. We shall appeal to our people to keep the peace, observe the law and calmly await the day of their deliverance."

On October 9 Chamberlain issued an address to the people of the United States, asserting that "the lawlessness, terrorism and violence far exceeded in extent and atrocity any statement yet made public." At the same time he appealed to President Grant for aid in "suppressing domestic violence in the State." The President issued an order that all "combinations and unlawful assemblages disperse to their homes," and General W. T. Sherman transferred all available troops into this State. The Democratic Committee published the following ironical response to these orders and proclamations:

HISTORIC CAMDEN

"We cannot disperse because we are not gathered together. We cannot retire peacably to our homes because we are in our homes in peace, disturbed alone by the political agitation created by the Governor and his minions.

"The 'Rifle Clubs' are associations formed for home protection. The politicians who are the authors of all our evils are teaching the colored race the use of the rifle and torch, we know that our homes are in peril and our women and children exposed to the horrors of ruthless butchery and barbarity."

The "Rifle Clubs" disbanded in appearance only. Their name was changed to "Democratic Precinct Clubs", the membership of which embraced every white male able to ride horseback and use a gun. Their arms they kept well concealed and accessible.

Some one now unknown, doubtless recalling Garibaldi, suggested a Red Shirt for these clubs. The idea took. It is said the Club of Geo. D. Tillman in Edgefield first wore it. The story is told that when a member of his club turned out in white homespun shirt, Tillman gathered poke-berries and daubed him red.

We venture to assert that this State has never before nor since been so highly wrought as in 1876. Hampton was received in every county with unparelleled ovations. When he reached Camden, rusty old Revolutionary cannon were mounted and thundered on the Park named in his honor on DeKalb Street between Lyttleton and Fair. On the occasion of Chamberlain's visit, throngs of negroes packed the sidewalks, and between these dark lanes, defiantly rode endless columns of mounted Red Shirts, gathered from this and all adjoining counties. Perfect bedlam reigned for hours. In his public speeches General Hampton recorded this pledge:

"In the presence of the people of South Carolina and in the presence of my God I pledge myself that if elected I shall know no party, no race, no color or condition in the administration of the laws."

At request of the Democratic State Committee, October 26 was observed as a day of prayer for redemption of the State and all business places were closed.

On election day, November 7, whites and blacks struggled madly for possession of the polls.

The whites would mass at the ballot box and strive to bar off the blacks, which led to a tug of war that lasted from day-break until dark, without interference from the Federal soldiers camped within rifle range. In most rural districts, however, the whites were too heavily outnumbered to use these tactics to any advantage.

By the utmost efforts and every known device, the State was carried for Hampton by only thirteen hundred and twenty-three (1,323) on the face of the returns. The day would have been lost had not Georgians crossed the Savannah on Election Day and joined the men of Abbeville, Aiken, Anderson and Edgefield Counties. As good news came over the wires that night Camden went into ecstasy. Barrels of rosin blazed in huge bonfires at every street corner; men embraced and leapt for joy. Not since Israel passed the Red Sea did such Hosannahs ascend.

But further probation was to be endured. Election returns were disputed, fraud and intimidation charged. The presidential election turned on the result in South Carolina. A dual State Government was organized. Federal soldiers filled the State House upholding Chamberlain. Red Shirts massed in Columbia to seat Hampton, and "Hunkidori" roughs marshaled to support Chamberlain. This dangerous tension, lasting for weeks, was finally composed. Federal Troops were withdrawn and Hampton took undisputed possession April 10, 1877, with a Legislature Democratic by one majority.

Half the counties of the State were still unredeemed. At Washington the "bloody shirt", and the red shirt in South Carolina, were rampant for another campaign. Division threatened to arise between the whites. Some original Straightouts took umbrage at seeing former "Conservatives" reap the rewards of offices. Some were bitter at what they deemed the "aristocratic" tendency of Hampton's administration. To quell this incipient revolt, General Hampton proclaimed:

"An Independent is worse than a Radical. He who sets up his individual opinion, and refuses to act in full accord with our platform is an independent."

This dictum became the political creed of South Carolina Democracy, and solidarity of the whites has since remained as an inflexible law and its violation the unpardonable political sin. Among the few who refused to surrender their individual views was Major L. W. R.

Blair. During 1874-1875 and 1876 his editorials in the *Kershaw Gazette* were marked by a virile and pithy style, always straightest of the straightout.

In December 1875 he wrote: "Is it not true that every white man should cease to talk this fusion gibberish? Credulous Conservatives must open their eyes to the fact that one or the other of the two races must rule the State of South Carolina."

In August 1876 he wrote: "Between the white man and the negro nature has imposed the impassable barrier of race; but to compensate for this she has woven between the two in this country the ties of a common interest. White and black are mutually dependent upon each other, and should respect, honor and observe the rights of each other."

After the over-turn of 1876 he doubtless felt that his services and ability were ignored in favor of former "Conservatives", a common grievance in politics. From his home at Paint Hill, where he depended on a small farm to support a large family, in those days a hard problem, he continued to expound his views in the Camden papers. He had always favored the Greenback doctrine, which had utterly been obscured in this State by local issues prior to 1877. The National Democracy was not harmonious on the subject. In South Carolina, the Democrats declared for "hard money", and the Greenback doctrine was condemned as heresy. Blair would not retract nor dissemble. At public meetings he would advocate his ideas, and in return was jeered as Independent! Radical! On one occasion jogging muleback through the main street in Camden, he was followed and hooted by a party of young men on horse-back. He made no reply whatsoever to these taunts of his persecutors.

About this time also an acute issue arose in the State over the Stock law, which from earliest days, allowed cattle to roam and required crops to be fenced. The right of pasturage was immemorial and vital to that sandy region in which Blair had been born and raised, and which composed the greater part of Kershaw County. Around Blair, as exponent of free pasturage and greenbacks, gathered quite a number of white supporters. These followers in a State Convention at Chester in 1880 made bold to put him forth as an *Independent* Candidate for Governor, with David C. Gist of York for Lieutenant

Governor. This ticket was supported by the solid negro element and by a small band of whites in each county.

Was Blair elected? It is only certain that the returns showed otherwise, and that ballot boxes were stuffed with tissue ballots against him—regarded then as proper means to defeat any one supported by the negro voters.

As the leading Independent in the State, he continued to be the object of violent attacks in the public print. The following is from one of his rejoinders in the *Camden Journal* of March 1882:

"The bugbear of negro supremacy is as groundless and absurd as the raw head and bloody bones with which crafty nurses frighten ignorant children. The fact is notorious that the negroes never did rule South Carolina; even in the darkest period of radicalism she was ruled by a few cunning and unscrupulous white men."

"As for the negro, his inferiority to the white man is universally conceded; yet with his acknowledged inferiority he has been endowed by his Maker and invested by the American people with the franchise of an American citizen. Of these no human power can lawfully deprive him, and the white man who would do it by fraud sinks far beneath the average negro in degredation. Now is there any reason to desire that he should be deprived of any rights or franchise? His interests are the same with the interests of the mass of the white citizens. Both must live by labor and self exertion; and so surely as the weaker follows the stronger, the negro will follow the lead and counsel of the white man as soon as the latter wins by deserving his confidence.

"This has not yet been done or attempted. On the contrary, though we swore solemnly with Hampton only six years ago that if we came into power all his rights should be sacredly respected, our legislature passes a registration and election law framed purposely to defraud more than half of the colored citizens of their vote."

Whether by his wish or not, he became a Moses to the negroes. The rankle of persecution doubtless led him to tolerate their support. He had come to be ostracised by all orthodox Democrats. On July 4, 1882 the streets of Camden were crowded. At the southwest corner of Rutledge and Broad, where there was then a vacant lot, in the midst of a throng of darkies, the white head and beard of L. W. R. Blair could be seen towering above the black mass. Before sun down that day he lay dead on

Rutledge Street pierced by five bullets from a rifle fired by Captain Jas. L. Haile. That evening he was taken to his home on "Paint Hill", wearing a shirt red with his own blood. Never was home more sorely stricken. In a spectacular trial Haile was acquitted—a foregone conclusion. There was testimony to the effect that Blair had advanced upon Haile apparently with hostile intent, with right hand in the breast of his coat, an attitude however, quite customary with him. It was believed by Blair's friends that his doom had been decreed at a political conference.

A few weeks after the foregoing event, the body of young Rochella Blair was found at the foot of the "precipice" at Paint Hill. Beside it a phial of white powder, marked "strychnine", told the story. The cause—grief at her father's death. The *Camden Journal* of August 31, 1882, relates over the appropriate caption: "A sad scene realized", that, being gifted as an artist, she had shortly before painted a scene, picturing the figure of a girl lying dead at that very spot, surrounded by three "hovering angels".

## CHAPTER XIX.

### THE IRON MAN.

In September 1804 the grand jury made presentment as follows: "We the grand Jurors for Kershaw District Present as a grievance the prevalence of Dueling; which contrary to all law Human and Divine, sweeps off many useful citizens. We present as a grievance the want of Public Schools throughout the State.

BURWELL BOYKIN,
Foreman."

Exploring still further into the past we find traces of some of those grievances alluded to by the Grand Jury, doubtless but samples of many similar instances lost in oblivion. Earliest and bloodiest recorded was the duel between Jacob Brown and Thomas Baker, found among the inquest papers of 1789. As an introduction to the principals it may be stated that Jacob Brown and his brother Daniel[1] appear to have been the first attorneys resident in Camden. The accomplishments of Baker in rowdyism will appear from the following affidavit of one John Havis (who was afterwards jailer at Camden), found in the old Court House rubbish:

"That on April 17th last (1788) he was in the house of Joseph Quarell, tavern keeper, in Fairfield County, setting in the porch, when he was violently assaulted by Capt. Thomas Baker, and kicked, knocked down and beaten and his ear dangerously bitten by him. And although James Douglas and John Bigham pulled deponent from under said Baker, he was a second time thrown down by him, violently beaten and both his eyes gouged, one in so dangerous a manner, that deponent has not recovered the full use thereof. Deponent alleges all this done without any provocation whatever given by him." James Douglas deposes that he saw John Havis beaten and gouged as aforesaid; that in the second encounter he could not pull Baker off as they were so closely engaged, "the thumb of the said Baker being in the mouth of the said John Havis."

[1] Daniel Brown was a graduate of Harvard.

HISTORIC CAMDEN

In April 1789 Jacob Brown swears out a peace warrant against the said Baker. A month later they made corpses of each other. From the old inquest papers we detail the following particulars. A challenge was sent by Baker to Brown, who was attending Court at Winnsboro. They met on the race course at Camden, Thursday morning, May 28th, 1789. Standing back to back, each stepped five paces, turned and fired, each receiving mortal wounds. Baker died in half hour; Brown that night. The "race course" in those days surrounded an area extending from the Court Inn to the Methodist Church and Hampton Park. Benjamin Carter acted as Brown's second, David Evans as Baker's.

The old files contain some details of another tragedy of this sort, reciting briefly that on the 24th day of April 1812, Timothy Spann "came to his death in consequence of a wound received by a shot in a duel with a certain Lavall and that a certain Doctor Gill and a certain Mayrant were seconds and that said duel took place this day about two miles below Camden." Signed, John Doby, foreman, Joseph Mickle, Coroner.

Captain James I. Villepigue told us of the tradition that as Lavall, wounded in the hip, was in the act of falling, Spann made some exulting exclamation, whereupon Lavall fired and hit Spann in the forehead, killing him instantly. He also stated that the scene of this affair was just a little east of the Taylor field, and was pointed out to him by General Chesnut.

Seldom has heavier news reached Camden than that of the fall of young Henry G. Nixon in the fatal duel with Thos. A. Hopkins in 1829. No native of the town, where he was born February 10, 1800, has ever been such a darling of the community. Mention of him will be found in various other portions of this volume. The granite wall enclosure surmounted by iron railing, at the rear of the old Presbyterian Cemetery, foot of Church Street, marks the place of his interment. This lamentable event occurred at the notorious Sand Bar Ferry near Augusta on January 15, 1829. An extra of the *Camden Journal* of the 17th contains the intelligence in these words: "With the sensation of unmingled horror do we perform the task this morning of announcing the death of Colonel Henry G. Nixon. He fell in a duel at one o'clock P. M. on Thursday last (15th) with Maj. Thos. Hopkins of this district. Nixon at the first fire received the ball of his antagonist in the right breast, and fell instantaneously dead, his own pistol going off harmlessly, while in the struggle of death. We have this moment conversed with Maj. McWillie, who with Ex-Gov. John L. Wilson acted as Col. Nixon's friend upon the ground. He states the conduct of the parties to have been in strict accordance with the laws of *honor* in such cases. Nixon sustained himself in the firmest manner. The corpse of poor Nixon arrived at Welsh's hotel in this town at 7 o'clock this morning."

"We have no time to give more particulars of this heart-rending affair, nor can we trust our feelings to do so, for he was our friend, and the present is a scene calculated to freeze up the sources of the heart. We say nothing of the grounds of the fatal controversy, but we feel deeply, deeply feel the event, and so does every citizen of the town. In the morning of life, and while his friends and his native state were anticipating the ripening honors which a vigorous and cultivated intellect had just budded forth, Henry Nixon is a cold and lifeless corpse."

"P. S. We have this moment seen a letter from Gov. Wilson to the father of the deceased and subjoin this paragraph: 'There was an incident of the contest I cannot fail to record. After your son received the most deadly and severe wound, he fired his pistol, and keeping erect, grasped the other pistol and died in the attitude of manly resistance and determined purpose of character. In life and death he was noble, brave, magnanimous'."

What was the cause of this duel? The *Charleston Gazette*, in publishing an account of the tragedy, said: "The dispute is said to have been one of long standing, originating in political competition." Very likely the origin is traceable to a lawsuit entered in 1824 by Elizabeth Hopkins (nee English) and her children, of whom Thos. A. Hopkins was one, against Wm. Nixon, father of Henry G. Nixon, for recovery of a valuable tract of land of which, they charge, Wm. Nixon had defrauded them. The attorneys in the case were ranged somewhat according to political lines of the day, John Carter and S. D. Miller representing the Hopkins, Chapman Levy and Wm. McWillie the Nixons.

In 1828 the case ended in favor of the Hopkins. The duel followed soon after. Hopkins was two years younger than Nixon, a rival for military honors, for in 1827 he was elected Major of militia. Nixon was on Governor Wilson's Staff, with rank of Colonel.

Bits of tradition have come down to the following effect; that the immediate *casus belli* was a critical remark of Nixon regarding the manoeuvers of Hopkins' regiment; that Hopkins, cool of nerve, slept soundly the night before the duel, while others of the party were up late carousing; that Nixon, quite a dude, wore a fancy coat, with the white of his handkerchief showing from the breast pocket, on seeing which Hopkins exclaimed: "The man has marked his heart for me to hit"; that Nixon, some say Hopkins, practised upon a tombstone in the Quaker Cemetery, head piece at the grave of "Neil Smith, merchant, and his wife Mary McLehose," bearing date 1822. Upon the back of it may still be seen pit marks as of bullets.

In "Sabine's Notes on Duelling" we find this item concerning the Nixon-Hopkins duel: "A gentleman at Augusta said in a letter to a correspondent: 'We had a show here two or three days ago. A party from Camden came here to fight a duel, and, after preparing themselves, went to the ground at noonday, through Broad Street with as much parade as if Lafayette had been coming, carriages, gigs, sulkies and horsemen following to witness the bloody deed. One of the combatants was killed instantly, the other ran as hard as he could to the river and crossed. The magistrates were close after to arrest him, and contemplated petitioning Gov. Forsyth to demand the gentleman from the Governor of South Carolina. The late Governor of that State was second to the deceased."

A sorrowful concourse attended Nixon's funeral January 18.[1] The Camden Bar met and published memorial resolutions drafted by Wm. B. Hart, Chapman Levy, Jno. M. DeSaussure, Wm. J. Grant, and C. F. Daniels. From a tribute which appeared in the *Camden Journal* the following is extracted:

---

[1] Captain Villepigue told us that as a boy he attended this funeral, he being so small that his father held him up for a last look at Nixon's face in the casket.

"His was a character which had sunk deep into all our hearts. At the early age of twenty-eight he had attained to a distinction and influence in the councils of our state which ordinary talents could not have acquired, and which is usually the reward of a long and arduous probation.

"The estimation of his services, which promised to extend to extraordinary usefulness with the increase of years, pervaded every portion of the State. The powers of rapid conception, a fruitful imagination and an extraordinary fluency eminently qualified him for the station to which he had been repeatedly elevated.

"The external graces of the orator he possessed to an unusual degree. Animated and vehement in gesture and delivery, his manner was admirably adapted to the strength and enterprise of his intellect. His ambition was an elevated passion, the burning impulse of a young and noble spirit. There was established in the public mind a confidence in his talents and integrity which every day strengthened.

"He was eminently strict in the performance of duty, and scrupulously observant of the moral obligations of life."

To this testimonial may be added the words of the celebrated Mrs. Anne Royall, who came to Camden in 1830:

"I have already remarked that a friend of mine, Henry G. Nixon, fell in a duel not long since. This gentleman was not only the pride of Camden, but the pride of mankind. Beloved he lived and lamented he died. He was polished, humane and generous as a prince, admired by all who knew him. The tear of the widow and orphan flowed for his fate. Alas that such a fate awaited such worth; cut off in the bloom of youth. My friends anticipating my wishes ordered the driver to proceed to the grave. The pang that wrung my heart, as my eyes rested upon the fresh looking earth, may easily be imagined."

Of Wm. Nixon the father she writes: "I mingled my tears with his. Oh, how I felt for him. I handed him a bottle of essence to revive him. He is still a young looking man, with a face of singular sweetness and expression. He is of good size, with a full, soft, black eye, round face, arched brow, his features without fault."

In 1832 this father erected around his son's grave the enclosing wall of granite with iron railing, above mentioned. It is said the only burial in the enclosure is that of Henry G. Nixon.

Hopkins soon followed Nixon to the grave. He rapidly pined away with grief. He lies at the old Swift Creek Church, ten miles below Camden. A stone slab marks the spot, which may be seen in the grove to the left of the public road, near Boykins Mill pond. A tree fell across the stone breaking it in half, but the following inscription is still legible on the fragments:

To the memory of<br>
THOMAS A. HOPKINS<br>
Who was born 29th Aug. 1803<br>
and died 10th Sept. 1831.

Fortunately we can subjoin here something on this subject from Colonel Shannon's pen, the more valuable as coming from contemporary sources. Says he: "Amid the stir and excitement of party strife, the hot blood of partizans, particularly among the young, produced frequent difficulties. One fatal duel resulted, that between Col. Henry G. Nixon and Mr. Thos. Hopkins, both young men of high position, each with many friends, and each regarded as somewhat representative of his party. Col. Nixon was one of the most gifted young men of the State. He was talented, sensitive and ambitious. Gentle and courteous to his friends, but haughty, dictatorial and overbearing to his foes, he was pledged to a series of duels when he fell dead on the field, under the unerring aim of the cool and imperturbable Thos. Hopkins. They were both fine specimens of elegant manhood. Hopkins was easy, graceful and much beloved by his friends and his very large family connections. He was a remarkable shot and felt confident that he would kill Nixon, was as amiable as he was brave, and would if it had been possible have avoided the issue forced upon him. We have often heard Col. Nixon's friends who stood to him through all his trials, even those who stood by him on the fatal field say, that Hopkins' whole conduct on the field was unexceptionable, perfectly self-possessed and cool. But his was a generous and noble spirit; he turned from that field a saddened man, and scarce a year had passed when he too, slept with his fathers.

## The Iron Man

"Col. Henry G. Nixon was succeeded (in the legislature) by his younger brother, Col. Wm. O. Nixon. Either of them would have filled a place in the Senate House of the United States in its palmy days, or would have graced positions in the highest Courts, to which our ministers are accredited.

" 'I have seen the cedars fall
And in their room a mushroom grow'."

The crude figure at the head of this chapter represents an old relic which has fortunately survived its former usage. It suggested the title for this chapter.

Its history is well authenticated. About the year 1845, when knighthood was in full flower, an encounter was pending between two Camden hotspurs, Colonel James P. Dickinson and Major John Smart. No published accounts of this affair have been found, and such as we here present are derived from conversations with aged contemporaries of those events.

Jim Lang, the faithful negro servant of Dickinson, told us that his master, in practising for the duel, had this figure wrought from iron as a target; that it was made just the size of Smart's side view; that he (Jim) procured metal from Matheson's store, then on the northwest corner of York and Broad Streets, and carried it to Shiver's blacksmith shop where the image was fashioned.

As related to us by Major E. B. Cantey, an exchange of shots between James Cantey of Camden and Pride of Chester had been narrowly averted by adjustment on the field. Dickinson, who had acted as Cantey's second, returning to Camden told Smart that a settlement had been reached very favorable to Cantey, but that Cantey had no fight in him, and had to be braced up by his seconds, or words to that effect. This Smart reported to Cantey, who demanded of Dickinson an explanation. Dickinson replied that Smart had told a "damned lie". Thereupon Smart challenged Dickinson, and they met in West Wateree in the vicinity of Lugoff.

Both were crack shots. Two fires were exchanged and neither hit. Smart being the challenger was thereupon asked according to code rules: "Are you satisfied?" "Disgusted", he replied—a response whose jocularity produced good humor and ended hostility. Smart further observed: "In practice I could hit a sapling the size of my wrist every fire, and Dickinson could too, but then the sapling was not armed."

Jim Lang who was present upon the ground told us he suspected that the pistols had not been loaded with balls, by connivance of the seconds. Mr. Henry Salmond, however, said that he and others had found bullet marks upon the timber in rear of the duellists. Jim further stated that Dickinson was dressed in green silk to match the background of the woods.

According to tradition, after this Smart-Dickinson affair, the iron man was dumped into the "Factory Pond", the body of water on the eastern edge of Camden. Years after, when the lake was drawn off to repair the flood gates, the iron man emerged as the water subsided, standing erect. He was brought to land by some enterprising person to complete his still unfinished mission.

For some time after the Civil War there seemed to exist a cordiality in the social life of Camden, due doubtless to the common misfortunes endured by all. But by degrees this good fellowship gave way to the poison of jealousies and feuds, leading to the epidemic of duels that for a time cursed this community. Here that hideous practice was revived and here it met its death blow.

In two years, 1878-1880, four of these affairs culminated here; several others were barely averted. In rehearsing for these combats the iron man was re-enlisted. He was daily peppered by bullets and the crack of the pistol resounded daily in the vicinity of Johnson's Pond where the figure was installed.

The first of the series occurred August 29, 1878, between S. Miller Williams of Camden, and Boggan Cash of Cheraw. These young men had been college friends. Some dispute arose between them in regard to a race horse, "Prussian" by name, and insults were exchanged, to be appeased only by resort to the duelling code. Both parties were of massive physique, and, at the ten paces assigned, should have presented ample marks to each other. But the two shots passing between them went astray, and composition followed. The bullets for Williams' pistol were moulded by his wife, who was Jane Petigrew, of the distinguished North Carolina family.

The next affair seems to have grown out of seeds sown by the preceding. The principals were the aforesaid W. B. Cash and James Cantey, a neighbor and cousin of John Manning Cantey who had acted as second for S. Miller Williams. It appears from a hand-bill circulated at the time, that James Cantey had denounced Robert G. Ellerbe, Cash's uncle, for remarks reported to Cantey as made by Ellerbe about Cantey's father. In a letter to Cantey, Ellerbe denied and disclaimed the remark attributed to him. Cantey wrote withdrawing his offensive comments. Ellerbe sent the following rather cryptic reply: "Your note of yesterday has been received, and while it was not all I could desire and had reason to expect, yet the circumstances in which I am at present situated render it necessary that I should say that I am satisfied." The very next day this "satisfaction" is followed by a letter from Ellerbe's nephew, W. B. Cash, to Cantey, renewing the trouble, terming Cantey's retraction a "mean and contemptible apology". The consequence was an appeal to the iron man. Their meeting was at DuBose's Bridge on the Darlington side of Lynches River, and was bloodless, but by a very close margin. Cantey, who was robust and burly, received a ball through his waistcoat across his breast. The articles of agreement under which the two above meetings were held are here reproduced:

*Articles of Agreement.*

Articles of agreement entered into between J. N. Weatherly and J. M. Cantey, the respective friends of W. B. Cash and S. M. Williams.

1.—It is agreed that there shall be a hostile meeting between W. B. Cash and S. M. Williams at the point where the plank road leading from Cheraw to Wadesboro crosses the State line, on Thursday the 29th day of August 1878 at 12 o'clock M.

2.—Weapons to be used shall be the ordinary duelling pistols, to be held in a perpendicular position, pointing muzzles down until the word "fire" has been given.

3.—Distance shall be ten (10) paces.

4.—Weapons used shall not be moved from a perpendicular position until the word "fire" has been given nor discharged after the word "halt" has been given.

5.—Weapons shall be wadded single and in the presence of the seconds.

6.—The right to give the word shall be decided by lot and the party winning the word shall have choice of position.

7.—The positions shall be agreed upon and staked off before it is decided to which party belongs choice of position.

8.—The word shall be given, "Gentlemen, are you ready (if both principals answer Yes) Fire, one, two, three, halt—and the firing must be made between the words "fire" and "halt".

9.—When the principals have been placed in position and before they are armed the party winning the word shall give them the word in the same manner, tone of voice and rapidity of delivery, as he intends to give them in the fight.

10.—There shall be no firing of weapons or popping of caps upon the ground by either party without the expressed consent of the opposite party.

11.—The principals shall not address each other nor use any remark intended to excite each other nor shall they leave their positions until directed to do so by the respective seconds in the fight.

12.—The seconds shall be armed with Colts pistols and it shall be their duty to secure a fair and equal fight—any point of difference arising and not settled by this agreement shall be decided by reference to the Code of Honor and the usages among gentlemen as practiced in South Carolina.

13.—There shall or may be present the following persons and no others to wit:—One surgeon and two friends besides the seconds of each party.

14.—Either party may change his second on the field by giving fifteen minutes previous notice of his desire to do so.

J. N. WEATHERLY.
J. M. CANTEY.

The undersigned, the respective friends of James Cantey and W. B. Cash, have agreed that there shall be a hostile meeting between Mr. Cantey and Mr. Cash in Darlington County, S. C. at the first high land North of Dubois bridge on the road leading from Bishopville to Darlington Court House, on the 30th day of December 1878 at 12 m. and they further agree to be governed in the fight by the above articles of agreement—They also stipulate and agree that neither party shall wear anything about the person which will be calculated to repel or resist a pistol ball and that the opposing surgeon shall have the liberty to examine the person of the opposing principal after he has been placed in his position.

ALFRED BREVARD.
W. B. SANDERS.

## The Iron Man

On what is now the golf field, just north of Hobkirk Hill, Mr. C. J. Shannon and Captain T. H. Clarke confronted each other in conformity with the Code on August 25, 1879. Their meeting resulted from offensive charges by Captain Clarke against Colonel W. M. Shannon in connection with the finances of the old Wateree River Bridge, published in the local papers. Mr. Shannon interposed and issued a challenge in order to forestall his father. Luckily the shots went wild and adjustment followed.

Alarmed by these distressing proceedings the Camden Anti-Duelling Society was formed, General J. B. Kershaw, President. A similar society had been formed in Camden in 1829 after the fall of young Nixon. But another victim had to be sacrificed before public opinion was mobilized to the point of suppressing the duelling practice forever.

In March 1878 Mr. Robert G. Ellerbe, having in possession a bottle of rum, on his way from Camden, stopped at the home of Conrad M. Weinges by the wayside. Both being appreciative of such wares imbibed freely. Words soon arose, then a fracas, in which Weinges was seriously battered by Ellerbe. In December 1878, Weinges, through his attorneys, Captain W. L. DePass and Colonel Wm. M. Shannon, sued Ellerbe for the battery inflicted upon him as aforesaid. The case was tried in 1879 and verdict for two thousand dollars was returned against Ellerbe. But Weinges could not collect his verdict, for Ellerbe had previously confessed judgment to his sister, Mrs. Allan E. Cash, wife of Colonel E. B. C. Cash, in the sum of fifteen thousand dollars, and Ellerbe's entire property was advertised for sale under the Cash judgment, immediately after rendition of the verdict in favor of Weinges.

Whereupon Weinges (by his attorneys, DePass and Shannon) brought suit against Robert G. Ellerbe and Allan E. Cash to restrain the sheriff from selling Ellerbe's property, and to set aside Ellerbe's confession of judgment. The pleadings were framed by Captain DePass. The first draft of the pleadings contained, upon the margin, the following clause: "That further the plaintiff alleges that the pretended confession of judgment has been made by the said defendant, Robert G. Ellerbe, to his own sister, who is the said Allan E. Cash, and thus by family arrangement the said defendant intends to defeat the plaintiff."

This clause was expunged from the revised pleading drawn for service upon Mrs. Cash. But by mistake the pleading as first drafted with the marginal clause got among the papers handed out to Sheriff Doby, on November 2, 1879, to be served upon the defendants. On the same day Colonel Cash was in Camden and asked the sheriff to let him examine the papers in his hands and thus by mischance got hold of the draft containing the offensive marginal clause. Becoming enraged thereby he remarked to his attorney, Major Leitner, that he would rather die than submit to such an insult. A day or two afterwards he prepared challenges to Colonel Shannon and Captain DePass, the delivery of which was deterred by friends whom he consulted, who pointed out that the clause was in the handwriting of Captain DePass, that Colonel Shannon had always been friendly and that he should be given an opportunity to explain. The result of this advice was the following correspondence:

"Cash's Depot, November 24, 1879.

"Col. Wm. M. Shannon:

"Colonel:—I have seen the original summons and complaint of a case entitled Conrad M. Wienges vs. Allan E. Cash and others, in which your name appears as one of the attorneys for the plaintiff. In the latter part of the instrument are the following words: 'That further, the plaintiff alleges that the pretended confession of judgment has been made by the said defendant, Robert G. Ellerbe, to his own sister, who is the said Allan E. Cash, and thus, by a family arrangement, the said defendant intends to defeat the recovery of the plaintiff'. These words are not in the body of the instrument, but are written on the margin of the summons, and may have been placed there after your signature had been affixed. These words have been erased from the copy on Mrs. Cash's attorney. When I consider the kindly relations that have existed between us for more than twenty years, in connection with circumstances and incidents of very recent date, I am induced to hope and believe that this charge of fraud against Mrs. Cash has not been made with your knowledge or approval.

"Please, Colonel, say if you have made the charge, or if you have advised or encouraged any one else to do so.

"Very respectfully,

"E. B. C. Cash."

# THE IRON MAN

"Camden, S. C., Nov. 25, 1879.
"Gen. E. B. C. Cash, Cash's Depot:

"Dear General—Your kindly and courteous note is just received, and amid pressing engagements, I reply at once without consultation with any one.

"I reciprocate the appreciation you express of 'kindly relations that have existed between us for more than twenty years' (you might have said thirty-five), and although I do not know what the 'circumstances and incidents of very recent date' you refer to in the same spirit may be, I yet know there has been no change in those relations, so far as I am informed. And your 'hope and belief' are reasonable that no charge whatsoever of 'fraud', in any offensive sense, was made or intended, either by me or any other counsel in the cause so far as I know.

"In both cases I was only assistant counsel, and it was only a courtesy towards me that induced the regular attorney in the causes to use my name as leading counsel. He prepared all the papers, and I only examined the witnesses and made an argument in the first cause, all of which you saw or heard.

"In the present suit I never read the papers at all. They were read to me just before they were filed, but I saw no marginal note, and knew nothing of either the margin being there or its being erased; nor did I have any thing to do with the erasure on the copy served on Mrs. Cash's attorney, knowing nothing of it one way or the other; but the erasure shows that the counsel who erased it withdrew it. I neither made it (and of course) nor withdrew it.

"I knew of course, that as counsel and as an individual, I would be responsible for anything I assented to in the papers, and surely I would not shirk it if I were. But I neither knew of the *existence* or *withdrawal* of the marginal clause. Don't know when it was put there or erased. But the copy shows that it was withdrawn by whoever put it there, for the copy served is the authorized copy.

"I am confident that the regular attorney said, and meant to say, nothing that could be regarded as a charge of fraud, in the sense you deem it as applicable. I *know* I was never rude to a lady in all these long years.

"I know nothing whatever of the rights Mrs. Cash has in the property of Mr. R. G. Ellerbe—whether her claims can be established or not. If they fail to be established, it would be because the law would hold that such a preference, as was thus made by the confession itself, is irregular, to one creditor over another, would work a legal *fraud*, not a fraud as you construe it; and

I judge that was all that the draughtsman of the complaint intended. That is matter of law and fact to be determined by the evidence, and is in no way offensive.

"I hope that you will find that this answer is as frank and kindly and satisfactory as you expected.

"Very truly yours,
"WM. M. SHANNON."

"Cash's Depot, Dec. 1, 1879.
"Col. Wm. M. Shannon, Camden, S. C.:

"Colonel—Your letter does not require a reply, but I wish to say it is substantially what I "hoped and believed" you would write me. I feel greatly relieved, for I have had no desire at any time to have rupture with you. It is true I felt very indignant at what *appeared* to be your course towards Mrs. Cash, and I sent a challenge to be delivered to you at Columbia, Fair Week, or at Camden on the following Saturday. Hagood wisely and prudently stopped the delivery of the challenge, and when I went to Camden on the 17th, persons mutually friendly to us expressed their belief that the imputations cast upon Mrs. Cash's character have been made without your knowledge or approval. It was then that I thought of "incidents of recent date" that appeared inconsistent with a want of proper respect on your part for me, and I determined to write you my last letter. In sending the challenge I acted from a sense of duty to myself and my family, and from no desire to injure you, and I am truly happy to know there is no cause for any change of the friendly relations that have existed between us for many years.

"Truly yours,
"E. B. C. CASH."

It would appear from the foregoing that Colonel Cash had been appeased. The case to set aside the Ellerbe confession of judgment to Mrs. Cash was tried before Judge Kershaw at Camden, in February, 1880. Colonel Cash was present as a witness and testified that Ellerbe's confession of judgment had been made upon his suggestion and urgency. He took no umbrage at anything he observed at the trial but states that his ire was revived by reports reaching him of certain questions addressed to Mr. Ellerbe by Colonel Shannon, not heard by Colonel Cash, who was partly deaf and not present during the examination of Mr. Ellerbe. The testimony was printed for appeal to the Supreme Court, and Cash states that upon thus having opportunity to consider it "understandingly" he became satisfied that a charge of fraud was intended to be imputed to Mrs. Cash by Colonel Shannon's questions. He himself avows that he then became bent upon forcing a fight.

The following extract from a memorandum found among Colonel Shannon's papers presents his attitude in his own words:

"At the January term 1880 the cause for injunction came to hearing at Camden before Judge Kershaw on complaint, answer, testimony, etc. The cause was earnestly conducted on both sides, but most harmoniously and pleasantly. Gen. Cash and myself cordial and kindly, and I might add, confidential, in our bearing and conduct towards each other. Judge Kershaw decreed, setting aside the confession of judgment from Mr. Ellerbe to Mrs. Cash, but entirely exonerating the defendants from legal or constructive fraud.

"Plaintiffs were content, of course, for they had gained their cause. Defendants appealed, and as Judge Kershaw, though deciding in favor of the plaintiff, had omitted to decide on one legal ground, plaintiff joined in appeal on two legal propositions and the facts constituting 'legal fraud'. Capt. DePass was absent at the time the appeal was completed and I drew these grounds of appeal—the only time I ever touched pen to paper in the cause, so far as I know and believe, and that was the only paper either original or copy I ever had charge, control or possession of in either cause. The cause went up to Supreme Court and I had no idea of any offense taken until about the 19th of May, Capt. DePass on his return from Supreme Court told me he had twice seen Col. Watts, who he said was a friend of his, who told him that Gen. Cash and Mr. Ellerbe were determined to hold us to account, and he (Capt. DePass) thought it his duty to inform me of it, though the cause of the offense was not referred to.

"Camden, S. C., June 5th, 1880."

Cash's bitterness became intensified upon the death of Mrs. Cash on April 19, 1880. On May 22 he was at the home of Mr. R. G. Ellerbe. On that day two challenges were sent, one by Mr. Ellerbe to Colonel W. M. Shannon, the other by Colonel Cash to Captain W. L. DePass, borne by Mr. W. B. Sanders and Colonel R. C. Watts, respectively. In these missives the "marginal clause" is revived and stressed as the special ground of grievance. Mr. Ellerbe's challenge was declined by Colonel

Shannon. That of Colonel Cash was accepted, and the meeting between him and Captain DePass was appointed for May 30, at DuBose's Bridge on Lynches River. But rumors of the affair having leaked out, Captain DePass and his second, Dr. T. Berwick Legare, were arrested on or about May 26. The next day Major L. W. R. Blair, representing Captain DePass, called upon Colonel Cash at his home (Cash's Depot, Chesterfield County), and there made new arrangements for a meeting at "Wright's Folly", Anson County, N. C., on June 3, 1880. On the way to the scene Captain DePass was again arrested by officials of Chesterfield County upon telegrams from Camden. Major Blair went forward to the place and, he states, found the Cash party on the ground, and an assemblage of some fifteen or twenty outsiders, waiting to witness the spectacle. He reported the detention of Captain DePass by officers of the law. Colonel Watts, a friend of Colonel Cash, suggested that Colonel Cash himself go security upon any bail bond required of DePass, thereby removing the obstacle to a meeting. Says Major Blair: "I promptly accepted the romantic and chivalrous proposal; but Colonel Watts requested time to consult General Cash, and on his return withdrew the proposition, informing me that General Cash took a different view of it." On June 5, Colonel Cash published a placard of the affair, characterized by the caustic and vivid style of which he was master. In similar vein on June 8 he published an arraignment of the Camden Anti-Duelling Society, from which the following sample is taken:

"Camden has grown pious very slow, very! As long as her men would fight we heard not one word about the 'criminal practise of duelling'. For years that section has been regarded as the Galway of the State, and only a short time ago Williams and Cantey were permitted to leave the town to fight duels; there was no howling on these occasions. Williams and Cantey were willing to fight and were not molested; but just as soon as two of the leading citizens of the town strike their colors and take to their heels, in order to hide their tracks, up pops an antiduelling society."

With Ellerbe's challenge spurned by Shannon, and DePass held under bond, a lull ensued, of short duration however. With inexorable purpose Cash continued to

## The Iron Man

assail Colonel Shannon in highly offensive circulars, until a condition was produced certain to bring on a bloody affray between the entire Cash and Shannon kindred. It was to avoid such a vendetta, that Colonel Shannon determined to challenge Cash, and the following correspondence resulted.[1]

"Camden, S. C., June 11, 1880.
"Gen. E. B. C. Cash, Cash's Depot, S. C.,
"Sir: In the correspondence between us from the 24th. November to 1st. December, 1879, and in subsequent personal interviews, you expressed yourself gratified and satisfied at the solution given to all matters involved, and yet, on the 20th. of May, 1880, in relation to the same matters, in your presence, and surely with your approval, Mr. R. G. Ellerbe addresses me a coarse, false and insulting letter based upon that correspondence, and the matters in it referred to, and containing a 'demand for redress and a hostile meeting'. For reasons satisfactory to myself I declined to accede to that demand, and with that correspondence I rest content.

"Yesterday there was shown me a circular containing that correspondence, endorsed by your son, W. B. Cash, in scurrilous, vulgar, libelous false and dirty language, in which the correspondence between you and me is referred to and threats issued as to what you will do with it, and you are held up as an ogre and cannibal to "fright me from my propriety."

"I have no issue with Mr. W. B. Cash, and the style and matter of that endorsement forbid my directly noticing that endorsement, but as all these things result from a present dissatisfaction with the correspondence between you and me, and as there has been no change in the condition of affairs since then, I ask to recall to your attention the fact that I held myself responsible in that correspondence for all that I had done, and I now add that I hold myself responsible to you for all the false positions you and yours have seen fit to assign me.

"Without investigation you have seen proper to place me there, and I see no reason for adjourning to others a difficulty which you inaugurated.

"Motives of convenience and privacy both induce me to forward this by mail.

"Respectfully,
"W. M. Shannon."

---

[1]Colonel Cash's son, W. B. (Boggan) Cash, had joined with his father in libelling Colonel Shannon, touching his most private concerns. He published a circular entitled "Camden Soliloquies", partly prose, and partly doggerel verse, so opprobrious and galling that endurance became impossible.

"Cash's Depot, S. C., June 15, 1880.
"Col. W. M. Shannon:
"Sir—Yours of the 11th. came to hand last night. In reply, I have to say that I have with *great* reluctance come to the settled conclusion that you are the unmitigated scoundrel you have been represented to be by those who have known you better than I did. When I called upon you in November for an explanation of your conduct toward Mrs. Cash you prefessed *entire ignorance* of the charge against her character, and most emphatically disavowed any intention of being offensive, and your deceitful and treacherous behavior to me on the day the injunction was served on your sheriff aided you in deceiving me, and inducing me to believe your false professions were sincere and true, and I was truly gratified to know there was to be no trouble between us, and I wrote you a candid and honest letter, expressing my pleasure that we were to remain friendly. But sir, I have since found that your assertions were basely false, and that you were acting the part of a hypocrite to avoid your responsibility to me." (There follows much more in the same strain, here omitted.)

"I think I have given you in this note ample and sufficient grounds to justify you in taking action against me, and should you determine to act on my suggestion allow me to assure you that *no friend* of mine will meanly resort to the law to punish you for sending me a challenge. Nor will *I attempt to array public opinion against you* by claiming that you have placed me in a false position.

"E. B. C. CASH."

"Camden, S. C., June 18, 1880.
"Gen. E. B. C. Cash, Cash's Depot.
"General: My absence from town for any noticeable period of time or my visit to your vicinity would, under existing circumstances, attract attention, and I therefore think it advisable to use the mail for this communication, and request that you name an early day, a convenient place midway between us, and a friend of yours with whom I may confer in reference to your communication of the 15th inst. to Colonel Shannon.
"Yours respectfully,
"W. E. JOHNSON."

"Cash's Depot, S. C., June 21, 1880.
"Mr. William E. Johnson:
"Dear Sir:—Yours of the 18th to hand yesterday. Your proposition is unusual, and I think impolitic and impracticable. In the face of the shameful action of *your* grand jury and the threats

## THE IRON MAN

of *your* Moody and Sankey clubs, it would be difficult to find a man (competent for such business) *in this section*, who would like to be connected in any way with a duel in this State, and really I would dislike to ask any friend (outside of my family) to make himself liable to the laws on this subject, and I therefore suggest that you take the train and come to my house, and I or my son will make all the arrangements with you for a meeting between Col. Shannon and myself, and our articles of agreement can be signed by the seconds who act upon the field. I think this plan will avoid suspicion, *save time*, and probably prove effectual. The trains reach my house at about 6 P. M. and we can arrange the business in time for you to take the return train, should you desire to do so. There is no danger of arrests in Chesterfield unless our people are forced to action from outsiders, and *not much danger then*. I think the argument between Col. Shannon and myself is fairly exhausted, and I am glad to know he is ready to take a vote on the questions at issue between us.
"Very respectfully yours,
"E. B. C. CASH."

"Camden, S. C., June 27, 1880.
"Sir: Your letter of the 15th was duly received. In reply to its insulting contents I have to demand of you that redress which is usual under such circumstances. My friend, Mr. W. E. Johnson, will make all necessary arrangements for a hostile meeting.
"Respectfully,
"WM. M. SHANNON.

"Gen. E. B. C. Cash, Cash's Depot, S. C."

"Cash's Depot, S. C., June 28, 1880.
"Col. W. M. Shannon, Camden, S. C.
"Your note of the 27th has been handed me by your friend, Mr. W. E. Johnson, and my friend, ——— has arranged with Mr. Johnson for a meeting between us, when I hope to be able to accord you the redress you demand.
"Respectfully,
E. B. C. CASH."

"Cash's Depot, S. C., June 28, 1880.
"This statement is intended to show that it is agreed between W. E. Johnson and W. B. Cash that a duel shall be fought between Col. William M. Shannon and Col. E. B. C. Cash at the first highland north of DuBois' Bridge, in Darlington County, S. C., (the same spot where W. B. Cash and James Cantey held their meeting), on Monday, the 5th day of July, 1880, between the

hours of 1 and 3 o'clock, P. M., and that they adopt the articles of agreement to govern the fight which were used beween W. B. Cash and S. Miller Williams, except in this, that instead of ten paces the parties shall be placed fifteen paces apart, and instead of the word "Fire", and in place thereof, the second winning the word shall raise his pistol and ask, are you ready, and then discharge his pistol in the air, and the parties may fire after such discharge, but not after the word halt. And it is further agreed that each party shall or may have three friends on the ground besides the second and surgeon.

"W. E. JOHNSON,
"W. B. Cash."

From a pamphlet published by Colonel Cash after the duel we here transcribe his own account of the meeting and tragic event:

"When I drove upon the ground I saw about one hundred persons standing in groups over the field. They were a motley mass of white people, mulattoes and freed negroes. I had never seen them before and did not address any remark to them individually or collectively, nor take any notice of them in any manner. So soon as I arrived upon the ground some of Col. Shannon's party advanced towards the center of the field, where I and some of my friends went to meet them. Here the pistols were loaded, and near by the pegs were set, and I was directed by my friend, Capt. William B. Sanders, to take my position. My brother-in-law, Capt. Ellerbe, and my son, W. B. Cash, came to bid me farewell. Our meeting was about one hundred yards from the group above referred to. Capt. Ellerbe said, 'Remember, old fellow, you are shooting at *long taw*,' and my son said, 'Father, remember *now* how poor mother was treated'. I replied, 'If Col. Shannon does not disable me before I shoot, I will send my bullet through his heart'. This is verbatim the conversation that passed between us. It was spoken in a low tone, and no one else heard it, and all statements to the contrary are absolutely false. When I took my position I drew from my pocket a photograph likeness of Mrs. Cash, and, while taking what I supposed might be my last look at the picture, Col. Shannon took his position, and, I am informed, saluted my friends and myself. I did not see his act, and therefore did not return the salute. To others this may appear a small matter, but the circumstance has annoyed me very much and I can't get over it.

"Mr. Johnson had won the word, and it was his duty to direct the fire. It would be impossible for any man to fill any position or to discharge any duty more *perfectly*, or more fairly, than he performed his part on that occasion. When asked 'Gentlemen, are you ready', Col. Shannon was the first to reply, and never can I forget his game cock crow of defiance. His voice was loud, clear and firm. A moment after I responded 'ready', and Mr. Johnson gave the signal. At 'one' Col. Shannon fired and I felt a burning sensation on my right cheek and neck and thought I was shot. The fire and smoke from Col. Shannon's pistol obscured the upper portion of his person and caused a moment's delay in my firing. I fired at 'two' and saw a white spot through his black coat precisely where I had aimed, and yet he stood firm and unmoved. The thought flashed upon me that I had been cheated. It was only for a moment— he stepped once forward (towards me), then turned to his right and staggered. I turned my eyes away, and saw no more. The friends of both parties seemed somewhat excited, and the seconds left their positions and approached the point where Col. Shannon had fallen, leaving me standing at my position. I called Mr. Sanders back and requested him to ask 'if the gentlemen were satisfied', (as the 'code' required he should do), to which Mr. Johnson replied, and I think said, 'My God, what more could we ask? Do you not see that Col. Shannon has been killed?' I then asked Mr. Sanders to take me off the field, and I rode off with my friend A. H. Waring in the first vehicle which was ready to move. No word was spoken for some considerable time, when I remarked to Mr. Waring: 'The powder from Col. Shannon's pistol struck me on the face.' He replied, 'No, it was the sand from his bullet which struck the ground near you'. That was the first idea I had as to where his ball had gone. I drove home, about forty miles, that night."

The fall of Colonel Shannon caused a profound sensation throughout the State, such perhaps as never produced by death of any other of her citizens, before or since. Public sentiment arose *en masse* in protest, making this the last instance of a duel in South Carolina.

It was realized that laws against that code were to become vital thereafter, and in the constitution of 1895 was inserted a provision disqualifying from office or membership at the bar any one who has participated in a duel as principal, second or otherwise, since January 1, 1881, a date subsequent to the Cash-Shannon duel.

Following this tragedy a storm of malediction broke upon Colonel Cash. Among many, Senator M. C. Butler came forward to hurl a stone, proclaiming against "border ruffianism", "blackguardism", suggesting that Cash was a lunatic. Colonel Cash retorted in a screed from which the following are some of the most civil expressions:

"I could not expect or wish, General, that a man of your soulless character could understand or in any manner appreciate the motives that actuate and sustain me in my present difficulties. It would surely appear presumptous in me to express any opinion as to my 'Lunacy', and I must let the General decide on that point for me. The term 'Blackguard' is an epithet indigenous to the lips of cowards, and is a shield for the dastard—it is the war whoop of the poltroon as he skirmishes *to the rear*, and it is croaked from the throat of the cackling craven as he wings his flight to arks of safety."

Colonel Cash was tried at Darlington for breach of the antiduelling laws, as were also others participating as seconds. The proceeding was perfunctory and acquittal resulted; for, while sentiment had become fixed against duelling for the future, these prosecutions were viewed as falling under the old regime when the law was a dead letter.

The Cashs, father and son, were powerful men physically and mentally. The son became violent and diabolical when under influence of strong drink. Yet, Henley, who in a pamphlet, branded them both unmercifully, has said of Boggan that in his young manhood he 'could not sufficiently praise his goodness of heart, his amiability, his generosity and his devotion to his friends."

On February 16, 1884, Richards, Marshal of the town of Cheraw had to give Boggan a severe beating in arresting him for disorder. On February 23, Boggan returned to Cheraw and deliberately shot and killed Richards and mortally wounded a bystander. He then mounted his horse, "Border Ruffian", and fled to his home and hid

COL. WM. M. SHANNON

COL. E. B. C. CASH

## The Iron Man

away. A reward was offered for his arrest. The County Sheriff made no effort to apprehend him. Finally Deputy Sheriff King, with a posse, surrounded Boggan in a barn in the Pedee Swamp just before day-light, and upon his refusal to surrender, indeed after he had fired twice upon the posse, riddled him with bullets.

Colonel Cash, the father, was born in Chesterfield County, his life-long home, in 1822, the same year as Colonel Shannon. He was active in formation of a regiment for the Confederate Service, was elected its Colonel, and was complimented by General Kershaw for his "Courageous bearing and able and efficient conduct" of the regiment during the whole day of the battle of First Manassas. He was not re-elected upon reorganization of the army, and returned home.

He took an ardent part in supporting Hampton during 1876 to redeem the State from Carpet-bag rule, and continued a cordial friend and supporter of Hampton and the State Democracy until embittered by the public odium, which followed his fatal duel with Colonel Shannon. In 1882 he joined the Greenback party, denounced Hampton and the Democratic leaders, ran for Congress on the Greenback ticket and was defeated. After this he kept in retirement at home, where he died of apoplexy on March 10, 1888. At his request his friend, General W. L. T. Prince read at his grave, Pope's "Universal Prayer."

We have space only for a bare outline of Colonel Shannon's career. He was born in Camden in 1822, a son of Chas. J. Shannon a prominent merchant and President of the Branch Bank of the State at Camden.

Colonel Shannon was a graduate of the South Carolina College, Class of 1841 and admitted to the bar in 1843. He married Henrietta McWillie, a daughter of Wm. McWillie (of whom see a sketch in another chapter). He was elected a member of the Legislature in 1857, serving until 1862, when he resigned and raised a cavalry company, the "Kirkwood Rangers", for the Confederate service. Of this Company, he was first Captain, and later rose to rank of Colonel. Upon his father's death in 1864, he succeeded to the Presidency of the Bank of Camden. His home, "Pine Flat" at the foot of Hobkirk Hill, with its beautiful premises, has since been converted into the tourist resort, known as "Hobkirk Inn".

Through marriage of his numerous children, he was allied with many families of the community. Of decided literary taste, with a wide acquaintance and genial interest in people, he contributed a valuable series of historical articles to the local papers, under the title "Old Times in Camden", which constitute the best reminiscences of his day and which this community should highly prize.

It may not be inappropriate to close this subject by quoting the following tribute to Colonel Shannon from his mortal antagonist. (At the head of which we retain the lines from Hamlet, as in the original.)

"O, God!—Horatio, what a wounded name,
Things standing thus unknown, shall live behind me!"

"At the solicitation of Col. William M. Shannon, a distinguished lawyer of Camden and a prominent citizen of South Carolina, I met that gentleman at DuBois' Bridge, Darlington County, S. C., on the 5th. day of July, 1880, for the purpose of settling a personal difficulty that had arisen between us. We fought in the usual manner of duelling. The fight was fair and equal, and there has been no complaint on the part of his friends that I sought or obtained any advantage over him. He fell at my fire, and I can honestly say, I do not believe a braver man ever bit the dust—He went down with his colors flying and fronting the foe. He died upon the ramparts of his enemy, and 'with a smile upon his face', he filled a hero's grave. Since my troubles with Col. Shannon began I have frequently heard him spoken of as a self-willed, imperious and intolerant man, who was often in difficulties with his associates. Of that I know nothing. For twenty-five or thirty years, he was to me the genial, cultivated gentleman, with whom it was a pleasure to meet. We were of the same age, and, when young, resembled each other so much that one was often taken for the other, and when we met we enjoyed these mistakes. I was fond of him, and the feeling seemed reciprocal. God forbid that I should now seek to cast reproach upon his memory. Most honorably has he settled his account with me, and we have passed receipts as to the affairs of this world."

# CHAPTER XX.

## THE COURT HOUSE.

For nearly a century after the settlement of the Province of South Carolina, the only Courts were held at Charleston. The consequence was that the inhabitants of the interior were practically without any administration of justice, except such as was dispensed by self constituted "Regulators", whose proceedings were liable to become as obnoxious as those of the regulated. Such a condition constituted one of the grievances of the colony against the Mother Country.

The earliest recognized division of the Colony was into three parts designated as Colleton, Berkeley and Craven Counties. Such was the ignorance prevailing in high places concerning the Back Country that the earliest maps show these three counties extending not more than about fifty miles from the Coast.

Nothing official could be found defining the limits of Craven County; but so far as can be gathered from the nebulous provisions of the old statutes creating Parishes in Craven County it may be regarded as all that part of the State lying east and north of the Santee River and its tributaries, Congaree and Saluda Rivers, from the Sea to North Carolina.

In 1757 the northern portion of Craven County was established as St. Marks Parish, embracing the locality now occupied by Camden with a radius of some fifty miles or more.

Parishes were formed from time to time for Church and political purposes, then very much one and the same. These subdivisions became obsolete after the Revolution.

Finally by the Statute of April 1768 the Colony was divided into several large Judicial Districts or Precincts, one of these being "Camden District", which included the present counties of Clarendon, Sumter, Lee, Richland, Fairfield, Chester, York, Lancaster and Kershaw. By the Act of 1770 appropriation was made for the erection of a Court House at Camden. The *Charleston Gazette* of May 1772 contains a statement that all of these District Court Houses had been built except the one at Georgetown. Hence we assign the year 1771 as the date of the building of the first Court House at Camden, to serve for the wide territory now embraced in the nine counties above named.

The first session of Court for Camden District was held here in November 1772 by Chief Justice Thomas Knox Gordon. All of the records prior to 1783 have entirely perished. This original Court House, located on lot No. 1, was burned in 1779, as appears from an old scrap of paper consisting of a claim of Joseph Kershaw against the State for reimbursement, which was as follows:

"March 11th. 1779—To cash paid for the apprehending and bringing to Gaol A. Westberry, who was supposed to be the person that burnt the Court House and set fire to the Gaol and other buildings at Camden—$100 Dolls."

As the fire occurred prior to 1780, in May of which year the British first entered Camden, it cannot be attributed to them, but was probably the work of Tories.

Fragments survive of the minutes of the Court held in November 1783, which bore the ponderous title of "Courts of General Sessions of Peace, Oyer and Terminer, Assigns, Gaol Delivery and Commons Pleas." For several terms all the attorneys in attendance were from Charleston, until 1786 when Daniel and Jacob Brown appear as resident attorneys, and about the same time Benj. Perkins, and one H. Beaumont.

In the year 1785 Camden District was subdivided into seven counties (Lancaster, York, Chester, Fairfield, Richland, Claremont and Clarendon), in each of which was established a County Court composed of three judges, combining the powers now vested in our present Probate Court, Register of Deeds, Magistrates and County Commissioners. Under the original subdivision Lancaster County extended down to Pine Tree Creek, just south of Camden, the Creek dividing it from Claremont County, the Wateree River dividing it from Richland and Fairfield.[1] Kershaw County was formed from parts of Lancaster, Claremont, Richland and Fairfield, so that conveyances of land now in Kershaw, between 1785 and 1791, were recorded in one or other of those four counties, from which it was composed. An old petition of

---

[1] The first recognition of "Kershaw" as a political district occurs in the Constitution of 1790, by which it is allowed two Representatives. But no legislative act defining its boundaries can be found prior to the Act of 1791.

## The Court House

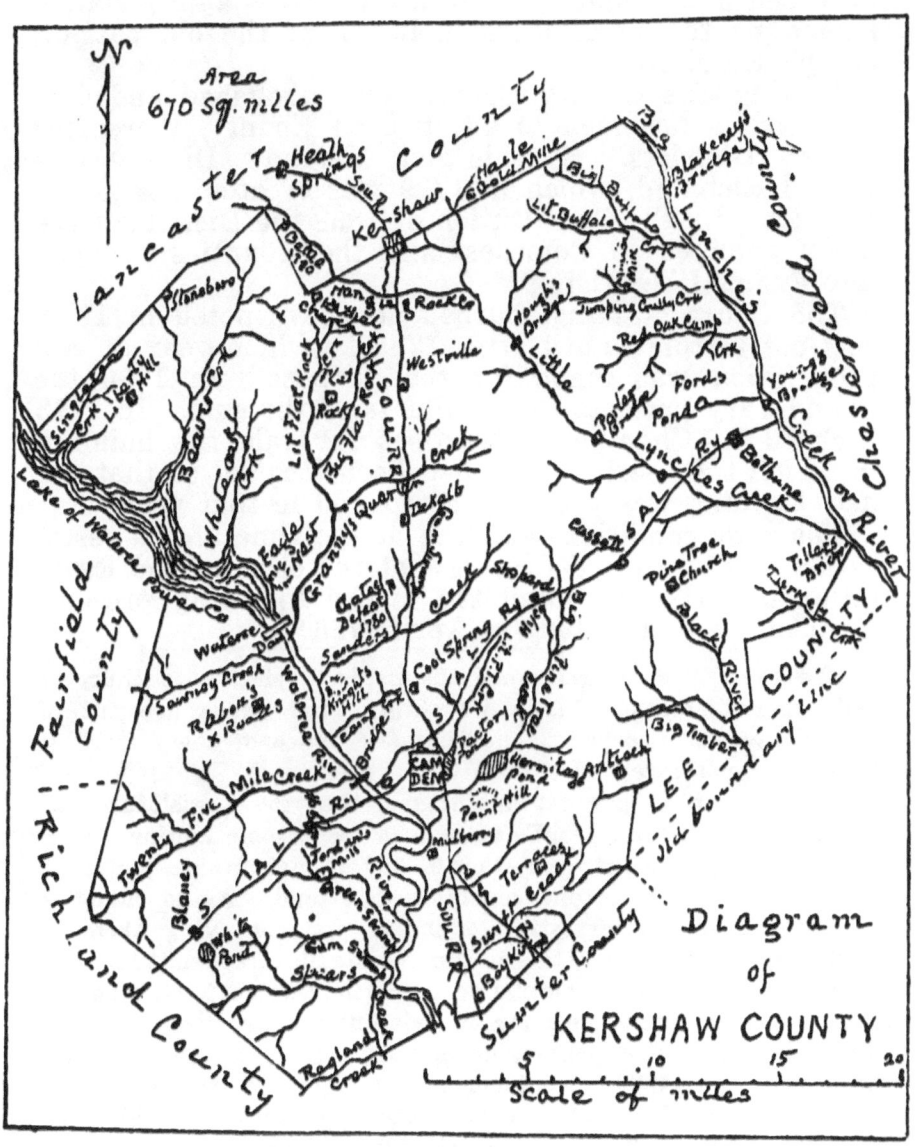

1788, unearthed among the State papers, addressed to the Legislature, suggests the name "DeKalb" for the proposed new County, which however was appropriately named by the Legislature in honor of the old patriot, Joseph Kershaw.

In 1798 the County Courts were abolished and Circuit Courts provided to sit in each County, thereafter termed Districts. By this Act, Kershaw District embraced Richland, which in 1799 was created a separate District. By the Constitution of 1868 the Districts were again changed to Counties, and the Counties grouped into Judicial Districts.

The Court building, burned as above noted in 1779, was not restored until after 1788 in which year an appropriation was made for the purpose. In 1790 the Grand Jury protests the smallness of the sum. In 1793 Richard L. Champion advertises for sale the building in which the Clerk's office had been located, so that the new building was probably completed in that year.

The rude conditions existing at the time of the restoration of Courts and Civil law at the close of the Revolution is strikingly exhibited in the following presentment of the Grand Jury in April 1786:

"We present as a grievance the neglect relative to churches and other places of Public Worship. That roads are out of repair, taverns disorderly, and that the police of the district is in general not attended to.

"We present as a great misfortune, that the Legislature has not hitherto put the Sheriff's office on a respectable footing. During the present court, the Sheriff had it not in his power to command so much as one constable to attend. As to funds to defray charges of arresting offenders for conveying them to gaol, supporting them there, summoning jurors, and for discharging other duties relative to the criminal court, we find the sheriff has no other funds for all this but his own private purse. As to keeping of prisoners, he is now obliged to use the most unjustifiable ways of confinement for want of the usual assistance about the gaol. Such is the degradation of this once respectable office. We fear that shortly no man of common pride or spirit will accept of it. In other counties that office is looked up to by the people, as holding the first rank and authority; but in this county, the place seems as if it has lost all estimation; and as to authority, he scarcely has that which a constable should have by law; for although the gentlemen hitherto holding the

## The Court House

office have the inclination to support the department at their own expense, yet the property of an individual is inadequate to the means. Thus offences are committed with impunity; every class of citizens know too well how easy it is to defy the Sheriff; to escape from him, or break prison, and to be screened from punishment by one means or another. And thus the officers of the law, which in a republic should alone bear rule are often insulted and bullied without the privilege of resisting. While we lament this, yet we have the consolation to know that the laws can be easily restored to full vigor and authority throughout this district, provided the wisdom of the Legislature will interfere, make the Sheriff's office once more respectable, and render it an object worthy the notice and rivalship of men of first distinction and abilities.

"The laws and constitution of the State are very dear to the freemen of Camden district; we value them the more, as they cost us so much of our property, our toils, and our best blood. And whatsoever misrepresentations some of our late good friends may have sent abroad to our prejudice, merely for the misconduct of one or two people at the Court before the last, the citizens of this district will unite with the Legislature in the same zeal and firmness to support the honor and authority of the Republic, which they formerly exerted in rooting its enemies out of the country. We return our warmest thanks to his Honor the Judge, for his excellent charge to us; he gave us much satisfaction by his information that a law which in Britain is called the Coventry Act is of force in this state, and that it takes in all such as are guilty of the barbarous, savage practice, called gouging, and we further express in a particular manner our full sense of his decided conduct and manly spirit, in bringing to immediate punishment the three gentlemen who were guilty of the riot the evening before last, and thus preventing any further violation of public peace and order. And we desire that the judge's charge to the Grand Jury, with these our Presentments, be published in the different Gazettes.

Joseph Kershaw, foreman
George Wright
William Whitacre
John McCay
Joshua Dinkins
John McNight
Thomas Duke
John Galbraith
Richard Sadler

Elijah McCay
Robert Reid
William Lang
Andrew Lister
John Frierson
James Cantey
Francis Boykin
George Ganter

HISTORIC CAMDEN

The *Charleston Gazette* notes the prosecution of three "Gougers" at this (1786) term in Camden, and says "It is hoped this will have a direct tendency to make men who boast of civilization desist from a practice which reduces them below the standards of brutes."

The gouger was at last suppressed, and his extinction is thus ironically lamented by a contributor signing "Pacificus", in a Camden paper of 1823:

"We hope to see those scenes which delighted our childhood just before and after the adoption of the Federal Constitution, and before the period when law and order, justice and honor (falsely so called we presume), began to assume their reign. Then the acts performed in the Court yard at one term furnished ample sources of litigation at the next; and numerous as well as delightful were the stabbing, the gouging and the fighting matches which came before the Court, accompanied by all the charming variety arising from those instructive scenes of intoxication and riot. The calm in our present court yards is really too uniform and disgusting."

While exploring the old Court records, items were noted some interesting, some quaint and curious, a few samples of which are here given. Among the earliest papers found was a batch of excuses by jurors for non attendance on Court in 1784. One pleads a lame knee, caused by slipping from a log.

The Court minutes of April 29, 1786, contain the following entry:

"The State
—vs—
Sam'l. Wilcox,
alias, Marygold.
Indictment.
Suspicion of Being a Scoundrel

Defendant was discharged at instance of Mr. Brown, Attorney on the ground that there was no such offense known to the law.

In those good old times horse stealing was very prevalent despite the death penalty.

The prince of horse thieves was Gray Briggs. The following account of his execution is found in a Charleston paper of December 13, 1794:

"On Friday Dec. 5th. was executed at Camden, pursuant to his sentence, Gray Briggs the noted horse thief. He died as he

## The Court House

lived a hardened wretch, for before he was turned off, he addressed himself to the surrounding spectators and told them he dared say that if a number of them had their dues, they deserved the punishment about to be inflicted on him."

The Grand Jury in 1809 recommends building of a fire proof Court House and in 1813 presents the "decayed State of the building". In 1826 a new building was completed on the original site (Lot No. 1), corner of King and Broad Streets. It still stands somewhat remodelled.[1] As constructed in 1826 the portico was supported by six columns, in the Ionic style, brown Sandstone. In 1847 considerable changes were made in the interior and porch, the six Ionic columns being replaced by four much larger ones, Doric order. The body of the building remains the same, measuring 43 by 62 feet. The old Ionic capitals are serving today as carriage landings at various points around town. In 1906 a new Court House building was erected up town on the site of the old LaFayette Hall which was burned in 1904. The old Court House was purchased by the Hobkirk Hill Chapter of the D. A. R. and is now in their custody.

A curious reminiscence of the fire of 1829 which demolished a great part of the Camden of that date and endangered the Court House consists of an affidavit of John J. Blair, then Clerk, who deposes: "that during the great fire in November last nearly all the records and other papers belonging to the Clerk's Office for said District, together with all the furniture were removed from the Court House into the Street; that the seal of the Court was lost, and after diligent search no traces of same can be found."

On Friday, March 2, 1827 James Barrentine was hung for the murder of Jesse Fley, presumably son of him of the same name who was hung in 1809 for the assasination of David Minton (see Chapter "Minton's Mill" in first volume of *Historic Camden*). Captain Jas. I. Villepigue told us that when a boy of six, he saw Barrentine being driven by to execution, seated on his coffin and heard some one in the crowd say, there goes the man who is to be hung for killing a fly.

A notable trial was that of L. W. R. Blair in 1853 for the death of Mrs. Young. Blair was defended by James

---

[1]The Act of December 1825 which provided for sale of the older building, directs that the foundation stones be reserved and probably are still a part of the structure.

Chesnut and Jas. L. Petigru. For the prosecution appeared A. P. Aldrich and B. F. Hunt. Blair was acquitted by a representative jury of which R. M. Kennedy was foreman. The tragedy occurred in the remote country district on Lynches Creek, where the Youngs and Blairs lived. Between these families there had existed an old feud. Hiram, the body-servant of Blair had been beaten up by slaves of the Youngs. Blair requested the Youngs to punish their offending slaves. It was said the Youngs wrote to Blair inviting him to come to their home to settle the matter. Blair went, taking his man Hiram and his gun. At the gate he left Hiram with the gun and entered the Youngs' premises. He was set upon by the four Young brothers with cudgels, and while being severely beaten, Hiram fired upon the Youngs in defense of his Master. At the moment the gun was discharged, Mrs. Young the mother appeared in the doorway and was mortally stricken by stray shot from Hiram's gun. As may be supposed this affair excited profound interest which lasted for a generation. Hiram was never tried.

We think worthy of presentation the brief reply of Neil Blair, when called upon, after conviction of murder in 1879, to say why sentence should not be passed upon him. In a fit of wild intoxication, while two of his friends, one on each side were trying to lead him home from the saloon, he drew a dirk and in a flash stabbed one mortally and the other desperately. It must be borne in mind that he was a mulatto and born a slave. His statement which he read and which was published in the *Camden Journal* was as follows:

"With me I suppose all is ended. If I killed Wm. Anderson I did not know it. My heart is innocent if my hands are guilty. In fact until I was told of it, I did not know that I had done it. I would not have harmed a hair of his head had I known what I was doing. I did not think the evidence sufficient to take my life, but the jury have seen fit to do otherwise, and I am willing to die. It is as natural to die as to be born. I leave them to their God and their conscience. To your Honor, I must thank for the impartial manner in which you have done your duty in the case. To the Solicitor I must say that I admire his great force and power, but I regret that his talent was against me. I have no hard feelings against him. To the noble and good men who have so ably defended me, may God bless them. My prayers will be

## The Court House

for them during what little life is left me. To the public I ask their forgiveness and their prayers."

His sentence was commuted to life imprisonment. After ten years of hard and faithful service he was pardoned on condition of leaving the State.

The most impressive incident in our Court House coming under our notice was the farewell spoken by Judge J. B. Kershaw, on retiring from the bench in 1893. His words then were not recorded, but the following sentences stuck in our memory and are very nearly as uttered:

"I have often in my career felt the hand of Providence lifting me up and sustaining me as plainly as the hand of a friend in the flesh. There is something higher and better in the world than position, power, money, little as some people may think; it is honor, truth, virtue, duty."

### Camden Attorneys.

In the following list the figures indicate the year of admission to the bar or of earliest appearance upon the Court records:

1786—Daniel Brown
— —Jacob Brown
— —H. Beaumont
1787—Benjamin Perkins
1790—Sam'l. Mathis
1792—Joseph Brevard
1798—John Brown
1800—Abram Blanding
1806—Chapman Levy
1808—James S. Deas
1809—F. A. DeLiesseline
1811—Stephen D. Miller
1813—Wyatt W. Starke
— —John S. Willett
1814—Royal Bullard
— —John Carter
1815—Benj. T. Elmore
1818—Wm. McWillie
— —John Boykin, Jr.
— —John C. Carter
— —Harris Hickman
1820—Chas. A. Bullard
1821—Geo. D. Blair

1822—Henry G. Nixon
— —Wm. B. Hart
— —Jas. C. Doby
1823—Adderton Boykin
1826—Wm. J. Grant
1828—Thos. J. Withers
— —John M. DeSaussure
1829—John C. Vaughan
— —Thos. B. Lee
1836—John Smart
— —J. G. Hall
1837—James Chesnut
1840—James P. Dickinson
1842—Jas. D. Blanding
1843—Jos. B. Kershaw
— —Wm. M. Shannon
— —B. B. Salmond
1845—Wilkes Thurlow Caston
— —W. B. Carlisle
1846—A. G. Baskin
1847—W. H. R. Workman
1851—Chas. S. West
1851—Chas. A. Price

1853—Wm. R. Taylor
—W. Z. Leitner
1857—W. L. DePass
—James M. Davis
1859—Arthur Lining
—John D. Kennedy
—Joseph D. Dunlap
1872—J. Thornwell Hay
—John Kershaw
—Junius Davis
—W. Randolph Withers
1878—Thos. Henry Clarke

## *Clerks of Court.*

Many of our oldest Court Records have been lost or destroyed, so that we have not been able to determine the name of any Clerk of our Court prior to 1789. Between 1791 and 1799 Francis Boykin was Clerk of the County Court and Register of Deeds. The following is a list of the Clerks of the Court of Common Pleas who after 1799 became also Registers of Deeds. Unless otherwise indicated the same officer served during the interims between the dates.

1789—Richard Lloyd Champion
1809—Thomas Salmond
1819—Thos. P. Evans
1829—Jno. J. Blair
1837—James W. Lang
1838—Geo. Q. McIntosh
1842—Benjamin Gass
1848—S. E. Capers
1851—Moreau Naudin
1856—Jno. R. Joy
1856—Wm. Clyburn
1868—C. Shiver
1872—R. E. Wall
1877—S. C. Clyburn
1888—Wm. Clyburn
1892—Joel Hough
1906—I. C. Hough
1912—J. H. Clyburn

## *Sheriffs.*
### Camden District.

1773—John Wyly
1783—Alexander Moore
1785—Hugh Milling
1788—Henry Hunter
1789—Joseph Brevard
1790—Wade Hampton
1794—Wm. Ransom Davis
1798—James Goodwyn

### Kershaw County.

1791—Joseph Kershaw
1798—John Fisher
1800—Benjamin Bineham
1804—Reuben Arthur
1808—Turner Starke
1812—Benjamin Bineham
—Francis S. Lee
1817—Matthew C. Wiggins
1821—J. W. Cantey
1823—J. S. Nettles
1828—John Goodwin
1834—John C. West
1837—Wm. Rosser
1840—Benj. Gass

## The Court House

1843—J. Baskin
1845—M. M. Levy
1847—Thos. J. Warren
1851—John Ingram
1853—Thos. Baskin
1855—E. Barnes
1859—E. E. Sill
1862—D. Sheorn
1866—E. E. Sill
1868—J. P. Boswell

1873—Sam'l. Place
1875—John Doby
1882—Jas. L. Haile
1892—R. B. Williams
1900—J. S. Thantham
1912—W. W. Huckabee
    (died in office 1917)
1917—I. C. Hough
1918—G. C. Welsh

# CHAPTER XXI.

### Schools and Schoolmasters.

No record has been found of a school in Camden or vicinity prior to the Revolution. That there were educational facilities of some sort can only be inferred from such evidence as the neatly written diary of Samuel Mathis,[1] "the first white child born in Camden", who grew to manhood there and certainly had some schooling. The character of the first settlers too was such that we cannot think they would have neglected some means of education for their children.

The two eldest sons of Colonel Kershaw, it is true, were sent to England to school; and Chief Justice Gordon, just returned from holding his first Court at Camden in 1770 lamented "the absence of good schools and school masters, churches and ministers"[2] in this section. The same year, Lieutenant Governor Bull called the attention of the Assembly to the fact that the "back-settlers" were destitute of even the rudiments of education and recommended the establishment of schools at the Waxhaws, Camden, Broad River, Ninety Six, New Bordeaux and the Congarees.

In 1778, a "Catholic Society" at Charleston was incorporated for the purpose of placing and maintaining a public school in the District of Camden, eastward of the Wateree River. We cannot find whether its purpose was ever put into effect.

Samuel Mathis records that on March 25, 1781, "Samuel and Burwell Boykin drank tea and we spoke about a school-master."[3]

In the *Charleston Morning Post and Daily Advertiser* of August 4, 1786, appears the following Camden notice: "To be rented—The Dwelling House of Eight-rooms, formerly a Boarding School for Young Ladies (which is at present much wanted there), known by the name of the Red House. For terms, apply to James Pearson in Camden, or, in Charleston, to Aaron Loocock." From a plat of the lower part of the town, made by James Ker-

---

[1] *Historic Camden—Colonial and Revolutionary*, Appendix.
[2] *South Carolina Gazette*.
[3] *Historic Camden—Colonial and Revolutionary*, Appendix.

shaw in 1811, we learn that this building stood on the east side of Broad Street, between the Central Square and Meeting Street. The lot just back of it, facing on Market Street, is designated on the plat "The Old Schoolhouse lot": on it was a building, perhaps our first seat of learning. Joseph Kershaw's will (1788) also mentions this lot as the site of an "old" schoolhouse.

A very notable work was done in South Carolina by the early educational and charitable societies; such as the South Carolina Society, at Charleston, founded in 1737; the Winyah Indigo Society, at Georgetown, 1740; Mt. Zion, at Winnsboro, 1777; St. David's, at Cheraw, 1778; and the Camden Orphan Society, which was organized July 4, 1786, and incorporated, by act of Assembly, February 27, 1788.

The application for a charter for the last-named institution was signed by Adam F. Brisbane, John Harker, John Kershaw, William Lang and Joseph Kershaw. It set forth "the great want of schools throughout the country, as well as the general inattention of most of the schoolmasters."

The constitution of the Society declared its purpose to be the founding and erecting of suitable buildings for the reception, education and support of "poor orphans and other poor children in distress within the state, and for the moderate relief of such members as may want it." The charter members were: Adam Fowler Brisbane, President; Isaac Alexander, William Lang, John Adamson, Benjamin Carter, Robert Reid, Joseph Brevard, James Cook, William Tate, William Carter, James Kerr, John Reid.

The seal bore the figure of "an orphan child in adversity", with the inscription: "I was a stranger and ye took me in."

Some of the provisions of the Rules are at least entertaining.

The annual meeting was set for July 4: the hours 11 A. M. to 5 P. M. It was customary, after the transaction of business on these occasions, to dine in state at Reid's (later Dinkins') Tavern, each member being assessed 3 shillings.

Rule 4 specifies that the President must sit at the head of the table, the Vice-President at the opposite end, the

Junior Warden in center of left side, the Treasurer in center of right side.

The duty of the Stewards seems, principally, to have been "to call for all liquors used by the Society."

Rule 15 provides that "Every member who shall attend the Society disguised in liquor shall, for every such offense, pay a fine of 10 shillings."

The indigent members were to be buried at the expense of the Society "in as frugal a style as propriety will admit."

The admission fee was fixed at 10 shillings for the first 25 members, 15 shillings for the next 10, and so on up to 40 shillings. Other funds were derived from donations, fines, forfeitures, and monthly assessments of two and quarterly of 5 shillings (later changed to an annual fee of $8.00), on each member. In addition, by legislative enactment in 1799, the proceeds of all escheated property in Kershaw District were vested in the Society, which, further, was authorized to establish one or more lotteries for the endowment and maintenance of a school in the town of Camden.

In 1788, four orphan children[1] were taken in charge and the same year eight lots facing on Campbell, York and Gordon Streets were deeded to the Society by William Lang as a site for the Orphan Houses and Academy.

By 1791, the school was opened, with Robert Dow as first principal. This gentleman was a native of Edinburgh, having come to this country in 1785. His wife was a Miss Richardson of this state.

He was succeeded, in 1793, by Rev. Thomas Adams, at the time also pastor of the Presbyterian Church here. His courses of study and rates of tuition, we learn from an old Charleston paper, were:

| Class | Per quarter pounds | shillings |
|---|---|---|
| 1. Rhetoric, Latin and Greek | 1 | 10 |
| 2. Arithmetic, Geography and Rhetoric | 1 | 5 |
| 3. Writing, English Grammar and Arithmetic | 1 | |
| 4. The Rudiments of Eng. language and writing | | 15 |
| 5. Mathematics, Elements of Geography & Surveying | 1 | 15 |

[1]The Society, in 1794, decided that not more than four orphans at a time should be educated at its expense.

## Schools and Schoolmasters

Mr. Dow was again put in charge in 1794. In his published announcements, the stress that he lays upon the practical English branches and his opinion that much time was wasted on the Dead Languages smack of modern ideas. His first honor roll, published in a Charleston paper, July 10, 1797, contains seventeen prominent family names, most of them now passed from this community: "Master Thomas Eveleigh, Master John Davis, Master Thomas Bevings, Master John Dinkins, Master William Lang, Miss Eliza Boykin, Miss Mary Martin, Miss Harriott Atkinson, Master Seré DuBose, Master Lawrence Manning, Miss Matilda Manning, Master Powell McRae, Master John Chesnut, Master Franklin Alexander, Miss Eliza Richardson, Miss Sarah Adamson, Miss Charlotte Cary and Master John Belton."

The minutes of the Society at that time afford a curious illustration of the transition from the old to the new currency. In 1797, the rates of tuition are announced in dollars and cents, with the proviso that, "any person paying paper money must allow the discount between specie and paper"; yet in 1801 we find that James Kershaw was paid "for a celestial and terrestial globe, £13—19—6." "June 4, 1802—To Monsieur Anone, for 4 maps of Assia, Africa, Europe and America @ 200¢ ($8.00)—£1—17—4." "Oct. 1, 1803,—To Thomas Berry for thunder-rod and fixing it—£4—6—11." "Apr. 9, 1803, To Mr. Slump, for inserting advertisement in his Gazette—175¢—8—2."

Mr. Dow[1] was succeeded in 1805 by Rev. Andrew Flinn, pastor of the Presbyterian Church. His salary was $1,000.00 per year, with the free use of schoolhouse, residence and boarding houses, on condition of teaching five indigent children without pay. A similar arrangement seems to have been made for many years with succeeding principals of the Society's schools.

The same year (1805) the grounds and buildings of the Orphan Society were reconveyed to Mr. Lang for $500.00 and the "Cornwallis House", then in a state of dilapidation, was purchased for $1,500.00 and converted into an Academy. For many years after, the Green in front was known as "Orphan House Square".

Rev. Samuel Brantley, a young Baptist divine, took charge of the school in 1809.

[1] He died in 1817 on his plantation at Jamesville, S. C.

HISTORIC CAMDEN

He was followed, next year, by Rev. B. R. Montgomery, D. D., of the Presbyterian Church.

It was the custom of that day for the pupils to make frequent exhibitions of their erudition before visiting Committees, by delivering "orations" in Latin or English in the Court House or one of the churches, "at early candlelight", as a quaint announcement puts it.

In 1810, the Society established a separate Free School, but this was discontinued two years later upon the inauguration of a Free School system by the State.

In 1811, Dr. Montgomery accepted a chair in the South Carolina College, and was succeeded in both school and church, by Rev. George Reid. Edwin J. Scott, in his "Random Recollections" leaves the following striking memorial of this gentleman:

"In 1811, my father removed to Camden, where I was sent for six years to an Academy for boys and girls, kept by Mr. George Reid, a portly, pock-marked Presbyterian clergyman of much experience and very superior attainments as a classical teacher; a rigid disciplinarian who used the rod and the ruler unsparingly and impartially whenever he thought it necessary. His favorite method of inflicting punishment was to lay the delinquent across his lap, face downward, and then paddle him with a broad flat ruler, leaving marks, in some cases, that were visible for weeks.[1] Under Mr. Reid I took his regular course in Latin—viz. from Rudiman's Grammar to Virgil and Horace, and was a year or so 'in the Creek', as my old friend, John Summer, said of his son Adam.

"He had as his assistant in the English department C. J. Shannon, subsequently a leading merchant and the father of the lamented Wm. M. Shannon.

"The boys in our Academy formed a uniformed artillery company, with two pieces, resembling cannon, turned out of wood, painted like brass and mounted on wheels, having musket barrels in the center and touchholes corresponding with those in the guns so that they fired very well; and we were highly complimented by the famous War-Governor, David R. Williams, on our appearance in line at a regiment or brigade reunion in Camden."

[1] In 1844, a rule was adopted that no boy above fourteen years of age was to be whipped by the teacher; it was rescinded the following year.

## Schools and Schoolmasters

From 1819 to 1823, John McEwen, a native of Edinboro, Scotland, was in charge of the school. After that he had a private school for young ladies (boarders taken), called the "Camden English Academy".

In 1820, Mr. James English purchased the "Cornwallis House", giving in exchange two lots on DeKalb Street just east of the Presbyterian Church, upon which the two Brick Academies, for males and females respectively, were built, being completed in 1822. They were one-story structures, each containing one very large classroom, with classic columns supporting the broad piazzas in front, and surrounded by a splendid Academic Grove of giant oak and hickory. Here many generations of Camden's youth drank more or less deeply at the Pierian Spring, and here for about seventy years that all-powerful autocrat, the school master of the olden time, held his mighty sway, ferule in hand.

Messrs. Thayer and Hart taught the school during the session 1823-4.

From January to June, 1825, Rev. Jonathan Whitaker and his son, Daniel K. Whitaker, both graduates of Harvard, were joint principals. Mrs. Whitaker had charge of the Female Department, and Mrs. and Miss Jumelle gave lessons in music. Daniel Whitaker later removed to Charleston, where he edited the *Southern Literary Journal*.

From 1825 to 1829, the academy was conducted successively by Rev. Raynolds Bascom and Ebenezer P. Niles.

In 1830, one of the ablest of the principals entered upon his work, Henry P. Hatfield, a native of New Jersey and graduate of the University of Virginia. He was noted as a scholar, and disciplinarian. His first wife was Miss Abigail Reed of Liberty Hill, Kershaw County, who died in 1839. Two years later, he married Miss Stella Phelps, at the time head of an excellent private school in Camden; of her we shall speak more fully later. In 1836, on account of failing health, Mr. Hatfield resigned, taking a school at Bradford Springs.[1]

The principal, from 1836-8, was Dr. Moses Holbrook, a former physician of Charleston. During his incumbency, the conduct of the boys became so objectionable

---

[1] An advertisement for a successor to Mr. Hatfield states that the institution "is endowed by the Legislature"; principal receives $1,200.00.

that a separate building for them was erected on what is now Hampton Grove, next to the Methodist Parsonage, and they were removed there in 1838. The gravest charge against them was gambling, the investigating committee reporting that they found forty-two packs of cards in the desks. Another offense was their playful custom of forming cordons across DeKalb Street, holding up even the most dignified citizens on their way down town.

The history of this "Pine Grove Academy", as it was called, is interesting. In the first place, it was the "Old Schoolhouse"[1] already mentioned, moved up presumably from Market Street and remodeled. In 1868, it was leased to and used by the Episcopal congregation for four years, at $50.00 per annum, after the destruction of their church on Main Street. In 1872, it was rented to the School Trustees of Kershaw County as a free school for girls, and, the same year, was sold to the Methodist congregation for $500.00, being again converted into a place of worship. Seven years later, it passed into private hands for a residence, and, in 1909, it was demolished.

In 1838, Henry P. Hatfield was recalled, and he and his wife presided over the two brick academies until 1845, when they left Camden for Augusta, Ga. After teaching there for two years, they removed to Perry County, Ala., becoming Associate Principals of the Marion Female Seminary. They died in Alabama, Mr. Hatfield in 1864; Mrs. Hatfield in 1876.[2]

During this period, from 1839 to about 1846, Mr. Leslie McCandless seems to have begun his long and distinguished career as a teacher, in the Pine Grove Academy, under a private lease and a new name, the "Classical English School".[3] The Orphan Society boys, with improved manners, we infer, were allowed once more in their old haunts on DeKalb Street.

In 1845-6, the brick academies were in the hands of George S. Walker and Miss C. W. Ellis (Female Department).

[1]Minutes of Society, December 22, 1838.
[2]Mrs. Anne B. Archibald, a daughter of Mr. Hatfield by his first marriage, now living in Meridian, Miss., furnishes this information.
[3]A Mr. Leland was associated with Mr. McCandless at first for a short time, probably John A. Leland, who became later a noted educator.

## SCHOOLS AND SCHOOLMASTERS

From 1846-9, Leslie McCandless seems to have conducted the O. S. Schools, with Mrs. A. H. Hart, Miss Fanny A. Coleman and Miss Clarissa Brittain, successively (it is assumed), in charge of the girls. In 1848, Miss Coleman became Mrs. Leslie McCandless. In 1849 Mr. and Mrs. McCandless resigned, the former renting the Male Academy for his private school.

In 1853, William Steadman appears as principal of the Female Department.

The minutes during these years from 1838 on are not clear. The school buildings apparently were leased for a small rental to the teachers, or they were required to give free instruction to from two to five indigent children in lieu of rent. The Society, however, elected the teachers, fixed the rate of tuition and otherwise acted as Trustees.[1]

From 1859-63, Charles H. Peck conducted a Semi-military school in the male (or Eastern) Academy. The war-fever was then strong even among the small boys, and several of them in their teens left the school for the army. Mr. Peck, though a Northern man, was an ardent sympathizer with the South. He died in 1863 and lies in our cemetery. Miss Maggie Denoon had charge of the girls' department at this period.

Though no minutes of the Society were kept during the War, we learn from old citizens that Mr. Peck's successors (1863-67) were low-country gentlemen of scholarly attainments refugeeing in Camden; to wit, Dr. Bruns and Dr. Matthews of Charleston, and Mr. Stuart of Beaufort.

In 1867-8, the Pine Grove Academy was again rented to Mr. McCandless, and the Eastern Brick Academy was leased to Miss Denoon.

From 1870 to 72, the Western Academy was in charge of W. Beaumont Clarkson.

His successor was Captain John W. Jamison, a gallant ex-Confederate soldier, bearing upon his body grievous wounds that necessitated his resignation in 1880.

The Western Academy had been leased to the County Commissioners for a free school in 1873, and in 1875 it was fitted up as a residence for Captain Jamison, who taught in the Eastern Academy.

[1]The holidays, in 1845, were fixed at "one week at Christmas, one week at 4th July and four weeks in summer months."

His successor (1881-83) was W. F. Schoenberg, a native German and an accomplished linguist.

He was followed (1883-84) by Aubrey Bourne, a scholarly and somewhat eccentric Irishman, who later entered the Episcopal ministry. Mr. Bourne married Miss Agnes Villepigue, of Camden.

Mr. Schoenberg was again called to the principalship in 1884 serving this time until 1886. During this period, in 1885, the modern Graded School system was partially inaugurated, the Orphan Society schoolhouses and the "McCandless" schoolhouse on Laurens Street being utilized and the private schools of Mrs. Mary A. Shannon and Mrs. Mary C. Thomasson, with their principals, being absorbed.

From 1886-88,—Turnipseed was in charge of the schools.

He was followed (1888-90) by A. C. Moore, later Professor of Botany in the University of South Carolina, who really first put the new (Graded School) scheme into effective operation.

His successors as Superintendent were:

Robert Morrison, 1890-91.
Clarendon R. Spencer, 1891-93.
Robert M. Kennedy, 1893-1912.
C. R. Legge, 1912-13 (Died in office).
R. F. Simpson, 1914-17.
J. G. Richards, Jr., 1917—

In 1893, those interesting old landmarks, the Orphan Society Academies on DeKalb Street and the almost equally famous "McCandless" schoolhouse on Laurens Street were deeded by the Societies controlling them respectively to the Trustees of the Camden Graded Schools.

The two former were sold to private parties: the eastern academy was remodeled as a home: the western was demolished, a residence being built on the site. The McCandless school building was moved across Laurens Street and made into a dwelling. On its former site the so-called "Graded School" was erected, at a cost of $11,000.00, being dedicated March 14, 1894.

In 1903, the property (four acres with buildings) of the late Major Zach Leitner on Monument Square was purchased for $5,000.00 and the substantial old residence was used as the High School. This was sold in 1920 and the splendid old mansion and grounds of the late Dr.

## Schools and Schoolmasters

George Reynolds, facing on Lyttleton, Laurens and Fair Streets, were acquired. The residence was utilized as the High School, but only for a few months, as it was burned to the ground on January 1, 1921.

The following year the present handsome Grammar School was built, at a cost of $125,000.00, on the Reynolds lot and the Laurens Street building was converted into a High School.

In 1867, through the efforts of Rev. B. F. Whittemore, a small frame schoolhouse for negroes was built on the southwestern Public Square, permission being granted by the city authorities.

This was replaced in 1893 by a larger frame building, still in use, when the negro school was taken into the Graded School system.

In 1923, a brick High School for negroes was put up on the same square.

In 1922, the present Factory School, midway between the two cotton mills, was erected, at a cost of $12,000.00. It too is a part of the city school system.

### *Private Schools.*

Only a few other of the more noteworthy Camden schools—"private" we may call them by the way of distinction—can be mentioned; of some of the earliest there unfortunately are no records.

Between 1815 and 1820, the local papers advertise the schools of Mr. Jesse Pope; of Mr. Joshua Reynolds (for young ladies); of the Misses Carpenter, a boarding school at the upper end of Broad Street; of Mrs. Langley,[1] "lately a preceptress in the famous Lodebar Academy"; and of Mr. A. Carpenter, under the auspices of "The Camden School Association", I. Smith, F. S. Lee, J. Brown, W. Blanding, R. Bullard, Trustees.

Between '20 and '30, the "Male and Female Academy of Dr. Cleary and Lady" was conducted "in Mr. Whitaker's rooms on Broad Street". Mrs. and Miss Clarkson had a school, which was discontinued on the marriage of the latter, Miss Esther Clarkson, to Mr. Ebenezer P. Niles, of the O. S. Academy. The Misses Salmon operated the "Female Seminary, opposite LaFayette Hall".

[1] Wife of Dr. Wm. Langley, Intendant of the town in 1817.

Between 1830 and '40, Mrs. Bascom (presumably the wife, or widow, of Rev. Raynolds Bascom) and "Miss Legare" had a winter school in Camden and a summer school in Kirkwood.[1] P. McCaskill ran an "English School in a "house of Mr. Douglas on DeKalb Street, recently occupied by Dr. Mills".

In 1833, one of the best schools for girls ever maintained in Camden was opened by Misses Stella Phelps and Mallory, "in Mr. Niles' schoolroom on Lyttleton street just above York, next to the residence of Mr. J. K. Douglas". Miss Phelps was a native of Brattleboro, Vt. Her father, Judge Phelps, was a member of Congress during the administration of John Quincy Adams. An elder sister was the first wife of Alonzo Taft, father of the ex-President. She was educated at Troy Female Seminary, Mrs. Emma Willard's famous school. Miss Phelps was a woman of decided literary ability, a frequent contributor in prose and verse to the leading periodicals of the day. In 1841, as stated, she became the wife of Henry P. Hatfield. Of this marriage two sons survived in 1910—John H., of St. Louis, Mo., and Charles Albert, Colonel 13th Reg't U. S. A. Miss Phelps was the originator of the beautiful May Day celebrations in the open air which enjoyed such long vogue in Camden. The most popular, usually the loveliest, girl was elected and crowned "Queen of the May", in the presence of a great throng. The honor was much coveted.

At this period, also, was established the excellent school of Misses Henrietta and Rebecca DeLeon, which stood on Broad Street, opposite old LaFayette Hall.

The notice, in 1831, of "Monsieur Godefroy's French School" recalls the fact that, prior to 1820, one Michael Rudolph, another Frenchman, opened a school here for boys. He was a fine linguist and an expert fencer. Indeed his skill in the latter art gave some color to his claim, when in his cups, that he was no less a personage than Marshal Ney. It so happened that certain French residents of the town, among them Mm. Meugy and Lemiere,[2] who had served under Napoleon, it is said,

---

[1]Probably in the schoolhouse that stood, until about 1860, on a three or four acre lot on the northwest corner of the present Bull place, "Holly Hedge". A public school is said to have been conducted there at one time.

[2]Jardin Constant Lemiere died in 1821. He was a captain of dragoons at Waterloo (Inscription on his tombstone, cemetery).

did not give much faith to such pretensions; so, constituting themselves a committee, they waited upon old Michael and advised him to "move on", which he did, to North Carolina.[1]

In 1842, a large school, with fifty boarders, was operated by Mrs. Charles Spann; for the summer months, a "large airy Kirkwood residence" was used. Her terms were $350.00 per session.

In 1849, the advertisements appear of the classical school conducted by Rev. Thos. B. Russell, in the "Cunningham" house opposite the Presbyterian Church on DeKalb Street.

Reference has been made to the connection of the greatest of our "Old Masters", Leslie McCandless, with the O. S. Schools, which, as seen, was brief. It has been stated that he opened a private school here in 1839 in connection with Mr. Leland, who soon withdrew. For more than fifty years, Mr. McCandless was the dominant figure in the educational life of this community. He had been taken from the Charleston Orphan House by those who perceived the latent talents of the boy and given a thorough education, graduating from the South Carolina College in 1838. When he began teaching in Camden, the next year, he was only about eighteen years old.

Ten years later, he married Miss Fanny A. Coleman, a native of West Haven, Vt., who had come, about 1845, to take charge of the school vacated by Miss Phelps (then Mrs. Hatfield).

The Academies, for boys and girls respectively, taught by Mr. and Mrs. McCandless, up to the Civil War enjoyed an unexcelled reputation in this and adjoining counties. Among the boys who attended from other sections may be mentioned John L. Manning and John P. Richardson, afterwards Governors of the State, and James H. Carlisle, destined to be known as "first citizen and foremost apostle of learning" in the State.

So remunerative was the work of Mr. and Mrs. McCandless that they could afford to limit their numbers and fix practically their own rates of tuition. Mrs. McCandless, at one time, would take only seven pupils, at $300.00 each without board. In the '50's, Mr. McCandless, it is

---

[1]This story was told by the late Captain James Villepigue, who had it from his father. It is possible that Rudolph was the same man who, as Peter Ney, more successfully advanced his pretensions, later, in North Carolina.

said, declined the Chair of Ancient Languages in his Alma Mater.

About 1854, they removed their schools to the new frame building erected by the Educational Association on Laurens Street which was ever after known as the "McCandless Schoolhouse". The War broke up the school. Mr. McCandless entered the Confederate service, serving for a while with Boykin's Rangers. Later he and his family removed to Atlanta, Ga. They returned to Camden at the close of hostilities, but the wife and children soon separated from him and returned to Atlanta; they were never reunited.

A proper tribute to Mr. McCandless is given in the family sketches, but it is only just to say that the fame of his wife in their common profession was no less than his. Her schoolhouse in the early '50's stood on DeKalb Street opposite the eastern (O. S.) Academy. One of her girls[1] says of this period: "Mr. McCandless gave our Latin a weekly test, with his terrible X-rays frightening Mrs. McCandless equally with her scholars. In 1854, the large school[2] was opened, Mr. and Mrs. McCandless teaching together. Our class was Mr. McC's. especially. He handled us without gloves, 100 lines of Virgil and as many in Racine or "DeL'Allemagne" for a lesson. This season must have nauseated him with girls, for he went back next fall to his boys."

Among the several assistants whom Mrs. McCandless found it necessary, at different times, to employ was a young foreigner, Von Fritz, who inherited a German estate and title while teaching here, at once resigning to enjoy his patrimony. His gallantry was so great that, when the girls were unprepared on their lessons, they would keep him busy during the entire recitation period with requests for water, which he was too polite to allow them to get for themselves. He returned to Camden on a visit in 1901, receiving a warm welcome from the grey-haired ladies who had been his mischievous pupils.

Mrs. McCandless conducted a small school in Atlanta after the War. Her death, in 1889, was deeply lamented wherever she was known. She was laid to rest in our peaceful City of the Dead, and her husband, from whom she was so long estranged in life, rests by her side.

---

[1] The late Miss Sue McDowall.
[2] On Laurens Street.

## Schools and Schoolmasters

Among popular private schools after the War may be mentioned those of Mrs. F. Bruce Davis and her sister, Miss Emma Reynolds, of Miss Emily Smith, of Mrs. Mary C. Thomasson and of Mrs. Mary A. Shannon, the two latter, as already stated, being absorbed by the Graded Schools in 1885. These cultivated ladies, having suffered crushing (?) losses of fortune as a result of the great conflict, maintained in their private residences excellent schools that are gratefully remembered by those who were so fortunate as to gain admission to them.

### Educational Notes.

As germane to our subject, it may be stated that the first Sunday school in Camden was organized in 1819. It was a Union, or undenominational, school, and was held in the Court House. The *Camden Journal* of August 21, 1822, says with pardonable pride: "In the last 12 months, 40 scholars have recited 17,720 verses of Scripture; answers to Catechism, 16,640, and 8,240 hymns; sum total of recitations, 42,600."

In 1822, J. Winship announces his academy for intruction in Stenography and Short Hand writing, in the ball-room of Mess. Welsh and Smyth's Tavern.

The importance attached to dancing as a polite art is evidenced by the number of dancing schools conducted in the early years of the 19th century. It is amusingly illustrated in the advertisement of one Kingsbury in 1824, in which he offers instruction in cotillions, set dances and a "variety of new and fashionable dances" and plumes himself on his long experience in "that elegant and necessary accomplishment."

A noted dancing master in Camden of an even earlier date was Pierre Laurent Jumelle, a refugee from San Domingo. It was not uncommon for French refugees, gentlemen of broken fortunes, to eke out a livelihood in this way. With fiddle under chin, they would to their own music teach the latest steps, the correct poise, the graceful bow and parlor manners.

Mr. Jumelle attained high social position and considerable means. The commanding elevation above Kirkwood Common still bears his name. He was the father of Mrs. John C. McRae and Mrs. Benjamin Perkins.

In 1831, A. McLaurin, styling himself "Writing master" advertises that he will teach "fancy and ornamental hands".

The DeKalb (Cotton) Factory, established in 1838, maintained a flourishing day school and Sunday school for its operatives (*Camden Journal*, June 30, 1849).

An editorial in the *Camden Journal and Southern Whig* of October 10, 1835, on the remodeling of the Free School system, makes the suggestion that the free academies be manual labor schools, fitting for mechanical and agricultural pursuits. John C. West was editor of the paper at the time.

In the *Camden Journal* of December 6, 1848, a writer signing himself "W" suggests that the State Academies at Columbia and Charleston be allowed to take a certain number of beneficiary students, on condition that they be required to teach in the state for five years after graduation, in order that "we might have better educated teachers." In the same paper of April 11, 1849, "R" advocates a state normal school and a school superintendent for each district, in addition to the state superintendent of education.

Whether or not in these proposals is the genesis of some of the similar provisions of our present educational system, we have here proof of the early working of these advanced ideas.

Mention may be made of a privately endowed institution in Camden for the education of negroes, the Browning Home and Mather Academy, which was founded in 1880. It is situated on the corner of DeKalb and Campbell Streets. The old Lang residence, a landmark on the site, was the nucleus about which has grown up an extensive plant of several well-appointed frame buildings. The school is supported by the Woman's Home Missionary Society of the Northern Methodist Church, whose headquarters are in Cincinnati, Ohio.

# CHAPTER XXII.
## CHURCHES.
### Baptist

The first services under Baptist auspices held in Camden seem to have been conducted by that distinguished exponent of the faith, the patriot preacher, Rev. Richard Furman, Sr., who became pastor of the Baptist Church at the High Hills of Santee, S. C., in 1775.

J. C. Furman, in his sketch of Richard Furman's career, says: "Near the commencement of the Revolution, an appointment had been made for him in the Court House in Camden, where the Gospel rarely if ever had been dispensed. A large audience assembled to hear the word of life, but were kept waiting out of doors. The sheriff, in whose custody was the key, refused to open the building or to give up the key, alleging as his reason that Mr. Furman was not a minister of the Established Church. A number of the most respectable citizens present were inclined to obtain an entrance by force, but the youthful messenger of peace begged them to desist, telling the congregation if they would retire to a spot at a little distance, where they could be accomodated better than where they stood, he would address them in the open air. He then preached on the vital doctrines of the Gospel, with a solemnity, pungency and pathos calculated to make a deep impression. And such was the effect: the discourse was long and affectionately remembered. The principal citizen of the place, by whose instigation, it was believed, the sheriff acted, was seen after the sermon coming from his house and showing the preacher marked attention. This he continued to do ever after, and the use of the Court House was not again refused."

After his return from exile, along with other notable patriots of the Revolution, Mr. Furman, it is stated, again visited Camden[1]; and it was doubtless through him that, on November 30, 1784, Colonel Joseph Kershaw, evidently the "principal citizen" referred to above, sold to the Incorporated Baptist Church at High Hills, Santee, for the purpose of building a daughter church in Camden,

---
[1]From sketch of Camden Baptist Church, by T. E. Goodale (1907).

lot 638, in the extended plan of the town, fronting on the east side of Fair Street, midway between King and York[1] The adjoining lot 637, was purchased also of Mr. Kershaw, in 1785.

There is no evidence of a house of worship having been erected on this site.

It is unfortunate that the old minute book of the Mother Church at the High Hills cannot be found. It would tell much of interest, no doubt, about her Camden offspring at that early period.

From the minutes of the Camden Orphan Society we learn that a Baptist Church was completed here in 1809, and that Rev. Sam'l Brantley, principal of the Orphan Society's School, officiated "at the new church". This building stood on the northwest corner of Market and York Streets, Lot 1069, which had been given to the congregation, in 1808, by Richard Lloyd Champion. It was a severely plain frame structure, on brick foundations.

In 1810, the Camden congregation was formally organized, with a membership of twenty-five, and admitted into the Charleston Baptist Association. The first pastor was Rev. Joseph B. Cook, son of Joseph Cook, of Bath, England, and a graduate of Rhode Island College, now Brown University.[2]

By act of the Legislature, "The Baptist Church of Camden" was incorporated, December 21, 1814.

"The greatest revival in the Church's history" occurred in 1832, resulting in 32 baptisms (increasing the membership to 100), the organization of a Sunday School and the "setting apart of two members to the Gospel ministry, W. F. Brasington and W. W. Childers."[3]

This impetus and increase caused the sale of the first church and the purchase of the second location, on the west side of Broad Street, just above DeKalb. The old house of worship, it is said, was bought by the town and used as a hall for theatrical entertainments until about 1850, when it was torn down, or burned. The corner stone of the second church was laid in 1834, and the house was dedicated in 1836.

[1] Record Book B., p. 49, office Clerk of Court, Camden.
[2] Furman's *Baptist Churches*, (1811).
[3] T. E. Goodale's Sketch.

## Churches

The lecture room at the rear was added in 1853, for the use of the negro Sunday School. The church membership then was 266, of whom 166 were slaves.

In 1863, during the War, there were only eight (white) male members at home, the rest being at the front, a notable testimonial to the patriotic spirit of the congregation.

After the War, with changed social conditions, the question was, what to do with the negro members. Though assisted to build churches of their own, as many as wished were allowed to retain their membership in the white church. Accordingly, that eminently useful and respectable negro, Rev. Monroe Boykin,[1] continued with the Camden Church until he was chosen first pastor of Mt. Moriah Baptist Church (colored), which was organized in 1866, and of which he was the faithful shepherd until his death in 1904.

In 1876, the Camden Congregation, with others, withdrew from the Charleston Association and formed the Santee Association, and from the latter they seceded, in 1905, to join the Kershaw Association.

In March, 1907, the church property was sold, and the present location, on the corner of Broad Street and LaFayette Avenue, was purchased. The old building was converted into an armory for the Kershaw Guards and was demolished in 1919. The McClelland house, perhaps the oldest residence in Camden, stood on the new site. This building used as a Parsonage was moved back to face the Avenue and the present church was erected in its place, being dedicated February 2, 1908.

*List of Pastors.*

| | |
|---|---|
| 1810-1812—Joseph B. Cook | 1832 ———— Barnes |
| 1814-1819—Jesse Pope | 1833-1835—J. H. Devotie |
| 1819-1827—Supplies | 1835-1836—Supplies |
| 1827-1829—Robert Missildine | 1836-1843—C. M. Breaker |
| 1829-1832—"Supplies" (Students of Roberts Academy, High Hills, Santee) | 1843-1847—B. M. Whilden |
| | 1848-1849—Samuel Furman (Supply) |

[1] As a missionary, Monroe Boykin established most of the older Baptist churches for negroes now existing in the counties of Kershaw, Lancaster, Sumter and Clarendon. A granite shaft to his memory, erected with the aid of many white citizens, stands in front of his church on lower Broad Street.

1849-1852—T. Mason (Supply)
1852-1860—J. K. Mendenhall
1860-1863—W. E. Hughson
1863-1870—J. E. Rodgers
1870-1873—A. K. Durham (Supply)
1873-1876—Robert Thompson
1876
W. W. Guinn
L. I. Foster
1877   —W. G. Rollins
1878   —W. A. Therrell
1879-1882—A. W. Lamar
1882
J. W. Wingo
D. M. Ramsey

1883-1885—M. E. Broaddus
1886-1888—C. A. Fulton
1888-1891—P. V. Bomar
1891-1894—M. W. Gordon
1894-1900—A. T. Jamison
1900-1902—A. E. Crane
1902-1905—Jabez Ferris
1905-1906—J. D. Moore
1906-1910—L. A. Mitchell, D. D.
1910-1913—M. L. Lawson
1913-1917—John A. Davison, D. D.
1917-1921—M. M. Benson
1922-1924—J. J. Johnson
1924   —John P. Graham

*Grace Church (Episcopal).*

In colonial days, Camden was in St. Mark's Parish, which was laid off, by act of assembly, in 1757, with boundaries not very clearly defined, being "the continuation of the Northwest line of Williamsburg Township to the Peedee and the Santee, and all the land situate Northward of said line." St. David's was cut off from it in 1768, extending from Lynches River to the North Carolina line, but St. Mark's was left still an abnormally large parish.

It is small wonder, therefore, that the Grand Jury, at the November session of Court in Camden, 1772, presented as a great grievance the extensive bounds of said Parish, which not only made it "difficult for the church wardens to collect the poor tax", but "hindered the spread of the Gospel in the Back Parts", some of the parishioners being 140 miles distant from "the comfort of the Preaching of the Gospel and divine service."

The mother church of St. Mark's was on the northern side of Santee River, about ten miles from Wright's Bluff. It was burned by Tarleton's cavalry during the Revolution.

Services of the Church of England were held in Camden prior to the Revolution by Rev. Theophilus Drage, but we are of the opinion that there was no Episcopal

Church here at that period,[1] despite the following testimony from the Records of Grace Church, taken by the Rector, Rev. Francis P. Lee, January 5, 1843: "I received yesterday from a niece of Miss (Mary) Kershaw, who is still alive, but who no longer sees strangers, the following account of a conversation she had just had with her aunt: 'The Episcopal Church, built before the war,[2] was situated on the corner lot, since used for a Presbyterian Meeting House, and where Mr. Nixon's grave now is. There was no church on the square given to the town by Colonel Kershaw, but it was intended to build a larger church on it when the congregation increased.

"'Colonel Kershaw's family, Mr. Champion's, Mr. Carey's, and several Englishmen and others were members. The Rev. Theophilus Drage was the minister. He left for England when Charleston was taken and never was heard from by any of his congregation. His books and mss. sermons were burned with Colonel K's library.

"'After he left, Mr. Logue, a Presbyterian, used the church until Cornwallis and his army entered Camden. The officers had the church pulled down to build barracks for the soldiers. My aunt says she distinctly remembers the destruction of the church and the row, or street, of huts occupied by the soldiers. She was then ten years of age, and remembers going to church with her parents, and of the minister's being often at her father's house. She is not certain but thinks Mr. Drage married her father and mother'."

Miss Kershaw, who gave the information, was at the time seventy-two years of age, having been born in 1771. Her memory was certainly at fault in regard to Mr. Drage, who died in Camden in 1775, as we see by the following communication[3] from her father, Colonel Joseph Kershaw, to Henry Laurens, of date, Camden, January 5, 1780: "The letter you forwarded to me was from a Mrs. Hannah Swain Drage, the widow

---

[1] Dalcho in his *Historical Account of the Protestant Episcopal Church in South Carolina* says that a regular congregation was not organized in Camden until 1808, though Episcopal clergymen had occasionally officiated there prior to that time, even before the Revolution (see also *Presbyterian Church*, for further discussion of this point).

[2] The Revolution.

[3] From *South Carolina Historical and Genealogical Magazine*. Miss Kershaw was four years old when Mr. Drage died.

of a very fine Old Gentleman who officiated as Preacher to this district and died here, something more than four years ago. His Books and apparel was sent by me to the Old Lady. His executor, John Rodgers, sold his trifling Household furniture and an ———,[1] which did not quite pay the demands against his Esta. here. There was due to him six months salary, or Fifty pounds sterling, which I endeavored to get from the Publick, but from the confusion of the times it could not be got in the usual way, so the account was layed before the Assembly, who thought proper to throw it out, tho' it was certainly due to him. I would recommend it to the executor to renew the application, but, as the money is reduced, it would scarcely be worth the Old Lady's acceptance."[2]

Colonel Kershaw, prior to 1774, gave the land, 330 feet square, on the northeast corner of Bull and Church Streets, extending to the old central Public Square, as a site for an Episcopal church and burying ground; but, as his daughter has testified, the church was never built. He himself, his son John and other members of his family are buried in the lot. Their graves are marked by handsome stones and a substantial brick wall surrounds the enclosure. In an adjacent plot were interred the early members of the families of Richard Champion and Wilie Vaughan: the bodies from this enclosure, however, were removed to the Quaker Cemetery about 1880,[3] owing to acts of vandalism committed by crowds attending circuses held on the once hallowed spot. Judge J. B. Kershaw in 1885 wrote to Dr. Burgess[4] that he remembered when there were hundreds of graves in the Episcopal burying ground, "now all entirely obliterated, except those of the writer's ancestors."

For half a century after the Revolution, the Episcopal Church, from its former connection with the British hierarchy, was looked upon with disfavor, even sus-

[1] Word illegible.

[2] The Bible and Book of Psalms, printed in 1635 and 1636 respectively, said to have been used by Mr. Drage in services here, are now in possession of the Kershaw family. The Book of Common Prayer (1764) also so used, as tradition has it, was owned by the late Henry K. DuBose, a descendant of Colonel Joseph Kershaw.

[3] One of them, that of Miss Virginia Vaughan, was found petrified, the hair, it is said, having grown almost to the feet.

[4] See his *Chronicles of St. Mark's.*

BISHOP THOS. F. DAVIS

## CHURCHES

picion, in the up-country of South Carolina; as a consequence, it did not grow as other denominations did.

In 1808, an effort was made to organize a congregation here. An old subscription list, of that date, containing thirty-three names, shows that $2,365.00 was raised for the building of a church; but the plan was abandoned, and there is no record of a minister having been called or of regular services having been held.

In 1813, Rev. Andrew Fowler was sent to Camden, as a missionary, by "The Protestant Episcopal Society for the Advancement of Christianity in South Carolina." He found but four communicants in the town. Services were held in the Court House. Mr. Fowler was withdrawn in 1817.

In 1830, Rev. Edward Phillips was sent here by the same society. The Masonic Hall was used for morning services and the "school-room in Kirkwood"[1] for the afternoons. A congregation was formed and incorporated, by Act of Legislature, under the title of "Grace Church", and Mr. Phillips was elected rector. Through the untiring efforts of this gentleman, a lot on the west side of Broad Street, below DeKalb, was acquired, on which a house of worship was erected and dedicated, by Bishop Bowen, in 1832. It was of brick, with a square turret and belfry in front, and contained forty-six pews.[2] The first vestry was as follows: John Boykin, Samuel Boykin, John Cantey, Daniel Carpenter, James C. Doby, Benj. T. Elmore, Edward Anderson, and James S. Deas.

During the next few years, this church, like all others in Camden, lost many useful members, who joined in the mad rush to the newly opened Indian lands of the Southwest. Many later came back, richer only in experience.

Mr. Phillips resigned, owing to failing health, in 1842, and was succeeded by Rev. Francis P. Lee, a native of Camden. After four years of faithful work, Mr. Lee accepted a call to Alabama.

In 1847, the vestry was fortunate in securing the services of Rev. Thomas Frederick Davis, that eminent churchman, who, in 1853, was elevated to the Bishopric

---

[1] On northwest corner of present Bull property, formerly of W. E. Johnson.
[2] The *Camden Journal* (1831) speaks of the building as a beautiful one, "in the most classic style of Gothic architecture."

of South Carolina. His life story is briefly told in an account of the Davis family.

Bishop Davis paid Camden the high compliment of continuing his connection with the church here after his election to the Episcopate—the first instance of a Bishop of this diocese residing elsewhere than in Charleston. His son, Rev. Thos. F. Davis, Jr., was chosen Assistant Rector, which position, virtually the rectorship, he filled most acceptably until his untimely death in 1865.

Mainly through the efforts of Bishop Davis, a Theological Seminary for the Diocese was created, in 1859, and, for his convenience, located in Camden, on the west side of Broad Street between Laurens and DeKalb, almost directly opposite his residence. The building was two-storied and of brick. The Faculty consisted of the Bishop, Rev. Paul Trapier and Rev. Thomas Hanckel.

There were ten students at the outbreak of the War, in 1861, and, almost to a man, they enlisted in the army. On March 31, 1865, just one month after Sherman's Raid, the Seminary was burned to the ground, the act of incendiaries. Later the institution was moved to Spartanburg, where, for a time, it occupied the present site of Converse College.

In 1866, Rev. John Johnson, a former student at the Seminary, who had greatly distinguished himself in the siege of Fort Sumter,[1] was called to this parish.

During his pastorate, the pretty little church on Broad Street was destroyed by fire, having caught from an adjacent frame building, on May 29, 1867. Some of the furniture was saved but the organ and bell were consumed, the latter wierdly tolling its own knell as the flames embraced it.

Coming just after the exhausting War, this was a heavy blow to the parish. For three years following, services were held in the Pine Grove Academy (facing Hampton Park); the house had been leased and consecrated as a chapel.

Efforts were soon made to rebuild. The lots on which both church and seminary had stood were sold, and the present site on the southwest corner of Laurens and Lyttleton Streets was purchased.

---

[1] Of which he has written a masterpiece of military history, *The Defense of Charleston Harbor*.

## Churches

Shortly after the new church was begun, Dr. Johnson accepted a call to St. Philips, Charleston. His ties to this community, however, had been cemented by his marriage to Floride, daughter of Gen. James W. Cantey.

Mr. Johnson was succeeded by Rev. J. S. Kidney, of Albany, N. Y., who remained but a few months. During his brief term, however, a gloom was thrown over the entire Diocese by the death of the Bishop, which occurred at his home here, December 2, 1871. The Sunday before, he had preached the first sermon in the still uncompleted church—his last words to his devoted flock.[1]

In 1873, under the rectorship of Rev. B. F. Dunkin Perry, the new church was consecrated by Bishop Howe. When built, it was a severely plain brick structure of Gothic style. The present imposing front, with corner tower, was added in 1908. A memorial window, in the rear of the chancel, to Bishop Davis, the side panels of which are dedicated to his two sons, Rev. T. F. Davis, Jr., and Rev. F. Bruce Davis, was put in by the congregation. Other handsome memorial windows and mural tablets adorn the walls.

The ornate marble font came from the old Plowden Weston Church near Georgetown.

Mr. Perry, who died in 1874, lies in our "God's Acre". He was succeeded by Rev. Edward R. Miles, who served for four years. Then came Rev. C. I. LaRoche, who, in 1881, gave place to Rev. W. J. Alger, of Maine.

Rev. James Moss Stoney's pastorate of thirteen years, 1884 to 1897, was one of the longest in the history of the parish. Mr. Stoney was much beloved, especially by the poor, among whom he did a fine missionary work. The chapels at Malvern Hill and Swift Creek were results of his efforts. He too was allied to Camden by the bonds of marriage; and here he rests from his labors. One of the fine stained glass windows in the church was erected to his memory by the Sunday School.

Rev. Wm. Baker Gordon of North Carolina succeeded him in 1897. To his untiring efforts are due most of the material improvements to the church property already mentioned. In addition, the neat frame Sunday School room, which stands among the splendid pines on the church lot, was built in 1900. Owing to advancing years, Dr. Gordon was retired, as pastor emeritus,

[1] See Davis Family.

in 1912, continuing his residence in Camden, honored by all her citizens, until called to his reward in 1921. He lies in our cemetery.

## Rectors.

1775—Theophilus Drage
1813-1817—Andrew Fowler
1830-1842—Edward Phillips
1842-1847—Francis P. Lee
1847-1853—Thomas Frederick Davis (Elected Bishop of the Diocese in 1853.)
1853-1865—Thomas F. Davis, Jr.
1866-1870—John Johnson
1870-1871—J. S. Kidney
1873-1874—B. F. Dunkin Perry
1875-1879—Edward R. Miles
1879-1881—C. I. LaRoche
1881-1884—W. J. Alger
1884-1897—James M. Stoney
1897-1912—Wm. B. Gordon
1912-1924—F. H. Harding
1924—I. DeL. Brayshaw

## Methodist.

At the famous "Christian Conference" held in Baltimore in January, 1785, the Methodist Episcopal Church was first formally organized in America.

From this assembly, Bishop Asbury hastened on his mission to establish the church in South Carolina. He held the first Methodist service in Camden on April 4, 1787.

In the same year, Rev. Isaac Smith was sent as minister to Camden, and, doubtless, neighboring communities, by the first annual Conference for South Carolina, which was held by Bishops Coke and Asbury at Charleston. Camden was then included in what was known as the Santee Circuit, which embraced the territory on both sides the Santee and Wateree Rivers, from Nelson's Ferry on the Santee nearly to Charlotte, N. C.[1]

From the Autobiography of Rev. James Jenkins we make the following extracts:

"Mr. Dan Carpenter was a pioneer of Camden Methodism. His house was the preacher's home, and, it is possible, was at first a place for preaching. Very early, persons of highest influence and social position in Camden became members." Again: "Before going to Conference" (in 1797), "I went home, and on my way passed through Camden, and preached in the house of Brother Isaac Smith, there being no church."

[1]Burgess' *Chronicles of St. Mark's Parish.*

CHURCHES

Mr. Jenkins, himself one of the earliest disciples of John Wesley in the State, was appointed to Camden in 1794 and again in 1800. Here, at the age of 83, he died in 1847, after an active service in the ministry of fifty-three years, and his body rests in our cemetery.[1]

The clever pen of Mrs. Isaac Alexander[2] pays the following glowing tribute to Rev. Isaac Smith and Dan Carpenter as she knew them in the early years of the 19th century: "Who recollects the good old Parson Smith? If any, they have not forgotten his house where the travelling preacher and the wanderer of whats'ever name found a welcome resting place, where none who craved assistance or sympathy applied in vain. Over the couch of the sick or dying, wherever or whoever they might be, there was his voice lifted up, * * * and when he committed their bodies dust to dust, ashes to ashes, all felt the peculiar solemnity of the scene. * * * Few men have lived in Camden whose memory will be cherished with more respect and affection, as long as there remains one to recollect the dear old man.

"Next, must not be forgotten one who was the first Methodist in Camden, from whose family altar arose the first prayers offered in Camden by that people— Dan Carpenter, a name long remembered and revered. He came here before Parson Smith and for some time stood alone. Religious meetings were held in his house. No man has ever lived in Camden who sacrificed more to private benevolence or public good. His house and heart were ever open to all who stood in need. He sacrificed all, even life, to public benefit, for he caught the fever of which he died in his attempts to render the river navigable."

Dr. Burgess (*Chronicles of St. Mark's Parish*) informs us that Isaac Smith was one of the founders of the Georgia Conference; also that he had been a Revolutionary soldier, fighting under LaFayette, who met and embraced him with the utmost tenderness on his visit to America in 1824. This incident occurred probably at Camden.

Rev. H. F. Chreitzberg, in an article[3] on the church in Camden, states that the first House of Worship here

[1] For his descendants, see Workman Family.
[2] Her *Camden Fifty Years Ago* (mss) was written about 1856.
[3] Published in the *Southern Christian Advocate*, 1879.

was erected in 1798. This can scarcely be credited if we accept the testimony of Mrs. Phineas Thornton, who came to Camden, a bride, in 1804. In her interesting Reminiscences (mss), written in 1856, she says: "Four years before I came, as I learned, the first Methodist Conference Camden ever saw was held. Bishop Asbury presided, I suppose. One important fact I well remember, that Mr. (Dan) Carpenter and Mr. (Isaac) Smith entertained the entire Conference with their horses. Mr. Carpenter had at his house thirty preachers, and his stables were filled to the very utmost. Conference was either held in the Court House or in a two-story house of one Fisher, called the Yellow House, standing on corner of jail square, where James Conner lives. Mr. Carpenter lived just below the present Market House, and Mr. Smith lived next to him just below."[1] Evidently there was no church building in 1800.

She further states that in 1804 the Methodists had the only house of worship in Camden. This would lead to the inference that it was reared between 1800 and 1804. It was a small frame structure, situated about three hundred yards due west of the old jail, on King Street, midway between Church and Campbell. For further information regarding it, we quote Mrs. Thornton again: "By advice and aid of Bishop Asbury, it was lengthened in the rear, making quite a walk to enter at one end and go up through to the other. At sacramental occasions, the first communicants would go out at side doors and come in again below, while the Second-Table communicants would approach in middle aisle. The whites would remain in until all the blacks would commune."

In 1828, a new Church was completed, on West DeKalb Street, facing Church Street, and dedicated during the Annual Conference in session here that year. This large frame structure, still standing, has been used, since 1872, by the (African) M. E. Church (North).[2]

In 1860, $10,000.00 was raised for the building of a much handsomer brick church on Monument Square. Work was actually begun, the walls being raised several feet above ground, when the undertaking was killed,

[1] Opposite the old Court House, corner Broad and King Streets.
[2] In 1925, it was demolished and an ornate brick structure is rising in its place.

CHURCHES

like so many others, by the outbreak of war. The lumber on the ground was burnt during Sherman's raid in 1865, and even the site was subsequently abandoned.[1]

As stated, in 1872, the DeKalb Street property was sold to the negroes, and the Pine Grove Academy,[2] which had been used as an Episcopal Chapel since 1868, was secured temporarily for services. Preparations were at once begun for the building of the present edifice on Lyttleton Street, which was dedicated in 1879. A tablet to the memory of Samuel Mathis, "the first white child born in Camden", is placed in the vestibule, having been removed from the old DeKalb Street Church. The annex for the Sunday School was added in 1900.

The building stands on a part of the ground presented to the "Methodist Society of Camden", in 1851, by Mrs. Sarah Ciples and Mrs. Amelia Haile, who also built and gave the commodious Parsonage, erected on the land, with several outbuildings as quarters for servants. There last-named were to accommodate the three negro slaves which, in 1852, Mrs. Ciples donated for the use of the minister: to wit: "one negro boy named John, aged about twenty years, one negro woman named Easter, aged about twenty-three years, and her boy child named Alex, about two years old, and their future issue and increase." Mrs. Ciples at the same time gave twenty shares of stock in the Bank of Camden, to be applied to the support of the parson, and specifically provided for the clothing of said servants.

A slave-holding church! What a howl the "Liberator" would have raised over this bit of information!

Camden was separated from the Santee Circuit and made a "station" in 1811, and has been an independent charge ever since.

*Ministers Who Have Served in Camden.*

(Up to 1811, these men served other churches in Santee Circuit besides Camden.)

1787—Isaac Smith
1788 { Isaac Smith
      { H. Herbert
1789 { M. Moore
      { J. Russell
1790 { L. Andrews
      { J. Askew

[1] From the article on *Camden Methodism*, by Rev. H. F. Chreitzberg.
[2] On Hampton Park; since converted into a residence.

1791 { J. Crawford / J. Tolleson
1792 { Isaac Smith / John Wood
1793—Tobias Gibson
1794—James Jenkins
1795—Isaac Smith
1796 { G. Clark / N. Williamson
1797—Tobias Gibson
1798 { I. Doughet / Geo. Dougherty / R. Grains
1799 { R. Wiley / T. Shaw
1800 { James Jenkins / L. Garrison
1801 { W. Gassaway / W. Avant
1802 { W. Gassaway / W. Jones
1803 { W. Gassaway / Thos. Shaw
1804 { S. Ansley / Jno. McVean
1805 { H. Ledbetter / Jno. McVean
1806—H. Porter
1807 { W. Warwick / B. Gordon
1808 { J. Jackson / W. Gassaway / Wm. B. Kennedy
1809 { I. Tarplay / N. Powers
1810 { John Hill / James Capers
1811 { S. Miles / G. D. Glenn
(Camden now separate "Station")
1812—S. Bryan
1813-1814—H. D. Green
1815 { T. Mason / D. McPhail
1816—Hilliard Judge
1817—Wm. Hollingsworth
1818—W. B. Kennedy
1819—Samuel Dunwoody
1820—W. C. Hill
1821—T. Sneed
1822—N. Talley
1823—R. Tucker
1824—J. N. Glenn
1825—Malcolm McPherson
1826—B. L. Hoskins
1827—J. Freeman
1828—Thos. L. Wynn
1829—Benj. H. Capers
1830-1831—Samuel W. Capers
1832—W. M. Wightman
1833—W. Murrah
1834—D. G. McDaniel
1835—Whitefoord Smith
1836-1837—James Stacey
1837—K. Murchison
1838—W. J. Jackson
1839—B. Thomason
1840—Samuel Townsend
1841-1842—W. C. Kirkland
1843-1844—C. H. Pritchard
1845—W. P. Mouzon
1846—Charles Taylor
1847-1848—S. M. Green
1849-1850—W. T. Capers
1851-1852—H. C. Parsons
1853-1854—William Martin
1855-1856—James Stacey
1857—W. A. Gamewell
1858—H. C. Parsons
1859—Robert J. Boyd
1860—E. J. Maynardie
1861 { E. J. Maynardie / Manning Brown
1862—Manning Brown
1863 { M. Brown / Robert Allston

PRESBYTERIAN CHURCH
DeKalb Monument in front.
One of Orphan Society Academies at right

## Churches

1864-1865—J. T. Wightman
1866—T. J. Clyde
1867-1868—C. Thomasson
1869—W. Thomas
1870—J. W. Humbert
1871-1872—A. J. Stokes
1873—R. L. Harper
1874—J. W. Kelley
1875-1876—H. F. Chreitzberg
1877—G. W. Whitman
1878-1880—John O. Willson
1881—D. Z. Dantzler
1882—D. D. Dantzler
1883-1884—H. M. Mood
1885-1886—W. T. Capers
1887-1888—P. A. Murray
1889—E. J. Maynardie
1890 { E. J. Maynardie / J. M. Rodgers
1891-1894—Mark L. Carlisle
1895—G. H. Waddell
1896-1899—J. Thos. Pate
1900—W. M. Duncan
1901-1902—J. L. Stokes
1903-1904—A. B. Earle
1905-1908—C. C. Herbert
1909—B. G. Murphy
1910-1913—H. Bascom Browne
1914-1915—Charles B. Smith
1916-1918—John H. Graves
1918-1920—W. W. Daniel
1920-1924—W. H. Hodges
1924—J. T. Peeler

*Presbyterian.*

As stated in our first volume, the Quakers had a Meeting House at this place, then Pinetree Hill, as early probably as 1759.

Of the orthodox churches, the Presbyterians are entitled, we believe, to the distinction of having the only House of Worship in Camden prior to the Revolution.

Miss Kershaw's testimony, given in the sketch of the Episcopal Church, would seem flatly to contradict this statement; but we believe that it will not hold in the face of the evidence to the contrary. Miss Kershaw, quite an old lady, was inaccurate, as shown, in her recollection of Mr. Drage: her memory alone, it is needless to say, therefore, is impeached.

That the ground on which stood the little church that she called "Episcopal" belonged to the Presbyterians certainly as early as 1774, the date of the first recorded plat of Camden, is proved by her father's[1] will, which was executed June 6, 1788: "To the Presbyterian Congregation, I devise lots No. 287 and 288, with all my right, title and property to that part of Church Street laying south of the *lot given to that congregation prior to the town of Camden being laid out in lots*, as far down as Wateree Street, not doubting but that ground will here-

[1] Colonel Joseph Kershaw.

after be vested in that Society by law, and that Church Street will not extend further south than the *Meeting House* ground." (The italics our own.)

Colonel Kershaw had given another site for an Episcopal Church also prior to 1774.[1] Is it likely that that congregation would have built upon the site owned by the Presbyterians? Is it not likely that the "Meeting House" on the Presbyterian lot was built by, or for, the Presbytertains; or perhaps as a house of worship for all demominations?

Mills, in his *Statistics* (1826), says that the Presbyterians had a place of worship in Camden some years before the Revolution. Dr. Furman, in his Appendix to Ramsay's *History of South Carolina*, says the same thing. Miss Kershaw states that the church was demolished to make barracks for the British soldiers.

Mouzon's map of South Carolina, made in 1775, shows that there was then a church in Camden, evidently only one.

Dr. Howe, in his *History of the Presbyterian Church in South Carolina*, says that Rev. John Logue, an aged preacher of Irish extraction, "preached statedly a part of his time in Camden for several years after the war", but that, as Camden was "the oldest inland town in the state", it may have had "occasional services of ministers of our church prior to the War". Miss Kershaw asserted that Mr. Logue "used the church" after the retirement of Mr. Drage (in 1775) until the occupation of the town by Cornwallis in June, 1780. As there is no evidence that a church was ever built on the site given by Colonel Kershaw to the Episcopal congregation, we can reconcile Miss Kershaw's statements with the seeming facts only by assuming that Mr. Drage, the clergyman of the English Church, made use, for his services, of the "Meeting House" on the Presbyterian lot.

The Presbyterians evidently rebuilt after the War, doubtless on the same site, prior to 1790. This is indicated by Colonel Kershaw's deed of assignment, dated February 4 of that year, in which he turns over to his creditors, among other possessions, "that tract of land containing twelve acres, which includes twenty-five lots, on part of which the *Meeting house now stands*."[2]

---

[1] See Diagram No. 3, *Historic Camden, Colonial and Revolutionary*.
[2] Records in Lancaster Court House.

## CHURCHES

As to what became of this second sanctuary, history is silent. Mrs. Phineas Thornton testifies that it was not standing in 1804.[1]

Colonel Kershaw's creditors, it appears, did not disturb the Presbyterians in the possession of their church property, nor was Church Street ever extended through it. The site is still occupied by what is known as the "old Presbyterian churchyard", containing many mossy graves and stones.

In 1789 Rev. John Logue was succeeded by Rev. Thomas Adams, a young Congregational minister from Roxbury, Mass. He was a son of Rev. Amos Adams and grandson of the noted Dr. Chauncey, was a recent graduate of Harvard and served here also as Principal of the Orphan Society's School. Mr. Adams married Dinah, daughter of the Quaker, Wm. Wylie, of Camden. He died here in 1797, and lies in our cemetery[2] by the side of his wife. The notice of his death, in a contemporary Charleston paper, speaks of his eloquence and unusual promise.

Dr. Howe's History, which is an accepted authority on South Carolina Presbyterianism, says of this place: "During the year 1804, a number of gentlemen united in the laudable effort of building a Presbyterian Church on the site assigned by the founder of Camden for that purpose, and, having finished the undertaking by voluntary subscription", Rev. Andrew Flinn was elected pastor, at a salary of $800.00 per annum, to be raised by assessments on pews.

On the fly-leaf of the Record Book of the Camden Church we find this entry: "The Presbyterian Church at Camden, South Carolina, called 'Bethesda', was first organized July 6, 1805." This organization was effected "in the Court House".

On January 1, 1806, Mr. Flinn entered upon the discharge of his duties, and on February 20, 1806, there is record of a second congregational meeting, this time "in the church", which, we therefore infer, was erected during the latter part of 1805, or the first part of 1806.

The first elected elders were: Dr. I. Alexander, John Kirkpatrick, James Syng Murray, and Zebulon Rudolph.

[1] See *Methodist Church*.
[2] In the Young enclosure.

HISTORIC CAMDEN

The signers of the call to Mr. Flinn were: Isaac Alexander, Isaac DuBose, Wm. Lang, Joseph Brevard, Zack Cantey, John Kershaw, Abram Blanding, John Adamson, James Clark, John McCaa, Ben Carter, Wm. Parker, Joseph Mickle, John Kirkpatrick, Francis S. Lee, Sam'l Bread, Jonathan Eccles, Henry H. Dickinson, Dan'l Rose, Wm. Hutchison, James Young, John Trent, J. D. Deveaux, Thomas Wilson, James W. Ker, Wm. Cloud, Jos. H. Howell, Reuben Arthur, Alexander Matheson, Wylie Vaughan.

That entertaining chronicler, Mrs. Thornton, frequently quoted in these pages, says: "I remember when the first Presbyterian Church was built near the grave of Colonel Dickinson. Mrs. Isaac Alexander[1] gave $1,000.00 to it, as stated on her tombstone. That church was torn down and removed. Part of it is McCreight's workshop."[2] At the time this was written (1856), Colonel Dickinson's remains had not been removed from the old Presbyterian cemetery, and McCreight's workshop was on Rutledge Street, north side, near Broad. Mrs. Thornton was evidently ignorant of the fact that this was the third church on the site. The inscription on Mrs. Alexander's tombstone alluded to speaks simply of "her unwearied and successful labors and liberal donations in founding the Presbyterian Church in Camden."

One of the first entries in the Record Book gives a faint but suggestive picture of this third little church; it is dated November, 1806, and is a resolution providing for a "Bell-ringer, who shall also do the duties of a sexton, open the church, light candles, etc.", said functionary to be supported "by a tax of 25¢ per quarter on the pews below stairs and 12½¢ per quarter on the pews or seats east end of the church."

On March 11, 1806, the church was taken under the care of the First Presbytery of South Carolina with the title, "Bethesda of Camden".

In 1820 the congregation had become so large that it was deemed necessary to erect a bigger church in a more central location. Accordingly, Messrs. Wm. Ancrum, Alexander Young and James K. Douglas, the com-

---

[1]First wife of Dr. I. Alexander and daughter of Dr. Wm. Brisbane, of Charleston.

[2]Captain Jas. I. Villepigue says the church stood just east of the Ancrum enclosure and was built of wood. He had been in it.

CHURCHES

mittee appointed for the purpose, secured the present site on DeKalb Street, and, under their supervision, the handsome brick building still in use was erected, at a cost of $14,000.00.[1] It was dedicated in October, 1822. In order to support the church, the pews were regularly sold, titles being given. The charges were $30.00 per year for the middle and double side pews, and $15.00 for the single side pews. The minister was to receive $1,000.00, with surplus from pew rents. From a plan of the church, recorded in our Court House, January 21, 1823, (Book K. p. 123), we learn that there were then the following pew holders: A. Young, H. R. Cook, W. McKain, James Clarke, Thos. Lang, B. Bineham, Wm. Daniel, John Kershaw, John Boykin, Jr., J. K. Douglas, D. L. DeSaussure, Jane Lane, C. E. Cattonet, J. C. Carter, E. C. Brevard, H. H. Dickinson, T. P. Evans, Wm. Ancrum, Joseph Goodman, Nancy Reid, C. A. Bullard, Mary Whitaker, W. W. Lang, Royal Bullard, J. W. Lang, J. J. Blair, Alex Matheson, J. C. McRae, H. McCall, Wm. B. Whitaker, Alfred Brevard, J. S. Murray, Wm. McWillie, J. Adamson, Lewis Ciples, James Chesnut, John Boykin, J. S. Deas, C. J. Shannon, Thos. Salmond, E. H. Anderson.

According to Dr. Howe, Rev. John Joyce, then pastor, was largely instrumental in securing the new building, and its somewhat remarkable arrangement was to meet his "peculiar views", to wit, the incongruous steeple in the rear, the pulpit between the two front doors, and the "five porches of Bethesda" on the outside in the rear, which were landings for stairs leading to the organ loft and gallery, one side of which was reserved for negroes. There were also a high quaint pulpit, standing well forward into the body of the church and entered by winding steps, and high backed pews with doors that closed each family within its own compartment. The interior of the building was modernized in 1890, losing all of its quaintness; even the Bethesda porches, the special glory of this sanctuary, were ruthlessly altered.

A deep sweet-toned bell used to hang in the spire. This was melted into cannon, during the War, for the Confederate service. In 1873, a new bell was put in by the Ladies' Society.

[1] It is said to have been built by the noted architect, Robert Mills.

HISTORIC CAMDEN

The monument to DeKalb was placed in front of the Church in 1825.

The longest pastorate in the history of the church was that of Rev. Samuel H. Hay, from 1851 to 1879, when, owing to advancing years, he retired from active work.[1]

In 1884, Rev. W. H. Mills, D. D., was called to Camden. His devoted ministry of twenty years, ending with his resignation at the close of 1904, on account of failing health, has left an impression that will long endure on both church and community. Dr. Mills was born in Sumter County in 1837. He graduated from the South Carolina College and intended entering the Theological Seminary at once. The outbreak of the War, however, caused him to enter the Confederate service instead, in 1861. On the retreat of Lee's army from Richmond he was seriously wounded through the body. Before entire recovery, he had entered the Seminary, from which he graduated in 1868. His health was never afterward robust. In 1868, he was married to Miss Sarah Edith Smith, of Pendleton District. Dr. Mills died at Camden in 1905, revered by the entire community.

The first Manse of which there is record or tradition, used from 1835 to 1851, was situated on the northeast corner of Mill and DeKalb Streets. In 1857 the Manse on the corner of Fair and Union Streets was acquired. It was a handsome residence surrounded by spacious grounds. In 1913 this property was sold to the Camden Hospital Association, the house, with a brick veneer, being converted into the central building of the present modern hospital. A new manse was built on Lyttleton Street opposite Rectory Park.

No history of Bethesda of Camden would be complete without mention of the remarkably long service of some of its Ruling Elders:

Daniel L. DeSaussure served 30 years; died in 1857.
James K. Douglas, 50 years; died, 1860.
John Rosser, 20 years; resigned, 1860.
Charles J. Shannon, 31 years; died, 1863.
John J. Workman, 32 years; died 1865.
Robert J. McCreight, 27 years; died, 1888.
Wm. H. R. Workman, 29 years; died, 1889.
Anthony M. Kennedy, 33 years; died, 1892.

[1] See Hay Family.

## Churches

### Pastors.

—John Logue
1789-1797—Thomas Adams
1806-1809—Andrew Flinn
1809-1810—W. Brantley of the Baptist Church (Temporary Supply)
1810-1811—B. R. Montgomery, D. D.
1811-1819—George Reid
1819-1820—Alfred Wright (Temporary Supply)
1820-1820—Austin Dickinson (Temporary Supply)
1820-1822—John Joyce
1823-1824—Samuel S. Davis, D. D.
1824-1825—R. B. McLeod
1825-1827—John Joyce
1827-1828—Raynolds Bascom (Temporary Supply)
1828-1832—S. S. Davis, D. D.
1833-1837—John Witherspoon, D. D., L. L.D.
1837-1844—R. B. Campbell
1845-1851—S. S. Davis, D. D.
1851-1879—Samuel H. Hay
1881-1883—A. M. Sale
1884-1904—W. H. Mills, D. D.
1905-1907—T. M. McConnell, D. D.
1908-1917—J. C. Rowan
1918—Edwin Muller, D. D.

### Roman Catholic.

Until very recent years, Camden was a mission station served by the pastors of the Columbia church.

According to Dr. O'Connell,[1] it was "one of the most barren spots in the entire mission. A church edifice was begun during the pastorship of Mr. Quigley", (1844-48), "and sold for debt before its completion. There were scarcely any Catholics of means in that place who felt the slightest interest in religious matters. Bishop Reynolds declined assuming the debt on his accession to the see of Charleston. The amount could not have been very large, for the building was wooden and of moderate size. There were some complications, which terminated in the sale of the church at public auction. It was bought in by a Frenchman, who converted it into a dwelling-house.

"In earlier times this place was repeatedly visited by Bishop England. He lectured on those occasions to the elite and wealthy people who possessed the surrounding fertile country and owned fancy residences in the town, which boasts of the DeKalb monument and preserves his remains. I subsequently preached in the Town Hall.

---

[1]*Catholicity in the Carolinas and Georgia* by Rev. Dr. J. J. O'Connell, Copyrighted, 1879.

"One family resided in the town who always adhered to the Faith—the Campbells. The father had not yet joined the Church; the mother, raised in Charleston, was a most excellent and pious woman, who taught her children their obligations to God and man."

The uncompleted church building, sold for debt, still stands on West DeKalb Street next to the county jail. It was bid in by Paul Francis Villepigue, who had advanced the money to put it up, and it has ever since been used as a residence. The high columns in front easily distinguish it as of ecclesiastical origin, though it was never consecrated or used as a church.

The second attempt to establish a mission church in Camden was more successful, the edifice, now a Jewish synagogue, on Lyttleton Street, being erected and dedicated in 1903, under the title of Sacred Heart Church. Reverend Thomas J. Hegerty of Columbia was the rector and Reverend B. W. Fleming, through whose efforts the little church was built, was the curate. "Being a frame structure", we are informed, the house was never consecrated.

Succeeding Father Fleming, the following clergymen served as Columbia parish curates in attendance upon Sacred Heart Church at Camden:

1909-1913—John J. Hughes     1913-1915—Nicholas A. Murphy

The present beautiful little church and rectory on upper Lyttleton Street, Kirkwood, was completed in 1914. It was a benefaction of Miss Charlotte de Macklot Thompson, a devout Romanist of Baltimore, who bought and occupied for several years the old Boykin homestead, "The Terraces", below Camden, now the Charlotte Thompson School. The church was consecrated by Bishop Northrop on February 28, 1915, under the title of Saint Mary of Perpetual Succour, more popularly styled St. Mary's.

The church was then separated from St. Peters at Columbia and has since had the following resident rectors:

1915-1918—Denis A. Lanigan     1920-1922—J. Alexis Westbury
1918-1920—Cornelius A. Kennedy     1922-1925—M. J. Reddin
                                   1925—Thomas J. Mackin

## Churches

St. Mary's is the chief church of the Camden Missions, which comprise all churches and missions in the counties of Chesterfield, Kershaw and Marlborough.

Reverend Thomas J. Mackin, the present rector, is our authority for the history of the parish since 1903.

The congregation of the Camden Church is locally small, but it is considerably augmented during the winter seasons by guests and employees of the tourist hotels.

# CHAPTER XXIII.

### NEWSPAPERS.

So far as research reveals the first newspaper published in Camden appeared in May 1802. But a single specimen (issue of October 19, 1802) has been discovered in the residence of Mr. S. J. T. Young, an old building about ten miles north of Camden. Its title was:

*The Carolina Journal or the Camden Advertiser.*—The caption is decorated with the strange device of an eagle with expanded wings; from the tip of one of which dangles an anchor, from the other a head of wheat. It was published by "J. Martin Slump at the corner of York and Church Streets" and bore this latin motto:

> "Omne tulit punctum, qui miscuit utile dulci,
> Lectorem delectando pariterque monendo."

Among its news items is found this morsel: "Married: on Thursday the 7th inst. Mr. Hugh McClester, butcher of this place to the amiable and accomplished Miss Sarah Drakeford, eldest daughter of Richard Drakeford. May all butchers make as good a choice in the purchase of beef cattle as they are apt to do in search of a partner and our citizens will never want for good marrow bones nor the community for good cooks to prepare wholesome and nourishing dishes."

How long this paper managed to subsist is unknown. No other specimen of any Camden newspaper could we discover between that of May 1802 and April 4, 1816, on which latter date appears the first issue of the

*Camden Gazette.*—"Printed by P. W. Johnson, King Street, Camden, S. C. for the proprietors." For some time prior to this, how long is not disclosed, there was no newspaper published in Camden, for the *Gazette* of May 2, 1816, says: "No event is more auspicious to the welfare of Camden and its vicinity than the acquisition of a paper."

The *Gazette* was for a time edited by Dr. Wm. Langley, an excellent citizen of old Camden. But his style seems to have been rather too drab and didactic for his patrons. He writes: "We have been lately told by a friend that our plan in conducting this paper is not well adapted to the understanding of a majority of our readers. We will observe that a little attention will not only render it palatable but interesting. That he who takes up a paper for amusement and not instruction will not be fully gratified is conceded." Dr. Langley continued the even tenor of his style which certainly had not the vice of levity.

In 1818 the paper was purchased by Wilie Vaughan, enlarged and the title extended into the

*Camden Gazette and Mercantile Advertiser.*—This was continued during 1819, 1820 and 1821 until February 1822 when it appears under the title of

*The Southern Chronicle and Camden Gazette.*—Published by Geo. Walter Tarbox. In September 1822 this title is changed to

*The Camden Chronicle.*—Was again changed in January 1824 and converted into

*The Southern Chronicle.*—Published by Tarbox and Addison. In February same year Chas. A. Bullard becomes editor and remodels the name into

*The Southern Chronicle and Camden Aegis.*—The public or the publishers must have been fickle, for in 1825 the heading appears as

*The Camden Literary and Political Register.*—This too falls by the wayside within a year and is replaced by the steady old *Camden Journal,* founded in January 1826 by Chas. A. Bullard. Concerning him we have been able to discover very little. Very likely he was from New England, for in 1823 he publishes a call for a meeting of the "Sons of Pilgrims" at McAdams and Drakefords Long Room, there being then in Camden a considerable colony of New Englanders.

Soon after this (1826) Bullard left Camden to edit the *Telescope,* a paper then published in Columbia, S. C. W. J. Grant took his place as editor of the *Journal.*

Shortly after this (in 1828) another New Englander, C. F. Daniels, a native of Connecticut, took charge of the *Journal,* and certainly made it an interesting paper. He became one of the celebrated Journalists of his day. He first appears in South Carolina at Cheraw as editor of the *Peedee Gazette* in May 1826, and a little later of the *Cheraw Spectator.* He came to Camden and assumed charge of the *Journal* September 1828.

He announces: "My politics are the politics of South Carolina", then deeply stirred by the anti-tariff, states-rights agitation. The so-called "peaceful remedy" of Nullification was in process of evolution. The Union element in the state while opposed to protective tariffs, were more hostile to the proposed Nullification remedy. Daniels made of the *Journal* a formidable weapon for the Union party.

As to the effectiveness of the *Journal* under Daniels, the *New England Review* of that day gives this testimonial: "We will say to the public respecting this paper (*Camden Journal*) what we have already said to the editor, it is worth more than all the other periodicals which we receive from the South of the Potomac." But in the next breath Daniels is most bitterly arraigned for recreancy to the land of his nativity as follows: "But we have some fault to find. The editor is a New Englander, and a traitor to the land of his fathers. He has gone to the South and Southern principles have taken the place of those of his native clime. Come home, friend Daniels."

Daniels stood between a cross fire from the radical Nullifiers in Carolina on one hand and the Abolitionists of his native New England on the other. If to the one he was a renegade, to the other he was (to quote one of them) "a hollow hearted hypocrite." While he possessed the friendship of Unionists, who always predominated in this district, such as McWillie, Levy, Blair, Chesnut, Nixon, yet he suffered anything but gentle treatment at the hands of the Nullifiers. In June 1831 Jas. H. Hammond (who afterwards became Governor of the State and United States Senator) then Editor of the *Columbia Times,* a fierce Nullification organ, resenting a bitter editorial in the *Journal,* came over to Camden, accompanied by a friend, and attacked Daniels on the street with a stick. In the scuffle which ensued Daniels fired a pistol without hitting his assailant. Citizens quickly interferred and stopped the fight.

The article by which Hammond was so wrought appeared in the *Camden Journal* of May 28, 1831. It sarcastically repels a charge of Hammond that the *Journal* had falsified in regard to an election then of exciting interest. It is headed by the couplet:

## NEWSPAPERS

"Good Mr. Muggins knew ye not,
Back through the vent would fly the shot."

It wound up with these words: "We will not bear the supercilious sneers of a pitiful political coxcomb; and if the Malvolio of the *Columbia Times* ceases not his unprovoked aspersions, we will show him up to the people of South Carolina in a new form of cookery that shall leave him no desire to meddle with us more."

At last finding such atmosphere too uncongenial, Daniels, in January 1833 retires and in his valedictory says:

"This number of the *Journal* closes my connexion with it, and an uninterrupted communion of something more than four years has ceased forever. I shall be succeeded by native Carolinians, by those who can advocate the principles of order, law and government without carrying dead weight. It has been a continuous source of ungenerous imputation upon me that I am a "Yankee", and therefore an alien enemy of South Carolina. I feel much pride in pleading guilty to the enormity of birthplace. I would not leave my post while a vestige of liberty lingered in South Carolina or while a single true hearted son of the soil was left alive to raise his voice for freedom, if I did not believe that it can be sustained with more effect by others."

Thus Camden lost a gifted and valuable citizen. He was born in Waterford, Connecticut, December 3, 1788; married Mary A. Prentis of New London, December 31, 1821. He studied law under Judge Griswold of Lynne, and begun practice in Haddam, an adjoining town of Connecticut. He moved to Cheraw, South Carolina, in 1825.

On leaving Camden in 1833 he went to New York City, and there became associate editor of the *Courier and Enquirer*, then a leading paper of the country. Subsequently he edited *The New York Gazette*. He moved to New London in 1848 and there edited the *New London Chronicle*, a daily paper embellished by his caustic wit and facile style. He died in New London, October 19, 1858.

When Daniels left Camden he carried with him a bound volume of the *Camden Journal* 1828-1833. Mr. Robert Coit of New London, who knew Daniels, being a connection of his family, most kindly sent us that old volume of the *Journal* and also some data regarding Daniels which have been inserted above. Between the leaves of that old volume was a clipping from some New York paper comparing Leggett, the famous editor of the *Evening Post*, with Daniels. From this contemporary estimate of Daniels we quote the following:

"We do not, however, consider Mr. Leggett so eminently *forcible* a writer as his occasional opponent, Mr. Daniels of the *Courier and Enquirer*. * * * Mr. Daniels can compress more concentrated wormwood into one of his sentences, can bring out the last word with more real scorpion tact, than any writer whom we know. But he can also sadly disorganise your intercostal muscles with imperative and cruel laughter. Some of his jokes are more drastic than a whole bottle of croton oil, and a fellow looks as completely flaccid and foolish as 'a purser's shirt upon a handspike'. But this gentleman's talents are so versatile, and so variously exercised, that only those who are acquainted with the interior of the office can possibly imagine the compass of his ability or the extent of his industry. He is the main pillar of the *Courier* establishment, and far better would it be both for it and the public if his highly honorable and generous mind were allowed to guide the moral and national influence of that journal."

In opposition to the *Journal* the Nullifiers in 1831 established

*The Camden and Lancaster Beacon.*—Conducted by Major J. D. Cocke, of fiery quality. This paper expired in two or three years. It is said that Cocke moved to Texas, and in the struggles of that State with Mexico was captured, drew the black bean and was shot. In 1833 is found mention of

*The Camden Republican.*—Published by Samuel Weir. This was successor to the *Beacon* and likewise a Nullification organ. No sample copy of this paper has been discovered. It was probably short-lived. In 1836 the title of the *Journal* is expanded into

*The Camden Journal and Southern Whig.*—Under editorship of J. C. West, who notes the recent happy compromise between the Union and Nullification parties. The same year Robert McKnight purchases the paper. His son, George McKnight, born in Camden 1833, of poetic tendencies, as Confederate prisoner at Johnson's

Island, emitted humorous verses under the signature "Asa Hartz".

In March 1837 publication of the *Journal* was suspended, and until May, Camden was without a paper. In that month however appeared the first issue of the

*Camden Commercial Courier.*—Edited by Mordecai M. Levy. It came to an end April 1838, and again Camden was devoid of a newspaper until December 1839, when emerged again

*The Camden Journal.*—Under conduct of Thos. W. Pegues, a faithful and estimable citizen. He was born October 2, 1808, in Marlboro District, and came from a family of Welsh settlers who figured in the Revolution. He followed C. F. Daniels to Camden in 1829. For forty-eight years, with a brief interval, he dedicated his time to printing the *Camden Journal* until his death in January 1878. It is enough to say of him what was truly said by one who knew him, "He was universally esteemed for all those virtues that ennoble humanity."

From its revival in 1839 down to 1848 the *Journal* was for most of that period edited by Wm. B. Johnston. He was a native of Lancashire, England, naturalized in Camden in 1832. He married a daughter of Dr. Joshua Reynolds of Camden. He moved from Camden to Columbia, where he conducted a paper, and in 1864 as state agent, was keeper of the Roll of Honor, which was a record of those who gave their lives in the Confederate service.

The *Journal* was edited during 1849 by Thurlow Caston.

From 1850 to 1861 Thos. J. Warren was proprietor and editor of the *Journal*. His name is to be preserved not so much for shining talent, though a respectable editor, as for sterling character and patriotic devotion. His ancestry it is said traces to the Warren of Bunker Hill. His father, Thomas James Warren, with a brother, Dr. Joseph Warren, came to Carolina from Boston. Joseph settled in Sumter, Thomas in Camden. Peter Warren, his uncle, was mayor of Camden in 1809 and also in 1823. Thomas Warren's articles in the *Journal* were extreme and fiery in advocacy of Southern Secession. When the war came his course conformed to his words. He raised a company and as captain carried it into many an ordeal of battle. At Gettysburg he fell dead on the field from a bullet which entered his eye, while commanding the regiment in place of Colonel Wm. F. DeSaussure who had fallen. The spot of his burial was marked, and in May 1871 his remains were interred with honors in Camden soil. The *Sumter Watchman* of that date said of him: "No more unflinching, self-sacrificing or heroic son of South Carolina buckled on his armor"; and said Dr. Meynardie: "At the age of 38 he has passed away; but the savor of his memory will ever be sweet, and the recollection of his piety and patriotism will be an incentive to imitate his brilliant example." He married a Miss Maxwell, of Pendleton, and his sister, Elizabeth, lived, unmarried and alone, to a great old age in the family home, still standing, on the north side of DeKalb Street between Fair and Mill Streets.

Besides the *Journal*, Warren also published in Camden for some years the

*South Carolina Temperance Advocate.*—The file of this paper for 1853 contains little of interest.

When Warren went to the front the *Journal* suffered another suspension. Its place was supplied by the

*Camden Confederate.*—The first issue appearing November 1, 1861, which during the war period, was ably conducted by J. T. Hershman.

In January 1864 a resident of Camden, one Daniel D. Hocott resurrected

*The Camden Weekly Journal.*—He was long celebrated in these parts as the hero of an "incident by flood and field", which he himself immortalized in his paper under the title *Forty-eight Hours in a Tree Top.*

It seems that on January 11, 1865, Hocott embarked with his servant in a bateau upon the inundated bottoms of the Wateree River to rescue his hogs. After proceeding far out on the waters a dike up stream broke. The rushing flood capsized the boat. Hocott and his man, thoroughly wet, managed to climb a small cotton-wood tree against which they were driven. Here they remained two days and nights in the cold of mid-winter. To keep from freezing they had to pummel each other, kick the tree, and climb up and down. When rescued they were well nigh exhausted. Ever afterwards this flood was referred to as the "Hocott freshet".

In January 1865 Hershman took over the *Journal* and made a combination of the

## Newspapers

*Journal and Confederate.*—The Confederate part of the caption expired of course with that cause and military occupation of Camden in 1865.

All the papers above mentioned were weekly publications, except the semi-weekly issue of the *Journal* for a time under Warren's management, but it remained for the aforesaid D. D. Hocott to perform the feat of producing from July to December 1864 a daily sheet under the caption of

*The Daily Journal.*—We have seen a few specimens printed upon rough, grey paper such as used for wrapping. It is a pathetic witness to the straits and hardships of those last months of the war. But Hocott was not alone as the proprietor of a daily. Another rival, W. K. Rodgers, during the latter half of the same eventful year, 1864, put forth

*The Daily Bulletin.*—A single sheet it was, even smaller than the *Daily Journal,* but a trifle more newsy. Thus we see, that for a brief season Camden could boast of two dailies and a weekly.

In 1866 *The Camden Journal* was revived under conduct of the above mentioned Thos. W. Pegues; in 1871 it was purchased and conducted by John Kershaw, who sold it to W. D. Trantham and J. T. Hay in 1873. They disposed of it to G. G. Alexander in 1878, by whom it was conducted until its expiration about the year 1890.

The *Wateree Messenger.*—Was established in October 1884 by C. W. Birchmore and the

*Camden Chronicle* by W. L. McDowell in May 1888. These papers have been continuously published to date (1926) by their original founders. In October 1925 the *Wateree Messenger* celebrated its forty-first anniversary, not having missed a single issue in all that time.

In 1873 the *Kershaw Gazette* was started by Frank P. Beard. For several years it was ably edited by L. W. R. Blair. It expired about 1888. For a short time a small daily edition of the *Kershaw Gazette* was published—soon coming to a close.

In 1904 *The People* appeared, conducted by W. A. Schrock. This paper was discontinued in 1909, and was replaced in July 1909 by the *Camden News* under auspices of J. W. Hamel, continuing until January 1913 when it was sold to the *Camden Chronicle.* This paper showed a spirit of enterprise and suggested many improvements around Camden which were realized. Mr. Hamel after disposing of the *News* established *The Era* at the town of Kershaw, his printing establishment being on the Kershaw County side of the boundary line which passes through that town.

# CHAPTER XXIV.
## LIBERTY HILL.

Immediately after crossing Saunders Creek, six miles above Camden, the wayfarer finds himself in a distinctly different region, the up-country of South Carolina.

The deep white sandbeds have abruptly ended and he is in the land of gravel and great rough red-clay hills.

Behind are left the scrubby black-jack and stately long-leaf pine; around him now the characteristic trees are the cedar, oak, holly and hickory. Among many varieties of oak, the white and the chestnut flourish: they are rarely found lower than Saunders Creek.

Cavernous gullies in which large houses might almost be lost to sight, huge boulders picturesquely piled, and vast exposed beds of lichen-covered rocks, are common sights. This was evidently a playground of youthful Titans.

The streams are clear and swift, purling over pebbly bottoms, sometimes dashing merrily around great heaps of stone. After a heavy shower, these pebbly brooks become roaring mountain torrents, suddenly submerging their narrow valleys and as suddenly returning within their proper channels when the storm is spent.

Passing the little settlement on Cantey Hill, ten miles above Camden, Granny's Quarter Creek is crossed and the road climbs through a rugged and sparsely-settled country, over two other pretty water courses, White Oak and Beaver Creeks. From every hill-top extensive and charming views are afforded of the country and of the great lake, formed by the impounded waters of the Wateree River, the great reservoir of the Southern Power Company, which covers for miles the old river-road. The upward grade is very marked from Beaver Creek to the summit of the considerable elevation on which Liberty Hill is perched.

Here one is twenty-two miles from the county courthouse, thirteen miles from the nearest railroad, and six hundred and sixty feet above the level of the sea, the highest point, so railroad engineers have pronounced, between Winnsboro and Charleston, Ridgeway excepted.

## Historic Camden

No village in the state is more finely placed. The narrow plateau on which it stands slopes gradually on every side to streams, beyond which rise the near green and distant blue hills in a vast amphitheatre as far as the eye can see. Those across the river to the west lie in Fairfield and Chester Counties; those to the north are in Lancaster; those to the east and south belong to Kershaw. On a crisp winter day, the naked eye can discern the far-away towns of Ridgway, Winnsboro, Longtown and Lancaster, none nearer than twenty miles, and the movement of trains on the Southern Railway between Charlotte and Columbia may be followed along the distant ridge by the trailing smoke. No shrieks or snortings of the "Iron Monster" have yet disturbed this peaceful Arcadia.

This section was once the abode of the Catawba Indians and their flint arrow-heads and tomahawks are still occasionally found: on the edge of the village is an Indian mortar perfectly hollowed in a granite boulder.

Attracted by the natural fertility of the soil, which along Beaver Creek produces cotton of the finest texture, the white man invaded these parts prior to and just after the Revolution. Among the pioneers may be mentioned Arthur Cunningham, Colonel Adam McWillie, Lewis Collins, Adam Thompson, Samuel Dixon, James Somerville, Reuben Patterson, Shaw Brown, Dr. David George and William Russell.

The Beaver Creek meeting house was the mother-church of the region. It was built in 1772. In the old burying ground attached to it repose the ashes of McWillies, Thompsons, Barbers, Hoods, and other early families, many now extinct. The McWillie plot, enclosed in massive granite walls, contains the handsomest monuments. The Patterson family cemetery nearby also had many fine memorial stones, now seriously disfigured by forest fires.

Later this church was torn down and rebuilt on the Lancaster stage road, where it still stands.

As a locality, Liberty Hill dates from the early years of the 19th century. Peter Garlick's store, which had long stood on the site, was the rendezvous of the farmers and young "sparks" of the neighborhood, and about it as a nucleus grew the little planter community. Garlick's advertisement appears in the *Camden Gazette* of 1817.

## Liberty Hill

He was a tinkerer at all trades,[1] even catering to the needs of the community as doctor and maker of coffins. Perhaps too to keep these professions active, he had a capacious rum cellar that added much to the popularity of his establishment.

The upper half of the Hill at first belonged to Wylie and Wyatt Patterson, twin brothers, while the lower half was the possession of Joseph Cunningham, son of Arthur. The first fine house in the locality was built by Joseph Cunningham, and the commanding view from it overlooked his vast estates that stretched from the headwaters of Beaver Creek on the east to the river on the west. It is now the home of Gov. John G. Richards.

Joseph Patterson, known as the "squire", was also a very large land-holder in the vicinity.

A Presbyterian church was built on the Hill about 1835, and a schoolhouse a few years later. In 1851, the latter was replaced by a two-storied Academy, presided over by a male principal and two female assistants.

Between 1840 and 1850, the wealthy planters of the neighboring country began moving their residences to Liberty Hill, building big typically Southern mansions, of which a few are still in evidence, though not maintained in their former style. The spacious grounds surrounding them were embellished by the skill of the landscape gardener with rare shrubs and flowers. The entrance gates were, in many instances, of wrought iron and the great pillars sustaining them, as well as all the fence posts, were of blue-gray granite quarried in the vicinity. Orchards supplied a variety of fine fruits.

A liberal hospitality was dispensed within those handsome homes. In summer, visitors were numerous and the Hill was gay, though the somewhat Calvanistic atmosphere discouraged dancing, drinking, card playing, racing, and other worldly amusements popular at the time in the lower section of the county.

Camden was the market for all this region, especially after the completion of the railroad from Charleston to that point in 1848. Previously, large rafts and "matchboats", capable of conveying 150 bales of cotton, were poled down the river direct to the seaport from Chesnut's Ferry. Smaller boats, carrying sixty bales, were

---

[1]Dr. J. Marion Sims, in his "Story of my Life", says that his father, in 1813, went to school to "Dr. Garlick, who lived at Liberty Hill".

taken down from Peay's Ferry and even higher up the stream.

Much of the rock used in the construction of the Catawba Canal was gotten from the Ciples place, five miles from the Hill, and conveyed to the river on a horse tram-way, said to have been the first railway in the state, thence to the canal by boat. The oxen used in hauling these tram-cars had to be shod for the very rough work.

Among the settlers of the middle of the century may be mentioned William Dixon, Robert and William Cunningham, Rowland Cornelius, Leroy and John L. Jones, George and John Perry, Jesse Kilgore, John Brown, James Thompson, Henry Brown, Abram Jones, James B. Cureton, Colonel Lewis Patterson, Dr. Robert Johnson, Dr. Pomeroy Bush and Dr. Thomas McDow.

At least four men of the neighborhood were veterans of the Florida War, Lewis Patterson, William Dixon, Ross Dye and John Thompson.

In 1846 a great barbecue was given at the church for the purpose of enlisting volunteers for the Mexican War and many men responded to the eloquent appeals to service made by Colonel Dickinson.

The Hill also furnished its full quota to the Confederate cause.

More than half of Sherman's entire army encamped at Liberty Hill for eight days in the last part of March, 1865, en route to North Carolina, after the burning of Columbia. The Wateree was swollen at the time by one of the biggest freshets on record, and the pontoon bridge at Peay's Ferry broke when half the Federal troops had crossed; the other half crossed at Rocky Mount, eight miles higher up—hence the long delay. Both divisions later united at Warrenton Place, five miles east of the Hill, heading towards Lynch's Creek.

A large raiding party was sent from Liberty Hill to Camden.

The "big houses" of the village, whose sole occupants were ladies, many of them refugees from Columbia, were taken over by the officers, and, as an old darkey described it to the writer, "de woods and hills was bilin over with soldiers." All live stock and provisions for miles around were seized and what could not be consumed or carried away was ruthlessly destroyed.

## Liberty Hill

Many buildings were burned, among them the Academy, the tannery which for years had supplied leather for the shoe factory of George Alden in Camden, and the beautiful homes of Joseph Patterson and Robert Cunningham. The last-named is said to have been fired by slaves at night and the doors and windows by which the terrified occupants sought escape were found barred on the outside. Many negroes followed the army on its march.

A purely agricultural community, Liberty Hill did not easily adjust itself to the new conditions after the War. The rolling soil had been well-nigh exhausted by the old-time system of farming with abundant slave labor. The people were somewhat disheartened and many young men left home for other fields. Times brightened after a long period and some men have prospered, but "the glory that was Rome's", whatever the developments of the future may bring to this beautiful locality, can never perhaps be fully restored.

Just after the Civil War two families established themselves on the Hill that later figured prominently in South Carolina politics—the Floyds and the Richards. The local progenitor of the former, Col. J. Walker Floyd, a one-armed Confederate Veteran from Maryland, served as Adjutant General of the State, 1899-1903. The head of the latter family, Rev. J. G. Richards, was pastor of the Presbyterian Church at Liberty Hill for many years. He left a large family, extensively connected. One of his sons, John G. Richards, was elected Governor of South Carolina in 1926.

# CHAPTER XXV.

### NOTES FROM NATURE.

Camden is situated in the midst of the Sand-hill region that stretches from Raleigh, N. C. to Montgomery, Ala. This sandy belt averages about twenty-five miles in width, and according to geologists marks the beach of the ancient sea. Its porous soil and growth of long leaf pine render the air of this district soothing and curative. It was Dr. Parker of New York who in 1872 first recognized and proclaimed the merits of the Camden climate, and Mrs. Parker has since then spent seventeen winters in Camden. Now that Camden has grown to a noted winter resort, its climate no longer needs puffing and can bear recital of the cold facts.

The latitude of Camden is 34 deg. 19 min. North; longitude 80 deg. 35 min. West; elevation above the sea level 222 feet. Hobkirk and Kirkwood Hills are about 50 feet higher. The average seasonal temperatures for Camden have been given as follows:

| | | | |
|---|---|---|---|
| Spring | 61.90 | Winter | 45.16 |
| Summer | 79.32 | Annual Average | 62.16 |
| Autumn | 62.26 | | |

These and all following readings are Farrenheit.

*Heat.*—The earliest record of temperature for Camden we could discover was that kept for June and July 1785 by Richard Lloyd Champion. He states that his thermometer "hung against the Southern wall of a room defended against the rays of the sun by a piazza." His highest reading is 91 deg. for July 7 and 9, the lowest, 64 deg. for July 1.

James Kershaw's Diary contains a systematic record of thermometer readings taken in the vicinity of Camden between June 1791 and August 1802; and between September 1808 and June 1815. His entries are of three daily observations at 7 to 8 A. M., Noon, and 9 to 11 P. M. The highest readings noted in the Kershaw records are 96 degrees on August 3 and 6, 1794; 98 degrees June 7 and July 7, 1812—observation at noon on those dates.

From Major DeSaussure's "Weather Book", covering a period of 19 years we select the following items as to

## Notes From Nature

Summer heat: "July 4th, 1858, very hot, ther. 90 at 2 o'clock in passage, door shut; July 18th, 1859 ther. 92 in passage, shut up; July 1st, 1860, ther. 92 in my shut up entry; 3rd and 4th, ther. 94; on the 4th, ther. 90 in my entry at eleven o'clock in the night, July 9th, 1869, ther. 90 to 96; Sept. 4th, 5th, 1875, intense heat, ther. 92 in window; July 3rd, 1876, ther. in entry 96, in window 98."

Some maximum readings recorded by the Weather Bureau are as follows:

| | | | | |
|---|---|---|---|---|
| June 4 1911 | 104 | June 24 1917 | | 99 |
| Sept. 1 1912 | 103 | Aug. 14 1918 | | 103 |
| July 6 1913 | 100 | July 14 1919 | | 102 |
| July 18 1913 | 100 | July 29 1922 | | 106 |
| July 26 1914 | 105 | Sept. 8 1925 | | 106 |

It must be borne in mind that early temperature records were made from observed readings of ordinary dry bulb thermometers at stated hours and that the maximum of these old records would rarely coincide with the true maximum for the day, which would often occur between hours of observation. Weather Bureau records for past two decades are made from standard maximum and minimum thermometers exposed in lattice shutters in free air.

*Cold.*—The most extreme cold ever experienced here occurred on the morning of February 13, 1899. The self-registering thermometer of Dr. J. W. Corbett recorded a minimum of ten (10) degrees below zero on that date; Dr. Leslie Zemp's, 12 below. While this was undoubtedly the coldest spell ever known here, the Wateree River was only partially frozen over at Camden, not sufficiently for one to walk across. The cold of 1827 and 1835 probably lasted longer. The lowest readings in James Kershaw's record are: 9 degrees December 23, 1796 and same January 22, 1910, observations at 7 to 8 A. M.

"Wateree River frozen over at Camden January 3rd, 1827, a circumstance which has not before happened in memory of the oldest inhabitants."—*Camden Journal*, January 6, 1827.

Captain James I. Villepigue relates that the Wateree River, at Camden, was frozen over in the year 1835, and that he, then a boy of fourteen, walked across it on the ice.

"The weather since our last has been extremely cold. The small ponds in the neighborhood have frozen over so hard that on Tuesday morning several gentlemen amused themselves in skating, but this is an amusement that but few can participate in, there not having been, we believe, a suitable pair of skates in town, until one of our blacksmiths fabricated a pair upon the spur of the moment."—*Camden Journal,* January 17, 1829.

"Since Tuesday last our weather would laugh a Laplander out of all countenance. Any man that sheds tears now will cause great disturbance upon the pavement, for it will evidently be a hail storm."—*Camden Journal,* December 25, 1830.

"During the past week the 'Factory Pond' was frozen sufficiently to admit skating and a large number of our citizens availed themselves of the opportunity seldom offered in this mild latitude." (Only one pair of skates in the crowd however, and among them all only Mr. R. M. Kennedy, a native of Scotland, could really skate.)—*Camden Journal,* January 10, 1877.

The freeze of January 1886, when the thermometer fell to one degree below zero, was in some respects more severe than any before or since, owing to the fierce gale by which it was ushered in.

*Frost.*—On May 23, 1883, frost fell in and around Camden, but did no permanent harm to crops. On Tuesday, April 26, 1873, a killing frost destroyed gardens and full grown foliage of the woods. On the morning of April 27, 1898, thin ice formed, but cloudy skies saved vegetation from serious damage. On October 7, 1889, occurred a killing frost, the earliest of such severity in the memory of the old.

*Dots From Major DeSaussure's Weather Book.*
"1858—Feby. 25th. Put in the ice-house 20 wagon loads of snow and sleet.

April 28th. Heavy frost. Ice today—murderous—corn much cut down—Grape shoots killed within six inches of the vine and bunches killed.

Sept. Comet in N. W. Tail immensely long, very brilliant.

## Notes From Nature

1859—Dec. 31st. Housed 400 wagon loads of corn.
1860—March 3rd. Heard blue Martin today first time this year. Few peach blooms show.
1862—Mar. 3rd. Blue Martin appeared today.
1863—Feby. 22nd. Freshet—wheat under water eight days.
1865—Jany. 31st. Filled ice house from McRae's old Mill—Ice 3 inches thick. Ther. 11.
    Mar. 30th. Ten freshets in River since Jany. 1st.
    July 10th. Excessive heat, 95 in passage.
1867—Mar. 16th. Peach trees in bloom encased in ice.
    Mar. 17th. Fruit not killed.
1871—April 1st. Spring unusually early. Dogwood full bloom.
    April 7th. Bee-Martins and Chimney Swallows arrive.
1872—May 3rd. Okra blossom.
    Oct. 15th. Heavy frost—cotton killed.
1873—April 26th. Heavy frost—young snow—Irish potatoes foot high killed.
1874—April 30th. Heavy frost—garden sick.
    May 7th. Smart frost.
1875—July 18th. Thermometer 100 in window."

*Rainfall.*—A table has been made up and here appended, showing the monthly rainfall at Camden, during seventy-four years, 1852 to 1925. A portion of this table is taken from Major DeSaussure's weather Book (1858-1865), another portion (1866-1893) is compiled from records kept by Mr. Colin McRae at Kirkwood, a suburb now included in the limits of Camden; the remainder reproduces figures of the Weather Bureau.

The monthly and annual rainfall averages for Camden according to the U. S. Weather Bureau, and that deduced from our tabular record of seventy-four years are herewith compared and as will be seen correspond within a slight fraction.

|  | Gov't. | Ours |  | Gov't. | Ours |
|---|---|---|---|---|---|
| January | 3.38 | 3.45 | July | 5.23 | 5.24 |
| February | 3.97 | 3.83 | August | 5.48 | 5.31 |
| March | 3.70 | 3.57 | September | 3.66 | 3.83 |
| April | 3.08 | 3.07 | October | 2.62 | 2.56 |
| May | 3.21 | 3.31 | November | 2.35 | 2.35 |
| June | 4.48 | 4.52 | December | 3.40 | 3.38 |
| Annual Average |  |  |  | 44.54 | 44.42 |

# HISTORIC CAMDEN

| Year | Jan | Feb | Mar | Apr | May | June | July | Aug | Sept | Oct | Nov | Dec | Totals |
|------|-----|-----|-----|-----|-----|------|------|-----|------|-----|-----|-----|--------|
| 1852 | 0.94 | 1.23 | 2.98 | 4.73 | 4.15 | 4.79 | 8.30 | 8.03 | 2.52 | 0.85 | 9.49 | 4.55 | 52.59 |
| 1853 | 1.31 | 4.61 | 6.90 | 1.02 | 0.51 | 2.31 | 7.16 | 5.76 | 6.22 | 2.92 | 2.64 | 4.74 | 46.10 |
| 1854 | 7.07 | 4.10 | 2.91 | 3.81 | 4.55 | 6.19 | 8.27 | 4.50 | 6.10 | 2.53 | 0.96 | 1.19 | 51.58 |
| 1855 | 1.32 | 1.06 | 4.40 | 0.65 | 5.22 | 2.74 | 7.49 | 7.29 | 5.22 | 0.72 | 1.64 | 4.65 | 42.60 |
| 1856 | 5.95 | 2.20 | 6.27 | 0.83 | 6.98 | 3.08 | 3.61 | 8.50 | 4.41 | 2.57 | 4.86 | 4.83 | 53.94 |
| 1857 | 4.07 | 1.93 | 2.78 | 2.63 | 3.33 | 2.67 | 6.10 | 8.40 | 0.90 | 1.30 | 1.08 | 4.83 | 41.68 |
| Rainfall — Major Desaussure's Record | | | | | | | | | | | | | |
| 1858 | 4.10 | 5.40 | 1.00 | 3.60 | 1.30 | 5.00 | 2.30 | 1.80 | 7.10 | 2.70 | 3.00 | 6.20 | 44.00 |
| 1859 | 2.70 | 5.00 | 3.40 | 3.70 | 5.10 | 3.00 | 2.30 | 10.30 | 4.00 | 0.70 | 2.00 | 3.10 | 45.30 |
| 1860 | 0.50 | 6.40 | 2.02 | 3.00 | 3.05 | 3.30 | 3.00 | 3.00 | 0.80 | 4.00 | 4.50 | 3.00 | 36.67 |
| 1861 | 6.00 | 5.52 | 1.07 | 5.00 | 2.00 | 6.00 | 3.50 | 4.50 | 4.30 | 4.10 | 1.50 | 1.00 | 45.47 |
| 1862 | 5.02 | 6.13 | 4.51 | 4.02 | 2.03 | 5.60 | 6.40 | 7.00 | 1.70 | 3.60 | 1.50 | 3.00 | 49.91 |
| 1863 | 3.50 | 4.50 | 4.50 | 2.00 | 2.70 | 7.00 | 9.50 | 2.40 | 3.00 | 2.00 | 2.00 | 2.30 | 48.19 |
| 1864 | 4.00 | 0.60 | 4.20 | 4.00 | 5.00 | 7.70 | 4.30 | 5.04 | 4.10 | 2.70 | 5.40 | 1.40 | 45.80 |
| 1865 | 10.70 | 3.20 | 5.10 | 4.00 | 5.50 | 3.40 | 5.00 | 2.40 | 1.00 | 1.40 | 9.20 | 5.10 | 53.90 |
| Rainfall — Colin McRae's Record | | | | | | | | | | | | | |
| 1866 | 1.43 | 2.43 | 1.43 | 4.89 | 5.61 | 4.00 | 2.52 | 3.20 | 0.80 | 2.62 | 1.46 | 2.69 | 33.08 |
| 1867 | 2.12 | 2.08 | 2.85 | 2.71 | 2.73 | 5.52 | 1.24 | 10.22 | 4.57 | 5.33 | 1.97 | 2.92 | 44.27 |
| 1868 | 5.89 | 4.65 | 1.76 | 6.40 | 1.61 | 1.84 | 8.40 | 7.86 | 4.61 | 3.47 | 0.00 | 5.21 | 51.10 |
| 1869 | 2.48 | 3.22 | 2.12 | 1.31 | 1.93 | 1.79 | 4.22 | 2.52 | 1.11 | 0.35 | 2.38 | 6.67 | 30.10 |
| 1870 | 7.85 | 3.83 | 6.60 | 3.40 | 0.57 | 4.68 | 4.64 | 5.27 | 1.22 | 5.60 | 1.52 | 2.98 | 45.83 |
| 1871 | 0.57 | 7.07 | 2.77 | 3.02 | 5.12 | 3.19 | 2.09 | 4.96 | 1.82 | 2.77 | 4.19 | 2.17 | 40.14 |
| 1872 | 2.44 | 6.28 | 5.51 | 1.05 | 1.70 | 4.41 | 4.63 | 3.20 | 2.47 | 1.83 | 2.23 | 2.00 | 38.55 |
| 1873 | 2.67 | 4.57 | 1.26 | 2.06 | 6.53 | 2.44 | 4.62 | 9.94 | 8.57 | 0.51 | 2.57 | 2.49 | 48.19 |
| 1874 | 2.36 | 4.82 | 3.78 | 7.70 | 1.80 | 6.27 | 7.22 | 2.36 | 5.03 | 1.40 | 1.42 | 2.71 | 47.41 |
| 1875 | 4.96 | 4.49 | 6.03 | 3.81 | 4.32 | 2.31 | 5.49 | 5.08 | 3.68 | 1.10 | 3.14 | 3.36 | 48.79 |
| 1876 | 0.60 | 3.60 | 2.83 | 3.46 | 2.66 | 7.43 | 6.60 | 1.82 | 4.46 | 1.78 | 2.61 | 3.33 | 41.58 |
| 1877 | 2.83 | 2.34 | 4.46 | 4.89 | 1.32 | 3.20 | 4.67 | 1.26 | 6.76 | 3.92 | 4.31 | 4.80 | 44.16 |
| 1878 | 4.41 | 0.76 | 0.63 | 2.41 | 1.53 | 1.90 | 6.46 | 1.47 | 12.70 | 1.68 | 2.31 | 3.11 | 38.98 |
| 1879 | 1.76 | 3.04 | 2.35 | 3.74 | 2.23 | 1.49 | 4.60 | 4.29 | 2.07 | 1.42 | 1.33 | 1.93 | 30.37 |
| 1880 | 4.65 | 2.65 | 5.32 | 4.72 | 0.48 | 1.96 | 7.30 | 2.29 | 4.13 | 1.24 | 4.03 | 2.67 | 39.04 |
| 1881 | 5.55 | 3.77 | 4.05 | 2.78 | 1.04 | 0.58 | 0.29 | 3.66 | 3.55 | 2.77 | 3.55 | 3.11 | 34.70 |
| 1882 | 3.13 | 2.11 | 4.18 | 3.78 | 3.86 | 3.98 | 2.98 | 8.43 | 3.87 | 2.71 | 2.97 | 5.23 | 47.23 |
| 1883 | 5.94 | 1.44 | 3.77 | 2.77 | 3.74 | 4.14 | 1.25 | 2.72 | 2.77 | 2.47 | 2.74 | 1.79 | 37.95 |
| 1884 | 5.35 | 2.73 | 4.73 | 3.82 | 3.50 | 5.19 | 5.54 | 1.77 | 4.71 | 0.04 | 1.11 | 4.02 | 40.55 |
| 1885 | 6.27 | 3.65 | 1.40 | 1.52 | 5.03 | 5.36 | 5.68 | 2.30 | 5.34 | 2.89 | 1.83 | 3.29 | 46.99 |
| 1886 | 2.61 | 1.69 | 3.40 | 2.01 | 5.46 | 7.07 | 4.78 | 2.78 | 2.19 | 0.39 | 0.42 | 2.19 | 35.59 |
| 1887 | 3.13 | 2.27 | 3.27 | 1.92 | 2.14 | 1.92 | 4.13 | 2.23 | 2.86 | 7.22 | 0.55 | 1.54 | 31.28 |
| 1888 | 3.25 | 3.24 | 6.23 | 2.30 | 2.70 | 6.15 | 2.30 | 7.20 | 2.00 | 1.52 | 3.67 | 1.50 | 46.71 |
| 1889 | 5.03 | 3.93 | 3.20 | 0.54 | 1.92 | 5.15 | 4.95 | 7.54 | 4.03 | 3.20 | 7.49 | 0.88 | 49.67 |
| 1890 | 0.86 | 2.29 | 2.32 | 1.74 | 4.19 | 2.27 | 6.32 | 5.75 | 6.12 | 2.40 | 1.05 | 2.02 | 35.53 |
| 1891 | 3.72 | 2.44 | 4.17 | 3.35 | 5.62 | 3.80 | 6.23 | 5.04 | 4.79 | 2.04 | 1.73 | 1.47 | 44.42 |
| 1892 | 7.33 | 6.57 | 3.91 | 1.23 | 1.61 | 2.73 | 4.00 | 2.74 | 4.02 | 0.57 | 0.93 | 2.52 | 38.28 |
| 1893 | 2.36 | 5.13 | 1.10 | 0.48 | 5.50 | 7.11 | 2.93 | 8.70 | 1.99 | 4.13 | 1.97 | 3.63 | 45.11 |
| U.S. Weather Bureau Record | | | | | | | | | | | | | |
| 1894 | 2.41 | 4.69 | 1.71 | 1.56 | 1.81 | 2.00 | 3.77 | 6.39 | 7.52 | 5.77 | 1.85 | 2.56 | 42.24 |
| 1895 | 8.09 | 3.12 | 6.36 | 6.05 | 3.05 | 7.04 | 2.68 | 7.48 | 0.92 | 1.66 | 1.79 | 2.94 | 51.20 |
| 1896 | 2.63 | 6.53 | 2.28 | 0.72 | 3.35 | 3.58 | 9.68 | 2.68 | 2.52 | 0.42 | 2.88 | 4.50 | 40.81 |
| 1897 | 1.73 | 8.12 | 3.23 | 3.13 | 3.68 | 7.03 | 5.24 | 3.18 | 3.33 | 2.09 | 2.11 | 1.92 | 45.54 |
| 1898 | 1.83 | 1.01 | 3.45 | 4.83 | 0.35 | 4.91 | 11.62 | 13.55 | 3.21 | 3.41 | 4.70 | 1.54 | 55.06 |
| 1899 | 5.82 | 9.28 | 4.23 | 2.76 | 0.23 | 3.14 | 5.20 | 6.42 | 2.34 | 4.26 | 6.75 | 2.50 | 54.54 |
| 1900 | 1.85 | 1.10 | 4.47 | 7.17 | 1.67 | 6.10 | 6.42 | 2.31 | 1.65 | 2.90 | 4.62 | 6.03 | 51.79 |
| 1901 | 3.75 | 2.52 | 6.44 | 5.14 | 6.28 | 6.34 | 3.69 | 9.75 | 5.24 | 0.45 | 0.43 | 5.37 | 58.65 |
| 1902 | 1.97 | 4.67 | 3.69 | 1.58 | 4.62 | 5.46 | 3.56 | 5.43 | 2.25 | 4.31 | 2.95 | 4.29 | 45.41 |
| 1903 | 2.94 | 7.97 | 6.49 | 2.85 | 3.50 | 9.55 | 2.26 | 7.77 | 4.21 | 3.49 | 1.22 | 1.91 | 55.31 |
| 1904 | 2.10 | 3.41 | 3.61 | 1.41 | 1.46 | 3.65 | 6.51 | 1.76 | 1.40 | 3.12 | 2.57 | 37.90 | |
| 1905 | 1.66 | 3.45 | 2.05 | 3.71 | 5.40 | 0.48 | 5.10 | 7.74 | 2.02 | 1.60 | 0.12 | 2.78 | 42.69 |
| 1906 | 4.55 | 2.34 | 5.87 | 1.70 | 4.30 | 8.13 | 6.94 | 4.92 | 4.40 | 5.58 | 0.71 | 2.24 | 51.68 |
| 1907 | 0.67 | 4.37 | 1.46 | 3.04 | 6.16 | 5.52 | 5.46 | 5.46 | 2.10 | 0.46 | 3.96 | 3.08 | 44.05 |
| 1908 | 4.36 | 4.78 | 4.83 | 2.19 | 1.72 | 9.12 | 5.90 | 14.02 | 6.40 | 4.43 | 1.41 | 2.69 | 57.25 |
| 1909 | 0.93 | 4.13 | 3.51 | 1.78 | 3.01 | 6.45 | 5.06 | 4.66 | 1.32 | 2.22 | 2.25 | 2.43 | 39.25 |
| 1910 | 3.64 | 5.13 | 1.62 | 1.26 | 3.27 | 7.91 | 4.06 | 4.24 | 3.72 | 2.76 | 0.01 | 1.58 | 39.29 |
| 1911 | 1.16 | 0.98 | 1.72 | 2.16 | 0.06 | 2.94 | 3.60 | 11.30 | 2.24 | 6.84 | 3.02 | 2.36 | 36.37 |
| 1912 | 4.27 | 7.41 | 6.04 | 2.74 | 2.08 | 7.38 | 3.87 | 2.46 | 8.26 | 1.45 | 2.28 | 1.95 | 51.70 |
| 1913 | 2.54 | 5.14 | 7.02 | 0.74 | 2.42 | 5.73 | 7.40 | 2.58 | 4.94 | 2.16 | 1.39 | 4.19 | 46.41 |
| 1914 | 2.62 | 4.47 | 4.56 | 2.81 | 3.90 | 0.41 | 4.47 | 2.10 | 8.84 | 3.14 | 2.44 | 1.45 | 42.74 |
| 1915 | 5.29 | 2.22 | 2.67 | 1.89 | 5.14 | 4.44 | 2.81 | 5.45 | 0.71 | 4.21 | 2.08 | 1.16 | 37.12 |
| 1916 | 1.57 | 4.23 | 2.21 | 0.54 | 0.57 | 6.43 | 14.99 | 2.34 | 1.83 | 2.14 | 0.54 | 1.89 | 39.31 |
| 1917 | 5.23 | 3.41 | 3.43 | 4.22 | 2.13 | 6.35 | 1.29 | 5.00 | 1.77 | 0.76 | 0.74 | 3.73 | 37.72 |
| 1918 | 1.63 | 1.65 | 1.81 | 5.58 | 6.11 | 1.75 | 3.04 | 3.28 | 4.72 | 3.38 | 1.28 | 2.51 | 37.42 |
| 1919 | 4.86 | 5.23 | 5.17 | 2.52 | 4.11 | 3.95 | 10.99 | 3.26 | 0.13 | 2.11 | 0.19 | 2.19 | 42.95 |
| 1920 | 4.59 | 2.11 | 3.85 | 5.27 | 0.65 | 8.38 | 5.58 | 6.05 | 2.73 | 4.11 | 4.91 | 49.06 | |
| 1921 | 3.69 | 5.32 | 2.08 | 1.99 | 6.04 | 3.21 | 10.38 | 1.21 | 1.82 | 1.54 | 3.11 | 2.14 | 42.47 |
| 1922 | 2.73 | 5.43 | 7.19 | 5.09 | 3.17 | 5.34 | 6.01 | 3.50 | 4.05 | 6.52 | 0.68 | 3.32 | 50.12 |
| 1923 | 2.19 | 5.15 | 5.95 | 2.67 | 2.32 | 3.82 | 4.58 | 10.53 | 4.85 | 0.62 | 1.70 | 3.63 | 45.12 |
| 1924 | 3.82 | 1.97 | 2.88 | 0.88 | 5.54 | 7.67 | 3.60 | 1.25 | 14.33 | 1.35 | 1.70 | 0.74 | 39.47 |
| 1925 | 11.84 | 1.24 | 0.50 | 2.27 | 1.71 | 3.48 | 5.67 | 2.78 | 1.41 | 2.27 | 2.53 | 3.26 | 39.16 |

## Notes From Nature

The only absolutely rainless month in our table was November, 1868.

The year 1925 broke two records of 74 years, with 11.84 inches of rain for January, and only 21.53 inches for the nine months between January and November. In September 1924 the astounding amount of 14.33 inches fell, exceeding beyond all comparison any previously recorded precipitation for that month.

"Three (3) inches of rain fell in 15 minutes with hail and wind on May 12th, 1823"—*Southern Chronicle and Camden Gazette*, 1823.

*Snow.*—Such records as we have indicate that in our locality snow falls two out of three years, on an average. It is seldom the ground remains white over twenty-four hours, and a fall of more than an inch or two is rare. However, falls of six, eight or even ten inches are not unknown. Sleet is more common than snow.

"Snow nine or ten inches deep Feby. 1st, 1818."—*Camden Gazette*, February, 1818.

"We will tell our Camden readers what they knew before, but what some other readers may not believe, that the snow at this present writing is eight inches deep."—*Camden Journal*, February 17, 1829.

"On April 15th, 1849, a snow fall whitened the ground at Camden, the crops much injured. This probably the *latest* snow ever known here."—*Camden Journal*, April 18, 1849.

Snow was twelve inches deep on the level, at Camden, February 13, 1899, probably the *heaviest* fall ever known here. Narcissus blooms were buried and after the thaw reappeared unhurt.

Entries in Major DeSaussure's Diary show that between 1858 and 1877, nineteen years, there were six winters without any snow, six in each of which snow fell once, three in each of which there were two snow falls, two with three snow falls, one with four falls, and one, 1871-1872, with eight snow falls. The heaviest snows he mentions during this period are as follows:

| | | | | | | |
|---|---|---|---|---|---|---|
| Mar. 19 1861........ | 3 | inches | Mar. 15 1867........ | 3 | inches |
| Dec. 29 1866........ | 2 | inches | Jany. 26 1872........ | 1½ | inches |

Mr. Colin McRae's notations of snow falls for seven years, 1885 to 1891, show two years, 1887 and 1891, without snow; in 1885 four falls; 1890, three; 1886 two; 1888 and 1889 one each.

*Drought.*—In the year 1845 the up-country of South Carolina, including Camden, suffered from extreme drought. The following is from the *Camden Journal* of July 9, 1845: "We are really threatened with a partial famine. Corn in some places has fallen down, in others drying up. Mills have ceased to grind for want of water; cattle suffering; cotton blossoming at height of three or four inches and from that to knee high." On August 6, the same paper records rains, too late to benfit crops except in some sections.

The drought of 1881 was memorable. For the months of May, June and July a total of only two (2) inches of rain fell at Camden, in such light and scattered sprinkles as to be of no benefit. Corn crops were ruined. The down pour which mercifully came on August 1, after twelve hot and parching weeks produced a magic effect upon cotton, which took on a new growth, marked by excrescenses around the stem, resembling the joint of a corn stalk.

In the year 1916 occurred perhaps the worst combination of dry and wet in sixty years. In the vicinity of Camden during April and May of that year, a total of but one inch of rain fell, so that crops were very late in starting. In June and July twenty-one inches fell, ruining the young crops and causing the greatest floods in memory of the living.

*Beaver Creek Dry.*—A plat of land granted by the State to Rush Hudson dated October 8, 1768, recorded in office of Secretary of State, Plat Book 9, page 320, shows "no water" in that stretch of Beaver Creek just above the point where the old Road from Camden to Liberty Hill crosses (now known as Hilton's Ford). If the surveyor's notation of "no water" was correct, a drought must have prevailed at that time equal to or exceeding any since. Can any one remember this Creek ever to have run out of water at that point?

*Aurora Borealis.*—"Brilliant aurora-borealis in North from 9 o'clock till day-light, Sept. 25th, 1870. Aurora brilliant Oct. 14th, 1870."—*Major J. M. DeSaussure's Weather Book.*

## Notes From Nature

*Falling Stars.*—"We were presented on the morning of the 13th (Nov. 1833), with a grand display of nature, in the descent of meteoric stars in such numbers as to fill the whole atmosphere with streaks and flashes of light. They were first observed after mid-night and continued until daylight obscured them."—*Camden Journal,* November 23, 1833.

*Earthquakes.*—A letter written from Stateburg, 18 miles south of Camden, to the *Charleston Gazette,* in April 1799, mentions an earthquake and states that it was much more violent at Camden. Recorded also in James Kershaw's Diary as occurring at 3 A. M., April 11, 1799.

Quite a decided earth shiver was felt in Camden on January 18, 1860. Crockery was rattled.

August 31, 1886, the severest earth quake ever felt in Camden occurred at 10 P. M. Buildings were shaken to the point of collapse, chimneys in places were broken off and walls cracked, producing mortal terror in man and beast. The first shock was succeeded in a few minutes by another, little less severe than the first, and the most alarming tremors continued all night. For weeks the earth seemed to shiver and everyone was at high tension, ready to rush out doors, and many a wild stampede occurred. There were constant muffled rumblings and the sensation under foot of a deep seated boiling cauldron, lasting for many days.

Mr. Colin McRae records very perceptible quakes beside the great one of August 31, on the following dates: (1886)—Oct. 9, 22, 31; Nov. 1, 5, 7, 9; (1887)—Mar. 4, 17; Apr. 11, 18; July 10; Aug. 10, 27; (1888)—Jany. 13; (1889)—July 11; (1890)—Mar. 5.

*Eagle.*—"Mr. R. B. Patterson kills huge eagle at Liberty Hill, eight feet between tip of wings."—*Kershaw Gazette,* April 18, 1878.

*Wild Pigeons.*—"These birds are more numerous in this neighborhood than they have been for many years. Some of the papers speak of flocks two or three miles long. They fly over this town in flocks larger than that we should think. One flock passed over Tuesday morning, which a friend of ours says, 'contained one million if it contained one'."—*Camden Journal,* February 14, 1828.

"Merchants, clerks, lawyers, trades-men, statesmen, financiers, school-boys and everybody who could manage to beg, borrow or steal anything in the shape of a gun, might be seen armed and equipped. This commotion was created by the appearance of innumerable multitudinous flocks of wild pigeons, compelled we presume by the recent severe weather at the North to pay us a foraging visit."—*Camden Journal*, February 26, 1845.

Appearance of wild pigeons at Camden mentioned, the last time in *Kershaw Gazette*, January 17, 1877.

*Whippoorwill.*—This bird seems to have disappeared from the vicinity of Camden. The writer has not heard one here for over forty years. It has been replaced by the Chuck-wills-widow. What has become of the plaintive cry of poor Will, so familiar to our childhood? The Chuck-widow is not a satisfactory substitute.

*Raccoons.*—"A few hundred raccoon skins for sale by P. Thornton."—*Camden Gazette*, 1817.

*Panther.*—"Panther killed at DuBois Ferry on Lynches Creek; few seen about here since the Revolution."—*Camden Journal*, January 28, 1826.

*Deer.*—"A fine buck was killed this week upon Dr. Anderson's lot on Rutledge Street in Camden. He was started upon Sanders Creek (about six miles above town) and after a very long chase sank down exhausted near the most populous spot in this town."—*Camden Journal*, September 18, 1830.

"A party of fifteen or twenty deer-hunting at Mr. Ario Niles', nine miles above Camden. One fine deer killed by Mr. J. M. Cantey, our City Marshal."—*Camden Journal*, September, 1872.

*Alligators.*—"Alligator captured at creek, just South of town limits, ten and half (10½) feet long, 346 lbs. weight."—*Camden Journal*, 1827.

"Alligator killed by Henry Wilson just below town limits, measuring eleven (11) feet, seven (7) inches long."—*Kershaw Gazette*, September, 1884.

*Sturgeon.*—"Two sturgeon caught in Wateree River, one 260 lbs., the other 250 lbs. weight."—*Camden Journal*, April, 1852.

*Turnipissimo.*—"Our chivalry has not been over ambitious, never having been engaged in a tournament for turkey, or run a tilt for a large turnip with our brother Editors. We have rarely vegetated to the extent of some of them. We have never even become the Chronicler of a cabbage but in one instance. We have generally left the glory of mammoth potatoes and gigantic cucumbers to loftier aspirants for fame and many a pre-eminent pumpkin has gone down to oblivion from sheer want of disposition to immortalize it. But we have lately received materials for "Memoirs of a Turnip", which we mean to make matter of history. The distinguished esculent is now in the hands of Dr. William Blanding of this town, and weighs about *nine pounds*. It was raised on Little Lynches Creek."—*C. F. Daniels in Camden Journal*, January 17, 1829.

"A Turnip still larger than the one we mentioned last week has been brought into town within a few days. Dr. S. Blanding has one which weighs *twelve pounds and two ounces*. This turnip was raised upon Gates Battle Ground."—*Camden Journal*, January 24, 1829.

"Turnip from L. W. R. Blair, 9 lbs."—*Camden Gazette*, January 6, 1875.

*Turpentine and Terebene.*—In the *Camden Journal* of January 31, 1862, Dr. I. B. Alexander offers to change "Kerosene, camphene or oil lamps" so as to burn Terebene, "the best light now used in the Confederacy." This oil used during the War for illuminating was made from the rosin and turpentine of the long leaf yellow pines, which covered all the sandy districts, over two-thirds of the area of this county. This process of turpentining, which began near Camden about 1854, in the course of thirty years resulted in the almost complete destruction of the magnificent forests of original pines, which many can remember as extending from the outskirts of town in every direction.

### River Freshets.

*The Southern Chronicle and Camden Aegis* of September 22, 1824, records a freshet in the river at Camden as the "Greatest since 1771." James Kershaw in his Diary mentions a freshet of April 8, 1791, as being supposed by many as equal to the "Great May Freshet of 1771." He also notes that seven "Freshets" during the year 1795 had destroyed all the corn and indigo. He records that a freshet of January 1796 swept away Wylie's Warehouse and 80 Hhds. of tobacco, and that a party went in "flatts to the Indian Mounts." There is no means of determining the height of the 1771 freshet.

The *Camden Journal* of August 27, 1831, tells of the "greatest freshet ever known, sweeping away the bridge at Camden." This bridge was constructed for the Camden Bridge Company in 1827 by Colonel William Nixon and was the first built across the Wateree River at Camden. It was finished about October 1828. The stone for masonry of the piers was quarried some miles up the river (probably at Eagles Nest) and transported down stream in flat boats. On January 6, 1829, Colonel Nixon advertises for sale "two flats used in raising the bridge and carrying rocks, also the tools used in quarrying the Rocks."

The *Camden Journal* of April 13, 1833, records a freshet " a few inches higher than that of 1831," and the paper of June 6, 1840 mentions a freshet "Nearly as high as that of 1831." The bridge which had been rebuilt safely withstood this flood.

The freshet of 1831 wrecked the bridge built in 1827, after which the Bridge Company conducted a Ferry until 1838, in which year the superstructure was rebuilt upon the original piers. On December 23, 1837, fourteen negro slaves were drowned while crossing on the ferry boat. These slaves were the property of James C. Doby who recovered a judgment of $14,000.00 against the Bridge Company for the loss.

The *Camden Journal* of August 31, 1852, tells of a freshet equal to or higher than that of 1831, causing great destruction of crops and endangering the bridge.

The *Camden Journal* of February 28, 1854, mentions "the highest freshet ever known in our river; Eastern abutment of bridge washed out."

Major J. M. DeSaussure in his Diary records a flood in February 1861, as "thought to be higher than 1854." This entry appears in the Diary under date of January 11, 1865: "Very heavy freshet—supposed higher than ever known by 2½ feet. It was four feet on floor of West End of River Bridge, but not on Water spans." This flood became celebrated as the "Hocott Freshet" by reason of the adventure therein of D. D. Hocott, related in another chapter.

## Notes From Nature

It seems that in February succeeding the Hocott freshet of January, high water prevailed again at the time of Sherman's approach to Camden, and subsequently a confusion arose between the "Sherman" and "Hocott" freshets.

In May 1886 previous high water records were broken, according to the *Camden Journal* of May 27, which states: "The freshet of this month was one (1) foot higher than the Sherman freshet of 1865; the Water rose one foot above spikes driven in a tree to mark the former." The *Kershaw Gazette* of same date said: "The rains of Thursday and Friday last (May 20 and 21, 1886) were so general as to cause the biggest freshet in the Wateree River which has been experienced within the recollection of the proverbial oldest inhabitant. In fact the 'Hocott' freshet is said to have been nowhere."

The old bridge built in 1827 and rebuilt in 1838 was burnt by Sherman in 1865. A ferry was operated at its site between 1865 and 1872, in which latter year the County erected wooden spans on the old piers which still stood. One of these spans fell in course of construction, costing the life of one of the workmen. By 1878 it had become so unsafe that it was abandoned and destroyed as a menace. Again a ferry was operated until 1883 when a steel bridge was constructed by a chartered Company about a mile up stream above the old site. In 1891 the United States Weather Bureau established a guage at this bridge for measuring the stages of the river. Although the water of May 1886 was regarded as the highest to that date, we find the following item in the *Camden Journal* of September 13, 1888: "On yesterday the 12th, the Wateree River was six inches higher than ever known. The gauge at the iron bridge registered 31.6." Hence we infer that the River in May 1886 reached 31 feet.

In a book kept by Mr. Colin McRae, we find the following entry under date of January 7, 1886: "High water at Railroad trestle 5 feet from top of cross ties, being four feet eight inches (4 ft. 8 in.) below Sherman freshet." This gives us some basis for comparison.

On May 24, 1901 high water mark of 32.5 feet was reached in the freshet of that date. On the 25th day of August 1908, the waters rose above that record, and by the afternoon of that day a huge drift of trees and wreckage piled against the bridge piers. Workers on the raft were striving desperately to break it loose. On the bridge were others attempting to cross. Suddenly the whole structure toppled over and the raft shot down stream. All those on the bridge and raft were cast into the raging current. Four were drowned. Ten were swept into trees on the bank and were saved. The most remarkable escape, was that of Mr. Henry Savage, who was on the raft directing the workers when the bridge went down. He floated on drift wood for ten miles below Camden and was rescued by a party who were working on a dike. To those knowing the conditions his survival was nothing less than miraculous. On the following morning (August 26, 1908) the waters reached a height of 39 feet 7 inches. It was generally predicted that such a flood would never again occur in this generation, a prophecy which was soon falsified, for the flood of July 18, 1916, reached the greatest height ever known, forty and four-tenths (40.4) feet, eight (8) inches above that of 1908.

The flood of water on July 18, 1916 entirely surrounded the old brick depot of the South Carolina Railway, built in 1848, and rose on the walls to a point three (3) feet above the ground, reaching almost to the window sills. This point was marked on the wall and by careful measurement is seven and one-half (7½) feet above the cross ties on the Railroad Trestle over Pine Tree Creek, above mentioned. It is quite certain that the level of this trestle has been practically the same since 1865, indeed since its first construction. It appearing from McRae's notes that the Sherman (or Hocott) freshet rose to a point four (4) inches below the top of the cross ties on this trestle, the water of July 1916 was at least seven (7) feet above the Sherman or Hocott freshet of 1865. It is a well known fact that from the time of its construction in 1848 the highest water had never come up to the old brick depot until the floods of 1908 and 1916, both of which, as above stated, rose three feet on the walls of that old building, and *seven feet above the rails on the aforesaid trestle*. Hence we conclude the Hocott freshet reached a height of 33 feet.

The Wateree River, about two miles from the town, is the same stream as the Catawba which rises in the mountains of North Carolina, the name changing to the

## Notes From Nature

Wateree at a point about twenty-five miles northwest of Camden where Wateree Creek, a tributary, enters it from the west. The lowest known water in the river at the bridge near Camden that of June 1884 is zero point for measuring stages of water, and is 132 feet above sea-level. Camden is, according to the U. S. Weather Bureau, 222 feet above sea-level and 90 feet above zero of the river. The Wateree is extremely violent in time of highest floods. On its headwaters, near Alta Pass, over twenty-two inches of rain fell in 24 hours on July 15, 1916, which is the record rain-fall in the United States for one day. It is not surprising that the resulting flood carried away all the bridges on the river from the mountains down to Camden.

The present highway bridge across the river is two miles from the city limits about a mile and a half above stream from the one destroyed in 1908 and was opened for traffic on March 16, 1920.

# CHAPTER XXVI.

## MISCELLANEOUS.

### Boykin's Mill Disaster.

May 5, 1860 was a dark day in the annals of Camden. At Boykin's Mill Pond on Swift Creek about nine miles south of Camden, a merry picnic party was gathered, young people from Camden and the vicinity of the Mill, which is located about two miles from the Sumter County line. Between four and five o'clock in the afternoon, some fifty or sixty of the party boarded a large flat boat for a pleasure trip on the pond. Soon after leaving shore the flat ran upon a snag and sprang a leak and began to sink. A wild panic seized the occupants, most of whom jumped overboard. Twenty-four were drowned. The sad story of the tragedy was related at the inquest by James Jones and E. E. Sill who were present. The following is a list of those who perished:

    Amelia A. Alexander, of Camden
    Selena Crosby, of Camden
    Mary Hinson, of Camden
    B. F. Hocott, of Arkansas
    Sarah Ann Howell, of Camden
    Joseph Huggins, of Sumter
    Mary C. Jenkins, of Clarksons
    Jane Kelley, of Boykins
    Lucius LeGrand, of Camden
    William LeGrand, of Camden
    Louise McKeown, of Camden
    Margaret McKeown, of Camden
    Elizabeth McKagen, of Camden
    William McKagen, of Camden
    Jeremiah R. McLeod, of Sumter
    Louisa Nettles, of Camden
    John Oaks, of Camden
    S. T. T. Richbourg, of Sumter
    Alice Robinson, of Camden
    Sam'l. H. Young, of Boykins
    Two Misses Young. Sisters of Sam'l. H. Young
    Dorcas Page, a free negro
    Pender Ciples, a negro slave

## Miscellaneous

### The Cleveland School Fire.

On the night of May 17, 1923, the pupils and teachers of the Cleveland School, located about six miles southeast of Camden, at "Sandy Hill", the old Chesnut summer home, were rendering a play to an audience of relatives and friends. The hall, about 20 by 40 feet, on the second floor of the wooden building, was crowded. The only exit was a stairway about four feet wide, walled up on both sides, landing with a right angle turn at the bottom, in a small cloak room which formed one side of a porch jutting from the main building.

In the midst of the proceedings a large pendant lamp broke from the ceiling, fell upon the stage, spread burning oil and ignited the inflammable fittings. Some time was lost in effort to subdue the flames, which made rapid head-way and uncontrollable panic ensued. Some leaping from the upper windows sustained injuries, others escaped upon the porch shed, tore away the flag pole and on this slid to the ground. The greater number rushed for the stairs, where those in front were overturned by the pressure behind, so that the stairway soon became a pit, packed with an inextricable mass of men, women and children, mostly prostrate, others erect held as in a vise against the walls. The frantic survivors struggled desperately, but vainly to release the jam. Tom Humphries was fatally burned in the effort to save his parents. In these appalling moments there was minifested by not a few that nobility of soul which only a supreme crisis reveals.

Few calamities have so profoundly moved the hearts of the whole land. A generous outpouring of contributions and tributes to the afflicted came from far and near. A massive granite monument marks the site of the school and records, on a bronze tablet, the following names of the seventy-seven who perished on that terrible occasion:

| Name | Age | Name | Age |
| --- | --- | --- | --- |
| Arrants, Grace | 7 | Bowen, Fannie | 16 |
| Arrants, Ima | 17 | Croft, Mrs. Lula | 37 |
| Brown, Mrs. Floride | 47 | Croft, Dorothy | 16 |
| Brown, Lottie | 9 | Croft, Hamilton | 6 |
| Brown, Eugene A. | 57 | Campbell, Mrs. Estelle | 20 |
| Brown, Mrs. Eugene A. | 49 | Campbell, Eoline | 14 |
| Barnes, Ellie | 17 | Davis, Ase R. | 37 |

## Historic Camden

| Name | Age | Name | Age |
|---|---|---|---|
| Davis, Mrs. Ase R. | 42 | Johnson, Wm. Jeter | 11 |
| Davis, Deila Mae | 14 | McCaskill, Mrs. Kate | 40 |
| Davis, Lina | 8 | McCaskill, Roy | 4 |
| Davis, Mrs. Lizzie | 34 | McCaskill, Adeline | 20 |
| Davis, Eva Mae | 16 | McCaskill, Colza | 12 |
| Davis, Fannie Lee | 7 | McCaskill, Grace | 5 |
| Davis, W. G., Jr. | 7 | McLeod, Miller L. | 39 |
| Dixon, C. Lucas | 42 | McLeod, Mrs. Miller L. | 33 |
| Dixon, Clara | 12 | McLeod, Lindsey | 5 |
| Dixon, Mrs. Nannie | 50 | McLeod, Milton | 1 |
| Dixon, Lenwood | 12 | McLeod, Burnel S. | 29 |
| Dixon, Sara | 9 | McLeod, Mrs. Burnel S. | 27 |
| Dixon, Mrs. Addie | 22 | McLeod, Bruce | 2 |
| Dixon, Margaret | 7 | McLeod, M. B. | 73 |
| Dixon, Mrs. Theresa | 32 | Pearce, Jessie E. | 40 |
| Dixon, Thelma | 9 | Phillips, Mrs. Dora | 45 |
| Dixon, Theda | 6 | Phillips, Ola | 17 |
| Dixon, Willene | 1 | Phillips, D. | 14 |
| Godwin, Mary Lynn | 1 | Phillips, Eva | 8 |
| Hendrix, Charles W. | 52 | Rhoden, Mrs. Grace | 32 |
| Hendrix, Mazie | 15 | Rush, Jack | 15 |
| Hendrix, Annie Lee | 13 | Sowell, Clara Mae | 13 |
| Hendrix, Wilbur | 10 | Sowell, Louise | 8 |
| Hendrix, Alva | 6 | Smith, Jessie | 13 |
| Hendrix, Wesley E. | 60 | Truesdel, D. | 23 |
| Hendrix, Bertie | 16 | Trapp, Emily | 10 |
| Hinson, Frank | 9 | Trapp, Vera | 9 |
| Hinson, J. C. | 9 | West, Shell J. | 37 |
| Hinson, Ora Belle | 11 | West, Thelma | 15 |
| Humphries, Chas. N. | 64 | West, Rebeckah | 11 |
| Humphries, Mrs. Chas. N. | 56 | Wade, Sadie (colored) | 11 |
| Humphries, Tom B. | 30 | | |

### *A Bloody Bayonet.*

On Friday night May 23, 1851 during the encampment of the Fifth Brigade of State troops at Camden, an officer became deranged and was placed under guard. The officer having apparently fallen asleep, the guard left him to answer roll call of his company. During the guard's absence the officer seized a gun with fixed bayonet, rushed out and stabbed severely six or seven of the campers before he could be subdued. The most dangerously injured was Dr. Chas. J. Shannon, who while sitting at his tent door received a thrust in his lungs. Fortunately all the wounded recovered. It is stated by the *Camden Journal* of that date that the officer's aberration was due to no dissipation or indulgence in stimulants, nor to any other delinquency on his part. His name was not mentioned.

*Anonymous Poem Written in a Camden Gaol, 1782.*

The following extracts are from a poem of forty-one stanzas, entitled *Sketches of Modern Improvements: a Poetical Essay*, composed by a British soldier in prison at Camden in 1782. They were published probably soon after that time, though the thin antiquated volume has no title page or indication of when or where printed.

A copy is in the Library of Congress: this was sent the writers with a request that they throw what light they could on the authorship. They regret that they cannot offer any, though the assistance of several well-known students and historians was sought.

The author was evidently an Englishman and a scholar, as well as a poet of promising talent.

The identity of the friend of his brighter days, "my Lucius", to whom he dedicates his composition, must also perhaps remain a mystery.

Rowland Rugeley, a brother of the famous Colonel Henry Rugeley, of "Clermont" above Camden, was a composer of verses, but, though he was born in England, we do not believe he was of sufficient poetic ability to write these lines, nor is there any evidence that he was ever a prisoner in Camden. He was a member of the Royal Council in Charleston and not a soldier.

The unfortunate Major Andre wrote inferior verses while in Charleston, but he had been executed in October, 1780.

Indeed it seems almost incredible that British soldiers were still languishing in a Camden prison as late as February 17, 1782, though peace was not finally declared by treaty until September 3, 1783.

We give the dedication and the first six stanzas of the poem, in the hope that some chance reader may solve the riddle of the authorship.

# Historic Camden

*"Dedicatory Sonnet.*

Friend of my brighter days, whose soul sincere
Hailed the fair prophets of the flattering morn,
O'er noontide clouds now drop the soothing tear,
And cheer the gloom of wretchedness forlorn:
Incumbent mists disperse, and blushing fly,
Soon as the sun's keen ray pervades the low'ring sky.
My Lucius, once I wept thy hapless fate,
By sorrow now allied, teach me thy art,
With dignity, to give this prison state,
And make affliction virtue's charms impart.
To thee this verse is due, whose patriotic mind
Exults in glories which thy country crown,
And ardent heaves to swell her high renown;
Triumphant by her arms, and by her arts refined.
                Camden, S. C., February 17, 1782."

"The following essay is but some outlines of an extensive work, wholly planned, though but in part executed; as it was written to dissipate the gloom of misfortune, which denies access to books, or the means of recent information: nor is it likely to be renewed by a mind, not given to studious pursuits, when the causes which have now induced it, are happily no more."

### 1.

"Tho' wakeful guards, and dreary walls surround,
And liberty with-holds her placid smile,
Yet shall my mind, triumphant, leap their bound;
And rising arts the tedious hours beguile.

### 2.

"Those arts which deck fair Albion pleased I sing,
Since fate denies me longer to defend
Her sacred laws, her empire, and her king;
To British themes, ye Britons then attend.

### 3.

"Let no debasing doubts that ardor damp,
Which slows, your country to improve or save:
Be yours the wish of fame's distinctive stamp:
'The paths of glory lead beyond the grave'.

## Miscellaneous

#### 4.

" 'Tis glorious in her injured cause to rise,
O'er ocean's billowy realms her rights sustain;
To brave surrounding foes, and fev'rish skies
Or bleed to serve her, on the hostile plain:

#### 5.

"Yet not less glorious is his peaceful meed
Who, with inventive mind, at early morn
Tries the new plough, or plants th' exotic seed,
And views fresh crops paternal fields adorn:

#### 6.

"And oft the civic and the martial crown
Their fragrant flow'rs and verdant foliage twine:
Where vict'ry bears her country's wide renown
The aiding arts in equal honours shine."

### *The Prison on Lake Erie.*
#### By Asa Hartz, February, 1864.

(Major Geo. McKnight, of General Loring's Staff, during the Civil War, under the *nom deplume* of Asa Hartz, wrote verses of some merit, especially those emanating from his prison on Johnson's Island, Lake Erie. Camden has the honor of his birth place and boyhood residence. Here Asa was born in 1833, his father, Robt. McKnight, for a time editor of *Camden Journal*. Asa tells that he was familiar with every foot of Camden "from the Indian to the Old Machine Creek.")

The full, round moon, in God's blue bend,
  Glides o'er her path so queenly—
Dark shadows creep, fade into light,
  And stars look down serenely.
A captive looks out on the scene—
  A scene so sad and dreary,
And thinks a weary captive's thoughts,
  In prison on Lake Erie.

## HISTORIC CAMDEN

> The happy, happy days of youth,
>   Flit by him fast and faster;
> The joys which gave no warning note
>   Of manhood's dire disaster;
> The days when joy, and peaceful homes
>   And firesides bright and cheery,
> Come back to find him sad and worn
>   In prison on Lake Erie.
>
> For many moons will rise and wane
>   How many months will languish—
> Ere peace, the white winged angel comes
>   To soothe a nation's anguish?
> God speed the long'd and pray'd for day,
>   When loved ones bright and cheery,
> Shall welcome us around the hearth,
>   From prison on Lake Erie.

*State Senators and Representatives.*

The following list is not entirely complete. The loss of records and the failure of the older reports to enumerate the members of the General Assembly, has rendered the compilation of these names difficult. With more opportunity for exhaustive research we might have supplied the omissions.

*Senators.*

(Term Four Years)

| | |
|---|---|
| 1792—John Chesnut | 1875—Frank Carter (col.) |
| 1804—Z. Cantey | 1878—L. J. Patterson |
| 1812—Reuben Starke | 1882—W. Z. Leitner |
| 1816—Chapman Levy | 1886—G. G. Alexander |
| 1828—Jas. S. Deas | 1890—James R. McGill |
| 1832—James Chesnut | 1894—T. J. Kirkland (resigned in 1896) |
| 1836—John Chesnut | |
| 1840—Wm. McWillie | 1896—J. T. Hay |
| 1844—Wm. McWillie | 1898—J. T. Hay |
| 1846—Wm. J. Taylor | 1906—W. R. Hough |
| 1848—James Chesnut, Jr. | 1910—W. R. Hough |
| 1860—A. Hamilton Boykin | 1914—A. J. Beattie |
| 1865—J. B. Kershaw | 1918—J. Cope Massey |
| 1868—Justus K. Jillson | 1922—L. O. Funderburk |
| 1871—Henry Cardozo (col.) | 1926—G. C. Welsh |

## Miscellaneous

*Representatives.*

(Term Two Years)

1793—Benj. Haile, John Kershaw
1794—Willis Whitaker, Geo. Ross
1796—Joseph Brevard, Isaac DuBose
1798—Joseph Brevard, S. Mathis
1800—John Kershaw, Isaac DuBose
1802—James Chesnut, Willis Whitaker
1804—Benjamin Bineham, James Chesnut
1807—Abram Blanding, Isaac DuBose
1808—James Chesnut, Reuben Arthur
1812—Samuel James, Chapman Levy
1814—James Chesnut, Samuel James
1816—W. W. Starke, Everard Cureton
1822—Joseph Patterson, John Boykin, Thos. Lang
1824—Thos. Lang, Jos. Patterson, H. G. Nixon
1826—H. G. Nixon, Thos. Lang, Jos. Patterson
1828—H. G. Nixon, Chapman Levy, Jos. Patterson
1832—Thos. Lang, Wm. McWillie, W. O. Nixon
1834—M. M. Levy, Jos. Cunningham, Ezekiel Mayhew
1836—J. D. Murray, L. J. Patterson
1840—Jas. Chesnut, Jr., L. J. Patterson
1842—Jas. Chesnut, Jr., J. P. Dickinson
1844—Jas. Chesnut, Jr., J. P. Dickinson
1846—A. H. Boykin, James Cantey, Jr.
1848—A. H. Boykin, James Cantey, Jr.
1850—A. H. Boykin, James Cantey, Jr.
1851—James Cantey, James Chesnut
1852-1856—J. B. Kershaw, A. H. Boykin
1857-1859—A. H. Boykin, Wm. Shannon
1860-1861—Wm. Shannon, J. M. DeSaussure
1862-1864—(No House or Senate Reports.) (J. M. DeSaussure served during these years.)
1865-1867—W. Z. Leitner, W. L. DePass. (Leitner resigned to become district judge.)
1868—John A. Chesnut (col.), John A. Boswell, Jonas W. Nash (col.)
1870-1871—F. Adamson (col.), Reuben Gaither (col.), S. Gary (col.)
1872-1874—F. Adamson (col.), Reuben Gaither (col.), Allison W. Hough (col.)
1875-1876—R. D. Gaither (col.), S. Gary (col.), E. F. George (col.)
1877—E. H. Dibble (col.)

1878—J. D. Kennedy, L. B. Stephenson, W. R. Nelson
1880—J. D. Kennedy, W. R. Nelson, W. D. Trantham
1882—J. T. Hay, A. A. Huckabee, L. L. Clyburn
1884—E. Miller Boykin, L. L. Clyburn, Neal A. Bethune
1886—W. A. Ancrum, Joel Hough, P. H. Nelson
1888—W. A. Ancrum, Joel Hough, James R. McGill
1890—J. T. Kirkland, G. W. Moseley, W. F. Russell
1892—J. T. Kirkland, W. R. Bruce
1894—C. L. Winkler, J. W. Floyd
(1895—Const. Convention; J. T. Hay, C. L. Winkler, J. W. Floyd, members)
1896—C. L. Winkler, J. W. Floyd
1898—C. L. Winkler, D. M. Bethune
1900—C. L. Winkler, J. G. Richards, Jr.
1902-1906—J. G. Richards, Jr., M. L. Smith
(M. L. Smith, Speaker, 1903-1906)
1908—J. G. Richards, Jr., D. M. Bethune
1910—J. G. Richards, Jr., M. L. Smith
1912—M. L. Smith, T. J. Kirkland
1913—M. L. Smith, Newton Kelly
(M. L. Smith again Speaker, 1911-1914)
1915—Laurens T. Mills, J. M. Martin
1917—H. T. Johnson, Norman S. Richards
1919—Murdock M. Johnson, Joe V. Young
1921—Murdock M. Johnson, G. G. Alexander
1923-1924—James B. Munn, Norman S. Richards
1925—M. L. Smith, W. L. DePass, Jr.

# CHAPTER XXVII.

## CURIOSITY SHOP.

### *Serug's Battle.*

This expression which seems to have been confined to Camden and once current here is now obsolete. It signified a conflict such as Kilkenny cats are supposed to indulge when they meet. Riding around town on November 27, 1901 with the venerable Captain James I. Villepigue, then eighty years of age, but with mind clear and vigorous, we came to the southwest corner of York and Campbell Streets. "Here" he said, "in my boyhood stood the 'Yellow House',[1] a tavern which used to furnish entertainment for the river boatmen. On Saturday nights the roughs there gathered used to engage in ferocious fisticuffs. The town boys used to steal down there to witness these bouts, which we called Serug's Battles. I never knew why."

He was pleased to learn that the term was familiar to the writer, who heard it often used at home when a boy. Here follows all that we could discover in regard to this curious old expression.

In our Court records was found the following queer entry of date April 3, 1790.

"William Serug of Claremont County[2] for sixteen guinneys paid by Olivine Serug conveys to her one sorrel horse, with a small star in his forehead, and a large white spot on his nose, branded on the near shoulder (1), on the near buttock (2) and on the off buttock (3) and on the off shoulder (H. S.) and twenty head of hogs, marked with a poplar leaf in one ear and a hole in the other."

This remarkable steed was no doubt the same as that described in the following indictment unearthed among the dusty documents of our Court:

"Personally appeared John Moore of Claremont County who maketh oath that on or about the 2nd. of June 1st. (1789) this deponent lost a bright bay guelding

---

[1] The Yellow House dates back as far as 1804 and is referred to in Mrs. Thornton's reminiscences of Camden.

[2] In those days Claremont County was closely adjacent to Camden on the south, the northern boundary of Claremont being Pine Tree Creek, just a few hundred yards beyond the southern limits of Camden.

about fourteen and half hands high neither docked nor branded when taken away; one foot white, a small star in his forehead and a small snip on his nose, having remarkable straight hind legs and that the said guelding was stolen and led away by William Serug, Junior."

At the trial in November 1789 John Chesnut was a witness. A verdict of guilty was signed by Richard Bettis, foreman. The penalty for horse stealing then was death by hanging. Whether the sentence was ever executed neither the record nor tradition discloses. For a similar offense we do know that Gray Briggs was actually hung at Camden in 1794. (See chapter on "Court House.")

Nor is this all. At the same term of Court was found an indictment against the same Serug for stealing cattle from Joseph Kershaw and others. Among those summoned to testify appears the name of Zerephia Serug, William's sister.

From all of which we conclude that Serug was no myth but a daring bandit, and possibly the hero of some desperate struggle against capture.

It appears further that prior to the Revolution, Wm. Serug was the owner of the "Cannon Field" just a mile south of Camden, and lying between Pine Tree Creek, the Railroad, the Black River Road and the Charleston Road. Here were buried some old Revolutionary Cannon (hence the name) and it was the scene of a sharp attack by Marion in 1781 upon the British, posted at the old Mill near by. The fight here which was short but sharp may have been locally known as Serug's Battle—owing to Serug's ownership of the spot—but this is mere speculation.

The name Serug will be found in Luke, Chapter 3, verse 35 (Revised Version). In the King James Version it is Saruch.

*Ap Dick, The Welsh Goat—A Revolutionary Relic.*

The following biographical sketch is reproduced from the *Camden Journal* of February 28, 1829, and is undoubtedly from the facile pen of the Editor, Constans Freeman Daniels.

"Memoirs of all sorts and of all qualities have been the rage for some years past, and I am determined to write

## Curiosity Shop

'memoirs' too. And what though they are but the memoirs of a Goat?

"I undertake the present task under great advantages, and promise with the utmost confidence, to do it faithfully; since I owe no obligations to the family, whose illustrious relative I am about to immortalize; and since the sources whence I draw my materials for this history, are of the most undoubted authenticity.

"The illustrious Cambrian whose exploits I now intend to immortalize, was born somewhere in Wales; but at what precise time, or in what particular spot, I shall be unable to satisfy my readers, for though a goat of very particular pre-eminence, his birth place is as dubious as old Homer's, and for ought I know as many cities will hereafter contend for the honor. Historians in general however, incline to the opinion that he was born somewhere in Brecknockshire. A fact which they infer principally from his great propensity in his mature years, for the *breaking of necks*. At all events, he evinced very early in life, a most martial disposition, and during the American revolution embarked with Gen. Burgoyne and the British Army, and arrived in Quebec; accompanied that General to Lake Champlain; was with him at Crown Point, Ticonderoga, Skeensborough, etc., etc., and was taken with Gen. B. at Saratoga. His exploits during this campaign must remain unrecorded for the present, and perhaps forever; unless my readers should call for a second and enlarged edition of this history. But after his capture, at Saratoga, his politics like those of many other individuals in the British service, underwent a very material change; and he joined the American army under the protection of Lieutenant Parker—became a staunch whig, and forever thereafter, hated a red coat, as a benedictine Monk hates the devil. The services which Dick rendered to the American cause while he remained with Lieut. Parker, cannot at this moment be detailed, as my principal object in these scanty memoirs, is as I have said before, to beget a curiosity in the public for a fuller biography in some future edition of this uncommonly interesting work.

"Lieut. Parker was killed at the battle under Gen. St. Clair; but our hero Dick, did not follow the fortunes of his master so far, having staid in Camden, and become the property of Col. Kershaw of this town, in whose ownership he continued until the year 1799, the unfortunate period of his death, as will appear in the sequel.

"During the march of the Army South, after the capture of Burgoyne on the 17th. of October, 1777, Dick endeared himself very much to the American officers, by his martial deportment, strict observance of military etiquette, and the lofty chivalry of his bearing upon all occasions. His knowledge of camp duties was as accurate, as his performance of them was exact and punctilious. At tattoo, he retired to his quarters with all the punctuality of a veteran, and he never failed to turn out and parade regularly at reveille. In action he was equally prompt—never failing to form himself in the rear of his master, and charging with him upon the enemy; and though expected to act merely as a *corps de reserve*, he was always first in action. At the capture of Cornwallis at Yorktown, he particularly distinguished himself. The artillery however, was his favorite corps, and he has been known to stand by his gun through a whole battle, and watch the effects of its fire upon the enemy with intense solicitude, and with the most imperturbable coolness and gravity, always sleeping under the gun carriage at night. But it is in *private life* after all, that Dick is best remembered; especially by the good people of Camden; for his arrival here was after military operations had ceased; and it was as a goat in the discharge of civil functions, that his biographer finds most to detail. In this period of his career, he was well known and appreciated, and but few persons can be found, who lived in Camden previously to the year '99, who cannot relate some exploit of Ap Dick, the Welsh goat.

"Though he had given up campaigning altogether, he never entirely threw off his military habits. Like the late Emperor Alexander, he was notorious for *mediation;* and like another great peace maker, he never suffered a fight to take place in his presence, without having a hand (or at least a horn) in it himself. Nor would he ever strike an antagonist while he was down; but waited like a true pugilist, for his enemy to rise; when he would with the utmost good nature knock him down again.

"Dick's antipathy to scarlet continued through life, as many an old woman with a red cloak, who happened unluckily to come in contact with him, can testify. Other biographers describe the *personal* appearance of their heroes, and I shall be accused of a fatal omission, I suppose, unless I follow the example; but here I am at fault somewhat: Dick's portrait never having been taken in his lifetime, and tradition being rather scanty upon the point of his *bodily* contour. It is understood however, that like modern Dandies, he wore *large mostachios*, somewhat in the fashion of his Prussian Majesty's chasseurs. His horns are all that have survived; one of which in the possession of Dr. William Blanding we have seen; and it proves him to have been a goat of most colossal dimensions, indeed his great strength is evidence of that; for Peter Francisco himself was scarcely more famed for a 'dead lift'. Dick frequently took up and carried between his horns a man of two hundred pounds weight. We must close however, for the present; and merely tell our readers that Dick like all other heroes died; and this is the most grievous spot in the whole of this most interesting of all possible histories, for Dick died ignominiously—being kicked to death by a mule."

*A Good Indian.*

From records in Clerk's Office, Camden Court House, Book A, page 232:

"I do herewith certify that the bearer Onaeh Kampae Oneyda is one of the Northern Indians of the Oneyda Nation—that he with consent of his parents and friends, and with permission of the Governor of the State of New York, went in the year 1784 with me to Europe as a servant, that in the year 1786 he returned with me to Albany again, where he saw his Mother and Relations— But not wishing to remain with his people he came with me, with their consent, to South Carolina, where he has ever since continued.

Santee Canal, in the State of South Carolina, the Sixth of February 1797
To all it may concern
Ch. Senf.
(LS) Colonel of Engineers and one of the Justices of the Quorum of this State."

*Elephant Hunting.*

As Bailey's Circus was wending its way from Camden to Columbia on August 26, 1855, on reaching the forks of McCords Ferry and Columbia Roads, just beyond Lang's Mill (later known as Jordan's Mill), the elephant Jumbo insisted on taking the McCord's Ferry Road to the left. When co-erced to the right he became enraged, killed his keeper and a horse and went at large. The Camden Light Infantry Company was summoned and under Lieutenant James I. Villepigue proceeded to hunt down the monster. He was found in the swamp above the Mill pond. Volleys were fired into him without effect, as his hide was immune against the rifles of that day. Finally a crack shot landed a bullet in his eye which brought him down. Lieutenant Villepigue, who obtained one of the tusks as a trophy, related the facts to us, and we have also the account contained in the *Camden Journal* of that date.

While the Coroner's jury was holding an inquest over the keeper at the scene of the tragedy, some one cried out: "Here comes the elephant." Whereupon the jury dispersed in a panic.

*Dicey Davis.*

"I see around me here
Things which you cannot see."
—*Wordsworth.*

As we recollect it was about the year 1865 when we first became aware of Miss Dicey Davis. She was heralded by the thuds of a ponderous stick which she carried and let fall on each of the front steps as she mounted. Her wrinkled face and wild eyes under an antediluvian bonnet in which she always wore a sprig of green pine bespoke a beauty seared by time and care. She was no suppliant but extracted contributions. She would trudge in to Kirkwood from her abode on the hill east of Dicey's Ford on Little Pine Tree Creek. Here in the woods two miles out she lived alone in a log hut of one room, perfectly fearless and perfectly content in this wilderness. She would sally forth to forage around with the said stick and a white cotton bag or wallet for supplies for herself and dogs. She would gather wild grapes and sloes, dry them in the sun, and in her outward voyages carry a cargo of this tart and bitter produce to bestow upon her benefactors.

Beside her cabin was a small garden, and in it one pear tree, a favorite perch for mocking birds and other warblers. To her the notes of these birds were the voices of spirits. Her lover, she called him Joseph Lepeace, —had long ago disappeared, and had never returned. In the midst of conversation, if she heard the note of a bird, for which she seemed always intent, she would break off and exclaim: "Don't you hear what he says? Joseph Lepeace, Joseph is coming! Uncovered! Uncovered!", and other such incoherences.

Her cabin was always neat and clean. She scoured the chairs and the outside of the pots. She was always busy washing, cooking and knitting socks and gloves which she hung on the pear tree for Joseph. There they would hang until they disappeared, probably stolen, but she would never doubt that Joseph had gotten them.

For years she stuck to that old cabin until one night a forest fire was raging out there. Some one thought of poor Dicey and hurried to her rescue. She lay in bed watching the flames serenely, saying to them: "Come on, I am not afraid of you." She had to be saved forcibly. The hut and dogs were consumed. She was taken to the County Poor House, where half demented she did not long survive. "Dicey's Ford" over Little Pine Tree Creek is a short distance down stream from the pumping station of the City Water Works.

## Daniels and the Lioness.

On Monday, March the 22nd, 1830, Mrs. Anne Royall, authoress of the *Black Book*, alighted from the Stage Coach in Camden.

It was fortunate for future generations that there then dwelt in Camden the talented Constans Freeman Daniels, Editor of the *Camden Journal*, who in the columns of that paper heralded her coming and recorded the incidents of her reception, stay and departure in matchless style.

Mrs. Royall had become notorious as publisher of a paper which she called *Paul Pry*, and for other reasons. Presbyterians were her pet aversion—termed by her "Blue Skins". She was violent against advocates of the U. S. Bank, those being the days of "Old Hickory". It has been told of her that, having vainly tried to get an interview with President Tyler for *Paul Pry*, she watched her chance, caught the President bathing in the Potomac according to a custom of his, and while she sat on his clothes she obtained an interview from him with only his head above water.

According to the Library of Southern Literature, she was born in Virginia in the year 1769; while very young, she was stolen by the Indians and lived with them in the forests for sixteen years. She survived until 1854. At the time of her visit to Camden in 1830, she was at the fascinating age of 61, and a powerful magnet for the sparks of the town.

In 1829 she was indicted in the District of Columbia as a common Scold. Daniels in the *Journal* advises her to plead that she was an "uncommon Scold". We read that she was convicted before Judge Cranch and sentenced to pay a fine and give security to keep the peace.

Daniels thus bemoans her grievous plight:

"Our grief is so over-powering upon this occasion, that we cannot of course be expected to say much, till the flood gates of our sorrow run off a little surplus melancholy, otherwise we should say a pathetic thing or two this week. Never since old Socrates was made to take hemlock, has there been seen in the world such judicial iniquity, and never since that amiable consort of his helped him to a domestic shower bath, has Mrs. Royall's peeress astonished the world. Judge Cranch will go down to posterity not many leaves behind Eratostratus. We are glad however, that he didn't send her to the ducking stool, for that would be an indignity not to be borne. If she don't put him and that whole caitiff jury who convicted her into her new *Black Book* for this, there is nothing amiable in Bedlam."

Mrs. Royall's fame has been perpetuated not only by Daniels but also by herself in the *Black Book*, which narrates in racy style her tour through the United States. Extracts from her chapter on Camden and from Daniel's columns in the *Journal*, will render unnecessary any further feeble efforts on our part to depict the stir produced by her visit to this community.

The coming advent of Mrs. Royall, announced by her in a letter to the Editor, is thus heralded by him in the *Camden Journal* of February 20, 1830:

"Mrs. Royall says she is about to make our beatitude perfect by coming South, nay, thanks be to the lucky stars which govern this year, she will shortly be in Camden!!! We shall be upon the spot to meet her if Providence permit—or we should not be away. Mrs. Royall's letter is made up in her usual 'cursory' and attractive style. All the readers of the *Journal* will acknowledge that we have been extra super-fine in our notices of that distinguished Sappho. Our friends of the Artillery propose to receive her *a la Suwarrow* and to fire seventy-five guns if they can procure wadding.

" 'The Campbells are coming Oho, Oho.' "

For a time it seemed that Camden would miss the felicity of her presence. But in the *Journal* of March 13, 1830, the public are reassured thus:

"She tells us however that she intends to be here before long. This is very happifying to us. She has sent us she says some twenty or thirty volumes of her books, which we intend to advertise in *Glaring Capitals*. Mrs. Royall, is without competition the greatest *Lioness* of the present day. There is an interest about her which is quite indescribable. Nay, what is more, she is comparatively quite young, for she tells us that she is twenty-three years younger than her husband, who was a gallant officer of the Revolution and fought in the battle of Camden. This new information of our 'dear friend's' juvenility will awaken troublesome sensations in many a bachelor bosom, we are afraid."

The auspicious event actually occurred, and Monday, March 22, 1830, Mrs. Royall arrived. The *Journal* of March 27 proceeds as follows:

"Mungo Park tells us, if we mistake not, that a certain people among whom he traveled in the interior of Africa, distinguished that portion of their Chronology in which he visited them, as 'the year the white man passed'. The annals of Camden will hereafter show a *black* mark in the record, in everlasting commemoration of 1830, as the year particularly glorified by the transit of Mrs. *Anne Royall*.

"That distinguished lady arrived here on Monday evening in the Charleston Stage, on her way to Savannah! This is an overwhelming proof of partiality in traveling a hundred or two miles out of her way.

"She is, without flattery, the most extraordinary woman we ever saw, as we took occasion more than once to say to her. But we are aware that our praise should be suspiciously received, in as much as Mrs. Royall has shed the benignity of her smiles upon our favored pericranium, in showers quite too copious to permit our pen to be entirely impartial. We had no idea that we had laid up for ourselves such a magazine of good will; but there is nothing like the return of a grateful heart! Mrs. Royall has remembered all our labours of love, and she has paid them all back with a Dutchman's generosity.

"She is indeed the *dearest* of women, as some of our friends will probably make solemn affidavit to. She tells us that she has pretty much done the work for the 'Blue Skins' of the North and all south of 'Mason's and Dixon's Line', may as well look out for squalls, for her pen is going in a ratio proportioned to the squares of her tongue, which we can tell them would leave a railroad 'locomotive' panting in the rear. 'Copperheads' and a certain other genus of bipeds called 'Missionaries', the objects of her especial ire, will do well to take sanctuary at once. She tells us she has determined to destroy one of our Senators in Congress, for a late obnoxious vote, and has actually *black booked* a brother Editor as the 'Pink of the South'.

"Well, so it is; she seems to be raised up for some mighty purpose. She has visited all our Lions (herself the greatest lion of all), and has traversed our Classic fields—now rendered still more extra-classic. Cornwallis, Lord Rawdon, and even the Baron DeKalb stood but sorry chance for immortality, till Mrs. Anne Royall visited the scene of their exploits, and determined to hand their names down to everlasting remembrance on the same page with her own.

"Farewell, dear Mrs. Royall.

"P. S. Mrs. Royall left us for Columbia at one o'clock on Thursday. It is due to her to say that her conduct here has been marked by none of the annoyances which have been charged upon her elsewhere. Mr. and Mrs. McAdams, her host and hostess, declare they never had a boarder who gave less trouble, and she pronounces them both to be the Prince and Princess of Tavern Keepers. On the whole; she considers Camden the garden spot of her travels, while our citizens look upon her as the very *Queen of Flowers*—and the nightshade of authors."

Now for Mrs. Royall herself—Thus she speaks at various points in her *Black Book*, Vol. 11.

"Camden was too strongly entwined round my heart ever to be separated. It had long been the subject of my too anxious thoughts!

"They had however, by some means heard I was to arrive in the Stage that evening, and a number of choice spirits were assembled at the stage house to receive me.

"I shall never forget that memorable evening—nor shall I ever forget the thrill of pleasure I felt when the gentleman who helped me out of the Stage said, 'I am Daniels!' Humble as the great

## CURIOSITY SHOP

may deem us, we yet have hearts, and hearts that feel. Mr. Daniels amidst a crowd, led me into the house and I was soon surrounded by as true hearts as ever beat in human breasts. We were in fact all crazy, and it was with great difficulty the most sane part of the citizens could restrain the other part from firing a salute, they actually had powder and guns ready. Though I begged them to retire, arguing my fatigue and want of refreshment, they being round me till I took tea, while their hearts as well as my own overflowed with joy. These were the happiest moments I ever felt! The dear creatures at length tore themselves away and I was about to retire.

"They all flocked in the next chamber, and after being introduced to several gentlemen not in the preceding night, arrangements were made for escorting me round the environs of the town, as I wished to view those places where the sons of freedom fought and bled, in which my husband bore his part.

"A carriage was provided, and, attended by Mr. Daniels and Col. McWillie, I passed through the principal streets. One object of remark is the splendid mansion of Dr. McCaa, a most superb building.

"We proceeded to the battle ground of Gen. Green and Lord Rawdon—a conical hill called 'Hobkirk Hill'. The remains of several redoubts are still to be seen, and the graves, mostly Americans, are visible!! These are on each side of the road, and though on a high barren soil, the graves are over grown with flowers, and a rich coat of fine grass, the only grass which I saw in the State, and mark the dimensions of the graves precisely!

"To begin with the citizens of Camden, one of the first as well as the best men in the place, is a Yankee, though he now unites all the warmness of heart of the true Yankee, with the refined urbanity of the South. Every one is aware I mean none other than Mr. Daniels of the *Camden Journal;* he has resided long in the Southern country, and is a real Southerner in every sense of the word; learned, liberal, polite and ingenious—he is beloved by all who know him. C. F. Daniels, Esq., is rather a small man, and light make, under middle age, a neat figure, with a thin, round face, neither fair nor dark, and a keen, dark grey eye; his countenance is staid, firm and steady, and upon the whole he would be taken for a stern philosopher. *I never saw the semblance of a smile upon his countenance in our many interviews,* but his language, his manners and his actions are all of a piece, and breathe the essence of philanthropy. He is not only all soul, as the phrase is here, but all heart, which overflows with the milk and honey of human kindness. I had long been an admirer of Mr. Daniels, having been familiar with his fame as a gentleman and an editor, and was disappointed in but one thing, viz.: he greatly exceeded my anticipation. He is an editor whom every one likes; never bitter, but often feeling, witty and sometimes sarcastic, and such are his talents and independence, that few care to engage with him. In short I know few men his superiors, take him on any ground, and if I were to trust my honor to the life of any man, he is the one. I am rather under the impression that his worth and honor constitute his earthly possession.

"Some ladies on horseback passed our carriage, during our excursion. I remarked to my friends, that their ladies rode well, and made some remarks on the beauty of their horses. 'Yes, Mrs. Royall, we have fine horses, and our South Carolina girls know how to ride them—we have the finest horses and the finest girls in the Union', said Colonel (McWillie) and upon reflection I think he is right, for I never saw ladies of greater beauty, or that rode with more grace.

"I shall be obliged to visit Camden again, as we were all in such a delirium of joy and uproar, myself not the least, that I find from the notes, my sketches of portraits in Camden are the most imperfect of any in my travels. This is perhaps, the best character, I mean the truest, I could give of this delightful spot.

"It so happened, that sundry gentlemen had been at a party in the neighborhood, and several of them called at Camden, and of course upon my *Royal-ty*. They were all young hot spurs, high-minded and full of glee, quizzing, and mischief, participating in the general joy; their urbanity knew no bounds. It was nothing but skipping and spouting, jesting and romping about, the whole time; we had a complete comedy of it. No wonder I forgot everything I ought to have remembered; these wild rogues said I 'must give my studies to the winds'. Of all people the Southerners are the closest followers of nature, gay, lofty, artless and candid, alike unawed and unaffected, they indulge in a freedom of thought and action unknown in our States.

"One H———, a blue skin, thought he might slip in unperceived, but I instantly challenged him, and expressed my surprise that such a man was countenanced. 'We did not know it, madam; how can you tell?' Any one might tell. Imagine my grief when informed he was at the head of an academy! To think that these refined people should be gulled by these traitors! These Presbyterians are in possession of all our strongholds, and if they give them up without blood-shed, I am much mistaken. They own all the cash, the United States Bank, and presses, and have put down the only periodical paper of any value in our Country, the *North American Review!*

"I fell upon another blue-skin, one D———. He looked vengeance at me, as I passed him by accident.

"Presbyterians! Bravo! they know how to clinch the *cash!* Shame on South Carolina going to the dogs like Virginia, and the *Christian Almanac* selling in Camden (by the Postmaster) for 12½ cents. The poor fellow was much alarmed when I detected him, and presented me with a treatise on gardening. It was inscribed as follows: 'Presented by J. Eccles to Mrs. Anne Royall, as a tribute of respect to her genius.' It containes twelve pages, and is no doubt a useful work—But, had he been a Blue-skin, all the tributes would not have saved him; he was a mighty Methodist. Strange that men want to be anything but honest men. I cannot see through it.

"A length the trying time arrived, when I had to part with friends dear to me as life. My bill was paid by the City Council, and on the third day, after dinner, my friends gathered around me, to take leave; my heart was pained to the core—the thought of being severed from souls of such feeling and worth, was bitter indeed! I could have expired amongst them—we pressed hands in silence and I stepped into the Stage! Imagine my feelings upon receiving a parting address on behalf of the town, delivered by the amiable and accomplished Daniels. The citizens, with hats off in deadly silence listened. The pathos, the eloquence, the depth of feeling, the warm sensibility, the touching strains in which the speaker portrayed the qualities and services of my deceased husband—the delicacy of terms in which he alluded to myself—the pleasure of my visit, and my arduous pursuits, entwined our hearts in the most indissoluble friendship. Tears dropped from several and, over-powered by my feelings, I waived my hand in silence, and the Stage moved off!"

# CHAPTER XXVIII.

### FAMILY HISTORIES.

No attempt is made to supply genealogical tables. It is enough for our purpose to give brief sketches, as accurate as we have been able to make, of those representative families that settled in Camden, or in Kershaw County but largely identified with the town, from about the beginning of the 19th Century through the War between the States. In our first volume we treated in the same way the families that were here during the colonial and Revolutionary periods.

We have had to rely principally on information obtained from descendants of these families, reinforced and corrected sometimes from public records of various kinds, including wills, newspapers and inscriptions on tombstones.

If some sketches are briefer than others, it is due in most instances to paucity of data procurable. In a few cases we have had to condense the information furnished, to conform to the general scheme.

It is quite probable that, without intention, we have omitted some Camden families that should have gone in; and we are aware that there are many old and highly respectable families outside the town that might have been treated had we undertaken to cover in this field the whole of Kershaw County—such names as Hough, West, Bethune, McCaskill, McLaurin, McLeod, McDowell, Humphries, Pearce, Peeples, Bell, Dunn, Smyrl, Joy, Vaughan, Stokes, Sowell, Truesdale, Huckabee, Brown, Dixon, Hilton,[1] Gaskins, Barnes, Baskin, Bradley, Fraser, Young, Brewer, Stover, Tiller, Hinson, Moseley, McCoy, Ratcliff, Horton, Rabon, Burdell, Massey, Fletcher, Catoe, Myers, Bowen, Gay, Cauthen, Sill, Owens, Kirkley, Elliott, King, Williams, Drakeford, Russell, Bateman, and a number of others that will readily occur to some minds.

Nor have we given accounts of the many worthy families that have settled in Camden since the Civil War. It was necessary to draw the line somewhere, so we fixed that epoch as our limit.

---

[1]From this family sprung Richmond Hobson Hilton, one of the Congressional Medal Heroes of the World War.

## Family Histories

It may be said here that practically every family name in Kershaw County, including the town, will be found figuring creditably in the rolls of soldiers appended to the accounts of the various wars in which our men have fought, especially in the Confederate rolls; and, had our space permitted their inclusion, in the World War rolls many of these names would have been repeated and many new ones added.

Without any idea of making invidious distinctions of relative importance, we have found it advisable to make two groups of families.

In the first group, we place those about whom, for one reason or another, our information is very meager, though many of them are of long standing in the community.

We know, for instance, that the families of Gayle, Latta, Baxley, Sheorn, Campbell, Malone, Brasington, Boswell, Meroney, Crosby, Morrell, Love, Walker, Shiver, Man, Billings, Sutherland, DeHay, Mathis, David Kennedy, Jones, were here in the early or middle 19th Century, yet these we can only name.

Of some others we can give but fragmentary information, as follows:

ALDEN.—George Alden was a familiar figure in mercantile circles in Camden from the middle of last century to the time of his death in the 80's.

He was a Northern man by birth, from Massachusetts we believe, but thoroughly identified with the South by long residence.

His first business advertisement appears in a local paper in 1845. At one time he operated a successful shoe factory.

Mr. Alden married Mary Wylie, of York County, a woman of social graces and talented as a pianist. Their home on Broad Street, opposite Bishop Davis', was the center of much musical and other entertaining.

Mrs. Alden died a few years before her husband. Their attractive home passed into other hands and was burned a few years later.

There were no descendants.

ARTHUR.—From a monument in our cemetery we learn that John W. Arthur was born in 1798 and died in 1862. He was the father of the late John and William Arthur, well-known Camden merchants.

John married Jessie Zemp of Camden.
William married June Weston, of Richland County.
A sister, Louise, became the wife of Frank Mitchell of Wilmington.
A brother, Jesse, early moved to California.
All of that generation have passed.

BIRCHMORE.—Thomas Birchmore was a member of Captain Francis Blair's company in the War of 1812.

Charles W. Birchmore, editor of a local paper, is a descendant.

BISSELL.—Dr. M. W. Bissell was long a practicing dentist of the town. His sons, Edward and Wyckam, and daughter, Mrs. Richardson, were once well-known citizens.

BRUNSON.—Sylvester and Edward M. Brunson were tinners in Camden in 1816. Their descendants were residents of the town until recent years.

BURNS.—James H. Burns (1802-1846) and his wife Mary (1813-1851) came to Camden from Cabarrus County, North Carolina. Both are interred in our cemetery. Their children were: Isaac, mortally wounded at Weldon Roads, 1864; Captain James H. (1841-1863), who was killed at Gettysburg; C. Benton (1835-1871), who succeeded Thomas J. Warren as Captain of the Kershaw Guards, Co. D., 15th Regiment; and four daughters, Elizabeth, Lucretia, Mary and Margaret.

After the War, Benton Burns was engaged in business in Camden up to the time of his death. His wife was Marietta McLaughlin, of Roanoke County, N. C. She survived to a great age, rearing her two sons to manhood in the homestead on Fair Street.

DICKINSON.—(See "Kershaw Volunteers in the Mexican War.")

GERALD.—W. J. Gerald was settled in mercantile business in Camden in the first half of the last century. He was intendant of the town in 1846. His wife was a Clarkson, sister, we believe to Mrs. Joseph Cunningham and Mrs. Barnes.

There were several children, but one of whom made his home in Camden, the late William C. Gerald, a well-known merchant and a worthy Confederate soldier in Hagood's brigade. He married Miss Frances Cuber, and left a number of descendants.

# Family Histories

The youngest son of W. J. Gerald, Reuben, was killed in the Civil War.

GOODALE.—Alexander Goodale, who died in 1798, was in the tailoring business in Camden. The family is still largely represented in the community. The late John R. Goodale was twice intendant of the town. His wife was Mary Arrants, a niece of Mrs. Charles McDonald.

The Lewis family also descends from Alexander Goodale.

LYLES.—James V. Lyles (1810-1863), a native of Fairfield County, married Mary, daughter of Major Joseph Mickle, and was in business in Camden for many years.

Their children were:

MARTHA, who married Dr. George Todd, a Confederate soldier from Kentucky, whose sister, Mary, much to his dislike it may be said, had become the wife of the "Great Emancipator", Abraham Lincoln. Dr. Todd remained through life an unreconstructed "rebel".

JOHN BELTON, who married Louisa, daughter of Wyatt Patterson.

SARAH, who married Dr. Edwin Hughes, a Confederate surgeon.

MARY; unmarried.

The Lyles home, formerly of Samuel Mathis, one of the oldest landmarks, still stands on the southeast corner of Broad Street and Monument Square.

MCDONALD.—Charles A. McDonald, (1802-1879), of Cumberland County, North Carolina, was a long-established Camden tailor. He married Mary Arrants, of an early Camden family, and their daughter, Sarah, married J. W. McCurry, a prominent Baptist and merchant of the town.

MCEWEN.—James McEwen, (1780-1864), took out naturalization papers in 1832, stating that he came from Scotland in 1820. He was a cotton buyer in Camden in 1831 and in 1843 was operating a stage line to Gadsden. One of his daughters married Robert L. Tweed; another married John Knox Witherspoon.

We do not know what relation, if any, he was to John McEwen, who was principal of the Orphan Society School in 1822. They were probably brothers.

MCQUEEN.—Donald McQueen (1818-1877) was born in Invernesshire, Scotland. When three years of age, he, an only child, was brought by his parents, Donald and Jean McQueen, to Charleston, S. C., where the family settled.

Shortly afterwards, both parents died of yellow fever. The son was educated in Charleston, married Estelle Boutan of that city, and lived there until 1862, when, with his wife and five children, he removed to Camden, being engaged in business there up to the time of his death.

He had recently been made Treasurer of the County.

The children of Donald and Estelle McQueen were:

CHARLES FARRAR, married Esther Whale, of Augusta, Ga.

DONALD, married Ellen Lynch, of Columbia, S. C.

He served as agent of the South Carolina Railroad at Camden, later removing to Columbia, where to the time of his death he was agent of the Southern Railway.

KATHERINE (1853-1912), unmarried.

JULIA COURTNEY (1855-1910), married Dr. I. H. Alexander, of Camden.

Mrs. McQueen died in 1906, in her 86th year.

MILLING.—Hugh Milling was appointed Sheriff of Camden District in 1785.

DR. JOHN MILLING (1790-1864), was probably a son of Hugh. He came from Fairfield District, married a daughter of Willis Whitaker and was for many years a planter on Saunder's Creek; a man held in high esteem in the county. He lies in our God's Acre.

His children, all daughters, were:

SARAH, who married John Belton Mickle.

MATILDA, who married Joseph Mickle, brother of John.

MARY, who married Dr. James Milling of Fairfield.

BELLE, who married John Starke.

HARRIET, who married Solomon Lorick.

There are quite a number of descendants of Dr. John Milling through these unions.

MOFFAT.—(See "Kershaw Volunteers in the Mexican War".)

NILES.—From Ebenezer P. Niles, who was principal of the Orphan Society Schools, 1825-29, through his marriage with Esther Clarkson, also a teacher in Camden in the "20's", are descended the families of a son, the late Ariovistus Niles, a soldier of the Confederacy, and of a daughter, the late Mrs. A. R. Goodwyn. After the death of Mr. Niles, his widow married the first Joseph Cunningham.

PEGUES.—T. W. Pegues was printer of the *Camden Journal* in 1831. His descendants lived here until after the Civil War. Their old house, a landmark, on the corner of DeKalb and Mill Streets, was burned in recent years.

ROSSER.—William Rosser (1813-1847) served under Captain John Chesnut in the Florida War. Afterwards he was Sheriff of Kershaw County.

JAMES PINCKNEY ROSSER (1819-1847) died while in service in Keith Moffat's company in the Mexican War and is buried in Puebla, Mexico.

MAJOR JOHN ROSSER settled in Camden in 1827. He served as mayor in 1857. Some of his anecdotes of Revolutionary soldiers he had known personally were given in our first volume. In 1860 he left Camden and of his subsequent career we are not informed.

These men were probably brothers.

SCHROCK.—David Schrock was paymaster of Captain Francis Blair's company in the War of 1812. From him descended William A. Schrock, until recently a citizen of Camden, and the late Mrs. Columbus Vaughan.

The family homestead, a very old one, stood on the southwest corner of DeKalb and Lyttleton Streets.

SENF.—In the *City Gazette and Daily Advertiser* (Charleston) of July 11, 1799, appears the following notice: "Died at Rocky Mount, on Catawba River, Mr. Lucas Senf, father of Colonel Senf, in his 78th year."

In the *Charleston Courier*, September 3, 1806, is this announcement: "Died at his Seat at Rocky Mount, on the 24th ult., of a lingering illness, in the 53rd year of his age, Col. Christian Senf, Chief Engineer of the State of South Carolina. He was an officer of merit and information, and had served with great applause in the Southern States as an engineer during our Revolutionary contest."

Colonel Senf was attached, as engineer, to the American Army at the Battle of Camden. He was also employed in the construction of the Catawba Canal and in other large engineering projects.

SHAW.—George W. Shaw (1820-1860), a Northerner by birth, was for a long time a resident merchant of Camden.

JOHN G. SHAW, probably a brother, was also in business here in 1840.

GEORGE SHAW married Mary, daughter of William McKain. She died at a great age in 1910.

Their children were:

JOHN, married Josie Jones, of Memphis, Tenn.; died 1889.

CAMILLE ADELE ("MATTIE"), married Mansfield McLaurin. Her death occurred in 1916.

MARY, died in 1879, aged 19 years.

GEORGE, married Frances Eleanor Alger; died 1890.

None of the married children settled in Camden.

The Shaw residence was on Fair Street, long afterwards the home of the late Major E. E. Sill.

SMART.—John Smart was a Marylander, who settled in Camden about the middle of the last century and practiced law for many years. The late Major E. B. Cantey remembered him as a man of fidelity, tenacity and courage, if very eccentric. An account of his duel with Dickinson is told in another chapter. He became insane over a suit at law that he was pressing and died in an asylum.

SMITH.—From Mendel Smith, who was in business in Camden in the early days of the 19th century, there are some descendants through his sons, LaFayette, Napoleon and William Smith, and a daughter, Mrs. Osteen. Judge Mendel L. Smith, son of the first-named, is one of these.

TEAM-GETTYS.—Adam Team died in Kershaw County in 1844, aged 85 years. In early life he settled in Salisbury, N. C. As a Revolutionary soldier, he participated in the battle of Stono Ferry, 1799, and in the battle of Camden under Gates. Afterwards he served under General Davie. The greater part of his life was spent farming in Kershaw County. At the time of his death there were three other veterans of the Revolution living in the county.

The late Benjamin Team, a large planter in West Wateree, and Mrs. James Gettys, were his descendants.

JAMES GETTYS was a son of John Gettys, who owned the lands on which the present power plant of the "Southern Power Company" is located, about eight miles north-

## Family Histories

west of Camden. The family is an old one in the county.

THOMPSON (NINIAN).—Ninian Thompson (1824-1881) and his wife came to Camden from Aberdeenshire, Scotland. Mr. Thompson was in the business of house painting. A son, Waddy Thompson, is a prominent banker and citizen of Lancaster. There were three daughters, one of whom married D. E. Hinson. The entire family has left Camden.

TWEED.—Robert L. Tweed (1815-1850), an old Camden merchant, was a native of County Antrim, Scotland. He married Susannah, daughter of James McEwen.

Mrs. Tweed (1818-1901), with her sister, Miss Dinah McEwen, for many years, conducted the leading millinery store of Camden, which was continued until recent years by her daughters, Misses Ellen and Elizabeth Tweed. The latter married Louis Brunson: no descendants.

The Tweed home, still standing, was on the northwest corner of DeKalb and Lyttleton Streets. The family is extinct.

WILSON.—Thomas MacCartney Wilson (1821-1870), was born in County Antrim, Ireland. He received his education at Dublin University, coming to Charleston, S. C. 1840, where in 1843 he was married to Miss Mary Doud and moved to Camden. Here he engaged in the hat and shoe business under the firm name of Wilson & Shegog. He helped organize and for a long time was captain of the first Volunteer Firemen's Company and was one of the three who organized the Order of Odd Fellows here. Entered the Confederate Army in 1860, in Captain Wm. Clyburn's Company. After the War he was in the shoe business here with two of his brothers, Samuel M. and Paul H. He left three children; the late George Charlesworth Wilson and Thomas MacCartney Wilson of Jacksonville, Fla., and Rose Emma Wilson, now Mrs. George Gilman Alexander.

Coming to Charleston and Camden, later, where all lived for a while, were Robert, James Young, George S., William, Samuel MacCartney, Paul H., brothers of Thomas M. Wilson, and a sister, Miss Matilda Wilson, later Mrs. T. B. Walker, who conducted a millinery store here for many years. All received their education before coming here under the direction of their uncle, Bishop MacCartney of the Church of England, and were confirmed by him in that Faith, a number never removing their membership from the little church in their native home.

William died of typhoid fever about 1854 and is buried in Camden. Robert, George and James opened a large grocery store here and did a good business until the Florida Boom about 1850, when they moved to Jacksonville, Fla. Samuel and Paul also went to Jacksonville but returned here and entered the Confederate Army; both were wounded. After the War, Paul went to Bishopville and died there. Samuel opened a grocery store here, married Mrs. Mary Louisa Hamilton, and died in 1917, leaving two children, Mrs. J. C. Nicholson and W. G. Wilson of this city.

Of the following families more detailed information has been available.

### ANDERSON (EDWARD).

Dr. Edward H. Anderson, (1st), (1781-1843), was born in Frederick County, Maryland. He came to Camden in 1810, and was a leading physician of the town to the time of his death. His wife was Catherine Pricilla Morris, of his native county. Her death, at Camden, occurred in 1824. Both lie in our cemetery. Their children who reached maturity were:

CATHERINE (1812-1873), second wife of Governor William McWillie.

RICHARD L., died at the age of 21.

DR. EDWARD H., (2nd).

THOMAS SALMOND.

In 1827, Dr. Anderson married Eliza, sister to Colonel Chapman Levy of Camden. Their children were:

CHAPMAN LEVY.

LUCY A., became the wife of Captain Adam McWillie, son of Governor McWillie.

Treating these in the order given above:

DR. EDWARD H. ANDERSON (2nd), (1817-1907), was born at Camden. He graduated in medicine at the University of Pennsylvania (1840), and practiced in Camden until 1845, when he removed to Canton, Miss., continuing in practice there. His second wife was Sarah McWillie McCulloch, a descendant of Colonel Adam McWillie.

THOMAS SALMOND ANDERSON (1819-1861) was also a native of Camden. In early life he too made his home in

## Family Histories

Mississippi. He married Flora, only daughter of Colonel Chapman Levy. Their eldest son, Edward (1843-1861) was killed at First Manassas. An incident in connection with his death is related by Mrs. Jefferson Davis in her life of her husband: "While in the agonies of pain and parched with thirst, some of the ambulance corps came to take private Edward Anderson to the hospital, but he pointed to a wounded man near him saying: 'Take him; he may recover, I cannot'." A knightly deed, suggestive of Sir Philip Sidney at Zutphen.

CHAPMAN LEVY ANDERSON entered the Confederate service at the age of 16, as an officer of the 39th Mississippi Regiment. He became a member of Congress and was a prominent lawyer in Mississippi. His wife was a daughter of Dr. R. B. Johnson, formerly of Camden.

The Anderson family, of good old Maryland stock, is more or less identified with Camden in other lines.

An uncle of the first Dr. Edward H. Anderson was the distinguished Revolutionary officer, Colonel Richard Anderson, of the Maryland line, who was wounded in the battles of Camden and Guilford. After the war, he visited Camden on more than one occasion, serving as a pall-bearer on the reinterment of DeKalb's remains in 1825, again responding to a very complimentary toast at a banquet given to General Blair in 1832. His son, Dr. William Wallace Anderson (1st), settled at Stateburg about 1820,[1] and was the father of General Richard H. Anderson (1821-1879), the ranking Confederate officer from South Carolina.

General Anderson, after the War, spent several years in Camden as agent of the South Carolina Railway. A man of infinite modesty, never obtruding himself in any way upon the public notice, it was hard to believe, except for his erect soldiery carriage, that this quiet unassuming gentleman had by his dashing gallantry won for himself the sobriquet of "Fighting Dick" Anderson.

DR. WILLIAM WALLACE ANDERSON (2nd), of Stateburg, a graduate of West Point, a surgeon in the old U. S. Army and ranking surgeon in the Confederate service, was a brother of General Dick Anderson. He was the father of Mrs. William Sanders, the present owner of "Hillcrest".

[1] His home there, "Hillcrest", is one of the famous colonial mansions of South Carolina.

DR. RICHARD ANDERSON (1796-?), fourth son of Colonel Richard Anderson of the Revolution and brother of the first Dr. William Wallace Anderson, practiced medicine in Camden in the first quarter of the last century, later removing to Stateburg. He was the father of Dr. William Wallace Anderson (3rd) born in 1844, a resident of Summerton, S. C.

The name has long since passed from this community.

## ANDERSON (WILLIAM)

William Anderson, one of Camden's early notable merchants of Scottish extraction—the full list of whom is both long and honorable—was born at Castle Douglas, a little Galloway town in Scotland, in 1806. His father, who bore the same name, was a soldier in the ranks of the famous regiment known as the "Scots Greys", and was killed at Waterloo.[1] His mother was Mary Kirkpatrick.

At the age of sixteen, he came to Charleston, South Carolina, where he was employed for some time by an uncle, John Kirkpatrick. About 1826, he settled in Camden, in business with Christopher Matheson. Three years later, he was married, at Morristown, N. J., to Sarah, eldest daughter of James K. Douglas, who, by the way, was a fellow townsman in Scotland of both the Andersons and McDowalls. Mr. Douglas was at the time a temporary resident of New Jersey.

Mr. Anderson's place of business in Camden, until his death in 1860, was on the northeast corner of Broad and DeKalb Streets, the present site of the Post Office.

He built, and occupied as long as he lived, the handsome residence in Kirkwood, later the property of the late Captain William L. DePass. He was an elder in the Presbyterian Church.

His children who lived to maturity were:

WILLIAM DOUGLAS (1828-1895), married Annie Douglas, of Charleston. Their children are the surviving representatives of the family.

MARGARET GORDON (1830-1908), unmarried.

JAMES KIRKPATRICK (1834-1875), who served in the War from 1861 to its close as Assistant Quartermaster in

---

[1] For this and other statements in regard to the family, we are indebted to the late Miss Ellen Anderson.

FAMILY HISTORIES

Stokes' Battalion, 4th Regiment, South Carolina Cavalry; unmarried.
CHARLOTTE ELLEN (1837-1913), unmarried.
SARAH KENNEDY (1840-1880), unmarried.

BLAIR-RAY-MCMILLAN-RUGELEY.

John J. Blair and his brother, Francis, natives of York County, were engaged in general merchandise business in Camden in 1817. They were cousins of General James Blair, long a representative of the District in Congress. John (1793-1844) was later a partner in business with William E. Johnson. He also served as Clerk of Court and many specimens of his exquisite penmanship are extant in the Court records. The late Captain James Villepigue related that he had seen him write his name perfectly on a wall with a 50-pound weight hanging from his little finger. He built and long occupied the large residence opposite the Presbyterian Church, known later as the Cunningham House.

Chagrined by his defeat for election as cashier of the Bank of Camden in 1836, he left the town forever, settling in Mobile, Ala.

Mr. Blair married Martha, a daughter of CAPTAIN PETER RAY, a native of St. John's, Berkeley, who died in Camden in 1814, aged fifty, as we learn from his monument in our cemetery. Another daughter, Elizabeth Ray, married, in 1816, JOSEPH GOODMAN, who conducted a well-known hotel of the old days in Camden. Still another daughter, Louisa Ray, married THOMAS MCMILLAN, a native of County Ayr, Scotland, who was for many years a cotton buyer in Camden and an elder in the Presbyterian Church, removing before the War to Mobile, where his descendants are prominent. He was a first cousin of Anthony M. and Robert M. Kennedy.

One of the daughters of John and Martha Ray Blair, Mary, was his assistant in the Clerk of Court's office. Another daughter, Ellen Blair, married JAMES RUGELEY, son of Colonel Henry Rugeley of Kershaw County. They also moved to Mobile. One of their sons, Edward Rugeley, was killed in the Civil War, leaving several daughters.

FRANCIS BLAIR was prominent in military affairs. He commanded a company from Kershaw County in the War of 1812, and in 1817 succeeded Adam McWillie as Colonel of the 35th Regiment, S. C. Volunteers. Colonel Francis Blair, in 1817, married Flora Lee, of Sumter District.

GENERAL JAMES BLAIR and his family are fully treated in another chapter.

## BROWN.

The Browns were farmers in the Liberty Hill section possibly as early as the Revolutionary period.

ROBERT BROWN (1774-1818) had his home on Still House Branch, a little south of Beaver Creek, and there, near the river, he lies buried. Close by are the unmarked graves of his parents, of whom there seem to be no records.

ROBERT BROWN married Elizabeth, eldest daughter of Arthur Cunningham, and left three children who lived to maturity:

MARY (1801-1888), who became the wife of Alexander Hodges, and, on his death, married William E. Johnson, Sr. (See Johnson.)

JOHN, who married; first Mrs. Jane Bailey, daughter of Robert Cunningham; second, Mrs. Martha Stinson (nee George). By the first union, there was one son who lived to manhood, William Brown (1828-1902), who married Elizabeth Perry and left several children. By the second, there was also one son, Arthur Pomeroy Brown, who married, first, Hannah, daughter of Wm. Curry Cunningham; second, Anne Wade.

HENRY (1805-1868), who married Elizabeth Reed; their children were:

SERENA (1831-1897), married Geo. R. Miller.
MARY (1835-1903), unmarried.
HENRY R. (1833-1890), married Sallie Hatfield.
LAURA (1839-1867), married Wm. Drakeford.
WILLIAM, married Frances Spurrier.
JANE (1844-1889), married John M. Perry.
EUGENIA, married Wm. F. Rutledge.
JAMES (1849-1905), married Catherine Barber.
EMMA (1851-1886), unmarried.

John and Henry Brown became large planters. The former built one of the handsomest houses on Liberty Hill; the latter built the house that crowned the elevation nearby, the highest point in that section. Both places passed into other hands after the War.

# Family Histories

## Capers-Zemp.

We link these families because the former is represented now in Camden only through the latter.

The Capers name is highly distinguished in both the ecclesiastical and military annals of South Carolina.

It is one of the oldest families in the state, having settled on St. Helena Island and in Christ Church Parish, Berkeley, prior to 1692.

Two Bishops and a great number of ministers, a few Episcopal but the large majority Methodist, bore the name; and thirty-seven men of the name fought under the banner of Dixie, eighteen of whom were officers, eleven of them having been promoted for gallantry on the field of battle. Two of these became Brigadier Generals.[1]

The Camden branch of the family was established by Reverend Samuel Wragg Capers, a Methodist minister who was stationed here in 1830-31. He was a son of Captain William Capers, a distinguished officer in the Revolution, who served both in the Continental Line and as one of Marion's Men. He was born on his father's plantation in Georgetown District, 1797. Mr. Capers was thrice married: First to Elizabeth Humphries; second to Sarah Brandt; third to Abathiah Harvey Thornton, of Camden. He was brother to Bishop William Capers of the Methodist Episcopal Church. His death occurred in 1855 and he is buried in Camden.

By his first wife, he left one son, Samuel (1818-1894); by his second wife, a child who died in infancy; and, by his third wife, the following issue:

RICHARD THORNTON, who was in the Methodist itinerary from 1854-6; married Mary Hard.

ABATHIAH ELIZABETH (1831-1909), who married Dr. F. L. Zemp.

SIDNEY, who married first, Jessie Darby; second, Edith, daughter of Bishop W. M. Wightman.

JOHN, killed at Appomattox, 1865, age 23.

MARY (1844-?), who married Reverend C. Thomasson, of the Methodist connection.

SARAH (1846-?), who married Dr. A. J. Stokes, of the Methodist Conference.

CAROLINE (1848-1890), unmarried.

[1]Our informant as to the family war record was Mrs. Mary Capers Thomasson.

EMMA (1850-1878), who became the wife of James Nelson, of Kershaw County.

EDWIN (1852-1901), died, unmarried. He was engaged in mercantile business in Camden for many years.

There were four others who died in infancy.

DR. FRANCIS LESLIE ZEMP (1819-1893) was brought to this country in 1825 by his father, who died of yellow fever the same year at Charleston, South Carolina. The lad, having apparently no other relatives, was placed in the Charleston Orphan Asylum. After some years he came to Camden where he worked and studied in Dr. Joshua Reynolds' Drug Store.

By his twentieth year, 1839, he was able to enter the Charleston Medical College. Next year he pursued his studies at the Medical College of what is now the University of Pennsylvania, in Philadelphia, qualifying as both physician and pharmacist. He practised first in Sumter County, soon removing to Camden, where, until his death, he was one of the town's most energetic and successful business men. When still a young man, Dr. Zemp had the misfortune of losing a leg in a railway accident near Marion, South Carolina. He recovered damages to the amount of $10,000.00, one of the earliest verdicts against a railroad for injury to passengers.

Being thus somewhat incapacitated for general practice, Dr. Zemp opened a Drug Store, where his ability and willingness to prescribe remedies were at once a boon to the poor and the means of his building up a large trade. He did, at the same time, quite a good office practice. At the time of his death, he had amassed considerable wealth, by dint of business sagacity, untiring activity and straight dealing. He was, at one time, owner of the Factory Pond where he conducted a flour mill, the products of which were shipped as far as North Carolina and Georgia. He also had a tannery that produced a fine grade of leather. He was president of our first Building and Loan Association and of the Wateree Bridge Company, both of which he was instrumental in organizing. He was a most devoted Methodist, the main prop of the church during his latter years; indeed the present church building was made possible, largely, by his liberality and labor. In appearance he was a typical Swiss, and it is easy to believe, as some of the descendants have

# Family Histories

seemed to establish, that he was a connection of a late President of the Swiss Republic of the same name.

Dr. Zemp was twice married. His first wife was Rebecca, daughter of Dr. Joshua Reynolds; of this union there was one child, Sophia (1844-1918). His second wife was, as stated, Abathiah, daughter of Rev. Samuel Wragg Capers, by whom he had the following issue:

LESLIE (1850-1915), married Emma Hamlin.
WILLIAM (1852-1912), married Alice Brunson.
EUGENE (1854-1903), married Mary Blakeney.
ELLA (1858-1920), married U. B. Rankin.
FRANCIS M. (1860-   ), married, first, Kate DeLoache; second, Nadine Dabney.
JESSIE (1862-1893), married, first John Arthur; second, L. Meares.
ANNIE (1867-   ), married Rev. W. S. Stokes.
SIDNEY (1868-   ), married, first, Hattie Truesdale; second, Gertrude Mitcham.
RUSSELL (1871-   ), married Kathleen Hunt, of Alabama.

## CARPENTER.

(See THORNTON).

## CIPLES.

Lewis Ciples (1775-1836) was for forty years a resident of Camden. He owned a large plantation on the old river road to Liberty Hill, between Granny's Quarter and White Oak Creeks. On this place was quarried the granite for the DeKalb monument in Camden. This stone, by the way, had a great reputation for its fine quality and is mentioned by Tuomey, the geologist, as "DeKalb" granite.

Mr. Ciples married Sarah (1788-1863), daughter of John Adamson. They left no children but adopted and raised Sarah, daughter of Ebenezer P. Niles, to whom they left their property. She married Colonel Artemas Goodwyn of Fort Motte and left one child, Elizabeth, who became the wife of Dr. T. Berwick Legare, for many years a prominent dentist in Camden and, later, Columbia.

Mrs. Legare gives the following interesting account of her mother's foster-father:

"Uncle Ciples was a very cultured as well as wealthy man. I've always been under the impression that he came from England and had no relatives in this country. In fact I never heard the name attached to any other than himself. His library for that time was quite large, showing him a man of letters. His books were frequently annotated in a small scholarly hand."

Lewis Ciples had an unfortunate difficulty with his wife's nephew, John Adamson, in which Adamson, who was insane, was killed. The trial of Mr. Ciples was a notable one: he was acquitted. The bail required of him was $60,000.00, the largest on record in the County Court: it was promptly furnished by the largest property holders in the community. He died at Red Sulphur Springs, Virginia.

His house is still standing, on lower Fair Street. It was inherited and occupied for years by Mrs. Legare.

## CLARK.

(See THORNTON).

## CLARKE.

Caleb Clarke (1777-1849), a Marylander by birth, was a prominent lawyer of Winnsboro, South Carolina, serving as solicitor of the middle circuit and as a member of the Legislature.

His wife was Julia Harrison, of Chester County.

One of their sons, Dr. Henry H. Clarke (1813-1864), a physician by profession, was a wealthy planter of Fairfield County. His residence at Longtown overlooked the Valley of the Wateree, with a magnificent prospect. Like the other old mansions of that locality, it fell a victim to the ravages of war.

Dr. Clarke married Louisa, daughter of James Goodwyn, of lower Richland County.

Their children were:

LUCY GOODWYN, who married Goodwyn Nixon, of Alabama.

JAMES CALEB (1839-1864), killed in the battle of Boonsboro.

MARY GOODWYN (1841-1924), unmarried; spent the greater part of her life in Camden, to which place her mother removed after the Civil War.

THOMAS HENRY (1844-1890), served in the 17th South Carolina Volunteers under Governor Means. After the war, he planted in West Wateree, and, in mid-

FAMILY HISTORIES

dle age, studied law, practicing for many years in Camden. "Hal" Clarke, as he was familiarly known, was a handsome man. He fought a duel with Charles J. Shannon, son of Colonel William Shannon, an account of which is to be found on other pages. Mr. Clarke married Sallie, daughter of the second Burwell Boykin, and they were the parents of six children, of whom but one remains in the community, B. Boykin Clarke, a practicing attorney-at-law. Their home in Camden was "Milbank", a lovely place on the lake.

CARRIE AIKEN (1846-1914), who married Dr. Albertus A. Moore, one of Camden's best-loved citizens.[1]

ELIZABETH PEAY (1847-    ), who married the second John Whitaker; of their union there were seven children, four of whom and their families are still living in Camden. Mrs. Whitaker is the sole surviving child of Dr. Henry Clarke.

## CLYBURN.

Louis and Mary Craig Clyburn removed from Virginia to South Carolina prior to 1800, settling in upper Kershaw, or possibly Lancaster County. The Court House records show that there was a William Clyburn in Kershaw County in 1795. What his connection was with Louis Clyburn we do not know.

WILLIAM CRAIG CLYBURN, a son of Louis and Mary Clyburn, born in 1802, had large farming interests in the northern part of Kershaw County and took an active part in public affairs. He died in 1886. His wife was Frances West, a member of another large Kershaw County family, many representatives of which are still living.

The children of William Craig and Frances West Clyburn were:

JAMES (1827-1853).

HENRY CRAIG (1829-1847).

WILLIAM CRAIG (1831-1900), Captain of the Moffat Rifles in the Civil War; Clerk of Court of Kershaw County in 1856 and again from 1888 to 1900.

SUSAN ANN (1834-1905).

THOMAS JEFFERSON (1836-1861), First Lieutenant in Captain C. C. Haile's company in the Civil War.

[1] See Moore.

STEPHEN CRAIG (1838-1904), in business in Camden prior to the War; sold out and entered the Confederate service as a private in his brother William's company, the Moffat Rifles, a part of Nelson's Battalion, later attached to Hagood's Brigade; was in service from 1862 to 1865. He married Margaret Smyrl, of the well-known family of that name in the northern section of the county. After the War, he planted until 1869, when he removed to Florida for several years. In 1877, he came back to South Carolina and was elected Clerk of Court of Kershaw County. In 1888, he retired on account of bad health.

LEWIS LEE (1840-1925), served as First Lieutenant in the Moffat Rifles, succeeding his brother William as Captain of the company. After the War, he became one of the largest planters in upper Kershaw County. At the time of his death, he was the last surviving Captain of all the companies that went out from the county in the Confederate service.

## COLLINS.
(See PATTERSON).

## COOK.
(See SALMOND).

## CUNNINGHAM.

The founder of this, one of the largest family connections in the county, was Arthur Cunningham, who emigrated from Ireland during the latter part of the 18th century, bringing with him his wife, Jane, and possibly the oldest children. They settled on Beaver Creek, near the Lancaster line, and Arthur lived to see his seed multiply about him and grow strong. He died in 1828, having reached, or passed, the centenary mark: family tradition has it that he was born in 1725, but this is not a matter of record. He is buried in the old Summerville enclosure, about three miles above Liberty Hill, and on his tombstone it is written that he was "about 100 years old". The contemporary notice of his death in the *Camden Journal* says that he had a son in the Revolutionary armies, but, if so, there is no mention of him in the family genealogy.[1] He was thrifty and pros-

---

[1] Compiled by the late Dr. R. B. Johnson, of Kosciuski, Miss., to whom we are indebted for much information.

## Family Histories

perous and of tremendous vigor. When more than eighty years of age he would ride horseback to and from Camden on the same day, a distance of more than forty-five miles. About this period of his life, too, he took unto himself a second wife, Mary Twaddle, and lived to see a daughter by this union grow to womanhood and marry.

The issue of the first marriage were:

I. ELIZABETH (1770-1822), who married Robert Brown.

II. JOSEPH (1772-1850), who married: (a) Jane Cunningham, his cousin, by whom he had (1) Nancy Louisa, who became the wife of Hon. Wm. McWillie; (2) Mary, who married James B. Cureton; (b) Mrs. Hester Niles (nee Clarkson), by whom there was one child, Elizabeth, who became the wife of General John D. Kennedy.

Of Joseph, as perhaps the foremost man of the name, we shall have more to say.

III. ROBERT (1778-1836). His first marriage was to Mary Stover. Issue:

1. SARAH, married David Miller.

2. JANE (1801-1851), married, first, a Bailey and had one daughter, Amanda, who married William Dixon; second, John Brown.

3. ELIZABETH, married Wylie Patterson.

4. MARY, became the wife of Wyatt Patterson.

5. JOHN S. (1807-1851). His first wife was Louisa, daughter of Dr. Robert D. Montgomery[1] and Sarah his wife, who was sister to the first Mrs. Joseph Cunningham. The children of this union were:

(a) ISABELLA, who married Dr. Thomas F. McDow.

(b) NANCY, who married her cousin, Cunningham B. Cureton.

His second wife was Mary Massey; no children.

6. ROBERT BROWN. He married, first, Jane Harrison, by whom he had issue:

(a) JOHN, married, first, Sue Dixon; second, Amanda Dixon.

(b) SALLIE, married Charles Dunlap, son of James Dunlap.[2]

---

[1] The Montgomerys lived on the Catawba River, in Kershaw County, five miles northwest of Liberty Hill; no descendants except through the family of Dr. McDow.

[2] See "Dunlap", Vol. I.

(c) MAGGIE, second wife of Charles Dunlap.
(d) LUCY, married Edward Dunlap, brother to Charles, above.
(e) CORNELIA, married N. A. Peay.
(f) SELWYN, married Adella Jones.

(6) ROBERT B., married, second, Mary Small, by whom there were four sons:
(g) WILLIAM.
(h) ROBERT.
(i) EDWARD.
(j) CHARLES.

7. WILLIAM C., married Rebecca Jones. Issue:
(a) MARY, second wife of Cunningham B. Cureton.
(b) ABRAM.
(c) ELIZABETH, married Austin Peay.
(d) WM. C., ("TUCK"), married Mollie Dixon.
(e) THOMAS.
(f) JOHN S., married Ida Brown.
(g) ROBERT, married Anne de Graffenried.
(h) REBECCA, married Louis Perry.
(i) JOSEPH, married Lydia Cunningham.
(j) SARAH.
(k) HANNAH, married A. Pomeroy Brown.
(l) NANCY, married Rev. W. L. Boggs.
(m) JAMES, married Jane Ferguson.

III. ROBERT CUNNINGHAM'S second wife was Martha Summerville (1803-1852). By this union his children were:

7. ANN AMELIA, married Wm. E. Johnson.
8. JOSEPH, killed at Gettysburg.
9. ROBERT J., married Antoinette Stinson.

IV. JAMES, married Nancy Thompson. They moved to Alabama, in the 30's, where they left many descendants. One of the sons, Joseph, married Elizabeth, daughter of Everard Cureton.

V. JANE, married Wm. Curry, of Lancaster County.

The Cunninghams were nearly all thrifty planters, of the Hill section of the county. Robert B. (III.6) and his brother, William C., (III.7) had handsome residences at Liberty Hill. That of the former, as well as the old home of his father on Cedar Creek, five miles above, were destroyed by Sherman's troops.

# Family Histories

Joseph (II), as said, merits special notice. He was, indeed, a remarkable man, of marvelous energy, industry, economy and business capacity. Before his death, in 1850, his fortune was perhaps the largest that has ever been accumulated in the county, approximating the million dollar mark, then very unusual in the United States; and his wealth was all from farming operations. He had a passion for land and had vast tracts in the northern section of the county, as well as "Betty Neck" and "Stockton" in the lower section, and large interests in Pickens County, Ala. He owned about 800 slaves, and it is said, never sold one. Many of them were trained mechanics and with them he built his fine house on "The Hill", and operated his saw, grist and flour mills, his looms, tanneries, cotton-gins and his boats on the Wateree that hauled his products to Charleston. He was of irreproachable moral character. His death occurred at his Camden home, opposite the Presbyterian Church, of which he was a member; and he was buried in the Summerville plot, above Liberty Hill, near his father's grave. He owed not a dollar, and left his three daughters great heiresses.

## Cureton.

This family is of Welsh origin. Two brothers of the name emigrated from Wales about the middle of the 18th century, settling first near Lancaster, Pa. Thence they moved southward to the vicinity of Petersburg, Virginia, where one of them, James (1), married a Heath and with the Dobies, Masseys and other families migrated to the Waxhaws, in the present Lancaster County, South Carolina, where they acquired lands.

The other brother settled in Greenville County, South Carolina, where his descendants still live.

This was, according to the family biographer,[1] about the close of the Revolution, but they were in South Carolina probably earlier, for Dr. J. Marion Sims, in his autobiography, says: "The Crawfords, Dunlaps, Jack-

---

[1] Captain T. J. Cureton of Winnsboro, himself an elderly man (1904) who got his facts from his uncle, Thomas Cureton, of the Waxhaws: the latter died, quite an old man, in 1857.

sons (General Jackson was then sixteen years old), Whites, Masseys, Dobys, Curetons, and others of the same stock, held the Waxhaws" (for the Whigs).

These families seem very much to have intermarried: indeed it is highly probable that they all came from the same section of Virginia. Branches of three of them—Cureton, Doby, Dunlap—were transplanted to Camden about the same time, the first years of the 19th cenutry.

This first James Cureton had four sons—Jeremiah, Thomas, William and Everard—and several daughters.

The two former remained in Lancaster County. William moved to Pike County, Alabama. Everard settled in Camden.

Of the daughters of James (1): Mary became the first wife of Benjamin Haile (1): Sarah, the first wife of John Doby (1): both of Camden. Another daughter married Henry Massey, a distinguished Revolutionary soldier of Lancaster stock, long a state senator of Mecklenburg County, North Carolina.

EVERARD CURETON, son of James (1), shortly after settling in Camden, married Rebecca, daughter of Abram Belton and sister of the second wife of John Doby (1). He was a planter on Twenty-five Mile and Horsepen Creeks, and, for a time, engaged in mercantile business in Camden. He was also prominent in the political movements of the time, serving in the Legislature and in the Union Convention of '32-'33. Two years later, in 1835, he joined in the westward migration that then so sapped this community, settling in Pickens County, Alabama, where he died in 1852. Colonel Shannon remembered him as "a courtly old gentleman, with silvery locks, ruddy cheeks, tall and erect form and polished manners."

His family consisted of four sons and five daughters. Of these:

JOHN, married Nancy, daughter of Hugh Cunningham of Liberty Hill, and left one child, who died without issue.

ANN DOBY, married Thomas Calvin March, and lived in Alabama, leaving descendants.

REBECCA, married the Reverend Mr. Murrah, a Methodist minister. Their son, Dr. William Belton Murrah, was elected, in 1910, a Bishop in the Southern Methodist Episcopal Church, a man of marked ability.

## Family Histories

ELIZABETH, married Joseph Cunningham.[1]

EVERARD (2nd), died a bachelor.

JAMES BELTON (1809-1884), in whose line alone the name is here perpetuated, married Mary, daughter of the first Joseph Cunningham, who left a very large estate. They remodeled and extended to the present proportions "Cool Spring", one of the most beautiful and noted homes in the county, where they lived in great affluence up to the time of the War.

Mr. Cureton was a storehouse of information on various subjects, especially our local history, and his help would have been most valuable had such a work as this been undertaken during his life. Mrs. Cureton died in 1890, in her 81st year.

Their children were:

ANN. (1829-1904), married Burwell Boykin McCaa.[2]

JANE (1833-1889), married Thomas Whitaker (3rd).

CUNNINGHAM (1835-1900), married, first, Nancy, daughter of John S. Cunningham; second, Mary, daughter of William C. Cunningham.

EVERARD (1837-1908), married Mary, daughter of Burwell Boykin (2nd). No issue.

JAMES BELTON (1840-1864), left South Carolina College in Sophomore year, 1861, to enter army; killed during Grant's approach to Richmond.

MINETTE (1845-1908), married Thomas Lang Boykin.

WILLIAM (1848-?), died in Mississippi.

JOHN (1849-1912), married Cornelia Corwin, of Ohio.

REBECCA (1850-    ), married William Lucas, of Charlotte, North Carolina.

### DAVIS.

From the admirable memorial sermon upon Bishop Davis, delivered in Camden by Rev. John Johnson, we learn that the ancestors of the Davis family settled for a while in Boston, removing thence, still in Colonial times, to the Parish of St. James, Goose Creek, in South Carolina. Among these ancestors were two of our Colonial Governors, Sir John Yeamans and James Moore.

[1] See CUNNINGHAM.
[2] See "MCCAA".

HISTORIC CAMDEN

The Right Reverend Thomas Frederick Davis, D. D., first of the name in Camden, was born on a plantation near Wilmington, North Carolina, February 8, 1804. He was the eldest child of Thomas Frederick Davis and Sarah Isabella Eagles, his wife.

At the early age of ten, he was sent to a preparatory school attached to the University of North Carolina, at Chapel Hill, where he remained four years, then for four more years he was a student in the University proper.

Returning to Wilmington he studied and entered upon the practice of law. About 1827, he married Elizabeth Fleming, who died the following year, soon after the birth of a son, later Reverend Thomas Frederick Davis, Jr.

The death of his wife seems to have determined Mr. Davis to abandon law for the ministry. He was ordained deacon in St. James' Church, Wilmington, in 1831, and priest the following year.

In 1832, he married Anne Ivie Moore, of Wilmington, North Carolina.

For a year he preached in Pittsboro and Wadesboro, North Carolina. Then, for three years, he served as rector of St. James' Church, Wilmington. Here his health failed, necessitating a year of rest. He then assumed charge of St. Luke's, Salisbury, where he remained ten years, during which he built up missions in several neighboring towns.

In 1846, he accepted the call to Grace Church, Camden, which town thenceforth was his home.

As an indication of the hold that he soon gained upon the affections of this community, when, later, he received, and was seriously considering, an invitation to accept a church at Fayetteville, North Carolina, citizens of Camden, irrespective of creed, came forward and pledged their support in the successful effort made to retain him here.

In 1853, he was elected Bishop of the Diocese of South Carolina, succeeding Bishop Gadsden. It was an open secret that at the time the Convention of North Carolina was on the eve of offering him the Bishopric of that state. He was consecrated in New York City.

A few years later, premonitions of his approaching blindness began to appear. Eminent specialists were

## FAMILY HISTORIES

consulted in this country, and, in 1858, he visited England and Paris for treatment. No relief was gained and by 1862 he entirely lost his eyesight. This terrible affliction did not interfere with the ministrations of his high office and seemed to enhance the veneration in which he was universally held—"the good blind Bishop", as the poor, among whom he did his great missionary work, henceforth called him. To quote Dr. John Johnson, "How often, in the services of the Sanctuary, have we not been touched by his appearance as he entered, leaning on some supporting arm, or guided, at Confirmation, so as to lay his hands on the heads of the candidates kneeling at the rail!" His devoted daughter, Lila, was his constant companion on his necessary visitations about the Parish.

His connection with the Theological Seminary here has been elsewhere mentioned.[1]

At the close of the War, realizing that his burdens were becoming more than his strength could stand, he asked for an assistant, and, in 1870, Bishop Howe was made Co-Adjutor.

His death occurred at his residence here on Broad Street, December 2, 1871, in the 68th year of his age. An impressive shaft marks his last resting place in our Cemetery. The handsome window in the chancel of Grace Church is also a memorial to him. His Episcopate was noted for its harmony and for the growth of the Church in the Up-Country.

The following tribute was paid his memory shortly after his death in a newspaper article by a writer from Abbeville signing himself "M. M.": "First the highly gifted, broad-minded Bishop Davis, the blind, eloquent old man, whose last speech on tolerance of opinion where non-essentials are concerned is still spoken of by his contemporaries as the noblest ever uttered before the House of Bishops. We all know that he was great in intellect and great in character. His presence won for him a sense of deep reverence, almost a feeling of awe, as we looked upon him, sightless himself, but glowing to us with the spiritual life so bright within his soul. This holy, consecrated man held his diocese a unit."

By his first marriage, Bishop Davis had, as indicated, one son:

[1]See "Episcopal Church".

HISTORIC CAMDEN

THOMAS FREDERICK (1828-1865), associate rector of Grace Church, Camden, from 1854-1865. He married Mary Boykin, daughter of the first Dr. John McCaa. She, with a son and daughter, survived him. The congregation of the church erected the monument over his grave in the cemetery.

By his second marriage, Bishop Davis left the following issue:

JAMES MOORE (1834-1878), a captain in the Confederate armies and a leading member of the Camden bar; married Mary, daughter of Major John M. DeSaussure.

ANN ELIZA ("LILA"), died 1923; unmarried.

SARAH EAGLES, married John Stoney Porcher.

JOHN TOOMER (1840-1882), unmarried; profession, law.

FREDERICK BRUCE (1843-1873), married Esther, daughter of Dr. George Reynolds; died as the result of a fall from a horse, just after assuming the rectorship of the Episcopal Church at Union, South Carolina.

JUNIUS (1846-1889), married Sarah, daughter of Major John M. DeSaussure.

## DEAS.

Two brothers, David and John, sons of David Deas, of Leith, Scotland, were the first of this prominent family to locate in this state. They became wealthy merchants in Charleston. The former left three daughters, only one of whom had children, and they were taken by their mother to live in England, so that John (1735-1790), who came over in 1749, (eleven years after his brother), was the real founder of the Carolina family.

He married Elizabeth, daughter of William Allen, of "Thoroughgood" plantation, St. James, Goose Creek, and was the father of eleven children.

The youngest of these, JAMES SUTHERLAND DEAS (1784-1864) came to live in Camden shortly after his admission to the bar in 1808, and married Margaret (1787-1874), daughter of the first John Chesnut.

For nearly thirty years, he was a leading lawyer and prominent figure in the county.

In 1823, he is recorded as president of the Orphan Society and about the same time served as colonel of a cavalry regiment. For several terms he was our representative in the lower branch of the State Legislature and

## Family Histories

served as a member of the Senate of the State from 1824-1832. He was one of the leading Nullifiers.

Smarting under defeat, after a heated contest for the Senate with his brother-in-law, Colonel James Chesnut, in 1832, he removed with his family, in 1835, to Mobile, Alabama, and never returned. His children were:

SARAH CANTEY, married Dr. Josiah Clarke Nott.

ELIZABETH ALLEN, married John Middleton Huger.

JOHN CHESNUT, married Adele Auzé, from France.

MARGARET, married Charles Auzé; victim of a terrible hotel fire in New York City in 1899; she was then eighty-four years old.

JAMES SUTHERLAND, died young.

ZACK CANTEY (1819-1882), General in the Confederate Army; treated in another chapter. General Deas married Helen Glover Lyon, of Alabama, who is still living, aged 98, in New York City (1926).

JAMES SUTHERLAND, also died young.

MARY CHESNUT, married N. Harleston Broun.

HENRY, unmarried.

SERENA CHESNUT (1829-1907), married Samuel Jennings Murphy.

All of them were natives of Camden, but left in early life. Not one now survives. There are numerous descendants.

LYNCH HORRY DEAS, M. D. (1807-1884) was born at Charleston, South Carolina. His father, a brother to James S. Deas, was Henry Deas, a prominent figure in Nullification times and for eight terms President of the State Senate, until his resignation in 1835. His mother, Margaret Horry, was of distinguished Revolutionary stock.

After preparation in the schools of his native city, he entered the South Carolina College, where he graduated in 1824. He then completed the course at the Medical College in Charleston, took a course of lectures in Philadelphia and finished off his excellent professional training with a year at Paris. Then followed a year of travel in Europe.

On a visit to his uncle in Camden, Dr. Deas met his future wife, Ellen, daughter of James K. Douglas. They were married in 1835. At first the young couple lived in Mobile, Alabama; then, for a short while, in Louisville, Kentucky. In 1837, on account of his wife's health, Dr.

Deas determined to locate in Camden, and, from that time until his death in 1883, he was one of the leading physicians of the place, honored and beloved. His successor both in the practice of his profession and in the universal esteem of our people, Dr. A. A. Moore, read, in 1907, before the Camden Historical Society, a fine and just tribute to Dr. Deas, from which we make a few brief extracts:

"On a few occasions it became the duty of the writer to be present in sick chambers in which he (Dr. Deas) was tenderly and faithfully ministering to the needs of ill patients, and it was indeed a pathetic picture to observe the pallor overspreading his benevolent face, the result of extreme anxiety and fatigue. In all such tests of his fidelity, patience and skill, his nature was ever responsive and true. He was the embodiment of truth and honor and therefore had a supreme contempt for anything mean or little. And so to the close of a long and useful career, obeying the precepts and following in the footsteps of the Master, 'He went about doing good'."

A mural tablet to his memory in Grace Church states that he was one of its wardens.

The children of Dr. Lynch and Ellen Douglas Deas were:

HENRY (1839-1894), served on General Kershaw's staff during the War; unmarried.

MARGARET (1843-1905), married John Manning Cantey.

LYNCH (1845-1879), entered the army at seventeen; wounded and captured at "Old Church"; imprisoned at Elmira, New York, where he endured hardships that permanently impaired his health; never married.

ALLEN (1846-191?), entered the army at fifteen and served to the end of hostilities; married Mary Richardson of Savannah.

ELLEN (1848-1914), married Franklyn W. Boykin.

CHARLOTTE (1851-1915), unmarried.

JAMES DOUGLAS (1853-191?), married Camilla Richardson, of Clarendon County.

Dr. Deas built the handsome residence on the northeast corner of Lyttleton and Chesnut Streets in 1848; it passed into other hands after his death. The family is represented now in the county only through the female lines.

# Family Histories

## DeLeon.

Family tradition has it that this quite distinguished Jewish family fled from Almeria, Spain, to Portugal during the reign of Philip II. Later they emigrated to England, thence, some of them, to Charleston, S. C., in 1721.

At least four descendants made their homes in Camden: to wit, Dr. Abraham DeLeon, his two sisters, Henrietta and Almeria (Mrs. Hayman Levy), and his brother, Dr. Mordecai H. DeLeon (for a few years).

They were children of Jacob DeLeon, of Charleston, and Hannah Hendricks, his wife, the latter, it is stated, of a prominent Dutch family of New York;[1] she died in Camden in 1839, aged 72 years.

DR. ABRAHAM DELEON was practicing medicine in Charleston in 1813.[2] He seems to have removed to Camden about 1815 (James Kershaw's Diary). In the *Camden Gazette* of 1816, "Dr. DeLeon (late of the Hospital Department of the U. S. Army) tenders his professional services." Elzas states that he had served as surgeon's mate in the War of 1812. "A. & M. DeLeon" were in the drug business here in 1816. In the *Camden Gazette* of 1818, "M. II. DeLeon" appears as a partner of Hayman Levy, general merchandise, the firm being dissolved in that year. This was, we take it, Dr. Mordecai H. DeLeon (1791-1848), later a leading physician of Columbia. Dr. Abraham DeLeon was prominent in both medicine and masonry. He officiated, as said in another chapter, as Worthy Grand Master in the Masonic ceremonies connected with the reinterment of DeKalb's remains, and we are informed that LaFayette presented him on that occasion with a beautiful Masonic emblem.

He married Isabel, daughter of Major Benjamin Nones of Philadelphia,[3] and they were the parents of the following children:

BENJAMIN NONES DELEON.
H. H. DELEON.
MIRIAM (MRS. COHEN). It may be of interest to state that the only son of this lady, Lawrence, was killed in a duel at Savannah in 1870. The seconds were indicted

---

[1] From a full account of the family supplied by the late Captain Perry M. DeLeon.
[2] Elzas: *Jews of South Carolina*.
[3] See "LaFayette's Visit".

for murder but acquitted. The tragic event, however, put an end to duelling in Georgia.[1]

HENRIETTA (MRS. SEIXAS).

ANNA (MRS. PERRY MOSES). A son, Perry Moses, Jr., was killed at Malvern Hill, aged 18 years.

None of these children of Abraham DeLeon settled in Camden, so far as we can learn.

Major Benjamin Nones, we are told, was a Frenchman, who came from Bordeaux to this country with Count Pulaski, under whom he served till Pulaski's death. He then was made major of a battalion under Baron DeKalb, and, as elsewhere stated, was present at DeKalb's first interment. He must, therefore, have been a prisoner of war at Camden.

HENRIETTA, sister to Dr. Abraham DeLeon, never married. For years she conducted an excellent private school at Camden. Her body was brought back to the town for burial about 1910. She had lived to a great age and it is doubtful if any of her old pupils survived her.

DR. MORDECAI H. DELEON removed from Camden to Columbia about 1822 (?). He married Rebecca Lopez of Charleston and three at least of their sons attained more than ordinary distinction, to wit:

DR. DAVID CAMDEN DELEON (1822-1872), surgeon, U. S. Army; twice received the thanks of Congress for gallantry in action in the Mexican War;[2] later first surgeon-general of the Confederacy and General Lee's medical director. He was serving under Kirby Smith, in the Trans-Mississippi department, at the close of the war. With General Smith he fled to Mexico to avoid surrender. On General Grant's invitation both later returned to the States and Dr. DeLeon practiced in New Mexico until his death. He probably owed his middle name to his having been born in Camden.

HON. EDWIN DELEON (1828-1891), author, diplomat, consul-general at Cairo under Pearce and Buchanan, and Confederate Commissioner to France. He brought from Egypt a splendid Arabian horse which he presented to President Jefferson Davis. This animal is said to have been taken by Sherman's Raiders in 1865 from General Chesnut's stables at Camden. It had probably been entrusted to General Chesnut's keeping during the war.

[1] From papers of Perry M. DeLeon.
[2] Appleton's *Cyclopedia of American Biography*.

# Family Histories

THOMAS COOPER DELEON, historian and novelist; prominent in the civil service of the Confederacy; known as the "Blind Author of the South"; died in 1914, at Mobile, Ala., in his 76th year.

CAPT. PERRY M. DELEON is our authority for the statement that of the eleven grandsons and great-grandsons of Jacob DeLeon, two served the Confederacy in civil positions, and eight in the field, four being killed; also that, through intermarriages, all of the Nones and four-fifths of the DeLeons have become Christians.

Capt. Perry DeLeon himself was an officer in the Confederate navy and later consul general of the United States in Ecuador.

## DePass.

Jacob Samuel DePass (1798-1869), the pioneer of this family in Camden, was born in Bordeaux, France.[1] He is said to have come over in 1819. For many years he was an active merchant of the town and, in his old age, served in the commissary department of the Confederacy.

He was twice married; first to Eliza Perriman (1810-1853), a native of Camden; then to Harriet Porter, who died in 1860, without issue.

By the former union, there were the following children:

MARGARET (1831-1832).

SAMUEL C. (1833-1906), a graduate of the Citadel Academy at Charleston; a lieutenant in the service of the Confederacy; after the war, removed to Memphis, Tenn., where he married and reared a large family.

MARY (1834-1835).

WILLIAM LAMBERT (1836-1881). Educated in the schools of Camden, he first taught for several years, then studied law and was admitted to the bar. At the commencement of the Civil War, he was commissioned first lieutenant in John D. Kennedy's company. He was wounded at Manassas, one of the first of our troops to be disabled, and again at Second Manassas. After recovery, he organized a company of light artillery, of which he was made captain. This battery served on the Coast of South Carolina under Colonel Charles J. Colcock. Just before the close of hostilities he was commissioned major.

---

[1] From a sketch of the family furnished by Alva C. DePass.

After the war, he resumed the practice of his profession in Camden, served several terms in the Legislature, and acted as chairman of the Democratic party in the County.

Captain DePass married Freelove P. DeLoache, (1839-1887), of Barnwell County, a sister of Elliott and James DeLoache and of Mrs. Reuben Patterson, all of whom came to live in Kershaw County shortly after the War.

There were ten children of this marriage, but five of whom survived to maturity.

JAMES P. (1839-1908), a minister in the Methodist Conference; served as chaplain in the Confederate army; married Anna Gunnels, of Laurens; died in Florida, leaving many descendants.

ELIZA P. (1842-1880), married Victor Manget. This family settled in Marietta, Ga.

JACOB WALTER (1844-1886), practiced dentistry for several years, then studied law; a well-known member of the Camden bar up to the time of his death.

Mr. DePass married Flora Mitchell (1847-1924). He left eight children, all of whom settled in other places.

SARAH KERSHAW (1846-1847).

SARAH J. (1848-1872), unmarried.

MARGARET ROSALINE (1849-1851).

Shortly after the War, Captain William DePass acquired the beautiful old home of the late William Anderson, in Kirkwood. Here a son, bearing his name, still resides, he and his children being the sole representatives of the family left in the county.

## DESAUSSURE.

No attempt will be made here to give a full sketch of this distinguished Carolina family, the branches that belong to Camden alone being treated with some degree of completeness.

The antecedents of the DeSaussures lived in Lausanne, Switzerland, whence Henry DeSaussure emigrated to America in the early years of the 18th Century, settling in Beaufort District, South Carolina.

Daniel, the son of Henry, was active in the Revolutionary struggle, being deported, with sixty or more other gentlemen of the low country, to St. Augustine, on the fall of Charleston. After the war, he served as a member

## Family Histories

of the Privy Council (1783), and was later the first President of the Senate of South Carolina.

His son, Henry William, bore arms at the siege of Charleston, though a mere lad of sixteen. He too was deported, being held for two months on a prison ship and finally, on exchange of prisoners, sent to Philadelphia. This youth became, in later life, the eminent jurist, Chancellor DeSaussure, whose name is writ large in the annals of the state. His service on the Bench extended over twenty-nine years. He left several daughters and six sons—Henry, William Ford, Charles, Louis McPherson, Daniel Louis, and John McPherson.

Of the daughters:

CAROLINE became, in 1815, the second wife of Abram Blanding.

ANNA FRANCES (1786-1878) married Wilmot S. Gibbes, and they were the parents of the late Miss Sue Gibbes of Camden.

Another daughter (SARAH?) married Bishop Boone (of China).

Of the sons:

WILLIAM F. (1792-1870), a fine scholar and one time United States Senator, was the father of Mrs. Hamilton Boykin, senior,[1] who died in 1893, aged seventy-six years. His home was in Columbia.

LOUIS MCPHERSON (1804-1870), a physician, was the father of Dr. Charles A. DeSaussure, for some years a resident of Camden (later of Memphis), who married Ella, daughter of Dr. George Reynolds. Dr. Louis DeSaussure is buried in Camden, where doubtless he once practiced, though of this we have no record.

DANIEL LOUIS and JOHN M., the two youngest, were sons of Camden by adoption and their records are a part of our history.

A. The former, Daniel Louis, (1796-1857), was a midshipman in the United States Navy, and served in the War of 1812, also in the War with the Barbary Pirates, along with Tatnall, Decatur and Farragut, who were his lifelong friends and correspondents. After seven years service afloat, he was honorably retired.

While on a visit to Camden he met his future wife, Frances, daughter of Dr. James Martin.[2] About 1820,

---

[1] See Vol. I, "BOYKIN".
[2] See Vol. I, "MARTIN".

after his marriage, he bought "Claremont", the famous old Rugeley place on Granny's Quarter Creek, and there settled and planted. In 1846, he removed with his family to Camden, occupying the house which he built on Mill Street, since occupied by his descendants.

His children, who lived to maturity, were:

CAROLINE (1824-1844), the first wife of Dr. Benjamin F. Watkins. No issue. Dr. Watkins (1815-1878), by a second marriage, left two children, now both dead. His old home is opposite "Bloomsbury".

SARAH (?-1898), who became the wife of her cousin, Louis Daniel DeSaussure, of Charleston.

OCTAVIA (1830-1905), unmarried.

DOUGLAS BLANDING (1832-1882), graduate of the University of Virginia; married Martha Lamar Stark, of Columbia.

DANIEL LOUIS (2nd) (1838-1909), a practicing physician and life-long resident of Camden. Dr. DeSaussure married Sarah, daughter of the Reverend W. A. Gamewell, of the Methodist Conference, and niece of John Gamewell, of Camden.

B. Major John McPherson DeSaussure, youngest of the Chancellor's sons, born in 1807, at Charleston, came to Camden, in 1828, to study law with Abram Blanding, his brother-in-law; later he was taken into co-partnership. Although successful in his practice and with a bright future at the Bar, he practically abandoned his profession on his marriage, in 1832, to Eliza (1812-1864), daughter of Richard Lloyd Champion, in order to attend to his wife's extensive plantations, among them the present State Farm, a few miles below Camden, long known as the DeSaussure plantation. His record books, relative to his farming operations and containing besides valuable meteorological observations, are models of care and neatness.

Besides being more than once Mayor of Camden, he served creditably in the State Legislature.

About 1835, he acquired from John McRae the uncompleted mansion on Mill Street, which he christened "Lausanne". Mr. McRae exchanged this handsome property for Mrs. DeSaussure's residence on Broad Street, later owned by Dr. A. A. Moore. Under Major DeSaussure's artistic direction, "Lausanne" became one of the most luxurious homes, and its gardens among the most beautiful, in the Up-Country. It is now, with spreading additions, "Court-Inn", a tourist resort of wide reputation.

The War left Major DeSaussure in greatly reduced circumstances. For many years he served as Probate Judge of the County. His large property, including "Lausanne", passed into other hands, and in 1883 he died, at the age of seventy-six.

Gradually, by death and removal to other fields of activity, the "Lausanne" family has completely passed from our midst; indeed there is not now a single bearer of the DeSaussure name in Kershaw County.

The children of Major John M. DeSaussure and Eliza, his wife, were:

CHAMPION, accidentally killed by his brother, Henry, while out hunting, in 1849; aged fifteen years.

HENRY W. (1835-1862), graduated at the South Carolina College in 1855; killed in the Seven Days' Fight around Richmond, while acting as Major of the Sixth South Carolina Volunteers. He married Mary, daughter of Dr. George Reynolds.

CAROLINE, died in 1864, unmarried; aged eighteen years.

JOHN M. (2nd), removed, with his family to Louisiana; married Alice Moise.

LOUISA (1839-1901), married Captain James M. Davis.

IDA (?-1906), married her cousin, Alexander DeSaussure.

SALLIE (1848-1888), married Junius Davis.

LLOYD (?-1888), educated at Washington and Lee University; unmarried.

In the little Alpine town of Chamonix, Switzerland, there stands a most impressive group in bronze, representing Balmat, the famous guide, pointing the way to the summit of Mount Blanc, which he first blazed in 1786, to the distinguished scientist, Horace Benedict DeSaussure, by whose long-standing offers of reward the "monarch of the Alps" had at last been conquered. This DeSaussure was of the parent Swiss stock, and his strong face is singularly suggestive of some of his distant South Carolina kinsmen.

## DOBY.

John Doby (1st) settled in the Waxhaws, Lancaster County, S. C., prior to, or during, the Revolutionary War. The first deed that we can find to him is of 514 acres on Cane Creek, of date 1778. These lands he left to his son, William, who deeded them, in 1793, to John Brown.

He came from Virginia with his wife, who was Elizabeth Massey, and certainly three sons, William, Joseph and John.

There are still Dobys (Dobies) of the original stock about Petersburg and Norfolk, Va. Along with John Doby and his family came probably one or more of his brothers and certainly some of the Masseys and Curetons to the Waxhaws from the Old Dominion about the same time. They were all Whigs in the Revolution.[1]

From what seems well-authorized family tradition, John Doby (1st) and his "eldest son", (certainly not William, Joseph or John, all of whom survived the War), were killed at the battle of Eutaw Springs. John Doby (2nd), born in 1776, told his wife and she, her daughter, from whom to the authors, that he remembered his father's horse being brought home with the news of his father's and brother's death.

William settled in York County and left two daughters who married Whites. The family later moved West.

JOSEPH and JOHN (2nd) conducted, as partners, a mercantile business in Camden prior to 1808. Joseph married Sarah White; he died in 1811, leaving six young children, none of whom seems to have remained long in the community. One of them, John M. Doby, born in Camden, a graduate of the South Carolina College (1818), was after 1824[2] a prosperous planter in the Waxhaws, and married, first, a sister of Governor Stephen D. Miller; second, a Miss Crawford. In 1856, he removed to Arkansas, where he amassed a large fortune from his plantations. He died in 1878, aged 77. His sons served in the Confederate armies. His sister, Mary, was the wife of Dr. Henry Miller, a brother of Governor Miller.

JOHN DOBY (2nd), (1776-1826), was an enterprising and useful citizen. Besides merchandising, he operated large planting interests in the Waxhaws and about Camden, owned a brickyard, and ran a line of boats on the Wateree to Charleston. He was one of our earliest cot-

---

[1] See extracts from Dr. J. Marion Sims in account of the Cureton family.
[2] See "Military".

## Family Histories

ton-buyers. In 1811, he was Ordinary of Kershaw County. In a notice of his death, we read: "All his public duties were discharged with manly independence and dignity and all his private engagements were fulfilled with scrupulous fidelity and honor."

He married, first, Sarah Cureton, sister to Everard; second, Ann Belton (1796-1848), daughter of the pioneer, Abram Belton. (Her only sister, Rebecca, became the wife of Everard Cureton).

By the first marriage, there was one child:

JAMES CURETON DOBY (1801-1850).

By the second:

ELIZABETH (1814-1869), who married James Dunlap.

BELTON (1816-1823).

JOSEPH WILLIAM (1818-1863).

SARAH (1821-1893), wife of Anthony M. Kennedy.

MARGARET (1827-1873), first wife of Robert M. Kennedy.

JAMES CURETON DOBY (1801-1850), born in the Waxhaws; graduate of the South Carolina College; studied law and became a partner of Hon. Stephen D. Miller, who expressed a high opinion of his legal abilities. On his marriage to Sarah, daughter of James and Ann Darrington English, Mr. Doby retired to his wife's plantation in West Wateree, where he became one of the largest slave-owners in the county.

His children were:

JAMES ENGLISH (1830-1865), planter; unmarried.

JOHN DOBY (1832-1852), unmarried.

EVERARD CURETON (1836-1877), unmarried; lived in Texas.

SARAH ENGLISH (1838-1860), married Alfred Brevard and left one child, the late Mrs. E. M. Boykin.

ALFRED ENGLISH (1840-1864), student at the South Carolina College and at the University of Virginia; later went on a European tour, with the intention of studying medicine at Paris; hastened back at the outbreak of the War, and was aide-de-camp to General J. B. Kershaw, with the rank of Captain. At the battle of the Wilderness, while rapidly advancing with General Longstreet and other officers, the party was fired on, through one of those terrible mischances, by our own men. General Longstreet was severely wounded, and General Micah Jenkins, Captain Doby and Orderly Marcus Baum (also of Camden) were instantly killed. Alfred Doby had recently married his cousin, Elizabeth, daughter of Anthony M. Kennedy. He left one child, now Mrs. Beverly M. English.

JOSEPH WILLIAM DOBY (1818-1863), after studying at the South Carolina College, engaged in agricultural and mercantile pursuits until chosen cashier of the Branch Bank of the State at Camden. Shortly before his death, he was made President of the Bank. He married Martha Gerald, of Sumter District.

Issue:

JAMES CURETON, captain of the Kirkwood Rangers, succeeding Colonel Wm. Shannon; later promoted major; died in 1890; unmarried.

JOHN, served in the Confederate army, a mere stripling; sheriff of Kershaw County for many years; removed with his family to Texas, where he died in 1910.

JOSEPH, died, a prisoner, at Fortress Monroe, in 1864; unmarried.

EVERARD, died in Texas; unmarried.

BELTON, died in Mississippi; unmarried.

There were also four daughters, three of whom married and all settled out of the county.

The following glowing tribute to Joseph William Doby may be added both as a memorial to one of the most popular men in the county in his time and as a specimen of the style of the scholarly Leslie McCandless:

"Possessing an august presence, his features still handsome retained the peculiar charm which characterized them through the different changes of childhood, youth and manhood—one of the few men to whom the words of Eüripides may be applied: 'The very autumn of a form once fine retains its beauties'. Doby was the 'pet' of the whole district and sincerely loved wherever he was personally known. Steady, solid, just, incapable of using falsehood, flattery or deceit, he was a man in whom all the virtues shone with congenial brightness."

## DOUGLAS.

James Kennedy Douglas (1780-1860), son of William Douglas and Sarah Kennedy, his wife, was born at Minnegaff, County Galloway, Scotland.

He came to America in 1800, on the inducement of a family friend, also a native Scotchman, John Kirkpat-

FAMILY HISTORIES

rick, then a successful merchant in Charleston, South Carolina, with whom at first he accepted employment.

Soon afterward he removed to Camden, where, until his death, he was one of the leading figures in both mercantile and social life. He was one of the mainstays of Bethesda (Presbyterian) Church, and was identified with the temperance and other great moral movements of his day.

Colonel Shannon says that he was courtly in manner, much travelled and possessed of a large fortune won by skill and integrity; and that a contemporary said of him: "Man and boy, I have known him for fifty years, and I have never known him for one moment anywhere else than on the side of virtue."[1]

Though he left no son, one of the largest and most influential family connections in Camden trace back to Mr. Douglas as their progenitor and bond of union. His home, one of the oldest houses in Camden, still stands on the north side of York Street, between Lyttleton and Fair.

He was married, in 1806, to Mary, daughter of Dr. James Martin.[2] Of this union, there were the following issue:

    I  SARAH (1810-18?), married William Douglas Anderson.

    II  ELLEN (1812-1872), married Dr. Lynch Horry Deas.

    III  CHARLOTTE (1819-1849), married William A. Ancrum.

    IV  MARGARET (1821-1887), married Thomas J. Ancrum.

    V  LUCRETIA (1824-1902), married General Joseph B. Kershaw.

The children of the first two are treated, in this volume, under the families of Anderson and Deas, respectively. The first generation of descendants of the last three may be here mentioned, to supplement the sketches of the families of Ancrum and Kershaw in our first volume.

Issue of William A. Ancrum and Charlotte Douglas, his wife (III):

MARY DOUGLAS (1840-1920), married Dr. Charles J. Shannon (II). (See SHANNON).

---

[1] *Old Times in Camden.*
[2] See Vol. I, "MARTIN".

## HISTORIC CAMDEN

THOMAS JAMES (1841-1900), worthy Confederate soldier; married Mary Cantey; planted in lower Kershaw.
ELIZABETH BRISBANE (1843-1905), married Samuel Boykin.
JAMES KENNEDY (1844-1864), died in service of the Confederacy.
ELLEN DEAS (1846-    ), married Major Francis D. Lee.
MARGARET DOUGLAS (1848-1883), married Samuel Francis Boykin.
Issue of Thomas J. Ancrum and Margaret Douglas, his wife (IV):
WILLIAM ALEXANDER (1843-1906), in service of the Confederacy throughout the War; on the Haskell ticket in 1890; married Anna Calhoun, of Abbeville.
MARY CAMBER (1843-1845).
CHARLOTTE DOUGLAS (1847-1909), married James Cantey.
THOMAS BRISBANE (1850-1911), unmarried; planted below Camden.
ELIZABETH BRISBANE (1852-1913), married John Boykin.
MARGARET FRANCES (1856-    ), married Robert C. Johnson.
JAMES DOUGLAS (1858-1866).
CATHERINE PORCHER (1860-1861).
MARY CATHERINE (1862-  ), married D. Blanding DeSaussure.
JESSIE DOUGLAS (1865-    ), married Clarendon R. Spencer.
Issue of General Joseph B. Kershaw and Lucretia Douglas, his wife (V):
JOHN (1847-1921), D. D.; distinguished rector of St. Michael's Church, Charleston; Confederate soldier, lawyer, clergyman; married Susan DeSaussure.
MARY MARTIN (1848-    ), married Charles J. Shannon (III).
HARRIET DuBOSE (1849-    ), married Thomas Lang.
CHARLOTTE DOUGLAS (1851-1923), unmarried.
JOSEPHINE (1867-    ), married W. Bratton deLoach.
The career of General J. B. Kershaw is given in other pages.

### ECCLES.

(See THORNTON).

# Family Histories

## Ellerbe.

(See Sanders).

## Gamewell.

(See Thornton).

## Hay.

The Reverend Samuel Hutson Hay, (1818-1886), was the much beloved pastor of the Presbyterian Church in Camden from 1853 to 1880, and he and his family were thoroughly identified with our people.

He was the fourth son of Colonel Frederick Jay and Susan Brown Hay, of Barnwell County, and was born at "The Boiling Springs" in that district, which was the site of his father's beautiful plantation home, burned by Sherman's raiders, and which is now a hamlet of families descended from Colonel Frederick Hay. The Hays have an extensive and influential connection in that section and indeed throughout the state.

The Rev. Samuel Hay was a distinguished alumnus of the South Carolina College and of the Presbyterian Theological Seminary at Columbia, S. C.

While a student at the former institution he met his future wife, Mary Peck, of the well-known Virginia family, who was visiting her grandfather, Thomas Park, for many years professor of philosophy and librarian of the college.

After serving charges at Beech Island and Winnsboro (1843-1845), he went back to Boiling Springs to assist his father in the management of the plantation. Eight years later, he accepted the call to Camden.

After a devoted ministry here of twenty-seven years, he removed to McClellanville. From 1883 to 1885 he served as Evangelist of the Charleston Presbytery at Allendale, and in the latter year he returned to his boyhood home at Boiling Springs, where he died in 1886.

Mr. Hay was a finished scholar and a devout Christian. It is said that he educated all of his children himself.

The issue of Rev. Samuel and Mary Peck Hay were:

Frances Snowden (1844-1888), married Colonel Del Kemper, a distinguished soldier of the Confederacy, at one time a professor at the Citadel, Charleston, S. C., and later United States Consul to China.

JAMES THORNWELL (1847-1907), a life-long resident of Camden, a leading lawyer, who served the county, as Representative and Senator, for many years in the Legislature. Mr. Hay was a soldier in the service of the Confederacy, Company D, 5th Battalion, South Carolina Reserves. He married his cousin, Josephine Oakman, of Barnwell County, and their two sons, with their descendants, are the sole representatives of the family left in the community.

FREDERICK JAY (1849-1922), a surveyor and civil engineer; married Jennie Richards, of Liberty Hill.

SAMUEL HUTSON (1852-1923), like his father, a minister of the Presbyterian Church; married his first cousin, Mary Louisa Gantt, of Barnwell County.

THOMAS PARK (1854-1921), also a Presbyterian divine; married, first, Susan Venning; second, Jennie Mikel.

MARY SUSAN (1856-1908), married her first cousin, Dr. Walter Hay.

BURWELL BOYKIN (1861-1925), on the publishing staff of a newspaper in Atlanta, Ga.; married Annie Winne.

ELLEN REYNOLDS (1864-   ), married her first cousin, John Mackall Gantt.

WILLIAM SMITH (1868-   ), a practicing physician at Allendale, S. C.; married Burney Clarke.

The descendants of these unions are numerous.

## JOHNSON.

William E. Johnson, founder of the family in Camden, was born in the Waxhaws in 1797. His father was John Johnson; his mother's maiden name was Jane Scott.

Mr. Johnson came to Camden about 1818 and engaged in mercantile business, at first in partnership with John J. Blair, on the site of the present Post Office; later, in his own name, in the old Samuel Mathis store, now a residence, southeast corner of Monument Square.

On Hon. Wm. McWillie's removal to Mississippi, he was, 1845, elected President of the Bank of Camden, which position he held until his death in 1871.

His first residence was in the Lee (now Baum house) on Broad Street. In 1824, he moved to Kirkwood and, about 1842, built there, at old Mortimer Springs (since called Johnson's Springs), an attractive home, on the surrounding grounds of which he lavished his fine taste

## Family Histories

and scrupulous care until the place became noted for its beauty.[1]

William E. Johnson was one of the "Worthies" who gave tone to Camden's business and social life before the war.

The following tribute, from a friendly pen, at the time of his death, appears to be a just estimate: "Of highly nervous organization, of close habit of thought and analysis, of indomitable will and energy, of gifted tongue and easy bearing and address, success attended his every effort, and, although an invalid for half a century, he was active and busy while life lasted. His business ability was great, his tastes cultured, his conversational powers unsurpassed—and yet he was, what might be called, a self-educated man."[2]

Mr. Johnson was married, in 1824, to Mrs. Mary Brown Hodges, daughter of Robert Brown, of Liberty Hill, and to them were born two sons:

DR. ROBERT B. (1825-1914), who married Jane, daughter of Honorable William McWillie. Dr. Johnson graduated at the Charleston Medical College in 1847. For five years he practiced at Liberty Hill, removing, in 1852, to Camden, where he was one of the prominent physicians until the outbreak of the war.

In 1866, he made his home at Kosciusko, Mississippi, where he raised a large family. In 1909, he revisited Camden, after an absence of more than forty years, and to his charming reminiscences the authors are indebted for many bits of information concerning our men of the past. He died in Camden.

WILLIAM E. JOHNSON, (II), (1827-1897), married Ann (1833-1910), daughter of Robert Cunningham (I). Mr. Johnson was a graduate of the South Carolina College (1857), and served through the War as Captain in the Second (South Carolina) Regiment. He acted as second to Colonel William Shannon in his duel with Colonel Cash. Inheriting his father's beautiful home in Camden, he gathered about him there a coterie of friends, mostly young men, who were deeply attached to him. Two sons survived him:

ROBERT (1850-1910), who married Fannie, daughter of Colonel Thomas Ancrum.

[1] Now the Bull place, "Holly Hedge".
[2] Colonel Wm. Shannon, in *Old Times in Camden*.

WILLIAM (1852-    ), who married Kate, daughter of Colonel William M. Shannon.

In each of these families there are among several children, two sons, a Robert and a William, just as in each of the two preceding generations.

## JONES.

Darling Jones, an early settler in the Liberty Hill section, is said to have figured as a Tory in the Revolution. He married Hannah Belton, of the old Quaker family of Camden.

ABRAM D. JONES, their son, was a large planter of Longtown, Fairfield County. He married Caroline, daughter of James Goodwyn of Richland County and sister to the wife of Dr. Henry Clarke, of Longtown.

The issue of this union were:

REBECCA, who married W. C. Cunningham of Liberty Hill.

THOMAS, who married Caroline Ellison, of Fairfield County.

ABRAM D. (II), who married Elizabeth, daughter of Wylie Patterson. Mr. Jones planted at Liberty Hill, where many of his descendants still live.

JAMES, unmarried.

WILLIAM, who married Catherine Matheson, of Kershaw County.

CAROLINE, who married Colonel Robert Lamar, of Beach Island, long a resident of Columbia.

HANNAH BELTON, who married Dr. Robert H. Edmunds, of Fairfield County.

Darling Jones had, by another union, one other son:

LEROY, who married Sarah Flake. They were the parents of the late Captain John L. Jones, of Liberty Hill.

## JORDAN.

Daniel William Jordan (1810-1883) was born in Pitt County, North Carolina, son of Valentine Smith and Sarah Jones Jordan. He was a descendant of Major John Jordan of the colonial militia, a member of the two provincial congresses in North Carolina, at Hillsboro and at Halifax (1774).

Daniel Jordan in early life removed to South Carolina, and became an extensive rice planter on Waccamaw Neck. Run out by the "Yankees", who shelled his plantation and burned his mills, he removed with his family

## Family Histories

to Camden in 1863, and there spent the remainder of his life, merchandising and operating a large farm in West Wateree. He had been a Colonel in the State Militia prior to the Civil War and the title stuck to him.

A man of fine business capacity and highly esteemed as a citizen, he died possessed of an ample estate. His home on upper Broad Street, now owned by his son-in-law, Henry G. Carrison, is one of the most beautiful in the town; it was built by Charles J. Shannon (I).

Colonel Jordan married Miss Emily Tuttle, of Mississippi, a woman of strong character, who long survived him.

Their children were:

VICTORIA (1841-1860), who married Ambrose Davie, of North Carolina. These young people were both drowned on their bridal tour in one of the most distressing tragedies of the Mississippi River. Their steamer, "The Charmer", went down, with a loss of seventeen passengers, among them several recently wedded couples.

VALENTINE SMITH (1843-1883). Val Jordan ran away from school to enter the Confederate army. Later, he was a large planter in West Wateree. His wife was Hallie Richardson, of Savannah.

CORA (1845-1919), married Colonel Ralph Nesbit, of Georgetown County.

MARGARET (1850-    ), married Henry G. Carrison, who later became a large merchant, planter, bank and mill president of Camden.

### KENNEDY (ANTHONY and ROBERT).

John and Anthony Kennedy came to seek their fortunes in the States in 1834, mere youths, being consigned to the care and training of a near kinsman, James Kennedy Douglas, at Camden. Ten years later, a younger brother, Robert, then twenty years of age, joined them here.

They were sons of Alexander Kennedy and Elizabeth MacMillan, his wife, of Ayrshire, Scotland, and were of the "Craig" branch of the family.[1] The Kennedy name is legion in Ayrshire.

John disapproved of the institution of slavery, and, in the early 30's, moved out West, taking lands on Fox

---

[1] The "Craig" and "Millenderdale" estates came, by entail, into possession of the eldest brother, David, in his 74th year. It was the good fortune of one of the authors to visit him there in 1900.

River, Illinois. The trip from Camden was made on horseback, with one companion, a young Witherspoon of Society Hill. Later he became a pioneer citizen of Chicago (then Fort Dearborn). On one occasion, we learned from his lips, he was offered a large slice of the Lake Front, about the site of the Auditorium Hotel, in exchange for his horse, but declined. The village then had small prospects. As an Indian fighter and as head of the police department of Chicago during the Civil War, he won the title of Captain. His death occurred in 1899 in his 84th year.

ANTHONY M. KENNEDY (1817-1892) was first taken into the family and employment of Mr. Douglas. Later he established an independent business. In 1844, he and his brother, Robert, formed a strong mercantile firm which continued in operation until shortly before the War, when it was taken over by Robert M. Kennedy alone, who conducted it until 1887.

Anthony served in the Florida War[1] and did Bureau work for the Confederacy, in connection with his brother Robert and Colonel Joseph Daniel Pope. At the close of hostilities, with fortune shattered, he farmed for some years. His home in Camden was the fine old brick house on Broad Street, built by James Clark, with its original spacious grounds one of the handsomest places in town; it was burned in 1884. Mr. Kennedy was most widely known, perhaps, for his work in the cause of temperance and of the Presbyterian Church, in whose councils he stood high.

He married Sarah, daughter of John and Ann Belton Doby. Mr. and Mrs. Kennedy celebrated their "golden wedding" in 1889, surrounded by numerous descendants. Mrs. Kennedy died in 1893, aged 72.

Issue:

JOHN DOBY (1840-1896), a Brigadier General in the service of the Confederacy. For a sketch of the life of General Kennedy, see other pages. He married, first, Elizabeth, daughter of Joseph Cunningham (I); second, Harriet, daughter of Burwell Boykin (II).

ELIZABETH MACMILLAN (1841-1917), wife of Captain Alfred English Doby.

ANN BELTON (1843-1852).

---

[1] In a Columbia company.

## Family Histories

ALEXANDER DALTON (1847-1922), student at South Carolina College; served in the Confederate armies; merchant and planter; married, first, Martha Bissell, of Selma, Ala.; second, Bettie Bissell, her sister.

SARAH DOBY (1851-     ), wife of Edward Flud Burrows, of Sumter County.

ROBERT M. KENNEDY (1821-1896) was, for quite a third of a century, perhaps the leading merchant of Camden. Of wide information through contact with the world of men and books, courteous and of fine appearance, of strictest business integrity, he was an interesting companion and enjoyed high credit in the Northern markets where he was a familiar figure. An anecdote may be pardoned.

On his first trip to New York after the War, to which he had contributed largely of his means and which had, of course, left him financially crippled, he was asked if he desired a compromise of his antebellum obligations, as practically all other Southern merchants had been compelled to seek. His reply was that, if allowed time, he would pay dollar for dollar, and this he literally did—a rare case, perhaps. The *News and Courier* published the notice of his death in Charleston under the caption "A Prince among Merchants".

Mr. Kennedy was in the civil service of the Confederacy, and was mayor of Camden at the time of Sherman's Raid. He was twice married; first to Margaret Doby (1827-1873), sister to his brother Anthony's wife; second to Anne (1837-1893), daughter of Judge Joseph H. Sherrard, of Winchester, Va.

By the former union there were the following children:

ANNE (1848-1880), wife of William K. Thompson, of Liberty Hill.

ELIZABETH D. ("NELLIE") (1850-     ), wife of Hunter R. Boykin.

BELTON O'NEALL (1852-1899), student at Washington and Lee University; assistant cashier of the Atlanta National Bank, of Atlanta; married Ellen Bissell, of Selma, Ala.; left three sons.

MARGARET (1854-1863).

AGNES (1857-1859).

SARAH (1860-     ), wife of James W. Blakeney.

JOHN DOBY (1862-     ), married Anne Kearney, of Illinois; lives in California.

ROBERT MACMILLAN (1866-    ), married Julia, daughter of Major R. W. Hunter, of Winchester, Va.

By the second marriage there was one son:

JOSEPH SHERRARD (1877-    ), married Julia, daughter of Dr. N. A. Pratt, of Atlanta, Ga.

Mr. Kennedy's residence, which he built, was on Lyttleton Street, adjoining Dr. George Reynolds'. He lavished much care on the extensive grounds, now much cut up. The fine gardens were laid out, as were those of several other old Camden homes just before the War, by Crammond, an artist in landscape gardening.

## KENNEDY. (WILLIAM).

William Kennedy,[1] a native of Dumbartonshire, Scotland, was naturalized in 1827. He had come over in 1822, his first employment being with Douglas, Kirkpatrick & Hall, commission merchants, in Charleston.

Later he settled in Kershaw County, and married Mary, daughter of the first Benjamin Haile. He operated his wife's plantation in West Wateree until the late 60's when he followed his sons to Texas, where he died soon after.

The late Major E. B. Cantey, who remembered him, described him as "a very genial old man". He is our authority for the following list of the children of William and Mary Kennedy:

WILLIAM, about Major Cantey's age; a very bright young man and a graduate of the South Carolina College; moved to Texas, where he became a distinguished lawyer.

KATE, first wife of the late John Whitaker.

ELLEN, married a Presbyterian minister, a brother of the eminent Dr. Palmer, and lived in Mississippi.

BENJAMIN, a fine Confederate soldier; lived in Texas after the War.

WALTER, served through the War in Major Cantey's and James Doby's companies; afterwards made his home in Texas.

EDWARD, also moved to Texas.

---

[1] The *Biography of James Kennedy Patterson, President of the University of Kentucky,* 1869-1910, published in 1925, reveals the fact that this distinguished educator was a nephew of William Kennedy of Camden and indeed owed his education largely to the help received from Mr. Kennedy and his wife, Mary Haile Kennedy.

# Family Histories

There are no representatives of the family left in this section, which accounts for our lack of information.

## Kilgore.

(See Patterson).

## Kirkland.

The first mention of the Kirkland name in South Carolina is found in an entry in the Register of St. Phillips Church at Charleston, S. C., which records the burial there of John Kirkland, September 18, 1728.

The next recorded mention is found in the old plats of land originally granted by the State to the first settlers, from which it would appear that a veritable colony of Kirklands arrived in the state during the twenty years prior to 1776. A list of their names is here given in the order of the dates of their respective land plats:

1—Edward Kirkland, 1753
2—Richard Kirkland, 1753
3—Moses Kirkland, 1753
4—Robert Kirkland, 1753
5—Joseph Kirkland, 1755
6—William Kirkland, 1755
7—Joshua Kirkland, 1762
8—James Kirkland, 1763
9—Snowden Kirkland, 1763
10—John Kirkland, 1764
11—Francis Kirkland, 1772
12—Thomas Kirkland, 1773
13—Benjamin Kirkland, 1774

What if any relationship existed between these individuals we have not been able to ascertain, but it is well nigh certain that Joseph and William were brothers.

John Kirkland (No. 10 above) settled near White Oak Creek in the northern part of this county. His son Moses in 1792 conveys a part of his father's land to Lewis Collins. The will of this John, probated 1772, of record in Charleston, leaves his land to his wife Jean for life and at her death to his sons Moses and William. This William was known as "William of the Wateree" and was not the William (No. 6 above) who settled on Cedar Creek in Fairfield County and was a captain in the Revolutionary War. Moses was certainly not the noted Tory of that name whose will was recorded in London in 1789 (see *South Carolina Historical Magazine*, Vol. XII, p. 218).

A deed from Anthony Wright conveying to Edward Kirkland lands near Lugoff, in Kershaw County, dated

April 2nd, 1753, is witnessed by Robert Kirkland, Moses Kirkland and William Harrison and probated by James McGirt.

Lands in this county were conveyed to Richard Kirkland by Sam'l Bacot in 1754, witnesses Josiah Cantey and William Cantey. Lands about seven miles south of Camden were granted to Joseph Kirkland in 1769, designated in the grant as "Woodyard", by which name it is still known.

The following items are gleaned from the Revolutionary Records in the State House:

"William Kirkland (of Cedar Creek), 261 pounds 16s 8d Currency, 37 pounds 8—1 sterling for 68 days as Captain of Horse in Gen. Williamson's Brigade at Augusta in 1779. Sworn to before John Winn, J. P., certified correct by Lieut-Col. Joseph Kirkland.

"William Kirkland (of the Wateree), for 191 days service as private and as Lieut. in 1781 and 1782 in Gen. Sumter's Brigade.

"Zachariah Kirkland, for 100 days service as horseman in Gen. Williamson's Brigade, certified by Lieut Col. Joseph Kirkland.

"Samuel Kirkland, for service in militia at Charleston.

"Reuben Kirkland, for 72 days militia service under Lieut. Jacob Buxton.

"Richard Kirkland, for 72 days service under Col. Jacob Buxton, also 153 days as Captain in 1781 and 1782 in Col. Hardin's Regt.

"Joseph Kirkland (Lieut-Col), account for high blooded stallion valued at 225 pounds.

"John Kirkland, for 7 days Militia service under Lieut. Jacob Buxton.

"Francis Kirkland in 1791 requests his indents for service as Revolutionary soldier—witness Richard Winn."

Two distinct families of the Kirkland name have figured in Kershaw County, the one tracing from Daniel, the other from William Kirkland (Number 6 above).

## I.

DANIEL KIRKLAND (AI). His will, of record in Kershaw County, dated October 20, 1820, probated July 8, 1828, leaves his lands on White Oak Creek to his wife

## Family Histories

Parmelia and his sons, Samuel and Joseph. His son Samuel was born in 1772, so that Daniel must have been fully 75 or 80 years of age at time of his death and probably among the early settlers of this County.

SAMUEL KIRKLAND (AII), son of Daniel (AI), died in Kershaw County, February 26, 1857, age 79. His children were John, William, Daniel and Amelia Hester Dunlap (wife of James J. Dunlap).

JOHN KIRKLAND (AIII), son of Samuel (AII), died October 1868. His children were Richard Rowland Kirkland, noted for his act of heroism in bearing water to the wounded enemy at Fredericksburg, Daniel P. Kirkland, Jesse A. Kirkland, William Kirkland, Mary Truesdale (wife of S. J. Truesdale), and James Kirkland. James was deceased in 1870, leaving three sons, Frederick, Henry and Richard. Shannon B. Kirkland who resides in Camden is a son of Daniel P. Kirkland.

WILLIAM KIRKLAND (AIV), son of Samuel (AII), left a will probated 1862, disposing of his property to his wife, Margaret, and four children, Powell, Willie, Mary and Sarah Caroline.

DANIEL KIRKLAND (AV), son of Samuel (AII), died October 4, 1843; left no descendants.

JOSEPH KIRKLAND (BI), son of Daniel (AI), left a will dated January 19, 1848, probated December 28, 1849, disposing of his estate to his wife, Mary, and to his children, Daniel D. Kirkland, John P. Kirkland, Joseph K. Kirkland, Wm. G. Kirkland and a grandson Daniel K. Price.

## II.

WILLIAM KIRKLAND (CI), served as Captain in the Revolution. He and Joseph Kirkland, who was probably his brother, settled on Cedar Creek in Fairfield County, near Richland County line, at least as early as 1753. He and Joseph are mentioned in Mills Statistics as brave fighters in the cause of the colonists. Both were members of the State Assembly of 1782 at Jacksonboro, which confiscated the property of many Tories, among them Moses Kirkland. As appears from the will of Benjamin McKinnie, dated August 24, 1759, found in Probate Court at Charleston, William had at that date married Elizabeth, daughter of said Benjamin and Joseph had married Lemender, another daughter. This Benjamin McKinnie was settled some eight miles south of Camden as early as 1746, the date of a conveyance of land to him by Charles Ratcliff. In his will he mentions his following children:

| | |
|---|---|
| Achelaus McKinnie | Fanny McKinnie |
| Penelope McKinnie | Christian McKinnie |
| Elizabeth Kirkland | Samuel McKinnie |
| Sarah Mackey | Michael McKinnie |
| John McKinnie | Pricilla McKinnie |
| Mary McKinnie | Lemender Kirkland |

The will of this William Kirkland is of record in Probate office at Winnsboro, dated December 1806, probated December 27th, 1806. It names his son Joseph as Executor and disposes of his property to his children, Sarah Taylor, Frances Alston (wife of James Alston), Archy, Mary Honor, John Debell, Martha Maria. The three last-named were almost certainly the children of a second marriage. A daughter, Elizabeth Sorsby, had probably predeceased her father.

JOSEPH KIRKLAND (CII), son of William (CI) was born in 1773, educated as a physician, and in 1795 married Marianne Guerard, the young widow of Governor Benj. Guerard. After his marriage he resided in Charleston, where he served through the yellow fever epidemic of 1817. On November 12, 1817, he died and was buried in the family cemetery on Cedar Creek in Fairfield County. His gravestone contains the following inscription:

> "Rest here the noblest work of God—a truly good man.
> Weep not my wife nor son most dear
> I am not dead but sleeping here.
> My debts are paid and I am free.
> Prepare to die and follow me."

Marianne, the wife of Joseph, was the daughter of Henry Kennan and Susannah Godin, who were married in 1751. Henry was among those imprisoned by the British on ships in Charleston harbor, suffering great hardships. His wife, Susannah, was the daughter of Benjamin Godin and Marianne Mazyck, both of the Huguenot Colony which came to Charleston about the year 1700.

WILLIAM LENNOX KIRKLAND (CIII), son of Joseph (CII), was born in 1797. He married Mary Anna Faber, widow of a Mr. Faber. She was a daughter of Dr.

FAMILY HISTORIES

Thomas E. Lynah, who was a son of Dr. James Lynah. Dr. James Lynah served as a surgeon in the Revolution and was originally from the Isle of Man. William died June 21, 1828, at the early age of 31, on a visit to the family home in Fairfield County, and lies in the family cemetery there near Cedar Creek.

WILLIAM LENNOX KIRKLAND (CIV), son of Wm. L. Kirkland (CIII), was born in 1828. Prior to the Civil War he resided in Charleston and on his rice plantation on the Combahee River. In 1859 he married Mary Miller Withers,[1] daughter of Judge T. J. Withers. During the Civil War his family was forced to reside in Camden, owing to military operations on the Coast. He was a member of the Charleston Light Dragoons and died in Richmond, June 1864, from a severe wound received in battle at Hawe's Shop, near Cold Harbor. He left three children, Thos. J. Kirkland, who married Fredricka Alexander; Mary Anna Kirkland; Elizabeth T. Kirkland (deceased), who married Thos. M. Trotter.

LEE.

The Lee family of Camden, now unrepresented in the county, claimed descent from one Thomas Lee, who emigrated from England in 1600 and, with a brother, settled in South Carolina. From another brother, who located in Virginia, descended the South's peerless chieftain, Robert E. Lee.

We may assume quite confidently that the Francis Lee who settled in 1752 on Beaver Dam, branch of Rocky Creek, in Chester County, a little south of the Waxhaws, was the ancestor of the Camden family.

It was probably his son, Joseph Lee, who was a member of the Jacksonboro Assembly in 1781 and of the House of Representatives from Camden District in 1784 and 1786.

[1] In a town noted for the comeliness and charm of its women, Mrs. Kirkland was famed for her unusual beauty and intellectuality. Before her marriage, she made a tour of Europe with Mr. and Mrs. David R. Williams, and there, as in this country, her vivid personality attracted widespread admiring comment. After the death of her husband she lead a secluded life in her delightful Kirkwood home, "Kamschatka," never however losing interest in people and affairs. Her death, at the age of 87, occurred November 7, 1925.

R. M. K.

HISTORIC CAMDEN

ROBERT LEE, possibly a brother of Joseph, was a justice of the peace in this district in 1791.[1]

JOSEPH LEE was the father of Francis Stephen Lee (1781-1822), whom we find living in Camden in the early years of the 19th century. He was sheriff of Kershaw District in 1816 and was probably a member of the firm of Lee & DeLeon, merchants here at that time.[2] He married Frances Broom, probably a daughter of Thomas Broom, of Camden. She survived her husband, the home of her old age being later the residence of Captain Joseph Mickle on Broad Street.

The children of Francis S. and Frances Broom Lee were:[3]

DR. JOSEPH LEE (1804-1859).
THOMAS BROOM LEE.
REV. FRANCIS P. LEE.
REBECCA.
ELIZA.

THOMAS BROOM LEE was a lawyer here in 1829, in partnership with John C. Vaughan. He removed to Louisiana, and died there, a wealthy bachelor.

REV. FRANCIS P. LEE was rector of Grace Church, Camden, from 1842 to 1846. He was educated in Morristown, N. J., and at a theological seminary in New York, graduating in 1835. He married Ann Cooper, of New Jersey, and is buried under the chancel of Grace Church, Mobile, of which he was rector. His son, John Boykin Lee, married a Miss Shipworth, of Baltimore (?), and their daughter, Emma, married Barnwell Stuart, of Beaufort, who conducted a school in Camden during the War.

REBECCA married E. W. Bonney, a Northern man, who was a successful merchant in Camden for many years. Their home was the old Bynum house on Broad Street, later the residence of Dr. A. A. Moore. A tradition that seems well founded has it that a daughter has never been born in this house. Mrs. Bonney used to say that she could not even raise a pullet on the place. There were two sons to the Bonneys, Usher and Frank, who both left Camden. Mrs. Bonney removed to Charlotte, N. C., where she died in 1876.

[1]*Charleston City Gazette and Daily Advertiser*, 1791.
[2]*Camden Gazette*, 1816.
[3]No attempt is made to list them by age.

## Family Histories

ELIZA married her cousin, Benjamin Lee, of Charleston. His brother, Major Francis Dickinson Lee, served as an engineer in the defense of Fort Sumter and was the inventor of a torpedo boat for the Confederate service. Major Frank Lee married Ellen, daughter of William Ancrum, of Camden. After the War, he went to France, on invitation of Napoleon III, to exhibit his torpedo boat, all expenses paid, and was royally entertained. With his family he spent the latter part of his life in St. Louis, where he won distinction as architect and engineer. He died about 1880.

GENERAL STEPHEN D. LEE, of Mississippi, we are informed, is also sprung from the Charleston branch of this family.

DR. JOSEPH LEE (1804-1859), we have reserved for the last because longest identified with our history. He was one of our earliest dentists. In 1826, he married Catherine, daughter of James Clarke. Their residence was "Greenleaf Villa" on Broad Street a handsome house with typically Southern grounds, now owned by the Baum family. Mrs. Lee (1806-1894) was an ardent Southern sympathizer, president at one time of the "Soldiers Rest Society", which cared for poor wounded Confederates returned from the scenes of war. Her beautiful home was fired by Sherman's raiders, but was saved by her cool direction of those who came to her assistance. She died in Anderson, S. C., at the home of her son, William.

The children of Dr. Joseph and Catherine Lee:

DR. FRANCIS S. LEE, a young dentist of Camden, who lies by his father's side in our cemetery.

WILLIAM S. LEE, died in 1907 at Anderson, where he lived for many years. A son, W. S. Lee, Jr., is Vice-President of the Southern Water Power Company, of Charlotte, N. C.

MAJOR FRANCIS BROOM LEE (1835—?), civil engineer and architect; married Miriam Earle, of Anderson; lived in Charlotte, N. C.

ALEXANDER YOUNG LEE, architect and civil engineer; married a Miss McDonald of Columbia; died about 1901.

REBECCA, married, first, Henry Howard; second, ——— Walker, both of Charleston; died shortly after the War.

ELIZA, married Howard Snowden, of Charleston; living (1909), a widow, at Elberton, Ga. To her and to the late Mrs. G. G. Young of Camden we are indebted for many of the statements here made as to the family.

## LEITNER.

Major William Zack Leitner (1830-1888) was born in Fairfield District. After a course at Mt. Zion Collegiate Institute, Winnsboro, he attended the South Carolina College, graduating in 1849. He was admitted to the bar in 1854, settling in Camden, where he practiced his profession for more than thirty years, at one time in partnership with his brother-in-law, Joseph Dunlap.

He entered the Confederate service at the beginning of the war as a lieutenant and rose to the rank of major. At Gettysburg he was severely wounded, necessitating the amputation of his right leg.

In 1865, he was sent to the Legislature. About this time he was elected a district judge and served until the office was abolished on the adoption of the Carpet-bag Constitution of 1868.

Major Leitner played a prominent part in the campaign to elect Hampton in 1876. He was sent to the State Senate in 1882, and in 1886 he was elected Secretary of State, in which office he died two years later.

He married Anne, daughter of James Dunlap, of Camden; she, with two sons and three daughters, survived him.

Their home, the old Gamewell house, on Monument Square, was sold, after his death, to the Trustees of the City Schools and was used as a High School until 1919.

The family left Camden. The sons were already in business elsewhere.

Mrs. Leitner died in 1916, in her 84th year.

An editorial in the *News and Courier*, at the time of Major Leitner's death, speaks of his courteous manners, absolute sincerity and downright honesty and adds that "beneath this gentle exterior there beat as brave and true a heart as ever throbbed with love for South Carolina."

## LEVY.

There were three families of this name in Camden during the first half of the 19th century, all of some

# Family Histories

prominence and connected by marriage, but of separate stock.[1]

The most conspicuous was that of Chapman Levy (1787-1749), a noted lawyer and politician. He was a son of Samuel Levy (1762-1842), an early merchant of Camden, and Sarah Moses, his wife. He was admitted to the Bar in 1806. In 1812 he was a Representative, and in 1818 State Senator, from Kershaw County. He was again in the Legislature from 1829-1833 and from 1836-1838. Colonel Levy was a strong Union man and was a member of the Nullification Convention of 1832. He was captain of a volunteer company in the War of 1812, and won his title of colonel probably in militia service. In the late 30's he removed to Mississippi, and died on his plantation in Attala County, that state.

He was twice married; first, to Flora Levy; second, to Rosina Levy, both sisters of Mordecai M. Levy. The latter (Rosina) died aged 18 years, without issue; the former, who died in her 21st year, left two children:

EDWARD ANDERSON LEVY, died, 1848, at Kirkwood, Miss.

FLORA (1823-1851), married Thomas Salmond Anderson, son of Dr. E. H. Anderson of Camden.

Chapman Levy's residence in Camden was later the home of Bishop Davis, still standing, on Broad Street.

HAYMAN LEVY was a large merchant and cotton factor, in partnership with M. H. DeLeon, at Camden, as early as 1818.[2] He was Intendant of the town in 1843, and a director of the Bank of Camden from 1842-1854. He fought a duel with Wiley McKain, because of an alleged insult to Levy's son, Saul, who, it may be added, died during the War of disease contracted while in the Confederate service.[3] Another son, Julian, was killed in the Seven Days fighting near Richmond. These are the only children of Hayman Levy about whom we have information. His wife was Almeria, daughter of Jacob DeLeon. Their home, now destroyed, was the former residence of Hon. William McWillie, just below the old Court House.

[1] Elzas, *The Jews of South Carolina*.
[2] *Camden Gazette*.
[3] McKain, an inveterate tease, tortured Saul Levy, with jibes over a game of cards. Saul challenged; McKain replied that he "would not fight a sick monkey." Hayman Levy took up his son's quarrel, with the duel as a result. Neither was hurt.

We are indebted to the late Captain Perry M. DeLeon for the following statements as to the ancestry of Hayman Levy. He was the son of Solomon Levy, and grandson of Hayman Levy, a fur dealer of New York City, in whose store the first Astor learned the trade, beating furs at $1.00 per day.

MORDECAI M. LEVY was also in the mercantile business at Camden, being at one time in partnership with Dr. Abraham DeLeon in the drug business. He was sheriff of the county in 1844, Representative in the Legislature from 1834-1838 and a candidate for Congress in 1836.[1] He engaged in a duel with John Hemphill, of Sumter in 1833. Hemphill lost the thumb of his right hand.

Of his family, further than what has been mentioned in connection with Chapman Levy, we have no data.

## LUCAS.

The first member of this old low-country family to settle in Kershaw County was Benjamin Simons Lucas, M. D. (1804-1890). He was a son of Jonathan J. Lucas, founder of West Point Rice Mill, Charleston, S. C., the first mill of the kind ever built. His mother was Lydia Simons.

Dr. Lucas was educated in medicine at Oxford University. On returning to this country he stood examination at the Charleston Medical College, securing a diploma from that institution. About 1828, he removed to Camden, where he practiced but a short time, then settling at Tiller's Ferry, Lynches River, in the eastern section of the county, where he farmed and practiced his profession till his death.

He married Miss Melita Tiller. Five sons were born of this union:

JONATHAN J. LUCAS, major in the Confederate service; married Miss Carrie McIver, of Society Hill, where Major Lucas made his home and was an honored citizen.

BENJAMIN SIMONS LUCAS, M. D. (II), graduate of the Citadel Academy; drill officer of 7th South Carolina battalion, Confederate Army; lost an arm at Cold Harbor. Two companies from Kershaw County were named for him. He was a graduate also of the Charleston Medical

[1]Elzas, *Jews of South Carolina.*

## Family Histories

College. Dr. Lucas married Miss Eleanor King, of Hartsville, S. C., where he settled and had a large practice. His two sons, Dr. T. C. Lucas, of Columbia, S. C. and E. R. Lucas, Vice-President of the Baldwin Cotton Mills, Chester, S. C., are our informants as to most of the facts about the family here given.

THOMAS E. LUCAS, M. D., graduate of the Citadel and of the Charleston Medical College; Major in the Confederate service; married Miss Dorothy Hanna, daughter of General Hanna; practiced medicine in Chesterfield, S. C.

SIMONS D. LUCAS, planter at Tiller's Ferry; married Miss Celia Fulton, of Williamsburg County. At his death the old home place on Tiller's Ferry passed into other hands; his descendants are the sole representatives of the family left in the county.

EDWARD B. LUCAS, unmarried; farmed at Tiller's Ferry.

All of the sons of the first Dr. Benjamin Lucas have passed away.

## McCAA.

The first of the name in this section seems to have been John McCaa, whose naturalization papers, obtained in 1804, show him to have been then a resident in the state for ten years. From entries in James Kershaw's Diary,[1] as well as from traditional evidence, we learn that in 1794 he kept an inn in Camden. A deed at the Court House, dated 1809, speaks of him as a planter.

In 1818, "Hodges and McCaa" advertise in the local paper as dealers in Dry Goods, etc. This may have been the first John McCaa or possibly one of his sons.

Of the family of the first John McCaa, we can secure no data further than that he left certainly three sons:

POSTELL, who was a steward of the Camden Jockey Club in 1819. He moved to Alabama, probably in the 30's, and raised a family there.

JOHN McCAA, M. D. (1793-1859), a graduate in medicine at the University of Pennsylvania in 1814. He was long a prominent physician of the town. His wife was Amelia, daughter of Burwell Boykin (I) and their home on Hobkirk Hill was one of the beautiful places crown-

---

[1] *Historic Camden—Colonial and Revolutionary.*

ing the ridge. It passed into the hands of Baron Von Tresckow, and was burned in 1910.

WILLIAM L., also a graduate of the Medical School of the University of Pennsylvania, class of 1823; removed to Alabama in 1833, and died there in 1853, aged 53 years.

The issue of Dr. John and Amelia (Boykin) McCaa:

BURWELL BOYKIN (1822-1863), was married in 1848 to Ann Elizabeth, daughter of James Belton Cureton; moved to Pickens County, Alabama, about 1855, to a plantation inherited by his wife. He was captain of a company, which he raised, in the Civil War, and was killed in battle in Virginia.

LOUISA, married Columbus Haile, who moved with his family first to Alabama, then to Staunton, Va. Their home in Camden was the (later) Presbyterian Manse on Fair Street, since converted into the city hospital.

THOMAS, a physician; married Mary, daughter of Christopher Matheson; practiced first in Camden, later in Gainesville, Florida, to which place he went before the Civil War. He was a surgeon in the Confederate army.

WILLIAM LOWNDES, a cotton factor in Charleston; married Mary Murray of Stateburg; died before the Civil War; no issue.

MARY (1832-1918), married Rev. Thomas F. Davis, son of the Bishop.

JOHN (III), (1835-1892), a physician; married, first, Rebecca, daughter of Wylie Patterson, of Liberty Hill; second, Mary, daughter of Lawrence Whitaker; several children by both unions. Dr. McCaa lived in West Wateree during the latter part of his life, doing a country practice.

AMELIA, married James, son of Colonel John Chesnut.[1] Lived in Gainesville, Florida, to which place the family removed in the 50's.

ELISE, married Charles Haile; also among the Camden colony living in Florida.

JAMES, served through the War in the Boykin Rangers. Later moved to Mobile, Alabama, where he married and was engaged in business as a cotton factor.

The late Major E. B. Cantey gave us most of the above information; it was impossible to secure more.

---

[1] See "Florida War".

## Family Histories

Of this large family, there are representatives now in Kershaw County only through the issue of the second Dr. John McCaa.

### McCandless.

No other individual has left so deep an impress upon the men of Camden as Leslie McCandless, for none has ever had so long and complete sway over its boys; three generations were subject to his iron discipline. That fact would entitle him to special mention, but his abilities as a scholar and teacher, his extended and devoted service to education, deserve a lasting memorial.

We shall only attempt to speak of him as personally known to us during the last third of his life. After several years absence he had come back in 1870 with his family to Camden where he had taught for over thirty years. His reputation was great and his return was hailed as a fortunate event. He opened school in his male academy and a full attendance gathered at his call.

The old field pay school was still in its vigor, and he belonged to the old style which spared not the rod yet often spoiled the boy. He was noted for severity and the faculty of imparting learning to a dunce by main force if necessary. Hence fathers would deliver over dull boys to his auspices to be dealt with at will. A term in purgatory would be about as inviting.

Upon this second advent of the great instructor, it was at once decreed that the writer hereof, then a timid boy of ten, should be put in his charge. The boy was ushered into his awful presence. On the platform or dais of the school-room (which some readers will recall), sat the monarch, with full beard, beetling brows, and austere features, like a veritable Rhadamanthus. But terror subsided by degrees, as he spoke very kindly, and the writer can testify that for five long years he experienced only gentle treatment, and has ever felt for his old tutor only the warmest attachment.

It was not long however before cuffs and buffets began to fall upon the unhappy wights, with such edifying epithets as, "You stupid jackass". The tyrant began to storm and rage. At the first outbreak it appeared that he had omitted to bring any instrument of torture. Perhaps he had formed a good resolution to leave it off;

but old habits were too strong. One Tom Oaks, a puny little fellow, was the first grave offender. He had proven impervious to the inculcation of a particular piece of information. He was summarily ordered out to get a switch for his own chastisement. There were only oaks on the grounds, no switches, so Tom climbed a tree, broke a limb and dragged it into the school-room, leaves and all. The merriment that arose was too much even for Mr. McCandless. Tom escaped his drubbing. Later a formidable palmetto stick was adopted as ferrule. For many years it served to punch up the fire as well as the boys.

His besetting sin was his temper, which was violent and ungoverned. This had not improved with age. When first known to us he was fifty or over. Dyspeptic and morose at times, he would be very cruel to some hapless fellow and arouse thereby bitter and lifelong resentment. It was hard to think he was ever young, for to the boys he was always "Old Mac", as far back as tradition goes. A boy was on good behavior when he said "Mr. McCandless" behind his back.

But the worst is said and the better part remains. For all his crabbed and ugly temper he had a warm heart, and often exhibited tender emotion. Sometimes for a whole day he would be in real sunny mood and laugh heartily at the humors of the school-room, the grim wrinkles of his face relaxing into smiles.

In school duties he was most thorough, systematic and faithful. His scholarship was superb. He had perfect mastery of the Greek and Latin classics, also of French, German, Italian and Spanish. A specimen or two from his pen, in another chapter, show great beauty of style.[1] It is doubtful if the State has produced a finer scholar. He was quite competent to have filled with distinction a seat in any University of the land. But strong ties seemed to bind him to the narrow field of the Camden Academy. It is not wholly strange that he should have been irascible and sour in the drudgery of drilling mere rudiments into dull boys.

As he declined in years the stream of progress left him stranded. The private school dwindled before the public. The academy building in which he had so long ruled

---

[1] See Doby Family.

was rolled off and converted to private uses and the Graded School reared in its stead. He shifted his quarters from place to place, attended by a small corps of boys, sons of some few of his former pupils who still believed in him. His family scattered, departed, he led a lonely life, and fell at last like an old horse in harness, September 27, 1898.

Could all the boys that passed under his rod be gathered before him on the academy campus, they would make a legion. Should one of the assemblage propose a tribute of affection to their harsh old master, the sweeter memories of that school boy spot would surely overcome the bitter and subdue all hard feelings. Probably there would not be a dissenting voice.

For further account of Leslie McCandless and his equally distinguished wife, who was Miss Fannie A. Coleman, of Vermont, see the chapter on "Schools and Schoolmasters".

Their children, affectionately remembered by the older citizens of Camden, were: Sidney; Mary, who taught with her mother in Atlanta; Linnie (Mrs. Wilson), a talented musician; John, a distinguished chemist in Atlanta.

## McCreight.

Robert McCreight (1819-1888), a native of Winnsboro, settled in Camden about 1846.

His father, Colonel William McCreight, a prominent man in his section, commanded a regiment from Fairfield County in the War of 1812. Colonel McCreight was one of the early makers of cotton gins.

ROBERT MCCREIGHT also manufactured cotton gins in Camden, and transmitted the business to his son, Oscar. He was for twenty-seven years an elder in the Presbyterian Church, a quiet, useful citizen.

His wife was Mary, daughter of Beverly Randolph of Fairfield County. She died in 1901.

There were but three children who lived to maturity:

WILLIAM RANDOLPH (1847-1904). As a boy of sixteen he ran away from home and entered the Confederate Army. He was a leader in musical organizations in Camden. His wife was Irene Whitney of Charleston.

EDWARD OSCAR (1849-1906), who married Margaret Alexander, of Camden. Mr. McCreight served as mayor of the town from 1900-1904.

LUCY AUSTIN (1854-1883), unmarried.
The children of William and Oscar McCreight, all sons, make their homes in other places.

## MCDOWALL.

William Douglas McDowall was born at Newton-Stewart, County Galloway, Scotland, in 1808. His father was Charles McDowall; his mother was Mary, daughter of William Douglas and Sarah Kennedy, his wife, and, therefore, sister to James Kennedy Douglas.[1]

On the death of his mother, in 1820, Mr. McDowall, then only twelve years old, came to Camden to be under the care of his uncle, Mr. Douglas, and here he spent the rest of his long active life. He was a large merchant, at one time in partnership with Charles J. Shannon, and served one term as mayor of the town.

Though of a somewhat reserved nature, he was thoroughly identified with the best business and social life of the community until his death in 1879.

In 1835 he married Susan, daughter of Dr. John Witherspoon, pastor at the time of the Presbyterian Church at Camden. Mrs. McDowall died in 1857, aged 40.. Their children were:

JOHN (1836-1870), served in the Western Army, C. S. A.

CHARLES (1839-1884), entered the army in Dr. E. M. Boykin's Company, and served through the war; married Fannie, daughter of Wylie Patterson; was engaged in mercantile business in Camden and planted at Liberty Hill, where he met his death in an unfortunate personal difficulty with Lewis Perry.[2] A strikingly handsome man, he was very popular with his intimate associates.

SUSAN (1840-1923), unmarried.

MARY (1841-1906), married George G. Young.

SARAH DOUGLAS (1843-1869), unmarried.

WILLIAM (1845-1912), married Ellen, daughter of John Whitaker; served in Kirkwood Rangers, C. S. A.; planted at Knight's Hill.

ELIZABETH (1847-1916), married Lawrence Whitaker, brother to Mrs. William McDowall.

---

[1] See DOUGLAS.
[2] Perry was tried and acquitted.

## Family Histories

FREDERICK (1850-1882), unmarried; planted above Camden; was killed by a negro farm hand.

JAMES DOUGLAS (1854-    ), married Anne, daughter of General John D. Kennedy; the family removed in recent years to Charleston, West Virginia.

### MCKAIN.

William McKain (1782-1852) is the first of this family of whom we have record. In 1816, the local paper advertised his tavern "near the big ditch". Later he ran the hotel on the southwest corner of Broad and DeKalb Streets, afterwards known as Robinson's hotel.

His wife was Elizabeth Stover (1787-1850), of Lancaster County.

Issue: '

I. JAMES R. MCKAIN (1812-1850), druggist; intendant of Camden at the time of his death. With his mother he was drowned in the Alabama River, on the burning of the steamship "Orline St. John". Mrs. Vaughan of Camden and her daughter, Virginia, were also lost.

Mr. McKain married Sarah Donaldson. Their children were:

JOHN J. (1837-1862), killed in the Peninsula campaign in Virginia.

WILLIAM (1839-1866), married a daughter of Wiley Patterson of Liberty Hill. Their daughter, Lily, married Steven Richards.

ELIZABETH (1841-1876), married Major E. E. Sill, a gallant Confederate soldier, for many years a county official.

HENRIETTA (1843-    ), second wife of Major Sill.

MARY (1844-1905), a well known teacher of Memphis, Tennessee.

II. JOHN, moved West in early life.

III. WILEY J. MCKAIN, M. D., graduate of the South Carolina Medical College; practiced in Liberty Hill and in Lancaster County, then in Camden; a man of talent whose career was ruined by the morphine habit. Dr. McKain was a daring wag and tease. He fought a duel with Hayman Levy, which has been mentioned in another place. He married Miss Kennedy, of Sumter County, and passed his last days on his wife's plantation.

IV. MARTHA, married a Frenchman, Alphonse Catonnet,[1] who had a confectionary store in Camden. They had two handsome daughters, Adele and Antoinette. The whole family removed to Mobile about 1836.

V. MARY (1824 (?)-1910), married George W. Shaw.

VI. SARAH (1826-1915), married the late Captain James I. Villepigue.

## MCMILLAN.

(See BLAIR).

## MCWILLIE.

An interesting family tradition worth recording has it that the father of Colonel Adam McWillie, the first representative of the family to settle in America, had, for political reasons, been compelled to change his name, Donald McDonald, to John McWillie. He had figured in the Rebellion of 1745, on the Stuart side, and had been wounded and captured at the battle of Clifton. His life had been spared on the condition that he assume another name, enlist in the British army and leave England forever. He is said to have fought in the battles of Camden and Guilford with his Majesty's troops. At Camden, it is related, he was wounded and allowed to return to England.

So much for tradition. It is stated as a fact that John McWillie died in County Armagh, Ireland, in 1804, at the age of 88. If so, he was 64 years of age at the period of his Revolutionary service in the Carolinas.

His wife was Margaret Davidson and one of their three children came to this country. This was Colonel Adam McWillie (1766-1827), who settled, about 1790,[2] on Beaver Creek above Camden. He had married, in Ireland, Anne McCullough, whose father is said to have been a settler upon Beaver Creek prior to the Revolution, after which, owing to his Royalist proclivities, he had returned to Ireland.

Adam McWillie is said to have been educated as a civil engineer. Many records of his work as a surveyor are found among old papers in the Court House. He

---

[1]Alphonse Cantonnet arrived in this country in 1819 and was admitted to citizenship in 1831.

[2]His naturalization papers (1807) state that he came over in 1789.

## Family Histories

also planted on a large scale and acquired considerable wealth.

Some account of his services as Lieutenant-Colonel of an Infantry Regiment in the War of 1812 has been given in another chapter.

He is buried in old Beaver Creek grave-yard. The Presbyterian Church that once stood there was the place of worship of the McWillies, Cunninghams, Pattersons, Thompsons and other early settlers of that section. There are many interesting monuments in the McWillie enclosure, which is surrounded by a massive stone wall.

Of the eleven children of Colonel McWillie, the following reached maturity and married:

SARAH (1788-1855), born in Ireland; married W. B. Stover, of the upper part of the county; the family removed in the 30's to Alabama.

JOHN (1791-?), married Mrs. Alice Woodward, (née Williamson), of Fairfield; settled in Louisianna.

WILLIAM (1795-1869), later Governor of Mississippi; his distinguished career is elsewhere told.

MARGARET (1798-1865), married, first, Dr. John Mackey, an Irishman, graduate of the University of Glasgow, who lies buried in Beaver Creek cemetery; second, Dr. William McCulloch; two children by the first union, four by the second.

TIRZAH ANN (1802-1869), married Thomas Taylor Williamson, of Fairfield; issue, seven children.

ABRAM (1811-1862), married Jane Andrews; no issue.

HON. WILLIAM MCWILLIE married, first, Nancy Louisa, daughter of Joseph Cunningham, of Liberty Hill.

Issue:

JOSEPH C. (1819-1892), unmarried; for more than fifty years an inmate of the Pennsylvania Hospital for the Insane.

ADAM (1821-1861), born at Camden; educated at the South Carolina College; planted in Mississippi, whither he removed about 1846. He commanded a Mississippi company in the Mexican War, and later entered the Confederate service as captain of the Camden (Miss.) Rifles; fell in the First Battle of Manassas and buried on the field. His wife was Lucy, daughter of Dr. E. H. Anderson, of Camden; she, with five children, survived him.

MARY (1823-?), married Thomas C. Richardson, of Clarendon. The late James Manning Richardson and

Elizabeth, first wife of A. H. Boykin (II), were her children.

MARGARET, twin sister to Mary.

HENRIETTA (1825-1891), married Colonel William M. Shannon.

NANCY LOUISA 1827-1900), married Burwell Boykin Salmond.

JANE (1827-1906), married Dr. R. B. Johnson.

Governor McWillie's second wife was Catherine, daughter of Dr. Edward H. Anderson. From this union there were fourteen children, nine of whom were born in Camden. They all, with their father, removed to Mississippi, where their descendants are numerous and prominent.

Governor McWillie as indicated was the father of 21 children, 12 daughters being born in succession. His winter residence in Camden was a large brick building next south of the old Court House on lower Broad Street. It was demolished about 45 years ago. His summer home, on Hobkirk Hill, was until recently the property of the late Allen Deas.

## MATHESON.

Our sources of information about this family, now without representatives here, are meagre.

*The Camden Journal* of May 13, 1826, announces the death of Alexander Matheson, "a native of Scotland, for many years a prominent merchant of Camden." His naturalization papers were taken out in 1804, ten years after his arrival in this country. Other records show that he was in Camden in 1795. He was a partner, in 1818, in the "new" firm of "C. Matheson & Co., Dry Goods and Groceries". The head of the firm was Christopher Matheson.

WILLIAM MATHESON opened a mercantile business here in 1818, "two doors from Masonic Hall".

From inscriptions in the cemetery we learn that Roderic Matheson (1789-1815) and Farquhar Matheson (1813-1845), both natives of Ross Shire, Scotland, were residents of Camden. Farquhar became a citizen in 1838, after seven years residence.

Of only two of these can we get information, from conversations with the late Major E. B. Cantey.

CHRISTOPHER MATHESON[1] was for many years a large

[1] His naturalization papers taken out in 1822 state that he came over in 1816.

## Family Histories

Camden merchant, genial, upright and highly respected. He married Catherine (1803-1858), daughter of the first Benjamin Haile. His death occurred in 1861, at Gainesville, Florida.

Issue:

ALEXANDER, a farmer; married Miss Perry of Liberty Hill; moved to Florida before the War; afterwards returned to the Hill, where he spent his last years.

MARY, married Dr. Thomas McCaa; died in Florida, at their home.

BENJAMIN, a physician; practiced here and in Alabama; returned to Camden for a few years; died in Florida, in 1910; unmarried.

ELIZABETH, married and lived in Florida.

SARAH, married Edward, son of William Adamson, of Camden. They also removed to Florida, after the War.

JAMES, in business with his father when the war broke out; served, with distinction, as lieutenant in a cavalry company; returned at the close of hostilities, closed up his father's business and moved to Gainesville, Florida, where he merchandized and married. He was elected County Treasurer and died in office, at Gainesville, 1911.

KATHERINE.

CHRISTOPHER, lived in Florida.

FARQUHAR MATHESON married Rebecca Haile, sister to Christopher's wife. He was in business with Christopher and died in 1845, of consumption, in his 33rd year. He left two daughters, Jeanette and Kate, who lived with their aunt, Mrs. William Kennedy.

While it cannot be stated as a fact, it is believed that Christopher, Alexander, Roderick, William and Farquhar Matheson were brothers.

### MOORE.

This prominent up-country family of South Carolina is identified with Camden in the person of one of its most estimable members.

ALBERTUS ADAIR MOORE, M. D., was born in York County in 1834. His father, James Moore, was a prominent planter of that section and had figured politically as a member of the State Legislature and of the Nullification Convention. His mother was Sophia Springs. There were ten sons and three daughters of this union.

Dr. Albertus Moore was educated at Ebenezer Academy and the University of Virginia, graduating in medicine at the University of New York in 1859. The next year he located in Camden to practice his profession, but the tocsin of war had sounded and in 1861 he enlisted as orderly sergeant, Co. C, 6th Regiment (the "Kershaw Troop"). In 1863 he became Assistant Surgeon of the 5th South Carolina Regiment and in this capacity served until the surrender at Appomattox.

Returning to Camden, he resumed his medical practice, which he continued until his death in 1910.

Dr. Moore served as a member of the State Board of Health and as President of the South Carolina Medical Society and was the author of several valuable contributions to medical journals. He was not only a leading physician of the town for half a century, but no man of his day was more honored and beloved for all the high qualities that betoken the true gentleman.

He was married, in 1865, to Sallie, daughter of James Dunlap; she died in 1867. In 1873, he married Carrie, daughter of Dr. Henry Clarke. Of the latter union there were two children, Dr. Albertus A. Moore, Jr., and Caleb C. Moore, both now residents of New York. The second Mrs. Moore died in 1914.

Their home in Camden was the old Bynum residence on Broad Street.

## NIXON.

The earliest known ancestor of this family was John Nixon, who settled at or near Fredericksburg, Va., prior to the Revolutionary War. His wife was Elizabeth Dinwiddie. Their two sons, William and Henry, left home upon their father's second marriage, and made their way to South Carolina.

HENRY, whose name was either George Henry or Henry George, served as Brigadier General under Andrew Jackson, at the battle of New Orleans. In the *Southern Chronicle and Camden Aegis* of October 20, 1824 we find this item: "Died August 19 last at his seat at Pearlington, Miss., General George Henry Nixon, formerly of Camden, aged 46."

WILLIAM, son of John and brother of Henry, located in Camden prior to 1800, going to work in the cotton fields and at other manual labor. By native ability and energy he accumulated considerable wealth. He built the first bridge at Camden across the Wateree River in 1827. He also built and operated for a time a large brick hotel, on the northeast corner of Broad and King Streets, which was burned in 1829. "Colonel Nixon's hotel" was a famous landmark in early times. His wife was Mary Owen, who died in 1817. About 1835, having married a second time, he left Camden and located at Vineville, Ga., where he died in May 1840, at the age of 67. The following were the children of the first marriage:

HENRY GEORGE, born in Camden, February 10, 1800. Many references to this brilliant young man are found in other chapters of this book; killed in duel, January 15, 1829 (see the chapter "Iron Man"); unmarried.

WILLIAM O., born in Camden, February 27, 1802; moved to Lowndes County, Alabama about 1833, where he purchased a large plantation, and built a mansion furnished with Italian marbles, and fitted with water works and plumbing in modern style. He was ardent in the Confederate cause but barred from military service by age and infirmity. His elegant home was burned by the Federal troops, also seven hundred bales of cotton. The family portraits were set up against trees on the lawn, used as targets and shot to pieces by the raiders. He died in a log cabin on his land May 28, 1868, and was buried nearby. He never married.

JOHN, born at Camden, June 24, 1804; died September 25, 1822. He is said to have been the most talented of the gifted Nixon brothers. When about to leave to attend a German University, he was stricken down with malarial fever and died under the barbarous treatment then practiced—drastic medicines, bleeding and no water to quench burning thirst.

BENJAMIN BINEHAM, born in Camden, May 12, 1811; died January 31, 1835, from a malady caused by exposure as a member of a military company which marched in 1832 from Camden to Charleston, where a body of State troops were marshaled to uphold the "Nullification" doctrine.

REBECCA BALLARD, born at Camden, June 27, 1813; died at Narragansett Pier, R. I., June 25, 1897. Her mother having died when Rebecca was but four years of age, she was placed with Mrs. Rebecca Ballard, a friend of the family. At nine she was sent to the Moravian school for girls at Salem, N. C. At twelve she was sent to a fashionable "finishing" school in New York, attended only by the wealthy. Here she spent four years, returning to Camden upon the eve of her brother Henry's fatal duel with Hopkins. On February 25, 1841, she was married at her plantation, "Prariewood", in Alabama, to Colonel Alfred Vernon Scott of that State. It is said that in 1854 she and Colonel Scott moved with all their slaves to Montpelier in Virginia, the former home of President Madison, which Colonel Scott purchased. In 1857 they sold Montpelier and moved to Washington, D. C., where they resided till the death of Colonel Scott in 1860. After the death of Colonel Scott, she travelled abroad, and was constantly roving. Never in her life had she lived over four years in any one place. With elegant homes in Baltimore, and New England, she would board at hotels. There were four children of her marriage to Colonel Scott.

COLUMBUS INDEPENDENCE, born at Camden, July 4, 1806 (whence his unusual name which he always disliked); died in Alabama, May 30, 1835, unmarried. He was orator on the "Fourth" at Camden in 1832. He was very handsome, high strung and sensitive.

MARY OWEN, born at Camden, March 13, 1809; died February 11, 1812. The family preserves an incident of the child's last illness, touching as the death of Paul Dombey. To her mother watching beside her bed, she said: "I hear such beautiful music and I see such beautiful little babies flying around the bed."

In our Court House is recorded the will of John Nixson, probated November 7, 1797, perhaps a different family from the preceding. Note the different spelling. The testator in this will mentions the following children: Travis, John, Elizabeth Ballard, William, Hannah Pendergrass. This family was settled on Beaver Creek, northern portion of the County, where "Nixson Spring" still preserves the name.

## PATTERSON-COLLINS-KILGORE.

The first authentic records of this influential family of the upper part of the County are of Reuben Patterson and his three sons, Joseph, Wyatt and Wylie, the two last-named being twins. They were large planters in the

## Family Histories

Liberty Hill section, the father having settled there before the beginning of the 19th century. Reuben died about 1803; he left also four daughters, Martha, Susannah, Mary and Jane.[1]

MARTHA, married Dr. George, of Russell Place.

I. JOSEPH, known locally as "Squire" Patterson, was a man of wealth, enlightenment and considerable political influence, having served many years in the State Legislature. He enjoyed the distinction of having introduced the first light vehicle, a two-wheeled sulky, into the county. Travel in those days was almost entirely by horseback. Mr. Patterson could remember seeing hogsheads of tobacco rolled down the road past his residence on White Oak Creek on the way from North Carolina to the Camden warehouses. His home, said to have contained fourteen rooms, was burned by Sherman's troops. He died in 1846.

His wife was Elizabeth, daughter of Lewis and Charlotte (Hammond) Collins, whom he married in 1808.

Their children were:

LEWIS JEFFERSON (1810-1892), a prominent figure in the county, having served for ten years in the Legislature, four as State Senator. In the Florida War, he was an officer in Chesnut's company.

His wife was Margaret, daughter of Judge D. Lewis Wardlaw, of Abbeville. Their beautiful home at Liberty Hill, since burned, was a centre of typical Southern hospitality, even after the War. Mrs. Patterson died in 1879, without issue.

MARY, married J. Ross Dye, a planter on Beaver Creek.

CHARLOTTE (1816-1890), married James S. Thompson, of Liberty Hill.

JOSEPH, died young.

Wylie and Wyatt Patterson had their residences on Liberty Hill, near their extensive lands.

II. WYLIE, married Elizabeth, daughter of Robert Cunningham (I). Their issue were:

SOPHIE, married Rev. W. L. McCormack.

ELIZABETH, married Abram D. Jones.

REUBEN, married Nean de Loach.

JANE, married first, John McKain; second, a Mr. Gibbs.

[1]Probate Court records.

REBECCA, first wife of Dr. John McCaa (II).
FANNIE, married Charles McDowall.

III. WYATT, married Mary, sister to his brother Wylie's wife. He died in 1866. Their children were:
ROBERT.
AURELIA, married Rev. Douglas Harrison.
FLORIDE, married Rufus Moore.
WYATT.
WILLIAM.
MARY, married Lewis Perry.
LOUISA, married John Belton Lyles.
JOSEPH.
SARAH, married Rev. Mr. De Graffenreid.

LEWIS COLLINS, to whom reference has been made, was born in Virginia in 1763. He removed to South Carolina, settling on the headwaters of White Oak Creek, Kershaw County. His house still stands, on old "Collin's Place", though in sad decay. He was a progressive man, having operated, it is said, the first mule, the first African slave (whom he bought from a shipload in Charleston), and the first Whitney cotton gin, in his section. His country-bred horse, "White Oak Split", created a sensation by winning the four-mile heat in the Camden races.

His wife was Charlotte, daughter of Captain Samuel Hammond, also a Virginian and a Revolutionary soldier, who died in South Carolina in 1806. "Hammond's Spring" is on a corner of the line between Kershaw and Lancaster Counties.

Lewis and Charlotte Collins had three children:
WILEY, died 1816.
ELIZABETH, married Joseph Patterson.
ALETHEA LOIS, married Jesse Kilgore.

Lewis Collins' death occurred in 1815. His widow, a most energetic woman, conducted the plantation until her death in 1862, at the age of 98. The cotton raised on her place was noted for its superior quality. Each bale was stamped with her initials, and "C. C." cotton was widely famous, even so far as the Liverpool market.

JESSE KILGORE was born in Greenville District in 1797. At the age of sixteen, he removed to Columbia where he served as secretary to his brother Josia Kilgore, Surveyor-General of the state. In 1819, he operated a gen-

## Family Histories

eral merchandise business with Robert Latta in Camden.

The same year he married Alethea Collins and settled on White Oak Creek, where for the rest of his life he was a successful planter and country merchant. His place was known as "Red Hill". He removed to Mississippi, about 1866, where he died shortly after.

One son, a student of the South Carolina College, left a daughter who married William McKain of Camden.

A daughter of Jesse Kilgore, Mrs. Charlotte Kilgore Wardlaw, writing from Oxford, Mississippi (1910), gave us the foregoing information.

### RAY.
(See BLAIR).

### REYNOLDS.

I. JOSHUA REYNOLDS (1787-1844), first representative of the name in Camden, took out his naturalization papers in 1815, stating that he had been seven years a resident of the state. He was a native of Armagh, Ireland. In the *Camden Gazette* of 1816 he advertises his "school for young ladies, limited to twenty-five." This was probably located in the old house on southeast corner of Broad Street and Monument Square, formerly the store of Samuel Mathis, who deeded it in 1816 to Joshua Reynolds. The latter had married Sophia Mathis, daughter of Samuel; she died in 1834, aged 39, leaving eight children:

ELIZABETH, born in 1814; married her cousin, Dr. Wm. Reynolds, of Columbia. Their daughter, Sophia, with her aunt, Jane, conducted for years a famous private school in Columbia.

MARGARET MILLER (1816-1844), married Wm. B. Johnstone, editor of the *Camden Journal*.

SOPHIA VOGAN (1818-?), married Samuel Elizabeth Capers.

REBECCA (1821-1847), married Dr. F. L. Zemp, leaving one daughter, Sophia.

SAMUEL MARK, born in 1823; married Miss Singletary.

MARY BLOUNT (1826-?), married Rev. Claudius Hornby Pritchard, who lived in Camden, 1865-1869, while serving as Presiding Elder of the Columbia District. Their son, Prof. Samuel R. Pritchard, of the Virginia Polytechnic Institute, is our informant as to the families of Joshua Reynolds and Samuel Mathis.

WILLIAM LISTER, born in 1828; married Miss Jane (?) Bell.

JANE HARPER, born in 1831; mentioned above as co-principal with her niece, Miss Sophia Reynolds, of a well-known school in Columbia. She never married.

II. DR. GEORGE REYNOLDS (1803-1847), nephew to Joshua, came to Camden by a remarkable chance. He was a son of William and Mary Reynolds, of Armagh, Ireland. In his 18th year, he went with a friend of his father to Demerara, South America. There he contracted yellow fever, and, on his father's command, set out, as soon as recovered, for home. This was in 1820. Off Cape Hatteras his ship was wrecked. Rescued from this peril of death, he made his way to his uncle at Camden. Here he was persuaded to remain and he pursued the study of medicine under Dr. E. H. Anderson. Later he attended lectures in Philadelphia, graduated in 1824 and returned to Camden where he was in active practice until his early death.

He was married, in 1834, to Mary Cox, daughter of Colonel James Chesnut. The next year, with his wife, he went to Europe and studied at the hospitals in Paris.

Of this union sprung the following issue, all daughters:

MARY (1837-1903), married Henry W. DeSaussure.

EMMA (1839-1917), unmarried.

SARAH (1840-1878), married Joseph J. Mackey, for several years a resident of Camden.

ELLEN (1842-1920), married Dr. Charles A. DeSaussure.

ESTHER (1845-1919), married Rev. F. Bruce Davis.

Mrs. Reynolds survived until 1899, having reached the unusual age of 97 years. Of this lovely old lady, the last of the immediate "Mulberry" family, in her serene latter days, truly it might be said that "Age could not wither her"; to the end her eyes were bright and her skin as soft and pink as a young girl's.

Dr. Reynolds built, about 1834, the handsome mansion on Lyttleton Street, which only passed out of the family on the death of his daughter, Mrs. Davis, in 1919. It was purchased by the public school trustees and converted into a high school. On January 1, 1921, it was burned to the ground. The new grammar school stands on the spacious grounds.

FAMILY HISTORIES

Two brothers of Dr. George Reynolds, William and Mark, followed him to Camden.

III. WILLIAM came over in 1828, studied medicine and practiced for some years in Camden. Later he went to Dublin where he fitted himself for the practice of dentistry. Returning, he located in Columbia where he practiced his profession till his death in 1871. As indicated he married a daughter of Joshua Reynolds. Their only child, Sophia, was long a well-beloved teacher in Columbia.

IV. DR. MARK REYNOLDS, the younger brother, came over in 1836. He received his medical education in Camden and Charleston, settling at Stateburg, where he married Julia Reese and enjoyed a large neighborhood practice. He died in 1883.

RUGELEY.

(See BLAIR).

SALMOND-COOK.

THOMAS DURHAM SALMOND (1783-1854) came to Camden from Scotland (Edinburgh) in the early years of the 19th Century. He was naturalized in 1807, after five years residence in this country.

A man of considerable force, he was a leading figure in business and social circles for nearly fifty years. On the establishment in Camden of the Branch of the Bank of the State, he was made its president, and held the office from that time (1822) till his death. Colonel Shannon[1] remembered him as "a jovial, august, accomplished, intelligent, venerable old gentleman", of the Federal School in politics, hostile to Jefferson and Calhoun. He was five times elected intendant of the town.

His wife was Margaret Irvin, widow of Adam F. Brisbane (II).

Issue:

ANN LOUISA (1817-1884), unmarried.

EDWARD ANDERSON, M. D. (1819-1858), graduate of the South Carolina College (Class 1838) and of the Charleston Medical College (1842); entered at once upon the practice of his profession in Camden; married Ann, daughter of Henry R. Cook. They had one son, the late Henry Cook Salmond.

[1] *Old Times in Camden.*

HISTORIC CAMDEN

BURWELL BOYKIN (1821-1862), studied law, but abandoned that profession to accept a position in his father's bank; married Nancy Louisa, daughter of Hon. William McWillie; removed, with his family, about 1855, to his wife's plantation in Pickens County, Alabama, inherited from her grandfather, Joseph Cunningham; enlisted at the beginning of the War, in Wheeler's Cavalry; accidentally killed, in 1862, near Tupelo, Miss. His commission as Captain was received by his company a few days after his death. His wife and six children survived him.

THOMAS WHITAKER, M. D. (1825-1869), graduate of the Charleston Medical College (1849); in active practice in Camden to the time of his death; entered the Confederate service in Kershaw's Regiment, as surgeon, with the rank of captain. In 1864, ill health forced his resignation. At that time, he held the office of Brigade surgeon. He was twice married; first, to Mary, daughter of John Whitaker; second, to Isabel Scota, sister to his first wife. There was no issue by the first marriage; one child (the late Mrs. S. Logan Lang) by the second.

HENRY COOK SALMOND (1843-1907), son of Dr. Edward and Ann (Cook) Salmond, planted near Camden; served through the War in the Kirkwood Rangers, being wounded at Cold Harbor; married Rebecca Valk of Charleston; several children.

HENRY RAINES COOK (1790-1844), came to Camden from Virginia when a young man. He was a wheelwright, and not only amassed considerable wealth, but, as Colonel Shannon expresses it,[1] "by sterling worth, public spirit and good deportment, attained high social position." His shop, where he manufactured excellent wagons and carriages, on lower Broad Street, was demolished in 1910. He married Eliza, daughter of the old surveyor, Josiah Cantey, and their only child, as previously stated, became the wife of Dr. E. A. Salmond.

Mr. Cook was four times intendant of the town.

He built two notable residences, that on DeKalb Street, next west to the Presbyterian Church, and "LaFayette Hall", sold before completion to Hon. John Carter (1823).

SANDERS-ELLERBE.

The family surname Sanders is also spelled Saunders. William Sanders was one of the earliest

[1] *Old Times in Camden.*

## Family Histories

pioneers of the interior of this State, engaging in trade with the Indians. "Sanders Creek", six miles north of Camden, derives its name from him and was so designated on the first survey, made in 1734, of Fredericksburg Township, which includes Camden. It is traditional that he first named the creeks south and north of Camden, which is highly probable. He was an Englishman, and in 1734 obtained a grant of land known as "Oakland" some miles south of Camden, now in Sumter County. Large adjacent tracts were acquired and have been occupied by his descendants to this day. While these lands are mostly in Sumter County, just across the Kershaw County line, the family has been so much identified and associated with Camden that we feel they belong at least as much to us as to Sumter.

WILLIAM (1), married Felicia Furguson. Their son:

WILLIAM (2), born in 1748, married Martha Cantey. Their son:

WILLIAM (3), married Sarah Ragan. He was a Revolutionary soldier, suffered as a prisoner of the British and died in 1810. His son:

WILLIAM (4), married Eunice Garner. Their children were:

JOHN, married Miss Allston.

GARNER, married Rebecca Osborne; parents of Richard and Thomas Osborne. (See below)

MARION, married Sarah Allston.

ELIZABETH, married Dr. Ballard.

EPATHA, married Dr. William E. Ellerbe; parents of W. C. S. Ellerbe. (See below)

WILLIAM (5), born 1804, married Sarah Gwinn Bracey.

The children of William (5) were:

SWEPSON HARRISON (M. D.), born 1826; married Harriet Rebecca McCall.

AUGUSTUS, born 1830; married Caroline McCall.

MARY EUNICE, born 1832; married Wm. C. S. Ellerbe.

CORNELIA HICKS, born 1834; married Thomas Osborne Sanders.

GEORGIANA UNDERHILL, born 1842; married Colonel J. D. Graham.

EMMA REBECCA, born 1854; married John Ashe Alston (M. D.).

WILLIAM BRACEY, born 1847; married Ella Frasier.

HISTORIC CAMDEN

The children of Dr. Swepson H. Sanders are: George McCall, whose residence, notable for a splendid avenue of oaks, is near Stateburg, married Louisa Wertenbaker; Caroline Leake, married Harris Hopkins; William Leonidas (see below); Sarah Louise, married Wm. P. Manning, M. D.; Swepson Harrison, married Jane S. Counts; Hannah Jane, married John Blair, M. D.; Amarintha Gibson, married Wm. Haynesworth; Marius B., married Annie Hartzog; Harriet Rebecca, married Thos. L. Eberhardt; Augustus Hicks.

WILLIAM LEONIDAS, above mentioned, resides at the historic home "Hill Crest", in Stateburg, about twenty miles south of Camden. He married Ann Catherine Anderson, daughter of Dr. Wm. Wallace Anderson. Their daughter, Mrs. Virginia S. White, furnished the data for this family, which we have condensed. Their son, the late Major William Harrison Saunders, accomplished the first mission in Observation Aviation from the United States Army over the German lines in the World War and at the time of his death in 1919 was considered the outstanding Observer of the United States Aviation.

RICHARD SANDERS,[1] married Elizabeth Lenoir. They were the parents of John, Richard, Thomas Polk, "Cap." (Isaac Lenoir), and Mrs. Williamson (afterwards Mrs. Spain).

THOMAS POLK SANDERS was a gallant Confederate soldier. His large planting interests were partly in Kershaw County and he was a familiar and popular figure on the streets of Camden.

THOMAS OSBORNE SANDERS,[2] was the father of Arthur K., Charles, Thomas ("T. O."), and Marion.

ARTHUR K., a prominent political figure in the State, served in the Legislature and as Superintendent of the Penitentiary.

WILLIAM CRAWFORD SANDERS ELLERBE, a son of Epatha Sanders and Dr. William E. Ellerbe, for many years resided in Kirkwood, whither he removed from Sumter County just after the Civil War. He was greatly esteemed in this community and in 1873 he was Intendant of the Town, which was extended, in 1872, to include Kirkwood. Later he removed again to his old Rafting

[1] Son of Garner and Rebecca Osborne Sanders.
[2] Son of Garner and Rebecca Osborne Sanders.

FAMILY HISTORIES

Creek home. He married Mary Eunice Sanders. Their children are:
FLORENCE BRACEY (deceased).
SARAH ELLEN.
ALLAN EUNICE (deceased).
WILLIAM ELLIOTT (deceased), married Miss Gaillard.
ROBERT GARNER (deceased).
NAPOLEON GRAVES, married Miss Sanders.
CLARENCE AUGUSTUS.
MARY ALDEN PORTER, married Dr. Marion Kirk.
ROBERT G. ELLERBE was a brother of Wm. C. S. Ellerbe; their sister, Allan, married Colonel E. B. C. Cash.

SHANNON.

The Shannon family, with its extensive connections, has held a place of influence in the history of Camden since the early years of the 19th century.

CHARLES JOHN SHANNON (1783-1863) was born in Winnsboro. His father, bearing the same full name, was one of a group of Irishmen who settled in Fairfield County about 1780; others of the colony were the forbears of the McMasters, Buchanans and McCreights.

He seems to have come to Camden between 1811 and 1817, for between those years he taught in the Orphan Society Schools.[1] In 1817, he was in partnership with John G. Ballard, and, in 1828, with Charles J. McDowall, in general merchandise business. His store and home were burned in the great fire of 1829. Later he built the fine residence on Upper Broad Street now owned by Henry G. Carrison.

For fifty years, Mr. Shannon was a leading merchant and citizen, interested in many public enterprises, and he amassed considerable wealth. From 1854 to 1863, he served as president of the Branch Bank of the State.

In 1818, he married Martha Allison, daughter of Colonel Thomas English. Their children were:

    I   THOMAS ENGLISH (1819-1881).
    II  JOHN JOYCE (1821-1822).
    III WILLIAM MCCREIGHT (1822-1880).
    IV  ALLISON (1824-1825).
    V   CHARLES JOHN (1826-1870).

[1] See "Schools and Schoolmasters".

HISTORIC CAMDEN

VI JOHN ALLISON (1828-1845), died at school, Mt. Zion Academy.

VII MARGARET ALLISON (1830-1832).

VIII MARTHA ALLISON ENGLISH (1833-1893), unmarried.

IX SAMUEL DAVIS (1833-1900).

X MARY MARGARET ALLISON (1833-1834).

The three last-named were triplets.

The first Mrs. Shannon died in 1833, and in 1834 Mr. Shannon married Harriet Letitia Winn, of Fairfield County, who left no descendants.

I THOMAS ENGLISH SHANNON (1819-1881) inherited a valuable plantation from his grandfather English, for whom he was named. He married Elizabeth, daughter of the first Benjamin Haile, herself heiress to a fine estate in West Wateree (now known as the Baum place). Both inheritances were lost after the Civil War. Mrs. Shannon died in 1908, aged 86.

Their children were:

ALLISON ENGLISH (1844-1865), killed in battle at Goldsboro, N. C.

CHARLES JOHN (1844-1869), served in the Confederate War.

BENJAMIN HAILE (1849-1878), also in Confederate service.

MARTHA ENGLISH (1851-    ), married Dr. J. C. Spann.

ENGLISH (1853-?), married Mary Welsh.

THOMAS ENGLISH (1858-1889), married Rose McFadden.

WILLIAM MCCREIGHT, died in infancy.

MARY LOUISA (1861-    ), married Edward C. DuBose.

ELIZABETH HAILE (1864-    ), married Thomas Perkins.

SALLY DOBY, died in infancy.

JOHN JOYCE, died in infancy.

III COLONEL WILLIAM M. SHANNON (1822-1880), was a distinguished member of the Camden bar for many years. He served as first captain of the Kirkwood Rangers, resigning in 1862. An account of his tragic death in the famous duel with Colonel Cash has been given in other pages.

## Family Histories

Colonel Shannon married Henrietta (1825-1891), daughter of Hon. William McWillie. They were the parents of thirteen children, all of whom were living at the time of his death:

HARRIET (1844-1908), married Dr. Andrew W. Burnet, for many years one of the leading physicians of Camden.

CHARLES JOHN (III) (1846-   ), married Mary Kershaw.

NANCY CUNNINGHAM (1847-1922), married Randolph Withers.

MARTHA ENGLISH (1849-1924), married, first, Arthur P. Lining, a member of the Camden bar; second, R. J. McGill.

MARY ("MINNIE") (1851-1890), unmarried.

CATHERINE MCWILLIE (1854-   ), married William E. Johnson (III).

WILLIAM MCWILLIE (1855-1921), a prominent lawyer and public spirited citizen of Camden; married Camilla Agnes Nelson.

HENRIETTA MCWILLIE (1857-   ), married P. H. Nelson.

ADAM MCWILLIE (1859-   ), married, first, Mrs. Alice Williams; second, Aubrey Brown.

JANE JOHNSON (1860-   ), married Rev. James M. Stoney, one time rector of Grace Church, Camden.

ALLISON ENGLISH (1863-1889), unmarried.

IDA MCWILLIE (1866-   ), married James M. Heath.

LUCY MCWILLIE (1869-   ), married Wm. DeSaussure Boykin.

V  CHARLES JOHN SHANNON (II), M. D., after travel and study abroad, settled in Camden to practice medicine. At one time, he and Dr. W. J. McKain, operated an infirmary in Camden for the treatment of chronic diseases. Shortly before the Civil War, he retired from practice to engage in farming. He acted as surgeon in the Kirkwood Rangers, Confederate service. Dr. Shannon married Mary, daughter of William Ancrum, who survived him until 1920, a noble matron and beloved teacher of the youth of Camden for more than thirty years. Their children were:

ELLEN DEAS (1860-1884), first wife of Wm. DeSaussure Boykin.

CHARLES JOHN (IV), (1863-    ), a prominent merchant and banker of Camden; married Emily Jordan Nesbit.

LEILA ANCRUM (1867-    ).

CHARLOTTE DOUGLAS (1869-    ).

IX SAMUEL DAVIS ("SAM") SHANNON (1833-1900), was a picturesque figure. Handsome, magnetic, with a certain dash of manner which he maintained through all the later vicissitudes of fortune, he was widely known in the Southern army, in which he served as a member of the Kirkwood Rangers and later on the staff of General Dick Anderson. A prime favorite with the gentler sex, he had many "affaires du coeur" in Virginia. Finally he captivated one of the belles and beauties of Richmond, Elizabeth Peyton Giles, their wedding being a conspicuous society event of the war period. His wife did not long live with him, securing a divorce and returning to her Virginia home. The grounds, it is said, was non-support. Without means, he had a sublime contempt for toil.

After that, he roamed from place to place, "visiting", for indefinite stays, his friends who were fond of him and took him into their homes. Often his former lady admirers came to his assistance in times of need. Always his wit and charm of manner served him in good stead.

Cleveland appointed him Secretary of State of Utah, and, for a brief space, he lived, it is said, like the proverbial grandee. It lasted but a year or two, and, once again, he was back on the world, in which, from experience, he apparently had great faith. Lamed by a fall, he was cared for by the unfailing friends till his death, which brought sad memories of more romantic days to hearts in many Southern homes. He left no descendants.

## THOMPSON.

This family has, for five generations, been prominently identified with the upper section of the County.

ADAM THOMPSON, an emigrant from Ireland, secured lands on Beaver Creek shortly after the Revolution. He died about 1817. His son, William[1], married Sarah, daughter of James and Elizabeth Shropshire and, dying

[1]There were three other sons, Peter, Adam and Alexander. (Probate Court Records). Of them we have no other information.

young, left two sons to the guardianship of Mr. Jesse Kilgore, a friend and neighbor.

These lads, James and John, remained under the care of their guardian until they reached the ages of sixteen and fourteen, respectively, when their quite extensive estates were turned over to their own management.

JOHN was a Captain in the Reserves, in the Confederate service. He died in 1868, unmarried.

JAMES, born in 1815, was married to Charlotte, daughter of Joseph Patterson (I). In 1850 he sold his Beaver Creek Plantation to his brother John and removed to Liberty Hill, where he built one of the fine houses which adorned that little community of rich planters. He died in 1897, seven years after the passing of his estimable wife.

Their children were:

JOSEPH, who died in 1858, two years after graduating at the South Carolina College.

SARAH ELIZABETH (1837-1885), married Major Andrew B. Wardlaw of Abbeville.

JOSEPHINE (1839-1888), married Dr. Wm. Clark Wardlaw, a Captain in the Confederate army.

WILLIAM KILGORE (1842-1913), a student at the South Carolina College in 1861; resigned his academic career to enter the army in the "Kirkwood Rangers"; served until the surrender, when he returned to the farm, living first at "Collins Place", then at Liberty Hill. In 1888 he was elected to the Legislature, serving one term. The same year he was chosen master of the State Grange, which position he held for more than twenty years. Mr. Thompson was married three times; first, to Ellen Blue, of Cheraw; died in 1870; second to Anne, daughter of Robert M. Kennedy of Camden; died in 1880; third, to Sallie Chesnut, daughter of John Whitaker, of Camden; died in 1909, aged 62.

LEWIS COLLINS (1846-1902); entered the army, 1863, under Captain E. M. Boykin; surrendered with Lee at Appomattox; married Mary, daughter of Colonel James Perrin of Abbeville; farmed at Liberty Hill; later removed to Atlanta, Georgia, where he died.

JOHN SHROPSHIRE (1850-1907); married Jane Perrin, sister to his brother Lewis' wife; practiced dentistry, first in Abbeville, then for many years in Atlanta.

MARNIE, died in 1870, at the age of eighteen years, shortly after leaving college.

JAMES (1854-     ), married Margaret Caldwell, of Greensboro, North Carolina; lives in Atlanta.

THORNTON-CARPENTER—CLARK-ECCLES-GAMEWELL

These five families may be treated together, as they were nearly allied by marriage, forming what may be called the Thornton Connection, not one of them being perpetuated in the male line and only through the descendants of Phineas Thornton being now represented here at all.

One of the oldest headstones in our cemetery is to the memory of Gilbert Thornton, who was born in Boston, Massachusetts in 1732 and died, evidently at Camden, in 1802. By his side rests Keziah, his wife. The death of the latter is recorded in the *Camden Gazette* of May 9, 1817, with the information that she was aged 73 years, that she was born in New Jersey, and that she left thirteen children, sixty-four grandchildren, and eighteen great-grandchildren.

Of these, four children at least settled in Camden: Lydia (Mrs. Dan Carpenter), Nancy (Mrs. James Clark), Phineas, and Catherine (Mrs. Jonathan Eccles). As Mrs. Clark was certainly married in Camden in 1798,[1] and Phineas was clerking here for Dan Carpenter in 1793,[2] Gilbert evidently settled in Camden prior to 1800. Of him even the descendants can give no information. Indeed it is only from the inscription on his daughter, Mrs. Eccles' tomb, that we can assert that he was the common ancestor of the connection mentioned.

PHINEAS THORNTON,[3] son of Gilbert, was born in New Jersey in 1779. He came to Camden, as said, when fourteen years old, in the employment of his brother-in-law, Dan Carpenter, whose partner he became later. In 1804, he was married to Elizabeth Williams, of Raynham, Massachusettes, bringing his wife directly to Camden. This lady wrote, in 1856, interesting reminiscences of Camden as she first knew it, from which we have quoted liberally in other chapters.

Phineas Thornton was a merchant on his own account for many years, and was postmaster here for twenty-three years, until his resignation in 1843, having had,

[1] See James Kershaw's Diary, *Historic Camden*, Vol. I.
[2] Mrs. Thornton's *Reminiscences*.
[3] Spelled "Phinehas" on his tombstone.

## Family Histories

as the local paper commented, "to rise at any hour of the night on sound of the mail-horn." He died in 1851.

Mrs. Thornton moved to New Jersey, in 1865, to live with her daughter, Mrs. Gamewell, and died there in 1884, aged *102 years and nine months*, having lived to see six generations of descendants.

She had two children—Abathiah (Mrs. Capers[1]) and Sarah (Mrs. Gamewell), 1819-1889.

DANIEL CARPENTER, who, as stated, married Lydia Thornton, was born in Massachusetts in 1768. As his marriage occurred in that state in 1789 and he was in business in Camden in 1793, we can come very near to the date of his locating here. It was possibly his coming that drew hither his wife's family. He was one of the first New Englanders to settle here, and was one of our earliest prominent Methodists.[2] Of his five children one, a second Dan, was "Secretary and Treasurer of the Handel and Haydn Society" in 1831;[3] he married, and left one son, Dan, who died without issue. The "Mrs. Carpenter and Daughters",[4] who had a school here in 1817, were doubtless the widow and children of the first Dan, whose death occurred in 1806.[5]

JAMES L. CLARK was a native of Scotland and a prominent merchant and Methodist of the early 19th century in Camden. He built, on upper Broad Street, the handsome brick house, later known, for years, as the home of Anthony M. Kennedy, more recently of William C. Gerald. It was burned in 1884, and the fine grounds were divided into three lots.

Mr. Clark's store was next below his residence. He and Samuel Mathis were the large "Log-Town" merchants. "Messrs. McRa, Cantey, Douglas and others held the fort downtown."[6] We shall let Colonel Shannon tell the following anecdote: "However well Mr. Clark understood finances practically, he had not much theoretic knowledge of 'cent, per cent'; for we remember often to have heard that he expostulated with his friend Mr. Douglas as to the high rates of profit made by the downtown

---
[1]See "CAPERS".
[2]See "Methodist Church".
[3]*Camden Journal*, January 8, 1831.
[4]See "Schools".
[5]*South Carolina Gazette.*
[6]*Old Times in Camden.*

merchants, telling him they were downright extortioners, often making thirty and fifty per cent profit while one per cent was enough for any man; 'Doubling is always my rule'."

Mr. Clark, as said, married Ann Thornton. They were the parents of three sons and several daughters, all of whom and their descendants have passed from among us. One daughter, Catherine, married Dr. Joseph Lee; another, Alexander Rutherford of Richmond, Virginia; a third, Colonel Augustine Leftwich of Lynchburg, Virginia. These ladies were noted for their beauty.

JONATHAN ECCLES[1] married Catherine Thornton in 1805. We learn, from the full inscription on their common tomb, that he was born in Roscommon Parish, Killukin, Ireland, 1776, dying at Camden in 1836; and that she was born in New York in 1784 and died here in 1830. Mr. Eccles was a considerable merchant of the town as early, perhaps, as 1800. Of their five children, but two lived to maturity; Nancy (Mrs. John C. West[2]) and Catherine.

There are no descendants now in our community.

JOHN M. GAMEWELL, who married Sarah, daughter of Phineas Thornton, was born in Cheraw, South Carolina, in 1822. He was the son of John Gamewell, a pioneer Methodist minister. He was engaged in mercantile business, first in Charleston, then in Camden, where he conducted a book store. In 1843, he was appointed Postmaster, to succeed his father-in-law, and, about the same time, was put in charge of the local office of the "Washington and New Orleans Telegraph Company."

Years afterwards, he resigned both positions to undertake the introduction of the "Gamewell Fire Alarm Telegraph", which he invented. James Dunlap of Camden was his partner. Patents were obtained in the United States, Canada and England.

At the close of the War, he removed, with his family, to New Jersey, recovering, through strong influence, his confiscated patents, and there he died in 1896, aged seventy-seven years.

Mr. Gamewell built and occupied the residence facing Monument Square, for many years the home of Major W. Z. Leitner, later the High School. There were nine

[1] Arrived in this country in 1802; naturalized in 1807.
[2] See "WEST".

FAMILY HISTORIES

children born to Mr. and Mrs. Gamewell. One of them, Dr. Frank Gamewell, was a missionary to China, conspicuous in the siege of Peking.

A correction may here be made of an error discovered in our first volume.[1] The second wife of Dr. Isaac Alexander was SARAH THOMPSON, of New York, said to have been a niece of Phineas, and therefore a granddaughter of Gilbert Thornton.

## VILLEPIGUE.

This family descends from one Francois Villepigue who emigrated from France in 1788 to the French colony of St. Domingo.

This unhappy man fell a victim, in 1800, of the terrible Slave Insurrection on his adopted island, being massacred by his own negroes. His wife, warned at the last moment, escaped with two sons, and, in company with Pierre Laurent Jumelle, to whom reference has been made in other pages, landed at Charleston, South Carolina, whence the party found their way to Camden.

PAUL FRANCIS, one of these sons, was for many years a prominent merchant of the town. His naturalization papers (1827) show that he came to this country in 1807. He was of the Romanist faith, and, on money advanced by him, the Roman Catholic "Church" on DeKalb Street was built in the 40's.[2] His wife was Agnes Mattuce, who died in 1860, one year before her husband's death. Their children were:

I  PAUL THOMAS, long a merchant in Camden. He married Martha (1832-1878), daughter of Philip Bracey of Stateburg.

Issue:

PHILIP BRACEY, who died in New York, 1895. As a boy, he left the Arsenal at Columbia to enlist in the Southern army.

FREDERICK, died at Macon, Georgia, 1898.

AGNES, married the Reverend Obre Bourne, an Episcopal clergyman, once Principal of the Camden School.

PAUL T. (1854-1911), married, first, Elise, daughter of Dr. John McCaa (II); second, Emma, daughter of John

[1] See "ALEXANDER" in Vol. I.
[2] See Roman Catholic Church.

Cantey.[1]  Mr. Villepigue was, for years, a prominent merchant of Camden, and at one time president of Hermiage Cotton Mill.

JOHN.

II  CHARLOTTE (1819-1852), married Robert Fletcher.

III  JAMES IRWIN (1821-1905), died in Camden at the ripe old age of eighty-four. As a young man, he was in the mercantile business with his father, later on his own account. He served gallantly through the War, as Quartermaster, Second South Carolina Volunteers.

No figure was more familiar on the streets of Camden than Captain Villepigue, and it may be said, no man had fewer enemies. Of large physique, his magnificent beard gave him a somewhat patriarchal look. Under rough externals of speech and manner, there beat a true big heart. He was married to Sarah (1826-1915), daughter of William McKain, and of this union sprang:

JAMES I. (II), married; a resident of New York.

FRANK, unmarried.

DAVIS, unmarried.

EUGENE (1856-1910), unmarried.

SARAH, who became the wife of Professor C. M. Furman, of Clemson College.

KATE, unmarried.

WALTER, unmarried.

Two of these children, Davis and Eugene, have died in recent years.

IV  FREDERICK, an honor graduate of the South Carolina College; removed to Florida before the War, from which state he entered the army as Captain of the "Villepigue Artillery". During the Reconstruction Period he was Secretary of State of Florida. His wife was a Miss Armstrong of that state.

V  AGNES, died; unmarried, at Memphis.

VI  PHILIP.

VII  JOHN BORDENAVE (1830-1862), Brigadier General, Confederate States army. His career is sketched in another chapter.

---

[1] A son of this marriage, John Cantey Villepigue, was one of the six young South Carolinians to whom was awarded the Congressional Medal, for heroic conduct in the European War (1914-1918).

# Family Histories

## West.

JOHN CHARLES WEST was born in 1801 at Fayetteville, North Carolina.

Says his son, John Camden West, in an admirable sketch of the family to which we are indebted for much of the information here given: "He came to Camden as a youth of seventeen, friendless and unknown, but soon exhibited a character and capacity which commanded the respect, esteem and admiration of the best and most influential citizens. After some experience as a clerk and salesman, he became a partner of Charles J. Shannon in the mercantile business and a strong and life-time friendship grew up between them.[1] He was fond of books and, by application and study in spare time, he soon attracted attention as a writer and speaker. He was an intimate friend of Honorable William McWillie and Judge John Belton O'Neall, and delivered temperance addresses from the same platform with them."

In 1833, he was elected Sheriff of the County on the Union ticket but refused to take the Test Oath, publishing an address to his constituents justifying his action. He was not then allowed to assume office but did so two years later on his triumphant re-election. In 1835, he became editor and manager of the *Camden Journal and Southern Whig*, which he conducted ably. The next year he was chosen teller of the Branch Bank of Camden, which position he held till his death in 1855. William E. Johnson, President of the Bank, paid him the following trubute: "Mr. West does not claim the infallibility of the Pope, but, in the examination of his books for many years we have never found even a clerical error. He is the most accurate man I ever knew."

Mr. West was Mayor of Camden in 1845. He was married, 1827, to Nancy Clark, daughter of Jonathan Eccles. Of this union the following children were born:

CHARLES SHANNON.
MARY (Mrs. Mary W. Moore, Austin, Texas).
CATHERINE (Mrs. Kate E. Green, San Antonio, Texas).
JOHN CAMDEN, a prominent lawyer and insurance man of Waco, Texas and the author of "A Texan in Search of a Fight".

---

[1] This was evinced by the unusual compliment of naming two of his sons for Mr. Shannon; one died in infancy.

JUDGE CHARLES SHANNON WEST (mentioned above), died in 1885, a member of the Supreme Court of Texas. He was born in Camden, September 25, 1829.

In the family sketch already referred to we learn that in early boyhood he was an omnivorous reader with a prodigious memory. To encourage this faculty his father gave him five cents per page for memorizing history and the same per hundred lines for repeating Milton's "Paradise Lost". When fourteen years old, he repeated, on one occasion, eight hundred lines of that great epic without a break. His teachers in the local schools were Miss Henrietta DeLeon, Miss Rebecca Reynolds and Leslie McCandless. In 1847 he attended Jefferson College, Pennsylvania and later the South Carolina College where he graduated in 1848.

Following this he taught school in the Boykin neighborhood seven miles below Camden, at the same time preparing himself for the Bar under Honorable James Chesnut. In 1850, he was successfully practicing law in Camden. The same year he moved to Texas, where, till his death, he rose steadily to the forefront as a man of mark in his adopted state.

He married in 1859 Florence, daughter of Judge Thomas H. Duvall of the Western Federal District of Texas, and left three sons all of whom rose to prominence.

His success in his early career in Texas drew thither in the 50's his sisters and brother, so that no descendants of the family remain in this community.

## WITHERS.

For a sketch of Judge Thos. J. Withers, ancestor of the Camden branch of this family, see Chapter XIV in this volume. As therein stated, Judge Withers was married in 1831 to Elizabeth T. Boykin. Between 1832 and 1838 they suffered the loss of their first four children when between the ages of one and three years. Their names were Mary, Amelia, Sarah and Burwell. Their children reaching adult age were:

MARY MILLER, who married Wm. Lennox Kirkland (See Kirkland family).

THOS. JEFFERSON (1841-1858), who was accidentally killed in riding a race with his friend Benj. Perkins.

KATHERINE (1845-1865), died unmarried.

Family Histories

WM. RANDOLPH WITHERS (1846-1877), who married Nancy C. Shannon (1847-1922).
The children of Wm. Randolph and his wife Nancy C. Shannon were:
MARY SHANNON (1873-    ), married Wm. G. Gambrell.
HENRIETTA MCWILLIE (1874-    ), married F. Barron Grier.
NANCY SHANNON (1876-    ), married John G. Chaffee.

## WITHERSPOON.

REV. JOHN WITHERSPOON, D. D. (1789-1853), son of John Witherspoon of "Pembroke", near Newbern, N. C., and grandson of Rev. John Witherspoon of Princeton College, signer of the Declaration of Independence, was pastor of the Presbyterian Church at Camden, (1833-1837). He was a man of much learning and was offered a professorship at the South Carolina College. After leaving Camden, he was pastor of the First Presbyterian Church in Columbia and later preached at Hillsborough, N. C., where he died. His sister was the wife of David Ramsay, historian of South Carolina.

Dr. Witherspoon's wife was Susan Kollock (1793-1854), of Elizabeth, N. J., a granddaughter of Hannah Arnett, a Revolutionary heroine.

Their children, who were long identified with Camden, were:
JOHN KNOX, who married Elizabeth McEwen.
SUSAN KOLLOCK (1817-1857), who married William Douglas McDowall.

JOHN KNOX WITHERSPOON was a well known life-long resident of Camden, an elder in the Presbyterian Church and owner of the telegraph line from Camden to Columbia.

His children were:
DENAH (1837-1859), first wife of James Jones.[1]
JAMES, died in the Confederate service.
JOHN, killed in the Confederate service.

---

[1] James and Thomas Jones, brothers, were well-known merchants of Camden for many years. The family of the former have long since left Camden. The widow of William, son of Thomas Jones, still occupies their old homestead on Lyttleton Street.

HENRY, married Jane Sadler.

SUSAN (1848-1909), wife of Dr. Eugene Daniels, a Presbyterian minister.

MARIA, wife of Rev. Wm. Dodge, of the Presbyterian Church.

AGNES, wife of Robert Shields, of Memphis.

DAVID (?-1918), who married Mary, daughter of William Douglas Anderson. David was the last of the family in Camden, removing, in 1912, to Columbia, where he died.

## WORKMAN.

From a sketch of the family furnished us by the Reverend W. H. Workman, we learn that the progenitor of the American branch was one John Workman, a sea-captain engaged in the linen trade between Belfast and Liverpool, who emigrated with his family to America prior to 1793. His wife was a Miss Clark.

Their daughter Elizabeth married her cousin, James Workman, who settled in Winnsboro, South Carolina.

Two sons of this couple removed in early manhood to Camden, John and William Clark Workman.

I. JOHN (1793-1865) learned the trade of gin-making, an occupation offering new and inviting prospects. It will be noted that he was born the year of Whitney's epoch-making invention. We find his advertisement, "Saw gins made and repaired", in the *Camden Gazette* of 1817. He was in partnership with William Atkinson, and they announce that "their shop in Winnsboro is in full operation". This, therefore, was probably the date of his advent in Camden.

In 1820 he married Rebecca Jackson.

John Workman later conducted a large general merchandise store, which stood on the southeast corner of Broad and Rutledge Streets and was familiarly known as "The Ark". It was one of a row of very quaint old wooden buildings that extended from the present Opera House site down to the bakery that used to be conducted by Mrs. Crosby, a pink-cheeked little Englishwoman, beloved of all children of the town for several generations. These interesting antique structures, full of equally curious and conglomerate stores, passed in the destructive fire of 1877.

Mr. Workman was for thirty-two years an elder in the Presbyterian Church. He was a large investor in Cam-

## Family Histories

den real estate, owning many town lots at the time of his death. He built and occupied the residence on Fair Street, now the property of L. A. Kirkland.

Issue of John and Rebecca Workman:

THOMAS J. (1822-1869), graduated in medicine, University of Pennsylvania, in 1846; a successful practitioner in Camden, and a surgeon in the Confederate service. Unmarried.

EDWARD E., also a physician; graduated at the same medical college in 1848; married a Miss Robinson of Virginia. Buried at Petersburg, Virginia.

JOHN J., graduate of the University of Virginia; practiced law in Camden; married Isabella Campbell, of Winnsboro. No issue.

WILLIAM H. R. (1825-1889), graduate of the University of Virginia ("first medal"); practiced law in Camden, at first as a partner of his brother John. Later, he served as Cashier of the Bank of Camden; resigned to go into the War; after which he returned to the Bar, being in partnership, successively, with General James Chesnut and General J. B. Kershaw. For twenty-nine years he was an elder in Bethesda (Presbyterian) Church.

He was twice married; first, to Maria Minor of Charlottsville, Virginia, then to Ketura Gatewood (1841-1894), of Charleston, South Carolina. Of the first union, there were two sons and two daughters; of the second, five sons and six daughters.

II WILLIAM C. WORKMAN (1804-1861), who followed his brother John to Camden from Winnsboro, was also a merchant here for many years. He married Sarah, daughter of the Reverend James Jenkins.[1] Five children survived him:

ELIZABETH (1833-1911), married William Wallace.

SARAH (1839-1879), married Major L. W. R. Blair.

JAMES J. (1841-1908), a Methodist minister; married Mary Sullivan.

WILLIAM C. (1846-1899), served in the 7th South Carolina Cavalry (Gary's Brigade); married Mary Germany; removed to Savannah, Georgia, where he died.

REBECCA (1849-1923), married W. Elliot DeLoach.

This line is represented here through the Wallace and DeLoach families.

[1] See "Methodist Church".

## YOUNG.

ALEXANDER YOUNG (1784-1856) was a native of Fifeshire, Scotland. His naturalization papers were taken out at Camden in 1811 and show that he had been ten years a resident of the state. His advertisement of jewelry, patent medicines, and so on, appears in the local paper in 1816; he had perhaps established his business many years earlier.

As jeweler, watchmaker and bookseller, he controlled the field for nearly a half century and passed the very respectable business on to his two sons, by whom it was continued for almost another half century.

To great mechanical skill and inventive genius, he united considerable knowledge of chemistry, metaphysics and natural philosophy. Mr. Young had a high rating among the early American silversmiths, having a recognized "hallmark". The silver trowel used by LaFayette in laying the cornerstone of the DeKalb monument was made by him. The mechanism for ringing the hours or a fire alarm was his invention.

Colonel Shannon says[1] that he was a lover of rare old books, not displaying them on the shelves of his store, but hiding them with other treasures in some private nook "where with mysterious and melting air of hospitality he would carry a willing listener (a great favor) and let him taste of them as an old 'bon vivant' would let one taste of his wine."

He was married in 1806, at Baltimore, to Elizabeth Kewe of English parentage.

Issue:
JAMES ANDREW (1808-1882), M. D.
MARY LAW (1813-1901).
ROBERT ALEXANDER (1811-1864).
EDWARD ANDERSON and
THOMAS SALMOND, twins, born in 1816. The former died in 1848, the latter in 1877.
MARGARET REID (1819-1822).
GEORGE GRAHAM (1823-1897).

Only two of the children were married, Robert[2] and George; the former to Mary Riley Kershaw, a sister of

---

[1] *Old Times in Camden.*

[2] Robert A. Young and his family removed early to other parts. Their home in Camden was the old residence at corner of Fair and Haile Streets.

FAMILY HISTORIES

General J. B. Kershaw; the latter to Mary Douglas McDowall.

DR. JAMES A. YOUNG (1808-1882), was a graduate of the South Carolina College and of the Medical College of Philadelphia, completing his professional studies in Paris. He practiced for some years in Camden and for a short period in Columbus, Georgia, returning to take charge, with his brother, George, of his father's business which he continued until five years before his death, when he retired on account of ill health. A man of the highest moral character, a vestryman for long years of Grace (Episcopal) Church, he was full of learning and most interesting in conversation.

GEORGE G. YOUNG (1823-1897) kept up the business for twenty years after his brother's retirement. At his death, it was closed. Young's Book Store was one of the landmarks of the old town, a noted resort for men of literary tastes.

ZEMP.

(See CAPERS).

*The Jewish Citizens of Camden.*

There must have been quite a number of Jews in Camden prior to 1788, in which year Joseph Kershaw made his will, for in it he says: "To God's Antient people the Jews I give and devise the lot 315 for a Burying ground and place of worship whenever they may incline to build upon the same."

This lot was on the east side of Market Street between York and King. It was never used for either purpose. The Jews were not strong enough to form a congregation until 1880, when they organized as "Gemilath Chasodim of Camden". They bought the land adjoining the Quaker Cemetery in 1877, which they have since used as their burying-ground. In 1921, they purchased the abandoned little Roman Catholic Chapel on Lyttleton Street and converted it into a synagogue.

Elzas, in his *Jews of South Carolina*, could find only four Jewish names in the Camden records prior to 1800; David and Isaiah Bush, Samuel Levy, and Moses Sarzedas, and he is uncertain whether the Bushes were Jews.

The DeLeons and the Levys were prominent Jewish families in the early years of the 19th Century. They have been treated in the family sketches and elsewhere in this volume.

The following representative Jewish families settled in Camden just before or immediately after the Civil War. Of those who came later we regret that our space will not permit discussion.

BARUCH.—The eminent American physician, Dr. Simon Baruch, was born in Prussia in 1840. Coming to this country in early manhood, he graduated in medicine at the Medical College of Virginia in 1862. For the next three years he served as a surgeon in the Army of Northern Virginia.

Immediately after the war he settled in Camden where he practiced his profession for fifteen years. He was president of the South Carolina Medical Society in 1873 and chairman of the State Board of Health in 1880.

His talents were of such a high order that in 1881 he removed to a larger field, settling in New York City, where he rose to the highest distinction in his profession and where he passed the rest of his long life.

He was physician and gynaecologist to the Northeastern Dispensary from 1883 to 1887, physician and surgeon to the New York Juvenile Asylum for the next thirteen years, chief of the Medical Staff of the Montefiore Home for Chronic Invalids for eight years, and professor of Hydrotherapy in the New York Post-Graduate Medical School and Hospital up to the time of his death in 1921.

Elzas says: "Dr. Baruch diagnosticated the first recorded case of perforating appendicitis successfully operated upon, and Dr. J. A. Wyeth stated in a discussion in the New York Academy of Medicine that 'the profession and humanity owe more to Dr. Baruch than to any other one man for the development of the surgery of appendicitis'."

The introduction of free municipal baths in the largest cities of the United States is also the result of Dr. Baruch's persistent efforts. He was the author of several medical books that were translated into both German and French.

Dr. Baruch married Miss Belle Wolfe, of Winnsboro, a very handsome and talented woman. They had two sons, Hartwell and Bernard M. Baruch, of New York City, the latter the eminent capitalist and publicist, in-

## Family Histories

timate friend and adviser of Woodrow Wilson in the World War period and chairman of the War Industries Board.

BERNARD BARUCH, as a memorial to his father and mother, built and endowed the present handsome Hospital in Camden.

HERMAN BARUCH, a brother of Dr. Simon Baruch, served as a courier on the staff of General Beauregard, Co. K., 7th Cavalry, in the Confederate War. Later he was a large merchant in Camden, removing in the 80's to Charlotte, N. C. Two of his sons returned to Camden and engaged in business.

BAUM.—Three brothers, Mannes, Herman and Marcus Baum, Germans by birth, settled in Camden shortly before the Civil War.

They were all soldiers in the service of the Confederacy. Marcus was killed by our own men at the battle of the Wilderness when on a reconnoitering expedition with General Longstreet. Captain Alfred Doby of Camden was killed at the same time.

After the War, Baum Bros. (Mannes and Herman) operated a large mercantile business up to the time of their deaths.

Herman also had large planting interests in West Wateree. His home, the old Lee place on Broad Street, is one of the handsomest in town, still occupied by his descendants. His wife, Miss Heyman of Chester, was very highly esteemed in the community.

WITTKOWSKY.—ADOLPH WITTKOWSKY, a native German, settled in Camden before 1860. He was a brave soldier of the Confederacy, serving in Anderson's Brigade, Longstreet's Division. He was wounded at Williamsburg, being permanently disabled. For four months he was a prisoner in Washington, D. C.

Later, up to the time of his death, he was in business in Camden.

His wife was Miss Hyams, of a well-known Jewish family of Charleston.

One of their sons is a prominent member of the Camden bar.

WOLFE AND RICH.—The families of Wolfe and Rich, it is believed, were both in Camden in business before the Civil War; certainly for many years after.

DAVID WOLFE is at present a considerable merchant and useful citizen of the town. His beautiful home on Lyttleton Street was formerly of the late Robert M. Kennedy; Mr. Wolfe has owned it since 1885.

WILLIAM GEISENHEIMER, a gallant soldier of the Confederacy (Washington Artillery), wounded at Shiloh, was also a merchant in Camden for many years immediately following the War.

Other names may unintentionally have been overlooked. The Jews have always been public spirited citizens.

## *Postscript to Family Histories*

It is a matter of increased regret, at the conclusion of our labors, that the limitations which we found necessary to fix in our treatment of families, confining ourselves to those settled in Camden not later than the Civil War, has excluded many excellent ones that have made this their home since that time.

Such names as the following occur at once to the mind: Barrett, Blakeney, Burnet, Carrison, DeLoach, DuBose, Dunn, Eldredge, Heath, Lindsay, Lining, Little, McDowell, Mills, Nelson, Phelps, Rhame, Savage, Sill, Stoney, Taylor, Trotter, Von Tresckow, Wallace, Whistler, Williams (two families), Wootten. The list is not complete, of course: omissions are faults of memory. Many of these have been mentioned in this volume or in our first. The residence of most of them in this community dates from the period immediately following the War and they have figured prominently in our later history. To have treated them with any degree of sufficiency would have made this volume much more bulky: hence the regrettable limitation.

# APPENDIX

### Confederate Soldiers From Kershaw County.

[The following lists are of course not free of errors and omissions. It would be utterly impracticable, indeed impossible, to make them so. The reason is obvious when it is realized that membership of a company during the four years of war was in continual transition owing to losses of battle, disease, discharge, transfer and accessions of recruits. A single roll represents only the composition of a company on a particular date. Of some companies as many as a dozen rolls survive, in the form of quarterly reports to the War Department in Richmond—none later than October 1864. Of other companies only two or three such reports are preserved; of others mere fragments, and none at all of still others. These military records were captured by the Federals upon the occupation of Richmond, and were long held inaccessible to all comers in Washington, until within recent years when photostatic copies were procured by Mr. A. S. Salley, Secretary of the State Historical Commission, and placed on file in that office. These constitute the most authentic lists of Confederate troops, but being made up in camp and field, often under stress of action, furnish few data beyond the names of those present for duty on certain dates.

Soon after redemption of the State from Carpetbag rule provision was made for compilation of the Confederate rolls and the office of State Historian established for the purpose, a position filled successively by prominent ex-Confederates. It is notorious that the rolls then collected are largely reproduced from memory and more or less defective, many exceedingly so. The compilers did not have the benefit of the captured Confederate records.

Beside the above sources of information we examined closely the reports and casualties contained in the newspapers published during the war of which we gathered somewhat broken files. The utmost diligence has been used to construct a record of our troops as nearly complete and accurate as possible.

Our greatest difficulty was encountered in trying to identify those belonging to Kershaw County. Most of our companies contained members from other counties, and many rolls failed to show the county of their residence or were very full of errors on this head, which years of inquiry and investigation could not fully rectify. Beside all this we have had to condense into a few pages material that would fill a large volume.]

# Appendix

The economy of space has compelled the adoption of abbreviations such as: killed (kd); wounded (wd); discharged (dschd); surrendered (srrd); captured (cap); prisoner (pris); died of disease (d); transferred to some other company (tr); and so on. In not a few cases a member was wounded more than once, and yet only noted as once wd, for the reason that the record of casualties is very imperfect and incomplete. It will also be observed that some names appear in two or more companies. This is in most cases owing to transfers. Those names marked with an asterisk (*) were not from Kershaw County.

These lists are swollen by many names of those who were merely temporary, casual members who were led by enthusiasm and patriotic fervor to join, but owing to age or other defects were unable to endure the service and were discharged or resigned. It was rare that a man of forty could stand the hardships. The Civil War, as every war before and since, was fought by young men. The real effectives in each company were not more than two-thirds of the total membership. Company E. 2nd Regt. (Camden Volunteers), see list below, may be taken as an example of the deductions to be made from the full roll for various reasons.

## DeKalb Rifle Guards.

### *Company J., Gregg's Regiment, South Carolina Volunteers.*

[This company is given first place in our list because of its long standing prior to 1861, and famous record as a member of the Palmetto Regiment in the Mexican War. It was the first to entrain April 24, 1861, at Camden for the front in Virginia, Co. E. (Capt. Kennedy) having departed on April 9 for Fort Sumter. During the battle of First Manassas this company guarded the camps and was not engaged. After the battle, owing to some disagreement, it was disbanded and its members joined other commands.[1]]

| | |
|---|---|
| Captain Thos. L. Boykin | *Privates* |
| 1st Lieut. James M. Davis | Bass, Eli |
| 2nd Lieut. Wm. Clyburn | Bass, James |
| 3rd Lieut. Thos. W. Bracey | Brannon, David |
| 1st Sergt. Eli W. Parker | Brannon, John |
| 2nd Sergt. Chas. J. McDowall | Cameron, W. J. |
| 3rd Sergt. Duncan Whitaker | Campbell, Chas. |
| 4th Sergt. U. P. Bonney | Coates, Sam'l |
| 5th Sergt. Joshua Josey | Copeland, L. P. |
| 1st Corp. W. J. Hatfield | Croft, Robt. |
| 2nd Corp. Anderson Stuckey | Davis, J. A. |
| 3rd Corp. M. G. Huckabee | Davis, S. T. |
| 4th Corp. J. L. Gettys | Dunlap, L. D. |
| 5th Corp. A. Kelley | Dunlap, W. D. |
| 6th Corp. Henry Davis | Erving, John |

[1] A roll of this company after years of inquiry was at last found in possession of Mr. J. F. Turner. None could be found among the Confederate Rolls collected by the State.

# Appendix

Estridge, James
Gardner, J. C.
Gardner, J. W.
Gardner, Thos.
Goff, John
Goff, Wm.
Griffin, Stephen
Hays, James
Hays, Joseph
Hall, J. Melvin
Harrell, James
Hatfield, S. B.
Hinson, Francis
Hinson, Isom
Holland, John
Huggins, C. R. E.
Jackson, Douglas
Jackson, J.
Jeffers, Osborn
Kelley, J. F.
Kemp, Warren
Kirby, T.
Kirby, T. W.
Marshall, John C.
Mathis, Wesley
Mattox, J.
Meyers, L. E.
McCaskill, C. W.
Outlaw, J. E.
Parker, John
Parker, Mason D.
Rush, J. J.
Richbourg, J. J.
Self, W. F.
Shiver, John
Shiver, Joseph
Smith, G. W.
Smith, J. J.
Spradley, W. J.
Tiller, H. D.
Truesdale, J. T.
Turner, J. F.
Watts, Columbus
Watts, Francis
Wilson, John
Yates, Samuel

## Camden Volunteers.

### Company E., 2nd Regiment, South Carolina Volunteers.

[Names marked * not from Kershaw County.]

Capt. Kennedy, Jno. D., pro. Col., Brig. Genl., wd 7 times.
Capt. Leitner, Wm. Z., wd Gettysburg, lost leg, pro. Major.
Lieut. Dunlap, Jos. D., wd Chickamauga.
Lieut. Doby, Alfred E., pro Aid to Kershaw, kd Spottsylvania.
Lieut. Sill, E. E., wd twice, pro. Adjt.
Lieut. Drakeford, Jos. J., retired '64, disability.
Lieut. DePass, Wm. L., wd 1st Manas., Captain Co. G., Pal. Bat., Art.
Lieut. McKain, John J., mort wd Warwick River.
Lieut. Riddle, James M., wd Chickamauga.
Sergt. Niles, Ed. E., Qmaster, died at Camden, '62.
Sergt. Dutton, Wm. C., kd Shpsbg.
Sergt. Pegues, Richard H., detailed Tel. Service.
Sergt. *Ryan, David R., (Charleston) wd twice, kd Gettysburg.
Sergt. Gerald, Reuben L., kd Chickamauga.
Sergt. Nettles, Hiram, wd Shpsbg, Deep Bottom.
Sergt. Hodgson, Henry F., wd Morris Island, lost arm.
Sergt. McKagen, Henry G., mort. wd Fredsbg.
Sergt. Small, Robt. F., mort. wd Gettysburg.
Sergt. Niles, Ario, transf to Cavalry.
Corpl. Boswell, Jas. P., transf to Co. G., Pal. Bat., Art.
Corpl. Perry, John A., dischd, ill health.
Corpl. Honnet, Benj., dschd, ill health.
Corpl. Devine, Frank G., kd Chickamauga.
Corpl. Gardner, E. T., wd Gettysburg, kd Spottsylvania.
Corpl. Polk, J. W., kd Gettysburg.

# APPENDIX

*Privates.*

Allen, W. J.
Allen, W. Riley, wd; kd.
Anerum, Thos. J., Sr., dschd.
Arrants, Benj., kd.
Arrants, Jas. R., wd.
Arrants, James H., (cas).
Arrants, Jos. H., kd.
Arrants, Robt. B., wd, kd.
Arrants, Wm. T.
Baer, B. M., dschd.
Baker, Malcolm L., kd.
Banks, T. (cas).
Barnes, J. Burgess, deserted.
Barnes, Sam'l Y.
Barnes, H. A., (cas).
Barrett, Edward, kd. 1st Manas.
Baum, Marcus, pro. Ker. staff, kd.
Bass, Eli (cas).
Beaver, John R., deserted.
Bowen, Anderson, dschd '62.
Bowen, Wm., d at Rchmd.
Boykin, James F., dschg, ill.
Brasington, Jas. F., (cas).
Brasington, John F., wd.
Browne, J. J. (cas).
Brown, James R., wd.
Brown, John S., d in Va.
Buchanan, Wm. L.
Burchfield, Ed. C., wd, trf.
*Chrestona, R. D., (cas).
Campbell, Alexr, d in Va.
Caston, G. W. (cas).
Coker, Reuben, wd.
Cook, James, d in Va.
Cook, John.
Cook, Joseph, d in Va.
Cook, Mathew, d in Va.
Cooper, John C., kd Shpsbg.
Cooper, J. D., kd Shpsbg.
*Crenshaw, W. J., wd.
Craft, J., wd, kd Ptrbg.
Craft, R., (cas).
Crump, T. M., dschd '62.
Cunningham, J. S., pr. Sergt.
Cusick, Patrick.
David, H. L. (cas).
Davis, John T., trf '61.
Dawkins, W. B. (cas).
DeBruhl, Benj., dschd, ill health.
DeLoach, Jas. R., dschd, joined Cav.
Dunlap, Chas. J., Med. Dept.
Dunlap, E. B., Q. M. Dept.
Durant, James A., d in Va.

Dutton, Benj. Z.
Easton, B. B. (cas).
Elkins, E., d at Rchmd.
Evans, Geo., kd Mal. H.
Evans, D. A., d in hosp.
*Fain, A. W., (Va.) (cas).
*Fain, J. T. (Va) (cas).
Ford, A.
Francis, John H., wd 1st Man.
Freeman, James, cut foot.
Freeman, Mathew, wd.
Fullerton, Geo. F., d in Va.
Gardner, Tim B., mort. wd.
Gerald, L. C. (cas).
Gibson, H. B., wd, lost leg.
Goens, E.
Graham, D., wd.
Graham John T.
Groom, John (cas).
Haile, Jas. L., trf Kirk. Ran.
Harrison, Benny.
Heath, B. D., wd.
Hinson, John E., wd.
Howell, M. (cas).
Jeffers, Lewis, d in Va.
Jackson, J. (cas).
Jinks, E. W., d in Va.
Johnson, W. E., trf Kirk Ran.
Jones, J. W.
Kelley, B. E., d in Va.
Kelley, D. H., wd.
*Kendrick, James, dschd.
King, Geo., d in Va.
Kirkland, R. R., trf Co. G.
Kirkley, Robt., prls Ft. Del.
Lawrence, J. H., wd.
LeGrand, L. (cas).
LeGrand, James M., wd.
Leitner, Benj. F., mort. wd.
Lemmond, M. L., wd.
Love, Lawrence W., kd.
Love, Wm., kd.
Maddox, Tom, d in Va.
Marsh, L. C. d in hosp.
Martin, W. (cas).
*Meares, S. B. (N. C.).
Mickle, J. P., dschd.
Middleton, David J., d hosp.
*Miller, J. A., d in Va.
Moore, Levi, d in Va.
Morrison, M. W., dschd '62.
Moseley, Levi (cas).
Munroe, Alexr., wd.

# APPENDIX

Munroe, Geo., fat. wd.
Munroe, James, d in hosp.
Munroe, John, wd.
Murchison, Alex. A., d in hosp.
McCain, S. H. (cas).
McCown, John.
McDaniel, J. B., d in Va.
McIntosh, T. R., dschd '62.
McKain, Wm., dschd '62.
McKagen, J. W. P., dschd '62.
McRae, Duncan, wd.
McMillan, Joel A., deserted.
Nelson, Geo., d in hosp.
Nettles, Jesse, kd 1st Man.
Nettles, Joseph E., wd, lost leg.
Nettles, Wm. A., pro. Corpl.
Onsted, T. M. (cas).
Outlaw, R (cas).
Parker, A. (cas).
Parker, G. (cas).
Peeples, L. W. (cas).
Pegues, Claudius J.
*Pennington, R. A.
Perry, J. A., dschd.
Phillips, R., wd.
Pickett, John R.
*Pierson, P. J., wd.
Pope, Thos. W., wd.
*Prescott, P. B. (cas).
Pritchard, David, trf Co. A.
Proctor, Robt. W., wd.
*Rembert, Thos. M., trf.
Robinson, R. A. (cas).
*Ryan, P. H., wd.
*Scarborough, H. G.
*Scarborough, L. W.
Scott, W. A.
Smith, Geo., wd, lost leg.
Smith, John, dschd '62.
Smyrl, James K., d in Va.
Stewart, W. M. (cas).
Stokes, Wesley, dschd '62.
Strawbridge, B. R.
Team, John W., d in Va.
Tidwell, David W., wd.
Truesdale, W. M. (cas).
Turner, Wm., d in Va.
Vaughan, Lewis, d in Va.
Warren, James O., d in Va.
Watkins, H (cas).
Watts, Wm. W.
Watts, D. (cas).
Watts, Dan'l (cas).
Watts, L. (cas).
Watts, W. R. (cas).
Wells, David E., kd.
Welsh, H. L.
Wethersbee, J. Alfred.
Wethersbee, Thos. C., d in Va.
Wilson, Roland R., dschd '62.
Wilson, J. S., dschd '62.
Wilson, T. R.
*Winder, J. R. (Va.).
Witherspoon, Jas. M., kd.
Wood, J. M., tr. to Cav.
Wood, John J.
Wood, Pinckney E.
Wright, W. H., d in Va.

[Total enrolled 198; from Kershaw County 186; killed or mort. wd. 24; wounded 48; died in service 31; total casualties 103. This company roll contains many names of those who served not more than thirty days, casuals marked (cas). From total membership must be deducted about 66 names, leaving only about 132 effectives. Sergt. Hiram Nettles still in 1926 surviving age 89, was of great assistance in revising this roll. He served throughout the war, was twice seriously wounded, and knew nearly every man in the company. He witnessed the act of Richard Kirkland in crossing the wall at Fredericksburg. While Capt. Leitner lay wounded on the field of Gettysburg, where he lost his leg above the knee, his friend Thos. W. Salmond, Surgeon of the Regiment went to him under the heaviest fire and took him to the camp hospital on his horse.]

## FLAT ROCK GUARDS.
### Company G., 2nd South Carolina Volunteers.
[Names marked * not from Kershaw County.]

Capt. Haile, Columbus Cureton.
Capt. Cunningham, Jos. P., kd Gettysburg.
Capt. Truesdel, Jesse E., wd Gettysburg, srrd Grsboro.

# APPENDIX

Lieut. Clyburn, Thos. J., d of disease Fairfax.
Lieut. Cantey, Thos. R., tr to Co. F., 7th Bat.
Lieut. Patterson, Wm. W., wd Sharpsburg, srrd Grsboro.
Lieut. Jones, Wm. J., resigned, ill health.
Lieut. Benton, Sam'l J., wd Gettbg, Fishers Hill, pro. Capt. Co. K., Br. Gds.
Sergt. Kirkland, Richard Rowland, kd Chickamauga.
Sergt. Murchison, Julius J., wd Wilderness.
Sergt. Cauthen, James T., tr to Co. G., Pal. Bat. Art.
Sergt. Cauthen, Andrew J., d of disease at home.
Sergt. Jones, Burwell N., wd 1st Man., tr to Cav.
Sergt. *Blackmon, Benj. J., (Lan.) wd Wilderness, srrd Grbro.
Sergt. McDowell, J. E. C., wd several times, srrd Grbro.
Sergt. Sowell, John A., wd Gettybg, srrd Gbro.
Sergt. Patterson, Reuben B., wd 1st Man., Gettybg, srrd Grbro.
Sergt. West, Sam'l, wd Cold Harbor, srrd Grbro.
Sergt. West, Thos. G., wd Gettysburg, srrd Grbro.
Sergt. Dixon, Sam'l L., served through war, srrd Grbro.
Corpl. West, Wm. S., died disease Bull Run.
Corpl. Coats, Sam'l W., d of dis. Bull Run.
Corpl. Williams, Richard H., wd 1st Man., tr to 4th Regt.

*Privates.*

Alexander, J H. R.
Baskin, C. Edward, d of disease
Baskin, John C., Sr.
Baskin, John C., Jr., kd.
Baskin, Robt. C., tr to Cav.
*Belk, J. M., d in hosp.
Bird, W. L., d of wd.
*Blackmon, J. C., kd.
Blackmon, W. M., wd 2 t, srd.
Blackwell, John A., d in Va.
Boone, James M., wd.
Boone, John, wd, captd.
Boone, Wm., wd 2 t.
Bowers, Geo. M., kd.
Bruce, Jas. H., d in Va.
Catoe, A. D., d in hosp.
Chaney, B., dschd.
*Clark, J. W. (Lan.).
Coats, Gabriel H., srrd.
Coats, Henry J., d in Va.
*Coon, S. C., mort. wd.
*Cook, J. E. (Lan.).
Cook, T., wd, srrd.
Copeland, W. M., tr to Cav.
Crawford, Sam'l H.
*Croxton, J. Q., mort. wd.
Davis, Dyson, wd, srrd.
Davis, H. G.
Deas, Henry.
Dixon, Bailey S., d in Va.
Dixon, G. L., dschd (Co. D. 7th B.).
Downs, And. J., srrd.

Dunn, W. J., wd 3 t, d in Va.
*Faile, John, dschd.
Falkenberry, John, wd.
Falkenberry, Wylie J., d in Va.
Falkenberry, Jos. W., kd.
Fletcher, David G., kd.
Fletcher, Wm. J., wd.
Gardner, Robt. C., mort. wd 1st Man.
Gaskin, Dan'l, miss. Winchtr.
Gaskin, John, kd.
Gaskin, J. B., dschd '62.
Graham, Jackson, d in Va.
Gray, Wm., srrd.
Haile, G. W., Miss. Wnchtr.
Hall, John B., wd, captd.
Holley, Joel, kd Bean Sta.
Honey, Elias.
Honey, Stephen D., d in Va.
Hough, Joel, wd, pris, exchd.
Hough, Nath., pris.
Hough, Wilson C., wd, srrd.
Hunter, W. J., srrd.
Johnson, Arch. A., dschd.
Johnson, W. M., tr to Cav.
Johnson, Witty, kd.
Jones, Sam. D., musician, kd 1st M.
Kelley, Mansel P., tr to Cav.
Kirby, John, wd.
Kirkley, Dan'l M., wd.
Knight, J. Allen, d in Va.
Knight, W. A., kd Knoxv.
Love, McDuffie Rutledge, kd.

# APPENDIX

*Mahaffey, Oliver C.
Mahaffey, Wm., wd.
Marshall, J. S., dschd '62.
Marshall, W. D., d in Va.
Martin, John S., wd.
Martin, Wm. H., srrd.
Mason, L. R., wd.
Mason, T. E., miss. Wnchstr.
Moseley, Craddock, kd.
Moseley, Frank, kd Knoxv.
*McKay, Henry C., dschd.
McLure, John, captd Gettybg.
*McManus, Amos W., srrd.
Nelson, Thos. J., tr to Cav.
Parker, B., wd, lost leg.
Peach, Wm., srrd.
Perry, Thos. J., d in service.
Phillips, W. T., wd.
Powers, W. T., kd Chickamauga.
Raley, Benj., wd.
Raley, Reddick, tr 7th Bat.
*Raysor, J. C., tr to Art.
Ray, Duncan, dschd.
Reaves, David R., dschd.
Robertson, Levi D., wd, captd.
Robinson, E. H., mort. wd.

Roe, John, wd, captd.
Sheorn, James, kd Sav. Sta.
Sheorn, Morris D., d in Va.
*Small, A. J., wd.
Stover, David G., kd Sav. St.
Suggs, Wm., died in service.
Sutton, E.
Taylor, W. L., died in service.
Trantham, W. D., dschd, youth.
Truesdel, Burwell, kd.
Truesdel, Jas. T., kd Shpsbg.
Truesdel, H., dschd.
Truesdel, Wm. J., kd.
Truesdel, Wm. M., wd on R. R.
West, Joseph A., tr to Art.
West, Wm. M., mort. wd.
Whitehead, S., miss in Tenn.
Williams, C. D., mort. wd.
Williams, John, wd, captd.
Williams, John N., mort. wd.
Wilkerson, J., miss Wchstr.
Young, Chas. P., srrd.
Young, Geo. W., dschd.
Young, Judson N., tr to Cav.
Young, Wm. C., tr to Cav.
Young, Wm. J., kd Malv. H.

[Total enrollment 139; from Kershaw County 114; killed or mortally wounded 31; wounded 43; died in service 20; total casualties 93. This company derived its name from its home headquarters at the Granite Hill known as "Flat Rock". Capt. Haile once showed us a pipe he framed from the clay of the "Crater" at Petersburg where he commanded a company of the 23rd Regiment, which was posted on the very edge of this great explosion. Sergt. Murchison cut and wore a pair of cuff buttons from a fragment of his own skull.]

## KERSHAW GUARDS.
### Company D., 15th Regiment Infantry.
[Names marked * not from Kershaw County.]

Capt. Warren, Thos. J., kd Gettysburg.
Capt. Burns, C. Benton.
Lieut. Davis, James M., wd Sharpsbg, Gettysbg, pro. Adjt.
Lieut. Lyles, James V., resigned, ill health.
Lieut. Kirkley, Dan'l C., wd Chickamauga, lost leg.
Lieut. Schrock, Joel A., resigned 1863.
Lieut. Crosby, George, wd Gettysburg.
Lieut. Fisher, Chas. A., wd 2nd Man., mort. wd Sharpsburg.
Sergt. Somers, Adolph, drowned Charleston Harbor.
Sergt. Huckabee, Jos. J., wd Gettysburg, Wilderness.
Sergt. Davis, John J.
Corpl. Springer, Rudolph.
Corpl. Stewman, P. A. H., d in camp.
Corpl. Wolfe, Eugene.
Corpl. Young, John W., wd in Virginia.

# APPENDIX

*Privates.*

Ammons, H.
Ammons, W. W.
Bradley, John, wd.
Brannon, David, captd Gettybg.
Brannon, John, kd Val. Va.
Brannon, Robt., d in Va.
Brannon, Wm. Sr., wd.
Brannon, Wm., Jr., wd.
Brown, Wm., wd, kd Spotsv.
Capell, J. B., miss. Bboro.
Capell, S. B., d hosp. Cola.
Capell, W H., wd B'boro.
Collier, Fred. J.
Corbett, H. F., d hosp. Cola.
Corbett, J. C., kd Gettybg.
Creighton, F. E., dschd '64.
Creighton, H. L.
Ervin, John, wd.
Ervin, Sam'l.
Falkenberry, John, dschd.
Fletcher, David G., miss. Bbro.
Ford, E. J., deserted.
Fulghum, James, dschd.
Gardner, Jas. L., wd.
Gardner, Lewis, wd.
*Gayman, John B., deserted.
Graham, Wm., dschd.
Griffin, Stephen, wd Gettybg.
Hall, Russell, Jr.
Harrall, James, d in Va. '62.
Harrall, John, d Camden '62.
Hays, Emanuel.
Hays, James, deserted.
Hays, Joseph, wd Spttsv.
Hinson, John, Sr., dschd.
Hinson, John, Jr., d Cola. '62.
Hornsby, Joseph.
Hornsby, S. Wyatt, wd, kd Wild.
Hornsby, Sam'l, mort. wd Shpsbg.
Hough, Hollis, dschd.
Hunter, A. A., insane on march.
Jackson, Douglas.
Johnson, Benj. F., wd.
Johnson, W. B.
Jordan, D., mort. wd Bnsbro.
Jordan, W. H., d in Va.
Kelley, B. P., kd Val. Va. '64.
Kemp, Tira, d hosp. '61.
Kemp, Warren.
Kirby, Absolom, wd 2 t.
Kirby, J. W., wd, captd Gtbg.
McCallum, Hugh, Chaplain.
McGuire, Henry.
McInnes, N. H., kd Chick. or Ptrsbg.
McLeod, Norman A., mort. wd.
Marsh, Gates, kd near Rich.
Marsh, James, dschd.
Mattox, Geo. W.
Mattox, James, wd.
Mattox, Isaac S., left at Gettysbg.
Mattox, Sam'l, dschd.
Minton, Columbus, kd Gettybg.
Minton, John B., kd Gettybg.
Moneyham, John, wd.
Morris, John.
Munn, Angus J., (Corpl.) wd.
Outlaw, John E., wd.
Parker, Benj. B., d in camp.
Parker, Redding, d in Va.
Parker, Wm. E., drummer.
Ray, James, d '62.
Richbourg, John J., d '62.
Scott, Hasting, wd.
Scott, Manning, wd.
Shaylor, C. H., wd.
Shaylor, T. S., left sick on march.
Shedd, J. P., wd, kd Spttsv.
Shiver, Joseph, d in Va. '63.
Smith, Jesse W., dschd.
Spradley, John, kd Wldness.
Spradley, W. James, wd miss. Shpsbg
Turner, John F., capt Knville.
Hasseln, Adolph von, deserted.
Waddell, N. T., left sick on march.
Ward, John.
Warren, Wm., mort. wd 2nd Man.
Watson, W. W., miss. Bnboro.
Watts, Columbus, miss Blbro.
Watts, Frank, wd, kd Getbg.
Watts, John.
Williams, A. W.
Williams, B. Frank.
Wilson, Henry.
Wilson, Joel.
Wilson, Paul H., wd.
Workman, W. H. R., dschd.
Yates, Sam'l, wd.
Yates, Willis, kd.

[Total in Company 113, all save one from Kershaw County. Deducting 26 discharged, captured and deserted leaves 87 total effectives. Casualties: killed 18, wounded 35, died in service 15; total casualties 68.

# APPENDIX

Mention of Capt. T. J. Warren, who was killed at Gettysburg will be found in other parts of this work. Mr. John F. Turner of this Company revised this roll with us very carefully.]

## KERSHAW TROOP.
### Company C., 6th Regiment, South Carolina Infantry.
[Names marked * not from Kershaw County.]

Capt. Cantey, E. B., wd Sharpsburg, pro. Major.
Capt. Cantey, R. M., wd 2nd Manassas
Lieut. DeSaussure, Henry W., kd Frayser's Farm.
Lieut. Brevard, Alfred, wd Frayser's Farm.
Sergt. Moore, Albertus A., Asst. Surg. 5th S. C. Regt.
Sergt. Whitaker, Thomas, kd Ft. Harrison, Va.
Sergt. Doby, John, wd Boonesboro, srr.
Sergt. Kennedy, Walter, tr. to Co. H. 7th Cav.
Corpl. Hough Wm., kd Frayser's Farm.
Corpl. McLeod, Jno. A., wd Shpsbg, Wilderness, Ptrsbrg, srrd.
Corpl. Yarborough, J. H., died Germantown, Va.
Corpl. McLeod, Thos. A., wd Spottsylvania.

*Privates.*

*Adams, Jesse R., tr. to Cav. (Rich.).
Albert, John C., dschd.
Allen, Thomas, kd.
Allen, Wm. J. wd 2 t, pro. Corp.
Ammons, Thos., d in Va.
Arrants, Jno. B., wd, pro. Corp.
Arrants, W. Johannes, wd.
Atkinson, E., dschd.
Banks, Thos., deserted.
Barfield, David, dschd.
Barnes, H. A., kd.
*Barwick, Robt. T., kd.
*Barwick, Robt. T., kd (Rich.).
Bass, E., d in hosp. Va.
Bass, W. J. C., wagonner.
Baum, Marcus, trf Co. E., 2nd Reg.
*Bedon, Josiah, wd, trf Cav. (Col.).
Bell, M. J., d camp in Va.
*Belvia, John W., d hosp Va. (Sum.).
*Blackwell, C. (Sptbg.).
Brown, J. J., wd.
Cahoon, Geo., d in Va.
Capell, W. H., trt Co. D., 15th.
Caston, B. B., dschd.
Caston, G W., wd.
Christmas, R. L., dschd.
Cook, W. L., wd.
*Cotton, Joab, wd.
Croft, Robt., see Co. G., P. Bat. A.
David, H. L., d in hosp Va.
Dean, Geo. A., dschd.

DeSaussure, J. M., tr. to Co. K. 7th Cav.
Dunn, Stephen, tr. to Co. G., Pal. Bat. A.
Dunlap, Frank, d camp Va.
*Evans, O., tr. to 9th Regt.
Fields, Alexr., wd, srr.
*Fields, Elijah, kd (Darl.).
*Fincher, C., dschd (Nor. Car.).
Folsom, J. B., dschd.
Ford, J. F., d hosp Va.
*Freeman, Jacob, deserted.
Galloway, John, deserted.
Galloway, J. E., deserted.
Gerald, Lewis, wd, srrd.
Groom, John, dschd.
Hinson, Frank, shoemaker.
Hinson, Isham, wd.
Hinson, Joshua, d in camp.
Holley, Geo. W., deserted.
Hough, Benj., wd.
Huckabee, M. G., tr. to Co. K., 7th Cav.
Jackson, Geo., captured.
Jackson, John, wd.
Jackson, Ransom, d hosp Va.
Jeffers, Osborne, wd, deserted.
*Justice, Thos. M., wd (Nor. Car.).
Knight, Wm. A., tr. to 5th Regt.
LeGrand, Lucius, d hosp Va.
*Linder, L., trt 9th Regt.
Lovett, W. J., wd 2 t.
Mahaffey, John, wd, srr.
Mahaffey, Wm. K., trt 9th Regt.

459

# Appendix

*Marco, M., srr (Darl.).
Mathis, Wesley, wd 2 t.
Maurice, J. Jr., dschd.
Maurice, Sidney, deserted.
Mickle, J. P., trt Co. K., 7th Cav.
Moseley, L., d in camp.
Moore, David.
Motley, J. J., wd.
Motley, Sam'l, dschd.
*Moye, W. L., dschd (Rich.).
*McCall, H. M., dschd (Sptbg.).
McDaniel, Isaac, d hosp Va.
McDaniel, T.
McDaniel, ———
McInnes, Nich. H., kd.
McKain, Hugh R., wd.
McKain, Jas. W., d hosp Va.
McKain, Sam'l H., missing.
McKenzie, J. B.
McKenzie, J. D.
Nicholson, Sam'l, dschd.
Oursel, J., wd.
*Oxendine, Rich'd, kd.
Parker, A., d hosp Va.
Parker, G.
Peebles, Lewis H., srr.
Phillips, R., wd.
*Pitman, Rich'd, wd.
Prescott, J. B., dschd.
Rabon, W., wd.
*Richbourg, Ellis, (Rich.).
*Richbourg, Fletcher, wd (Rich.).
*Richbourg, Wash (Rich.).
*Robins, J. F., trt 9th Regt. (Sptbg.).
*Robinson, B. E., d in hosp.
Rogers, M., dschd.
*Russell, J., trt 9th Regt. (Sptbg.).
Scott, A., tr to Co.
*Seay, Robt., wd 2 t pr. Sergt.
Sessions, John, srr.
Shaylor, John O., dschd.
Sheorn, A. C., wd.
Sheorn, A. F., trt Regt.
Shiver, Joseph, trt Co. D., 15th Regt.
Shiver, Z.
Smith, David R., dschd.
Stewart, C. J., wd 2 t.
Stewart, N.
Stewart, Rich'd, wd.
Stokes, F. Marion, kd.
Stokes, Isaac, wd.
Stokes, R. K., srr.
Stroud, John, dschd.
Stuckey, Chris. C., kd.
Thomasson, Wm., srr.
Tidwell, Thos., d hosp Va.
Truesdale, Wm., dschd.
Warren, Henry, wd.
Watkins, Thos., dschd.
Watts, Adam, wd.
Watts, Dan'l, dschd.
Watts, David, dschd.
Watts, Levi, wd.
Watts, Lewis M., captured.
Watts, Owen, dschd.
Watts, Wm. R., deserted.
Westberry, J. P., wd.
*Williams, G. W.
Wittkowsky, Adolph, wd.
*Zimmerman, J. W., trt 9th Regt.

[Total enrollment 144; from Kershaw County 117; deduct for transfers, discharged, etc., 52, leaving 91 effectives; killed 11; wounded 48; died in service 18; total casualties 77. This company at the beginning of the war was a Cavalry troop. It volunteered promptly as infantry, retaining its long standing name. At Sharpsburg, Capt. E. B. Cantey was wounded through both thighs and could not walk for two years. At Seven Pines the company went into action with 31 men, losing 17 killed and wounded.]

## Lucas Guards.

### Company A., 7th Battalion.

[Names marked * not from Kershaw County.]

Capt. L. W. R. Blair, pro. Major, resigned ill health.
Capt. Lucas, Benj. S, wd Cold Harbor, lost arm
Lieut. McCaskill, Finley, kd Petersburg.
Lieut. Gardner, J. W., surrendered Grboro.
Lieut. McCaskill, Allen, wd Petersburg.
Lieut. Hough, Moses, wd Petersburg, srrd Grbro.

# APPENDIX

Sergt. Hargreaves, J. E.
Sergt. Newman, B. S., wd Petersburg, srrd Grboro.
Sergt. Burns, Isaac W., mort wd Petersburg.
Sergt. Outlaw, M. J., wd Drewrys Bluff, Bentonville.
Sergt. Outlaw, B. F., wd Cold Harbor, surrendered Grbro.
Sergt. Bethune, Dan'l M., wd Dr. Bluff, Ptrsbrg.
Sergt. Clyburn, John H., surrendered Grsboro.
Corpl. McLaurin, Dan'l M., wd Cold Harbor, srrd Grbro.
Corpl. Pitts, J. C., wd Cold Harbor, srrd Grboro.
Corpl. Campbell, John, d Adams Run.
Corpl. Yarborough, W. A.
Corpl. McLaurin, J. A.
Corpl. Atkinson, W. H., color br., kd Drewrys Bluff.

*Privates.*

Allen, Elias, dschd.
Allen, W. A., wd, srrd Grbro.
Allen, W. W., mort wd.
Anderson, John.
Atkinson, J. J., d Bentonville.
Bateman, W. J. T., srrd Grbro.
Beasley, S., dschd.
Berry, J. W., mort wd.
Bethune, Neil A., srrd Grbro.
Blackwell, M. T., kd.
Blackwell, T. J., srrd Grbro.
Blackwell, Uriah A., wd, cptd.
Bone, J. W., d in Va.
Brannon, Elias, wd.
Brannon, J. E., d in Va.
Cameron, W. J., srrd Grboro.
Clyburn, J. Henry, wd, lost arm.
Clyburn, W. A., wd, srrd Grbro.
Copeland, Moses.
Daniels, W. N., tr to 20th Rgt.
DeBruhl, Jesse, kd.
Douglas, Ed., captd on picket.
Douglas, James, captd on picket.
Evans, T. P.
Gardner, Sam'l T., srrd Grbro.
Hall, Chapman L., srrd Grbro.
Hall, Finley, d in service.
Hall, J. Melvin, srrd Grbro.
Hall, John J., kd.
Hall, L. M. C., d Adams Run.
Hammeslaugh, S., srrd Gbro.
*Harris, A. T. (Dar.), captd.
Horton, Ransom, dschd '62.
Hough, Amos, srrd Gbro.
Hyatt, C. W. H., wd, captd.
Hyatt, J. W., srrd Grbro.
Johnson, Noel, d 1862.
Jones, Calvin, dschd '61.
Jordan, Colin, d in Va.

King, G. B., srrd Grbro.
King, J. E., dschd.
Leach, John, d Adams Run.
Lucas, S. D., srrd Grbro.
Marshall, A. C., srrd Grbro.
McCaskill, J. D., wd.
McLaurin, Angus, kd.
McPherson, L. B., wd, srrd Gbro.
Mixon, J. S., mort wd.
Mixon, L. S., d Adams R.
Moseley, Isaac, wd, captd.
Moseley, Reddick, wd.
Murchison, D. P. C., srrd Gbro.
Newman, Nelson, srrd Gbro.
Nichols, Isaac, mort wd.
Norris, A. C., d Adams R.
Norris, Geo., d in Va.
Outlaw, Curtis, dschd '62.
Parker, Michael, dschd '62.
Randolph, Thos., mort wd .
Randolph, W. F., dschd '62.
Rodgers, J. D., mort wd.
Rodgers, S. C., mort wd.
Rodgers, W. J., wd, srrd Gbro.
Scarborough, B. J., d at Chsn.
Shaw, Wm., dschd, d '62.
Shirley, J. E., srrd Gbro.
Sinclair, James, wd 2 t.
Sinclair, John, srrd Gbro.
Stein, Henry, captd.
Stokes, E. E., served '61 to '65.
Stokes, E. J.
Stokes, Ephraim, dschd '62.
Stokes, Simeon, wd.
Stokes, W. J., mort wd.
Tiller, J. M., wd, srrd Gbro.
Tiller, John, srrd Gbro.
Tiller, W. P. C., dschd '62.
Waters, Thos., wd, srrd Gbro.

# APPENDIX

Watkins, E. M., d in Va.
Watkins, J. A., srrd Gbro.
Watkins, P. H., srrd Gbro.
Watson, James, wd, srrd Gbro.

Webb, Sam'l, kd.
Yarborough, J. C., d in ser.
Yarborough, Wilson, wd, srd Gbro.

[Total membership 104; Kershaw County furnished 103; killed and mort. wounded 15; wounded 31; died in service 15; total casualties 61. Capt. Lucas of this company was greatly idolized by his men and deservedly so. He appeared for the last time at the re-union of the 7th Battalion held at Bethune, in Kershaw County, Oct. 1914. Then past eighty, with the empty sleeve of an arm lost at Cold Harbor, too feeble to walk, he was lifted on the shoulders of his grizzly old comrades—a beautiful and refined old gentleman. This and Company F., composing originally one company, were both named in his honor—Thirty-six members of this company were under twenty-one years of age.]

## KERSHAW GREYS.
### Company D., 7th Battalion.

Capt. Jones, Jno. L., wd, captured Petersburg.
Lieut. Clyburn, Wm. (trfrd to Co. G., 7th Bat.).
Lieut. Young, Eugene A., wd, captured Petersburg.
Lieut. Moseley, R., resigned 1862.
Lieut. Cunningham, Robt. J., wd Richmond.
Sergt. Young, Rich'd W., wd Drewry's Bluff.
Sergt. Malone, Wm. R., never sick or absent.
Sergt. Clyburn, Lewis L. (see Co. G., 7th Bat.).
Sergt. Goodale, John R. (see Co. E., 7th Bat.).
Sergt. Wilson, Thos., served through war.
Sergt. Jones, Wm. J., wd Drewry's Bluff.
Sergt. Cauthen, W. C.
Corpl. Bell, L. C., wd and captd Petersburg.
Corpl. Young, M. J., died Adams Run.
Corpl. Young, G. W., died Petersburg.
Corpl. Lewis, Robt. T., wd Cold Harbor.
Corpl. Twitty, L. M.
Corpl. Young, W. J., wd Petersburg.
Corpl. Sheorn, John A., wd Cold Harbor.
Corpl. Cauthen, Lewis M.

### Privates.

Adams, W., wd, lost leg
Allen, J. W., kd.
Atkinson, R. R.
Bailey, D., wd, d in pris.
Ballard, J. F., wd.
Banks, J. M., kd.
Barnes, G. W.
Bell, J. L., wd.
Billings, C. T., mort wd.
Boone, J. W.
Boone, S., d at Chasn '64.
Boone, Z., wd.
Bruce, J. T., dschd '64.
Brazil, L., transferred.
Brown, J. T.
Brown, T. W.
Bryant, W.
Bullock, G. N., d Chasn '64.
Capell, H., d Mor. Isd.
Carroll, J., d Petrsbg.
Carter, J. F.
Cauthen, J. M., wd, d in pris.
Cauthen, L. M., wd, captd.
Cauthen, W. B., wd, captd.
Clyburn, J. C., d Ptrsbg.
Clyburn, J. N., wd, dschd.
Copeland, D. J.
Copeland, G. B., wd, captd.
Coward, J. H., wd, captd.
Dabney, J. A.

# APPENDIX

Dabney, J. H.
Davis, A. E., d Ptrsbg '64.
Denton, W. C., wd.
Dixon, G. L., wd.
Dunlap, R. M.
Duren, W. R., wd, lost arm.
Elmore, A., served to end.
Elmore, D., served to end.
Falkenberry, J. A.
Farmer, E. J., d Adams R. '62.
Farmer, J. A., d Adams R. '62.
Ferrell, J. R.
Fitzpatrick, T., wd, captd.
Gardner, R. J., d Ptrsbg.
Gardner, W. R.
Gaskins, J. B., wd, captd.
Gaskins, J. G.
Gaskins, R., kd.
Gillrane, M.
Gray, S. F., wd.
Green, J., wd.
Griggs, J.
Henderson, J., kd.
Henderson, W. M., kd.
Herbert, S., wd, captd.
Holland, J. C.
Holland, J. R.
Horton, Thos. C.
Kelley, H., wd, captd.
Kirby, F.
Latta, R.
Lewis, W. H., d Petrsbg.
Marshall, J. C.
McNaughton, W. D., kd.
McNeill, Dan'l.
Meggs, S.
Mickle, J. (youth of 15).
Moseley, C. L.
Moseley, J. C.

Moore, W.
Munn, D. A., dschd.
Munn, D. M., wd.
Outlaw, Richard.
Pate, B. M., captd.
Peach, Dan'l, wd, captd.
Pendergrass, J.
Price, D. K., dschd.
Quinlan, G. M.
Randolph, Hugh.
Ray Neil.
Reaves, David, kd.
Reaves, D. R., wd.
Rider, L. F.
Roe, Absalom, d Chasn.
Rutledge, J. E.
Rutledge, W. F.
Ryan, G. R., wd.
Sanders, P., d Ptrsbg.
Self, Stephen, wd, lost arm.
Self, W. F.
Smith, D. R.
Smith, Wm., Sr.
Smith, W. Jr., wd, drummer.
Smyrl, Thos. J., wd.
Spears, Benj. F., tr G. 7th B.
Stokes, W. C. J., wd, captd.
Stuckey, A.
Sutton, T. G.
Thomas, J. H., wd, lost arm.
Thorne, Jas. R., dschd.
Wall, W.
Warren, J. M.
White, R. J., wd, d Ptrsbg.
Williams, J. B.
Williams, J. N.
Wilson, J.
Young, Archy, d Adams R.
Vincent, Josiah, wd.

[Total membership 128 all of Kershaw County; killed and mortally wounded 8; wounded 40; died in service 17; total casualties 65. Capt. J. L. Jones, of Liberty Hill, was notable not only as a good soldier, but as a comedian. The song he sang on one occasion, at a "penny-reading" in Camden, created the most unbounded merriment.

## *Company E., 7th Battalion.*

[The following names all from Kershaw County.]

Capt. Boykin, Burwell E., resigned 1863.
Lieut. Goodale, John R., wd Petersburg.
Sergt. Fox, Thomas.

*Privates.*

Allen, James A., captured.
Allen, J. P., captured.

Anderson, W. E., captured.
Berry, James J. (Corpl.), kd.

# APPENDIX

Brown, Rich'd C., wd.
Brunson, Bernadotte D.
Chewning, James H.
Deas, Henry, wd.
Gerald, W. C., wd.
Goodale, Joseph, captured.
Leach, Wm. F., kd.

Moore, L. A.
McIntosh, James.
Meyers, Thos. S.
Thompson, John A., d 1863.
Wilson, S. G., captured.
Wilson, John, dschd '64.

[Only those members of the company who were from Kershaw County have been listed, twenty (20) in number. Of these killed 2; wounded 4; died 1, total casualties among Kershaw members 7, aside from captured 5. The total membership was 108, of whom fifty (50) were from Sumter County. Capt. Boykin resigned in 1863 and was succeeded by Capt. Philip P. Gaillard of Sumter.]

## LUCAS RIFLES.
### Company F., 7th Battalion.
[Names marked * not from Kershaw County.]

Capt. Dove Segars, wd Petersburg, surrendered Gbro.
Lieut. *McSween, Wm. (Chesterfield), mort wd Dr. Bluff.
Lieut. Horton, James Erwin, died at Adams Run.
Lieut. Tiller, Henry D., wd Petersburg, surrd Grboro.
Lieut. Raley, Andrew W., wd Petersburg, surrd Grboro.
Lieut. King, Gillam P., wd Dr. Bluff, Petrsbg, surrd Grboro.
Sergt. Gardner, Stephen L., wd Drewry's Bluff.
Sergt. Kelley, James F., surrendered Greensboro.
Sergt. Hough, Sampson, surrendered Greensboro.
Sergt. Pate, Henry, surrendered Greensboro.
Sergt. Phillips, Stephen F., kd Petersburg.
Sergt. McCaskill, James H., wd twice, Petersburg.
Sergt. Gardner, Thos. D., surrendered Greensboro.
Sergt. Sowell, James E., surrendered Greensboro.
Corpl. Turner, Benj. J., kd Petersburg.
Corpl. Folsom, Stephen T., kd Pocotaligo.
Corpl. Dunn, Thos. P., surrendered Greensboro.
Corpl. Horton, James S., surrendered Greensboro.
Corpl. West, Joseph, surrendered Greensboro.
Corpl. Raley, Reddick, surrendered Greensboro.
Corpl. Newman, John T., surrendered Greensboro.

### Privates.

Barnes, Reddin E., wd, kd.
Barnes, Wm., srrd Gbro.
*Bell, Robt. J., wd, srrd Gbro.
*Bennin, Neil J., srrd Gbro.
*Blackwell, Geo. P., srrd Gbro.
Boone, Jas. E., srrd Grbo.
Boone, Wm. W., wd.
*Bruce, James, mort wd.
*Campbell, Benj., srrd Gbro.
*Campbell, James, srrd Gbro.
Cantey, Thos. R., srrd Gbro.
*Caston, John W., d in serv.
*Catoe, James, srrd Gbro.
*Catoe, Wm.
*Catoe, Wm. T., d Chasn.
*Clanton, Lovick, wd, sr Gbro.
Copeland, Thos. R., srrd Gbro.
*Culpepper, John H., srrd Gbro.
*Davis, Thos. R., srrd Gbro.
*Dickson, Jesse, srrd Gbro.
*Elliott, Wm., srrd Gbro.
Folsom, John J., wd.
Folsom, Wm. Wesley, srrd Gbro.
Gardner, D. Whitfield, srrd Gbro.
*Gardner, Milus, tr 22nd Regt.
Gardner, Wm. J., wd.

# Appendix

*Gee, W. N., srrd Gbro.
*Gibson, Nath. W., srrd Gbro.
*Hagood, Jesse M., wd, kd.
Hall, Jacob Riley, wd, srrd Gbro.
*Hall, James, kd Pocot.
Hall, James E., kd Dr. B.
Hall, Francis, wd.
Hall, Wm. Ellison, wd, srrd Gbro.
*Herron, Sam'l S., kd.
*Herron, James E., wd.
*Holland, James, srrd Gbro.
*Holland, Thos., srrd Gbro.
Holland, Thos. R., wd Dr. B.
*Holleyman, Geo. W.
*Hollis, Hiram, srrd Gbro.
*Hopkins, James, wd, srrd Gbro.
*Hopkins, Lucius, kd.
*Hopkins, Malcolm, wd, srrd Gbro.
*Hornsby, Jesse, d in Va.
*Horton, Jas. W., wd.
*Horton, Ransom, kd.
*Horton, Thos. R., srrd Gbro.
*Hough, I. S., wd, srrd Gbro.
Hough, Laban C., wd 2 t, srrd Gbro.
*Ingram, Moody, d in Va.
*Jamison, C. Alex., wd.
*Jones, John T., srrd Gbro.
Jones, Nath. W., wd, srrd Gbro.
*Jones, Sam. N., srrd Gbro.
*Kennington, G. W., wd, srrd Gbro.
King, Geo., wd, srrd Gbro.
McCaskill, Chas. W. W., srrd Gbro.
*McCaskill, Wm. P., sr Gbro.
McCoy, Benj., srrd Gbro.
McGougan, Angus, wd, srd Gbro.
McGougan, Arch., mort wd.
McGougan, John, mort wd.
McLendon, Elias, wd, srd Gbro.
McLendon, Gillis, wd, srd Gbro.
McLendon, Wm., wd, d in Va.
*Miller, R. Peel, srrd Gbro.
Moseley, Milberry.
Munn, Henry J., wd, srd Gbro.
*Newman, Wylie B., wd 2 t, srd Gbro.
Newman, John H., srrd Gbro.
Newman, M. W., d Adams R.
*Newsom, Henry, srrd Gbro.
Norris, Hubert, wd, captd.
Outlaw, Curtis, wd, srd Gbro.
Pace, J. L., d Chsn.
Pate, Chapman, wd, srd Gbro.
Pate, Levi, d in Va.
Phillips, Chas. I., wd, srd Gbro.
Phillips, Geo. W., srd Gbro.
Phillips, Robt. J., srd Gbro.
Phillips, W. Riley, srd Gbro.
Phillips, S. F.
Ratcliff, W. C., wd, srd Gbro.
*Rains, Muses B., wd.
*Raley, Dove, d in Va.
*Raley, Wm., wd, srd Gbro.
*Robinson, Hilton, srd Gbro.
Robinson, James, wd, srd Gbro.
*Scott, Timothy, wd, srd Gbro.
*Searles, Ed. M., wd.
*Shaw, J. Duncan, wd, srd Gbro.
Shumake, Geo. N., d in serv.
Smith, John, srrd Gbro.
*Sowell, Wylie, wd, srd Gbro.
Stokes, C. Spencer, mort wd.
*Stroud, Lilly T., wd.
*Stroud, John, transferred to
Sullivan, Jas., wd, srd Gbro.
*Sutton, J. Fred., srrd Gbro.
*Thompson, Henry, wd, srd Gbro.
*Thompson, Wm. B., srd Gbro.
Thorne, Thos. S., srd Grbro.
*Tiller, Jos. J., srrd Grbro.
Turner, Ben D., srrd Gbro.
Turner, Robt. J., wd.
Warley, B. M.
Ware, Henry L., wd, captd.
*Warren, Wylie, d in Va.
Watkins, Jas J., wd, srd Grbro.
Watkins, Jesse E,. wd, srd Gbro.
Watkins, John E., wd, srd Gbro.
West, Rich'd E., kd.
Williams, Alexr. N., srd Gbro.
*Williams, Jas. E., wd, srd Gbro.
Woodham, J. W., surrd Grbro.
Yarborough, E. N., wd, srd Gbro.
Yarborough, T. G., wd, srd Gbro.
Young, Sam'l, srrd Gbro.

[Total membership 140; Kershaw County furnished 80; killed and mortally wounded 16; wounded 58; died in service 17; total casualties 91. Fifty-eight (58) enlisted when under twenty-one years of age, many but sixteen. Co. A. contributed 56 members to the formation of this company, both being named in honor of Capt. B. S. Lucas.]

# APPENDIX

## MOFFAT RIFLES.
### Company G., 7th Battalion.
[Names marked * from County other than Kershaw.]

Capt. Clyburn, Wm., tr from Co. D., surrendered Grbro.
Lieut. Clyburn, L. L., tr from Co. D., wd Petersburg, srd Grbro.
Lieut. *Sligh, Thos. W. (Fairfield), wd Petrsbrg, captured.
Lieut. *Taylor, W. J. (Richland), wd Drewry's B., srd Gbro.
Sergt. Clyburn, S. C., wd Drewry's Bluff, srd Grbro.
Sergt. *Rabb, James K. (Fairfield), wd Petersbrg, srd Gbro.
Sergt. *Mayrant, J. G. (Richland), mort wd Drewry's Bluff.
Sergt. Smyrl, Thos. J., wd Drewry's Bluff, srd Grbro.
Sergt. *Smith, Joel A. (Fairfield), wd Drewry's Bluff.
Sergt. *Murray, Wm. B. (Fairfield), wd Ptrsbrg, srd Gbro.
Sergt. *Cooper, Pres. (Fairfield), kd Petrsbrg.
Corpl. Spears, B. F. (tr from Co. D.), wd Dr. B., srd Grbro.
Corpl. Daniels, Edmund, captured.
Corpl. *Cooper, W. J. (Fairfield), wd Dr. B., captured.
Corpl. *Horton, Thos. C. (Lancaster), wd, Dr. B. captd.

### Privates.

*Augustine, S., kd, Dr. B.
*Bagley, W. L., kd, Dr. B.
*Baskins, W. D., wd, srd Gbro.
*Bradley, D. F., wd, srd Gbro.
*Broughton, E. L., srd Gbro.
Brown, E. T., kd Dr. B.
*Cooper, P., captd.
*Corder, James A., wd, srd Gbro.
Clyburn, J. N., kd Dr. B.
*Dean, G. A., srd Gbro.
*Dickey, C. A., srd Gbro.
Drakeford, W. H., srd Gbro.
*Fields, R. H., srd Gbro.
*Gardner, C. L., kd Dr. B.
*Gardner, H. N., wd, srd Gbro.
*Gardner, W. R., wd, srd Gbro.
Gaskins, G. W., kd Dr. B.
Gaskins, J. D., srd Gbro.
Gay, C. B., kd Dr. B.
Gillrain, M., wd, srd Gbro.
*Hall, H. H., srd Gbro.
*Hays, James, srd Gbro.
*Henson, Henry, srd Gbro.
Hill, J., mort wd Dr. B.
*Hocott, Rich'd, srd Gbro.
Holland, J., srd Gbro.
Holland, John C., kd Dr. B.
*Honey, Henry, srd Gbro.
*Hornsby, J. D., wd.
*Horton, J. C., srd Gbro.
*Hughes, A. F., wd, srd Gbro.
*Jeffers, Thomas, wd, srd Gbro.
Jones, L. C., wd, srd Gbro.
*Justice, Hilliard, srd Gbro.
Justice, Wm., wd 2 t, srd Gbro.
*King, Benj., srd Gbro.
*King, Edmund, srd Gbro.
Kirby, John, kd Dr. B.
Kirby, T., kd Dr. B.
Latta, Robt., srd Gbro.
*McDowell, A. J., srd Gbro.
McKinnon, L., srd Gbro.
McMullen, A. L., srd Gbro.
McNeill, Henry, kd Dr. B.
Marsh, James, srd Gbro.
Marshall, J. C., srd Gbro.
Martin, Philip, wd, captd.
Martin, Thomas, srrd Gbro.
*Medlin, C., d Chstn '64.
Mickle, Joseph, kd Ptrsbg.
Morris, J. J., srd Gbro.
Motley, Sam'l, wd.
Munn, D. D., d in Va.
Nelson, Columbus, srd Gbro.
Nelson, Francis, srd Gbro.
Outlaw, Bentley, kd Dr. B.
*Outlaw, Rich'd, wd.
*Outlaw, Rozier, srd Gbro.
Peach, Wm., wd.
*Pendergrass, Jos., d burnt boat.
*Perry, John J., kd Dr. B.
Phillips, E. D., wd, captd.
*Price, Thos. N., srd Gbro.
Quinlan, G. W., srd Gbro.
*Rabon, John, srd Gbro.
*Robinson, J. W., srd Gbro.

# Appendix

*Roe, J. W., wd, srd Gbro.
*Ryder, L. F., srd Grbro.
Self, G. W., srd Gbro.
*Smith, Henry, wd.
*Smith, W. L., captd.
Smyrl, J. N., wd, srd Gbro.
Stuckey, Anderson, d Chstn.
Sutton, G., wd, srd Gbro.
Sutton, T., kd Dr. B.
Thorne, J. R., srd Gbro.

Tiller, H. A., w 2 t, captd.
Villepigue, ———, wd, captd.
Ward, Allen, wd.
West, Joseph, kd Dr. B.
Wilkes, Wm., wd, srd Gbro.
Williams, J. B., wd 2 t, captd.
Williams, J. N., kd Dr. Bluff.
*Wilson, James, srd Gbro.
*Wilson, John, mort wd Dr. B.
*Wilson, W. M., wd, srd Gbro.

[Total membership 101; Kershaw County furnished 50; killed 22; wounded 38; died 3; total casualties 63. Of this company 58 surrendered at Greensboro, of whom 21 had been wounded. It suffered terribly at Drewry's Bluff.]

## Wateree Mounted Rifles.
### Company K., 7th Cavalry, Colonel Haskell.
[Names marked * not of Kershaw County.]

Capt. Boykin, Ed. M., wd old church, srd Ap.
Capt. *DuBose, D. St. Pierre, wd old church, srd Ap.
Lieut. Ancrum, Thos. J., orderly, discharged.
Lieut. Cantey, John M., trf to Western army.
Lieut. Whitaker, Duncan M., discharged.
Lieut. Arrants, James W., wd O. church, srd Ap.
Lieut. Johnson, Wm. E., wd O. church, captured.
Lieut. Truesdel, James T., resigned.
Sergt. *Sumter, Sebastian, srd Appomattox.
Sergt. Kirkland, J. P.
Sergt. McCoy, Chapman L., discharged.
Sergt. Boykin, Thos. L., kd Old church.
Sergt. Shannon, Kirkland, wd.
Sergt. Douglas, Robt. B., srd Appomattox.
Sergt. *Covington, B. H., tr to N. C. regt.
Corpl. Boykin, W. Frank, srd Appomattox.
Corpl. Truesdel, Henry T., srd Appomattox.
Corpl. *Allen, John W.
Corpl. *Rembert, Thos. M.

*Privates.*

Alexander, George G.
*Anderson, D. J., d in Va.
*Anderson, G. W., captured.
Arrants, Harmon, d in serv.
Arthur, Jess., captured.
*Atkinson, W. J.,
*Baker, B. J., d in Va.
Baruch, Herman, srd Ap.
Barfield, Sam'l, dschd.
*Beaty, J., kd Atlanta.
*Beckham, Simon, wd.
*Boyle, ———, kd.
Boykin, A. H., Jr.
Brown, Wash., wd.
*Brown, W. C.

*Brown, R. Sebastian.
*Burgess, J.
Campbell, B. J.
Christmas, Wm.
Clyburn, James, dschd.
*Cole, E. C., wd, tr N. C. Cav.
*Cole, J. W., tr N. C. Cav.
Collins, Reuben, captd.
Cook, D. J., d in pris.
Davis, E. W.
Davis, J. R., d in service.
Deas, Lynch H., wd, sr Ap.
Deas, Allen, captd.
DeBruhl, Geo. A., sr Ap.
DeBruhl, Benj.

# Appendix

*Dennis, J. M.
*Dennis, R. E.
DeSaussure, J. M., wd.
Doby, Jos. W., d in pris.
*DuBose, H. T.
*Duncan, D. A.
Duncan, G. W., dschd.
*Dusenberry, L. H., wd.
Elliott, Thomas, captured.
Evans, Moody, srd App.
*Fudge, D. R.
Gamewell, J. M.
*Garner, John, d in Va.
George, Darling J., dschd.
Hall, Shelton B.
*Harris, John.
Hilton, W. Hursh, deserted.
Hilton, S. Leonard, srd App.
Huckabee, Minton G., srd Ap.
Huggins, Frank A., kd.
*Huggins, ———, from Richland.
*Johnson, J. J.
Johnson, Wm. M.
*Jones, R. F., from Laurens.
Jordan, Zebedee, d in Va.
*Jordan, G (Horry Co.).
Kennedy, A. Dalton.
Kirkland, Sam'l R., wd.
*Lark, Cullen (Laurens).
*Lenoir, John J. (Sumter).
Marshall, Wiley S.
*Matheson, Benj. H.
*Myers, G. J., d in pris.
Meyers, Washington, d in serv.
Mickle, John P.
McDowell, W. D., srd App.
*McLeod, Thos. D. (Sumt.).
McMullen, Arch. L.
Nelson, Thos. J., d in pris.

*Nelson, Sam'l E., (Sum.).
*Neuffer, Abe, kd O. ch.
Nunnery, Ben.
Nunnery, Wm. E.
Owen, A. C.
Perry, B. J.
Pickett, John R., srd App.
Ratcliff, B. J., srd App.
Ratcliff, W. H., srd App.
Russell, Wm. F.
Sanders, E. R., srd App.
Sloan, Elam H.
*Springfield, H.
*Stevenson, Jas. E., srd App.
Stokes, Joseph, srd App.
Stokes, Wesley W.
*Stolvey, George (Horry).
*Stolvey, J. M. (Horry).
*Stolvey, W. B. (Horry).
Stover, Jas. L., srd App.
Strother, D. P., srd App.
Team, Wiley W.
Thompson, R.
Thompson, Lewis C., wd sr Ap.
Tryon, Dan'l C.
Turner, Silas B.
Veal, Wm. R.
Watts, Owen W.
Williams, John C. P.
*Wilson, Jos. S. (Sumter).
Woods, P. E., captured.
*Woodberry, James (Marion).
Workman, W. C.
Yarborough, Wilson.
Young, G. G., wd O. ch.
Young, Judson H.
Young, John N.
*Young, Chas. S., kd Deep Run.

[Total enrollment 126; from Kershaw County 82; killed 6; wounded 15; died in service 11; total casualties 32. Surrendered 21. Corpl. Henry Truesdel called the last roll at Appomattox. Capt. E. M. Boykin was promoted Lieut.-Col. His son Thos. L. Boykin was killed at Old Church where this company sustained nearly all its casualties. Col. Boykin's booklet "The Falling Flag" is a graphic sketch of his experience in the war.]

## Kirkwood Rangers.

### Company H., 7th South Carolina Cavalry Regiment.

Capt. W. M. Shannon, resigned 1862.
Capt. James Doby, wd Old Church, pro Major.
Lieut. Ed. M. Boykin, wd Old Church, pro Capt. Co. K.
Lieut. Zack Cantey, resigned 1862.
Lieut. Robert Johnson, resigned 1862.

# APPENDIX

Lieut. Usher P. Bonney, died in prison Johnson Isd.
Lieut. James G. Jones, resigned 1862.
Lieut. James D. Matheson, srd.
Sergt. Thos. J. Ancrum, tr to 2nd S. C. Inf.
Sergt. Chas. J. McDowall, tr to 2nd S. C. Cav.
Sergt. Wm. Johnson, dischd 1862.
Sergt. Chas J. Shannon.
Sergt. Geo. W. Barnes, dischd 1862.
Sergt. Jas. L. Haile, pro 2nd Lieut., srd.
Sergt. Jno. B. Lee, wd Old Church.
Sergt. *James A. McRae, kd White Oak Swamp.
Sergt. N. W. Thames.
Sergt. *John Parker, died of wounds.
Corpl. John Murray, over age, dischd 1862.
Corpl. S. Watt Wardlaw, pro Adjt. Holcomb Legion.
Corpl. William Whitaker, wd Old Church.
Corpl. James B. Cureton, kd Old Church.
Corpl. Daniel Kirkland.
Corpl. H. C. Salmond, wd Old Church.

*Privates.*

Aldrich, T. P., srd.
Arrants, James W.
Adamson, Edward E., srd.
Ancrum, Douglas, tr to 2nd S. C. Cav.
Baskins, Jno. A., srd.
Bonney, Chas. L., srd.
*Bright, Arthur G., srd (Chestfd).
Brannon, Allen.
Brennan, Thos. J., srd.
Brown, Henry R.
Brown, Wm. C.
*Burch, James F. (Chestfd).
*Burch, Tristram (Chestfd).
Capers, John S., kd.
Capers, Sidney W.
Clarke, T. H., wd.
*Charles, R. Kelso (Darlgtn).
Crampton, Z. C., srd.
Cureton, Cunningham B., srd.
Davis, John A., kd.
Davis, John T., wd.
Deas, Henry, tr to 2nd Cav.
Dunlap, Chas. J.
Dye, Wm. R.
Edwards, Scenas B., kd.
Graham, Wm. A.
Griffin, John, srd.
Hancock, Thos. L.
Haile, Chas. E., dischgd.
Haile, Thos. C., srd.
*Hemingway, David (Mississippi).
Hinson, Tilman (Henry), srd.
Hocott, Wm. H.

Hunnicut, J. M., srd.
Jones, Wm. F.
Keith, Thos. J.
Kennedy, Edward, wd.
Kennedy, Walter.
Kinard, A. L. C., srd.
Kirkland, William, srd.
Koon, Lewis, srd.
*Lucas, Francis, tr to 2nd Cav.
Lumpkin, Sam'l B.
*Massey, Austin H., srd (Chstfd).
*Massey, Reuben M., srd.
Matheson, Wm.
Moffatt, James G.
*Mulholland, Jno., wd.
Murphy, Thomas S.
McCaa, John.
McCoy, Robt. E., srd.
McCoy, Wm. W.
McKain, Wm.
*McPriest, Peter (Chestfd).
*McRae, Dan'l (Chestfd).
*McRae, Virgil, d in pris (Chestfd).
Parker, Eli W., wd.
Perkins, Benj., wd, srd.
Perkins, Roger, wd.
Player, John, srd, wd.
Player, Thomas.
*Rivers, David T. (Chestfd).
*Robinson, David (Fairfd).
Rosser, Sam'l A.
*Sanders, Thos. P., wd, srd (Sumter).
*Scott, David B., srd (Ala.).

# APPENDIX

Shannon, Joseph A., srd.
Shannon, Allison E., tr to 2nd Cav.
Shannon, Sam'l D., pro Staff Gen. R. H. Anderson.
*Sanders, John.
Scott, Walter.
*Singleton, Jno. (Rich'd).
Smith, David H., surrd.
Smith, Henry, srrd.
Stokes, Wesley.
Sykes, Wm.
Team, Powell M.
Thompson, John, srd.
Thompson, W. K., surrd.
Turnbull, John, srd, wd.
*Tradewell, James W., wd (Rich'd).
Watts, L. H., srd.
*Watson, Allen, srd (Chtfd).
Watson, L. A., srd.
Whitaker, Duncan, pro Lt.
Whitaker, Wm., wd.
Wilson, Raphael.
Wilson, Sam'l.
Wilson, Elias J.
Wilson, Jesse V.
Williams, John C.
Withers, Anthony G., wd, srd.
Witherspoon, John K., kd.
Wright, John, kd.
Young, John H.

[Total membership 119; Kershaw County furnished 97; killed 8; wounded 13; died 3; total casualties 24; surrendered 33. Nearly all the casualties of this company were suffered at Old Church. Astersks mark those members who were not residents of Kershaw County.]

## BOYKIN RANGERS.
### Company A., 2nd South Carolina Cavalry Regiment.

Capt. A. H. Boykin.
Capt. John Chesnut.
Lieut. J. T. McCaa.
Lieut. R. G. Ellerbe.

Sergt. Thos. L. Boykin.
Corpl. T. J. Ancrum.
Corpl. E. B. Cureton.

*Privates.*

Ancrum, W. A., wd 2 t.
Ancrum, Douglas, d.
Boykin, John, d in pris.
Boykin, Sam'l, pris Ft. Del.
Gerald, E. J.
Harris, J. N.
McDowall, C. J., wd, cap.
McCandless, Leslie, dschd.

Shannon, Allison E., kd.
Shannon, C. J.
Shannon, C. J., Jr.
Shiver, R. C.
Young, G. G., wd.
Whitaker, J. C.
Young, Allen.

[Total number in this company is by our count 128 from all parts of the State, of whom the foregoing 22 were from Kershaw County. This company was originally organized by A. H. Boykin and equipped largely at his expense with shot-guns, Enfield rifles and bowie knives. Capt. Boykin resigned owing to ill health. He was succeeded by the gallant young John Chesnut who died June 15, 1868 at the age of 31.]

## DeSaussure Artillery.
### Company G., Palmetto Battery Light Artillery.

Capt. DePass, W. L.
Lieut. Manget, J. A.
Sergt. Robinson, E. G.
Sergt. Holland, Isaac F.
Sergt. DePass, Jacob W.
Corpl. Boswell, J. P.
Corpl. Parker, John.

Sergt. Bradley, Wiley.
Sergt. DeLoach, W. E.
Corpl. Umphries, B. J.
Corpl. Goff, John.
Corpl. Dunn, A. M.
Bugler. Bowen, C. P.

# APPENDIX

*Privates.*

Arrants, W. J.
Alexander, J. H.
Arthur, John.
Atkinson, Jesse.
Atkinson, Thos.
Barnes, Adville L.
Barnes, Wm.
Barnes, H. A.
Barnes, W. C.
Bordenave, J. N.
Bowen, F.
Bowen, W.
Campbell, J. J.
Capel, John J.
Cauthen, J. C.
Cauthen, J. T.
Cauthen, T. A.
Cauthen, Wm. J.
Croft, J.
Croft, W.
DePass, James P., trf.
Dunn, J. Alfred.
Dunn, Stephen.
Griffin, Stephen.
Gillis, James.
Gillis, John.
Goff, W.
Hayden, Chas.
Holland, John.
Kennedy, D. R.
Langley, James.
Malone, Geo.
Marsh, Alfred.
McCoy, J. A.
McDonald, Elijah.
Moore, Wiley.
Myers, John.
Potee, Richard.
Pearce, B. M.
Rush, S. H.
Tiller, P. W. C.
Twitty, P. B.
Twitty, P. T.
Wilson, Judge.
Williams, R. H.
Williams, R. R.
Wooten, John.
Yates, Jesse L.

[The above 60 members of this Company of Artillery were all of Kershaw County. The names of the others from various parts of the State and quite numerous have been omitted. We could find no record of casualties or special data concerning this company. It served on the Coast of South Carolina during the latter part of the war and did effective service in stemming the invasion especially at Honey Hill. Capt. W. L. DePass was the active organizer of this company, the name of which was given in compliment to Maj. Jno. M. DeSaussure of Camden. Capt. DePass had been wounded at First Manassas while an officer of Co. E., 2nd Regt.]

## Company D., 5th Battalion Reserves.

Capt. John Thompson.
Lieut. Thos. J. Ancrum.
Lieut. T. J. Cauthen.
Sergt. R. B. Cunningham.
Sergt. R. Mickle.
Sergt. R. C. Drakeford.
Sergt. J. G. Bruce.
Sergt. A. Owens.
Corpl. R. McKee.
Corpl. T. L. Dixon.
Corpl. A. J. Falkenberry.
Corpl. J. W. Ford.
Corpl. Wm. Catoe.
Corpl. Angus McLeod.

*Privates.*

Arrants, H.
Atkerson, E.
Baker, Dan'l.
Barfield, David.
Barfield, W. A.
Baker, T. J.
Barnes, Geo.
Barnes, T. H.
Bass, Henry.
Bass, W.
Beaver, W.
Berkett, Thos.
Berry, J. A. W.
Billings, W. M.
Bolger, ———
Boswell L. B.

# Appendix

Bowers, J. T.
Bradley, Wm.
Branham, Wm.
Brannum, Robert.
Brannum, Warren.
Brannum, Wiley.
Brewer, M. N.
Brown, Joel H.
Catoe, Henry.
Christmas, Wm.
Clyburn, James.
Cooper, John.
Cunningham, W. C.
Davis, Alfred.
Dawson, Thos.
Deas, E.
Denton, W. C.
Doby, J. W.
Dowie, R. J.
English, Thos.
English, W. J.
Folsom, S. T.
Gamewell, Jno. N.
Goff, Wm.
Graham, John.
Hale, W. J.
Hamilton, Reuben.
Harrell, E.
Hay, J. Thornwell.
Hays, James.
Hinson, Reuben.
Hocott, R.
Hogan, W. D.
Holland, James.
Holland, Thos.
Holley, John.
Hough, Joel.
Humphries, Nathan.
Humphries, Nathaniel.
James, George.
Johnson, Wm.
Jones, Burwell.
Jones, Calvin.
Jungbluth, F. W.
Justice, John.
Kennington, Levi.
King, Wm.
Kirkland, J. R.
Kirkland, Powell.
Malone, Geo.
Mahaffey, George.
Man, Robert.
Mickle, Thos.
Munn, Henry.

McCaskill, Dan'l.
McCaskill, John.
McCoy, B. F.
McCoy, J. N.
McCreight, B. J.
McDowell, J. A.
McGougan, Dan'l.
McLester, A.
Nelson, Richard.
Newman, Jonathan.
Newman, W. W.
Nichols, W. F.
Norris, George.
Norris, H.
Nunnery, D. F.
Oakes, F. J.
Outlaw, Geo.
Outlaw, Wiley.
Pace, J. R.
Page, Jonathan.
Peake, Thos.
Pearce, B. M.
Perry, D. D.
Pettigrew, Geo.
Phillips, Lewis.
Price, Wm.
Rabon, A.
Rabon, John.
Reynolds, W. J.
Roach, J. J.
Robertson, Wm. K.
Ross, Calvin.
Ross, J. J.
Ross, Wm.
Rush, John.
Sessions, Thos.
Shannon, S. A. B.
Shannon, Thos. E.
Shehan, John.
Shiver, C. I., Jr.
Shiver, Isaac.
Simmons, Jas.
Spradley, John.
Steen, Wilson.
Stokes, Jno. J.
Thomas, R. D.
Thompson, J. S.
Thorn, Henry.
Thorn, Thomas.
Trantham, W. D.
Trapier, B. D.
Truesdel, Zack.
Turner, W. F.
Warren, H. F.

# APPENDIX

Watkins, B. E.  
Watkins, D. A.  
Watkins, Thos.  
Watkins, Wiley.  
West, H. C.  
Weinges, C. M.  
Weinges, Jacob.  
Wilson, Jas.  
Wilson, Joseph.  
Wilson, John W.  
Wilson, W. J.  
Wood, M. D.  
Wood, Wiley.  
Young, John.

[Total listed 152. Many never reported for duty. This company composed in 1864-5 of youths, old men, soldiers furloughed or discharged from active service because of physical infirmity or wounds, performed guard duty as part of the Reserves, commanded by Gen. James Chesnut. It was never in any actual engagement.]

## *Additional Names in Various Commands.*

Thos. W. Salmond, Surgeon 2nd Regt., Kershaw's Brig.
E. J. Meynardie, Chaplain, 2nd Regt., Kershaw's Brig.
James I. Villepigue, Commissary 2nd Regt., Kershaw's Brig.
McCreight, Wm., Co. A., 23rd Regt.
Owens, Archibald, captured, Co. A., 23rd Regt.
Roache, J. J., Co. A., 23rd Regt.
Sill, John H., kd Petersburg, Co. A., 23rd Regt.
Sessions, J. G., Co. D., Hampton Leg.
Bracey, T. W., Co. G., Hampton Leg.
Owens, J. J., Co. G., Hampton Leg.
Smith, J. J., Co. G., Hampton Leg.
Massey, W. R.
Moore, J., wd Wilderness, Co. G., Hampton Leg.
Dye, Henry, kd Reames St., Co. H., 13th Regt.
Robertson, R. D., wd Cold Harbor, Co. C., 2nd Regt.
DeSaussure, Doug. B., Co. C., Regulars.
Gaskins, Benj., Co. G., Regulars.
Meyers, C. R., Co. F., Regulars.
Polson, Abel, Co. E., Regulars.
Yarborough, James M., Co. A., Regulars.
Kirkland, Wm. L., mort wd Hawes Shop, Co. K., 4th Cav.
Sowell, Geo. R., Co. A., 4th Cav.
Withers, W. R., Co. K., 4th Cav.
Bonney, F. L. B., S. C. Mil. Acad. Cadet.
Johnson, W E., S. C. College Cadet.
Kershaw, John, S. C. College Cadet.
King, J. W., S. C. College Cadet.
Villepigue, J. F., S. C. Mil. Acad. Cadet.
Bowen, Anderson, Garden's Battery.
Darby, Frank, Marion Light Art.
Davis, John, Marion Light Art.
Davis, Junius, Marion Light Art.
Honey, Elias, Bachman's Bat.
Lyles, J. Belton, McBeth's Bat.
McNeal, Archibald, Bachman's Bat.
Reeves, John H., Bachman's Bat.
Boykin, John, skirmishing South of Camden 1865.

# APPENDIX

Boykin, B. H., skirmishing South of Camden 1865.
Boykin, E. M., Jr., skirmishing South of Camden 1865.

[Thirty-nine names. Doubtless other names belong in the list, undiscoverable amid the imperfect and confused mass of rolls and military reports not only of this but of other states.]

# INDEX

[Names of private soldiers in Confederate service from Kershaw County, will be found in the Appendix listed by companies alphabetically and have not been repeated in this Index. As the names of officers from, Corporal to Captain head the rolls according to rank and not alphabetically, they have been rearranged in this Index for ready reference.]

Abbott, Henry, 22.
Abernathy, Mr., 37.
Adams, Rev. Thos., 264, 293.
Adams, Wm., 104.
Adamson, Frank, 210, 335.
Adamson, John, 15, 19, 263, 294.
Alden, Geo., 31, 313, 351.
Alexander, Amelia A., 328.
Alexander, G. G., 307, 334.
Alexander, Isaac (I), 18, 263, 293, 294.
Alexander, Mrs. Isaac, 18, 287, 294.
Alexander, I. B., 323.
Allen, Corp. J. W., 467.
Alligators, 103, 322.
Allison, Andrew, 35.
Ancrum, (Thos.) family, 390.
Ancrum, (W. A.) family, 389.
Ancrum, Thos. J., 142, 467.
Ancrum, Wm. (II), 294.
Ancrum, Wm. A., Sr., 143, 389.
Ancrum, Wm. A., Jr., 336.
Anderson, Dr. E. H., 3, 21, 24, 42, 65, 75, 119, 283.
Anderson, (E. H.), family, 358.
Anderson, Col. Richd., 74.
Anderson, Wm., 30, 32.
Anderson, Wm., family, 360.
Antioch, 253.
Ap Dick, Welsh Goat, 338.
Arrants, Lieut. J. W., 467.
Arrants, N. B., 31.
Arsenal, 190.
Arthur, family, 351.
Arthur, Reuben, 260, 294, 335.
Artillery, DeSaussure, 470.
Atkinson, Corp. J. W., 31, 467.
Atkinson, Wm., 23.
Attorneys at Law, 259.
Aurora Borealis, 320.
Bailey, John, 45.

Ballard, John G., 44.
Ballard, Thos., 49.
Baker, Thos., 227.
Banks, 42-44.
Baptist Church, 277-280.
Barillon, C., 20.
Barnes, E., 261.
Barnes, Sergt. Geo. W., 469.
Bartlett, H., 31.
Baruch, Bernard M., 54, 55.
Baruch, family, 448.
Baruch, M., 55.
Baruch, Dr. Simon, 54.
Bascom, Rev. R., 267.
Baskin, A. G., 259.
Baskin, J., 261.
Baskin, Thos., 261.
Battlefield of Camden, 11, 12.
Baum, family, 449.
Baum, Marcus, 182.
Baxley, Neil W., 43.
Beard, Frank P., 307.
Beattie, A J., 334.
Beaumont, H., 259.
Beaver Creek, 320.
Bell, Conway, 167.
Bell, Corp. L. C.
Benton, Lieut. Saml. J., 456.
Bethune, Sergt. D. M., 461.
Bethune, Neal A., 336.
Bineham, Benj., 189, 260, 335.
Birchmore, C. W., 307.
Birchmore, family, 352.
Bissell, family, 352.
Blackmon, Sergt. B. J., 456.
Blair, family, 361.
Blair, Capt. Francis, 63.
Blair, Geo. D., 259.
Blair, Gen. James, 69, 86, 88, 91-99.
Blair, John J., 258, 260.
Blair, Neil, 258.

475

Blair, Maj. L. W. R., 99, 198, 215, 224-226, 242, 257, 307, 460.
Blair, Rochella, 226.
Blakeney, 253, 365, 397.
Blanding, Abram, 20, 23, 74, 79, 100-103, 188, 259, 294, 335.
Blanding, Col. J. D., 106, 259.
Blanding, Dr. Sam'l, 24, 103.
Blanding, Wm., 103, 105.
Blanding, Shubel, 103.
Bonanza Bills, 217.
Bonds, fraudulent, 203, 204.
Bonney, Eli W., 30, 104.
Bonney, F. L., 473.
Bonney, Lieut. U. P., 452, 469.
Boswell, J. P., 261, 453.
Bourne, Aubrey, 270.
Boykin, Adderton, 259.
Boykin, Capt. A. Hamilton, 334, 335, 470.
Boykin, Burwell, 142, 189, 227.
Boykin, Capt. B. E., 463.
Boykin's Depot, 41.
Boykin, E. Miller, 34, 40, 336.
Boykin, Dr. E. M., 78, 206, 467, 468.
Boykin, Elizabeth T., 152.
Boykin, John (Sr.), 20, 50, 52, 85, 86, 283, 335.
Boykin, John (Jr.), 259.
Boykin, Mary, 108.
Boykin's Mill, 174, 328.
Boykin, Monroe, 193, 209, 279.
Boykin, Rangers, 470.
Boykin, Capt. T. L., 159, 452.
Boykin, Sergt. Thos. L., 467.
Boykin, Corp. W. Frank., 467.
Bracey, Lieut. Thos. W., 452.
Bradley, Levi, 128.
Bradley, Sergt. Wiley, 470.
Brantley, Rev. S., 265, 278.
Brasington, Dr. S. F., 10.
Brasington, W. F., 278.
Bread, Sam'l, 294.
Breaker, L. F., 24.
Brevard, Dr. Alfred, 21, 24, 132.
Brevard, Lieut. Alfred, 459.
Brevard, Judge Jos., 92, 100, 108, 189, 259, 260, 263, 335.
Brewer, N. A. F., 30.
Bridges, River, 324-326.
Briggs, Gray, 256.

Brisbane, Adam F., 263.
Bronson, family, 352.
Brown, Dan'l, 227, 259.
Brown, family, 362.
Brown, Jacob, 227, 259.
Browning Home, 276.
Brown, John, 259.
Brown, Shaw, 310.
Bruce, Sergt. J. G., 471.
Bruce, W. R., 336.
Bullard, Chas. A., 104, 105, 259, 301.
Bullard, Royal, 104, 259.
Burdell, John, 54.
Burnet, Dr. A. W., 79, 433.
Burr, Aaron, 24.
Burns, Capt. Benton, 457.
Burns, family, 352.
Burns, Sergt. Isaac W., 461.
Bush, David, 49.
Bush, Dr. Pomeroy, 312.
Cain, Jas., 49.
Camden District, 251.
Camden Chronicle, 301, 307.
Camden Confederate, 306.
Camden Country Club, 47.
Camden Ferry, 324.
Camden Garrisoned, 196.
Camden Journal, 301.
Camden Medical Ass'n, 23.
Camden Volunteers, 453.
Camden Extended, 1.
Canals, 37, 38.
Campbell, Drewry, 23.
Campbell, Corp. John, 461.
Cantey, Maj. E. B., 233, 459, 460.
Cantey, Miss Floride, 168.
Cantey, James, 235.
Cantey, Gen. James, 125, 129, 130, 176, 335.
Cantey, Gen. James W., 50, 120, 143.
Cantey, James Willis, Jr., 127, 130.
Cantey, Maj. John, 47, 141, 145.
Cantey, Lieut. Jno. M., 467.
Cantey, Lieut. R. M., 459.
Cantey, Lieut. Thos. R., 456.
Cantey, Zack, 49, 52, 334.
Cantey, Lieut. Zack, 468.
Capers, family, 363.
Capers, S. E., 260.
Cardozo, Henry, 334.

# INDEX

Carpenter, Dan, 18, 286, 436.
Carpenter, Mrs. Lucy, 103.
Carpetbaggers, 201.
Carlisle, Dr. Jas. H., 27, 273.
Carlisle, W. B., 28, 259.
Carrison, H. G., 10, 34, 43, 395.
Carrison, H. G., Jr., 10.
Carter, Benj., 23, 79, 189.
Carter, Dr. B. W., 24.
Carter, Frank, 334.
Carter, John, 65, 259.
Carter, John C., 259.
Carter, R. W., 50, 180.
Cash, Col. E. B. C., 237-249.
Cash, W. Boggan, 234, 235, 243, 248, 249.
Caston, W. Thurlow, 259, 305.
Catawba Company, 37.
Catholic Society, 262.
Catholic Church, 279-299.
Catoe, Corp. Wm., 471.
Catonnet, Alphonse, 416.
Catonnet, C. Emile, 23.
Cauthen, Sergt. Andrew J., 456.
Cauthen, Corp. Lewis M., 462.
Cauthen, Sergt. Jas. T., 456.
Cauthen, Lieut. T. J., 471.
Cauthen, Sergt. W. C., 462.
Chamberlain, D. H., 203, 206, 209, 221.
Champion, Rich'd, 14.
Champion, R. L., 254, 260, 314.
Charlotte Thompson School, 13, 298.
Charlton, Thos., 15.
Chesnut, Col. James, 85, 86, 97, 189, 334, 335.
Chesnut, Gen. James, 5, 70, 141, 142, 145, 146, 149, 176-179, 200, 206, 209, 215, 218, 258, 259, 334, 335.
Chesnut, John (I), 334.
Chesnut, John (II), 85, 120-122, 334.
Chesnut, Capt. John (III), 470.
Chesnut, John A., 200.
Chesnut, Mrs. M. B., 179.
Chesnut, Miss Sally, 70.
Chuck-Wills-Widow, 322.
Ciples, Lewis, 79, 365.
Ciples, Sarah, 289.
Claremont County, 108, 337.
Clark, Catherine, 70.
Clark, family, 436.

Clark, James, 23, 294.
Clarke, family, 366.
Clarke, T. H., 206, 237, 260.
Clarkson, Hester, 70, 271.
Clerks of Court, 260.
Cleveland School Fire, 329.
Cloud, Wm., 294.
Clyburn, family, 367.
Clyburn, Jas. H., 260.
Clyburn, Sergt. Jno. H., 461.
Clyburn, Lieut. L. L., 462, 466.
Clyburn, Sergt. S. C., 260. 466.
Clyburn, Lieut. Thos. J., 456.
Clyburn, Capt. Wm., 260, 452, 466.
Coats, Corp. Sam'l, 456.
Colclough, Capt., 165, 174.
Cold, 315.
Collins, family, 422.
Confederate Congress, 154.
Confederate Flag, 159.
Confederate Soldiers, 451-474.
Confederate War, 159-175, 176-186.
Congressional Medals, 52.
Cool Spring, 11.
Cook, Ann, 69.
Cook, Henry R., 24, 82, 428.
Cook, James, 263.
Cooper, Dr. Thos., 83, 95.
Corbett, Dr. J. W., 54, 315.
Cornelius, Roland, 312.
Cornwallis House, 165, 265.
Cotton Mills, 31-35.
Court House, 251.
Court Inn, 47.
Craven County, 251.
Crosby, Lieut. Geo., 457.
Crosby, Selena, 328.
Cummings, Hetty, 78.
Cunningham, family, 368.
Cunningham, Jos., 96, 335.
Cunningham, Capt. J. P., 455.
Cunningham, Jno. S., 143.
Cunningham, Lt. Robt. J., 462.
Cureton, Corp. E. B., 470.
Cureton, Everard, 85, 335.
Cureton, family, 371.
Cureton, Jas. B., 11.
Cureton, Corp. Jas. B., 469.
Daniels, C. F., 85, 86, 105, 139, 301, 343.
Daniels, Corp. Edmund, 466.
Darby, Frank, 473.

477

Davie, Gen. W. R., 101.
Davis, Miss A. E., 167.
Davis, Mrs. F. Bruce, 161, 275.
Davis, Dicey, 342.
Davis, family, 373.
Davis, Corp. Henry, 452.
Davis, Lieut. Jas. M., 260, 452, 457.
Davis, Sergt. Jno. J., 457.
Davis, Junius, 260, 473.
Davis, Rev. Thos. F., 283.
Davis, W. Ransom, 260.
Deas, family, 376.
Deas, Jas. S., 50, 68, 85, 86, 259, 334.
Deas, Dr. L. H., 144, 197.
Deas, Gen. Zack C., 179.
Deer, 322.
DeKalb Lyceum, 28, 55.
DeKalb Rifle Guards, 51, 124, 159, 452.
DeLeon, Dr. Abraham, 24, 73.
DeLeon, family, 376.
Deliesseline, F. A., 45, 259.
DeLoach, Sergt. W. E., 470.
DeNoon, Maggie, 269.
DePass, family, 381.
DePass, Sergt. J. W., 470.
DePass, Capt. W. L., 199, 220, 237, 241, 260, 335, 470, 471.
DePass, W. L., Jr., 336.
Devereux, Capt. J. H., 164.
Devine, Corp. Frank G., 453.
DeSaussure Artillery Co., 470.
DeSaussure, D. L., 43, 144, 296.
DeSaussure, family, 382.
DeSaussure, Lieut. H. W., 459.
DeSaussure, Maj. J. M., 47, 141, 143, 160, 259, 314, 316, 317, 319, 324, 335, 471.
Diary from Dixie, 179.
Diceys Ford, 343.
Dickinson, family, 352.
Dickinson, Col. J. P., 106, 131-135, 141, 233, 259, 335.
Dill, S. G. W., 200, 201.
Dinkins Tavern, 18, 44.
Dixon, Sam'l, 310.
Dixon, Wm., 312.
Dixon, Tilman L., 143.
Dixon, Corp. T. L., 471.
Doby, Alfred E., 182.
Doby, Elizabeth, 70.
Doby, family, 385.

Doby, Capt. James, 468.
Doby, Jas. C., 259.
Doby, Sergt. John, 238, 261, 459.
Douglas, family, 388.
Douglas, Jas. K., 23, 296.
Douglas, Sergt. Robt. B., 467.
Dow, Robert, 264, 265.
Drage, Rev. Theophilus, 280.
Drakeford, Lieut. J., Jr., 453.
Drakeford, Capt. R. C., 471.
Drakeford, Col. Wm., 143.
Drought, 320.
Drucker, Moses, 31.
Dubose, C. P., 10.
Dubose, Capt. D. St. P., 467.
Dubose, Henry, 44.
Dubose, Henry K., 282.
Dubose, Isaac, 335.
Dunlap, James, 82.
Dunlap, Lieut. Jos. D., 260, 453.
Dunn, Corp. A. M., 470.
Dunn, Corp. Thos. P., 464.
Dunn, Dr. W. J., 10.
Dutton, Sergt. W. C., 453.
Duelling, 227-250.
Dye, Henry, 473.
Dye, J. Ross, 312.
Eagle, 321.
Eagle Nest, 324, 253.
Earthquakes, 321.
Eccles, family, 436.
Eccles, Jonathan, 23, 349.
Eldredge, F. W., 6, 47.
Ellerbe, family, 428.
Ellerbe, Robt. G., 235, 237, 470.
Elephant Hunting, 341.
Elmore, Benj. T., 85, 259.
English, James, 267.
English, Thos., 50.
Episcopal Church, 280, 286.
Evans, Thos. P., 93, 260.
European War, 52.
Factory Pond, 234.
"Falling Flag", 468.
Falling Stars, 321.
Falkenberry, Corp. J., 471.
Ferguson, Capt. C. W., 196.
Ferry, Camden, 324, Peay's, 163, Jones', 163, Tiller's, 218.
Fisher, Lieut. Chas. A., 457.
Fisher, John, 260.
Fiske, Capt. E. A., 198.

# INDEX

Flag, Confederate, 159.
Flat Rock, 13.
Flat Rock Guards, 159, 455.
Fletcher, John, 48, 50.
Fletcher, W. B., 143.
Fley, Jesse, 257.
Florida War, 120-123.
Floyd, Gen. J. W., 33, 336.
Folsom, Corp. S. T., 464.
Forbes, Geo., 23.
Force Bill, 87.
Ford, Capt. J. W., 471.
Fox, Sergt. Thos., 463.
Fraudulent Bonds, 203, 204.
Frauds Committee, 204, 206.
Freshets, 323.
Frogden, 178.
Frost, 316.
Funderburk, L. O., 334.
Furman, Rich'd, Sr., 277.
Gardiner, Wm., 32.
Gardner, Corp. E. T., 453.
Gardner, Lieut. J. W., 460.
Gardner, Sergt. S. L., 464.
Gardner, Sergt. T. D., 464.
Gamewell, family, 436.
Garlick, Peter, 310.
Gass, Benj., 260.
Gaskins, Benj., Jr., 473.
Gazettes, 300.
Geisenheimer, Wm., 450.
George, Dr. David, 310.
Gerald, family, 352.
Gerald, Sergt. Reuben L., 453.
Gettys, family, 356.
Gettys, Corp. J. L., 452.
Goff, Corp. John, 470.
Goodale, family, 353.
Goodale, Lt. Jno. R., 463.
Goodie Castle, 5.
Goodman, Jos., 45, 361.
Goodwin, John, 260.
Goodwyn, Col. A. D., 199.
Goodwyn, James, 260.
Gordon, Rev. W. B., 285.
Gouging, 256.
Grant, W. J., 9, 259, 301.
Greene's Spring, 8.
Haiglar, King, 191.
Haile, Amelia, 289.
Haile, Benj., 335.
Haile, Capt. C. C., 159, 455, 457.
Haile, Jas. C., 143.

Haile, J. L., 226, 261.
Hall, J. G., 259.
Hamilton, Reuben, 11.
Hammond, Jas. H., 176, 302.
Hammond, Capt. S., 424.
Hampton, Wade (I), 260.
Hampton, Gen. Wade, 220-224.
Harker, John, 263.
Hargreaves, Sergt. J. E., 461.
Hart, Chas. M., 112.
Hart, Wm. B., 115, 259.
Hartz, Asa, 305.
Hatfield, Henry P., 267, 268.
Hatfield, Corp. W. J., 452.
Havis, John, 44, 227.
Hay, family, 391.
Hay, J. T., 260, 307, 334, 336.
Hay, Rev. S. H., 149, 296.
Heat, 314.
Hershman, J. T., 306.
Hickman, Harris, 259.
Hilton, R. Hobson, 52.
Hobkirk Hill, 1.
Hobkirk Inn, 6, 46.
Hocott, D. D., 306.
Hodges, A., 52.
Hodgson, Sergt. H. F., 453.
Holbrook, Dr. Moses, 267.
Holmes, Jas. G., 23.
Honnet, Corp. Benj., 453.
Hopkins, Thos. A., 228, 232.
Hopkins, Gen. Wm., 21.
Horton, Lieut. Jas. E., 464.
Horton, Corp. Jas. S., 464.
Horton, Corp. Thos. C., 466.
Hospital, Camden, 54.
Hotels, 44.
Hough, I. C., 260, 261.
Hough, Joel, 236, 260.
Hough, Lieut. Moses, 460.
Hough, Sergt. Sampson, 464.
Hough, Corp. Wm., 459.
Hough, W. R., 334.
Huckabee, A. A., 336.
Huckabee, Sergt. Jos. J., 457.
Huckabee, Corp. M. G., 452.
Huckabee, W. W., 261.
Huger, Maj. Benj., 65.
Huger, Col. F. R., 71.
Hughson, J., 44.
Hughson, W. E., 31.
Hunkidori roughs, 223.
Hunter, Henry, 260.
Hurley, E., 24.

Hyco, 11.
Indian, Oneyda, 341.
Ingram, John, 261.
Inns, 44.
Iron Man, 233.
Insurrection, Slave, 187.
James, Sam'l, 335.
Jamison, Capt. J. W., 269.
Jenkins, Rev. James, 286.
Jillson, J. K., 200, 213, 334.
Johnson, Alexander, 43.
Johnson, family, 392.
Johnson, H. T., 336.
Johnson, Rev. John, 168, 284.
Johnson, M. M., 336.
Johnson, P. W., 300.
Johnson, Lieut. Robt., 468.
Johnson, Wm. E. (I), 5, 6, 24, 43, 143, 197.
Johnson, Wm. E. (II), 244, 247, 467.
Johnson, Sergt. Wm., 469.
Johnston, W. B., 124, 305.
Jones, A. D., 142.
Jones, A. Osceola, 202, 211.
Jones, Capt. B., 143.
Jones, Sergt. B. N., 456.
Jones, Lieut. Jas. G., 469.
Jones, Capt. Jno. L., 462, 463.
Jones, Maj. Sam'l, 52.
Jones, Lieut. W. J., 456, 462.
Jordan, family, 394.
Josey, Sergt. Joshua, 452.
Joy, John R., 260.
Joyce, Rev. John, 295.
Jugnot, Charles, 24.
Jumelle Hill, 1.
Jumelle, P. L., 275.
Jumelle Spring, 8.
Kamtchatka, 5, 178.
Kelley, Corp. A., 452.
Kelley, Sergt. Jas. F., 464.
Kelley, Newton, 336.
Kelley, Capt. Wiley, 143.
Kennedy, A. D., 34.
Kennedy, A. M., 30, 143, 296.
Kennedy, (A. M.), family, 395.
Kennedy, Gen. J. D., 159, 185-186, 199, 200, 218, 260, 336, 453.
Kennedy, R. M., 28, 316.
Kennedy, R. M. (II), 270.
Kennedy, R. M. (III), 55.
Kennedy, (R. M.), family, 395.

Kennedy, Sergt. Walter, 459.
Kennedy, Wm., 40, 143.
Kennedy, (Wm.), family, 398.
Kerr, James, 263, 294.
Kershaw County, 252, 253, 254.
Kershaw Era, 308.
Kershaw Gazette, 307.
Kershaw Greys, 462.
Kershaw Guards, 457.
Kershaw, James, 58, 315.
Kershaw, John (I), 189, 260, 335.
Kershaw, Gen. J. B., 125, 149, 180-185, 199, 207, 213, 215, 218, 237, 259, 334, 335.
Kershaw, (J. B.), family, 390.
Kershaw, Joseph, 254, 255, 260, 263, 277, 281, 291.
Kershaw, Town, 253.
Kershaw Troop, 459.
Kilgore, family, 422.
Kimpton, H. H., 203, 206.
King, Lieut. Gillam P., 464.
Kirkley, Lieut. D. C., 457.
Kirkland, Dan 49.
Kirkland, Corp. D., 469.
Kirkland, Maj. D. B., 143.
Kirkland, family, 399.
Kirkland, Sergt. J. P., 467.
Kirkland, Rich'd R., 183-185, 455.
Kirkland, Sergt. Shannon, 467.
Kirkland, Thos. J., 44, 334, 336.
Kirkland, Wm. L., 194, 473.
Kirkpatrick, John, 293, 294.
Kirkwood, 1-10, 25.
Kirkwood Common, 1, 2, 7.
Kirkwood Hotel, 47.
Kirkwood Rangers, 249, 268.
Knights Hill, 11, 179.
Knox, Jno. P., 143.
Krumbholz, T. E., 47.
Ku Klux, 201, 208, 209.
Lafayette Hall, 69-82.
Lafayette's Visit, 64-82.
Lang, Jas. W., 260.
Lang, Jim, 106, 193, 233.
Lang, Thos., 89, 145, 335.
Langley, Dr. Wm., 187, 300.
Latta, 23.
Lausanne, 47.
Lavall ———, 228.
Lee, family, 403.
Lee, Rev. F. P., 283.

480

# INDEX

Lee, Francis S., 260, 271.
Lee, Sergt. J. B., 469.
Lee, Dr. Jos., 17, 143.
Lee, Thos. B., 259.
Legare, Dr. T. B., 242.
Leitner, family, 406.
Leitner, Maj. W. Z., 199, 209.
Lemiere, J. C., 272.
Levy, Chapman, 58, 60, 85, 115, 259, 334, 335.
Levy, family, 406.
Levy, Hayman, 23, 142.
Levy, M. M., 140, 261, 305, 335.
Lewis, Capt. Rob't T., 462.
Library, Camden, 22, 255.
Lining, Arthur, 260.
Logtown, 18, 135.
Logue, Rev. John, 281, 292.
Lucas, Capt. B. S., 460, 462.
Lucas, family, 408.
Lucas Guards, 464.
Lucas Rifles, 464.
Lyles, family, 353.
Lyles, J. Belton, 473.
Lyles, Lieut. Jas. V., 457.
Lynches Creek, 173, 253.
Lyon, J., 23.
McAdams, 44, 45.
McCaa, family, 409.
McCaa, Dr. John, 24.
McCaa, Lieut. J. T., 470.
McCall, Hugh, 23.
McCandless, 150, 268, 273, 274.
McCandless, family, 411.
McCants, Hiram, 45.
McCaskill, A., 96, 460.
McCaskill, Lieut. Finley, 460.
McCaskill, Sergt. Jas. H., 464.
McCaskill, Kenneth, 143.
McCaskill, P., 272.
McClelland House, 18, 279.
MacColl, John, 45.
McCown, Anne, 70.
McCoy, Benj., 143.
McCoy, Sergt. Chap. L., 467.
McCreight, family, 413.
McCreight, R. J., 296.
McCulloch, M. M., 45, 50.
McCurry, J. W., 353.
McDonald, family, 353.
McDow, Dr. T. F., 206, 312, 369.
McDowall, Sergt. C. J., 452, 469.
McDowall, family, 414.
McDowell, Sergt. J. E. C., 456.
McDowell, W. L., 307.
McDuffie, Geo. 84, 140, 145.
McEwen, family, 353.
McEwen, James, 40.
McEwen, John, 267.
McGill, Jas. R., 214, 334, 336.
McIntosh, G. Q., 260.
McKagen, Sergt. H. G., 453.
McKain, 31, 45, 142.
McKain, family, 415.
McKain, Lieut. John, 453.
McKee, Corp. R., 471.
McKnight, Geo., 304.
McKnight, Robert, 304.
McLaurin, Corp. D. M., 461.
McLaurin, Corp. J. A., 461.
McLeod, Corp. A., 471.
McLeod, Corp. Jno. A., 459.
McLeod, Rev. Robt., 74.
McLeod, Corp. Thos. A., 459.
McMillan, family, 361.
McQueen, family, 353.
McQueen, Lieut. J. A., 170-174.
McRae, Colin, 1, 317, 319, 321, 325.
McRae, Capt. John, 47, 50.
McSween, Lieut. Wm., 464.
McWillie, Col. Adam, 59, 91.
McWillie, Capt. Adam, 119.
McWillie, family, 416.
McWillie, Wm., 85, 114-119, 141, 229, 334, 335.
Magazine, 190.
Magazine Spring, 51.
Magill, J. R., 214, 334.
Malone, Sergt. W. R., 462.
Malvern Hill, 11.
Man, Robert, 167.
Manget, Lieut. J. A., 470.
Manning, Rich'd I., 66, 93.
Marengo Mill, 11.
Martin, Dr. James, 101.
Martin, J. M., 336.
Martin's Branch, 3.
Massey, J. Cope, 334.
Matheson, Alex'r, 18, 24, 27, 167.
Matheson, C., 30, 142.
Matheson, family, 418.
Matheson, Lt. Jas. D., 469.
Matheson, Wm., 23.
Mathieu, J. B., 22, 44, 191.
Mathis, Sam'l, 15, 259, 425.

## HISTORIC CAMDEN

Mayhew, Ezekiel, 335.
Mayors of Camden, 10.
Mayrant, Capt., 74.
Mayrant, Sergt. J. G., 466.
Meroney, J. S., 166.
Methodist Church, 286-291.
Meugy, 22, 272.
Mexican War, 124-138.
Meynardie, Rev. E. J., 306, 473.
Mickle, 19, 23, 354.
Mickle, Joseph, 228.
Mickle, Sergt. R., 471.
Milhous, Robert, 15.
Military, 48-52.
Miller, Stephen D., 83, 88, 95, 107, 259.
Milling, family, 354.
Milling, Hugh, 260.
Mills, Laurens T., 336.
Mills, Robert, 25, 74.
Mills, Rev. W. H., 295.
Minton, David, 257.
Moffat, family, 130.
Moffat, K. S., 125, 130.
Moffat Rifles, 466.
Montgomery, Dr. B. R., 266.
Moore, Dr. A. A., 459.
Moore, Alexander, 260.
Moore, Prof. A. C., 270.
Moore, family, 419.
Montagu, Lord Chas., 15.
Morin, J. B., 23.
Morrison, Robert, 270.
Mortimer, Edward, 3.
Mortimer Spring, 3.
Moseley, G. W., 336.
Moseley, Lieut. R., 462.
Moses, Gov. F. J., 202, 205, 210, 211, 214, 217.
Mount Zion Academy, 263.
Mulberry, 13, 178.
Munn, Jas. B., 336.
Murchison, Sergt. J. J., 456.
Murray, Corp. John, 469.
Murray, J. D., 335.
Murray, J. S., 293.
Muster Spring, 13.
Naudin, Moreau, 260.
Nelson, Col. P. H., 181.
Nelson, P. H. (II), 336.
Nelson, W. R., 336.
Nesbit, Sarah, 11.
Nettles, Louise, 55.
Nettles, Sergt. Hiram, 453, 455.

Nettles, J. S., 43, 260.
Nettles, Capt. Wm., 74.
Newman, Sergt. B. S., 461.
Newman, Corp. J. T., 464.
Newspapers, 300.
Niles, Sergt. Ario, 453.
Niles, Ebenezer P., 267, 271.
Niles, Sergt. E. E., 453.
Niles, family, 354.
Nixon, family, 420.
Nixon, Henry G., 70, 84, 228, 259, 335.
Nixon, Wm. O., 85, 233.
Nones, Maj. Benj., 78.
Nullification Times, 83.
Nunn, Ilai, 24.
O'Cain, Wm. G., 24.
Olds, W., 24.
"Old Times in Camden", 16.
Orphan Academy, 24, 263-271.
Orphan Society, 263-271.
Outlaw, Sergt. B. F., 471.
Outlaw, Sergt. M. J., 461.
Owens, Sergt. A., 471.
Owens, Isaac, 180.
Paint Hill, 11, 224.
Panther, 322.
Parker, Doctor, 314.
Parker, Sergt. Eli W., 452.
Parker, Sergt. John, 469.
Parker, Wm., 23, 294.
Pate, Sergt. Henry, 464.
Patterson, family, 422.
Patterson, Joseph, 85, 335.
Patterson, Col. L. J., 143, 145, 334, 335.
Patterson, R. B., 321, 456.
Patterson, Lieut. W. W., 456.
Pearson, James, 262.
Peay's Ferry, 163.
Peck, Chas. A. H., 159, 269.
Pegues, family, 355.
Pegues, Sergt. Rich'd, 453.
Pegues, Thos. W., 305.
Perkins, Benj., 5, 66, 100, 144, 259.
Perkins, Chas., 31.
Perkins, Caroline J., 47.
Perry, Gov. B. F., 155, 197.
Perry, Corp. Jno. A., 453.
Perry, Geo. and John, 312.
Phelps, Stella, 267, 272.
Phillips, Sergt. S. F., 464.
Pigeons, wild, 321.

# INDEX

Pilgrims, 100.
Pine Flat, 6.
Pine Grove Academy, 267, 289.
Pitts, Corp. J. C., 461.
Place, Capt. Sam'l, 198, 261.
Plane Hill, 13, 109.
Poinsett, Joel R., 101.
Polk, Corp. J. W., 453.
Pope, Jesse, 271.
Potter's Raid, 174.
Price, Chas. A., 145, 259.
Presbyterian Church, 291-297.
Preston, Wm. C., 66, 67.
Public Works, 101.
Punch, N. S., 31.
Rabb, Sergt. Jas. K., 466.
Racing, 52.
Raccoons, 322.
Railroads, 41, 102, 118, 205.
Rainfall, 317, 318.
Raley, Lieut. A. W., 464.
Raley, Corp. Reddick, 464.
Ray, family, 361.
Reconstruction and Red Shirt, 196.
Reed, 42, 188, 267.
Reid, 213, 266.
Rembert, Corp. T. M., 467.
Representatives, House, 335.
Reserves, Co. D., 471.
Revolutionary remains, 26, 51, 69.
Reynolds, Emma, 275.
Reynolds, family, 425.
Reynolds, Joshua, 42, 271.
Richards, Gov. J. G., 313, 336.
Richards, Rev. J. G., 313.
Richards, Norman S., 336.
Riddle, Lieut. Jas. M., 453.
River, Wateree, 323.
Robinson, Eleven, 194.
Robinson, Sergt. E. G., 46, 470.
Rochelle, Charlotte, 92.
Rodgers, W. K., 307.
Rogers, A. S., 46.
Roman Catholic Church, 297-299.
Ross, Geo., 335.
Rose, Dan'l, 294.
Rosser, family, 355.
Rosser, John, 296.
Rosser, Wm., 31, 260.
Royall, Anne, 119, 231.
Rudolph, Zebulon, 16, 293.

Ruffin, A. R., 45.
Rugeley, James, 361.
Russell, Wm., 310.
Russell, W. F., 336.
Ryan, Sergt. D. B., 453.
Salmond, Dr. E. A., 143.
Salmond, B. B., 259.
Salmond, family, 427.
Salmond, H. C., 234, 469.
Salmond, Louisa, 70.
Salmond, Thos., 5, 43, 69, 144, 189, 260.
Salmond, Dr. Thos. W., 166, 473.
Sanders Creek, 253.
Sanders, family, 428.
Sarsfield, 178.
Savage, Henry, 326.
Scalawags, 201.
Schoenberg, W. F., 270.
School, Cleveland, 329.
Schools, 262-276.
Schrock, family, 355.
Schrock, Lieut. Joel A., 45.
Schrock, W. A., 307.
Scott, Edwin J., 76, 112.
Scott, Gov. R. K., 201, 206.
Seegers, Capt. Dove, 464.
Seminole War, 120-123.
Senf, Col. C., 36, 37, 341, 355.
Senators, State, 334.
Serugs Battle, 337.
Sessions, J. G., 473.
Shannon, Chas. J. (I), 27, 43, 85, 266, 296.
Shannon, Dr. C. J. (II), 31, 330.
Shannon, C. J. (III), 237, 469.
Shannon, C. J. (IV), 43, 434.
Shannon, family, 431.
Shannon, Mrs. Mary A., 433.
Shannon, Col. Wm. M., 3, 6, 91, 174, 180, 198, 206, 218, 232, 237, 249, 259, 335, 468.
Shannon, W. M. (II), 54, 433.
Shaw, family, 356.
Shaw, J. Duncan, 220.
Sheorn, Duncan, 261.
Sheorn, Corp. Jno. A., 462.
Sheriffs, 260.
Sherman freshet, 325.
Sherman's invasion, 162-174.
Shiver, C., 208, 260.
Sill, Lieut. E. E., 261, 415, 453.
Sims, Dr. J. Marion, 311.

Slaves, 187.
Sligh, Lieut. Thos. W., 466.
Slump, J. Martin, 300.
Small, Sergt. Rob't F., 453.
Smart, Maj. John, 143, 233, 259, 356.
Smith, Emily, 275.
Smith, Rev. Isaac, 18, 271, 286.
Smith, Josiah, 22.
Smith, Judge M. L., 336.
Smith, Judge Wm., 107, 108, 109.
Smyrl, John, 208.
Smyrl, Sergt. Thos. J., 466.
Snow, 319.
Solomon, Levi, 23.
Somers, Sergt. Adolph, 457.
Sowell, Sergt. Jas. E., 464.
Sowell, Sergt. Jno. A., 456.
Spann, James, 42.
Spann, Timothy, 228.
Spears, Corp. B. F., 466.
Spencer, C. R., 270.
Springdale, 13.
Springer, Corp. Rudolph, 457.
Starke, Capt., 74.
Starke, Reuben, 334.
Starke, Turner, 260.
Starke, Wyatt, 188, 259, 335.
Star Redoubt, 51, 69.
Stars, falling, 321.
Stateburg, 174.
Stephenson, L. B., 220, 336.
Stewman, Corp. P. A. H., 457.
Stoney, Rev. J. W., 285.
"Straightout", 219.
Stuckey, Corp. Anderson, 452.
Sturgeon, 322.
Summerville, Capt. H., 143.
Summerville, James, 310.
Sumter, Fort, 150.
Sumter, Sergt. Sebastian, 467.
Sutherland, J. F., 30.
Tarbox, G. Walter, 301.
Tate, Wm., 263.
Taverns, 44.
Taxahaw, 88.
Taxpayers Convention, 209.
Taylor field, 228.
Taylor, Lieut. W. J., 334, 466.
Taylor, Wm. R., 260.
Teamboats, 37.
Team, family, 356.
Team, James, 143.

Telegraph line, first, 41.
Telescope (n'paper), 151.
Temperatures, 314, 315.
Terebene oil, 323.
Terraces, The, 13, 109, 298.
Test Oath, 87, 112, 116.
Thames, Sergt. N. W., 469.
Thomasson, Mary C., 275.
Thompson, Charlotte, 13, 298.
Thompson, (Liberty Hill), family, 434.
Thompson, (Ninian), family, 357.
Thompson, Capt. John, 471.
Thornton, Abathiah, 70.
Thornton, family, 436.
Thornton, Joseph, 23.
Thornton, Phineas, 22, 104.
Thornton, Mrs. P., 17, 288, 294.
Ticknor, Caleb and Ben, 47.
Tiller, Lieut. H. D., 464.
Tillers ferry, 218, bridge, 253.
Todd, Dr., 161.
Trantham, J. S., 261.
Trantham, W. D., 219, 307, 336.
Transportation, 35-41.
Trent Hill, 11.
Trent, Dr. John, 294.
Truesdel, Henry T., 467, 468.
Truesdel, Lieut. Jas. T., 467.
Truesdel, Lieut. Jesse E., 455.
Tucker, Rev. Reuben, 95.
Turf, The, 52.
Turner, Corp. B. J., 464.
Turner, J. F., 452.
Turnips, 322.
Turpentine, 323.
Tweed, family, 357.
Twitty, Corp. L. M., 462.
Uphton (Upton) Court, 47.
Vaughan, John C., 259.
Vaughan, Wilie, 23, 301.
Vaux, E. S., 43.
Villepigue, family, 439.
Villepigue, Capt. Jas. I., 109, 228, 230, 257, 315, 342, 473.
Villepigue, Gen. J. B., 179.
Villepigue, K. S., 166.
Villepigue, John Cantey, 52.
Villepigue, Paul T., 34.
Von Tresckow, Mrs. E. C., 56.
Von Tresckow, Baron, 82.
Wall, R. E., 260.

# Index

War, 1812, 57-63, Seminole, 120-123, Mexican, 124-138, Confederate, 159-175, 176-186.
Wardlaw, Corp. S. Watt, 469.
Warren, Elizabeth, 306.
Warren, Peter, 23, 104, 105.
Warren, Thos., 104.
Warren, Capt. Thos. J., 105, 149, 261, 305.
War Rolls, 1812, 61-63, Seminole, 122-123, Mexican, 135-138, Confederate, 451-474.
Wateree Ag. Society, 27.
Wateree Messenger, 307.
Wateree Mounted Rifles, 467.
Wateree River, 323-327.
Water Powers, 41-42.
Watkins, W. B., 143.
Watson, Elkanah, 77.
Waxhaws, 91, 107.
Weems, Parson, 77.
Weinges, Conrad, 237.
Welsh, G. C., 261, 334.
Welsh, Thos., 45.
West, Chas. S., 259.
West, family, 441.
West, J. C., 89, 260.
West, Corp. Joseph, 464.
West, Sergt. Thos. G., 456.
West, Corp. Wm. S., 456.
Whippoorwill, 322.
Whitaker, Dan'l K., 267.
Whitaker, Lieut. Duncan, 452, 467.
Whitaker, Rev. Jonathan, 70, 267.
Whitaker, Maj. John, 21.
Whitaker, L. L., 142.
Whitaker, Thos., 122, 189.
Whitaker, Sergt. Thos., 459.
Whitaker, Corp. Wm., 469.
Whitaker, Dr. Wm., 21, 24.
Whitaker, Willis, 335.
Whitaker, Maj. Willis, 49, 74.
Whittemore, B. F., 201, 211, 213.

Wiggins, M. C., 260.
Willet, John S., 103, 259.
Willet, Susan, 103.
Williams, Gov. D. R., 65, 68, 100, 113.
Williams, D. R. (III), 121.
Williams, S. Miller, 234.
Williams, R. B., 261.
Williams, Corp. R. H., 456.
Wilson, family, 357.
Wilson, Paul, 209.
Wilson, Sergt. Thos., 462.
Winkler, C. L., 336.
Withers, family, 442.
Withers, Thos. J., 85, 139, 143, 145, 146, 149, 151-159, 259.
Witherspoon, family, 443.
Wittkowsky, family, 449.
Wittkowsky, L. A., 55, 197.
Wolfe, family, 449.
Wolfe, Corp. Eugene, 457.
Woodruff, Josephus, 202, 211.
Workman, family, 444.
Workman, John, 23, 31, 143, 296.
Workman, W. H. R., 259, 296.
Wylie, Capt. J. D., 159.
Wyly, John, 260.
Wyly, Sam'l, 15.
Yarborough, Corp. J. H., 459.
Yarborough, Corp. W. A., 461.
Yates, C. H., 10, 34.
Young, Alexander, 23, 27, 30, 81.
Young's bridge, 253.
Young, family, 446.
Young, James A., 79, 294.
Young, J. V., 336.
Young, Lovick, 68, 93.
Young, Mary, 70.
Young, S. J. T., 300.
Zemp, family, 364.
Zemp, F. M., 10, 34.
Zemp, Dr. Leslie, 315.
Zemp, Dr. S. C., 55.
Zemp, W. R., 55.

# INDEX TO ILLUSTRATIONS AND DIAGRAMS

|  | Facing Page |
|---|---|
| Folder—Extended Plan of Camden, 1926 | 1 |
| Diagram No. 1—Plat of Kirkwood, 1818 | 3 |
| Diagram No. 2—Kirkwood | 6 |
| Diagram No. 3—Localities in Vicinity of Camden | 13 |
| Illustration—Abram Blanding | 100 |
| Illustration—Stephen D. Miller | 109 |
| Illustration—Wm. McWillie | 115 |
| Illustration—Col. J. P. Dickinson | 131 |
| Illustration—Thomas J. Withers | 153 |
| Illustration—Generals Chesnut, Cantey and Deas | 177 |
| Illustration—Generals Kershaw, Kennedy and Villepigue | 181 |
| Illustration—Col. Shannon; Col. Cash | 249 |
| Diagram of Kershaw County | 252 |
| Illustration—Bishop Thomas F. Davis | 283 |
| Illustration—Presbyterian Church | 291 |
| Chart—Rainfall at Camden, 1852-1925 | 319 |

www.ingramcontent.com/pod-product-compliance
Lightning Source LLC
Chambersburg PA
CBHW030900080526
44589CB00010B/87